Writing & Reporting
FOR THE MEDIA

Writing & Reporting
FOR THE MEDIA

TWELFTH EDITION

JOHN R. BENDER
UNIVERSITY OF NEBRASKA-LINCOLN

LUCINDA D. DAVENPORT
MICHIGAN STATE UNIVERSITY

MICHAEL W. DRAGER
SHIPPENSBURG UNIVERSITY OF PENNSYLVANIA

FRED FEDLER
UNIVERSITY OF CENTRAL FLORIDA

NEW YORK   OXFORD
OXFORD UNIVERSITY PRESS

Oxford University Press is a department of the University of Oxford.
It furthers the University's objective of excellence in research, scholarship,
and education by publishing worldwide. Oxford is a registered trade mark of
Oxford University Press in the UK and certain other countries.

Published in the United States of America by Oxford University Press
198 Madison Avenue, New York, NY 10016, United States of America.

For titles covered by Section 112 of the US Higher Education
Opportunity Act, please visit www.oup.com/us/he for the latest
information about pricing and alternate formats.

Library of Congress Cataloging-in-Publication Data
Names: Bender, John R., author. | Davenport, Lucinda, author. | Drager,
  Michael W., author. | Fedler, Fred, author.
Title: Writing & reporting for the media / John R. Bender, University of
  Nebraska-Lincoln ; Lucinda D. Davenport, Michigan State University ;
  Michael W. Drager, Shippensburg University of Pennsylvania ; Fred Fedler,
  University of Central Florida.
Other titles: Writing and reporting for the media
Description: Twelfth edition. | New York : Oxford University Press, [2018] |
  Includes index.
Identifiers: LCCN 2018019923 | ISBN 9780190649425 (pbk. text)
Subjects: LCSH: Reporters and reporting—Problems, exercises, etc.
Classification: LCC PN4781 .B385 2018 | DDC 070.4/3—dc23
LC record available at https://lccn.loc.gov/2018019923

9 8 7 6 5 4
Printed by LSC Communications, United States of America

BRIEF CONTENTS

CONTENTS

Chapter 3   Newswriting Style   29

Chapter 4   The Language of News   47

Chapter 6   Ethics   106

SECTION III   THE BASIC SKILLS OF JOURNALISM   129

Chapter 7   Basic News Leads   131

PREFACE

You might think the news business is in trouble if you look only at the traditional measures of success: circulation and advertising revenue. The New York Times' daily circulation has dropped to about 570,000 printed copies, and its advertising revenue from the print edition was $64 million for the third quarter of 2017. But these numbers do not reflect the new realities of U.S. journalism. While the Times has lost print subscribers, it has rapidly gained digital subscribers. It now has 2.5 million people who pay to read the newspaper online. The Times' overall subscriber base has more than doubled over the last four years. For the 2017 third quarter, digital subscription revenue was $86 million. The transition from a print advertising revenue base to a digital subscription revenue base has been a rocky one for the news business, and it is not complete. But the Times and many other newspapers are profitable and are looking to expand.

The readership and revenue numbers for the Times and for most other news organizations reflect a changing industry. More and more Americans turn to digital devices—computers, tablets, smartphones—for news. In the digital world, however, advertisers depend less on traditional news and entertainment media for access to the consumers they want to attract than they did in the print world.

As the news business has changed, so have the expectations for the men and women starting careers in journalism. Journalism schools and departments are rethinking their curriculums as they try to figure out what sets of skills will best prepare their graduates for finding and holding jobs. At some schools, students are learning how to write HTML code, tell stories visually, develop and manage databases and even design video games. Other schools want students to become proficient in multiple skills, such as shooting still and video images and creating webpages, as well as the more traditional journalistic skills. A few schools have closed their journalism programs or merged them with other departments and majors.

At the same time, news editors and producers who hire journalism graduates want employees with solid skills in the core of writing, editing and researching. They want reporters who can think critically to evaluate information and work in teams to develop and present stories.

Just as the news business and journalism education have been changing, this textbook has been changing. We have added material on such things as writing for digital media and visual journalism. At the same time, we remain committed to emphasizing the basic skills of journalism, skills that will be demanded of all reporters, no matter whether they are writing for a traditional newspaper, a television station, an online news organization, a blog or a public relations organization. Every journalist must be able to write clearly and correctly and make complicated issues understandable and interesting.

The function of journalism that sets it apart from other jobs and communication businesses is its role in providing citizens in a democracy with the information they need to govern their society. As James Madison said nearly 200 years ago, "Popular government without popular information, or the means of acquiring it, is but a prologue to a farce or a tragedy or perhaps both. Knowledge will forever govern ignorance. And a people who mean to be their own governors must arm themselves with the power that knowledge gives."

Self-government in the 21st century requires citizens to confront such issues as health care, global warming, criminal justice, economic stability, international trade, war and diplomacy. The catalogue of issues is long and daunting. To make sound decisions about these issues, people need reliable information. And most will get the bulk of it from journalists. The reporters who are best able to provide that information will be ones who have a broad understanding of how society works and the ability to explain the issues and how they affect citizens in an understandable and interesting manner.

The task of journalism is an important one, but much of the public doubts journalists and the news they provide. Complaints of bias and fakery are common. Some people call news biased because it does not agree with their beliefs and ideologies. Public officials often complain about unfairness or inaccuracies when they are the target of critical coverage, even when the reports are accurate. But journalists have contributed to the public's distrust by making mistakes, failing to put events into context and ignoring important points of view. In a few instances, reporters have made up stories, quotations and sources. Although journalists who do this are fired when they are discovered, their actions taint the entire profession.

Dealing with public distrust is a challenge that young journalists will have to confront. And the distrusts probably will linger for many years. No simple solution exists. The best course is to concentrate on presenting the news as thoroughly, accurately and fairly as possible. Cultivating two traits can help journalists achieve those goals:

1. Be engaged in the world around you.
2. Be articulate.

Being engaged in the world means reporters have a high degree of curiosity about their beats and life in general and they feel empathy for the subjects of their stories. Curiosity helps reporters see story ideas in almost everything around them and develop the stories assigned to them:

● Many communities have charter schools, which are supported with tax money but exempt from some of the requirements placed on public schools.

Do students in charter schools perform as well as students in ordinary public schools? Do charter schools enroll the same proportion of students with disabilities or students whose native language is not English as public schools?

- Civil forfeiture laws allow states to confiscate money and property obtained illegally, as through the sale of illegal drugs, and use the money to finance law enforcement. What do state and local governments do with the money and property they confiscate? Are the people whose property is confiscated always convicted of crimes?
- States offer tax incentives to lure businesses to provide more jobs for their citizens. What businesses are getting these tax incentives? How much do they cost and how many jobs do they create?

These are just a few examples of the kinds of questions and stories journalists can generate if they are curious. Reporters must constantly ask about the details of their beats, even when they have no expectation the answers will lead to stories. No reporter can predict what tidbit of information may help unravel a great story. Even the information that yields no story might help the journalist understand and explain events to an audience.

Being engaged also means having empathy for the sources and subjects of news stories. People in the news often confront highly emotional situations. They may be victims of crime or the relatives of a victim; they may have lost loved ones in a plane crash; they may be athletes who have just suffered a defeat; or they may be community residents worried about how a proposed development might affect their lives and their property. A story about a knife attack by a male employee on a female supervisor is not just an antiseptic crime story or an exercise in deductive logic. It is a story about anger, frustration, betrayal, terror and humiliation. A reporter who cannot empathize with the people involved cannot truly understand their experiences or tell their stories.

The ability to empathize does not require reporters to abandon objectivity and impartiality. Empathy differs from sympathy. Sympathy requires one to have the same feelings as another or to achieve a mutual understanding with another. Empathy involves projecting one's personality into that of another to understand the other person better. Journalists who have empathy for others can understand them without embracing or approving their emotions. Empathy is consistent with objectivity; it also is indispensable for producing a truly objective and thorough story. If reporters cannot understand the emotional states of the people they write about or assess the emotional changes events inflict on sources, they will fail to report the full story.

Curiosity and empathy enable reporters to get the who, what, when, where, why and how of a story. Putting those elements into a coherent, interesting and readable story requires that journalists be articulate, which combines at least two skills. One is the ability to use words effectively, to select the appropriate words and use them correctly and to arrange them in sentences that are grammatically correct and properly punctuated. The other skill is the ability to organize the elements of the story—the facts, the quotations and the anecdotes—in a manner that is captivating, informative and dramatic.

Reporters who understand grammar and diction can construct sentences that are clear and precise. The following sentences contain the same words but mean different things, simply because one word is in a different location:

> She kissed only him on the lips.
> She kissed him only on the lips.

A skillful writer understands that in the first sentence, "only" limits whom she kissed, and in the second sentence, it limits where she kissed.

A skillful writer also knows that one of these sentences accuses the subject of a crime:

> Wanda sent her husband Bob to the store.
> Wanda sent her husband, Bob, to the store.

The first sentence uses "Bob" as an essential modifier of "husband," meaning that Wanda has more than one husband and the one she sent to the store is Bob. The sentence implies Wanda has committed bigamy. The second sentence, because it uses commas before and after "Bob," makes it clear that Wanda has only one husband, and his name is Bob.

The ability to construct clear, correct sentences is fundamental. But a news story may contain nothing but clear, correct sentences and still be impossible to understand because the writer has failed to organize the material. Readers, listeners and viewers crave organization; if they do not find it, they give up. A story that jumps from one topic to another and back to the first without any sense of direction will confuse people and drive them elsewhere for information. Reporters need to know how to organize information so its significance and drama become clear.

All of the skills one needs to become a great reporter—curiosity, empathy, knowledge of grammar and the ability to organize stories—are skills a student can learn. Some students may learn them more easily than others, or some may develop one set of skills more than the others. But anybody who can handle college-level course work can cultivate the skills a professional reporter needs. The 12th edition of this textbook offers many features—some new to this edition— to help students master the skills of news reporting.

New Features in the 12th Edition

As with the previous editions of this textbook, the 12th edition contains several changes. It also adheres to the approach and practice Fred Fedler developed when he created this textbook nearly 40 years ago. The co-authors, who have taken over much of the responsibility for this book, hope longtime users will be comfortable with it and new users will find it attractive.

Although the 12th edition contains many changes, some major ones are worth noting:

- Foremost is the addition of a workbook separate from the textbook. The textbook still contains exercises for students, but the addition of the workbook has allowed us to expand the number of exercises from which instructors may choose.

- For the past two editions, the book contained a separate chapter on the practice of digital journalism. Because all journalists now need skills in preparing digital content, this information has been spread throughout the textbook. The chapter on visual journalism, which was new with the last edition, has been retained (Chapter 14).
- The summary of Associated Press style has been returned to the textbook as Appendix B. Students can now find and refer to the summary quickly and easily.
- The book contains many visual elements, including full-color photographs and colorful graphics. New visuals and expanded captions reflect more recent events and correspond to and supplement the text.
- Many of the sidebars from the previous edition have been reorganized into two new boxes, "Hot Tip" and "From the News." These boxes provide students with important do's and don'ts and examples from specific news stories, respectively.
- The text includes many new examples on events that current and future students will likely remember. These include the election of Donald J. Trump as president, the controversy over the use of lethal force by police against minority citizens, and protests by athletes against such police killings.

Other Features of Interest

Appendices

This book provides three appendices: a city directory, a summary of Associated Press style, and rules for forming possessives.

Reporter's Guides

Nearly every chapter ends with a reporter's guide (e.g., "Reporter's Guide to Accuracy" in Chapter 2) that summarizes the major points covered in the chapter and helps students organize their writing assignments and make sure they are including all important information.

Flexibility

"Writing and Reporting for the Media" is flexible. Teachers can assign the chapters in almost any order. Moreover, the book and workbook provide enough exercises that instructors can assign their favorites and then assign extra exercises for students who need more help. Some teachers use the book for two semesters: for basic and advanced reporting classes. There are enough exercises for both terms.

   The book can be used in general media writing classes and those specific to newswriting and reporting. Still, those who prefer the book's traditional emphasis on the print media can assign the chapters on public relations and writing for broadcast media as optional readings.

Hundreds of Examples

The text contains hundreds of examples from the work of students and professionals. Each new topic or discussion of errors typically includes examples. Students are also shown how to avoid or correct errors.

Some examples have been written by prize-winning professionals, and students can use their stories as models. For instance, examples from The Associated Press, The New York Times, The Washington Post and several other U.S. newspapers, large and small, illustrate many of the concepts discussed in the text.

Realistic and Often Genuine Exercises

Many of the exercises in this book are from real events. Chapter 15 ("Speeches and Meetings") includes President Trump's speech announcing the decision to withdraw from the Paris climate change agreement. Chapter 17 includes exercises based on real traffic accidents, crimes and fires. Exercises in other chapters, although fictionalized, are drawn from real events.

To add to the realism, many of the exercises contain ethical problems: profanities, sexist comments, the names of rape victims, bloody details and other material that many editors would be reluctant to publish. Students completing those exercises will have to deal with the problems, and their decisions are likely to provoke class discussion.

Instructor's Manual

The authors provide a detailed Instructor's Manual that includes ideas and recommendations and discusses accuracy, grades, suggested policies and assignments. These sections are followed by sample course outlines and lists of the exercises that contain ethical dilemmas and sexist remarks. The manual also includes tests covering AP style, vocabulary, attribution and spelling.

Practical Approach

Like previous editions, the 12th edition is concrete, not abstract or theoretical. Its tone is practical and realistic. Its language is clear, concise, simple and direct. Because of the book's realism, students will encounter the types of problems and assignments they are likely to find after they graduate and begin entry-level jobs with the media.

Pro Challenge

A few exercises in the chapters about leads and the body of news stories have been completed by professional journalists. With these exercises, students can compare their work to that of the professionals.

A Note of Thanks

Journalists are wonderful people: enthusiastic, interesting and helpful. While working on this book, we wrote to dozens of them. Reporters, photographers and editors from Portland to Philadelphia, from Miami to New York, answered our letters and provided advice and samples of their work.

The authors wish to thank Joe Weber, an associate professor of journalism at the University of Nebraska-Lincoln and a former bureau chief for Business Week, who extensively revised and rewrote Chapter 16.

We would especially like to thank the many professionals who have given us permission to quote their work: Tom Rosenstiel, the executive director of the American Press Institute; Craig Silverman of the Toronto Star; Steve Buttry, digital transformation editor of Digital First Media; Sue Hadden Beard, retired editor of the Waynesboro (Pennsylvania) Record Herald; Henry McNulty, owner of Henry McNulty Communication Services and a former associate editor of the Hartford (Connecticut) Courant; David Cullier, an assistant professor of journalism at the University of Arizona; Matthew Stibbe, freelance journalist and CEO of Articulate and Turbine; Roy Peter Clark, senior scholar and vice president of the Poynter Institute for Media Studies; Don Fry, an affiliate of the Poynter Institute for Media Studies; Andrew J. Nelson, a reporter for the Omaha (Nebraska) World-Herald; Don Stacom, a reporter for the Hartford (Connecticut) Courant; Joe Hight, former editor of the Colorado Springs (Colorado) Gazette and The Oklahoman of Oklahoma City; Paula Lavigne, a reporter for ESPN's Enterprise and Investigative Unit; Jack Hart, former managing editor of The Oregonian in Portland; Scott Pohl, a radio news reporter for WKAR in East Lansing, Michigan; Robert Gould, television journalist and instructor at Michigan State University; and Naomi Creason, city editor for the Carlisle (Pennsylvania) Sentinel.

Numerous organizations, publications and news services gave us permission to quote their stories or republish their photographs: Aaron Bagley, Alamy Stock Photo, American Horse Publications, Andrews McMeel Syndication, AP Photo, Associated Press, The Bakersfield Californian, Biloxi Sun Herald, Brooklyn Daily/Brooklyn Courier, Bruce de Silva, Cagle Cartoons, Cartoonstock, Charleston Gazette, Chicago Tribune, CNN, Daily Bruin, The Daily Pennsylvanian, Delaware Online, The Denver Post, The Detroit News, Dizzi Globile Pty Ltd., Don Stacom, Earthworks, Fairbanks Daily News-Miner, Franklin and Marshall College, Getty Images, The Image Works, International Consortium of Investigative Journalists, iStockphoto, Jarrett Hill, Jennifer Bogo, Joe Hight, John Atkinson, John Guilfoil, Kentucky Kernel, LA Times, Lansing State Journal, Lincoln Journal, Mark Anderson, Mercury News, The Morning Call, National Press Photographers Association, NME, NPR News Now, The Oklahoman, Omaha World-Herald, Pew Research Center, The New York Times, The New Yorker, NY Daily News, The Philadelphia Inquirer, Politifact, The Poynter Institute, Portland Press Herald, Press Institute, Reporter's Committee for Freedom of the Press, Reuters, San Francisco Chronicle, Shutterstock, Society of Professional Journalism, Tampa Bay Times, TBC Media, Texas Monthly, Toronto Star, University of Washington, The Washington Post, Western Morning News, WildJunket.com, ZUMA Press, Inc.

The following professionals completed the "Pro Challenge" exercises: Naomi Creason of The Sentinel in Carlisle, Pennsylvania; Leah Farr, director of strategic communications for ABWE International in New Cumberland, Pennsylvania; Ryan Marshall, reporter for the Frederick (Maryland) News Post; Carolyn Swift Lasako, formerly of The (Easton, Maryland) Star Democrat; Liz Vargo Kemmery, formerly of the Waynesboro (Pennsylvania) Record Herald and now director of creative services at Shippensburg University of Pennsylvania; and Brendan deRoode West, formerly of The Times-Tribune in Scranton, Pennsylvania and now an editorial manager for Penn Foster.

Additional thanks for reviews and editing go to colleagues Geri Alumit Zeldes, Michigan State University, and Patricia Mills, independent writing professional and formerly of Ball State University; and to Serena Carpenter, Nicholas J. Robinson and Julie Goldsmith, while they were students at Michigan State University. Thanks also to Jason Greene for reviews, Rachael Greene for pop culture examples, Duygu Kanver for research and Jen Ware for contributing augmented content in the prior (11th) edition.

For their insightful comments and useful suggestions during the development process, thanks go to Marie Carey, University of Massachusetts; Michael A. Deas, Northwestern University; Mark Grabowski, Adelphi University; Catherine M. Hastings, Susquehanna University; Holly Hepp-Galvan, Fordham University and College of Mount Saint Vincent; Roberta Kelly, Washington State University; Tim Nicholas, Mississippi College; Emmanuel U. Onyedike, Virginia Union University; Lisa Pecot-Hebert, University of Southern California; John Roche, Marist College; Merwin Sigale, Miami Dade College; Maggie Lamond Simone, SUNY Oswego; Robert D. Spurrier, Endicott College; Stan Zoller, Lake Forest College; and, all of those reviewers who have chosen to remain anonymous.

We would also like to thank the staff at Oxford University Press. They have worked wonders with making the text more visual, colorful, rigorous and intellectually challenging for instructors and their students. Our thanks go to Acquisitions Editor Toni Magyar, Development Editor Janna Green, Assistant Editor Katlin Kocher, Editorial Director Petra Recter, Senior Production Editor William Murray, Production Manager Lisa Grzan, Art Director Michele Laseau, Marketing Manager Braylee Kremer, and Vice President and Publisher John Challice.

About the Authors

John R. Bender is a professor in the College of Journalism and Mass Communications at the University of Nebraska–Lincoln. Bender worked for six years for the Pittsburg (Kansas) Morning Sun, starting as a reporter covering local government and politics. He became the paper's assignment editor, news editor and then managing editor. During his term as managing editor, the Morning Sun won awards for farm coverage, photography and editorial writing. He has taught at the college or university level for more than 30 years. He was an assistant professor of journalism at Culver-Stockton College in Canton, Missouri, for five years, and he joined the faculty of the University of Nebraska in 1990. His teaching and research areas include news reporting and writing, communications law, media history and controls of information. In 2007, he won a College Award for Distinguished Teaching, and in 2011, he received UNL's James A. Lake Award for his work in promoting academic freedom. He is also a past executive director of the Nebraska High School Press Association. Bender has held a number of faculty governance positions at UNL, including president of the Faculty Senate. His bachelor's degree is in sociology from Westminster College in Fulton, Missouri.

He holds a master's degree in journalism from the University of Kansas and a doctorate in journalism from the University of Missouri at Columbia.

Lucinda D. Davenport is the director of the School of Journalism at Michigan State University, and was a former dean of Graduate Education and Research for the College of Communication Arts and Sciences. She recently received recognition as the Outstanding Woman in Journalism and Mass Communication Education from the Association for Education in Journalism and Mass Communication (AEJMC) Commission on the Status of Women. Teaching awards include the College of Communication Arts and Sciences Faculty Impact Award and the Michigan State University Excellence in Teaching Award. Davenport participates on numerous committees concerning journalism education and has been president of the board of directors for MSU's independent student newspaper. She has several Top Faculty AEJMC awards for her research that focuses on innovative technologies, journalism ethics, data analytics and media history. Davenport has worked as a reporter, broadcast journalist and announcer, public relations practitioner and online news editor. As an undergraduate at Baylor University, she earned a double major in journalism and radio/TV/film. She earned a master's degree in journalism from the University of Iowa and a doctorate in mass media from Ohio University. Both her thesis and dissertation were firsts about online news and information.

Michael W. Drager is an associate professor in the Department of Communication/Journalism at Shippensburg University of Pennsylvania. He graduated with a bachelor's degree in art from Millersville University in Pennsylvania. While working as a newspaper reporter, he earned a master's degree in communication at Shippensburg University. Drager received his doctorate in mass media from Michigan State University. As a journalist, Drager has worked as a reporter, copy editor, editorial writer, columnist and photographer. He has also worked in public relations as a writer and publications designer. As an educator, Drager has 31 years of experience in both public and higher education. He has taught courses in news writing and reporting, news editing and design, digital journalism, public relations writing, photography, photojournalism, magazine design, and media law and ethics. His research explores the relationship between mass media and public policy, and pedagogical approaches to basic writing and editing instruction. In addition, he has conducted workshops and seminars on the relationship between journalism and public institutions. In 2011, Shippensburg University recognized his commitment to diversity by presenting to him the Dr. Martin Luther King Jr. Humanitarian Award.

Fred Fedler taught journalism at the University of Central Florida for 38 years until his retirement in 2008. For 16 years he was the head of the UCF School of Communication's Journalism Division. Fedler received his bachelor's degree from the University of Wisconsin in Madison and then worked as a newspaper reporter in Dubuque and Davenport, Iowa, and as a copy editor in Sacramento, California. He received his master's degree from the University of Kentucky and doctorate from the University of Minnesota. He conducted research in the field of journalism but also wrote freelance for popular publications. Fedler's other books include "Introduction to the Mass Media," "Media Hoaxes" and "Lessons from the Past: Journalists' Lives and Work—1850–1950." In addition, Fedler served on numerous committees concerned with journalism education.

Many students and teachers have written us over the years telling us what they like and dislike about this book and suggesting new features. We have adopted many of those ideas, and we would like to hear from you. If you have a comment or suggestion, please write one of us:

John R. Bender
College of Journalism and Mass Communications
University of Nebraska–Lincoln
Lincoln, Nebraska 68588-0474
jbender1@unl.edu

Lucinda D. Davenport
School of Journalism
Michigan State University
East Lansing, Michigan 48824-1212
ludavenp@msu.edu

Michael W. Drager
Department of Communication/Journalism
Shippensburg University of Pennsylvania
1871 Old Main Drive
Shippensburg, Pennsylvania 17257
mwdrag@ship.edu

THE TOOLS OF JOURNALISM

JOURNALISM TODAY

Any discussion about journalism must include democracy because the history of journalism is intertwined with the history of the United States and its road to liberty for all. Since its birth, America's democratic society and its notion of a free press have served as role models for other countries. "Western thought probably created one idea that was more powerful and enduring than any other," said Tom Rosenstiel, the executive director of the American Press Institute. "It is that people can self-govern. We can be free and lead ourselves. Journalism evolved out of that idea."

The First Amendment states that we are more likely to find truth from a greater diversity of views and information, and the truth shall rise above. However, in today's world, people are exposed to more information than ever before, and they sometimes struggle to sift through the rumors, gossip and facts. It is reporters who make sense of it all and provide knowledge. As Rosenstiel told students at Michigan State University, journalists supply the road map that we can use to navigate civic life.

Journalism is the way in which people learn what is going on in their communities and across the world. It creates our common vocabulary and enriches social connectivity. It provides the foundation of facts by which we think about things. It gives information accurately and in context so that citizens can make good decisions to lead productive lives and compromise with one another. Journalists and the social flow they create are a part of that democratic process. Journalism is an enduring, noble calling.

Technology and Journalism

The fundamental skills of journalists are knowing how to think and distilling information. Reporters' intellectual discipline, their skills and their use of technology have moved them to a higher position than in the past, according

> "The press should be considered not as a fourth branch of government but as an essential counterweight to government, the basic check against abuse of official power."
>
> *Katharine Graham, newspaper publisher*

The People for a Free Press rally was one of several marches held early in Trump's presidency; it responded to his apparent intolerance of news stories and outlets that disagree with his views.

to Rosenstiel. Technology allows us to access mountains of information, and reporters navigate through them to provide knowledge and truth in a context that helps people understand the world and their role in it. Journalists develop an intellectual rigor of looking at the world to uncover truth and can use technology to their advantage.

The basic foundation and principles of journalism have remained constant even while the tools and technologies have changed: Journalists provide news to audiences accurately and ethically. Technology simply provides reporters with different ways to gather, organize, present and distribute information efficiently.

The journalism industry has always applied the strengths of developing technologies to its advantage. The printing press gave people greater access to information than handwritten translations and provided it more quickly and broadly, making it cheaper and improving literacy. The telegraph sent information to distant places more rapidly than carrier pigeons could fly. Typewriters replaced handwritten copy. Trains distributed newspapers to communities faster than the Pony Express or stagecoach did. Photography helped people see events more realistically than drawings; color photos appeared truer to life than black-and-white images; drones captured hard-to-reach images; and 360° cameras gave viewers control over what they saw. The telephone enabled the exchange of information more swiftly than

A typesetter (or compositor) proofs a page of metal type for the Los Angeles Mirror-News in the 1950s.

The publishing process is all computerized today.

letters or personal visits. Radio helped people hear events immediately instead of reading about them later. Television allowed people to watch events as they unfolded; satellite brought global issues into our living rooms 24/7.

As time passed, the internet eliminated the expense of printer's ink and newsprint. Tweets helped gather information and send updates, while reader comments and posts strengthened stories. Today, augmented content offers audiences additional information that is embedded in stories. Virtual reality (VR) and immersive journalism puts audiences inside the story, and live video sharing on social media carries breaking news as it happens.

As these examples show, new forms of journalism emerge as the media landscape constantly evolves. Traditional and newer media continue to compete, then make room for each other and find their niche. Whatever the form—text, audio, video, photograph, documentaries, design, 3-D information graphics, comics, augmented content or VR—journalists provide professionally reported, fact-based content.

Most Americans use multiple devices—television, radio, printed newspapers and magazines, computers, smartphones and tablets—to keep up with the news (see Figure 1.1). The more devices people use, the more they usually follow the news. Consumers turn to digital and printed newspapers and TV more than any other source for reliable news. They often learn about an event from family, friends or social media and then follow up on it with a reputable news outlet. Interestingly, a Pew Research Center study shows that tech-savvy people use traditional media just as much as non-tech-savvy people.

About 40 percent of American adults often get their news from an online source, such as news websites, news apps and social media. Half of the news consumers between the ages of 18 and 49 often get their news online. Facebook and YouTube are the most popular social media sites to find news, according to a Pew study in 2017. The study also found that most social media news consumers still get most of their news from traditional sources.

Information found on social media is problematic. Anyone can say anything, and people often do, to carry out an agenda. For example, "fake news" on social media is usually "click bait." In other words, it is intentionally provocative in order to entice people to click on the story and thus increase the number of views on the website. As Figure 1.2 shows, many people do not trust the news they find on social media. To ensure that online information is reliable, users should always check the original source to confirm it is from a professional journalist and a credible news outlet.

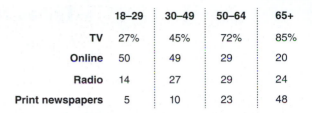

	18–29	30–49	50–64	65+
TV	27%	45%	72%	85%
Online	50	49	29	20
Radio	14	27	29	24
Print newspapers	5	10	23	48

Figure 1.1   Use of News Platforms, by Age Group and Percentage   The majority of Americans across generations use multiple devices to get news. Note: Just 1 percent said they never got news on any platform (not shown).

Source: http://www.journalism.org/2016/07/07/pathways-to-news/

	A lot	Some	Net
Local news orgs	22%	60%	82%
National news orgs	18	59	76
Family, friends & acquaintances	14	63	77

But social media garners less trust than either
% of web-using U.S. adults who trust the information they get from ...

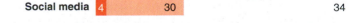

Social media	4	30	34

Figure 1.2   Percentage of People Who Trust the News, by Source
Factors such as fake news and click bait make news from social media sites the least trustworthy format.

Source: http://www.journalism.org/2016/07/07/trust-and-accuracy/

Types of News

Regardless of the medium or technology people use, virtually everyone looks for news. About 75 percent of Americans want news every day, according to the American Press Institute. While people use various devices (e.g., radio, TV, newspapers, laptops) to access news, they turn to four to five different sources. They might go to separate sources for weather (NOAA), sports (ESPN), science (National Geographic), entertainment (TMZ), community news (hometown weekly) and national news stories (NPR), for example.

The source a person uses may depend on the nature of the news, such as a quickly changing event (hurricane), a slow-moving issue (tax reform) or a specific topic (health). Most news topics hold similar interest levels to everyone, regardless of the source and the person's age, socioeconomic status or political leanings (see Table 1.1).

Evolution of the News Business

News is a business. It takes income to pay journalists, buy supplies and maintain equipment to produce the news. Before the 1900s, readers supported newspapers and magazines through circulation (subscriptions and single copy sales). Then advertising became the major revenue source for printed media, TV and radio. Your grandparents and maybe your parents can remember when all radio and television were free. While certain news sources, such as many online newspapers, are free today, the business model of consumers supporting the media is returning. News organizations no longer want to rely on unpredictable

TABLE 1.1 Percentage of People Who Follow News, by Topic and Age Group

Topic	% Who Follow News on This Topic			
	18–29	30–39	40–59	60 and older
Traffic and weather	71	93	81	95
Environment and natural disasters	69	78	74	87
Your local town or city	57	77	79	83
National government and politics	57	79	73	79
Business and the economy	62	67	69	80
Crime and public safety	64	68	62	80
Foreign or international issues	59	78	63	79
Health and medicine	62	57	68	69
Schools and education	49	67	66	56
Science and technology	59	69	53	58
Social issues	64	56	51	54
Sports	41	65	41	50
Lifestyle topics	40	48	45	45
Entertainment and celebrities	58	46	28	31
Art and culture	30	35	27	46

Source: http://www.americanpressinstitute.org/publications/reports/survey-research/personal-news-cycle/

advertisers who can place ads with the competition or eliminate advertising when their budgets are tight.

People are now accustomed to paying for their favorite channel options on cable and satellite TV. They have become familiar with being charged a fee for satellite radio. And they are getting used to the idea that they must pay for news if they want professional and ethical journalists investigating stories—not fake news possibly written by illegitimate sources. For many young people, paying for news is a way of life.

A top reason that consumers pay for news is that the publication excels at covering important subjects. Since the 2016 presidential election, legacy news publications (print and/or digital) have seen dramatic increases in subscriptions. The New York Times experienced record circulation growth—100 percent from the prior year, the best in its history for growth in one quarter—in the months following Trump's election. The Washington Post, The Wall Street Journal and The Atlantic also have experienced continuing upward swings.

Legacy publications are only part of the picture. A national study from the Media Insight Project found that more than half of Americans pay for their news by subscribing to (print or digital) newspapers or magazines, buying news apps or making donations to news media. Specifically, almost 40 percent of millennials (ages 18–34) pay for news. This statistic is supported by a 2017 Reuters digital news report in Politico, which states that millennials are the driving force in this area. Both studies focused on news publications, but the numbers would certainly have been much higher if radio or TV news had been included.

A lot has happened in the news business recently. Some newspapers folded during the Great Recession (2007–2009). Others with economic challenges transitioned from print to digital. Printed community newspapers generally continue to do well because they do not compete for national advertisers or with the internet. Some daily newspapers have private owners, such as Warren Buffett and Jeff Bezos, who invested in the newsroom to improve the product. Others prosper as solely digital products and have hired many full-time journalists, such as HuffPost (started in 2005 and awarded a Pulitzer in 2012) with its many international editions and BuzzFeed (begun in 2006) with about 1,300 employees in 18 cities worldwide. Bloomberg News (started in 1990), which reports on business and finance, began with six people and is now in 72 countries, has 146 news bureaus and employs almost 20,000 people. Barcroft Media (started in the British owner's back bedroom in 2003) pays its journalists an above-average salary of $99,000 and has 2.8 million paid subscribers and 60 million viewers of its Barcroft TV. De Correspondent, a Dutch publication that focuses on investigative reporting, was launched in 2013 by raising $1.7 million in eight days through a crowdfunding campaign. The money came from people who believe professional journalism is important.

Journalism as a Profession

All news outlets need trained journalists with high standards. Reporters are professionals who cover topics with truth, passion and authority. It is a great responsibility to accurately and ethically report news to members of society. People need journalists to sift through mountains of information to report news honestly and in context so that the public knows what is happening and can make informed choices. In order to work together successfully in a democracy,

Reporters work from the makeshift media desk at the Occupy Wall Street protest in New York City.

people need to know the opinions of politicians and others, as well as the effects that issues have on citizens.

The most essential tools for journalists are not dependent on a computer but on their minds and hearts. They are the very human qualities of curiosity, integrity and empathy, coupled with the storyteller's tools—scene, metaphor and imagery, said Poynter Institute's Chip Scanlon. Furthermore, managers of online websites told researcher Max Magee that the top requirements for story editing are news judgment and knowledge of grammar and style; for content creation, the ability to report and write original stories and edit visuals; and for attitudes and overall skills, attention to detail, communication skills, the ability to multitask and an awareness or ability to learn new technologies.

Journalism Competencies

The Poynter Institute developed a pyramid of journalism competencies that identifies the ideal attributes of a journalist (see Figure 1.3). Reporters do not need to be experts in all the areas included, but they should be versatile and conversant in them. The following list takes a closer look at each element.

- **Judgment:** Along with evidence, this competency is the cornerstone of the pyramid. Decisions on what to publish are generally based on two questions: Is it important? And, is it interesting? Some stories are important but not immediately interesting or vice versa, and other stories fall into both areas. Journalists become experts in recognizing the stories that matter and that are sometimes invisible to others. They make their stories relevant to audiences so that consumers understand the impact of the information.

- **Evidence:** Reporters gather and verify information and present stories of public interest. They collect information through various methods, including examining documents, interviewing, observing and analyzing data. Journalists verify information through triangulation, which means using more than one source to determine whether something is true.

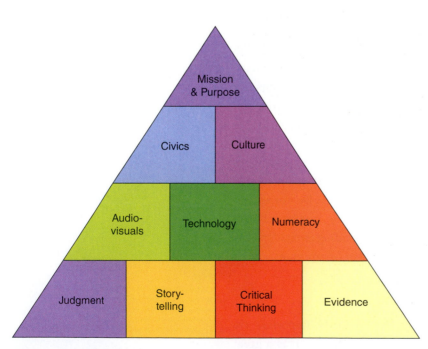

Figure 1.3   The Pyramid of Journalism Competence   This diagram encapsulates the various skills journalists need.

Source: https://www.poynter.org/news/pyramid-journalism-competence-what-journalists-need-know

- **Storytelling:** The best storytellers are those who give audiences a unique experience. Journalists are versatile in telling stories in different genres and forms for different media and audiences. They know grammar and punctuation rules and use news elements to transform information into narratives. Stories are not simply reports.
- **Critical thinking:** Journalists look at patterns and trends as they interpret information for audiences. They give context to facts by asking such questions as, "Why is this person saying this?" and "Why now?"
- **Numeracy:** Numbers help make sense of the world. Knowing how to adjust for inflation, break down tax increases and use spreadsheets enables reporters to perform their watchdog role. Many corrupt politicians and corporations have been exposed through the use of numbers.
- **Technology:** Technology provides different ways to gather, organize, present and disseminate information. Journalists use technology to do their jobs better. They also think about the ways that people use media.
- **Audiovisuals** (multimedia journalism): Journalists are able to shoot video, interview sources and write with just their cellphone. Some reporters combine these elements in a story. Being versatile with audio and visuals enables journalists to improve storytelling. Photography, video, sound bites, data visualization and design are all elements to consider when gathering information in the field and presenting the story in different media.
- **Civics:** Knowledge about the foundations of democracy, government processes, politics, history and power within communities helps journalists to ask the right questions and put information into context for audiences.
- **Culture:** Society is made up of all types of people whose points of view should be represented in the news. Journalists are sensitive to including diversity and respectful of different points of view. Understanding others—different genders, ages, races, religions, ethnicities, abilities, sexual orientations and socioeconomic levels—is as important when reporting within a local community as it is when working as a foreign correspondent in another country.
- **Mission and purpose:** This element represents the pyramid's apex. A clear sense of the purpose of journalism determines its relevancy in society. Knowledge about ethics, standards, journalism history, the First Amendment, democracy, law and social contracts informs the role of journalism in local communities and in the global village.

The Modern Journalist

Journalists have the option to provide news in more formats and platforms than ever before. As more people access news online, journalists learn web publishing software, record and edit audio and visual clips and use social media. In traditional reporting, journalists gather information from documents, interview sources, write the story and publish it in print or broadcast. While the writing process is essentially the same, the advent of digital media opened new avenues in storytelling. Digital media allow journalists to combine more text and visual elements to create story packages. Stories can include various combinations of text, audio, video, photo slideshows with music or narration, 3-D information graphics, animation, comics and virtual reality.

The Modern Journalist

For instance, a newspaper journalist covering a state Senate race writes stories about the campaign and the candidates as they give speeches and meet voters. The stories appear in both print and web editions. The print story may run with a photograph or illustration of a candidate or a bar chart of candidates' popularity among various communities. In the not-too-far future, audiences will be able to scan the printed text with their smartphone for audio or video that demonstrates or supplements what the text describes. This is called augmented content.

The web package includes all the elements of the print edition and can augment its story (without scanning) with audio and video podcasts of an interview with each candidate. It can link to the candidates' websites with their party platforms, to a government site with voter registration information, to a nonpartisan site with the incumbent's voting record, to sites representing issues the candidates support or oppose and to their blogs. The package also may contain a 3-D map of communities that candidates visited, an animated timeline of the election race, a photo slideshow and more. A comment section allows readers to post their thoughts on the story or the candidates. Tweeting the story alerts followers about election coverage updates.

Regardless of the platform, journalists never lose sight of the most important element: the story. And, the most important part of the story is the writing. Reporters write effectively for a standard story in print and broadcast, a digital news package, a blog or a tweet. Versatility is a key skill for today's journalists—this textbook examines the breadth and depth of news reporting and writing across storytelling forms and media platforms, giving a full picture of the modern journalist.

Journalism Style

Journalism graduates should be able to walk into any newsroom and immediately write a story using standard guidelines that professionals follow. This textbook and your instructor will show you the standard Associated Press (AP)-style copy-editing symbols and format generally accepted by news organizations all over the world. (Please see the inside front cover for these symbols.) Knowing the guidelines makes it possible for journalists to move seamlessly from one news organization to another.

AP Stylebook

The reason professional news stories from across the country can be read easily is they are written in a consistent style. This consistency helps journalists in any news organization know, for example, when the street suffix should be spelled out or abbreviated (Avenue or Ave.) and how to correctly write and punctuate times (two o'clock, 2 o'clock, 2:00 p.m. or 2 p.m.) and dates (January 3, 2015, or Jan. 3, 2015).

The Associated Press Stylebook and Briefing on Media Law is the style reference for journalists—writers, reporters, editors and students. Learning the guidelines becomes easy with practice. (The most common ones are included in Appendix B.)

Journalism Terms

Journalists do not use jargon—terminology specific to a field—in their stories, but there is journalism jargon used within the profession. For example, if reporters talk about "the third graph," they are referring to a third paragraph of text and not a visual information graphic within the story. Here are some other common terms and their definitions:

Byline: Name of the journalist(s) who reported and wrote the story.

Copy: Written version or draft of the story. This term is a holdover from when reporters would keep an original of the story and give editors a copy to review.

Dateline: City or town, if outside the local area, where the story took place, followed by an em dash (e.g., "AUSTIN, Texas—").

Graph or graf: Abbreviation of "paragraph."

Headline: Title that summarizes the story, usually written by the editor before the story is published.

Lead or lede: News peg. This is the sentence(s) that encapsulates why the story is worthwhile. It is often the first sentence that summarizes the who, what, where, when, why and how. Students frequently confuse the lead with the headline.

Slug: Two or three words to describe the story uniquely, placed in the top left corner of the copy's first page. The second line is the journalist's name, and the third line is the date. The slug might be duplicated on each page of the story.

Copy-Editing

Reporters edit and correct their stories on computers before sending the final version to an editor. Sometimes the editor prints out the story (or "copy") to review it. The corrections are inserted in the digital copy or the printed story, and it is returned to the reporter for revisions. The process of reviewing, revising and proofreading stories is called "editing." Many instructors require students to print out and edit their stories using standard copy-editing symbols.

Copy Format

Journalists have developed a unique format for their stories that is relatively consistent from one newsroom to another (Figure 1.4). Instructors require students to follow the same format with minor variations. For example, some who review printed copy may require students to begin stories one-third of the way

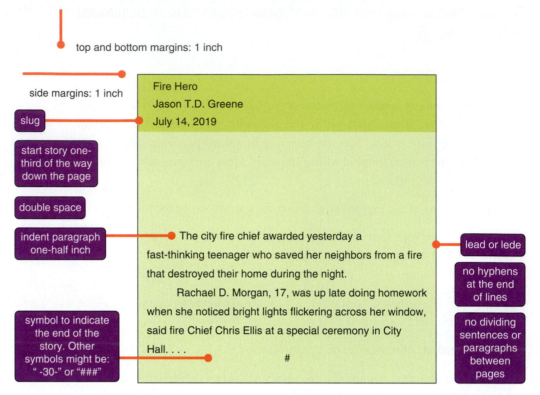

top and bottom margins: 1 inch

side margins: 1 inch

slug

start story one-third of the way down the page

double space

indent paragraph one-half inch

symbol to indicate the end of the story. Other symbols might be: " -30-" or "###"

Fire Hero
Jason T.D. Greene
July 14, 2019

    The city fire chief awarded yesterday a fast-thinking teenager who saved her neighbors from a fire that destroyed their home during the night.
    Rachael D. Morgan, 17, was up late doing homework when she noticed bright lights flickering across her window, said fire Chief Chris Ellis at a special ceremony in City Hall. . . .

#

lead or lede

no hyphens at the end of lines

no dividing sentences or paragraphs between pages

Figure 1.4   Journalists format their copy so that it can be edited and read easily.

down the page; they use the blank space for their comments. They might also ask students to type the word "more" at the end of the first page (to indicate that the story continues on another page), head the additional pages with the slug and a page number and type an end symbol at the bottom of the story. Other instructors might review the story electronically and not need these considerations.

The objective of this textbook is to act as a springboard, training students in the fundamentals of news judgment, critical thinking and writing. Students who are thoroughly practiced in these fundamentals adapt their knowledge and expertise to all forms of news and media that they might experience as they move from one interesting job to another during their journalism career.

The Writing Coach

The "N.E.R.D." Factor in Getting a Job

BY JOE HIGHT

When you graduate from college, it's important that you gain the "N.E.R.D. I.Q." in your job search.

That means:

N—Networking/names. Get to know people in your career field and the place where you want to work.

E—Earn awards and seek additional training. Develop skills that will enable you to win or place in awards contests. Then attend the awards ceremonies if at all possible. People who do hiring attend these ceremonies or hear about people who win awards. And *never* stop learning! Seek training that will enable you to pick up new skills or improve current ones.

R—Resume. You need a short cover letter, one-page resume and five to seven examples of your work neatly packaged together. Put phone numbers, email address and mailing on both the cover letter and resume. The purpose: To get a phone call for an interview.

D—Determination. Call if you don't hear from the person to whom you sent your job application (or send a polite email). Don't give up. If you don't get a job immediately, keep trying and ask the paper to keep your resume on file. Send a new one every year or after a significant change (award, major job, etc.). You'll have an advantage.

I—Interview skills. Wear nice clothes that are appropriate to the particular workplace. Don't slump in the chair. Talk about what makes you the best candidate for the job. Make eye contact. Send a thank-you note afterward.

Q—Questions. Be prepared to ask them. Never, never forget to ask questions when you're asked. Let the interviewer know that you know about the company.

Joe Hight has been editor of the Colorado Springs (Colorado) Gazette and the Oklahoman of Oklahoma City. He is now the owner and president of Best of Books, Inc.

SELECTING AND REPORTING THE NEWS

At the 2013 Boston Marathon, bombs exploded amid thousands of shocked spectators as they cheered runners to the finish line. Runners' legs fell out from under them from the force of the blast and bystanders crumpled to the sidewalk after being hit with shrapnel. Pandemonium broke out as shop windows burst, screaming people ran and frantic police searched for the source of the explosions, which killed three people and injured 264 others. Three days later, the FBI identified brothers Tamerlan and Dzhokhar Tsarnaev as suspects. Tamerlan was killed during police pursuit; Dzhokhar was arrested after a four-day manhunt, when police found him hiding inside a boat in a Bostonian's backyard.

The bombing touched many lives and captured top headlines all over the world for weeks. Six million people watched television news immediately after the bombing and more than 40 million tuned in to the last three hours of the manhunt. Millions more turned to their mobile devices and computers to read journalists' tweets, blogs and stories on news websites, while others read text messages from friends or relatives in Boston. Some news seekers connected with friends on social media, such as Facebook or Twitter, to discuss what they read or saw on websites or television. The event continues to be in the news, with stories on the survivors, plans for a memorial and the release of two movies about the attack.

Editors and news producers from all over the country had no difficulty determining what to cover the day after the bombing: There was only one news story. Even when the following days brought many compelling stories, editors emphasized similar ones because they applied the same sets of news values— values they developed through years of experience. As time went on, many perspectives emerged. Using their news judgment, journalists filed thousands

When major events such as the Boston Marathon bombing happen, there is little doubt as to the importance of the story. The question becomes how to tell it.

of stories with local and national angles, focusing on the significant and interesting details.

News judgment is a learned art. Journalists select stories from the many events and issues happening locally and globally. These stories inform, educate or entertain their particular readers, viewers or listeners. Editors determine the angle or element of the story that is most important to this audience.

News Characteristics and News Elements

Newsworthiness can vary from small towns to metropolitan areas. Although no single definition acknowledges all the factors affecting the selection process, journalists agree that news stories possess certain values. Jack Hart, former managing editor of The (Portland) Oregonian, says a good story should have the following characteristics: (1) an interesting central character who (2) faces a challenge or is caught up in a conflict and (3) whose situation changes as (4) action takes place in (5) an engaging setting.

Most journalists say that newsworthy stories possess the classic news values (or news elements) of timeliness, impact or magnitude, prominence, proximity, unusualness, and conflict.

Timeliness

News is so named because it is information about an issue or event that has just happened (e.g., minimum wage increases going into effect) or that is new to audiences (e.g., city council members taking extravagant trips on taxpayers' dime). Reporters stress current information—stories occurring today or yesterday, not

Bottled water is delivered to a fire station in Flint, Michigan. Lawsuits regarding the state's and city's roles in the water crisis continue to be filed.

several days or weeks ago—and report it accurately. For example, residents of Flint, Michigan, wanted up-to-the-minute information on why the water in their homes was brown and what the health ramifications were. They looked to journalists to tell them where to buy bottled water, how lead poisoned the water, how long they would be without tap water and who was responsible for the crisis.

Radio, TV and the web are ideal media for publishing the latest information while newspapers and magazines offer new, in-depth information with more developed angles and added content. No matter the medium, reporters always look for fresh angles and new details to build their stories. They feature the newest information early in the story and keep older, background information to a minimum, weaving it throughout or adding it at the end.

Journalism students often borrow ideas from existing stories. However, the original idea has probably lost its timeliness and is no longer new to the public. And "borrowing" is a slippery slope. In addition to borrowing other people's ideas, students may be tempted to use or paraphrase quotes from a published story or press release. This practice is unethical if it appears as though the student interviewed the source. It is plagiarism if he or she presents the work as his or her own and does not attribute it to the original reporter or news source.

Impact or Magnitude

Journalists choose stories that affect (impact) large numbers of people (magnitude). An international agreement to collaborate in the fight against ISIS is important news because the group's terrorist acts affect many countries and people around the world. The disappearance of a plane with 239 people on board is more newsworthy than the story of one missing person because more families and friends are involved. Similarly, a new state law prohibiting the use of mobile devices while driving affects more people than a law restricting anyone under 18 from using tanning salons.

Prominence

Routine events can become newsworthy when they involve prominent individuals, such as state senators, business leaders or celebrities. For example, if a classmate appeared drunk at a party and stated that cocaine ought to be legalized, it would not be as newsworthy as if your governor did so. That's a double whammy.

Ordinary people may become prominent when they are involved in a news event. When a crime is committed or an accident occurs, the media will name the adult suspects or victims. Once the story runs through a news cycle and is no longer considered newsworthy, the subject's status usually diminishes. The Elizabethan phrase "nine-days wonder" and Andy Warhol's reference to "15 minutes of fame" refer to short-lived publicity. The news story might be short-lived to audiences, but it might have a life-long effect on the people involved; therefore, journalists treat subjects with sensitivity.

Proximity

Proximity may be geographic or psychological. In terms of the former, an event becomes more newsworthy the more local it is. Readers, viewers and listeners are most interested in and affected by stories about their own communities and people they know. The Boston Marathon bombing was covered more extensively—with more in-depth stories and for a longer period of time—in Boston and the surrounding New England area than in other parts of the United States and the world. Residents in other states were intensely interested in the event, but fewer were as likely to be personally affected as those in Boston. Other news organizations did not cover up-to-the-minute events as they unfolded in the city, but they found local angles to connect their communities to the tragedy, such as a resident who ran in the marathon or the relative of a victim.

Psychological proximity refers to an emotional connection to an event. For example, audiences throughout the world are riveted to news stories about school shootings because they also have families and worry that their children's school could be next. Two individuals separated by thousands of miles but sharing a characteristic or an interest may want to know more about each other. An American mother may sympathize with the problems of a mother in a distant country. College students everywhere often have similar concerns.

Prince Harry and Meghan Markle pose for photos after announcing their engagement. Although engagements are a common occurrence, those involving royalty and celebrities garner more attention from the public and the press.

Unusualness

Deviations from the norm—unexpected or unusual events, drama or change—are more newsworthy than the commonplace. A story of a robber who returned a victim's cellphone because he did not like the model is more newsworthy than one about a robber who simply stole a phone.

Journalists are alert for the unusual twists in otherwise mundane stories. For example, fires might receive only a brief mention if there is no significant damage and no one is harmed. However, the circumstances surrounding a house fire in rural Pennsylvania captured attention: A member of a conservative religious sect set the fire to punish three people from his church because he thought they were sinners. In an editor's mind, this story does not occur every day, and it was front-page news.

Critics charge that the media's emphasis on the unusual gives audiences a distorted view of the world. They say that the media fail to portray the lives of normal people on a typical day in a typical community. Editors respond that, because it is impossible to cover every piece of news, they report issues requiring the public's attention. Even so, journalists also report on more common events, such as individuals helping others in need, organizations striving to improve literacy rates and programs working to reduce or defeat domestic violence.

Conflict

Conflict is apparent when people have different points of view. Their reasons for disagreeing about a social issue or government policy are more informative than the reasons of people who agree on everything. Conflict among government officials or agencies, private organizations or individuals often provides readers, viewers and listeners with different opinions about issues or resolutions that might affect them. Furthermore, it makes a story more interesting.

Conflict may also be internal to an individual. The student secretly living out of her car while working her way through college may face personal embarrassment and time and resource conflicts. A war amputee may struggle to live his life differently than before the war. In each of these stories, the conflict can be positive. Conflict can exist in any story.

Other Characteristics

Dozens of other factors affect journalists' selection of news and their efforts to inform, educate or entertain audiences. You probably recognize the following types of news stories.

- Reporters look for humorous stories—anything that will make the audience laugh.
- They report straightforward events—storms, earthquakes, assassinations—to help audiences learn more about what is happening in the community and elsewhere.
- They investigate complex issues that affect individuals and communities, such as the risks and benefits of opening a halfway house for former prison inmates. Journalists use their professional training to gather, sift through, organize and clearly explain complicated phenomena. The internet and computer-assisted reporting (CAR) skills help them access and analyze information to present it concisely, and their ability to identify and interview people affected differently by an issue brings the data to life.

The Nature of the Medium and the Community

Other news characteristics are shaped by the type of medium. Printed daily newspapers emphasize local events occurring during the last 24 hours but provide updates on their website. Large metropolitan dailies cover their communities but may also include extensive national and international coverage. Weekly community newspapers focus on local news that has happened in the last seven days. Some weekly news magazines report events of national interest in more depth and explain an event's significance; others summarize interesting and important news events that happened in the past week. Television reports headline news—pertinent information about the day's major stories. Broadcasters also favor visual stories (ones with strong, dramatic pictures) over stories that are complicated and difficult to illustrate. Commercial radio reports the news in a few sentences, while public radio gives news more airtime to cover stories in greater depth. All types of news organizations use social media to share quick updates on breaking news. Journalists tweet a new story in 280 characters, and they blog to add fresh perspectives on the beat they cover.

A news organization's size and the community it serves also influence news selection. A news organization in a small town may report several local traffic accidents; one in a medium-sized city may cover only those that cause serious injury; and one in a big city may report only those that involve prominent people or tie up traffic for several hours. Community or weekly newspapers often publish news of all sports events, from little tyke to high school competitions, and every wedding and engagement announcement. Metropolitan newspapers may report only professional and major college sports teams and may be more selective about what social announcements they publish.

News organizations also develop tendencies and traditions to emphasize some types of news stories over others. The New York Post traditionally focuses on crime, sports and photographs. The New York Times, which appeals to a wealthier, better educated audience than the Post, places a greater emphasis on political, business and foreign news.

Many people subscribe to several news sources to get comprehensive news. Their community newspaper and local TV offer local news; the nearby metropolitan newspaper and website provide state and regional news; and national news organizations, such as the Wall Street Journal, USA Today or National Public Radio, cover events unfolding across the United States and in other countries.

Types of News

Journalists recognize two major types of news: hard and soft. "Hard news" usually refers to serious and timely stories about important topics that inform or educate. These stories may describe an accident, major crime, fire, speech or press conference. Journalists sometimes call hard news "spot news" (reporting it on the spot), "straight news" (not fluff), or "breaking news" (events occurring or "breaking" now).

"Soft news" usually refers to feature or human-interest stories. Soft news entertains as well as informs; it may make readers laugh or cry, love or hate, envy or pity. Soft news might be a profile of a local person who has risen to prominence or a story about an unusual hobby (teaching dogs to "talk"), a "how to" (have a successful job interview), home decor (front-yard snow sculptures), or history (the first newspaper in the state was started in your town). Although still newsworthy, soft news often is less timely than breaking news. Consequently, editors can delay soft stories to make room for more timely items. See Table 2.1 for examples of hard and soft news, as well as the other characteristics discussed so far in this chapter.

Neil Maes (left) prepares for the Scripps National Spelling Bee with the help of his parents, Peter and Christy. Eleven-year-old Maes, who is deaf, uses bilateral cochlear implants and other assistive devices in his spelling competitions. Stories on Maes' experience are examples of soft news pieces.

TABLE 2.1 Applying the Elements of News

Element	Example
Timeliness	Two bombs exploded at the finish line of the Boston Marathon earlier today.
Impact or magnitude	About 27,000 runners and 500,000 spectators from across the globe attended the Boston Marathon.
Prominence	President Obama at the White House reassured Americans that all questions about the bombings would be answered. "We will get to the bottom of this. And we will find out who did this; we'll find out why they did this. Any responsible individuals, any responsible groups will feel the full weight of justice," he said.
Proximity	Two sisters from our city who ran in the Boston Marathon are coming home today.
Unusualness	While thousands of spectators ran away from the explosions, many others ran toward the chaos to help others.
Conflict	President Obama called the bombings an act of terrorism.
Hard news	Dzhokhar Tsarnaev pleaded not guilty to 30 federal counts in his first court appearance today.
Soft news	The Boston Marathon is the world's oldest annual sporting event and is held on Patriot's Day, the third Monday in April.

🔥 HOT TIP

Public Journalism

In covering public affairs, or civic events and issues, reporters engage audiences in public debate by asking the following questions, sometimes called the five W's and H. The why and how of a story sometimes are not confirmed until later:

- **Who** is involved, cares, is affected, needs to be included, has a stake, is missing from this discussion?

- **What** happened, are the consequences, does it mean to citizens, would this accomplish, values are at work?

- **When** did this happen, were things different, can things be different, should talk lead to action?

- **Where** did it happen, are we headed, is the common ground, should debate take place, is the best entry point for citizens?

- **Why** did it happen, is this happening, do we need discussion, are things not happening, should we care?

- **How** did it happen, does it affect civic life, did the community cope, does my story encourage action or help the public decide?

The Concept of Objectivity

News stories must be objective, or free of any reporter bias or opinion. Journalists gather information and report it as accurately as possible—they should not comment, interpret or evaluate. If an issue is controversial, they interview representatives of all sides involved and include as many views as possible. Some sources may make mistakes, and some may lie. Journalists may point out inconsistencies or inaccuracies in sources' statements, but they should not call people liars.

Biases, whether intentional or not, often appear in a story when a reporter covers only one side of an issue or gives one side more space or time than others. By going beyond one or two sources and treating all sides of an issue fairly, journalists provide their audiences with the facts they need to understand a story more fully. Total objectivity is an ideal; nonetheless, balance and fairness can be achieved through thorough reporting and clear writing.

Routine newsroom practices encourage impartiality. For example, several reporters may contribute information to a story another reporter writes. Several editors may then evaluate and edit the story. Team members serve as checks on one another: If one expresses an opinion in a story, another has a chance to detect and eliminate that bias.

Objectivity is important in public affairs, or civic, journalism. Supporters base public journalism on a fundamental concept of democracy espoused by former president James Madison: By participating in the governing of themselves, people preserve democracy. To achieve this kind of democracy, the press must inform the citizenry. This process allows the public to decide what is important. Professor Jay Rosen, a leading advocate of public journalism, has a philosophy about the field's proper task: Journalists should do what they can to support public life. The press should help citizens participate in public life and take them seriously when they do. It should create and nourish the sort of public talk some might call a deliberative dialogue. Most important, perhaps, journalists must see hope as an essential resource that they cannot deplete indefinitely without costs to the community.

To accomplish these goals, journalists must listen to all voices, not just the loudest, and listen particularly to those people whose views on issues fall near the center, not just those at the extremes. The routine five W and H questions (who, what, when, where, why and how) work well, but they may not be the only ones to ask.

Reporters explore the layers of civic life in their communities and are aware of the different neighborhoods because people in these areas may have various experiences and opinions regarding issues. Finally, reporters identify the community leaders who can be engaged as sources. Community leaders are not limited to elected officials: Private citizens can also be knowledgeable sources regarding issues facing a community.

What Is Not Newsworthy?

Reporters recognize what information is newsworthy as well as what is not. They rarely mention routine or expected procedures, such as that a city council met in a city hall and began its meeting with the Pledge of Allegiance. They also delete the obvious and the irrelevant, for example, that police officers rushed to the scene of a traffic accident or an ambulance carried the injured to a hospital. In most of the following cases, journalists ask if the information is central to the story.

Offensive Details

Editors generally omit material that is obscene, gruesome or in poor taste, usually on the grounds that their stories reach children as well as adults. What is the purpose of showing grisly photographs or video of a victim if the item's focus is to bring attention to a fourth accident at a particular intersection with a broken traffic light?, for example. Normally, news organizations avoid specifics about sexual assaults and omit most graphic or bloody details about accidents because they do not add to the point of the story.

Sensationalism

Most news organizations avoid sensationalism but not sensational stories. Historically, the word "sensationalism" has described an emphasis on or exaggeration of stories dealing with crime, sex and oddities. However, some events—presidential assassinations, wars and disasters—are inherently sensational and legitimate news.

Despite its motto of being fair and balanced, Fox News has been criticized for being biased. In 2017, the network changed its slogan to "Most Watched, Most Trusted."

Journalists evaluating a potentially sensational story, or potentially scandalous information to include within a story, ask themselves the following questions:

- Is the story newsworthy and important to the community? If so, how?
- Does each piece of information add to the reason for writing the story?
- Does the public need and have a right to this information?
- Whom will this story or piece of information help, and how many?
- Whom will this story or piece of information harm, and how many?
- How will people react to the information?

Rumors

Social media gaffes have reinforced the need for professional journalists. Anyone can tweet a comment or rumor—if it is repeated enough times, people assume it must be true. Journalists do not assume; instead, they investigate the veracity of rumors. If they find no evidence that one is true, they usually conclude that there is no story. However, editors may decide that a story exposing a prevalent false rumor will be more helpful to the people involved (e.g., by clearing a person's reputation) or the community (e.g., by eliminating general anxiety) than if they remained silent. If a rumor is true and important to the public, editors may run it as a well-researched story.

Sexual Assault

Most news organizations refuse to identify victims of sexual assault, even when they have a legal right to do so. Some journalists believe that publishing the names of victims may discourage others from reporting assaults.

At the time of writing, more than 80 women have accused film producer Harvey Weinstein of sexual assault. Whereas victims usually prefer privacy, most of these women are celebrities and accustomed to public attention. They have also come forward to encourage and support other women who have been assaulted.

Names of Juveniles

The news media generally do not identify juveniles accused or convicted of a crime unless they are tried as adults for a serious offense, such as murder. In many cases, the names are withheld until authorities have filed charges and prosecutors have decided to try juvenile defendants as adults. However, high-profile mass shootings receive so much media attention that the victims and shooters often are quickly identified.

Trade Names

Some editors hesitate to mention trade names because they think it is unnecessary and provides free advertising for the products. Although specific names can add detail, which is important to a story, reporters should use generic names unless a trade name is pertinent or helps readers gain understanding. "Soft drink" is an acceptable generic term for Dr Pepper or Sierra Mist. Similarly, a journalist should report that someone used a "tissue" rather than a Kleenex or made a "photocopy" rather than a Xerox.

The Importance of Accuracy

Errors affect the public's perception of the media and ultimately the media's credibility with the public. Editors, instructors and the public do not tolerate sloppiness of any kind, and they are particularly critical of errors in spelling, names and facts because there is rarely any excuse for them. Reporters who repeatedly submit stories with errors may be suspended or fired and have a hard time finding another job.

Accuracy in Facts

Professional journalists do their best to report the news as fairly and accurately as possible. And they do a good job: The information appearing daily in the various media across the globe is overwhelmingly accurate. Still, errors do get reported, and they can hurt the people involved in a story.

For example, three days after the Boston Marathon bombing, the front page of the New York Post featured a photograph showing two men with backpacks; the accompanying story said they were suspects. In fact, the photo was of Salaheddin Barhoum, 16, and Yassine Zaimi, 24, who were simply spectators and avid runners. Their backpacks were filled with running gear. Yet both men say that they suffered emotional and reputational injury as a result of being falsely identified as suspects. Inaccuracies can also be costly: The newspaper settled a defamation suit with both men for an undisclosed amount.

Carelessness, laziness and hurrying through a story cause most factual errors. After finishing a news story, reporters must recheck their notes to be sure it is accurate. Journalists never guess or assume the facts. If they lack some information, they consult their sources again. If the sources are unavailable or unable to provide the information, reporters may have to delete portions of the story or, in extreme cases, kill the entire item.

"Fake news" has become a catch-all phrase that frequently is used incorrectly. President Trump uses the term in attempts to discredit news outlets and stories he does not like. Journalists do not participate in fake news or alternative facts, which is deliberate misinformation. They do not use quotes from sources in their stories without checking the veracity of the information and the reliability of the source. Their job is to pursue accuracy; otherwise, mistakes can lead to incorrect labels of "fake news" or "alternative facts."

Journalists research and learn a topic in order to write about it. Too often, when asked about a fuzzy sentence or paragraph, beginners respond, "I really didn't understand that myself." If the reporter does not understand something he or she has written, neither will the audience. Reporters who do not understand information return to their source and ask for a better explanation or find a source who can explain it.

Journalists also use words they know. Sometimes students incorrectly repeat words or phrases they do not understand but have obtained from a document, website or interview. For example, if a reporter uses the word "decibel," he or she should

Infowars.com, a site managed by Alex Jones, features fake news and conspiracy theories.

know exactly how loud a decibel is in order to put the word in context for audiences.

Accurate writing requires specifics instead of generalities. Getting specifics requires more effort, but in the end the story will be clearer, more accurate and more interesting to readers, viewers and listeners. Journalists ask sources, "How do you know?" and they ask for examples. The response may provide additional sources for information.

Reporters are vulnerable to misinformation because many people want to publicize their views. Journalists might interview sources who have impressive titles or sound as if they know what they are talking about. But some sources may be ignorant of the facts, and others may lie. The reporter's job is to separate assertions from facts. A news organization's most important asset is its credibility, and managers protect that asset.

Accuracy in Names

Many people—including the authors of this textbook and, perhaps, you—have something in common: Their names are frequently misspelled. Dozens of names have different spellings, such as Ali/Allee, Rachael/Rachel, Jason/Jayson, and Fredrick/Fredric/Frederic/Frederick. Reporters confirm the spelling of names and the use of nicknames.

Most misspellings anger two sets of people—those who were intended to be named and those who are inadvertently named. Reporters verify the spelling of names by consulting a second source, usually a document (such as the telephone book or a city directory) or the internet. Some journalists ask sources to write their name and title, but they always confirm the spelling of both before ending an interview.

Accuracy Is a Priority

Some news organizations maintain a fact database composed of names, places, businesses, dates, and numbers that have all been verified and run in prior stories. Their journalists turn to these databases to check similar facts that appear in new stories.

In an effort to eliminate errors, a few editors may give the people named in news stories an opportunity to read and correct the item before publication. Although science writers and other journalists who deal with complex issues often follow this practice, most prohibit it because sources usually try to change statements they disagree with, not just factual errors. Other editors might ask sources to verify only their statements.

Another practice to prevent errors is to use a checklist such as the one in "The Reporter's Guide" box, on p. 26. Craig Silverman, fake news expert and Buzz-Feed's media editor, has led accuracy workshops at the Poynter Institute and encourages journalists to make up a best practices "to-do" list for news writing. After all, airline pilots review a checklist before every takeoff and travelers often use a checklist for packing.

Guest Columnist

Why I Stayed at a Small-Town Newspaper

BY SUE HADDEN

I'm one of the lucky ones. After 35 years, I still actually enjoy coming to work.

That's because I work for a small-town newspaper (circulation 9,000) that cares about its community. Every single day, my fellow newsroom employees and I have a brand new chance to inform, to inspire and to bring a smile to those who read The Record Herald.

I interview a lot of college graduates eager to land their first jobs. When I ask where they envision themselves in the next five years, most say they hope to land a spot on a big-city daily newspaper, move on to a public relations firm or go to work at a glossy magazine.

That's sad . . . not just for them, but also for small-town journalism.

I grew up in the town that is today such a vital part of my life. Like those fresh graduates, I had my eyes focused on big horizons when I set out to make my mark on the world. But a marriage, a daughter and lots of pleasure trips to far-off places big and small convinced me that the grass is pretty green in my own backyard.

My 17 years as a beat reporter gave me the opportunity to meet people and walk into environments I never knew existed, to ferret out violations of the open records law, to expose skullduggery in public office and to write about wrongs that needed to be righted.

It also gave me the opportunity to spotlight the small-town heroes who quietly meet the needs of those less fortunate, to bring a smile with just three paragraphs and to put everyday people on the front page.

When I learned about an asthmatic who lived in public housing and couldn't afford an air conditioner, I picked up the phone and talked with a human services worker with whom I was on a first-name basis. Now our town has a program that provides fans and air conditioners to the less fortunate.

A story about the poor attendance records of several members of the school board led to an overhaul at election time.

I got to write a feature story about the long-retired fourth-grade teacher who had inspired me to become a writer . . . returning the favor by telling her story using the words she taught me to love.

After an industry that had been in town for more than a century announced plans to build elsewhere, readers told me my commentary captured the emotions of losing an icon that had given employment to grandfathers, fathers, husbands and sons.

It concerns me that fewer and fewer young writers are interested in "paying their dues" at small-town papers like this one. It concerns me even more to see the brightest of them leave for higher paying jobs in bigger places where they'll go from being hometown writers to just another cog in a very big wheel.

Who will write and edit local stories 20 years from now? I fear it will be fleeting journalists who will have very little connection to this community, its history, its places and its people.

The opportunities are huge for those who manage to "catch" small-town journalism fever. At a small paper, you can learn all there is to know about interviewing, writing, layout, photography and copy editing. You have a really good chance of seeing your byline on the front page each and every day.

Complete strangers will feel comfortable about picking up the phone and calling you to offer criticism, advice and tips, and perhaps set you straight on something you missed.

A publisher once told me a good newspaper is one that is in conversation with the community it serves.

I worry that conversation will one day turn to deafening silence.

Sue Hadden worked for 36 years as a staff writer and then editor for The Record Herald in her hometown of Waynesboro, Pennsylvania, until her retirement.

The Reporter's Guide to Accuracy

While Reporting

- Ask sources to spell or write down their names and titles; verify the spellings.
- Record or transcribe interviews.
- When someone cites numbers, ask for (and check) the source.
- Ask, "How do you know that?"
- Seek documentation.
- Verify claims with reliable sources.
- Save links and other research.
- Ask sources what other reports on the subject are wrong.

While Writing

- Note facts that need further verification (highlight, circle, etc.).

Before Submitting (Final Checks)

- Verify numbers and math (have someone else check your math).
- Check names with more than just your notes and one other source.

- Confirm titles (people, books, places, businesses).
- Validate locations.
- Verify quotes with your notes/recording/transcript.
- Confirm attributions.
- Check definitions.
- Confirm that URLs are correct and that the cited content is still there.
- Call phone numbers.
- Ensure that spelling and grammar are correct.
- Look for spell-checker errors.
- Verify or remove assumptions.
- Consult the original source if you have any doubts.
- Clarify by reading the final copy to someone who understands portions where your understanding is weak.

After Filing

- Correct any errors you found in your archives, databases or other resources you control (but be certain you verified the new information).

Adapted from http://stevebuttry.wordpress.com/2011/01/04/ MY-VERSION-OF-CRAIG-SILVERMANS-ACCURACY-CHECKLIST/. Steve Buttry was director of student media at Louisiana State from 2015 until his death in 2017.

Review Exercises

After you complete the following exercises, compare your answers with those of your classmates.

1. News Judgment

You are the editor of a news outlet in your city and have space for one more photo. For each of the following pairs, select the image you would use and explain your choice.

1. a. Kate Middleton visiting a local hospital.

   or

   b. College students protesting the local university's fourth tuition increase in five years.

2. a. Two students from one of your city's elementary schools participating in the semifinals of a national spelling bee.

   or

   b. Three high school seniors being led away in handcuffs after being charged with causing nearly $80,000 in damage to the school, allegedly by spraying fire extinguishers onto computers and into file cabinets and smashing computer monitors and other equipment.

3. a. A young child in Afghanistan handing a bunch of flowers to a U.S. soldier.

   or

   b. The bodies of an Afghan father and his four children killed in a suicide bombing near an American compound in Afghanistan.

2. Newsworthiness

1. Rank the following stories by their newsworthiness for your local news outlet, using 1 for the most newsworthy and 10 for the least newsworthy. You can assume the stories are current. Be prepared to explain your choices.

   1. A large real estate agency in your community has hired two new vice presidents.

   2. The U.S. Department of Education released a report today that shows high school students in your city reached an all-time high in their SAT exam scores.

   3. The state approved a plan to build a six-lane bypass around your city that will cost $584 million and destroy thousands of acres of prime agricultural and developable land.

   4. A city man was charged in an arson fire that destroyed an apartment building and killed eight people, including five children.

   5. FBI investigators visited the public libraries in your city to check on the reading records of several local residents they believe may be linked to terrorism.

   6. Three Israelis and 10 Palestinians were killed in a suicide bombing at a bus stop in a suburb of Tel Aviv.

   7. The parents of quintuplets in your city saw their five children off to school for the first time, as the three boys and two girls were picked up by a bus that took them to kindergarten.

   8. More than 100 people were killed and another 800 injured when a runaway passenger train collided with a freight train in Tanzania.

   9. Tennis star Serena Williams married Reddit founder Alex Ohanian in a fairy-tale wedding.

   10. City officials agreed at the regular council meeting to spend $228 million to build a new trash incinerator that would burn trash from the city as well as from six surrounding counties.

2. Rank the following stories by their newsworthiness for your local news outlet, using 1 for the most newsworthy and 9 for the least newsworthy. Be prepared to explain your choices.

   1. A controversial painting called "The da Vinci Male Mona Lisa," was sold in New York for $450.3 million, the highest amount ever bid for an auctioned work of art.

   2. The driver of a compact car escaped injury early today when her car was struck by a freight train at a railroad crossing.

   3. Police and prison officials in your city were conducting a mock prison escape when three inmates walked out of the prison and disappeared.

   4. A new senior citizens center opened on the east side of the city offering nearby residents a place to get a hot meal at lunchtime, participate in games

and educational programs and pass time with friends.

5. Several long-time residents in the city are being deported, as they are technically undocumented immigrants.

6. An Arkansas woman was convicted in the deaths of her four children who were drowned in the family's bathtub. She was found guilty of four counts of second-degree murder.

7. Your state's Department of Labor and Industry announced today that the unemployment rate rose to 7.5 percent despite a rally that saw significant increases in the stock market.

8. A city police officer was arrested and charged with aggravated assault and using undue force after he broke the leg of a man who was attending a concert. The officer who was on duty patrolling the stadium parking lot mistook the man for a scalper, got into an argument with him and threw him to the ground.

9. A group of teenagers from a nondenominational church youth organization volunteered to help two elderly sisters maintain their home so that they would not be fined by the city for having a blighted property. The youths mowed grass, trimmed hedges and painted the sisters' house.

3. Patricia Richards, a 52-year-old businessperson in your city, today announced that she is running for mayor. You know and can prove all the following facts, but you have never reported them because she was a private citizen. Which ones would you include in your announcement story?

1. She is a cancer survivor.

2. At the age of 17, she and two friends were charged with stealing a car. The charges were dropped because the car was recovered undamaged and the car's owner, a neighbor, declined to prosecute.

3. She established, owns and manages the city's largest chain of furniture stores.

4. She has diabetes.

5. She has been divorced three times.

6. Each year, she donates more than $1 million to local charities that help troubled young women, but always avoids publicity and insists that the charities never mention her donations.

7. She is a recovering alcoholic; she has not had a drink in 20 years.

8. Before going into business for herself, she was fired from two other jobs because of her drinking.

9. Her campaign literature says she attended the University of Iowa, yet you find that she never graduated.

10. Various tax and other public records reveal that her chain of furniture stores is valued at $20 million and, last year, earned a profit of $2.3 million.

4. One of your state representatives, Joseph Collins, was involved in a traffic accident that resulted in the death of another driver and his passenger. Collins had minor injuries. Which of the following details would you use in a story on the accident and which would you discard?

1. Collins is married and has two children.

2. As an attorney, Collins successfully defended two people who had been accused of vehicular manslaughter.

3. Collins was speeding and ran a red light.

4. A woman, who didn't want to be identified, called your newsroom and said the minivan she and her children were riding in was almost struck at an intersection one time by a car driven by Collins.

5. Friends of Collins said he often joked about having a "lead foot."

6. Police said alcohol was not a variable in this accident.

7. Collins has had five tickets in the past four years for speeding and reckless driving.

8. Collins was first elected to office nine years ago.

9. The driver of the other car often said he did not vote for Collins.

10. Two people, a male and a female, in response to the accident, called police to accuse Collins of sexual harassment.

NEWSWRITING STYLE

Unlike other forms of writing, journalism is fact-based storytelling to an audience with varied interests, education levels, ages and other demographics. With their good news judgment, journalists identify immediately the importance of a story and its supporting elements. They then communicate how the event is significant to the individual. They present complex information in a way that allows almost everyone to understand it easily. Furthermore, their writing makes audiences want to continue reading, watching or hearing the story.

> "It's as interesting and as difficult to say a thing well as to paint it. There is the art of lines and colours, but the art of words exists too, and will never be less important."
>
> *Vincent van Gogh, artist*

Text and visual journalists achieve this goal by using newswriting style. This method lets them present factual information succinctly and clearly. It also ensures that they follow basic reporting principles: Separate fact and opinion, and remain impartial.

Simplify Words, Sentences and Paragraphs

Table 3.1 provides examples of different writing types: news, fiction and academic. Each is distinctive by its respective style.

A major part of newswriting style is simple language. George Orwell, in his classic "Politics and the English Language," complained that too often writers replace strong verbs and concrete nouns with abstract phrases. Such phrases tend to obscure facts and confuse media audiences. No one wants frustrated readers who must untangle the vague meaning of a word. Similarly, listeners and viewers who are stuck on a phrase miss important information while the news story continues.

CNN's Don Lemon reviews his story before going on air.

Another practice that can cause confusion or missed information is packing too many ideas into a single sentence. Consider the following example:

> The mayor said he was happy that the council had passed the resolution to increase the public library tax to provide more funds to expand the library's book collection, to build a website and to add a new wing to house government documents, but that the amount of the increase was not enough to do everything that has to be done because repairs are needed to the roof of the public library building and facilities must be improved for the disabled.

Now read the revised, clearer version:

> The mayor said he was happy the council passed the resolution increasing the public library tax. The amount of the increase, however, was not enough to do everything that has to be done, he said. The tax increase will

TABLE 3.1 Types of Writing

News story	A third robbery this month at the Starlite Apartments on Washington Street has tenants worried about their safety and building security.
	Two robbers with nylon stocking face masks stole a cellphone, a computer, DVDs and possibly other items at about 11 p.m. yesterday, according to Police Sgt. Katharine Jordan.
	"This has never happened to me before, and it's frightening," said Lyle Bagley, the tenant of the apartment, as he wiped his sweaty palms on his jeans a fourth time in as many minutes. "I thought a deadbolt would keep my stuff and me safe."
Fiction excerpt	Lyle's mind was whirling as he waited for the police to arrive. He was nervous and panicky as he wondered what he could tell them about the robbery. Was it his phone, computer and four DVDs that were stolen . . . or was it five? Were they really taken or had he just left them someplace? Maybe he had left one in his car. Didn't he let his sister borrow a couple? Too bad he hadn't renewed the insurance on his phone—where was he going to get the money for a new one? Was there anything else? He thought he saw the burglars—two guys with masks—he was sure of that—right? Who could it have been? Was it Megan's ex-boyfriend, who always glared at him, and the guy's smarmy younger brother, who tagged along everywhere?
	Lyle collapsed on the bed because he was feeling nauseous and needed to think. Should he move someplace else? Was someone out to get him? Was this just random? It was such a violation of his personal space. Nothing like this had ever happened before.
Academic article	Previous literature has shown that occupants whose homes are vandalized feel a disruptive sense of emotion similar to that of post-traumatic stress disorder (PTSD). The current study used a triangulation of methodologies, such as statistical survey, content analysis and qualitative in-depth interviewing. The researchers analyzed results, taking into account stratified sampling, demographics, dependent and independent variables, standard deviation of probability distribution and margin of error.

provide funds to expand the library's book collection, build a website and add a new wing to house government documents. Other needed work includes repairs to the library's roof and building access for the disabled, the mayor said.

Journalists use short sentences and short paragraphs. They focus on one idea within a sentence or even a paragraph. They rewrite long or awkward sentences and divide them into shorter ones that are easier to read and understand. Research has consistently found a strong correlation between readability and sentence length: The longer the sentence, the more difficult it is to understand. Put another way, more words mean more things to remember and connect. One survey found that 75 percent of readers understood sentences containing an average of 20 words, but comprehension dropped rapidly as the sentences became longer.

This statistic does not mean all stories should have only short sentences. Too many short sentences strung together makes the writing sound choppy. Long sentences, constructed well and used sparingly, can be effective tools for the writer. Moreover, sentences that vary in length make the writing more interesting. Here is an example written by Anne Hull, a former reporter at the St. Petersburg (Florida) Times. The story is about a police officer who defended herself when a teenager pulled a gun that evidently had no bullets.

> The sound she heard from the gun would reverberate for months.
>
> Click.
>
> It was the same sound the key in the lock makes as the father comes home now to the empty apartment, greeted by the boy in the golden frame.

Notice the construction of these sentences. One is the ultimate of brevity—only one word—and the other two are 11 and 29 words, respectively. The combination creates a vivid picture for the reader, as well as a rhythm that creates drama and touches the emotions of the officer, the father and the reader.

Journalists write for the eye and also the ear, listening to the natural flow of the words and sentences they write. They test their stories by reading them aloud to themselves or to a friend. If the sentences sound awkward or unsuitable for a conversation, reporters rewrite them to eliminate complex phrases and long or awkward sentences. They also remove ambiguities and vague terms by being direct and factual.

One way to keep sentences short, clear and conversational is to use standard word order: subject, verb and direct object. Notice how explicit and concise the

in other words

cubic containment system

misapplication elimination device

follicle redistribution mechanism

vermin de-infestation apparatus

horizontal tranquility terminal

©John Atkinson, Wrong Hands · wronghands1.com

Simplify Language

To simplify stories, avoid long, unfamiliar words. Whenever possible, substitute common shorter and simpler ones (known as nickel-and-dime words) that convey the same meaning, such as the following examples:

"about" not "approximately"

"home" not "residence"

"bruises" not "contusions"

"cuts" not "lacerations"

And to eliminate confusion, keep together words that belong in one phrase:

➤ She threw ˄ᵒᵘᵗ the baby ~~out~~ with the bathwater.

➤ He picked ˄ᵘᵖ the dog ~~up~~ from the kennel.

Reporters from the International Consortium of Investigative Journalists, the McClatchey Company and the Miami Herald collaborated to write a series of articles on the Panama Papers, leaked documents that exposed off-shore tax havens. The team shared the 2017 Pulitzer Prize in Explanatory Reporting. The prize board describes the award as recognition of reporting that "illuminates a significant and complex subject, demonstrating mastery of the subject, lucid writing and clear presentation."

following sentence becomes when it uses this sequence:

➤ ~~The half-time show at Super Bowl 51~~ *received* ~~was performed by~~ Lady Gaga ~~and~~ six *for her half-time show at Super Bowl 51* Emmy nominations ^ ~~were given to her because of it~~.

Be certain that each sentence contains related ideas. If not, parts can be eliminated or go elsewhere in the story.

➤ ~~A former student at Echo Elementary School,~~ he was elected president of the college's student senate.

➤ ^ *She succeeded in getting tickets by being* ~~Having been~~ the first person in line ~~for the concert, she wanted to show she could succeed at anything she put her mind to, such as buying her first car when she was 16~~.

Words that form sentences should flow smoothly, and the sentences that form paragraphs also should flow together, logically combining similar thoughts or ideas. The common practice in journalism is to start a new paragraph with each shift in topic, no matter how slight. Paragraphs in news stories often are one sentence because nothing more is needed to get a point across. But ideas that are related or belong together should not be artificially separated just to create shorter paragraphs. Needlessly separating ideas yields choppy writing.

Another reason to write in short paragraphs is that large, dense blocks of text discourage readers. Short paragraphs are best also when writing for audio or video. Journalists divide stories into bite-sized chunks that are easy to read, hear and understand.

Eliminate Unnecessary Words

Unnecessary words confuse audiences and make reading and listening more difficult. Journalists use brevity to help people grasp the main idea of a story and retain enough detail to make stories interesting and informative. Some words—"that," "then," "currently," "now" and "presently," for example—are almost always unnecessary. Writers who use two or more words when only one is needed waste time and space. For instance, eliminate redundant words referring to time, such as "*past* history," "is *now*" and "*future* plans."

Notice how easily unnecessary words can be deleted from the following sentences without changing their meaning:

➤ She *began* ~~was able to begin starting~~ college classes her ~~last and~~ senior year in high school.

➤ *He plans*
~~At the present time he is planning~~ ∧ to leave for ~~the state of~~ New York at 3 p.m. ~~in the afternoon next~~ Thursday.

➤ *One death occurs*
~~Deaths are extremely rare, with only one fatality occurring~~ ∧ in every 663,000 cases.

➤ ~~This is not the first elected office she has held in the city.~~ She ~~also~~ has been a city council member, a member of the library board and a tax collector.

Journalists also eliminate clichés so closely associated with newswriting that they are called "journalese." The term identifies phrases journalists use to dramatize the events they describe. Avoid the following clichés:

fires rage

temperatures soar

earthquakes rumble

floods go on a rampage

developing countries are war-torn, much-troubled or oil-rich

Some words repeat the same idea. The following phrases contain only two or three words, yet at least one—marked in italics—is unnecessary:

in fact	*armed* gunman	*completely* demolished
exactly identical	split *apart*	*brand* new
hurry *up*	*unexpected* surprise	more *and more*
mutual cooperation	*past* experiences	*fellow* colleague
reason *why*	free *of charge*	*needless to say*

Although it is easy to overwrite, journalists try to avoid using too many words when just one or two will do. Here are examples of wordy phrases and their more concise replacements:

conduct an investigation into	investigate
appoint to the post of	appoint
rose to the defense of	defended
succeed in doing	do
came to a stop	stopped
devoured by flames	burned
shot to death	shot/killed
have a need for	need
made contact with	met
proceeded to interrogate	interrogated/questioned
promoted to the rank of	promoted

Quiz

Are you ready for a quiz? Cross out the unnecessary words in the following sentences. Think about the words as you read them.

1. Although he was in a really very quick hurry, he stopped to warn that, in the future, he will seek out textbooks that are sexist and demand that they be totally banned.

2. As it now stands, three separate and different members of the committee said they will try to prevent the city from closing down the park during the cold winter months.

3. Her nice convertible was totally destroyed and, in order to obtain the money necessary to buy a new car, she now plans to ask a personal friend for a loan to help her along.

4. After police found the lifeless body, the medical doctor conducted an autopsy to determine the cause of death and concluded that the dead man had been strangled to death.

5. In the past, the professor often met and talked with the students at the computer lab and, because of their future potential, invited them to attend the convention.

6. Based upon her previous experience as an architect, she warned the committee members that constructing the new hospital facility will be pretty expensive and suggested that they step in and seek more donors.

7. The two men were hunting in a very wooded forest a total of 12 miles away from the nearest hospital in the region when both fell down in a very steep ravine and suffered really severe bodily injuries.

8. Based upon the results of several studies conducted in the past, she firmly believed that the newly prescribed medication will help people with bad liver problems and aid them in their progress toward improvement.

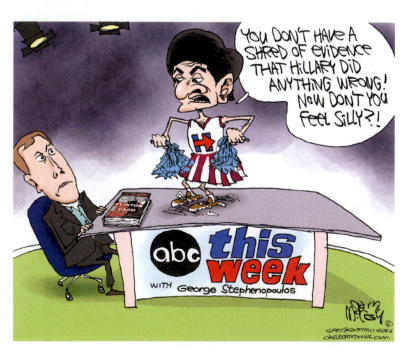

Remain Objective

Journalists are neutral observers who relate what happened. They are not advocates or participants. They strive to be as impartial as possible, reporting the facts and details of their stories, not their opinions about the issues and events. Journalists express their views only in editorials and commentaries, which are clearly labeled as such.

Reporters who inject their opinions into a story may appear to have also been biased when choosing sources and people to interview. Audiences cannot be certain the story is complete, and they may question if the news is one-sided. This taints the story and the journalist who wrote it, as well as the public's reactions to the news organization and journalism generally. When audience members are given all of the information, they are informed and capable of reaching their own conclusions about issues in the news.

One way journalists keep their opinions out of stories is by avoiding loaded words, for example, "extremist," "radical," "fanatic," and "zealot." Such words are often unnecessary and inaccurate. Furthermore, not everyone thinks the same way. A "cute kitty" to some people may be a "nasty-looking tom cat" to others. Many times, loaded words state the obvious: An argument was "heated" or a death "unfortunate." Reporters can eliminate the opinions in some sentences by simply deleting a single adjective or adverb: "famous actor," "gala reception," "thoughtful reply." Here are two more examples:

➤ ∧ ~~The price of tickets is inexpensive~~.
       Tickets are $5

➤ The ~~tragic~~ accident killed ∧ ~~several people unexpectedly~~.
                       three people

Entire sentences sometimes convey opinions, unsupported by facts. Editors (and instructors) will eliminate those statements. Notice how the second sentence in each of the following pairs contains a fact, not a personal view:

Opinion: The candidate looks like a winner.

Fact: CNN exit polls show the incumbent is ahead by six points.

Opinion: Everyone is angry about the mayor's decision.

Fact: About 400 people demonstrated in front of city hall to protest the mayor's decision.

Newswriters can report the opinions expressed by other people—the sources for their stories—but must clearly attribute those opinions to the source. If journalists fail to provide the proper attribution, audiences may think the reporters are expressing their own opinions or agreeing with the source. Consider the following example—the second statement correctly credits the speaker:

Opinion: Obamacare is great.

Fact: The Patient Protection and Affordable Care Act, commonly known as Obamacare, lets children stay on their parents' health plans until they are 26, said Ali Hussain, the president of the University Student Senate.

Respecting Diversity

Journalists avoid generalizing and stereotyping. They do not use offensive, condescending or patronizing terms or phrases in describing other individuals, especially women, people of color, older people and people with disabilities. Good writers are attuned to the "-isms"—racism, sexism, ageism—that can appear in a story even unintentionally. They understand the negative impact their words may have on audiences.

Racism

Journalists mention a person's race, religion or ethnic background only when the fact is clearly relevant to a story. Employees at The New York Times are told, "The writer—or the [sources] quoted in the story—must demonstrate the relevance of ethnic background or religion. It isn't enough to assume that readers will find the fact interesting or evocative; experience shows that many will find it offensive and suspect us of relying on stereotypes."

A criminal's race is usually irrelevant to a story. Identifying a criminal by race, when that is the only characteristic known, is especially harmful because it casts suspicion on every member of the race. Henry McNulty, a former associate editor of The Hartford (Connecticut) Courant, explained his paper's policy on racial identification:

> A long-standing Courant policy states that race and sex alone do not constitute an adequate description. For instance, if the only thing a witness tells police is that a "white woman" or "black man" committed the crime, the Courant will not use any description. Only when such things as height, weight, hair length, scars, clothing and so forth are given will the newspaper print the information.

By that policy, the following description makes appropriate use of a person's race to describe a specific individual whom some audiences might be able to identify:

> Witnesses said the bank robber was a white man, about 50 years old and 6 feet tall. He weighed about 250 pounds, wore a blue suit and escaped on a Honda motorcycle.

Sexism

All genders should be treated equally in news stories. Most of the time, a person's gender is not central to a story and does not need to be pointed out.

Journalists who are writing about a female ask themselves whether they would write the same words if the subject were a male (and vice versa). A headline that announces "Woman Exec Slain in Waldorf-Astoria" is inappropriate because no journalist would write "Male Exec Slain." Gender is irrelevant to this story, and the wording suggests that it is unusual for a woman to achieve a position of importance. Sexism can go both ways, however. The headline "Male Nurse Runs for Secretary of State" implies that this man's occupation is unusual.

Journalists avoid occupational terms that note only one gender: "fireman," "mailman," "policeman" and "cameraman," for example. Instead, they use "firefighter," "letter carrier," "police officer" and "camera operator." The Associated Press Stylebook recommends journalists use "spokeswoman" when referring to a woman and "spokesman" when referring to a man—or "spokesperson" if it is the preference of the individual or organization. Journalists often use "spokesperson," "leader" or "representative" to avoid awkwardness.

If it is not central to the story, journalists avoid writing about the attire of men or women. The clothing and hairstyles of all genders should be equally interesting or equally unimportant.

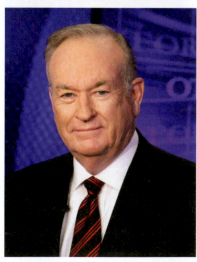

Bill O'Reilly, formerly of the Fox News show The O'Reilly Factor, was admonished for comparing Rep. Maxine Waters' [D-Calif.] hair to a "James Brown wig." O'Reilly later apologized for the comment.

Journalists use "woman" or "man" when an adult's gender is important. The words "female" and "male" are too general because they include all ages. "Lady" is a specific class of woman, just as "gentleman" is for a man.

Men and women should be referred to by their last names, rarely their first, except in stories in which multiple members of the same family are quoted as sources, and first names are necessary to clarify who is being quoted.

Too often news stories identify a spouse only in relationship to the subject: "Justin Timberlake's wife" or "Hillary Clinton's husband." It appears that one person is important and the other is not; it also connotes that the spouse is only a possession. People should be identified by first and last names (not "Mrs. Donald Trump," but "Melania Trump").

Writers eschew using the pronoun "he" as a general reference to men and women. Yet "he/she" or "he and/or she" can become so cumbersome that it distracts audiences. Writers use the following strategies to avoid this problem:

Substitute an article for gender-specific pronouns.

➤ An architect must always consult ~~his~~ *the* plans when designing a bridge.

Use no pronoun in place of "he" or "she."

➤ A nurse will always tell ~~her~~ patients to get some rest.

Substitute plural nouns and pronouns for gender-specific ones.

➤ ~~An emergency~~ *Emergency* medic*s* must train ~~himself~~ *themselves* to be ready at all times.

The Associated Press has guidelines when referring to LGBTQ people, issues and events, but this information is included only if it is central to the story. Not every person falls under the same categories when it comes to gender (social designation) and sex (biological determinant). Whereas transgender is an umbrella term for people who have an identity different from that which was assigned at birth, transsexuals have physically transitioned from one gender to another. For pronoun references, AP style recommends using either third-person or a plural pronoun.

Ageism

There is no magical age at which one becomes "old." For example, a 60-year-old may be considered a youngster when compared to a centenarian. Two-thirds of major U.S. corporations have boards of directors whose ages average older than 60. Many people are active and continue to work into their late 70s and beyond. When asked to describe their health, a majority of older Americans responded "good" to "excellent." Yet impractical stereotypes suggest they are all lonely, unproductive, poor, passive, weak and sick.

Journalists avoid using special terms when describing older people. For example, using the word "spry" gives the impression that some older people are unusually active for their age. Age should not be a factor in a story about an accomplishment—getting elected to office, winning an award—unless it is relevant to the story. The fact that a 70-year-old grandmother wins an election for state senator should not be treated any differently from the election of a

Mercury News ✔
@mercnews

Olympics: Michael Phelps shares historic night with African-American
bayareane.ws/2aQpPhv

8/11/16, 10:02 PM

See a problem with this headline? Michael Phelps gets his name publicized while Simone Manuel (left) is not named but is described by her appearance/ethnicity. Penny Oleksiak (right), who tied Manuel for the gold medal in freestyle swimming, is not mentioned. The story tries to do too much and should have been split into two stories—one featuring Manuel and the other on Phelps. The Cosmopolitan article "The Most Sexist Moments from the 2016 Olympics (So Far)" details additional sexist faux pas in the Olympics coverage.

40-year-old father. Neither one's age nor gender should appear in the headline or the lead of the story.

Avoid Stereotyping Other Groups

Many people with physical and mental disabilities lead active lives and contribute to society both professionally and personally. The terms "disabled" and "challenged" have replaced "handicapped." More acceptable is "person with a disability," "person who is blind" and so forth. Such phrasing emphasizes the individual before the condition. As always, reference a disability only if it is relevant to the story.

Religious groups sometimes accuse the media of bias in the portrayal of members of their faiths. Journalists are careful to avoid stereotyping all followers of a faith because of the actions of a few members.

Additional Newswriting Considerations for Digital Media

Newswriting for digital media (web, mobile, social media) has added considerations because digital stories have more elements and methods of dissemination than print stories do. Whereas print can accommodate text and still visuals (photos and information graphics), digital media includes audio and video podcasts, animation and virtual reality, for example. Reporters use Twitter to announce breaking news and write blogs for an additional perspective to a story. Thus, reporters think of digital stories as a package of elements. As in all types of journalism, reporters identify the central point of the story. For digital newswriting, this part is also the anchor for all components of the package. Journalists thus consider what to include, how it will be assembled and how it will be displayed in various digital formats (see Chapter 14 for more on visual journalism).

Information is presented differently in various media, usually based on how people interact with a medium. For example, text on a monitor is formatted differently from text on paper because of readability (and a few other reasons). Reading text on a computer monitor fatigues the eye more quickly than reading text printed on paper does. If the monitor's resolution is low, the text will not appear sharp, which also decreases readability and the time one spends reading news.

News stories published on the web usually are in sans serif typeface, such as Arial or Helvetica, because they are less elaborate, sharper and easier to read on a computer monitor. Paragraphs are not indented, but separated by extra space to give eyes a quick rest before starting the next section of information. News stories printed on paper often have a serif typeface, such as Times New Roman or New Century Schoolbook. Paragraphs follow one another in sequence without any additional spacing, and the first line of each paragraph is indented.

The Reporter's Guide to Newswriting Style

As you begin to write stories, make sure you follow these guidelines:

1. Identify the central point of the story.

2. Prepare a brief outline of the three or four major parts of the story.

3. Use short, familiar words.

4. Use short sentences and concise paragraphs.

5. Eliminate unnecessary words.

6. Remove unrelated ideas within sentences.

7. Keep sentences with one idea together in one paragraph.

8. Use relatively simple sentences that follow normal word order: subject, verb, direct object.

9. Avoid statements of opinion.

10. Avoid generalizing and stereotyping.

Review Exercises

1. Discussion Questions

1. Some people feel that journalists should use long or uncommon words to educate audiences and raise their reading level. Others feel that short, common words help audiences understand stories quickly and easily. What do you think? Give reasons to support your view.

2. You have just been named editor of your college news site. Formulate a policy that specifies when your staff can report that a person is "adopted," "biracial," "receiving welfare," "gay" or an "ex-convict."

3. Melania Trump is often described by her physical appearance, and her clothes are often the central idea of news stories. As a journalist, what do you think about this treatment?

4. Your city's new mayor, elected today, has never met her father and does not even know his identity. She was raised by her mother, who never married. Would you report that fact and discuss the circumstances while describing the new mayor? Why or why not? What is important to know about a new mayor?

5. A source you are interviewing uses an offensive stereotypical term about senior citizens. Would you print the word? Why or why not?

6. A bank in your city has named a new president; she is the first woman and first African American to hold the position. Should your story about her promotion emphasize these details? Why or why not?

7. For one week, examine news stories in any medium. Look for sentences or phrases that are not objective. Why is the sentence or phrase not objective? How would you rewrite it?

8. How do your favorite TV shows portray gender, age, people of color and people with disabilities? How do the portrayals foster or break stereotypical images?

9. For one week, examine every story published on the homepage of your campus or community newspaper. Identify or highlight words and phrases that you could replace with simpler ones. Do the simpler words and phrases change the meaning of the story? If so, how?

10. Book authors often use the first name for a woman and the last name for a man. They take more time describing a woman's physical appearance and detailing her clothing than a man's. (If they describe the man at all—for example, rarely are men's chests described.) Check the next five novels you read. How does the author introduce a new character and refer to him or her later? Is it fair and balanced? Why or why not? What should journalists do in news stories, and why?

2. Being Concise
Section I: Using Simple Words

Substitute simpler and more common words for each of the following.

1. obliterate
2. objective
3. utilize
4. negligent
5. imbibe
6. duplicate
7. gargantuan
8. remainder
9. eccentric
10. abandon
11. deceased
12. cognizant
13. lacerations
14. presently
15. stated
16. manufacture
17. loathe
18. component
19. obtain
20. relocate

Section II: Avoiding Redundant Phrases

A. Cross out the unnecessary words in these phrases.

1. totally destroyed
2. really big
3. postponed until later
4. freak accident
5. seldom ever
6. major breakthrough
7. dead body
8. qualified expert
9. dangerous weapon
10. armed gunman
11. honest truth
12. future plans
13. awkward predicament
14. fully engulfed
15. lag behind
16. write down
17. free of charge
18. maximum possible
19. foreseeable future
20. lose out

B. Cross out the unnecessary words in these phrases.

1. necessary requirement
2. young girl
3. duplicate copy
4. shot to death
5. underground subway
6. both alike
7. underlying purpose
8. narrow down
9. broad daylight
10. calm down
11. divide up
12. front headlight
13. true fact

14. common accord
15. false pretense
16. radical transformation
17. blazing inferno
18. perfectly clear
19. entwined together
20. died suddenly

C. Cross out the unnecessary words in these phrases.

1. small in size
2. join together
3. general public
4. honest truth
5. acute crisis
6. fell down
7. lag behind
8. protrude out
9. resume again
10. usual custom

Section III: Avoiding Wordy Phrases

A. Use a single word to replace each of these phrases.

1. on the occasion of
2. despite the fact that
3. at an earlier date
4. is going to
5. tender his/her resignation
6. united together in holy matrimony
7. give instruction to
8. on account of
9. was in possession of
10. register approval of
11. due to the fact that
12. exceeding the speed limit
13. made the acquaintance of
14. stated the point that
15. file a lawsuit against

16. be acquainted with

17. came to a stop

18. rose to the defense

19. draw to a close

20. arrived at a decision

B. Use a single word to replace each of these phrases.

1. raze to the ground

2. made contact with

3. bring to a conclusion

4. on a few occasions

5. for the reason that

6. made an escape

7. give encouragement to

8. file a lawsuit against

9. conducted an investigation of

10. summoned to the scene

Section IV: Eliminating Unnecessary Words

Eliminate the unnecessary words from the following sentences.

1. Kate Middleton talked to each and every child individually in the classroom.

2. The candidate running for the office of mayor will conduct a poll of the residents.

3. The North Korean president showed he was upset over the miserably failed missile launch that did not go as planned.

4. He said the birthday party was an unexpected surprise.

5. The police officer tried to calm down the accident victim, who was hurt.

6. The woman, who is a lesbian, said the old habit her daughter had of sleepwalking in the middle of the night was a really unique pattern that would take a qualified sleep expert to break.

7. The female state governor said there was an absolute guarantee that federal and local officials would cooperate together so that local residents would have utility services exactly identical to the ones they had before the storm.

8. If past experience is any indication, the car club members will polish up the antique vehicles no matter whether or not they can predict rain in the foreseeable future.

9. The mayor asked the council members to make a definite decision about the ordinance even though those who support the measure are few in number and flatly reject any compromise.

10. U.S. Vice President Mike Pence said that important essentials are being infringed upon in regard to the contract negotiations between North Korea and South Korea, the two countries involved in the talks.

11. The hockey player said she was acquainted with the author of the book about concussions on account of the fact they had made contact with each other years ago when she was experiencing post-traumatic concussion symptoms while he was doing research for the book.

12. The university's board of directors wanted to wait until later a decision on the project until the board received definite proposals from the contractors.

13. The mayor said the physical size of the new amphitheater was somewhat small, but it would have the maximum possible impact on the city's future plans.

14. Police have the belief that it was a freak accident that allowed the deadly poison to seep out of the tanker truck and cause the worst ever chemical spill in the country's history.

15. Firemen responding to the scene of the house fire were confronted with a blazing inferno and succeeded in doing their best to contain the flames.

Section V: Rewriting Wordy Sentences

A. Remove all redundancies and unnecessary words from the following sentences, eliminating as many words as possible and correcting any other errors.

1. The mayor said everyone had to cooperate together or someone would file a lawsuit against the city.

2. It would appear that the new school mascot, which got a stamp of approval from alumni, will make an appearance at Saturday's game.

3. As a matter of fact, some of the tickets were free of charge to the contest winners while other tickets cost the sum of $50 for handling fees.

4. Police claimed the armed gunman was carrying a dangerous weapon when he entered the bank with the underlying purpose of robbing it.

5. Local residents said they planned to evacuate in the event that the floodwaters reached the banks of the river and completely destroyed the town.

B. Remove all redundancies and unnecessary words from the following sentences, eliminating as many words as possible and correcting any other errors.

1. When the Wonder Woman movie came to an end, audience members commented to the effect that they liked the film.

2. The mayor said the issue in question is not being dealt with on the grounds that her opponent is not taking into consideration the feelings of voters.

3. The professor asked the student to make an approximation of how many people in the state would enter into bonds of matrimony this year and how many would postpone the decision until later.

4. The business owner said his equipment would depreciate in value due to the fact that the warehouse in which it was stored went up in flames.

5. All of a sudden, the motorist realized just now that she was exceeding the speed limit and came to a stop just before she saw the policeman on duty.

C. Remove all redundancies and unnecessary words from the following sentences, eliminating as many words as possible and correcting any other errors.

1. While they had not come to a final conclusion in regard to the plans for the new educational program, the members of the school board said that tentatively a total of about more than 800 students ultimately would be served.

2. According to the currently held belief on the part of the design engineer, Jonathan Emory, who is 56 years old and Hispanic, the important essentials for completing the construction project on time will require check points between the design phase and the actual construction.

3. Doctors rushed the boy who had been injured in the collision between two cars at the intersection of Main and King streets into the emergency ward and later said the boy currently was in critically serious condition.

4. Policemen chased the suspects vehicle through town at a speed estimated to be in the vicinity of approximately 80 miles per hour after it sped away when the officers arrived at the scene of the accident.

5. The attorney for the perpetrator said despite the fact that a dangerous weapon had been found at the scene of the crime it did not necessarily mean that the weapon happened to belong to her current client.

Section VI: Simplifying Overloaded Sentences

Shorten and simplify the following and correct any other errors.

1. Two university students, Jonathan Colson and Marie Parkinson, both seniors and both majoring in business in the Department of Economic Sciences, were driving south on Addison Drive during a thunderstorm when a tree, which was blown down by strong winds, fell across the road in front of them and Colson swerved to avoid the tree before hitting a utility pole with his car and causing more than 10,000 people to lose electricity to their homes.

2. Police officers chased the suspect, who had attempted to rob Robert Ames and his wife, who live at 1345 Grassland Avenue, of $3,500 in cash and jewelry that was in a small safe in their home, into the park where he tried to climb through the window of a childrens playhouse and got stuck in the window because his belt buckle caught on a protruding nail and officers had to cut the man's belt in order to get him out of the window and charge him with robbery, burglary and resisting arrest.

3. Mary Johnson, who is 51 and lives at 414 West Coast Boulevard and who is an emergency room nurse at Mercy Hospital and was on duty at 3 p.m. yesterday, was surprised when a woman who looked just like her was brought into the

emergency room after a minor traffic accident at the intersection of Lakeview Drive and Darlington Avenue in which the woman's car was struck in the rear by a pickup truck while she was stopped at an intersection and Mary began asking the woman questions about her family and past history, discovering that the woman had been adopted, but had been told she had a twin sister who had been adopted by another family when the sisters were three years old, so Mary introduced herself to her long-lost twin sister.

4. The mayor said she was more than willing to support the ordinance the city council was proposing to begin the building of a new facility to house elderly city residents who needed to have a place they could go when they could no longer live independently in their own homes, but the cost of such a facility had to fall within the current fiscal realities of the revenue stream city taxes could generate to support such a building program without raising taxes for city residents, which the mayor knows will upset city residents who will hold her responsible for any proposal the city counsel approves in the long run.

3. –Isms

Section I: Avoiding Sexual Stereotypes

Remove sexist language and comments from the following sentences.

1. The policeman told the cameraman that the accident occurred when the car swerved to avoid an old lady who stepped off the curb.

2. Congressman Janice Byron, a petite 38-year-old mother with a sunny disposition, voted in favor of the education bill, probably because her kids are of school age.

3. The men and their girl friends were expecting the concert tickets to arrive an hour before the show started.

4. The postman told the co-eds that she did not have a package for them today.

5. The author, Oliver Brooks, was in an attractive open-necked, blue shirt that showed off his sweaty, heaving chest and tousled blond hair as he rushed in late to the book signing, around 3:20 p.m.

Section II: Avoiding Exclusively Gender-Specific Nouns and Pronouns

Replace the gender-specific language in these sentences with gender-neutral terms, reduce wordiness and correct any other errors.

1. A policeman has to inspect his weapons before going on patrol.

2. The secretary said she couldn't find the papers before the meeting that her boss incorrectly filed before that.

3. The councilman said it is a fact that the average man will not understand the ordinance.

4. The teacher wrote a letter to each of her students, welcoming them to her class.

5. Encounters with dogs can be frightening experiences for a mailman as he makes his rounds delivering mail to his customers each day.

Section III: Avoiding Stereotypes

Ensure that the following sentences contain no stereotypical language or comments. Correct any other errors.

1. Jackson Smith, a spry 86-year-old resident of Greeley Court, is a real old-timer when it comes to cars because everyday he drives a 1936 Chevrolet coupe that he amazingly restored just last year.

2. The spunky newsboy dropped the paper on the porch just as the pretty housewife lazily opened the front door.

4. Margaret Adams, an attractive woman dressed in a knee-length gray business suit and black high-heeled shoes, became the first woman president and chief executive officer of the male-dominated Hudson Industries.

3. As pressure increased from 20 men and 60 ladies protesting the club's policies, the spokesman for the club said she had reached a gentleman's agreement with the protesters.

4. Members of the American Indian Movement went on the warpath today when federal agents attempted to interrupt a powwow of tribal elders.

Section IV: Remaining Objective

Eliminate the words and phrases that reveal opinions, stereotypes or –isms.

1. The surprisingly good student choral group from Central High won first place at the state conference.

2. Three soldiers training at a nearby army base died tragically in the helicopter accident despite heroic efforts to save them.

3. The female president of the board, who is a 68-year-old grandmother and the matriarch of the family-owned company, wanted to expand the business, but did not believe there were enough extra funds to do it at this time.

4. Tickets for a game at the new stadium will cost only $30 per person, which is really reasonable.

5. It was miraculous that only three people were injured in the 20-vehicle, chain-reaction collision on the fog-bound interstate.

6. The famous speaker, who truly will delight her audience, will discuss the relationship of economics and poverty at tonight's interesting presentation.

7. In a startling discovery, police claimed to have identified the despicable man who attacked the poor, defenseless 65-year-old man.

8. The tall master-of-ceremony towered over the buxom matron as he presented her with the prestigious award for her efforts on behalf of the animal shelter.

9. Theater-goers are urged to buy their tickets early, at a cost of only $20, for the sensational community theater production of "Wicked," which can look forward to a long run in the city.

10. The city council did a good thing when they voted to make it legal to manufacture medical marijuana in the zoned industrial parts of the city.

4. Testing All Your Skills

Correct all errors in these sentences.

1. It was an impetuous decision, but the 20-year-old surfer boy commented to the effect that he planned to purchase a new car when he graduated from college.

2. The students future plans for the recreation center would require university officials to reconstruct the entire facility at a cost of two million dollars, something the university president, a divorced father named Jim Smith, flatly rejected.

3. The church's layman committee, which was made up of four men and three girls, two of whom were Hispanic and one who was Asian, anticipated in advance that a reason for the construction of the new church would help more people be able to attend the services.

4. Adam Levine, the good lead singer for Maroon 5, stated the fact that the concert would be free and open to the public, and he had the belief that the number of attendees would be really a lot.

5. The incumbent senator, a man with a questionable past, planned to introduce legislation in the not-too-distant future on the grounds that the poor needed jobs.

6. Mike Deacosta, his wife and their two children, Mark and Amy, were invited to the congressmans reception along with several other local residents.

7. The police officer made it perfectly clear to the motorist that he had been exceeding the speed limit and would face the maximum possible fine if he did not locate his drivers license presently.

8. Before a young child can begin school, they must be able to read and write their name.

9. The informative information was presented at this point in time because all the members of the board, including Chairman Maggy Baille, were present and accounted for and would be able to vote on the proposal to increase contributions to the employees retirement accounts.

10. An attractive young brunette, Donna Moronesi, seemed to be an unlikely candidate for the office, but she has surprisingly raised more than 1 million dollars before the campaign has even begun.

11. He sustained the loss of his right eye, had lacerations and contusions and broke his leg in the unfortunate accident.

12. As a matter of fact, the mayor claimed she had already considered the attorneys proposal, but the terms of the agreement to settle with the bitter old man who filed a lawsuit against the city over the

death of his dog which had been taken to the city pound was not in accordance with the best interests of the city and its local residents.

13. The attorney was in possession of evidence that helped the jury to arrive at a decision.

14. It was the consensus of opinion of the board and chairman Jane Abbott that the impetuous offer by the other company would be a hindrance to negotiating a fair and equitable contract with her employees on the grounds that the massive increase would create an acute crisis of confidence among the employees and change the ground rules of the negotiations.

15. He stated that the important essential thing to remember is that the deficit was then not nearly as large as it is today.

"The romance between Andrew and Marion was truly magic," he said. Actually, the relationship was "magical." What's the difference? "Magic" is a noun meaning the "use of charms and spells to control events or the art of producing illusions by sleight of hand." "Magical" is an adjective meaning "producing extraordinary results as if by magic." But what about a similar pair of words, such as "tragic" and "tragical"? In this case, "tragical" is a noun meaning "the tragic element in art or life," whereas "tragic" is an adjective meaning "of or having to do with tragedy."

> "In the English language, it all comes down to this: Twenty-six letters, when combined correctly can create magic. Twenty-six letters form the foundation of a free, informed society."
>
> *John Grogan, journalist/writer*

The Effectiveness of Words

Writers sometimes misunderstand the words they use. Other times they fail to express their ideas clearly and precisely. In such cases, their sentences may state the obvious or impossible or carry unintended, often comical, meanings. Consider these examples:

The patient refused an autopsy.

Getting into the bathtub, the phone rang.

The girl wore a hat on her head made of straw.

Before the age of reason men took everything for granite.

She carried her broken leg in a casket for six weeks.

People expect journalists to have mastered the English language. When news organizations hire a reporter, they look for someone who understands and respects the language, knows spelling and grammar, possesses an extensive vocabulary and writes in a clear and interesting manner. Those who devote their

Newspapers from around the world covered the election and inauguration of Donald Trump. In whatever language they write, reporters follow the rules of grammar, spelling and punctuation.

lives to journalism strive to select the exact word needed to convey an idea, use the word properly and place it in a sentence that is grammatically correct. Of course, even careful writers make mistakes, sometimes hilarious ones. But if the errors become too numerous, they can damage a news organization's credibility and require costly and embarrassing corrections.

When a major event occurs, such as the election of a new president, a terrorist attack, the shutdown of a government, or the death of a celebrity, dozens and sometimes hundreds of journalists rush to the scene, gather information and then transmit it to the public. They write about the same event, but some stories are much better than others. Why?

Some reporters are particularly adept at gathering the information needed to write exceptional stories. Others produce exceptional stories because of their command of the English language. Their language is forceful, and their stories are written so clearly and simply that everyone can understand them. These reporters describe people, places and events involved in news stories and use quotations that enable the people involved to speak directly to the public. Skilled reporters can transform even routine events into front-page stories.

Mastering Grammar

Since the development of written languages, humans have created rules governing their usage. Basic understanding of English grammar begins with knowing the parts of speech and how they are used (see Table 4.1). All words are classified as one or more parts of speech. The rules and principles used to combine these parts into sentences are called syntax. Successful writers learn syntax and understand the importance of good sentence structure for conciseness and clarity.

Sentences can be either simple or complex. Simple sentences usually include a subject, a verb and a direct object. The subject is the person or thing doing the action; the verb describes the action; and the direct object is the person or thing acted on. Consider this sentence:

The batter hit the ball.

"Batter" is the actor (the subject of the sentence). "Hit" is the action (the verb), and "ball" is the thing acted on (the object).

Sometimes sentences include indirect objects, which tell who received the action. To test for an indirect object, place "to" or "for" before the word. The following sentences have both direct and indirect objects:

Paul gave Jennifer the tickets.

Gail showed her sister the letter.

TABLE 4.1   Parts of Speech

Nouns	Words that name any animate or inanimate thing: people, animals, places, qualities, acts or ideas.
Verbs	Words that describe action; they tell what things and people do.
Adjectives	Words that describe or modify nouns and pronouns.
Adverbs	Words that describe or modify verbs, adjectives and other adverbs.
Articles	The words "a," "an" or "the" and their equivalents used as adjectives.
Pronouns	Words that replace proper or common nouns to avoid needless and confusing repetition of a noun.
Prepositions	Words that show a relationship between a word or phrase that comes before a preposition, called an antecedent, and a word or phrase that follows, called an object or a subsequent.
Conjunctions	Words or phrases that connect other words, phrases, clauses or sentences.
Interjections	Words or short phrases that express strong, sudden emotions.

Subject	Verb	Indirect object	Direct object
Paul	gave	Jennifer	the tickets
Gail	showed	her sister	the letter

When a noun alone is used as an indirect object, it usually comes between the verb and the direct object, as in the preceding examples. But when the indirect object follows the direct object, it takes the form of a prepositional phrase.

Paul gave the tickets to Jennifer.

Gail showed the letter to her sister.

Nouns

The subject of a sentence can be a noun, pronoun, gerund or infinitive. A gerund is a verbal noun, formed by adding "-ing" to the base form. The infinitive is the basic dictionary form of the verb, appearing with or without the particle "to," which can stand as a noun phrase (among numerous other uses).

Noun subject: *Bill* threw the ball.

Pronoun subject: *He* threw the ball.

Gerund subject: *Throwing* the ball is tiresome.

Infinitive subject: *To throw* the ball all day is tiresome.

Verbs

There are three types of verbs: transitive, intransitive and linking. Transitive verbs propel the action in the sentence from the subject to the object. They are always followed by a direct object.

© MARK ANDERSON, WWW.ANDERTOONS.COM

The boy hated grammar.

"Well, you have a subject and a predicate,
so, content aside, nice job."

People believed the mayor when he said the water was safe to drink.

"Mayor" is the object of "believed."

Intransitive verbs also show action, but they are not followed by a direct object. They can also describe an action or provide a sense of location and are often followed by prepositional phrases or adverbs.

People believed fervently in the mayor.

Or simply,

People believed.

In the first sentence, "fervently" is an adverb that describes "believed." The second example is a complete verb because it takes neither a direct object nor a predicate complement.

Linking verbs express a state or condition and link a noun, pronoun or adjective that describes or identifies the subject. The most common linking verb is "to be."

The man with the snake tattoo on his arm *is* the only suspect in the case.

Other verbs may be used as linking verbs, as in these sentences:

He *looks* guilty.

The bridge *seems* sturdy.

In both examples the verb links the idea in the subject to the idea in the predicate (the part of the sentence containing the verb), stating that the subject possesses the condition described in the predicate.

Independent and Dependent Clauses

A clause is a group of words containing a subject and verb and is used as part of a sentence. An independent clause is a complete sentence; it can stand independently. A dependent clause, on the other hand, is an incomplete thought. Consider the following two sentences:

The senior trip to the museum was very popular, but many parents complained about the cost.

We ordered pizza for the meeting, which everyone on the news staff likes.

Both sentences contain two clauses. However, one sentence contains two independent clauses and the other contains an independent clause and a dependent clause. How can you tell? Separate the two clauses and see whether they make sense on their own.

The senior trip to the museum was very popular. Many parents complained about the cost.

We ordered pizza for the meeting. Which everyone on the news staff likes.

If you picked the first sentence as the one that contains two independent clauses, you are correct. Both are complete sentences, joined by the conjunction "but." The first part of the second sentence is also an independent clause because it can stand alone. However, the second half, "which everyone likes," makes no sense if it is disconnected from the other clause. Its clarity and meaning depend on the first part of the sentence.

Dependent clauses can come at the beginning, in the middle or at the end of a sentence. In the following examples, the dependent clauses are in italics:

When the sun came out, everyone felt more cheerful.

Typewriters, *which were once state-of-the-art word-processing machines*, disappeared when personal computers arrived.

You need to install an underground sprinkler system, *if you are planning to create a lawn in the desert*.

Writers can combine independent and dependent clauses in a number of ways. One way is to combine an independent clause with a dependent one to make a complex sentence.

I eat dinner after my last class is over.

Another is to combine two independent clauses to make a compound sentence.

Ice skating is her favorite sport, but she enjoys roller skating, too.

And yet another way is to string one or more dependent clauses together with two or more independent clauses to create compound-complex sentences.

I visit my aunt whenever I go home for the holidays, but I call her almost every week.

Sentences can also contain phrases, which are related groups of words that lack a subject, verb, or both. Prepositional phrases and verbal phrases are common types. They may be incorporated into the body of the sentence or introduce the main clause. The first of the following sentences ends with a prepositional phrase, and the second begins with a verbal phrase (both are italicized).

People spend more time outdoors *in the springtime*.

Tired from his bicycle ride, Michael took a nap.

Sentence parts can be combined and arranged in endless ways. Writers vary sentence structure to keep their prose from becoming too predictable and simplistic, but simple sentences that stick to subject-verb-object order are the clearest and most easily understood.

Active and Passive Voice

Sentences that use the subject-verb-object order are active-voice sentences; the subject performs the action. A passive-voice sentence reverses the structure so that the action is done to the subject: the direct object of the active-voice sentence becomes the subject; the subject becomes part of a prepositional phrase; and the verb is replaced with its past participle and a form of the verb "to be."

In the following example, the passive-voice sentence is two words longer than the active-voice sentence, but it says the same thing. Those extra words are unnecessary stumbling blocks for readers.

Active Voice: The batter hit the ball.

Passive Voice: The ball was hit by the batter.

The actor or subject can disappear from a passive-voice sentence:

Active Voice: The mayor gave Alex an award.

Passive Voice: An award was given to Alex.

Writers should avoid the passive voice not only because it is wordier than the active voice but also because it often camouflages responsibility. If a disaster strikes or a defective product harms someone, government or business officials may admit "mistakes were made," but the passive construction reveals nothing about who made the mistakes or why. The passive voice is the ally of all who seek to evade responsibility; it is the enemy of all who seek clarity.

Appositives

An appositive is a noun or noun phrase that renames, identifies, explains or in some way supplements the meaning of another noun or noun phrase. An appositive that is accompanied by modifiers is called an appositive phrase.

Appositives may be either essential or nonessential. An essential appositive defines the noun or noun phrase it accompanies. It is not set off with punctuation. A nonessential appositive adds supplemental information and is set off from the rest of the sentence with punctuation, usually commas or dashes. In the following examples, the appositive or appositive phrase is in italics.

Essential appositives:

The required class *Organic Chemistry 101* is one of the most difficult in the program.

The film *"Moonlight"* won three Academy Awards.

Team captain *Ronald Stevens* called for a meeting of the players.

Nonessential appositives:

"Gone with the Wind," *a novel about the Civil War era*, is laden with subtle racism.

My car—*a real lemon*—is in the repair shop again.

That blouse is the same color as my living room curtains, *dark green*.

Common Grammatical Errors

Run-on Sentences

A run-on sentence contains two or more independent clauses with no punctuation separating them. The following are run-on sentences:

I love to read books I would read a new one every day if I could.

We did not know which restaurant we wanted to eat at we drove for hours until we found one we all agreed to eat fast food.

To correct this type of error, add punctuation in the appropriate places, separate the clauses into separate sentences, or rewrite the sentence:

I love to read books; I would read a new one every day if I could.

We did not know which restaurant we wanted to eat at, so we drove for hours until we found a fast-food place we all agreed on.

Good writers carefully edit their stories to eliminate any run-on sentences.

Comma Splices

Some writers attempt to fix a run-on sentence by inserting a comma between the two independent clauses. Doing so creates another type of error known as the comma splice. Here is an example:

The purchase of a used car is hard, there are many good ones available.

There are four ways to fix this sentence:

The purchase of a used car is hard. There are many good ones available.

The purchase of a used car is hard, but there are many good ones available.

The purchase of a used car is hard because there are many good ones available.

The purchase of a used car is hard; there are many good ones available.

Agreement Errors

A basic principle of grammar is that nouns and verbs should agree with each other, as should nouns and pronouns. The principle is simple, but the opportunities for error are numerous.

Wednesday 14 March 2012

The Telegraph

HOME   NEWS   SPORT   FINANCE   COMMENT   BLOGS   **CULTURE**   TRAVEL   LIFESTYLE   F...

Film   Music   Art   **Books**   TV and Radio   Theatre   Hay Festival   Dance   Opera   Photography

Charles Dickens   Book Reviews   Fiction   Non-Fiction   Children's Books   Short Story Club   Book...

HOME » CULTURE » BOOKS » BOOK NEWS

How should Shakespeare really sound?

Audio: The British Library have released the first audio guide to how Shakespeare's plays would have sounded in the original pronunciation.

If The Telegraph were an American newspaper, this would violate subject-verb agreement. But British writers often use plural verbs for collective nouns.

SUBJECTS AND VERBS

If the subject of a sentence is singular, use a singular verb; if the subject is plural, use a plural verb. Getting subjects and verbs to agree is easy when sentences are simple. But when prepositional phrases separate subjects and verbs or when the subject is a collective noun, agreement becomes trickier. In the next example, the singular noun "team" is the subject, and the prepositional phrase "of researchers" describes the subject. The verb should agree with the singular "team," not the plural "researchers."

➤ A team of researchers ~~have~~ *has* gathered the information.

Some nouns—such as "economics," "politics" and "physics"—may appear to be plural because they end in "s," but they are considered singular in certain senses.

➤ Economics ~~are~~ *is* a required course.

Nouns that refer to a group or a collection of individuals as a whole are called collective nouns. Examples include "committee," "club," "jury," "regiment" and "team." Proper nouns that identify organizations—"Congress" and "Microsoft," for instance—also are collective nouns. In American English, collective nouns are considered singular and require singular verbs and pronouns:

➤ The jury ~~announce~~ *announces* ~~their~~ *its* verdict.

Note the change in pronoun, from "their" to "its."

➤ The American Society of Newspaper Editors ~~have~~ *has* begun a program to help journalists with their writing.

NOUNS AND PRONOUNS

Not only must pronouns agree with verbs, but they also must have the same number and gender as their antecedents. A singular feminine noun requires a singular feminine pronoun, and a plural neuter noun requires a plural neuter pronoun. In the following examples, the pronouns are underlined and their antecedents are in italics.

> *Rachael* took <u>her</u> work with <u>her</u> when <u>she</u> visited New York.

> The carpenter replaced the *nails* in <u>their</u> container.

Collective nouns cause the most problems with noun–pronoun agreement. When beginning writers are unsure whether a collective noun is singular or plural, they often try to have it both ways. They use singular verbs with collective nouns but plural pronouns to take their place:

> ➤ General Motors is expanding *their* product line.   *its*

> ➤ The faculty gave *their* vote to the director.   *its*

However, if the subject is a plural collective noun, a plural pronoun is needed:

> ➤ The committees reviewed *its* goal of curbing children's access to internet pornography.   *their*

"That"-"Which" Confusion

"That" and "which" are relative pronouns that introduce clauses referring to ideas, inanimate objects or animals without names. They are little words, but they can make a big difference in the meaning of a sentence. The following sentences illustrate this point:

> Jason used the lawn mower that is in the garage.

> Jason used the lawn mower, which is in the garage.

In the first sentence, "that" implies many lawn mowers exist on the property—in the yard, the garage and the barn—but Jason took the one from the garage. In the second sentence, the clause introduced by "which" is not essential. There is only one lawn mower on the property, so it is the only one Jason could use. It helps to know where the lawn mower is, but the information is not necessary to understand the sentence.

Here's a rule that can help decide between "that" and "which": If the sentence is read without the subordinate clause and the meaning does not change, "which" should introduce the clause. Otherwise, use "that."

"Who"-"Whom" Confusion

"Who" and "whom" are also relative pronouns, but they begin clauses that refer to people and animals with names.

> ➤ It was Morgan *that* came by the house yesterday.   *who*

> ➤ It was a stray cat *who* ate the bird.   *that*

The distinction between "who" and "whom" torments some writers. "Who" is the subject of a clause; "whom" is the object of a verb or a preposition ("Who tweeted whom?"). Whether a word is a subject or an object might not always be clear in relative clauses or questions, both of which may depart from normal word order.

Either "who" or "whom" may appear as the first word in a question, depending on its grammatical relationship to the rest of the sentence. These two sentences illustrate the difference:

> Who gave you the Kindle?

> Whom do you prefer as your district's legislator?

In the first example, "who" is the subject of the clause, the initiator of the action "gave." In the second, "whom" is the direct object of the verb "prefer." Here are two more examples:

> *To whom*
> ➤ ~~Who~~ did you speak ~~to~~?

> *whom*
> ➤ The report names the man ~~who~~ the police suspect of the crime.

In the first sentence, the relative pronoun is the object of the preposition "to." In the second, it is the direct object; it refers to the person the police suspect. Both should be "whom."

One way to avoid or reduce confusion over these words is to replace them with a personal pronoun. Isolate the "who" or "whom" phrase. If "he" or "she" sounds right, use "who." If "him" or "her" would be more natural, use "whom." Do that in the following sentence and it is easy to see that "whom" is wrong:

> The candidates argued about whom was responsible for the tax increase.

At first, the relative pronoun "whom" appears to be the object of the preposition "about," but it doesn't sound right when replaced with "him" or "her." That's because the relative pronoun is the subject of the clause "was responsible for the tax increase." No one would say "her was responsible," but "she was responsible" makes sense. Therefore, the relative pronoun to use here is "who."

Misplaced Modifiers

Modifiers are words or phrases that limit, restrict or qualify some other word or phrase. Modifiers should appear as close as possible to the word or phrase they modify. Misplaced modifiers can make sentences ambiguous, confusing or nonsensical:

> She retold the ordeal of being held hostage with tears running down her cheeks.

Readers might think the phrase "with tears running down her cheeks" modifies "hostage"—that she was crying while she was a hostage. But the phrase really tells how the woman behaved as she talked about her ordeal. The following version is clearer:

> With tears running down her cheeks, she retold the ordeal of being held hostage.

In the next example, the revision clarifies that the victim is left lying on the back seat, not just his hands and feet:

➤ The gunmen tied the victim ⌃and left him ~~with his hands and feet taped and~~ lying on the back seat.

, taped his hands and feet

Dangling Modifiers

Modifiers dangle when the word or phrase they are supposed to modify does not appear in the sentence. This error may happen when a thoughtless or hurried writer starts a sentence intending to state an idea one way and then switches in midsentence to express it in another way:

➤ Pleased with everyone's papers, ~~the class received congratulations~~.

the teacher congratulated the class

➤ ~~Angered by the unannounced closure of the plant,~~ security guards hurriedly cleared the area ⌃.

of employees who were angered by the unannounced closure of the plant

Readers understand that introductory words and phrases modify the subject of the sentence. If that is not the case, the modifiers are either misplaced or dangling.

Personification

Avoid treating inanimate objects or abstractions as if they were human. Objects such as buildings, cars, stores and trees cannot hear, think, feel or talk. Yet some writers see—and repeat—the error so often they fail to recognize it and continue to personify such things as corporations, countries and machines.

Memorial Hospital treated her for shock and a broken arm.

She was driving west on Hullett Avenue when two cars in front of her slammed on their brakes.

Can a hospital treat patients, or is that the job of a hospital's staff? Can a car slam on its own brakes? Of course not.

Luckily, personifications are easy to correct:

➤ The ⌃store said ~~it~~ will not reopen ⌃.

owner of the *she* *it*

➤ ~~The intention of the road was~~ to help farmers transport their crops to market.

Highway planners intended the road

Personification also contributes to two other problems. First, audiences cannot determine a story's credibility if reporters fail to identify their sources. The public can assess the credibility of a statement attributed to a mayor or governor, but not the credibility of a statement attributed to a city or state. Second, personification allows people to escape responsibility for their actions. Officials cannot be held accountable if reporters attribute their activities to a business or government.

Parallelism

When writers connect similar ideas, they do so with parallel structures. Grammatically parallel structures create harmony and balance in writing, and they help readers compare and contrast the ideas that are linked within the sentence.

The principle of parallelism requires that items in a series take the same grammatical form: for example, all are nouns, all are verbs or all are prepositional phrases. If the first verb in a series uses the past tense, every verb in the series uses the past tense. If the first verb ends in "-ing," all must end in "-ing."

If reporters fail to express like ideas in the same grammatical form, their sentences become convoluted and confusing:

➤ Police said the plastic handcuffs are less bulky, ~~not as~~ *less* expensive and ~~no key is needed~~ *less difficult* to remove ~~them~~ from a suspect's wrists than metal handcuffs.

➤ The Greenes have three children: ~~4-year-old~~ Gordon,*4;*∧ Andrea, ~~who is~~ *;* 3~~,~~ and ~~little~~ Fielding ~~is not quite 25 months~~ *,2*.

Syntax

As mentioned earlier, syntax refers to the arrangement and relationships of the words and phrases in a sentence. If parts of the sentence are disjointed or improperly arranged, the sentence will confuse readers.

Sometimes, the syntax error is simply the misplacement or omission of words:

➤ Hill said people cannot afford to be partisan but, instead, ~~will~~ *should* work ∧ *with* each other to help fix the world.

Other times, the syntax errors are more extensive, requiring a rewrite:

Wrong: Church said she was certain that her many years of attempts at being a creative writer, would be her calling, but found it was not.

Better: Church said she spent years trying to become a creative writer but discovered it was not her calling.

Three practices can help writers avoid syntax errors: (1) Keep sentences as simple as possible. Sentences that follow the subject-verb-object order are least likely to have syntax problems. (2) Think about what you want to say before writing the sentence. Planning the sentence forces you to think about the selection and arrangement of the words and phrases. (3) Reread and edit what you have written. Reading your writing aloud is especially helpful. Often the ears can detect syntax problems the eyes overlook.

Spelling

When readers complain about inaccuracies in news stories, they are often referring to spelling errors. Misspellings reflect laziness on the part of the writer, and they sometimes cause readers to doubt the facts in the story.

Correct spelling is as important for writers in broadcast journalism as it is for those in print. News announcers often lack time to review the reporter's copy for misspelled words, and misspellings may cause them to make mistakes on air.

Common phrases such as "a lot" and "all right" are frequently misspelled. Confusing words that look or sound alike but have different meanings, such as "accept/except" and "capital/capitol," are another common source of spelling errors. (See the vocabulary exercise at the end of this chapter.) Reporters usually follow formal rules for spelling. For example, they normally use "until" rather than "till" and "although" rather than "though."

A final point about spelling: Spell-check programs for computers help many writers. However, a computer program can look only at the spelling of a word, not how it is used. If you were to write, "There cat's name is Savannah," the spell-checker would not catch that "there" should be "their." No one should depend solely on a spell-check program.

Spelling errors such as this one are not only embarrassing for the journalist and news organization but also make people distrust the story's content.

Punctuation

Punctuation marks (see Table 4.2) help make the meaning of a sentence clear to a reader. Some punctuation marks indicate the pauses and stops that the voice makes when speaking. They specify not only where the pause goes, but the length of the pause as well. Other marks indicate inflections in the voice, such as questions or exclamatory remarks. Taken together, a sentence is only as clear as effective punctuation can make it. A misplaced punctuation mark can completely change the meaning of a sentence. Therefore, mastering punctuation is essential for anyone who aspires to write clearly.

Writing Like a Pro

Diction

Writing like a professional is hard work. It requires practice and an understanding of the effectiveness of the words selected to convey a thought or idea. A writer's choice of words and style of expressing them is called diction.

Diction in writing can be either formal or informal. By choosing one type, a writer establishes a tone for the story and the characterization of the subjects.

TABLE 4.2   Punctuation Marks

Period (.)	A period ends a sentence—period. Without a period, thoughts and ideas in sentences would collide and confuse the reader.
Comma (,)	A comma creates a short pause within a sentence.
Semicolon (;)	The semicolon is often used to connect two independent clauses without using a conjunction.
Colon (:)	The colon lets the reader know that a list, a sentence fragment, a sentence or a quotation follows.
Hyphen (-)	The hyphen is a connector and often is used to join words to form compound modifiers.
Dash (– or —)	An en dash (–) is primarily used to show a range between dates or numbers. The em dash (—) is used to create an abrupt and longer pause than a comma. It often is used to highlight an aside or brief change in thought that accompanies a sentence.
Parentheses ( )	Like an em dash, parentheses are used to set off additional information.
Quotation marks (". . .")	Quotation marks enclose the exact words spoken or written by someone else.
Apostrophe (')	The apostrophe is used to form possessives and contractions.
Question mark (?)	The question mark ends any sentence that is a question.
Exclamation point (!)	The exclamation point ends sentences uttered with great emotion or emphasis.

Lynn Truss, author of "Eats, Shoots & Leaves: A Zero Tolerance Approach to Punctuation," points out an error in a Toronto Star headline.

A light, breezy feature story may use informal language and contractions, setting a conversational tone. A news story about the president may use more formal language and set a more serious tone.

When in doubt, stick with formal diction. As William Safire notes in his book "How Not to Write: The Essential Rules of Grammar," contractions are not as powerful. The word "not" is strong. Safire says, "'I won't' sounds stubborn, but 'I will not' sounds determined and slightly more emphatic."

Precision

To communicate effectively, reporters must be precise, particularly in their selection of words. Mark Twain wrote, "The difference between the right word and the almost right word is the difference between lightning and the lightning bug." The perfect choice makes a sentence crackle; imprecision creates mush.

Some errors occur because the reporter is unaware of a word's exact meaning. Few journalists would report that a car "collided" with a tree, a "funeral service" was held, a gunman "executed" his victim or a child "was drowned" in a lake. Why? Two objects collide only if both are moving; thus, a car can strike a tree, but never collide with one. A funeral is a service; therefore, "funeral service" is redundant. "Executed" means put to death in accordance with a legally imposed sentence;

only a state—never a murderer—can execute anyone. A report that a child "was drowned" would imply that someone held the child's head underwater until the victim died.

Such considerations are not trivial. Journalists who fail to use words correctly can undermine their credibility and the accuracy of their stories and confuse or irritate their audience. Thus, instructors will object when students use language that is sloppy and inaccurate.

When reporters fail to express ideas clearly and precisely, audiences can derive meanings different from the ones intended. The unintended meanings may be difficult for the writer to detect. Double meanings in the following headlines, all of which appeared in newspapers, illustrate the problem:

Police Begin Campaign to Run Down Jaywalkers

Farmer Bill Dies in House

Queen Mary Having Bottom Scraped

Lawmen From Mexico Barbecue Guests

Iraqi Head Seeks Arms

Confusion sometimes arises because words look or sound alike. College students often confuse words such as "buses" and "busses," "naval" and "navel," and "reckless" and "wreckless." The word "busses" refers to kisses, not the vehicles people ride in. A "navel" is a belly button, and some motorists drive "wrecks" but are convicted of "reckless" driving.

Some words are simply inappropriate in news stories. Few editors or news directors permit the use of words such as "cop" or "kid" (they prefer the more formal and proper "police officer" and "child") or derogatory terms about a person's race or religion.

Editors and news directors also prefer the word "woman" to the archaic "lady." Many ban the use of contractions except in direct quotations. Professional journalists object to using nouns as verbs. They would not write that someone "authored" or "penned" a book, a city "headquartered" a company or an event "impacted" a community. Nor would they allow a reporter to write that food prices were "upped," plans "finalized" or children "parented."

Use Strong Verbs

Verbs can transform a drab sentence into an interesting and powerfully descriptive one. Notice the impact of the underlined words in a paragraph from a New York Times story about opioid addiction in America:

Once a popular honors student, Katie Harvey became addicted to heroin and has entered rehab several times. In telling Harvey's story, the reporter used active and powerful verbs in the lead to help set the scene and hook the reader.

Katie Harvey <u>walked</u> out of the house where she lived with friends, <u>shoved</u> her duffle bag into her mother's car and <u>burst</u> into tears.

By comparison, the following original sentences are weak and bland, yet it is easy to improve them. Simply add a strong verb and change them from passive to active voice.

➤ ~~The bodies were located by~~ *found the bodies* rescue workers ∧ shortly after 6:00 p.m.

➤ *Blustery thunderstorms sweeping across the state Monday afternoon toppled a* ~~A~~ ∧ historic railroad bridge that was once the tallest and largest in the world ~~was destroyed by strong thunderstorms that crossed the state Monday afternoon~~.

Strong verbs describe one specific action. Weak verbs cover a number of different actions. The first sentence in the following example is ambiguous because it uses a weak verb. The last three use specific, descriptive verbs and are more informative:

His brother got a personal computer.

His brother bought a personal computer.

His brother won a personal computer.

His brother stole a personal computer.

Avoid the repeated use of forms of the verb "to be," such as "is," "are," "was" and "were." These verbs are overused, weak and dull, especially when a writer uses them in combination with a past participle to form a passive-voice verb, such as "was captured." As noted earlier, sentences using passive verbs are also wordier than those with active ones. Both revisions cut five words from the original sentence:

➤ ~~It was discovered by the company's~~ *Company* lawyers ~~that~~ *discovered* the financial records were incorrect.

➤ *A neighbor called the* ∧ Police ~~officers were summoned to the scene by a neighbor~~.

Problems to Avoid

Overuse of Adjectives and Adverbs

News writers avoid adverbs and adjectives because they lack the force and specificity of nouns and verbs. William Strunk Jr. and E. B. White, authors of the influential book "The Elements of Style," wrote, "The adjective hasn't been built that can pull a weak or inaccurate noun out of a tight place." Along the same lines, Mark Twain warned, "When you catch an adjective, kill it."

Most adverbs and adjectives waste space by stating the obvious. They may also unintentionally inject a reporter's opinion into the story. If you write about a child's funeral, you do not have to comment that the mourners were "sad-faced," the scene "grim" and the parents "grief-stricken." Nor is there reason to report that an author is "famous," a witness "alert" or an accident "tragic."

Editorial comments can often be removed by eliminating adverbs and adjectives:

➤ ~~It was not until Monday that~~ university officials ~~finally~~ released the

  Monday
  report‸.

➤ Upon hearing about the ~~frivolous~~ lawsuit, the mayor ~~made it quite~~ *promised to fight it*
  ~~clear that she plans to fight the outrageous complaint~~.

The word "finally" in the first sentence implies that university officials were negligent and should have released the report sooner. Similarly, reporting the facts in the second story clearly and concisely eliminates the need for words like "frivolous" or "outrageous." And saying the mayor made something "clear" implies she is stating a fact, not an opinion.

Clichés

Clichés are words or phrases that writers have heard and copied over and over. Many are so old and overused that they have lost their original impact and meaning. Clichés do not startle, amuse or interest the public.

The news media can overuse a fresh phrase so much that it quickly becomes a cliché. The U.S. invasion of Iraq began with an intensive barrage of bombs and missiles designed, as military leaders described it, to produce "shock and awe" among the residents of Baghdad. After the attack, the phrase started appearing in stories dealing with such topics as football, the economy and insect invasions. Soon, "shock and awe" aroused only disgust and boredom.

Journalists employ clichés when they lack the time or talent to find words more specific, descriptive or original. A reporter under deadline pressure may say

that a fire "swept through" a building, an explosion "rocked" a city, police officers gave a suspect a "spirited chase" or protesters were an "angry mob."

Other clichés exaggerate. Few people are really as "blind as a bat," "cool as a cucumber," "light as a feather," "neat as a pin," "straight as an arrow," "thin as a rail" or "white as a sheet."

Political reporting is especially susceptible to clichés. It seems as though candidates always are nominated in "smoke-filled rooms," or they "test the waters" before "tossing their hats into the ring." Other candidates launch "whirlwind campaigns" and "hammer away" at their opponents, or they employ "spin doctors" to control unfavorable news. Some candidates "straddle the fence" on the "burning issues of the day." However, few "give up without a fight."

Slang

Journalists avoid slang, which tends to be more faddish than clichés. Some words that started out as slang have won acceptance as standard English. "Blizzard," "flabbergast" and "GI" (for soldier) are among such terms. Most slang never makes the transition, however.

Feature stories and personality profiles sometimes employ slang effectively, but it is inappropriate in straight news stories because it is too informal and annoying. Moreover, slang may baffle readers who are not of the right age or ethnic group to understand it. Slang is often specific to each generation and rapidly becomes dated so that a term used in a story may already be obsolete. During the 1990s, young people developed a set of "slammin'" slang terms and "dissed" anyone still using the slang of the 1980s as a "Melvin." In the early 2000s someone may have shown "props" to friends who knew the "off the hook" films showing at the "grind-house" and gotten "stoked" about "poppin' tags" and looking for "lollipops" at the mall.

Slang also conveys meanings or attitudes journalists may want to avoid. Terms such as "flaky," "ego trip" and "flatfoot" convey evaluations—often negative and stereotypical—of the things described. Reporters, however, leave such comments to editorial writers or readers and viewers.

Technical Language and Jargon

People in trades and professions develop their own technical language or jargon. When professionals use jargon to impress or mislead the public, critics call it gobbledygook, bafflegab, doublespeak or bureaucratese. Most jargon is abstract, wordy, repetitious and confusing. For example, a government agency warned, "There exists at the intersection a traffic condition which constitutes an intolerable, dangerous hazard to the health and safety of property and persons utilizing such intersection for pedestrian and vehicular movement." That sentence contains 31 words. A good journalist could summarize it in four: "The intersection is dangerous."

Many of the sources reporters routinely use—doctors, lawyers, business people, press releases, technical reports, and police and court records—speak in or contain jargon. Journalists must translate such language into plain English. Consider this quote:

> Dr. Stewart McKay said, "Ethnic groups that subsist on a vegetarian diet and practically no meat products seem to have a much lower level of serum cholesterol and a very low incidence of ischemic diseases arising from atherosclerotic disease."

The statement can be clarified by removing the jargon:

> Dr. Stewart McKay said ethnic groups that eat little meat have low rates of coronary heart disease and related illnesses.

Technical language may be appropriate in some specialized publications or broadcasts intended for experts in a particular field, such as medicine, business or engineering. It is not appropriate in pieces aimed at a mass audience.

Euphemisms

Euphemisms are vague expressions used in place of harsher, more offensive terms. They often are used by journalists, public relations professionals, industrial and corporate leaders—as well as ordinary people—to soften blunt language, but they sometimes can lead to unintended consequences.

Social media exploded in April 2017 when a video showing Dr. David Dao being dragged from a United Airlines flight was posted. The flight was overbooked, but Dao had refused to give up his seat; the airline officials had police forcefully remove him. United Airlines CEO Oscar Munoz apologized for having to "re-accommodate" the passenger. This term became a euphemism for physically assaulting him.

Some etiquette experts say that good manners require the use of euphemisms. Prudishly, Americans often say that a woman is "expecting" rather than "pregnant," and that they have to go to the "restroom" rather than the "toilet." Whatever value euphemisms have for etiquette, they detract from good news writing, in which clarity and precision are the most important goals. But sometimes news events force reporters to use descriptive words in place of confusing and awkward euphemisms. One of the more famous examples is the 1993 story of Lorena Bobbitt, a Virginia woman who used a kitchen knife to cut off her husband's penis after he allegedly raped her. The word "penis" rarely had appeared in news stories, and some organizations were squeamish about using it, especially in headlines. Euphemisms like "member," "organ" or "offending organ" appeared instead. The widespread coverage the Bobbitt case received apparently diminished journalistic sensitivity to the word. A computer search found more than 1,000 news stories that used the word "penis" in the six months after the Bobbitt story broke, compared to only 20 mentions in the previous six months.

As with sex, Americans often employ euphemisms when talking about death. They say that a friend or relative "passed on" or is "no longer with us," not that he or she has died and been buried or cremated. Hospitals report a "negative patient outcome," not a death. Funeral directors object to being called "morticians," a word that itself was originally a euphemism for "undertakers."

During a recession, major companies lay off thousands of employees without admitting it. Instead, corporate executives say they are "restructuring," "downsizing" or "rightsizing" to get rid of "excess workers."

War spawns grotesque euphemisms, perhaps, as some critics say, to hide the human pain and suffering every war causes. Killing the enemy has become "servicing the target." Airplanes no longer bomb enemy soldiers; they "visit a site." Civilians who are killed during attacks are called "collateral damage."

Profanity

News executives allow profanity only when it is essential to a story's meaning; even then, they refuse to publish the most offensive terms. In 2014, leaked audio conversations between Victoria Nuland, U.S. assistant secretary of state for European and Eurasian affairs, and Geoffrey Pyatt, U.S. ambassador to the Ukraine, included profanity. In an opinion piece in The New York Times, Jesse Sheidlower noted that most major news organizations, including The Washington Post, Associated Press, The Wall Street Journal and CNN replaced some letters of the profane expression with dashes or asterisks. The Los Angeles Times said that Nuland used "a blunt expletive when expressing frustration." The New York Times noted that she had "profanely dismissed" European efforts in Ukraine. However, Reuters used the profanity in a direct quote: "'So that would be great, I think, to help glue this thing and have the U.N. help glue it and you know . . . fuck the EU,' she said."

To understand why writers and editors at newspapers, television news programs and their online and social media versions avoid profanity, one has to look only at their audience. They provide information to a wide general public—one that encompasses many age, cultural and social groups—unlike the magazine industry, which often targets a specific audience. "Rolling Stone" readers can expect profanity in a story, but readers of The New York Times do not.

Stating the Obvious

Dull, trite, obvious remarks are called "platitudes," and journalists must learn to avoid them. The following sentence appeared in a story about technological changes that had occurred during the life of a 100-year-old woman:

> Superhighways, high-speed automobiles and jet planes are common objects of the modern era.

The sentence would have been more interesting if it had described the changes in more detail and clearly related them to the woman's life, such as the following:

> Lila Hansen once spent three days on a train to visit relatives in California. Now, she flies there in three hours every Christmas.

When people stop reading, watching or listening to a story, they rarely think about why it bored them. Perhaps it is just a series of platitudes, which say nothing new. Thus, people sometimes quit reading the story because it is no longer interesting or newsworthy.

To avoid repeating platitudes, reporters must recognize them when they conduct interviews. If a bartender is robbed at gunpoint, there is no reason to quote him saying he was scared. Most people confronted by guns are scared, and they often say so. If journalists want to quote the bartender—or any other source—they should ask more penetrating questions until they receive more specific, interesting or unusual details.

First-Person References

Except in extraordinary circumstances, journalists should remain neutral observers. They should not mention themselves in news stories. Journalists avoid the words "I," "me," "we," "our" or "us," except when they are directly quoting some other person.

Beginning reporters sometimes use these words when referring to the community in which they work or the United States. Use of first person pronouns implies the writer and the news organization endorse what is said. When the story involves political situations or actions, that implication undermines the objectivity of the news organization. Consider this example:

> ➤ The governor said ~~our~~ *the* state ~~demands that we take action to~~ *must* curb ~~our government~~ *its* spending.

The pronouns "our" and "we" in the first version suggest the writer agrees with the governor, but others may think the amount the state spends is just right or too low.

Negative Constructions

For clarity, avoid negative constructions. Sentences should be cast in positive form, as in the following examples:

> ➤ The student ~~did not often come~~ *rarely came* to class.

> ➤ The defense attorney tried to ~~disprove her client's sanity~~ *prove her client was insane*.

Sentences containing two or three negatives are wordy and even more difficult to decipher. These negative constructions force the reader to pause to determine their meaning:

> ➤ The women said they ~~are not against~~ *favor* the change.

> ➤ The senator said she would ~~not~~ accept ~~any~~ campaign contributions
> ∧ *only* from people ~~who do not live~~ *living* in her district.

Echo

An echo is the unnecessary repetition of a word. Good writing avoids an echo by eliminating redundant words or phrases.

➤   Her annual salary was $29,000 ~~a year~~.

➤   In Japan, ~~cancer~~ patients are rarely told they have cancer.

Writers sometimes repeat a key word or phrase for emphasis or to demonstrate an important similarity. If the repetition is needless, however, the result is likely to be awkward, distracting or confusing.

Gush

Reporters also avoid "gush"—writing with exaggerated enthusiasm. They write news stories to inform members of a community, not to please their sources. News stories should report useful information. They should not praise or advocate.

One way to avoid gush is always to use more than one source for a story. Another is to demand that sources provide specific details to support their generalizations. Using multiple sources who are independent of one another prevents reporters from being misled or manipulated by sources seeking favorable publicity. By insisting that sources provide details and specific examples to support their claims, reporters can minimize sources' tendency to engage in the kind of self-praise found in these sentences:

> "We feel we are providing quality recreational programs for both adults and children," Holden said.

> Police Chief Barry Kopperud said the city's mounted horse patrol, which began one year ago, has become a great success.

When a journalist finishes an article, it should sound like a news story, not a press release. Yet one travel story gushed that Mexico is "a land of lush valleys and marvelous people." Gush cannot be rewritten because there is nothing of substance to rewrite. It should simply be deleted.

There is a second type of gush—an escalation in modifiers. Columnist Donna Neely explains that what used to be called "funny" is now called "hilarious" and what used to be "great" is now "fantastic" or "incredible." Advertisers call their inventories "fabulous" and their sales "gigantic." Delete all such modifiers or replace them with facts and details and let readers and viewers decide for themselves what adjectives are appropriate.

Vague Time References

Unless your instructor tells you otherwise, use "today" and "tonight" to refer only to the day of publication and do not use "yesterday" or "tomorrow" to refer to a specific day. Instead, use the day of the week to date events that occur within seven days before or after the day of publication. For events that are more than seven days in the past or future, use a specific date, such as July 23 or March 4.

Using the date or day of the week eliminates the confusion that might arise with the use of "today," "tomorrow" or "yesterday" in news stories that are written a day or more in advance of their publication. For example, if a fire destroyed a home at 5 p.m. Tuesday, a reporter would write the story later that evening for publication in the Wednesday newspaper. If the reporter wrote that the fire happened "today," readers would think the fire occurred on Wednesday. If the reporter is writing about an event that will happen on the day of publication, the use of "today" is appropriate, as in this sentence in a morning newspaper: "The concert will begin at 3 p.m. today."

"Yesterday," "today" and "tomorrow" may be used in direct quotations or to refer to the past, present or future in general and not to specific days. Journalists also avoid the word "recently" because it is too vague.

Use of the Present Tense

Print reporters avoid the present tense and terms such as "at the present time" in stories for the printed newspaper because many of the events they report end before readers receive the paper. A reporter working on deadline should not say, "A fire at the Grand Hotel threatens to destroy the entire block." Firefighters almost certainly would have extinguished the blaze before readers receive the paper hours later. For the same reason, a reporter covering a fatal accident should not say, "The victim's identity is not known." Police might learn the victim's identity in a few hours, and local radio and television stations might broadcast the person's name before subscribers receive their papers. Consequently, print journalists must use the past tense:

> A fire at the Grand Hotel was threatening to destroy the entire block at 11:30 p.m.

> Police were unable to learn the victim's identity immediately.

Stories written for broadcast or for immediate publication on a website or social media are more likely to use the present tense. When the story is likely to reach readers or viewers as the events are unfolding, the present tense may be more accurate and more compelling than the past tense.

Excessive Punctuation

Journalists avoid excessive punctuation, particularly exclamation points, dashes and parentheses. Exclamation points are rarely necessary and should never be used after every sentence in a story, regardless of that story's importance. Parentheses interrupt the flow of ideas and force people to pause and assimilate some additional, often jarring, bit of information:

> She (the governor) said the elderly population (people 65 and older) had grown twice as fast as any other segment of the state's population during the last 20 years.

Removing the parentheses makes the sentence easier to read:

> The governor said the percentage of people 65 and older had grown twice as fast as any other segment of the state's population during the last 20 years.

If a source says something that is vague or convoluted, the writer should paraphrase or use a partial quotation rather than insert explanations in parentheses. Here is an example, followed by the revision:

> "I wish they (school administrators) would quit fooling around," she said. "They say they don't have enough money (to hire more teachers), but I don't believe that. I know they have it (the money); it's just a matter of priorities—of using their money more wisely."

> She said the school administrators should "quit fooling around." They say they do not have enough money to hire more teachers, but she does not believe that. "It's just a matter of priorities—of using their money more wisely," she said.

The Writing Coach

Become a Power Lifter When Picking Verbs

BY JOE HIGHT

Consider stronger verbs in your sentences if you want to become a Hercules, or Hemingway, of writers.

These are verbs that are specific, active and descriptive. They pace your sentence like a smoothly running engine in a Corvette. They strengthen your voice in writing. As Gary Provost writes in "100 Ways to Improve Your Writing," they are the executives of sentences—the primary source of energy in your sentences.

This means writers should avoid the passive voice whenever possible. In "On Writing Well," William Zinsser writes, "The difference between the active-verb style and the passive-verb style—in pace, clarity and vigor—is the difference between life and death for a writer."

Likewise, avoid weak linking verbs such as "is" ("there is," for example) and "has." Avoid verbal phrases that carry unnecessary prepositional phrases, abstract nouns or adjectives. Avoid extending verbs with the suffix "-ize." Avoid tagging "very" to a verb when a stronger word would be better.

Often, reporters think they can strengthen their sentences by substituting longer verbs such as "purchase" for "buy" or "conclude" for "end." However, they're mistaken, writes Jeffrey McQuain in "Power Language." He quotes poet Oliver Wendell Holmes Sr., father of the Supreme Court justice, as saying a long word should never be used when a shorter word serves the purpose. McQuain, who also writes a column called "Our Language," adds that the most inspiring verbs often are the simplest.

Watch how these three sets of verbs grow in power as they shrink in syllables:

Initiate—introduce—begin—start.

Accentuate—emphasize—highlight—stress.

Communicate—dialogue—discuss—talk.

Long verbs are not necessarily strong verbs. Jack Hart, who formerly wrote "Writers Workshop" for Editor & Publisher, recommends that writers devote part of their self-editing time to strengthen their verbs. He also recommends they use transitive verbs that create the most ruckus. Those are ones that require direct objects and generate casual flow: "Its claws raked her back." Or strong intransitive verbs, as in "The skier plunged into empty space."

"Nothing injects energy like action. And only verbs describe action. They deserve a lot of end-stage attention," Hart wrote.

But the question remains: How do you develop the ability to strengthen verbs in your sentences? By practice. By reading. By exercising your language skills as a bodybuilder lifts weights.

Author John Gardner was a powerful fiction writer who was known for his many passions, including motorcycles—he died in an accident in 1982—and writing. A friend, Charles Johnson, tells a story in "On Writers and Writing" of how at dinner one evening Joan Gardner teased her husband about the archaic language he used in "Jason and Medeia." The upset Gardner then took a magnifying glass and pored over every word in a dictionary so he could find stronger words to revise his story.

Perhaps Gardner was a man of extremes, but the story about him does make a point: that writers must seek the right words, the right verbs, to rank among the strongest of all.

Joe Hight has been editor of the Colorado Springs (Colorado) Gazette and the Oklahoman of Oklahoma City. He is now the owner and president of Best of Books, Inc.

The Reporter's Guide to the Language of News

1. Use subject-verb-object order for sentences.

2. Use singular subjects with singular verbs, and plural subjects with plural verbs.

3. Make sure pronouns agree with their antecedents.

4. Use "that," "which," "who" and "whom" correctly.

5. Place modifiers immediately before or after the noun they describe.

6. Do not depend on spell-check programs to find all misspelled words.

7. Choose words that convey your meaning as precisely as possible. Write your story with detail and explanation so it answers all the questions one logically might ask about the topic.

8. Use active verbs and vivid nouns.

9. Prune adjectives and adverbs from your sentences.

10. Avoid clichés, journalese, slang and euphemisms.

11. Avoid loaded words and opinionated or artificial labels.

12. Avoid mentioning yourself in the story and using the words "I," "me," "we," "us" and "our," except in direct quotations from a source.

13. Avoid misleading statements about the time of the story. Use the specific day of the week or the date—not "yesterday," "today" or "tomorrow."

14. Avoid gush, exaggeration, contrived labels and excessive punctuation.

15. Avoid an echo: Do not unnecessarily repeat the same word in a sentence.

16. Avoid platitudes: Do not state the obvious, such as the fact that a government official was happy to be elected.

17. Avoid the present tense when writing for print media; most events you write about already will have occurred. But for web or broadcast news stories, the present tense may be appropriate.

18. Cast your sentences in positive rather than negative form.

Review Exercises

1. Vocabulary

Choose the correct words in the following sentences and fix any errors in style and possessives. Consult The Associated Press Stylebook for preferred usage and Appendix B for the rules for forming possessives.

1. The news media are a (phenomena/phenomenon) of modern technology that have (altered/altared) the communication landscape.

2. The (envelop/envelope) the treasurer misplaced contained (about/around) $1,000 in contributions.

3. A large (bloc/block) of voters (alluded/eluded) to pollsters that the candidate was (elusive/illusive) when discussing (their/there/they're) views on foreign affairs.

4. She said rather (than/then) trying to (convince/persuade) the board of (trusties/trustees) to vote on the measure, she would work with the president and his (aids/aides).

5. They (hanged/hung) the new banner from a (pole/poll) and invited (more than/over) 200 (people/persons) to the ceremony.

6. Students are (liable/libel/likely) (to/too/two) demand (less/fewer) regulations (regardless/irregardless) what rules the committee might (adapt/adept/adopt).

7. The defendants (consul/council/counsel) (waived/waved) her right to a jury trial, saying he (adviced/advised) the defendant not to (chose/choose) that option.

8. The fire commissioner said the (forth/fourth) option to (reign/rein) in the cost of the firehouse expansion would be to (altar/alter) the (alley/ally) that is located behind the existing firehouse.

9. The woman, an (alumna/alumnae/alumni/alumnus) of the university, (implied/inferred) that the restrictions she placed on her donation may seem (bizarre/bazaar), but eventually they would be (cited/sited/sighted) as revolutionary.

10. The teacher was (discreet/discrete) when he (complemented/complimented) the group (composed/comprised/constituted) of six students for their paper (entitled/titled) "News and Social Media in the Modern World."

2. Active and Passive Voice

Rewrite the following sentences, changing active to passive voice and correcting other errors.

1. The students said there are some healthy choices in the cafeteria.

2. Most shoplifting by teenagers is done on impulse.

3. The robber was described by witnesses as a 20 year old male.

4. The car was destroyed by the flood waters.

5. The goal of the fundraisers is to have the public contribute to the organization.

3. Agreement

Correct all agreement errors in the following sentences. Rewrite the sentence if necessary.

1. The judge ruled that the committee acted within their rights when they voted to close the factory.

2. If a student under 21 has alcohol in student housing, they will be cited for underage drinking.

3. The jury said they could not reach a decision, leading to a mistrial.

4. The performance of the first three musical acts were very good.

5. Every one of the students want the exam postponed a week.

4. Plurals and Possessives

Edit the following sentences, correcting for plurals, possessives and other errors.

1. The womens car was parked nearby, and sheriffs deputies asked to see the owners drivers license.

2. The juror said she opposes assisted suicide "because a doctors job is to save peoples lives, not end them."

3. Last years outstanding teacher insisted that peoples complaints about the schools problems are mistaken.

4. Manvel Jones parents said there younger childrens teacher earned her bachelors degree in philosophy and her masters degree in education.

5. Everyones money was stolen, and the neighborhood associations president warned that the police are no longer able to guarantee peoples safety in the citys poorest neighborhoods.

5. Who and Whom

Choose the correct relative pronoun in the following sentences.

1. You went with (who/whom) to cover Hurricane Katrina?

2. He pushed (who/whom) off of the moving truck?

3. With (who/whom) did you go to the movies yesterday?

4. (Who/Whom) ate at the five-star restaurant with the senator last week?

5. (Who/Whom) told (who/whom) to call if there were an emergency?

6. Modifiers

Edit the following sentences, correcting for misplaced or dangling modifiers.

1. Touched and emotional, the letters to the soldiers were appreciated.

2. The child opened the toy truck he received from his mother painted red.

3. Coming in soaking wet from the rain, the clothes were thrown in the dryer.

4. Having begged for bicycles for months, the father was thanked by his children.

5. While eating the hotdog, the ketchup and mustard tasted great to the boy.

7. Personification

Rewrite the following sentences, eliminating personification and other errors.

1. The medicine bottle warns that its adverse effects include slowed heart beat, decreased respiratory function, sweating and nausea.

2. The accident occurred when the car driving east in the 100-block of Main St. collided with a dump truck that was driving west.

3. The meeting will decide whether the students have a right to protest the tuition increase.

4. Several vehicles pulled off the highway to assist police during the incident.

5. The witness told the jury he saw the vehicle driving recklessly with its headlights off.

8. Parallelism

Rewrite these sentences in parallel form and correct all errors.

1. She said after paying their rent, tuition and shopping for food, students have little money left.

2. To be admitted to the program, students must submit a written application, a portfolio and complete a 500-word essay.

3. The accident victim sustained a broken right arm, a fractured pelvis and his right lung was punctured.

4. Police said the robber was in his mid 20s, medium build, with dark blonde hair, wearing blue jeans, a green t-shirt and a blue cap.

5. Doctors said when the man was brought to the emergency room he was unconscious, blue and had stopped breathing.

9. Strong Verbs and Sentence Structure

Rewrite the following sentences, using stronger verbs and normal word order (subject, verb, direct object).

1. The best that can be hoped for is that the decision to postpone construction of the building by university officials will come soon.

2. Sitting across from me at the cafe dressed in a green hoodie and black hat, he ordered an espresso from the waitress.

3. More than 10 student residences have been broken into and have had things taken in the last two weeks.

4. Patients in dire need of treatment for serious injuries or illnesses are required to be taken to the nearest hospital by paramedics.

5. The three-vehicle accident that closed Main Street for two hours so authorities could investigate was witnessed by a bystander who called police to the scene.

10. Complete the Cliché

Fill in the missing word from the following clichés.

1. a close brush with _____
2. a step in the right _____
3. could not believe her _____
4. evidence of foul _____
5. fell into the wrong _____
6. has a nose for _____
7. last but not _____
8. left holding the _____
9. lived to a ripe old _____
10. lying in a pool of _____

11. Clichés and Slang

Rewrite the following sentences, eliminating any clichés and slang.

1. The president of the company asked employees to give the benefit of the doubt to his restructuring plan, but his plea fell on deaf ears.
2. The crowd erupted in violence when the doors to the club were closed, leaving them outside.
3. The governor said the election had tipped the scales in favor of his party.
4. The students believed the program was doomed to failure because few supported it.
5. Soldiers fought a pitched battle with a group of guerrilla fighters.

12. Jargon

Rewrite the following sentences, eliminating jargon.

1. Police said the perpetrators of the burglary would be arraigned later in the week.
2. Teresea Phillips, a/k/a Marie Phillips, testified that she entered the store and helped the defendant steal an unknown quantity of jewelry from the premises on or about the 9th day of last month.
3. The company said it would maximize efforts and utilize every department it had available to overcome the budget crisis.
4. The mayor said if the sanitation engineers went on strike, he would be forced to have other city workers drive the trucks.
5. Brown's lawsuit charges that, as a result of the auto accident, he suffered from bodily injury, disability, disfigurement and mental anguish. Brown's lawsuit also charges that he has lost his ability to earn a living and that the accident aggravated a previous condition.

13. Placement

Rewrite the following sentences, moving the related words and ideas as close together as possible. Correct any style or grammatical errors.

1. A 45-year-old man was sentenced to five years in prison after being convicted of embezzling $250,000 in Circuit Court on Monday.
2. The city counsel raised the parking fees on streets around campus from 35 cents to 50 cents an hour and restricted parking to two hours Tuesday afternoon.
3. The police arrested the man outside the bank standing near a telephone booth.
4. Born in Los Angeles, she moved with her family to Philadelphia where they opened a real estate business.
5. The principle suspended the student for possessing alcohol for one week.
6. The 16-year-old girl was driving home after school when her car struck the bridge traveling an estimated 50 mph.
7. He is making a list of the empty lots in the neighborhood so he can find the owners and ask if he can plant them next summer.
8. The police said the suspect shot the victim in a deserted section of the development.
9. The new university president met to discuss student concerns with the board.
10. Over $5 million was needed in order to begin construction of the new arts center by the city.

14. Multiple Errors

Rewrite the following sentences, correcting all errors. Most sentences contain more than one error.

1. A sheriffs deputy saw the teenagers Chevrolet pull out of the alley, driving recklessly without its headlines on, and arrested it's driver.

2. The city also said that they cannot silence Zheng Chen, the woman that fears pollution is likely to effect the neighborhoods 300 residents.

3. Seeking more money, publicity, and to help the poor, the churchs members said it wants the city to help it by providing food and offer housing for the homeless.

4. The Public Works Department said they could pave the developments road themselves for less than $1.2 million, the Roess Company submitted a bid of $2.74 million.

5. A jury awarded almost $10.5 million to the operators of an abortion clinic that charged that picketers tormented them and there clients. The clinics operators praised the jury's verdict, saying their courage and understanding set a needed precedent.

6. The committee said they feel the program is a beneficial one because a student can get class credit for all he does at the internship.

7. She laid on the beach from 8 AM in the morning until 3 PM in the afternoon realizing what a beautiful day it was.

8. The policeman told the jury that they needed to understand police procedures on investigations to understand how the robbery occurred during the trial.

9. The consensus of opinion among participants in the workshop is that a pay raise of 15 to 20 % should be received by the nurses.

10. The woman said her son, who she considered to be a budding genius, was champing at the bit to get to college next year.

THE LAW AND ETHICS OF JOURNALISM

5

LIBEL, PRIVACY AND NEWSGATHERING ISSUES

D o you recognize the name Leah Manzari? Probably not, but she is a celebrity in one segment of the entertainment industry. Performing under the name Danni Ashe, she was a pioneer in the online adult entertainment business. Her website, Danni.com, began operation in 1995 and by the early 2000s was generating multimillion-dollar revenues. She retired from the soft-core pornography business in 2004 and sold her website, although it remains active.

Nine years after Manzari retired, the Daily Mail Online, the internet companion to the London-based Daily Mail tabloid, published a story reporting that the porn industry in California had been shut down because an unidentified female actor had tested positive for HIV. The reporter who wrote the story suggested using a photo that would portray the porn industry without having any nudity. The photo the Daily Mail editors selected came from the Corbis Images database and showed Manzari in lingerie on a bed. Behind her, but visible, was a neon sign saying "In Bed With Danni." The story and the cutline for the photo contained no reference to Manzari or an explanation that the photo was nearly 13 years old.

As soon as she learned about the story, Manzari demanded that the Daily Mail remove her photo, which it did. But by that time, the story and photo had spread across the internet. Manzari sued for libel in U.S. district court in California. Associated News Ltd., owner of the Daily Mail Online, moved to dismiss the case under California's anti-SLAPP law. "SLAPP" stands for strategic lawsuits against public participation. The law deters suits intended solely to silence comment on matters of public importance. When the judge denied the motion, the company appealed to the 9th U.S. Circuit Court of Appeals.

The appellate court considered two issues: Could the story and photo be considered defamatory toward Manzari? Could she prove that Associated News published the story with actual malice, meaning the company knew the story was false or published with reckless disregard for whether it was false? In July 2016, the court ruled that the answer to both questions was yes. Even though the

"To courageous, self-reliant men, with confidence in the power of free and fearless reasoning applied through the processes of popular government, no danger flowing from speech can be deemed clear and present, unless the incidence of the evil apprehended is so imminent that it may befall before there is opportunity for full discussion. If there be time to expose through discussion the falsehood and fallacies, to avert the evil by the processes of education, the remedy to be applied is more speech, not enforced silence."

Louis Brandeis, U.S. Supreme Court justice

Former soft porn actor Leah Manzari (aka Danni Ashe) poses for her website in 2000.

story never used Manzari's real or stage name, the photo implied that the story was about her. Reasonable readers could easily conclude that she was the actor who tested HIV-positive. Her face was recognizable in the photo, and her stage name was visible in the sign. The court also said Manzari might persuade a jury that the Daily Mail published with actual malice. The Corbis Images database from which the Daily Mail obtained the photo clearly stated that the photo had been taken in 2000. Therefore, the publishers knew the photo was unrelated to the HIV issue, yet they failed to explain that to readers.

This case illustrates some points about libel law that even beginning journalists should know. One is that publishers are responsible not only for what they say explicitly but also for any implications readers, viewers or listeners might reasonably draw from a news story. Another is that, although there was no evidence the Daily Mail intended to defame Manzari, it could still be held responsible for any injury to her reputation. Finally, even though public figures have to meet a heavy burden to win a libel suit, it is not an impossible one. Under the right circumstances, public figures can and do win libel suits.

Journalism students usually investigate legal restraints on the media in specialized media law courses. This chapter introduces three areas that affect reporters almost daily: libel, privacy and access to news. The first two are covered more extensively because the danger of a lawsuit is high and the cost of defending or losing one can be great.

Libel

"Libel" is defamation by written words or by communication in some other tangible form, whereas "slander" is defamation by spoken words or gestures. Traditionally, the law has treated libel more harshly because the written word was more permanent and could reach more people than the spoken word. However, broadcasting blurred that line long ago because it can reach millions of people instantly. Many states now consider broadcast defamation libel rather than slander. The internet further erodes the distinction: Words, moving images and sounds can reach millions through the web, where they can remain almost indefinitely.

Libel is a major concern for the mass media. Juries sometimes award millions of dollars to successful plaintiffs. The Media Law Resource Center surveyed 557 libel trial verdicts over a 26-year period and found that the average damage award by a jury to a plaintiff was $2.85 million. Often that figure was reduced by the trial judge or an appeals court. The average final award was a little more than $560,000. Even when media organizations win libel suits, they still might spend millions on court costs and attorneys' fees.

Libel suits jeopardize not only the news organization's pocketbook but also its reputation. News organizations build their reputations on fairness and accuracy.

A libel judgment blemishes that status, sometimes irreparably. Individual journalists involved in libel suits may also lose their reputations or their jobs. Therefore, journalists must know what constitutes libel and what defenses can protect them in a suit.

The Elements of a Libel Suit

A person who files a libel suit involving a statement published in the mass media must prove certain elements. Different authorities have different requirements, but here are six generally recognized parts of a libel suit:

1. Defamation: A communication is defamatory if it is likely to injure the plaintiff's reputation among upstanding members of the community.
2. Identification: The defamatory communication is either explicitly or implicitly about the plaintiff.
3. Publication: The defamatory communication has been distributed to at least one person other than the plaintiff.
4. Falsity: The plaintiff must present credible evidence that the defamatory communication is false.
5. Injury: The plaintiff must present evidence that he or she has suffered some actual injury, which may be emotional or reputational as well as physical or economic. Plaintiffs who can prove the defendant published the statement with actual malice do not have to prove actual injury.
6. Fault: The plaintiff must prove the defendant was negligent (failed to act reasonably in the circumstances) in publishing the defamatory communication or published it with actual malice. In most states, private individuals who sue for libel must prove only negligence. Public officials and public figures must prove actual malice.

DEFAMATION

Proving that a statement is defamatory involves two steps. The first requires a judge to determine that the statement is capable of a defamatory meaning; in the second, a jury decides whether a substantial segment of the respectable public understood the statement as defaming the plaintiff.

Some statements obviously have the power to injure reputations—for example, statements that a person has committed a crime, has a terrible disease, has been incompetent in business or has engaged in serious sexual misconduct. Arthur Snyder, a former Los Angeles County supervisor, was the subject of emails written by Steve Lamb, a member of the Altadena, California, Town Council, and sent to other officials. The emails said Snyder had sexually abused his daughter, participated in a satanic ritual and made his daughter available for abuse by others participating in the ritual. Snyder and his daughter sued for libel, and the California Court of Appeals had no trouble concluding the allegations were capable of injuring their reputations.

But not every unflattering or even offensive statement is legally capable of a defamatory meaning. A statement has to sound factual and believable. Calling a person a "scumbag," for instance, is too vague and imprecise to be defamatory. Sometimes, the context in which the statement appears determines how recipients are likely to understand it. Before he died, the former Beatle George Harrison and the Honolulu Advertiser were sued by two of Harrison's neighbors. The newspaper had reported on Harrison's objections to a court order allowing his neighbors to cross parts of his property. "Have you ever been raped?" Harrison asked the Advertiser. "I'm being raped by all these people.... My privacy is being violated. The whole issue is my privacy." The neighbors claimed Harrison's remarks accused them of the crime of rape, but the Hawaii Supreme Court concluded "rape" was being used in a metaphorical rather than a literal sense and reasonable readers would understand it as such.

Sometimes, a statement conveys no obviously defamatory meaning. Instead, readers, viewers or listeners must combine the statement with known facts to find the defamation. Max Braun sued Armour & Co. over an advertisement that said his meat market carried Armour bacon. There's nothing obviously defamatory about selling bacon, but Braun ran a kosher store catering largely to Orthodox Jews. Many of Braun's customers who saw the ad stopped coming to the store. The New York Court of Appeals agreed that he had a case for libel.

Sometimes publications contain no explicitly defamatory statements, but they create defamatory implications by omitting key facts or by using certain combinations of words and pictures. When James Humphreys, a criminal defense lawyer, ran as a Democrat for a West Virginia congressional seat, he asked his former neighbors Harry Bell and his wife to endorse him and appear in a photograph with him. The photo ran in a Humphreys campaign brochure and on his website; it also appeared in an attack pamphlet prepared by the National Republican Congressional Committee, with the headline "Humphreys Defended Sex Offenders as a Criminal Defense Lawyer." Next to the heading was the photo of Humphreys and Harry Bell, with Bell's wife cropped from the picture. Bell claimed the brochure defamed him because the juxtaposition of the headline and the photograph created the impression he was a sex offender. A federal district judge agreed.

IDENTIFICATION

Libel plaintiffs have no trouble establishing identification in cases involving the news media. News stories usually identify sources or subjects clearly by name. In fact, detailed identification protects reporters against libel suits.

Many suits arise from situations in which similar names create confusion. If a Sam Johnson is arrested for selling cocaine, the commonness of the name creates the possibility of misunderstanding. By identifying the person arrested as Samuel H. Johnson Jr. of 3517 N. Forest St., Apt. 303, the reporter eliminates the possibility of inadvertently defaming other Sam Johnsons in town.

The publication can identify a plaintiff without using a name. In response to a lawsuit, a New York hospital issued a press release that referred to "misconduct carried out by former executives." Joseph A. Pisani, a former vice president of the hospital, sued for libel. The press release never used Pisani's name, but a federal district court held that the hospital's statement did identify him: the press release contained a hyperlink to the complaint in the original lawsuit, which mentioned him in connection with the misconduct, and he was fired on the day the hospital issued the press release.

PUBLICATION

Obviously, when a statement has appeared in a newspaper or on a television broadcast, it has been published. However, a statement does not have to be so widely disseminated for a person to sue for libel. The law requires only that the defendant made the statement to someone other than the person defamed. For example, Greenmoss Builders sued business services company Dun & Bradstreet for releasing a credit report with erroneous and damaging information about the contractor. Greenmoss won, even though only five clients received the report.

Once a libel is published, the plaintiff must sue within the time specified by the state's statute of limitations. In most states, the statute of limitations is one or two years. A few allow as many as three years. In all states, the statute of limitations runs from the most recent publication; republishing a defamatory statement extends the time during which the plaintiff may sue. Courts have held that the statute of limitations for online publications begins when the content is posted, while updates to the page and hyperlinks to an older page are not considered new publications that restart the clock.

Another issue connected with the internet is the liability of interactive service providers. Ordinarily a publisher is responsible for any material it publishes, but a federal law, Section 230 of the Communications Decency Act, protects interactive service providers. The case of Sarah Jones, a high school teacher and cheerleader for the Cincinnati Bengals football team, illustrates the protection that this federal law offers. Jones sued TheDirty.com for libel when Nik Lamas-Richie, the manager of the company that owns the site, refused to remove user posts suggesting that (among other things) Jones had had sexual relations with Bengals players and had contracted sexually transmitted diseases from a former lover. A jury awarded her $38,000 in compensatory damages and $300,000 in punitive damages. But a federal appeals court overturned the verdict on the basis that The Dirty.com is primarily a platform for content created by others and thus falls under Section 230 protection. The court said the remedy for Jones and people in her situation would be to subpoena Richie and TheDirty.com for information that would help her identify the people who posted the defamatory statements.

FALSITY

Some students confuse falsity and defamation. A statement may be false but not defamatory. Falsely saying someone is a war hero, for instance, does not defame that person. Conversely, a true statement may be defamatory. Saying someone was arrested for selling cocaine would defame that person, but he or she must be able to present evidence of falsity to sue for libel. The U.S. Supreme Court imposed this burden on all plaintiffs when the allegedly defamatory statements involve a matter of public concern. Making plaintiffs prove falsity means some defamed persons might not recover damages, but making defendants prove truth means some truthful publications will be punished. The court decided that, when the mass media publish statements about matters of public concern, the First Amendment requires tipping the balance in favor of freedom of the press.

Although the plaintiffs must prove falsity only when the defamatory statement involves a matter of public concern, the requirement applies in most cases involving the mass media. Courts usually conclude that statements appearing in the news media involve matters of public concern.

INJURY

Under traditional libel law, courts presumed obviously defamatory statements had injured the plaintiff. He or she did not have to produce any evidence of injury to reputation, monetary loss or emotional suffering unless the defamatory nature of the statement was not readily apparent. In 1974, the U.S. Supreme Court said the presumption of injury was incompatible with the First Amendment. Since then libel plaintiffs usually have had to prove "actual injury," meaning damage to reputation, humiliation and mental anguish to recover damages. There are two exceptions to this requirement: if the plaintiff can prove the defendant made the defamatory statements with actual malice or if the defamatory statements do not involve a matter of public concern.

A case requiring proof of injury involved former Chicago Bull Scottie Pippen, who lost much of his fortune because he received bad financial advice. When news organizations learned of his financial problems, some falsely reported he had filed for bankruptcy. Pippen sued for libel, even though the statement is not clearly defamatory; many people go bankrupt through no fault of their own. Pippen contended he had lost business opportunities after the publication, but a federal appeals court said Pippen would have difficulty showing the false news stories were the cause. In any event, the court said, he would lose his lawsuit because he could not prove actual malice.

FAULT

The most crucial issue in modern libel cases is fault, which refers to the state of mind of the person who uttered the allegedly defamatory statement. In other words, did the publisher knowingly, recklessly or negligently say something false and defamatory? Before 1964, many states said publishers of defamatory statements would have to pay damages even if they had taken every reasonable step to ensure the accuracy of the story. The Supreme Court changed that rule in 1964 for public officials who sue for libel and changed it further in cases decided in 1967 and 1974.

Public officials and public figures must prove that a defamatory statement was published with actual malice. The term causes confusion because many people think it means ill will, but whether the defendant disliked or wanted to harm the plaintiff is not an issue. All that matters is whether the defendant knew the statement was false or had a high degree of awareness of the statement's probable falsity when it was published. Proving actual malice can be difficult, as the plaintiff must produce evidence about the defendant's state of mind.

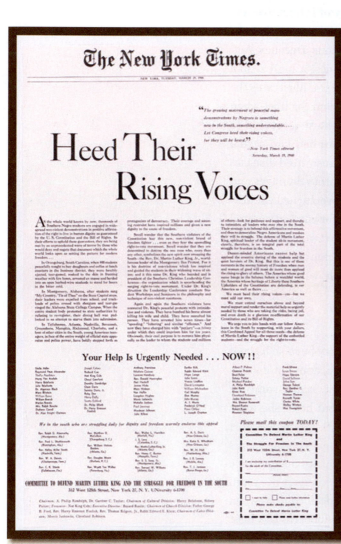

This March 1960 advertisement initiated the lawsuit that led to the Supreme Court's ruling that public officials must prove actual malice to recover damages for libel.

Since 1964, courts have handed down hundreds of decisions elaborating on what is and is not evidence of actual malice. The following list is not exhaustive but indicates the factors the courts consider.

It may be evidence of actual malice if the news organization:

- Simply made up a story or parts of it that are defamatory, such as fabricating quotations that make the source look immoral, incompetent or criminal.
- Published without investigating allegations from a source known to be unreliable or biased against the person defamed.
- Published an unverified story that is so inherently improbable that only a reckless person would believe it.
- Failed to check known sources that could conclusively confirm or deny a defamatory allegation.
- Published information from a source who, prior to the publication, had disavowed what she or he had said and the reporter was aware of the situation.

It generally is not evidence of actual malice if a news organization:

- Displayed ill will toward or an intent to harm the subject. A news organization's editorials against a political candidate, for instance, are not evidence by themselves that it published a defamatory news story with awareness of its falsity.
- Failed to investigate a story when the journalists responsible had no reason to doubt its truthfulness.
- Failed to investigate all the facts in a breaking news story—a story that had to be published quickly—and had no reason to doubt the truthfulness of what it was publishing.
- Made negligent errors in reporting a story, such as confusing or misspelling names or reporting complicated statistics incorrectly.
- Selected a reasonable, but mistaken, interpretation of a complicated or ambiguous document.
- Adopted an adversarial or investigative stance in reporting a topic.
- Published allegations even though the subject of the story denied them but failed to offer any evidence that they were false.

Private individuals have less difficulty winning libel suits. In most states, they must prove only that the defendant acted with negligence to recover actual damages. As previously noted, "negligence" essentially means acting unreasonably under the circumstances. Usually, the jury decides whether a defendant's actions were unreasonable. In a libel case, an error such as failing to check public records, misspelling or confusing names or accidentally transposing dates or figures might be considered negligence.

Who Is a Public Official? Who Is a Public Figure?

Because public officials and public figures must prove actual malice to win a libel suit, determining whether a plaintiff qualifies as either type often decides the outcome of a case. The Supreme Court has provided only hazy guidelines for distinguishing public officials and public figures from private individuals, leaving states with plenty of room to expand or contract the categories.

Paul Ryan, a former Republican representative from Wisconsin and Speaker of the House, was a public official.

The more clearly defined category is that of public official. The Supreme Court has said public officials must hold some government position. The category includes not only elected officials, such as U.S. senators, state legislators and city council members, but also appointed officials and government employees. Even unpaid government officials can be public officials for purposes of libel law. But being on the government payroll is not enough. While upper echelon officials such as governors and school superintendents are clearly public officials, a low-ranking worker in the city sanitation department or a secretary in the city attorney's office probably would not be one. A gray area exists between the top and the bottom levels, with the state courts deciding who belongs where. Most courts have found law enforcement officers and others who make decisions that affect the rights, liberty, health and safety of the public to be public officials.

Identifying public figures is even more difficult than identifying public officials. The Supreme Court tried to define "public figure" in a way that would keep the category small. It recognized three types: involuntary, general-purpose and limited-purpose. The court said the essence of public-figure status is that a person has voluntarily assumed some special prominence or role in society; therefore, the group of involuntary public figures must necessarily be very small, almost to the point of being nonexistent. The other two groups are somewhat larger.

The general-purpose public figure has such persuasive power and influence as to be a public figure for all occasions. Celebrities from entertainment and sports, such as Ansel Elgort, Taylor Swift, Denzel Washington, Lady Gaga, LeBron James and Richard Sherman, would probably fit this definition. So would people from other walks of life who have become unusually prominent—people like Elon Musk, Ann Coulter and Neil deGrasse Tyson. The Supreme Court said this group must also be small because few people attain such widespread notoriety.

The largest category of public figures consists of those who hold that status for the limited purpose of commenting on some particular topic or issue. These public figures have thrust themselves to the forefront of a controversy to affect its resolution. People who organize an abortion-rights march, lead an effort to persuade a school board to change the curriculum in history classes, or argue publicly for laws allowing people to carry concealed weapons are limited-purpose public figures.

Journalists need to remember that just being involved in a newsworthy event does not make a

Beyoncé and Jay-Z, seen here at the Metropolitan Museum of Art Costume Institute Gala, are public figures for the purposes of libel law.

person a public figure. The Supreme Court has said that people involved in civil court cases, criminal suspects and defendants, individuals and businesses who receive money from the government, and lawyers representing people in court are not automatically public figures. Such people have not necessarily stepped forward to influence the resolution of a public controversy.

Major Defenses to Libel Suits

The difficulty of proving actual malice has become media organizations' major defense in libel cases. Other defenses are available, and they can be important in some cases. The main ones are truth, fair-report privilege and fair comment and criticism.

TRUTH

The use of truth as a defense arose when courts presumed defamatory statements were false. Although plaintiffs must now prove falsity, proving a statement true can still defeat a libel claim.

Proving truth does not mean proving a news report accurate in every detail. Most courts require only proof that the sting or the gist of the charge is true. For example, a television news report about four Florida teenagers being arrested for bullying and defaming other teens on Facebook said "dozens" had been victimized, implying there were at least 24 victims. The parents of one plaintiff sued for libel, arguing that this number was incorrect and the police had never said how many teens were defamed. But a Florida court said the sting of the charge was that the girl had been arrested for cyberbullying. The precise number of victims did not affect the truth of that charge.

The defense of truth does not protect the accurate republication of defamatory charges made by other people. A news organization that reports a defamatory statement a bank president makes about a competitor cannot escape liability by demonstrating that it accurately quoted the speaker—it is also responsible for proving that the underlying statement is true. There are some exceptions to this rule; the main one is the fair-report privilege, which allows news organizations to report on official proceedings and documents.

FAIR-REPORT PRIVILEGE

The law recognizes certain occasions when people need absolute protection from libel suits. People called to testify in court, for example, cannot be sued for defamation because of what they say on the witness stand. Members of legislative bodies, such as Congress and state legislatures, cannot be sued over remarks they make in the course of their official duties. News organizations enjoy a similar privilege to report on what happens in courtrooms and legislative chambers and on what official documents say. As a result, a reporter covering a trial cannot be sued for reporting false and defamatory statements made by a witness so long as the story accurately summarizes the testimony.

This defense is powerful, but it can lead to injustices. New Jersey resident Janice Lee, a sales account manager for a distributor of hair products, was arrested by New York police during their bust of an alleged sex and prostitution ring. The New York attorney general's office announced at a press

Justin Bieber's arrest report in Miami on January 23, 2014, for suspicion of drunk driving. News reports based on official documents like this one are protected from libel suits so long as they fairly and accurately describe the documents, even if those documents contain defamatory falsehoods.

conference and in a press release that Lee had been arrested along with several other suspects. News of the arrest was disseminated by media in both states. Lee was innocent of all charges filed against her. Nevertheless, she spent nearly a week in jail and several more days getting the charges dropped. She later sued several news organizations for libel for having publicized her arrest. The federal district court that heard her case ruled that the fair-report privilege protected the news stories because they were "full, fair and accurate."

Journalists have the fair-report privilege when describing such governmental proceedings as court hearings, administrative agency meetings and legislative sessions at all levels of government, from town council to Congress. In most states, the privilege extends to official documents, such as police reports, health inspection reports, official government correspondence and court records. In some states, the privilege also applies to reports of nongovernmental meetings open to the public for discussion of matters of public concern.

A news organization loses the protection of the fair-report privilege if its story contains errors that would injure the plaintiff's reputation. Also, the privilege does not apply to information obtained from sources other than official documents or proceedings.

FAIR COMMENT AND CRITICISM

Everyone has the right to an opinion. The fair comment and criticism defense protects people who express their opinions about matters of legitimate public interest from libel suits. Usually, the defense applies only if the opinions are based on true facts, are the sincere opinions of the speakers and are not motivated solely by ill will.

Courts have struggled with how to separate statements of fact from statements of opinion. As the Supreme Court observed in one case, inserting "in my opinion" before a factual statement does not diminish the statement's power to defame. Furthermore, most of what is published in newspapers, magazines, TV news broadcasts and blogs blends fact and opinion. Editorials may state opinions, but they also contain facts. News stories may report facts, but they also report the opinions of the journalist's sources. A persistent issue is how much emphasis courts should give to the context in which a defamatory statement appears.

A case involving a book review published in The New York Times illustrates the difficulties courts have with the fair-comment defense. In his review of "Interference," a book on organized crime's influence on professional football, Gerald Eskenazi concluded that the work contained "too much sloppy journalism." The book's author, investigative reporter Dan Moldea, thought the remark libeled him and sued. After a federal district court granted The Times' motion to dismiss the case, Moldea appealed to the U.S. Court of Appeals for the District of Columbia Circuit. At first, the appeals court ruled that the statement was sufficiently factual that a jury could decide whether it was true. Furthermore, Supreme Court precedents prevented it from attaching much weight to the fact that the statement appeared in a book review.

A short time later, however, the court reconsidered its decision and concluded that the Supreme Court's rulings did not prevent courts from considering context in libel cases. When context is relevant, it helps indicate whether people will understand a statement as factual. The court said that, in the context of a book review, the accusation of sloppy journalism was exactly the kind of thing a reader would interpret as opinion and not as something that could be proved true or false.

Steps for Avoiding Libel Suits

No checklist or set of steps can guarantee that a news organization will never face a libel suit. Some have been sued even after they have checked stories and found evidence for every potentially defamatory statement. Usually, the conscientious news organization will win, but the cost of defending against the suit can be daunting.

Here are some things journalists can do to limit their risk:

1. Make sure everything in the story, especially any potentially defamatory statement, is newsworthy. Nothing is gained by risking a lawsuit over a statement that has no news value.
2. Identify everyone mentioned in the story as fully as possible.
3. Ask people who are attacked or criticized in news stories to respond, and include the response, even if it is just a flat denial. If a person refuses to respond, say so in the story.
4. If a person who has been attacked or criticized presents credible evidence to support his or her denials, check out that evidence.
5. Interview every relevant source and read every relevant document; do not ignore sources or information that might contradict any potentially defamatory statements.
6. Find out what basis a source has for making a defamatory charge and what the source's motives might be.
7. If a source for a story has credibility problems, explain them in the story.

8. Avoid confidential or anonymous sources. Reporters might be asked to reveal their sources at a libel trial. If they refuse to do so, judges may tell jurors to assume the reporters made up the information.

9. Never use confidential or anonymous sources for making attacks on a subject. Use them only for factual information that can be verified by other sources or documents.

10. If a story uses documentary sources, make sure the documents are understood and quoted accurately. Double-check the information in any documents; even official records may have errors.

11. If a story is not breaking news, take additional time to make sure the investigation is thorough and the story is accurate.

12. Adhere to organizational policies regarding keeping notes, tapes and other materials. If the policy is to keep all such materials, be sure everything is kept. If the policy is to destroy materials, make sure all are destroyed. Do not destroy some and keep others.

Privacy

At not quite 130 years old, the right to sue for invasion of privacy is relatively new in terms of legal history. Yet lawsuits over various forms of this type of offense have become a major concern to media organizations because people are more concerned about their privacy.

The law recognizes four kinds of invasion of privacy: intruding on a person's seclusion or solitude, giving publicity to private facts, placing a person in a false light and appropriating a person's name or likeness for one's own benefit (see Table 5.1). The last is primarily a concern for advertisers, although news and advertising messages could be the basis for a lawsuit over any of the four forms. The status of these four ways of invading privacy varies from state to state. Some states have recognized them in statutes; in others, court decisions have recognized privacy rights even in the absence of specific statutes. Some states do not recognize all four forms. Nebraska, for example, does not recognize a right to sue for giving publicity to private facts, and Texas does not recognize false-light actions.

Intrusion

Intrusion represents what most people think of as invasion of privacy. Barging into a person's home without permission or rummaging through someone's private desk is intrusion. But one does not have to enter another's space physically to commit intrusion. One could intrude by technological means, such as using a powerful telephoto lens to see someone in a private location or using highly sensitive microphones to pick up a private conversation.

A plaintiff in an intrusion case must be able to show that the defendant intruded into an area where the former had a reasonable expectation of privacy. Some places obviously are private: a person's home, a hotel room, a hospital room, a handbag or a briefcase. Even if a newsworthy event is happening on private property, a journalist may not enter without the owner's or legal occupant's permission.

TABLE 5.1   Types of Privacy Invasion

Type	Legal Requirement
Intrusion	To establish a case for invasion of privacy by intrusion, the plaintiff must show that a. the defendant intentionally intruded, physically or otherwise, on the plaintiff's solitude or seclusion, and b. the intrusion would be highly offensive to a reasonable person in the plaintiff's situation.
Publicity to private facts	A plaintiff suing over publicity given to private facts must prove a. the defendant gave publicity to b. private facts about the plaintiff, c. the disclosure of which would be highly offensive to a reasonable person in the plaintiff's situation, and the facts disclosed are not a matter of public concern.
False light	The plaintiff in a false-light lawsuit must prove a. the defendant portrayed the plaintiff in a false light b. that would be highly offensive to a reasonable person in the plaintiff's situation. In some states, all false-light plaintiffs must prove the defendant portrayed the plaintiff in a false light with the knowledge of its falsity or reckless disregard for whether it was false (actual malice). Some states say only public figures who sue for false light must prove actual malice. Private individuals can win by proving the defendant was negligent.
Appropriation	A person suing for appropriation (sometimes called misappropriation) must prove that a. the defendant used the plaintiff's name or likeness b. without consent c. for the defendant's benefit (usually meaning some kind of commercial benefit). A similar type of lawsuit, usually brought by a celebrity, is over infringement on one's right of publicity. This requires the plaintiff to show that the defendant a. used some distinctive element of the plaintiff's identity b. without consent and c. caused injury to the plaintiff (which may simply be the loss of an opportunity to capitalize on one's fame).

The California Supreme Court has also found that the reasonable expectation of privacy extends to at least some workplace situations. An ABC reporter, Stacy Lescht, worked undercover at a company that offered psychic readings by telephone. While on the job, Lescht wore a hidden microphone and camera. She recorded conversations she had with some of her co-workers, among them Mark Sanders. After ABC aired a story about the telepsychic business, Sanders sued for invasion of privacy. A jury awarded him $1.2 million in damages. An appeals court reversed the award, but the California Supreme Court reinstated it. ABC contended Sanders had no expectation of privacy because the telepsychics worked in open cubicles and could hear one another's conversations. However, the Supreme Court noted the office was not open to the general public; therefore, Sanders had a reasonable expectation that his conversations with colleagues would not be recorded or photographed surreptitiously and broadcast. Patrons and employees of businesses that are open to the public, such as restaurants and stores, may also have some reasonable privacy expectations.

As this case shows, the surreptitious recording of conversations is an issue closely related to intrusion. Reporters should always ask sources for permission to record conversations with them, even though recording without permission is legal in most states if one party consents. The consenting party may be the journalist who is doing the recording. However, 11 states—California, Delaware, Florida, Hawaii, Maryland, Massachusetts, Montana, Nevada, New Hampshire, Pennsylvania and Washington—currently require the consent of all parties, at least in situations where there is an expectation of privacy.

Surreptitiously photographing people also presents legal problems. At least 24 states outlaw using hidden cameras in private places. The laws vary widely: Some apply only to unattended cameras; others prohibit only attempts to use hidden cameras to photograph people in the nude. Dani Mathers, a former Playboy Playmate of the Year, was charged with a misdemeanor after she took a photo of a nude 71-year-old woman in a Los Angeles fitness club locker room. Mathers posted the photo on Snapchat, along with the comment, "If I can't unsee this then you can't either." After changing her initial not-guilty plea to no contest, she was sentenced to 30 days' community service and three years' probation; the fitness club also banned her from all 800 of its U.S. facilities.

While someone on a public street or in a public park has no expectation of privacy, there are limits to what reporters can do even in public places. Photographers or reporters who become so aggressive that they place their subjects in danger may be committing intrusion or some other tort. Courts do not consider ordinary newsgathering techniques—examining public records; interviewing someone's friends, relatives, enemies and associates; and interviewing or attempting to interview a person—intrusive.

Giving Publicity to Private Facts

Everybody has secrets, and most people would be upset if theirs were made public. Lawsuits for publicizing private facts allow people to receive compensation for injuries when their secrets are revealed. This form of privacy lawsuit, however, presents a potential for conflict with the First Amendment because an unfavorable judgment may punish someone who published the truth.

For such a case to be successful, the information disclosed must be truly private. Publicizing—meaning disseminating widely—facts that appear in public records, even if they are not generally known, cannot be the basis for a lawsuit. For example, property tax information is public record in most states. If a news organization publishes a list of the most valuable homes in the community, who owns them and how much the owners pay in property taxes, the people named cannot sue for invasion of privacy. Even if the information is not in a public record but is merely known to a large number of people, publicizing it does not invade that person's privacy.

The information that is publicized must also be highly offensive to a reasonable person. Disclosure of information that is merely embarrassing cannot be the basis for a lawsuit. The "reasonable person" standard is imprecise, but it asks juries to decide not by what would be offensive to the most sensitive or insensitive individual but by what a reasonable person in the plaintiff's situation would find highly offensive. Not surprisingly, many of the cases involve sex or nudity. Publicizing private medical information, relationships with spouses or children and personal financial information might also be highly offensive.

Even if the matter publicized is highly offensive to a reasonable person, the plaintiff still must prove there is no legitimate public interest in the information. Courts have generally held that news organizations may publish private facts about people so long as they bear some logical connection to a matter of public concern, such as information about people who are victims of accidents or crimes.

Gawker Media pushed the limit of what is newsworthy when it posted portions of a video of Terry Bollea, better known as former wrestling star Hulk Hogan, having sex with Heather Clem. Bollea sued Gawker for invasion of privacy. Lawyers for the website argued that, as Hulk Hogan, the plaintiff had bragged about his sexual prowess and penis size; thus, he could not claim that his sexual activities were private. Bollea said that Hulk Hogan was a public character, but the video showed a private moment. A Florida jury concluded the video was not newsworthy and awarded Bollea $115 million in actual damages and $25 million in punitive damages. The award drove Gawker Media and its founder, Nick Denton, into bankruptcy.

Courts generally have interpreted the phrase "matter of public concern" to include not only political and governmental information but also news of sports, entertainment, fashion and other matters likely to engage popular attention. The public interest is broader in people who are public figures—movie stars, sports heroes and important political figures—but it may also include private individuals who have been caught up in newsworthy events. Moreover, this interest extends beyond the specific event or situation and includes other aspects of the subject's life and information about his or her relatives, so long as those facts have some bearing on the matter of public concern.

False Light

A false-light invasion of privacy lawsuit resembles a libel suit in many respects. In fact, a person often may sue for either or both on the same evidence. The major difference between them is that a libel suit redresses injury to a person's reputation, whereas a false-light suit protects a person's interest in being let alone.

Actor José Solano Jr., who played Manny Gutierrez on the TV show "Baywatch," sued Playgirl magazine after it used his picture, without permission, on its cover. Solano said the picture and accompanying headlines gave the false

Terry Bollea (aka Hulk Hogan) testifies against Gawker at the Pinellas County Courthouse in St. Petersburg, Florida.

impression he had posed nude for the magazine. The headlines said things like "12 Sizzling Centerfolds Ready to Score With You," "TV Guys: Prime Time's Sexy Young Stars Exposed" and "'Baywatch's' Best Body: José Solano." A federal appeals court said the juxtaposition of the photo and the headlines could convey the false and highly offensive impression that Solano had posed nude for the magazine. Furthermore, there was evidence the editors knew they were conveying a false impression. The magazine's senior vice president had ordered the editors to "sex up" the January 1999 issue. And subordinate editors were aware the headline about the centerfolds was positioned where headlines about the person pictured on the cover normally run.

Appropriation

Anyone who uses the name or likeness of another for his or her own use or benefit may be sued for invasion of privacy by appropriation. This was the first form of invasion of privacy to win recognition in a statute. The most common form of appropriation is the use of a person's name or likeness in an advertisement.

Retired basketball star Michael Jordan received substantial payouts from two grocery chains when their advertisements featuring his name and jersey number appeared in a commemorative issue of Sports Illustrated recognizing his induction into the Naismith Memorial Basketball Hall of Fame. Jewel-Osco argued that its ad was not a commercial advertisement, but a federal appeals court said such images advanced the company's commercial interests. Dominick's Finer Foods admitted liability but contested the amount of damages the plaintiff wanted. After a jury awarded Jordan $8.9 million, Jewel-Osco reached an out-of-court settlement with him.

The use of a person's name or likeness in a news story is not considered appropriation, even though it might benefit the newspaper, magazine or broadcast by attracting readers, viewers, listeners and advertisers. The use must have some reasonably direct connection to a matter of public interest. Generally courts have considered the public interest to include a broad range of topics and have been reluctant to second-guess journalists as to what is newsworthy and relevant.

The exemption from misappropriation lawsuits for news publications and broadcasts extends to advertisements promoting them. A news interview program can include the name and likeness of a future guest in ads promoting the broadcast. However, the promotional material must not suggest that the person is endorsing that program, network or station. Nor can a broadcast or publication encroach on a performer's right to make money from his or her act. The U.S. Supreme Court upheld a judgment against an Ohio television station that broadcast a human cannonball's act in its entirety, ruling that the station had infringed on this right.

Newsgathering Issues

The First Amendment expressly protects the right to speak and to publish, but it says nothing about the right to gather information. The Supreme Court has recognized that freedom of the press means very little without this right, but the rights reporters have to information are largely defined by a hodgepodge of state and federal statutes and court opinions. This section covers three newsgathering issues: access to nonjudicial events and records, access to judicial proceedings and confidentiality for sources and information.

Reporters should always remember that the First Amendment does not protect them from prosecution if they engage in illegal conduct to gather news. Posing as a police officer, buying drugs and stealing documents are all illegal activities, and reporters who are prosecuted for crimes cannot plead that they were doing so to gather information for a news story.

Access to Nonjudicial Events and Records

NEWS SCENES

When a river floods a city, police discover a murder or a fire destroys a building, police, rescue workers and firefighters try to control the area to save lives and protect property. Some officials, however, worry as much about their images and how they will appear in news accounts as they do about citizens and their property. They may try to control what reporters and photographers see and how they report what they see.

When Hurricane Katrina hit New Orleans, journalists rushed to the city to report on the extensive damage, the plight of the victims and the rescue efforts. But officials for the Federal Emergency Management Agency and the Army Corps of Engineers tried to prevent some of the reporting. At one point, FEMA tried to impose a "zero access" policy to block coverage of the recovery of bodies. Photographers for Bloomberg News and the Miami Herald were escorted away from a recovery site, and other reporters were harassed while trying to gather information. Eventually, CNN obtained a restraining order from a federal district court, preventing FEMA from enforcing its policy. Yet even after the restraining order had been issued, soldiers threatened to revoke the credentials of a reporter and a photographer from the San Francisco Chronicle if they wrote about or took photographs of the recovery of bodies.

The protests and demonstrations that broke out in Ferguson, Missouri, following the fatal shooting of a young black man by a police officer brought news reporters from around the country. During one evening's protest, which degenerated into a riot, reporters Wesley Lowery of The Washington Post and Ryan Reilly of HuffPost were ordered by police to leave the McDonald's where the pair had been working on their stories. The reporters tried to take video of the confrontation, but they were arrested. One officer slammed Lowery into a soda machine and then handcuffed him. Although the reporters were soon released from custody, news organizations and even President Obama objected to what seemed an unjustified interference in newsgathering.

Some journalists are worried that the climate for newsgathering is worsening. Washington, D.C., police arrested nine reporters who were covering protests at the inauguration of Donald Trump. Prosecutors dropped charges against seven of them. Of the remaining two, one was acquitted of all charges after a trial. The other was awaiting trial as this book was being written. Several reporters who were trying to cover protests following the acquittal of a white police officer

Reilly's and Lowery's regular tweets from the scene of their arrest kept their followers updated on the situation in Ferguson.

Ryan J. Reilly ✓
@ryanjreilly

SWAT just invade McDonald's where I'm working/recharging. Asked for ID when I took photo.

4:53 PM - 13 Aug 2014

Wesley Lowery ✓
@WesleyLowery

Officers decided we weren't leaving McDonalds quickly enough, shouldn't have been taping them.

1:40am · 14 Aug 2014 · Cloudhopper

4,799   926
RETWEETS   FAVORITES

> ## 🔥 HOT TIP
>
> ## Covering News Scenes
>
> The Reporters Committee for Freedom of the Press recommends reporters and photographers do the following to minimize the risk of being harassed by police when covering protests, crimes or disasters:
>
> - Always carry press credentials.
>
> - Don't trespass on private property or cross clearly marked police lines.
>
> - Don't take anything from a crime scene.
>
> - Obey all orders from police officers, even if doing so interferes with getting the story or the photo. (The alternative might be going to jail.)
>
> - Don't argue with arresting officers.
>
> - Have $50 to $100 on hand to purchase bail bond.
>
> - Have a government-issued photo ID.

who had killed a black man were arrested. One, a reporter for the St. Louis Post-Dispatch, was knocked to the ground and pepper-sprayed, even though he was carrying press credentials. And Ben Jacobs, a reporter for The Guardian, tried to ask Republican congressional candidate Greg Gianforte about the cost of a GOP health care plan. Gianforte responded by body-slamming Jacobs. Gianforte's campaign initially blamed the reporter for the incident, but eventually the candidate was charged with misdemeanor assault. He pleaded guilty and was sentenced to 40 hours of community service and 20 hours of anger management classes.

RECORDS AND MEETINGS

All states and the federal government have laws that help citizens and reporters access government records. The main federal law is the Freedom of Information Act (FOIA, which can be pronounced as FOY-ya and is used as both a noun and a verb). This law has given the public access to such things as documents showing that the FBI has targeted groups such as Greenpeace and People for the Ethical Treatment of Animals for surveillance in the name of fighting terrorism and to National Security Agency files on the alleged UFO crash near Roswell, New Mexico, in 1947. Basically, the FOIA opens to public inspection all records held by agencies of the federal executive branch, unless the records fall into one of nine exempt categories (see Table 5.2). If a record is exempt, the agency may still release it but is not required to do so. Much litigation under the FOIA concerns whether records are exempt.

Since passing the FOIA, Congress has amended it several times. It has excluded information about foreign intelligence, counterintelligence and terrorism. It has also made it easier for law enforcement agencies to withhold information about their investigative procedures and techniques. When Congress created the Department of Homeland Security, it exempted from disclosure information that the department receives from private businesses about weaknesses in the country's critical infrastructure.

The FOIA says federal agencies should release nonexempt information in response to any written request that reasonably identifies the records. The relevant agency is supposed to respond within 20 working days, but it may have 10 additional days if a request involves unusual circumstances. Actually getting the information, however, could take much longer. The National Security Archive, a private organization that frequently uses the FOIA, discovered that some requests had been pending for more than 20 years. Most agencies have backlogs of requests—Congress has encouraged them to reduce this problem by making more information available online. The change has dramatically reduced backlogs at some agencies like the National Aeronautics and Space Administration, but the impact at others, such as the Department of Justice, has been minimal.

Univision anchor Jorge Ramos is physically removed from a news conference held in Iowa during the 2016 election campaign, where he attempted to ask Donald Trump about his immigration proposal.

State and District of Columbia laws about opening government records and meetings to the public and the press vary considerably. Some are very broad and have few exemptions. Others exempt dozens of kinds of records or meetings or have other qualifications that limit access.

Some public officials flout or ignore the law because they dislike having their records opened to public inspection. News organizations in most states have conducted statewide surveys of official compliance with public records laws and have found many instances of withheld records. New Jersey reporters discovered that, although they had no trouble getting local budgets, they received only 22 percent of their requests for police logs and 31 percent of school superintendents' contracts. In spite of such noncompliance, reporters rely on state open records laws almost daily because they apply to local governments, like cities, counties and school boards, as well as to state agencies.

TABLE 5.2   FOIA Record Exemptions

1. Classified information.

2. Information related solely to internal personnel rules and practices.

3. Information exempted by other statutes.

4. Trade secrets and confidential commercial information.

5. Interagency and intra-agency memoranda that would reveal decision-making processes.

6. Information that would be a clearly unwarranted invasion of personal privacy.

7. Law enforcement investigative files, the disclosure of which would or could cause certain harms.

8. Information about financial institutions.

9. Geological and geophysical information such as maps showing the locations of oil and mineral deposits.

When embarrassing information gets out, states sometimes amend their laws to limit disclosure. During a court hearing on the manner in which Missouri administered lethal injections to execute prisoners, the doctor who supervised executions admitted he was dyslexic, sometimes confused the dosages of the drugs used to kill the prisoners and had been sued for malpractice so often that two hospitals had revoked his privileges to practice. If the drugs used in the lethal injection procedure are not administered properly and in the right dosages, the prisoner can suffer excruciating pain. The doctor was identified as "John Doe" during the hearing, but the St. Louis Post-Dispatch later identified him as Dr. Alan R. Doerhoff. The response of the Missouri General Assembly was not to require more training or competence on the part of its executioners. Instead it passed a law making it illegal to disclose the identities of those who assist in the execution process. It also prohibited medical licensing boards from taking disciplinary action against any members who participate in executions.

Access to Judicial Proceedings

Freedom of the press is just one of many rights the Constitution guarantees to people in the United States. The Constitution also says a person accused of a crime has the right to a trial by an impartial jury. These two rights appear to conflict when news organizations publish information that might sway potential jurors. Some authorities have labeled this problem "free press vs. fair trial," suggesting one right must be sacrificed to the other. Fortunately, most judges, including those on the U.S. Supreme Court, reject that view. Instead, a judge presiding over a trial must protect both the right of a defendant to a fair trial and the freedom of the press.

In the 1960s, the Supreme Court said trial judges must protect judicial proceedings when there is a reasonable likelihood that news coverage could prejudice the trial. The court did not say how a judge should curb prejudicial publicity but focused on steps he or she could take to protect the trial without interfering with the news media. For example, a judge could sequester jurors, move trials to new locations if publicity becomes too intense, delay a trial or limit the kinds of statements prosecutors and defense attorneys may make to the press about a pending trial.

Although the Supreme Court said nothing about restraining what journalists say about court proceedings, judges in the 1970s started issuing "gag" orders prohibiting reporters from publishing certain information even when they learned it in open court. The court declared this kind of limitation on the press a prior restraint. It is unconstitutional unless the nature and extent of the news coverage threatens the fairness of a trial, no alternative to a prior restraint would protect the trial and a prior restraint would be effective in preventing prejudice.

After the Supreme Court sharply limited judges' ability to impose gag orders, trial courts started denying journalists access to information by closing the courtroom door. Again, the court stepped in to restrict what judges can do. The high court declared in 1980 that the press and the public have a First Amendment right to attend court proceedings that historically have been open to the public and where public observation is beneficial to the proceeding. That right is not absolute, however, and may be curtailed when necessary to protect a fair trial. Judges may close a proceeding if they find a substantial likelihood of prejudice that closure would prevent and alternatives to closure would not work. This is a very difficult standard to meet because it requires the court to find facts establishing both conditions.

Access to one particular court proceeding—jury selection—has become especially contentious. Jury selection is considered part of the trial; some attorneys consider it the most important step. But concerns for juror privacy and safety have persuaded some judges to close access to the selection process or prohibit release of jurors' names. Ronell Wilson, who had the nickname "Rated R," was accused of killing two undercover police officers. Prosecutors persuaded the federal trial judge that Wilson presented such a threat that the jurors should be selected in sequestered sessions and their identities, addresses and occupations should be kept confidential.

Occasionally, courts have closed jury selection even in cases where their safety was not threatened. The court that tried Martha Stewart on charges she had lied about insider stock trading barred news organizations from the jury selection process. News organizations objected, and a federal appeals court said the trial court had failed to show that closure of jury selection was necessary to protect Stewart's right to a fair trial.

Some states close or limit access to proceedings in juvenile, family or divorce courts. Other states allow public access to such courts. The U.S. Supreme Court has not specifically ruled on the matter.

The problems with gag orders and court closures became so severe in the 1970s that some state press and bar groups collaborated to write guidelines for dealing with each other during trials. These voluntary guidelines, which are also supposed to protect the interests of news organizations and criminal defendants, generally say the media should be free to report the following:

● Basic information about a suspect, such as name, age, address and marital status.
● The charges against the suspect.
● The circumstances under which the suspect was arrested, including whether any weapons were used.
● The names of those who have filed complaints against the suspect.
● If the crime involved a death, who died and how.
● The identities of the investigating agencies and officers.

The following information should not be published under most bar-press guidelines:

● The existence and nature of any statement or confession the suspect made to authorities.
● The results of any tests.
● Opinions on the credibility of the suspect, any witnesses or any evidence.
● Opinions about the outcome of the trial.
● Any other statements made outside the presence of the jury that might be highly prejudicial.

Furthermore, the guidelines strongly discourage publishing a suspect's criminal record because such information is considered highly prejudicial. However, preventing its disclosure might be impossible, given that it is a matter of open record in many states and could be in a newspaper's clip file.

Although bar-press guidelines are voluntary, reporters should pay attention to them and think carefully about the risks that publishing certain information may pose to criminal defendants. Many people think a person who has been charged with a crime is guilty, even before a trial. The National Registry of Exonerations, a joint project between the University of Michigan and Northwestern University law schools, lists more than 2,200 cases in which a person who was convicted of a crime was later found to have been innocent, often because of DNA evidence that was tested years later.

In many of these cases, the people who were later exonerated seemed clearly guilty at the time of their trials. A well-known example is the 1990 trials of the Central Park Five, which drew national attention. Teenagers Yusef Salaam, Kevin Richardson, Antron McCray, Raymond Santana and Korey Wise were arrested for the brutal rape and assault of a 28-year-old woman in New York's Central Park. Under intense and possibly coercive interrogations, all confessed to the crime. Although they recanted their statements, the fact they had confessed convinced the jury—and most of the press and public—of their guilt. Even before their trials began, many presumed the youths were guilty. All five served time in prison. Nearly 13 years after the crime, Matias Reyes said he alone was responsible; DNA evidence confirmed his confession.

Confidentiality for Sources and Information

For almost as long as reporters have written news, they have used confidential sources. Reporters depend on such people for some of their best stories. Because many sources will provide information only if they know they are safe, reporters routinely promise to protect their identities.

Law enforcement officials, grand juries, courts, legislative bodies or administrative agencies sometimes demand the names of confidential sources or other information the reporter wants to protect. The lawyers and judges want this information because they think it is relevant to a criminal or civil case. Reporters may receive subpoenas ordering them to testify before an official body. The subpoena may also direct them to bring their notes, photographs, tapes and other materials they collected. A person who fails to comply can be cited for contempt of court and sent to jail, fined or both.

Several major cases have underscored the dilemma reporters sometimes face. Judith Miller, a former reporter at The New York Times, spent 85 days in jail for contempt of court when she refused to disclose who had leaked the identity of covert CIA agent Valerie Plame Wilson to the media. Although Miller never published a story naming Wilson, the agent's name had been revealed to her in conversations with White House officials. Eventually, Miller's source, I. Lewis ("Scooter") Libby released her from her pledge to keep his name secret, and she testified to the grand jury. Libby eventually was convicted of perjury.

In another case, freelance video blogger Josh Wolf recorded a demonstration by anarchists in San Francisco that turned violent. A police officer was injured and a police car damaged during the protests. Wolf sold some of his footage to a local television station and posted edited clips of the rest on his website. Federal prosecutors thought Wolf might be able to identify some of the demonstrators who had committed crimes; they subpoenaed him to testify and turn over all of his tapes, including the unpublished portions, to a grand jury. Wolf refused and was held in contempt of court. He spent 226 days in jail, the longest term ever served by a journalist for refusing to reveal confidential sources or information. He was released after mediation resulted in an agreement with the federal government. Wolf persuaded prosecutors he had no information relevant to their investigation, and he agreed to post all of his videotapes on his website, making them available to prosecutors and the general public.

Subpoenas are a common problem for news reporters. Generally, broadcast news organizations receive more subpoenas than print news outlets. Most of the orders to radio and television stations ask for video or audio recordings, both outtakes and portions aired. Newspapers are more likely to receive subpoenas demanding that reporters reveal confidential information or sources.

Reporters have had mixed success resisting subpoenas. Some state and federal courts have recognized a reporters' privilege to protect confidential sources and information. The extent of this protection varies greatly, but usually it allows reporters to shield their sources except when the information is essential to a case, can be obtained in no other way and would serve a compelling governmental interest. Courts generally have held that this privilege does not apply to nonconfidential information and sources or to actions a reporter or photographer might have witnessed firsthand. Even in states that recognize a privilege, news organizations sued for libel must disclose confidential sources or information that the plaintiffs might need to make their case.

In addition to the privilege recognized by some state and federal courts, 40 states and the District of Columbia have shield laws that specifically guarantee a journalist's right to protect confidential sources or information. Again, the laws vary: some let journalists protect confidential sources and unpublished information; others limit the protection to confidential sources. State laws also differ in who is protected. Some shield laws apply to anyone engaged in gathering and disseminating information to the public. Others cover only professional journalists, often meaning people associated with traditional media. Such laws may leave bloggers and other nontraditional journalists unprotected. Furthermore, some states grant reporters a nearly absolute privilege to refuse to testify, whereas others qualify the privilege. Yet even in states that recognize an absolute privilege, journalists are required to provide information vital for securing a criminal defendant's constitutional right to a fair trial. Congress has refused so far to pass a federal shield law.

Former Fox News reporter Jana Winter covered a shooting in an Aurora, Colorado, movie theater that left 12 dead. Sources told her the suspect had filled a notebook with violent images and notes and sent it to a psychiatrist days before the shooting. The Colorado court issued a subpoena for her to reveal her sources, but this order also had to be enforced by the state of New York, where Winter was based. The state refused on the grounds that its reporter's shield law protected journalists' sources. The defense's attorney appealed to the Supreme Court but lost.

The Reporter's Guide to Libel, Privacy and Newsgathering Issues

Defamation

1. "Libel" is defamation by written words or communication in another tangible form; "slander" is defamation by spoken words or gestures.

2. Libel plaintiffs often must prove six elements: defamation, identification, publication, falsity, injury and fault.

3. Fault is often the most important issue in a libel case. Public officials and public figures who sue for libel must prove actual malice (knowledge that the information is false or reckless disregard for its probable falsity). Private individuals must prove only negligence.

4. "Negligence" means the publisher failed to do what a reasonable and prudent person would have done in the same circumstances.

5. Public officials are people in government who hold positions high enough that they have or appear to have influence over public affairs.

6. Public figures are people who are widely known and influential or who have taken a leadership role in trying to influence decisions about issues of public concern.

7. The major common-law defenses to libel suits are truth, fair-report privilege and fair-comment privilege.

Privacy

1. Invasion of privacy comprises four types of lawsuits: intrusion, publicity to private facts, false light and appropriation.

2. Intrusion is one person intentionally intruding on the privacy of another, by physical or other means, in a manner that would be highly offensive to a reasonable person. To sue for intrusion, the plaintiff must show that the defendant intruded on an area where the former had a reasonable expectation of privacy.

3. In most states, reporters may surreptitiously record conversations with a source without his or her consent. Eleven states require the consent of all parties, at least where there is an expectation of privacy.

4. Publicity to private facts involves publicizing private information about another person, the disclosure of which would be highly offensive to a reasonable person and which is not of legitimate public concern.

5. False light involves portraying another person in a way that is false and highly offensive (but not necessarily defamatory) to a reasonable person.

6. Appropriation is the use of another person's name or likeness for one's own benefit, usually meaning some kind of commercial use. Using a person's name or likeness in a news story is not considered appropriation if it bears some connection to a matter of public interest.

Newsgathering Issues

1. Journalists gather information at scenes of crimes, fires and natural disasters.

2. Reporters should never interfere with the work of police, firefighters, medical personnel or other officials. Police or other authorities sometimes object to the presence of news gatherers.

3. Access to meetings and records is governed by state and federal laws.

4. The U.S. Freedom of Information Act opens the records of the federal executive branch to public inspection, but nine categories of records are exempt from disclosure.

5. The Sunshine Act opens meetings of some federal agencies, such as the Federal Communications Commission and the Federal Trade Commission, to the public.

6. State open records laws require disclosure of the records of most state and local governmental bodies. The agencies and governmental units covered and the exempt records vary from state to state.

7. State open meetings laws require that the meetings and associated records of various governmental units be open to the public. Some meetings may be exempt, and most state laws allow for executive sessions under some circumstances.

8. Court proceedings are generally open to the public. Limited closures to prevent news coverage that might prejudice potential jurors against a defendant are permissible, especially during pretrial hearings.

9. Judges may not impose prior restraints on what news organizations may report about criminal proceedings unless the news coverage has been extensive and highly prejudicial, alternatives to a prior restraint would be ineffective or a prior restraint would be effective.

10. Journalists need confidential sources to report some stories, but if a grand jury or a trial court wants to know the identity of a confidential source, the reporter must either reveal the source or face the possibility of going to jail for contempt of court.

11. Forty states and the District of Columbia have shield laws, which allow journalists to withhold the names of confidential sources and other confidential information. The laws vary greatly in what is protected and how strongly. The federal government has no shield law.

Review Exercises

1. Libel

Decide which of the following sentences and paragraphs are potentially libelous. Label each statement that is dangerous for the media with a D and each statement that is safe with an S.

1. Police officers said they shot and wounded Ira Andrews, a 41-year-old auto mechanic, because he was rushing toward them with a knife.

2. Testifying during the second day of the trial, Mrs. Andrea Cross said her husband, Lee, never intended to embezzle the $70,000, but that a secretary, Allison O'Hara, persuaded him that their actions were legal. Her husband thought they were borrowing the money, she said, and that they would double it by investing in real estate.

3. A 72-year-old woman, Kelli Kasandra of 9847 Eastbrook Lane, has been charged with attempting to pass a counterfeit $20 bill. A convenience store clerk called the police shortly after 8 a.m. today and said that she had received "a suspicious-looking bill." The clerk added that she had written down the license number of a car leaving the store. The police confirmed the fact that the $20 bill was counterfeit and arrested Mrs. Kasandra at her home about an hour later.

4. Margaret Dwyer said a thief, a boy about 14, grabbed her purse as she was walking to her car in a parking lot behind Memorial Hospital. The boy punched her in the face, apparently because she began to scream and refused to let go of her purse. She said he was blond, wore glasses, weighed about 120 pounds and was about 5 feet 6 inches tall.

5. "I've never lived in a city where the officials are so corrupt," Joyce Andrews, a Cleveland developer, complained. "If you don't contribute to their campaigns, they won't do anything for you or even talk to you. You have to buy their support."

6. The political scientist said that Americans seem unable to elect a competent president. "Look at whom they've elected," she said. "I'm convinced that Carter was incompetent, Reagan was too lazy and senile to be even a mediocre president, the first George Bush cared nothing about the people, Clinton was a scoundrel and the second George Bush—the worst of the bunch—was a liar and a buffoon."

7. Police Chief Barry Kopperud said: "We've been after Guiterman for years. He's the biggest drug dealer in the city, but it took months to gather the evidence and infiltrate his operations. His arrest last night was the result of good police work, and we've got the evidence to send him away for 20 or 30 years."

8. Officer George Ruiz filed a $100,000 personal injury suit against Albert Tifton, charging that Tifton punched him in the nose last month while the police were responding to a call about a domestic dispute at Tifton's home. "It's the third time I've been hit this year," Ruiz said. "I'm tired of being used as a punching bag by these criminals, and I'm doing what I can to stop it."

9. Ruth Howland of 1808 Gladsen Blvd. is running for president of the local coin collectors society. Her opponent is Thomas C. Paddock of 1736 Hinkley Road. Howland has sent a letter to all members of the local society saying Paddock is a communist and an anarchist.

10. A prosecuting attorney, who asked not to be identified, said charges would be filed within the week against Mayor Sabrina Datolli, accusing her of having accepted bribes.

11. The firefighters union held a no-confidence vote on Fire Chief Tony Sullivan. The president of the union said Sullivan had been arbitrary and capricious in his decisions about layoffs resulting from budget cuts.

12. An activist for a local animal-rights organization, Julie Allyn, said she had investigated a fire at Weston's Pet Hotel that had killed 19 dogs and had smelled fire accelerant on the bodies.

13. Suzanne Kopp, whose husband died of lung cancer, is the president of a local group advocating tougher regulation of tobacco products. In a speech to high school students, Kopp said, "Tobacco company executives are nothing but

murderers. Morally, they stand no better than the paid assassin."

14. Officer Daniel G. Silverbach is investigating a convenience store robbery. Silverbach said of the store clerk, Wayne Brayton, 410 University Ave., Apt. 279, "He's acting suspiciously and is not able to give a coherent account of the robbery. I think he's doing drugs of some kind."

15. Professor Ahmad Aneesa, a microbiologist, said of a paper published by Professor William Baxter, a microbiologist at another university, "These results run contrary to everything we know about microorganisms. I know Baxter has a great reputation, but only a fool would accept his findings without more investigation."

2. Privacy

For each of the following passages, choose the form of invasion of privacy that fits best. Write I for intrusion, P for publicity to private facts, A for appropriation and F for false light.

1. A story describes a man as a veteran of combat in Iraq who has received a Purple Heart and medals for valor. In fact, the man served in the military during the Iraq War but was never in Iraq or in combat.

2. A local car dealer wants to run an advertisement that promotes the low prices for his vehicles with the headline "Bargains That Outshine the Stars." To illustrate the advertisement, he wants to use photos of famous Hollywood stars such as Jennifer Aniston and Matt Damon.

3. A news story reports that a member of the city council is having a romantic affair with a local business executive. Both the council member and the business executive are married to others.

4. A newspaper reporter follows up on the story of the affair between the council member and the business executive. The reporter follows the business executive to a motel. When she sees the council member arrive, she takes photographs of him getting out of his car in the motel parking lot. Although the reporter is some distance away, she is using a powerful telephoto lens that allows her to photograph the executive and the council member in their room.

5. An in-depth news story reports on a local family whose members have been involved in a number of crimes over the years. The story describes each family member and the crimes they have committed. The story also mentions in passing a member of the family who has never committed a crime.

6. A reporter is investigating a local judge who is reported to have accepted bribes from people accused of crimes in return for lenient sentencing. The reporter tries to interview the judge as he is getting out of his car to go to work, but the judge refuses to talk. However, the reporter sees the judge put an envelope in the glove compartment of his car, which he leaves unlocked. After the judge has left, the reporter opens the car and the glove box to find the envelope, which holds $1,000 in cash and a thank-you note from a defendant in a recent criminal case.

7. A television station reports that police are concerned about the rash of accidents, injuries and even deaths involving children playing in the streets. The station illustrates its story with some video footage of children playing in streets, some of whom are identifiable, and titles its story "They Beg to Be Killed."

8. A private college in the community recently hired a new dean of students, the first woman to hold the position at that college. A reporter, while preparing a profile of the new dean, discovers that she was born a male and underwent gender reassignment surgery 15 years ago. She told the college officials of her gender reassignment when she interviewed for the job, but she has not made that information public. The profile the reporter writes includes the gender change.

6

ETHICS

The importance of good journalism, professional journalists, ethics and the responsibilities of a free press in a democratic society has become prominent in the election of Trump and the rise of "fake news" as a popular term. Ethical reporting is a major part of the issue. Journalists research, analyze and provide the information people need to make good decisions and lead productive lives. Therefore, they must make the right choices when working on a story.

Thousands of professional reporters make many good decisions every day. They use critical thinking and informed decision-making processes when determining which story is more important to report, whom to interview, what questions to ask, what angle to take, whom to quote, which side to present first, how long to make the story, what visuals to use, where to place the story among other stories, and so forth. Even thinking about where and when to interview someone has potential ramifications.

Every choice a journalist makes when gathering, organizing and presenting the news—with text or images—requires value judgments. These choices have consequences that are direct and indirect, intended and unintended, short-term and long-term. They also affect others; for example, they may influence thousands of people's opinions on a political issue or a person's choice to remain in his or her community after being the subject of a story. Reporters examine their actions on the basis of professional and personal standards. They abide by the ethical codes of their organization, industry, community and society. If they are unsure of a decision, they always take the high road, the morally superior way to deal with something.

Above all other principles, journalists must:

- act and think morally;
- distinguish between right and wrong; and
- stay within the bounds of fairness, good taste and common decency.

Codes of Ethics

Major professional journalism organizations have adopted codes of ethics. An organization encourages its members to adhere to its guidelines, which can also be used by individual media companies to set their own policies. News outlets adapt ethics codes to reflect local standards, as what is acceptable in a metropolitan area might not be permissible in a rural community.

News agencies also employ codes of ethics to discourage the most obvious abuses, especially freebies, junkets and conflicts of interest (discussed later in this chapter). Yet some exceptional cases arise; thus, decisions will vary from one news organization to another, which might be one of the system's great strengths. After considering their news organization's code of ethics, journalists decide the proper (i.e., ethical) course of action. But any effort to change the system—to force every reporter in various situations to conform to an identical predetermined standard—would limit the media's diversity and freedom, as well as the public's access to information.

The American Society of Newspaper Editors (ASNE) adopted one of the industry's first codes, the Canons of Journalism, in 1923. Among other things, the ASNE declared that newspapers should act responsibly by being truthful, sincere, impartial, decent and fair. The Society of Professional Journalists (SPJ) has a well-known code. The National Press Photographers Association (NPPA) provides ethical guidelines for visual journalists who produce video and still images, and the Radio, Television, Digital News Association (RTDNA) has a code for broadcast journalists. There are others; for example, National Public Radio (NPR) has a social media code of ethics for their reporters, available at ethics.npr.org/tag/social-media/.

Ethical Decision Making

In addition to following the standards of their news outlet and professional organizations, reporters learn a set of decision-making questions to help them make good, ethical choices. A few decision-making processes are offered in the following sections.

Legitimate news publications, such as these magazines, must include only articles that adhere to the organization's and the industry's ethics.

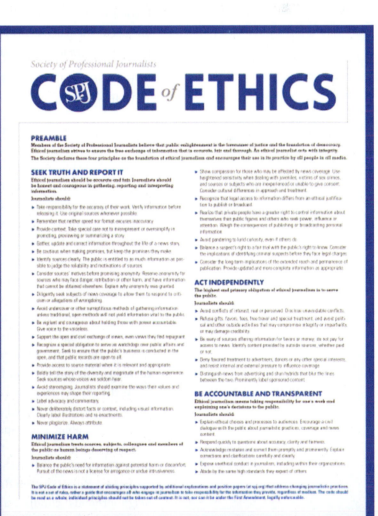

The Society of Professional Journalism (SPJ) adopted its current code of ethics in 1996 and revised it in 2014.

Who and How Many? (Two Questions)

Two fundamental questions that a journalist should ask when facing an ethical decision are:

- Who will be hurt, and how many?
- Who will be helped, and how many?

News stories sometimes hurt someone or some group. If the story hurts a few people and helps several hundred, then publishing it is most likely justified. Perhaps a local doctor has been accused of misdiagnosing symptoms, which has led to unnecessary surgeries and uncured ailments. The story would hurt the doctor and his family, but it would help many people when choosing a physician.

What Is the Purpose of the Story? (Two Follow-Up Questions)

Once the decision to publish a story has been made, journalists sometimes get too involved with the micro issues, such as the wording of a story or its headline, the visuals or the placement. While these details are important, reporters must also consider the macro issues by asking a second set of questions:

- What is the objective of the story?
- Will my decision contribute to the reason for writing the story?

The answers will help a reporter decide, for example, not to include how a teenager committed suicide because that would not be the purpose of the story. The objective most likely would be to either celebrate the teenager's life or to reference the incident while educating the community about the increase of teenage suicides and the signs of teenage depression.

Here is another example. In some cities, coalitions of merchants, homeowners and government officials combat prostitution by encouraging the police to make more arrests and asking news organizations to publish the names of both prostitutes and their customers. Editors realize that such publicity could ruin reputations, marriages and careers. Both clients and prostitutes often have spouses, children and colleagues who know nothing of their outside activities or criminal actions. In a big bust of 20 accused, one john was a scout leader and another was in a seminary. One of the prostitutes attended law school and another was trying to make ends meet for her family.

As the editors discussed the story, they initially focused on several micro issues: placement—a story placed on a jump page is less damaging to the accused than a story on the home page; space—a short story is not as noticeable as a longer one; and graphics and visuals—the type and number of illustrations, if any, can set the tone. They then revisited the macro issue—ridding the community of an unsavory business associated with drugs, violence and disease and other threats to family neighborhoods, children and businesses. Once they clarified their reasons for running the story, they were able to resolve the micro issues more easily. They put the story on the home page with a list of the names and mug shots of both the accused customers and prostitutes.

Can I Explain My Decision? (Six Questions)

Former journalist and professor H. Eugene Goodwin advised journalists and students to ask themselves six guiding questions while making an ethical decision. These are in addition to the four already discussed.

1. What do we usually do in cases like this? (What is the news organization's policy on this type of situation, and is it a good policy?)

2. Is there a better alternative? (Harmful results often can be avoided or eased by trying something different.)

3. Can I look myself in the mirror tomorrow? (You must think about how you feel and whether you can live with your decision.)

4. Can I justify this to family, friends and the public? (If we know we have to explain our decisions to our family—such as, what would Mom think?—or to the public in an editor's column, we might be more careful about our decisions.) Try listening to yourself out loud.

5. What principles or values can I apply? (Some overarching principles, such as truth, justice or fairness, will take priority over others.)

6. Does this decision fit the kind of journalism I believe in and the way people should treat one another? (Our judgments should correspond with the way we believe the media ought to be and the way people in a civilized society ought to behave. Take the high road.)

The Potter Box

The Potter Box, shown in Table 6.1, is a moral reasoning framework that a person can complete multiple times in any order to make a decision. It is based on the four categories that its creator, social ethicist and theologian Ralph Potter, believed were universal to ethical dilemmas.

A reporter might use the Potter Box when experiencing inner turmoil on running a story about a personal friend and beloved community member who embezzled from the local elementary school. This process is shown in Table 6.2.

News Media Credibility Considerations

Professional journalists are trained to think ethically and act responsibly. However, when a story is wrong or the journalist is unethical, the news outlet suffers a

TABLE 6.1 The Potter Box

Facts, without judgments	Values, such as personal, moral, professional and societal
Principles or classic ethical philosophies	Loyalties, such as whom you care most about

TABLE 6.2 Using a Potter Box

Facts, without judgments:	Values, such as personal, moral, professional and societal:
A staff member embezzled thousands of dollars.	The story would help parents understand why the school cannot provide as many supplies and services for children as it had in the past.
The school does not have any extra money in its budget. The loss will affect the business of running the school.	
Principles or classic ethical philosophies:	Loyalties, such as whom you care most about:
Rawls' veil of ignorance, which states that we should remove our personal interests and treat everyone the same way. (Thus, we cover an embezzler who is a family friend the same way we cover an embezzler we do not know.)	The public and the overriding principle for the greater good.

NBC Nightly News demoted news anchor Brian Williams after he embellished a story by stating on-air that he had been in a helicopter hit by a rocket-propelled grenade while in Iraq in 2003. (He had not been.)

blow to its reputation, and sometimes the whole industry suffers. If it is a large or repeated error, the organization may dismiss the reporter or editor responsible. This alone gives journalists a powerful reason to think through ethical issues.

Ethical and accurate credibility is important to news organizations for two main reasons:

1. People depend on news media for their information. Unlike bloggers and everyone else who writes online, professional journalists are trained in news judgment, vet their sources and report news accurately. News stories influence audiences, helping them form opinions ("Trump says LGBTQ soldiers are an issue in the military, but why?") and decide on activities ("I will choose a country other than North Korea for a study abroad experience") that can have a great impact on their quality of life.

2. News media must be credible to succeed as businesses. They need audiences for financial support. If people doubt the credibility of a particular news outlet, they will change websites, channels or newspapers. When audiences turn away, advertising and subscription revenues decline, news budgets shrink and comprehensive coverage diminishes, which drives away more audiences. The downward spiral usually continues until the outlet ceases business.

Ethics Issues Regarding Conduct

Some ethics issues arise from a journalist's conduct—his or her decisions, behaviors and practices. Journalists are aware that their personal actions affect other people and influence how the public sees the news media.

Plagiarizing and Fabricating Information: Never Acceptable

"Plagiarism" is copying somebody else's work or taking somebody else's ideas and passing them off as one's own. Copying and pasting quotes and other passages from the internet have made plagiarizing easy, but it is also illegal. Journalists who are caught plagiarizing or fabricating information often are dismissed. Some complain that deadlines and competition forced them to act unethically. However, legions of other reporters work under the same deadlines and uphold high principles. They understand that the reason doesn't matter—if journalists plagiarize or make up information, they are lying to the public. The Boston Globe argued in an editorial that journalists who fabricate or plagiarize stories are stealing something more valuable than money: They are stealing the public's trust and the news organization's credibility.

In this digital age, it is quick and easy to detect and expose plagiarism. As reporter Jarrett Hill listened to Melania Trump's 2016 National Republican Convention speech, he recognized words from an address that Michelle Obama gave eight years earlier. He compared the two speeches and found that Trump's included an entire paragraph from Obama's. Hill tweeted his findings to friends and fellow journalists, who soon retweeted the message thousands of times, and CNN televised a split screen with both women giving their speeches.

Jarrett Hill
@JarrettHill

CORRECTION: Melania stole a whole graph from Michelle's speech. #GOPConvention🎸
WATCH: youtu.be/53Ei2dSDsFY?t=...

And you know, what struck me when I first met Barack was that even though he had this funny name, even though he'd grown up all the way across the continent in Hawaii, his family was so much like mine. He was raised by grandparents who were working-class folks just like my parents, and by a single mother who struggled to pay the bills just like we did. Like my family, they scrimped and saved so that he could have opportunities they never had themselves. And Barack and I were raised with so many of the same values: that you work hard for what you want in life; that your word is your bond and you do what you say you're going to do; that you treat people with dignity and respect, even if you don't know them, and even if you don't agree with them.

And Barack and I set out to build lives guided by these values, and pass them on to the next generation. Because we want our children — and all children in this nation — to know that the only limit to the height of your achievements is the reach of your dreams and your willingness to work for them.

Jarrett Hill's tweet identifies the text from Michelle Obama's 2008 speech that also appeared in Melania Trump's 2016 address.

Finding Sources

Journalists search for and interview people who can be good sources for their stories. For example, sources for a story on diversity at a university include current students with different demographics, former students, an administrator who tracks diversity and perhaps faculty members who have been at the university for a long time. Journalists seek people with different opinions so that various angles of an issue are presented. Some instructors require three different types of sources instead of similar ones, such as all current students.

FRIENDS AND RELATIVES

Journalism students often want to use friends and relatives as sources in their stories. This is a bad idea because it lessens the story's credibility. Sources should be varied and come from backgrounds different from the reporter. The practice also compromises a journalist's integrity because a relative or friend usually will not mind if the reporter makes up or changes a quote to fit the story. Furthermore, when a journalist uses a friend as a source, he or she expects to be presented in a positive manner, or the journalist tries to make him or her look good in exchange for being in the story.

SCRATCHING BACKS AND BECOMING TOO CHUMMY

Journalists need to know where to draw the line between being friendly and being friends with sources. Once that line is crossed, it becomes harder for them to remain objective. Also, sources who become friends expect preferential treatment. They may assume journalists will clean up their bad language or omit quotes that would reflect badly on them.

The old adage "You scratch my back and I'll scratch yours" applies here. Sources give credibility to stories, offer ideas, add a different perspective and help with leads for more information. However, they do not consistently offer their time and information freely or out of the goodness of their hearts. They usually expect something in return, such as having only their point of view published or receiving publicity in another story to further their own interests.

A reporter's job is to be honest and objective. They should not fear or ignore stories that cast sources, particularly political or governmental ones, in a negative light. The informant might freeze the journalist out for a while, but not forever. If reporters cultivate a variety of sources representing different opinions, they can continue to do their job. Reputation is important: Journalists gain respect for writing balanced, fair stories. To avoid problems, they might request that a particularly negative story about an important source be assigned to another reporter or ask their editor for a change in beats if they become too chummy with a contact.

CURBING ANONYMOUS SOURCES

Reporters make clear at the beginning of an interview that everything is on the record and attributable. The public doubts sources who do not want to be named or held accountable for what they say. The credibility of the story and the journalist diminishes when no one is named to back up assertions. If a source for an important story supplies initial information but does not want to be attributed, the journalist finds someone willing to talk on the record. For some beats, such as national security, reporters must deal with anonymous sources, but these are rare (see Chapter 10). Most newsrooms have a two-source rule to confirm reports—and more is better, especially when the source is anonymous.

Recording Interviews: Audio Recorders and Video Cameras

Journalists often record interviews so that they can refer to the audio when their notes are confusing. They also use recorders to prove their stories are accurate and to protect themselves: Sources might claim the reporter misquoted them or even fabricated the entire interview. Some honestly forget what they said.

Journalists do not secretly record interviews without their editor's approval because that tactic is devious and unfair (but see Chapters 5 and 11). The use of hidden video cameras raises additional issues. While audio recordings capture only a person's voice, videos—which often end up on television or the internet—also include people's faces, clothing and actions. Many people consider hidden cameras a greater intrusion than hidden audio recorders.

Lawsuits for invasion of privacy can arise when journalists hide recording devices in places where people can reasonably expect their words and actions to be private. The threat of lawsuits discourages reporters from using hidden cameras or audio recorders unless the story is extraordinarily important and they have exhausted all other means of getting the information they need.

'Isn't That the Trump Lawyer?': A Reporter's Accidental Scoop

By KENNETH P. VOGEL   SEPT. 19, 2017

Reporter Kenneth Vogel got a scoop when, at a Washington restaurant, he overheard Trump's lawyers discussing the investigation of Russian election meddling. Vogel took notes on his phone and also shot a photo of the men. Taking notes of a public conversation is legal whereas recording without permission is not.

Eliminating Conflicts of Interest

A conflict of interest exists when journalists, their friends and relatives, or news organizations are in a position to benefit directly from a story. Reporters want to avoid even the appearance of such conflicts, which compromise their objectivity. In an effort to be transparent, they disclose any conflicts of interest in their stories. Audiences will decide if an issue exists and if it caused any bias.

ACCEPTING GIFTS: "FREEBIES"

Journalists refuse to accept money or anything else of value from the people they write about—before or after the story is published. Businesses do not give gifts without expecting something in return, whether it is currying favor for a current story or greasing the wheels for any potential stories. Gifts could subconsciously bias a journalist's story, and the appearance of giving/receiving such items may cause the public to suspect they have influenced the coverage. An editor at The Washington Post has said, "On some newspapers (this one included), the acceptance of a bribe—for that is what it is—is a firing offense."

Unless it is worth only a few dollars—a cup of coffee, for example—journalists refuse gifts. They tell the giver that the item cannot be accepted because of their organization's policies. Other newsroom guidelines require journalists to return the gift or send it to a charity. For example, reporters at the Detroit Free Press auction the amassed gifts annually and give the proceeds to charity.

ACCEPTING TRIPS: "JUNKETS"

Free trips, called "junkets," were once common. Fashion writers were invited to New York and television critics to Hollywood, with all of their expenses paid. Sports writers might accompany their local teams to games in distant cities, with the teams paying all the writers' expenses.

Many travel writers insist they could not afford to travel if hotels, airlines or other sponsors did not pay for them. Their stories are often compromised and unrealistic, however, because most people do not get complimentary trips with first-class transportation and managers' red-carpet treatment. Thus, the writer's experience neither resembles that of most travelers nor helps them decide how to spend their vacations.

PARTICIPATING IN THE NEWS

Journalists have lives outside of the newsroom, and those activities sometimes turn them into newsmakers. When that happens, editors worry that their journalists' involvement in events might undermine public confidence in the news organization's objectivity. Editors insist journalists' first obligation is to their primary employer. Reporters continue to represent their employers as objective news gatherers even after they leave work for the day; therefore, as stated in the SPJ's Code of Ethics, they should "remain free of associations and activities that may compromise integrity or damage credibility."

News executives generally agree that reporters should not hold public office (either elected or appointed), serve as party officials or help with anyone's election campaign. When in doubt about a possible conflict, journalists talk with their supervisors. A journalist is perceived as having a conflict when the official or candidate is his or her spouse or a family member. In these cases, editors often move the reporter to another beat or he or she takes a leave of absence until the election or term ends.

FREELANCING

At most news organizations, journalists are free to accept outside jobs, provided these roles do not conflict with their regular work. Typically, reporters can work as freelancers, but they cannot sell their work to their employers' competitors, such as other media in the same market.

Maintaining Objectivity

One component of objectivity, as discussed in the previous sections, is absence of bias. Everyone has biases and opinions, but journalists' can greatly affect a story. They may influence selection of story topics, sources, questions asked, story angle, organization and presentation. For instance, reporters who are passionate about the illegal immigrant issue might have difficulty writing objectively about Trump's proposed wall between Mexico and the United States. They might unintentionally interview only sources who share their opinions. Those aware of their prejudices might overcompensate in the opposite direction to present an impartial story. Journalists let their supervisors know when they cannot cover a subject objectively, and the editor or news director will assign the story to another reporter.

Objectivity also means integrating balance, fairness and accuracy within stories. Impartial facts without context can create inaccurate impressions. In Quill magazine, science reporter and educator Sally Lehrman criticized journalists who simply repeated a scientist's claim that the Maori, the native people of New Zealand, carried a "warrior" gene that promoted aggressiveness and violence and was linked to their high rates of alcoholism and smoking. Other journalists examined crime rates among the group, which seemed to support the findings. If journalists had been independent, critical thinkers, they would have looked at the Maori in a social context to interpret the scientist's findings. For example, the Maori, descendants of the Polynesians, generally experience discrimination. A well-established link exists among violence, poverty and lack of opportunity, which creates high unemployment, low education levels, low incomes and health disparities. Lehrman argued that, instead of automatically reinforcing a stereotype, these journalists needed to dig deeper to explain the context. Doing so would have exposed and possibly helped the Maoris' situation by giving the issue greater understanding.

Interviewing Victims

Journalists are sensitive to victims and the public's sense of decency as they photograph and interview victims and grieving relatives. They avoid having victims and their families relive a horrific event. Yet few journalists are psychologists. They may not realize many disaster victims and family members are in shock, which can affect people in different ways, for several days or even months after an event. People in shock sometimes inadvertently twist or forget facts. They may later recant their stories or accuse journalists of making up the interview. Many reporters obtain more accurate and complete stories if they wait several days to speak to victims. Although hard news stories can be written immediately after an event without these interviews, stories with more context and facts from the victim's family can follow later.

Victims or their family members sometimes choose to speak to only one journalist during their time of grief. And, families may have a representative, who might be a relative or close friend. In this case, journalists give their names and telephone numbers to the representative, and they ask the victim to call if and when he or she feels ready to talk. Compassionate, respectful journalists who do not pressure victims and their families receive more in-depth information.

Respecting Privacy of Sources

The media sometimes intrude on the privacy of individuals. Although journalists are often within their legal rights, they are not necessarily proceeding ethically. Some people who become involved in major lawsuits, crimes and accidents may expect to be mentioned in news stories about them, but others might be surprised or confused about being in the media spotlight. Reporters are sensitive to individuals who have been thrust into the news. The coverage of private citizens is often different from that of celebrities and politicians, who seek publicity.

Avoiding Deceit: Posing and Misrepresentation

Journalists strive to be trusted. They believe that deceit is a form of lying and that lying is unethical, even though a few may think deceit is the only way to get some stories. Yet most experts say the press should not criticize deceitfulness by public officials or businesses if reporters are also being devious while pursuing a story. An investigative story with many in-depth interviews and extensive background research provides a better story than one in which journalists use deception.

"Actually I'm not the queen - I'm undercover
for the Daily Mirror..."

Passive posing, where the reporter might appear to a business owner or government official as simply another member of the public, presents few ethical problems. He or she may experience a situation as an average citizen and gather information available to any person. Restaurant reviewers would be ineffective if everyone knew their identities. Restaurant owners, eager to obtain favorable publicity, would offer reviewers special meals and service, making them unable to describe what the average customer receives. Another example is a journalist who wants to cover a protest rally: If protesters realize a reporter is present, they might either act more cautiously or perform for him or her, behaving more angrily or violently to ensure that they got into the news.

More serious ethical—and legal—problems arise when journalists actively misrepresent themselves in order to gain access to places and information closed to the general public. For instance, a student reporter might want to investigate how his or her university handles sexual assault claims by posing as a victim or an accused person. Although it might be exciting and easier to write a story in the first-person, it is not a good idea. Journalists should not misrepresent themselves; it is a form of lying. In this case, the reporters should review the reason for the story. If the macro issue is to inform young women and men about the university's system, researching campus sexual assault policies and interviewing students who experienced the process, university officials, parents and lawyers would be helpful. Finding data on universities nationally would put the individual school into context.

In the past, journalists have posed as patients to gather information about a mental hospital or as laborers to write about migrant workers' exposure to pesticides. Although reporters could be exposing a social ill, the public disapproves of their conduct. They may even face legal penalties because of their dubious methods of gathering information.

Journalists talk to their supervisors before they use any form of deceit. News executives might allow their staff to pose only when no other safe way exists to obtain an important story. In addition, journalists state their use of deception in their stories and explain why it was necessary; they also call all people criticized in their stories and give them an opportunity to respond.

Witnessing Crimes and Disasters

Journalists and photographers might witness terrible tragedies, such as people drowning, falling to their deaths or fleeing from fire. They react in the same way they would if a member of their family was in physical danger—they help the person, particularly if they are the only ones on the scene. But when a victim is already receiving help from rescue workers, police officers, firefighters or medical technicians, journalists stay out of the rescuers' way and concentrate on reporting the event.

Reporters occasionally learn about a crime or hostage situation while it is in progress and are tempted to interview the suspect, who often has a weapon. However, the potential risk to the hostage outweighs the value of the information gleaned. Audiences will be informed just as well, if not more comprehensively, if the reporter learns information later from police. Furthermore, if he or she interrupts first responders trying to do their jobs, they may be unable to stop the suspect from killing someone or from escaping. Journalists are not hostage negotiators.

Ethics Issues Regarding Content

News executives consider the best ways to inform, educate or entertain their audiences. As the fourth estate, news media are respectful and considerate to sources, subjects and audiences while balancing society's need to know. Audiences might ignore an important story if the reporter obtained or presented the content in a controversial or unethical manner.

Avoiding Speculation: Get the Facts and Provide Accurate Context

When reporters do not know why things happen, they sometimes want to speculate in an effort to explain it to audiences. Their conjectures, however, mislead the public. Journalists refrain from guessing the "why" or "how" until the information is known for a follow-up story. Instead, they steer clear of sensationalism, respect an individual's privacy and focus on the objective of the story.

Journalists can inadvertently transform heroes and victims into bad guys and vice versa by presenting allusions and incomplete facts. When a teenage boy was killed while he and a friend tried to stop a burglar from getting into a neighbor's home, one newspaper stated that he was out at 4 a.m., smoking, had a gun and was a high school dropout. An anonymous source said the boy "liked to party." Very little information was presented about the burglar. A different newspaper called the boy a hero and quoted the positive things his family and friends had to say. This story noted that, at the time of the incident, the teenagers were sitting on the porch of one of the boys' homes because they were minding the rule that smoking was not allowed in the house. The victim was enrolled at an alternative school for dropouts because he was determined to get a GED and he had a job. The gun belonged to the other boy, whom the victim was defending when the burglar stabbed him. The burglar had been arrested several times for burglary and aggravated assault with a deadly weapon.

Using Visuals: Newsworthy or Sensational?

Editors and producers run photographs and videos because they tell a story. But the visual coverage of disasters, including civil wars, bombings, hate crimes, mass shootings and natural disasters challenge many news executives. They seek the proper balance between giving the public what it needs to see without presenting unnecessarily gory images, descending into sensationalism or being accused of running the visual for shock value. Too much repetition of the same graphic can distract people from the purpose of the story and, as researchers explain, numb viewers' reaction to the horrific events.

Sometimes, however, words alone cannot convey the situation as well as a photograph or video can. All journalists make decisions about whether to shield the public from unpleasantness or to educate them on a case-by-case basis. They use their ethical decision-making processes to discuss publishing an image or finding a middle ground by cropping it or giving a long view instead of a close-up. But reporters who cover a lot of murders and accidental deaths might not be able over time to objectively judge what an audience will find appropriate. Thus, news organizations keep in touch with the public's attitudes—what is acceptable to city dwellers in the East might not be acceptable to rural folks in the Midwest.

Altering Images

Photojournalists are loath to change the content of their photos in newspapers or online because it is dishonest and unethical. Just as writers do not lie about the content of their stories, photographers do not lie about the content of their captured images. Still, they have always been able to alter their photos. In the days of 35 mm prints, photos could be cropped, enlarged or burned to provide more contrast. With digital imaging software, photojournalists can remove a distracting object in the background of a photo without changing the essence and meaning of the picture. (For more on photojournalism and manipulating images, see Chapter 14.)

Deciding When to Name Names

News organizations have policies requiring journalists to fully identify everyone mentioned in their stories. However, some participants might make forceful claims for anonymity.

NAMING JUVENILES

Journalists usually do not name children who are connected to a crime. Children are not capable of dealing with the associated infamy, which might affect them for the rest of their lives. Traditionally, the criminal justice system has also shielded children under 18 who are accused or convicted of a crime. This protection has been explained on the grounds that juveniles understand neither what they did nor the consequences of their actions.

The main exception occurs when juveniles are tried in adult court because the charge is a serious crime or the suspects have already been punished for earlier serious offenses. If several teenagers are charged with committing crimes that terrorized a neighborhood, news executives might feel a need to identify them and perhaps their parents as well. Journalists might decide their obligation to calm people's fears by informing the community about the arrests outweighs their normal obligation to protect the accused and their families.

WRITING ABOUT VICTIMS OF SEXUAL ASSAULT

A national study of news executives showed that most news organizations withhold the names of rape victims. The nature of the crime and the subsequent attention traumatizes and stigmatizes victims in unique ways. Sexual assault is an underreported crime, and news coverage discourages some from going to the police. A study on rape victims showed that most were angry about being identified, and a few said they would not have reported the crime if they had known news media would name them. As a result of being named, most victims reported emotional trauma as well as embarrassment, shame and difficulties in their relationships.

Although the media does not usually name people who report a sexual assault, they do for those charged. Another study showed that audiences wanted to know the accused's name but felt that news organizations should not identify victims. Sexual assault suspects, like those in other crimes, are always identified so the public has full knowledge about the situation. Moreover, bystanders might come forward with information about the accused, and his or her neighbors can take steps to protect themselves. Thus, identifying a victim has little effect on audiences but may have negative effects on the individual.

Covering Killers

People remember events based on how the media covered them. When the news focuses on killers—their backgrounds and their families—and not the victims, some critics say the media glorify killers and imply that they are important and victims are not. For example, many people who saw news coverage of a man ramming his vehicle into anti-racist protesters in Charlottesville, Virginia, say they remember the perpetrator better than they do the person killed and 19 others injured. Were repeated stories about the driver's background verging on sensationalism? Was his story more important than those of the victims? Who should be remembered?

Reporting on Public Figures and Celebrities

The public's right to know often outweighs a government official's or public figure's right to privacy. Most Americans seem to agree that journalists should expose government officials who abuse their power, such as those who steer lucrative contracts to cronies, or who have personal problems, such as alcoholism, that affect their work.

But does the public have a right to know about a public figure's private affairs, such as adultery? Proponents argue that if a politician breaks a solemn promise, such as a wedding vow, pledges to his or her constituency might also be meaningless. The public has a right to know about the character of the person who represents them. Another variable is whether the affair is with a member of the government, which could lead to abuse of power or favoritism.

On the one hand, public figures and celebrities want to be the center of attention when promoting their causes, such as a new policy or an upcoming movie. When Angelina Jolie visited a refugee camp in Jordan as a special envoy for the United Nations High Commissioner for Refugees, she welcomed the publicity she drew to those displaced by the civil war in Syria. On the other hand, she was reticent to discuss her divorce from Brad Pitt, just as most celebrities do not want the public to know personal things that might be damaging to their image or causes. Critics say those in the public eye cannot have it both ways. Journalists use their professional news judgment to consider carefully whether a topic will affect the lives of their audiences.

Journalists identify the purpose of a story and what audiences need to know, such as in the case of New York City mayoral candidate Anthony Weiner, who was sexting explicit photos to several women, including a minor. Coverage of former Democratic Rep. Weiner's multiple sex scandals and sentencing were important because of his political career.

Reporting Rumors and Speculation

Journalists publish established and investigated facts, but the temptation to run unsubstantiated stories grows with the oft-repeated rumors that quickly fly across Instagram, Twitter, Facebook and other social media. Nonetheless, news organizations risk their reputations by publishing false information. All information should be checked out.

When an event occurs, some news elements—such as the who, what, where and when—are readily available. However, it might take days or weeks to find out the why or how. Journalists do not provide the why through speculation and interpretation, which could mislead audiences. Theories and conjectures are not news.

Reporting on Terrorism

Terrorists want credit for violent acts. Media coverage makes them feel important, and they think it legitimizes their cause. To attract even more publicity, terrorists conduct press conferences. Some want journalists to photograph and interview their captives. Others make videos that show hostages pleading for their lives, reading the terrorists' demands and warning that they will be killed if the conditions are not met.

Terrorists are responsible for bombings, hijackings and mass murders—events that news organizations cannot ignore. Yet some critics insist the media coverage encourages terrorists. They believe that if the media ignored terrorists, they would become discouraged and abandon their acts of violence. Former British Prime Minister Margaret Thatcher urged journalists to stop the coverage, to starve terrorists of "the oxygen of publicity." Other critics note that Americans have a right to know what is happening in the world, and a news blackout might result in rumors about the terrorists' activities that are more frightening than the truth. They also fear terrorists would escalate their violence if journalists tried to ignore them.

The World Press's Photo of the Year for 2017 prompted this type of debate among the judges, who were split on their decision. The photo showed the moment after Mevlut Mert Altintas assassinated Andrei Karlov, the Russian ambassador to Turkey, in protest of Russia's military presence in Syria. One of the judges said he had a "moral concern" that celebrating the photo would magnify attention to a successful terrorist act. Another judge focused on the bravery of the photographer, who shot the image from 15 feet away.

Publishing Ads

News organizations are under no obligation to publish advertisements. Many outlets refuse to publish ads for products and services—tobacco products, alcoholic beverages, happy hours, movies rated NC-17 (adults only), sexual aids, abortion services, handguns, massage parlors and escort services—that may be harmful to members of their community.

Some advertisers want to dictate news content and placement of their ads to be close to particular stories. Others may threaten to pull their advertising if news stories reflect negatively on their company's image or products.

AP photographer Burhan Ozbilici happened to be at the Ankara, Turkey, art gallery when Mevlut Mert Altintas killed Andrei Karlov. Ozbilici took about 100 photos of the incident; this image quickly went viral.

The Writing Coach

Journalists Should Understand: Victims Face Wall of Grief

BY JOE HIGHT

Most victims or victims' relatives face a wall of grief in the aftermath of a death or disaster. The wall blocks them from seeing that their lives may improve tomorrow. They don't see into the past or future; they see the present and feel the pain of the moment.

Then the reporter approaches them and violates their grieving space. Or, in a disaster, several journalists approach them.

So it's important to learn about coverage of victims. Here are several tips:

- When approaching a victim, politely and clearly identify yourself before asking questions.
- Treat each victim with dignity and respect. Veteran AP correspondent George Esper has said, "We should frame our questions with respect and research. We must be sensitive but not timid."
- Treat each person as an individual, not as part of an overall number. Each person is different and should be treated that way.
- Never ask "How do you feel?" or say "I understand how you feel." Simply say, "My name is . . ." and "I am sorry for what happened." Then ask questions such as "Could you tell me about your relative's life?" or "How did this occur?"

- Realize that you are violating the victim's space and may receive a harsh or emotional reaction at first. Don't react harshly if you receive this reaction.
- Allow the victim to say "no" after you make the approach and he or she refuses to answer your question.
- If the answer is "no," simply leave a card or number so the victim can call you later. Sometimes the best stories come this way.
- Know that little things count. Call the victims back to verify quotes and facts. Ensure photos are returned immediately.
- Try to call funeral homes or family representatives first to connect with a victim's family member. In most cases, relatives will want to talk about the victims' lives. In some cases, these may lead to bigger stories.
- Avoid words such as "closure" to indicate that victims or members of the community have overcome the trauma connected with a death or disaster. After her husband, Secret Service agent Donald Leonard, was killed in the Oklahoma City bombing, Diane Leonard said, "This will be a journey we'll be taking the rest of our lives. It's part of us, and always will be."

Joe Hight has been editor of the Colorado Springs (Colorado) Gazette and the Oklahoman of Oklahoma City. He is now the owner and president of Best of Books, Inc.

The Reporter's Guide to Ethics

1. The major principles guiding a journalist's decisions are to act and think morally; distinguish between right and wrong; and stay within the bounds of fairness, good taste and common decency.

2. Many professional journalism organizations—such as the American Society of Newspaper Editors, the Society of Professional Journalists, and the Radio, Television, Digital News Association—have codes of ethics.

3. When considering a story, reporters should ask themselves who and how many will be hurt by the publication and who and how many will be helped.

4. A Potter Box can help journalists to not only separate facts, values, principles and loyalties, but also lead them to an ethical decision.

5. Plagiarizing another person's work is never permissible and often results in a journalist's firing.

6. Reporters should avoid using friends or relatives as sources and should avoid becoming too friendly with sources.

7. Electronically recording an interview without the interviewee's consent may be legal in most jurisdictions, but it is unethical.

8. Journalists should not accept gifts or junkets from the people or organizations they cover.

9. Journalists, like everyone, have biases, but they should be aware of them and compensate for them by selecting sources with different views. When reporters feel they cannot set aside their biases on a particular story, they should ask their supervisors for reassignment.

10. Journalists need to be especially sensitive when interviewing victims of crimes or disasters.

11. Journalists should not misrepresent themselves to their sources; they should always reveal that they are reporters working on a news story.

12. News stories should be free from speculation and should present facts accurately and in context.

13. Photographs and videos should provide audiences with helpful information but avoid gore and sensationalism. They should never be altered.

14. Generally the subjects of and sources for news stories should be fully identified, but news organizations usually avoid identifying juveniles who have been accused of crimes and the victims of sexual assaults.

15. The public has an interest in knowing what celebrities and public officials are doing, but public figures still have some expectation of privacy. That expectation is even greater for private individuals who become entangled in news events.

16. Crimes and acts of terrorism are of public concern, but news organizations should avoid giving the perpetrators excessive publicity.

Review Exercises

1. Ethical Decision-Making Processes

1. Many journalists memorize a set of ethical decision-making questions that they use regularly. Which ones would you use most often? Would you use different ones in different cases? Give examples.

2. Choose a local issue that presents an ethical dilemma. Use the Potter Box to help you determine a solution.

3. An alum who is a frequent visitor, guest speaker and donor of an accumulated $500,000 to your journalism school referred to President Trump as a white supremacist in a tweet. Is this a story? If so, list any possible ethical dilemmas and the process you would use to find an ethical course of action.

2. Discussion Questions

After completing the following questions, discuss your decisions with the class.

1. Which of these actions is plagiarism? Add a few words to explain your answer.

   A. To sell the notes you took in class.

   B. To turn in a paper purchased online.

   C. To use, without attribution, a five-word phrase from a tweet.

   D. To use, without attribution, a 20-word paragraph from a magazine app.

   E. While writing about a celebrity, to copy a quote you found online.

   F. To use your own words, but another writer's ideas, that appeared in a TV newscast.

   G. To use, but totally rewrite without attribution, a story from another newspaper.

   H. To use, but totally rewrite with attribution, a story from a webpage.

   I. To use a press release without changing a word.

   J. For background while working under deadline pressure, to reprint verbatim several paragraphs from an old story written by another reporter at your news organization.

   K. While working for a radio or television station, to read your city's daily newspaper to determine what's happening in your community and what stories you should cover.

   L. While working for a radio or television station, to broadcast news stories published by your local paper or online without rewriting or attribution.

   M. While working for a radio or television station, to rewrite stories from your local newspaper or from online and attribute them to the newspaper.

   N. To duplicate the organization of a story, but not copy the words, from another source, such as Wikipedia.

   O. While working for a television station, to reuse footage shot by another reporter in a previous story.

2. Aside from the scenarios in the previous questions, what other examples of plagiarism have you experienced?

3. As editor of your student news organization (radio, TV, newspaper, online), you receive an anonymous letter that accuses a faculty member of repeatedly making sexist remarks. Would you publish the letter? If your answer is "no," at which point would you change your mind? (You can choose more than one response.)

   A. The student who wrote the letter identifies herself but, because she fears retaliation, insists that you keep her name a secret.

   B. Two more women come in and corroborate the letter's content but also insist that you keep their names a secret.

   C. All three students agree to let you quote them and publish their names.

   D. The three students play a recording they secretly made in class, one that clearly documents their complaints.

   E. The students complain that the faculty member also touched them.

4. As editor of your student news organization, which of the following gifts would you allow members of your staff to accept? Explain your decision.

   A. Free tickets to local plays, movies and concerts for your entertainment editor.

   B. Free meals at local restaurants for your food critic.

C. Free trips to out-of-town games with your college team for your sports editor.

D. Free loan of a sophisticated computer that a manufacturer offers to your technology editor for the school year so she can test new games and software.

E. Free one-week trip to Daytona Beach, Florida, for your entertainment writer and a friend to write about the popular spring break destination.

5. As editor of your student news organization, indicate the products and services you would be willing to advertise. Explain your reasoning.

A. Hate letters

B. Medical marijuana or cannabis clinics

C. Guns

D. E-cigarettes or cigarettes

E. An essay claiming the Holocaust is a hoax

F. Fortune tellers

G. Abortion clinics

H. Couples who want to adopt newborns of only a certain race

I. Escort services, massage parlors, nude dancers

6. If you had to write a policy as to the type of ad you would accept, what would you include, and why?

7. As editor of your student news organization, which of the following cases of deception would you permit? Discuss your reasoning.

A. After hearing complaints that the university is going overboard on the number and type of penalties regarding Title IX, allow a reporter to pose as a student with a complaint and another reporter to pose as the accused.

B. Allow a reporter using a fake identity to join a rebellious group that often marches and holds rallies in the region.

C. After hearing that some people may be cheating local charities by collecting food and money from several simultaneously, allow a reporter to pose as a destitute mother to see how much food and money she can collect in one day. The reporter promises to return everything after her story's publication.

D. Allow two journalists to pose as a same-sex couple and try to rent an apartment. Friends have told members of your staff about instances of discrimination.

E. A reporter informs you that his brother is opening a bar, and that city inspectors seem to be asking for bribes to approve the building's plumbing, electrical and health inspections. The reporter suggests that you notify the district attorney, install hidden cameras in the bar and begin to pay the bribes.

8. As editor of your student news organization, choose the practices you would permit. Justify your decisions.

A. Allow the sports editor to host a daily program on a local radio station.

B. Allow the sports editor to appear in television advertisements for a chain of sports stores in the city.

C. Allow the business editor to own stock in local companies.

D. Allow a popular columnist, a local celebrity, to charge $1,000 for each one-hour speech she gives.

E. Allow a local freelance cartoonist, whose cartoons your newspaper has agreed to publish regularly on the editorial page, to donate money to local politicians.

3. Discussion Questions

Read the following situations and decide what actions you would take. Discuss your choices with the class.

1. Without your knowledge, a talented young reporter on your staff hacks into the computer system at a competing news organization. The reporter gives you a list of all the stories the rival's staff is working on. Would you

A. Compliment the reporter on her initiative and quickly assign your own staff to cover the stories so you are not scooped?

B. Destroy the list and tell the reporter to never again enter the rival's computer system?

C. Reprimand the reporter, suspending her for a week?

D. Notify your rival and apologize for the reporter's actions?

E. Notify the police that the reporter may have unknowingly violated a state law?

2. One of your journalists is writing about a local country club that, she learns, excludes certain cultures. The reporter also learns that your publisher and other influential members of your community are members of the club. Would you

A. Abandon the story?

B. Inform your publisher about the story and suggest that she resign from the club?

C. Tell your reporter to interview the publisher and give her an opportunity to explain her membership in the club?

D. Publish the story but never identify any of the club's members?

E. Publish the story, listing your publisher and other prominent citizens who belong to the club?

F. List all 1,200 of the club's members?

3. As editor of your local daily, you learn that the next day's installment of Doonesbury, a popular comic strip, shows a political bias that might offend many readers. Would you

A. Publish the strip without change or comment?

B. Kill that day's strip?

C. Stop publishing the strip forever?

D. Change any wording to something less offensive?

E. Move the strip to your newspaper's editorial page and publish an editorial explaining that, although you dislike its content, you believe in freedom of speech?

F. Kill that day's strip but, in its place, publish a brief explanation and offer to mail copies of the strip to any readers who request it?

4. Each year, the SPJ in your state sponsors an awards competition. Minutes ago, you learned that a reporter on your staff won first place in feature writing and that your chief photographer won second place in sports. However, another newspaper in the city won five awards, a local

television station won four, and a citizen journalism site won three. How would you handle the story?

A. Ignore the story.

B. Report all the awards.

C. Report only the two awards won by your staff.

5. You run the evening news, and a sports reporter mistakenly credited the wrong football player with scoring two game-winning touchdowns. Would you:

A. Broadcast a correction the next evening?

B. Broadcast a correction and identify the reporter responsible for the error?

C. Broadcast a correction and punish the reporter, placing him on probation?

D. Broadcast a correction that identifies the reporter and reports his punishment?

E. Order the reporter to write a letter to the school, apologizing for his error?

F. Privately punish the reporter, placing him on probation, but publish nothing, treating the incident as a private personnel matter?

G. Do nothing, hoping nobody noticed?

6. Decide how you would respond in each of the following situations. Discuss your reasoning.

A. As news director of a local television station, you think an emphasis on crime and violence is bad journalism but don't know if it affects your newscasts' ratings. Would you continue to emphasize crime and violence?

B. A reporter on your staff has terrible vision, undergoes a new laser procedure to correct her nearsightedness and wants to write a series about the operation and the doctor who successfully performed it. The story is likely to interest thousands of readers, but you learn that the reporter's operation was performed for free. Would you let her write the series?

C. After serving three terms, your city's mayor—a popular and successful Republican—decides to step down. She then applies for a job as a political columnist for your editorial page and is obviously a good writer. Would you hire her?

D. Thousands of people live in your city's low-income areas. Advertisers prefer reaching people who are wealthy and well-educated. To improve your newspaper's demographics would you, as publisher, instruct your circulation staff to ignore your city's low-income areas and their residents?

E. A member of your state legislature proposes applying your state sales tax to advertisements, a policy that would cost the news site, of which you are publisher, millions of dollars a year. When asked, would you contribute $50,000 to a campaign your state press association is waging against the tax? Would you report your decision and the size of any contribution?

F. An extortionist says he has poisoned groceries in your town's largest chain of supermarkets. Customers continue to shop in the stores. Police say the threat is almost certainly a hoax, and that it will be easier for them to catch the extortionist in a day or two if you delay publishing the story. Would you immediately run the story?

4. Ethical Dilemmas

Read the following ethical dilemmas and answer the related questions, giving support for your answers. Discuss your responses with the class.

1. A student at a local high school brought his father's gun to school and shot another student. The school security guard killed the shooter. In an interview, the principal tells you that the student with the gun was "a troubled child"; she immediately asks you to please not run this statement, that she shouldn't have said it. Would you run it? Why or why not?

2. After a deadly car accident occurs, you interview the mother of a deceased driver. She tells you that he would have lived if the hospital had not acted so slowly. In describing the hospital, she uses several expletives. For your small-town paper, would you use the expletives? What about in a bigger paper like The New York Times? Does it make a difference that it might appear online for the Huffington Post? Are the expletives necessary? Does including them support the objective of the story?

3. While listening to a police scanner, you hear that a man has been arrested for raping a 16-year-old girl. You go to the police station and talk to the arresting officer. While discussing the case, he says he believes that "this man should fry." Is it ethical to publish this, or is it editorializing? Is there a better way to use the quote? Is the quote necessary? Does it support the objective of the story?

4. You are assigned to do a profile of a local African-American businessman who has just donated a large amount of money to a fund helping the urban black community. While discussing it, he drops a racial slur. Should you use it in your story, even though it takes away from the good deed he has done?

5. Your regular beat includes stopping by the mayor's office most days of the week, and you regularly talk with the mayor's secretary. One day she says that she will treat you to lunch and the two of you can discuss what goes on "behind the scenes." Should you accept the offer of the free lunch, even though she says that it is the only way you will get the information?

6. A local soldier was killed in Afghanistan and brought home. During the woman's funeral, your videographer captured the deceased's 5-year-old son wiping away a tear and holding a stuffed bear dressed like Uncle Sam. Should you use the video in your story? Does the decision change, depending on the medium, such as TV or internet or as a photo in print? Should a journalist be at the funeral, or is that invading the family's privacy?

5. Stories That Raise Ethical Concerns

Each of the following stories involves several ethical dilemmas. Write a news story based on each set of facts, thoughtfully deciding which ones to use and which to discard. Correct any errors you might find.

1. Nursing Home Employees

It's a shocking tale and an exclusive for your newspaper, revealed by a diligent and exhaustive month-long investigation by a team of 5 journalists and one editor on your staff. While visiting a nursing home where her mother is currently living, your police reporter recognized three faces, all ex-cons. The investigation revealed that felons have daily contact with the most frail and defenseless of your citys elderly residents. No one can say how many nursing home employees have been convicted of theft, prostitution, domestic violence, or other crimes because people in those jobs don't have to undergo a criminal background check. Using city directories and a multitude of other sources, the team learned the names of 412 nursing home employees and found that 1 in 5 had an arrest or conviction for a felony. Esther Onn, president of the state Coalition to Protect Elders, told one of the reporters that she wants and is fighting for all nursing home employees to be screened: "Our parents deserve the best care society can give them. They shouldn't have to worry about being robbed or beaten. In some nursing homes in the city we've found evidence of real brutality, of residents being terrorized by these thugs. These people work in nursing homes because they can get jobs there. The operators of the places know if they hire ex-cons, they don't have to pay them much. Giving them jobs at low wages increases the owners profits, and they're already exorbitant." But on the other hand Beatrice Rosolowski, spokesman for the State Federation of Nursing Homes, says checking on everyone goes too far and they themselves are pushing other reforms to the system they agree is flawed. "The cracks are there and they are big enough for people to be slipping through," Rosolowski admits. Theft is the most common crime against nursing home patients, and they are vulnerable because many residents are incapable of even reporting crimes against them, whether theft, brutality, intimidation or neglect. At least some of those crimes are committed by nursing home staffers, which is why people residing in nursing homes everywhere are told to keep their valuables hidden and drawers and doors locked. Even if background investigations of nursing home employees are conducted, the team learned they could be far from adequate since people convicted in other states would likely not be detected and background checks often are not run on people until after they have begun to work. And employees arrested or convicted after their initial check may not be detected until they apply for a job at another nursing home. Blanket screening would be expensive and not likely to make homes much safer. Another source, Atty. Harold Murray, represents 150 clients currently suing nursing homes in and around the state. Some have been abused, he said, while others have had their possessions stolen by nursing home workers. "You've got housekeepers, custodians, dieticians, and a host of employees who go into these rooms every day and who have contact with residents. Who are these people?" Murray asks. While pursuing the lawsuits Murray obtained records of nursing home workers and did his own background check. Of 378 employee names he submitted, 76 had been arrested for or convicted of felonies. The convictions included prostitution, assault and spousal abuse. Two former prostitutes work at Elder Haven, 3110 East River Parkway, and so does a bank robber released after 14 years in prison. A convicted child molester, Grady Smith, was found by Murray working at Sunnyview Nursing Home, 1012 Peters Dr. Smith was in prison from 1981 to 1993, when he got his current job as a janitor at Sunnyview and, according to police, has been in no trouble since then. The reporters also heard—but have been unable to document—allegations that some nursing home employees strap some residents difficult to handle to their chairs or beds, leaving them in such condition for prolonged periods of time on a daily basis. Unhappy residents families allege but have no proof that some residents are kept heavily sedated even when there is no clear medical or physical reason to do so simply because it makes residents easier to handle.

2. Teen Gang

Beginning at the start of last year the police in your city noticed an abrupt increase in crime, especially car thefts and residential burglaries, in the Oakwood Subdivision. As dawn broke early today police went to the homes of 4 teenagers, all students currently at Oakwood high school. The teens were arrested by police, who now say they were part of a ring suspected of involvement in a total of approximately 100 to 150 or more car and home burglaries. Police are looking for two other teens but did not identify them. All are white. All are male. Two of the 6 are on the schools honor roll, which requires a 3.5 gpa or higher. All are between the ages of 16 to 18 yrs of age. In a press conference today your citys police chief said the students apparently took orders from fellow students. His officers recovered property valued at $15,000, including radar detectors, televisions, stereos, cassette players, guns, cameras, stamp and coin collections, games, compact disc players and a trash bag full of cassette tapes. "Some of these kids were making a lot of bucks," the chief said. The youngest students, one age 16 and one age 17, were immediately taken to the county juvenile detention center for incarceration and were subsequently released to their parents. The other two, both 18, were charged with multiple counts of burglary, possession of stolen goods, and contributing to the delinquency of a minor, and are being held in the county jail with their bail set at $50,000. Because of the seriousness of their crimes, police charged all 4 as adults and identified them as:

Claude Nunziata, 16, son of Carmen Nunziata

Burt Dolmovich, 17, son of Sandra M. Dolomovich

Michael Gandolf, 18, son of Sandra Gandolf

Giles Grauman, 18, son of Alyce and Samuel Graumann

The police chief, who personally released the youths names to the press today, said, "The information our investigation is uncovering is that they've done a lot more than what we know. One of these punks told my men he'd been involved in at least 80 burglaries himself. What's worse, what's really depressing here, is that we think dozens of students at the school knew what they were doing and, because it was cheap, were buying things from them, things they knew were stolen." Police chief Barry Kopperud added that the parents of three of the boys voluntarily cooperated by allowing police to search their homes for stolen property taken in the crimes. Carmen Nunziata, the mother of Claude, refused to let the police into her home and refused to talk to the press when you called her today. Police subsequently obtained a search warrant, then proceeded to search the premises. She is divorced and on welfare, with a total of four children to support and is not currently working, having been on welfare for 11 years according to public records maintained by the city that you were able to see. The whereabouts of Nunziatas father is unknown at this point in time. "Some parents were aware their sons were wheeling and dealing with property, but they figured they were just swapping with one another," Kopperudd said. "I don't know, maybe some knew their kids were crooks." Some of the recovered property has been returned to its owners. For people who may be wondering whether or not some of the property could be theirs, Kopperud expressed that most of that which was recovered was stolen in the past 30 days and a lot of the rest was sold to other students and at flea markets, so its mostly now all gone.

THE BASIC SKILLS OF JOURNALISM

BASIC NEWS LEADS

A story—whether fiction or nonfiction—has to begin somewhere. The opening of a story needs to grab people's attention and hold it. The rest has to flow logically to its conclusion. The easiest thing for anyone to do is stop reading, watching or listening, and if the story fails to attract the person's attention at the beginning, he or she may ignore it. Just as a story needs a beginning, the process of writing must have one. Few writers can sit at a keyboard and tap out a story without first planning it.

> "If you don't hit a newspaper reader between the eyes with your first sentence, there is no need of writing a second one."
>
> *Arthur Brisbane, newspaper editor and columnist*

Prewriting

Identifying the Central Point

Writing requires preparation and organization. The preparation begins before gathering information, when the story is just an idea in the mind of the reporter, editor or producer. Earlier chapters of this textbook explained the changing nature of journalism and the concepts of digital journalism, which requires much more planning and organization to deliver content across multiple platforms. The story tree is a helpful tool for organizing and gathering information for a story (see Figure 7.1).

When reporters have gathered all the information they think they need for a story, they still face the task of organizing. The best way to start this process is to find the central point, a one- or two-sentence summary of what the story is about and why it is newsworthy. It is a statement of the topic and more. Several stories may have the same subject, but the central point of each should be unique.

When Hurricane Harvey struck the Gulf Coast of Texas and Louisiana, people turned to newspapers, television, news websites and social media to find out as much as they could about the catastrophe. Audiences wanted to know what areas were affected and how many people had died or were injured. They wanted to

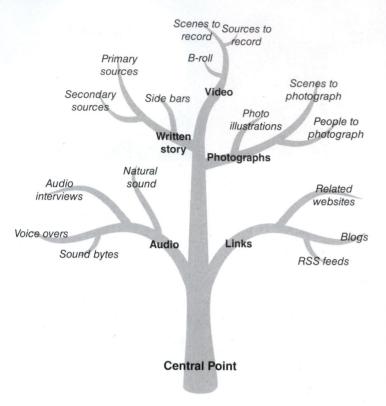

Figure 7.1   The Story Tree   A story tree can help journalists organize information for story packages.

know the status of local, state and federal government relief and recovery efforts, as well as ways to prevent the magnitude of the damage and loss of life from happening again. Every story about Harvey—whether from the view of the rescue and recovery agencies, government officials, witnesses or victims and their families—had its particular central point that distinguished it from all other stories on the same subject.

Reporters usually have a good idea what the central point of their stories will be even as they begin gathering information. However, unexpected details may emerge and force them to rethink this element. Therefore, journalists always review their notes and other materials before they start writing. Doing so ensures that they have identified the most newsworthy central point and have the information they need to develop it. It also helps them decide what the major sections of their stories will be. Reporters who fail to identify a central point or who lose sight of it risk writing incoherent and incomplete stories.

Every well-written news story contains a clear statement of its central point. It may be in the first paragraph, called the "lead," or in a later paragraph, called a "nut graph," that follows an anecdote, describes a scene or uses some other storytelling device to entice the audience into the story. By including the central point, writers clearly tell people what they will learn from the entire story.

Story Outlines

The next step in organizing a news story is to create an outline. A reporter covering a shooting and robbery at a local convenience store might draft this central-point statement: "A convenience store clerk was shot by a robber who escaped with only $15." The outline might have these major sections:

Victim and injuries

Police identify suspect

Witnesses' descriptions of robber

With this skeleton, the reporter needs only to develop each section.

Once reporters select a central point and write a brief outline, they go through their notes again to decide what information belongs where. Some number passages; others use colored pens, markers or highlighters to indicate where to put particular facts, quotes or anecdotes. They omit information that does not fit in any of the sections.

Donald L. Barlett and James B. Steele, investigative reporters who have written several stories for The Philadelphia Inquirer, Time magazine, and Vanity Fair, as well as eight books, say one of the keys to their success is organizing information.

They spend months gathering documents and conducting interviews, all of which are filed by topic or name of individual, agency or corporation. Then they read the material several times because important issues and ideas often become clear only after time. Once they have an outline of the story's major parts, they start drafting it section by section. Finally, they polish sections and spend most of their time working on leads and transitions between parts. Barlett and Steele's description of their process confirms what most writers say: No one sits down and writes great stories. Writers must plan their work.

Collaborators for over 30 years, Donald L. Barlett (right) and James B. Steele have won two Pulitzer Prizes, two National Magazine Awards, and five George Polk Awards together.

Planning the Digital Story

Even when developing a story for distribution across multiple digital platforms, reporters first establish a central point. If the story is about an increase in property taxes proposed by local government officials, the central point might be the effect the change will have on local residents. Using the story tree, reporters would begin by developing a list of sources to interview—government officials, local residents, business owners and others affected by the increase. They would also develop a list of government databases to scan for information on current tax rates, property values and local government spending.

THE VIDEO STORY

Digital journalists need to consider how best to use video with their story. Will it be a highlight segment with quotes from someone who is a source or subject of the story? Will it be a several-minute analysis with comments by several people involved in the story, with voice-over narration and b-roll? Or will it be a mini-documentary with multiple long interviews, interspersed with environmental shots to give viewers a sense of place, and voice-over narration and music? It often depends on the type of story and the amount of time the reporter has to write the story and to edit and prepare the video. Video is often used to explain a complex aspect of a story, which can be done better visually, or to emphasize and dramatize something in the story, but it also can be used to tell the entire story.

In planning video for a property tax increase story, reporters would first determine whom they want to record. From government officials, they would learn why the increase is needed and perhaps how the additional revenue will be spent. They would then record interviews with business leaders and local residents for reactions to the proposal. They also would determine what b-roll sequences they would have to record to add context to the story. If a reporter plans to attend a meeting where the matter will be discussed, he or she would want to capture video of the meeting in progress and any reaction from the audience. If there is no meeting planned, he or she might shoot video that includes areas of the community that will be affected by the increase, such as a shopping mall or business district and the homes in a local subdivision. He or she also may include video of locations where the increased tax revenue will be spent, such as local schools or road construction. (See Chapter 13 for more on video journalism.)

THE AUDIO ELEMENT

Journalists have been recording their interviews since the invention of small compact tape recorders and microcassette recorders. With small digital audio recorders, the process is easier than ever before. And the digitally recorded interviews can be uploaded to a computer to be edited and added to the digital news package (see Chapter 13).

In planning the story package, reporters have to decide how to use audio clips. As with video, the package could use brief statements from someone being interviewed to explain, emphasize or dramatize a point, or it could use a long interview that tells the entire story. It is important to determine how audio will be used in order to know how much has to be recorded.

Audio may also accompany photographic slideshows. This audio may be a narrator explaining what the images represent or music or natural sounds in the background as the viewer reads the captions, or cutlines, beneath each photo.

Planning for audio requires reporters to determine whom they want to record; where they want to record; what natural, or environmental, sound they need; and what music, if any, is appropriate. If reporters use any words, images or music others have created, aside from sources' quotes, they may need to get permission to use them in their stories. Failure to do so could violate copyright law.

PHOTOGRAPHS AND PHOTO SLIDESHOWS

Reporters also need to think about still photographs. For example, a newspaper story might appear both in print and online. While the former version may publish one or two photographs, the latter can accommodate as many photos as the editor wants to use. Slideshows often range from six to 15 photographs and may be accompanied by music and/or voice-over narration.

Many news organizations have staff photographers who are assigned to stories and take the shots that reporters need. At smaller news organizations, reporters often carry digital cameras to take their own photographs. And most news organizations have their reporters carry digital video recorders because staff photographers are often too busy to hang around for an entire interview.

Much like planning for the video story, reporters must take time to think about the photographs they will need. Using the example of the proposed tax increase, photos may include close-up, or mug, shots of the major players, such as the mayor of the community or other government officials; people who spoke at a meeting; or the community leaders who support or are against the change. The reporter also may want to include crowd or background shots if the story is taking place at a meeting.

Today's digital audiences expect reporters to provide visual content that will explain and enhance news stories.

The Summary News Lead

As mentioned at the beginning of this chapter, the first paragraph or two in a news story is called the "lead" (also spelled "lede"). The lead is the most important part of a story—and the hardest part to write. Like the opening paragraphs of a short story or novel, the lead attracts the audience and, if well written, arouses interest. It should reveal the story's central point, not hide the subject with unnecessary or ambiguous words and phrases.

Every news story must answer six questions: Who? What? When? Where? Why? How? The lead, however, should answer only the one or two that are most interesting, newsworthy and unusual. For example, few urban residents know the ordinary citizens involved in news stories, so the names of those people—the "who"—rarely appear in leads. The exact time and place at which a story occurred may also be unimportant.

When writers try to answer all six questions in one paragraph, they create complicated and confusing leads. Here's an example of an overloaded lead and a possible revision:

> Charles E. Vickers, 47, of 1521 Yarmouth Drive, died and John Aston Walters, 39, of 1867 Colonial Ave., was severely injured Sunday afternoon when the bicycles they were riding were struck near the intersection of Weston and Falmouth roads by a car driven by a man police said had a blood alcohol count of nearly .23 percent and was driving without a license because it had been revoked last year after his fourth conviction for driving under the influence of alcohol.

> One Mechanicsburg man is dead and another severely injured after the bicycles they were riding were struck by a drunken driver Sunday afternoon near the intersection of Weston and Falmouth roads.

Because people and what they do are central to many news stories, some journalists recognize two variations on the summary news lead: the immediate-identification lead and the delayed-identification lead. Reporters use the first type when the identities of the story's major subjects are important or are well known:

> President Barack Obama will personally welcome Pope Francis at the airport when he arrives for his first U.S. tour, a change for a protocol operation that normally only rolls out the red carpet at the White House.
> *(The [Harrisburg, Pennsylvania] Patriot-News)*

> Citing a recent ruling over custody of livestock seized from a Boonsboro farmer in 2014, Washington County Circuit Court

FROM THE NEWS

Leads and the Basic Questions

Each of the following leads answers the basic question that seems most important for the story.

Who	Warren Buffett's Berkshire Hathaway Inc. is nearing a deal to buy one of the country's biggest power-transmission companies, which would cement electricity as one of the conglomerate's largest businesses, people familiar with the matter said. (*The Wall Street Journal*)
What	Maryland regulators have allowed the state's first medical-marijuana dispensary to open its doors immediately, even though the drug will not be available for months. (*The Associated Press*)
When	William C. Morva was scheduled to be executed Thursday night in Virginia, after supporters failed to convince Gov. Terry McAuliffe (D) that Morva's mental illness merited clemency and a life sentence in the 2006 murders of a sheriff's deputy and an unarmed hospital security guard. (*The Washington Post*)
Where	Ukraine has dodged a second cyberattack, officials said Wednesday, suggesting the digital campaign that paralyzed computers across the country and around the world is ongoing. (*The Associated Press*)
Why	The dismal fiscal situation in many states is forcing governors, despite their party affiliation, toward a consensus on what medicine is needed going forward. (*The New York Times*)
How	A nearby resident pulled an Antrim Township milk truck driver from his crumpled tanker Tuesday morning after a Norfolk Southern train crashed into the rig at the Milnor Road railroad crossing. (*The [Waynesboro, Pennsylvania] Record Herald*)

> Judge Mark K. Boyer on Thursday denied a prosecution motion that could have resulted in euthanizing 14 pitbulls held in a pending dogfighting case. [The [Hagerstown, Maryland] Herald-Mail]

In many stories, the names of the main subjects are not as important as what occurred. For those stories, reporters use delayed-identification leads, which withhold complete identification of the people involved until the second or third paragraph. Here are two examples:

> An east Philadelphia man held his girlfriend's baby at knife point for more than two hours Saturday night before police officers captured him after shooting him with a stun gun.

> An 82-year-old Dallas woman is slowly recovering from a gunshot wound to the head, and police say they may be on the verge of charging a suspect with attempted murder.

Leads that hold back details so the reporter can get to the central point of the article more quickly are called "blind leads." Beginners should not misinterpret the terminology. A blind lead does not hide the central point of the story, only information that the audience does not need immediately. Blind leads let the journalist tell people what the story is about, to pique their interest and get them into the story.

A "catchall graph" usually follows the blind lead to identify sources and answer questions created by the lead. Missing details can be placed in subsequent paragraphs. Here's an example of a blind lead:

> It was an Altoona company that lost its appeal to Commonwealth Court, but it's the state agency charged with overseeing construction matters that's feeling the pain.
>
> *(The [Harrisburg, Pennsylvania] Patriot-News)*

In its second paragraph, the article identified the company and what the case involved. In the third paragraph, the article identified the state agency involved and what it had done wrong.

Before reporters can write effective leads, however, they must learn to recognize what is news. After selecting the most newsworthy facts, journalists must summarize those facts in sharp, clear sentences, giving a simple, straightforward account of what happened. Examine these leads, which provide clear, concise summaries of momentous events in the nation's history:

> Washington—Supreme Court justices revealed sharp and passionately held differences Tuesday as they confronted California's ban on gay marriages.
>
> *(McClatchy Newspapers)*

> Denver—Timothy McVeigh, the decorated soldier who turned his killing skills against the people of Oklahoma City, was condemned Friday to die.
>
> *(The Dallas Morning News)*

> Dallas, Nov. 22—A sniper armed with a high-powered rifle assassinated President Kennedy today. Barely two hours after Mr. Kennedy's death, Vice President Johnson took the oath of office as the thirty-sixth President of the United States.
>
> *(The Associated Press)*

Leads that fail to emphasize the news—the most interesting and important details—are sometimes described as burying the lead. Here's an example of an unsuccessful lead:

> Wentworth County is required to give inmates the same level of medical treatment the general public receives, Corrections Director Maria Sanchez said.

The news in the story, however, was not the level of medical care the county provides inmates. It was the financial problems the county was facing because of the requirement. This rewritten lead makes the significance of the story clearer:

> Wentworth County's costs for medical care for jail inmates doubled—from $50,000 to $100,000—last year because of a new state regulation. Friday morning, county and state officials gathered to find a way to pay the bill.

The Poynter Institute gives an "invisible prize" for the best leads in Pulitzer-winning stories. The 2016 winners were AP's Robin McDowell, Margie Mason and Martha Mendoza for the leads in their stories on slavery in the seafood industry.

Sentence Structure in Leads

Most leads are a single sentence. They must be complete sentences and follow all the normal rules for punctuation, grammar, word usage and verb tense. For example, if an event occurred in the past, the lead must use the past tense, not the present. Leads should also include all the necessary articles.

Some problems with sentence structure arise because beginners confuse a story's lead with its headline. The lead is the first paragraph of a news story; the headline is a brief summary that appears in larger type above the story. To save space, editors use only a few key words in each headline. However, that style of writing is not appropriate for leads.

Headline: Microsoft begins latest layoffs

Lead: Microsoft has started cutting thousands of positions, mostly in its sales department, days after announcing it would shift its sales strategy to focus more on cloud services than on its traditional server and desktop businesses.
(The Washington Post)

Most leads begin with the subject, which is closely followed by an active verb and then by the object of the verb (i.e., subject-verb-object order; see Chapter 4). Reporters deviate from that style only in the rare case that a different sentence structure better tells the news. Leads that begin with long qualifying clauses and phrases lack the clarity of simpler, more direct sentences. Long introductory clauses also clutter leads, burying the news amid a jumble of less significant details. Author and writing coach Paula LaRocque calls these "backed-into leads." She describes them as "one of the most pervasive and uninviting habits a writer can fall into." Consider the following example:

➤ Washington—~~In the most significant court case dealing with money and politics since 1976, a~~ ^A^ special three-judge panel today upheld ~~several~~ major ~~provisions~~ ^portions^ of a ~~sweeping~~ new ^federal^ law limiting political ~~donations~~ ^campaign contributions,^ but ^it also^ found ~~that~~ some ^parts of the law^ ~~of its measures were~~ unconstitutional.
(The New York Times)

The original lead delayed the news—information about the court's decision—until after a 13-word introductory phrase containing information that probably could have gone in the story's second or third paragraph.

Guidelines for Writing Effective Leads

Be Concise

The concise style of writing found in journalism makes it easy for the public to understand leads but difficult for reporters to write them. Two- or three-sentence leads often become wordy, repetitious and choppy, particularly when all the sentences are very short. Like most multisentence leads, the following example can be made more concise as a single sentence:

> Two women ∧ ~~robbed~~ *stole a purse containing $50 from* a shopper in a local supermarket Tuesday. ~~One woman distracted the shopper, and the second woman grabbed her purse, which contained about $50.~~

The original lead was redundant. It reported two women robbed a shopper, and then described the robbery. Reporters use two-sentence leads only when there is a compelling need to do so. Often, the second sentence emphasizes an interesting or unusual fact of lesser importance. Other times, the second sentence is necessary because it is impossible to summarize all the necessary information about a complex topic in a single sentence.

The lead in the accompanying article on brain trauma uses a second sentence to illustrate and explain the first. Many readers would find this 26-word lead difficult to read—a better average would be 18 to 20 words. Reporters should examine their leads critically to determine whether they are wordy or repetitious or contain facts that could be shifted to later paragraphs.

Journalists shorten leads by eliminating unnecessary background information—dates, names, locations—or the description of routine procedures. Leads should omit many names, particularly those the public is unlikely to recognize or those who played minor or routine roles in a story. Including someone's name may also require identifying him or her, which uses more words. Descriptive phrases can substitute for names. Similarly, a story's precise time and location could be reported in a later paragraph. A lead should report a story's highlights, not all its minor details, as concisely as possible:

> A ∧ *The FBI on Wednesday arrested a* former Roxbury woman~~,~~ who has eluded ~~federal law enforcement~~ authorities since ∧ *1983, when* she ∧ *was accused of hijacking an airplane* ~~allegedly hijacked a flight from San Juan to Cuba using a plastic flare gun in 1983, was arrested Wednesday as she stood alone on Union Street in Boston, according to the Federal Bureau of Investigation~~.

Although leads can be too long, they cannot be too short. An effective lead may contain only four to six words: "The president is dead," "Americans landed on the moon" or "There's new hope for couch potatoes."

Be Specific

Good leads contain interesting details and are so specific that the audience can visualize the events they describe. As you read the following lead from The Tampa (Florida) Tribune, you should be able to imagine the dramatic scene it describes:

At 59, she'd never touched a gun—until someone held one to her head.

Key Iraq wound: Brain trauma

By Gregg Zoroya, USA TODAY

A growing number of U.S. troops whose body armor helped them survive bomb and rocket attacks are suffering brain damage as a result of the blasts. It's a type of injury some military doctors say has become the signature wound of the Iraq war.

The second sentence in this lead is not only required to include additional information, but it also gives a compelling detail regarding the topic.

Reporters can easily transform vague, dull leads into interesting ones by adding more specific details. The second of the following leads is more successful:

> The City Council passed an ordinance that will affect all parents and teenagers living within city limits.

> The City Council ignored the objections of the mayor and numerous parents and voted 6–1 Monday to enact a dusk-to-dawn curfew to keep youngsters off city streets.

Some leads use worn-out clichés—a lazy way of summarizing a story. Avoid saying that "a step has been taken" or that someone has moved "one step closer" to a goal. Present specific details:

> ➤ *The university's Board of Governors voted Tuesday to increase* ^~~University officials moved one step closer to increasing~~ tuition
>
> *10 percent next year to offset cuts in state funding*
> and fees ^ ~~for the upcoming school year, leaving students up in the air~~.

Avoid "iffy" leads that say one thing may happen if another happens. In addition to being too vague, "iffy" leads are too abstract, tentative and qualified. Report the story's more immediate and concrete details.

Use Strong, Active Verbs

A single descriptive verb can transform a routine lead into a dramatic one. As you read the following lead, you may be able to picture what happened:

> Deland—After rushing her 7-year-old daughter to safety, Ann Murray raced back to the docks and pounded on her friends' boats while flames and explosions tore through Boat Show Marina early Friday morning.
> *(The Orlando [Florida] Sentinel)*

Strong, active verbs, such as "rushing," "raced," "pounded" and "tore," paint a vivid picture of the scene. They capture the drama and emotion of a news event and help the reader understand the impact of the story. The following lead uses several colorful verbs to describe the capture of a wayward Angus steer that escaped his handlers:

> The suspect tore through a homeowner's fence, ripped the wires from a satellite dish with his teeth, slammed head-on into a travel trailer, then bolted down the street on his way to a weird encounter with a canoe.
> *(The Orlando [Florida] Sentinel)*

Avoid passive-voice constructions, which combine the past participle of a verb with some form of the verb "to be," such as "is," "are," "was" and "were" (see Chapter 4). Compare the italicized verbs in these two leads:

Passive Verbs: One person *was killed* and four others *were injured* Sunday morning when their car, which *was traveling* west on Interstate 80, hit a concrete bridge pillar and *was engulfed* in flames.

Active Verbs: A car traveling west on Interstate 80 *swerved* across two eastbound lanes, *slammed* into a concrete bridge pillar and *burst* into flames, killing one person and injuring four others Sunday morning.

Writers can easily convert passive voice to the active voice. Simply rearrange the words so the sentence reports who did what to whom. Instead of reporting "Rocks and bottles were thrown at firefighters," report "Rioters threw rocks and bottles at firefighters."

Emphasize the Magnitude of the Story

If a story is important, reporters emphasize its magnitude in the lead. Most good leads focus on the impact stories have on people. When describing natural disasters or man-made catastrophes, such as airplane crashes, tornadoes or major fires, journalists emphasize the number of people killed, injured and left homeless, as well as the financial cost of the damage to buildings or other objects. When describing a storm, reporters may highlight the amount of rain or snow that fell. The following lead shows how magnitude can be emphasized in a story:

New York (AP)—Secondhand cigarette smoke will cause an estimated 47,000 deaths and about 150,000 nonfatal heart attacks in U.S. nonsmokers this year, a study says. That's as much as 50 percent higher than previous estimates.

Stress the Unusual

Leads also emphasize the unusual. By definition, news involves deviations from the norm. Consider this lead:

Oelwein, Iowa—Two men have been arrested for stealing a man's clothes and leaving him to wander around naked, officials said.
      (The Associated Press)

A lead about a board of education meeting or other governmental agency should not report "The board met at 8 p.m. at a local school and began its meeting with roll call." Those facts are routine and not newsworthy. Most school boards meet every couple of weeks, usually at the same time and place, and many begin their meetings with roll call. Leads should stress the unique—the action that follows those routine formalities.

Bank robberies are so common in big cities that newspapers normally devote only a few paragraphs to them. Yet a robbery at the Burlington National Bank in Columbus, Ohio, became a front-page story, published by newspapers throughout the United States. A story transmitted by The Associated Press (AP) explained:

A 61-year-old man says he robbed an Ohio bank with a toy gun—he even told the FBI ahead of time when and where—because he wants to spend his golden years in federal prison.

After his arrest, the bank robber insisted he did not want a lawyer. Instead, he wanted to immediately "plead guilty to anything." The man explained he recently was divorced, had no family ties and was disabled with arthritis. He had spent time in at least three federal prisons and wanted to return to one of them. "I knew what I was doing," he insisted. "I wanted to get arrested, and I proceeded about it the best way I knew how."

Reporters must learn to recognize and emphasize a story's unusual details.

Localize and Update

Reporters localize their leads whenever possible by highlighting their communities' involvement in stories. Audiences are most interested in stories affecting their own lives and the lives of people they know.

Reporters also try to localize stories from other parts of the world. When a bomb exploded in a Pan Am plane over Lockerbie, Scotland, newspapers across the United States not only ran the story of the bombing but localized it on the basis of where the passengers had lived. The Gazette in Delaware, Ohio, focused on the death of a student from Ohio Wesleyan University, which is located in the town. Similarly, when the FBI reports on the number of violent crimes committed in the United States, reporters stress the statistics for their communities:

> The number of violent crimes committed in the city last year rose 5.4 percent, compared to a national average of 8.3 percent, the FBI reported Tuesday.

Reporters update a lead by highlighting the latest developments in the story. The adoption of digital media platforms—both web and social media—have allowed news organizations to become 24/7 operations, capable of updating information throughout the day. By posting a story online, journalists can retain much of the original story but update the lead with new information as often as necessary.

Before the digital revolution, if a breaking story appeared in an early edition of a newspaper, a writer would gather new information and rewrite the story for publication the next day. Instead of saying a fire destroyed a store the previous day, reporters may stress that authorities have since learned the fire's cause, identified the victims, arrested an arsonist or estimated the monetary loss. In today's digital media environment, stories may be updated within minutes or a few hours after first appearing on social media or the web. Stories are updated so they offer the public something new—facts not already reported by other news outlets. Major stories about such topics as economic trends, natural disasters, wars and political upheavals often remain in the news for months and must be updated regularly.

Sean O'Sullivan's story on the bust of a drug cartel focuses on the work of local investigators, making the story particularly relevant to readers.

Not every lead can be updated or localized. If a story has no new or local angles, report it in a simple, straightforward manner. Do not distort the story in any way or fabricate any information.

Be Objective and Attribute Opinions

The lead of a news story, like the rest of the piece, must be objective. Reporters are expected to gather and convey facts, not commentary, interpretation or advocacy. They may anger or offend an audience when they insert their opinions in stories.

Calling the people involved in news stories "alert," "heroic" or "quick-thinking" or describing facts as "interesting" or "startling" is never justified. When accurate, these comments usually state the obvious. Leads that include opinion or interpretation must be rewritten to provide more factual accounts of the news:

➤ ~~Speaking to the Downtown Rotary Club last night,~~ Emil Plambeck,
superintendent of the City Park Commission, ∧ *wants developers to set aside* ~~discussed a topic of~~
5 percent of the land in new subdivisions for parks
∧~~concern to all of us—the city's park system~~.

The original lead is weak because it refers to "a topic of concern to all of us." The reporter does not identify "us" and is wrong to assert that any topic concerns everyone.

Here are other examples of leads that state an opinion or conclusion:

Adult entertainment establishments have fallen victim to another attempt at censorship.

Recycling does not pay, at least not economically. However, the environmental benefits make the city's new recycling program worthwhile at any cost.

To demonstrate that both leads are statements of opinion, ask your friends and classmates about them. Do they all agree that the regulation of adult entertainment establishments is "censorship"? Do they all think that recycling programs are "worthwhile at any cost"?

Although journalists cannot express their own opinions in stories, they often include the opinions of people involved in the news. A lead containing a statement of opinion must be attributed so that the audience clearly understands the opinion is not the reporter's.

A lead containing an obvious fact or a fact the reporter has witnessed or verified by other means generally does not require attribution. An editor at The New York Times, instructing reporters to "make the lead of a story as brief and clear as possible," noted, "One thing that obstructs that aim is the inclusion of an unnecessary source of attribution. . . . If the lead is controversial, an attribution is imperative. But if the lead is innocuous, forget it." Thus, if a lead states undisputed facts, the attribution can be placed in a later paragraph:

Washington—Cars and motorcycles crash into deer more than 4,000 times a day, and it's taking an increasingly deadly toll—on people.
(The Associated Press)

Strive for Simplicity

Every lead should be clear, simple and to the point. Here is an example:

> A party-crasher shot a 26-year-old woman to death at a surprise birthday bash in Queens early Sunday, police and witnesses said.
> *(New York Daily News)*

The next lead suffers from far too much detail:

> Officials of the city and the Gladstone School District are breathing sighs of relief following the Clackamas County Housing Authority's decision to pull out of a plan to build an apartment complex for moderate-income people on 11 acres of land between Southeast Oatfield and Webster roads.

The lead could be rewritten any number of ways. The reporter must decide what the important point is. Here are two versions of a simple blind lead for the same story:

> Several city and school district officials applauded the county's decision to scrap plans for a subsidized housing complex.

> A new subsidized housing complex will not be built, and city and school district officials are relieved.

Some Common Errors

Beginning with the Attribution

Avoid beginning a lead with the attribution. Names and titles are dull and seldom important. Moreover, if all leads started this way, they would sound too much alike. Place an attribution at the beginning of a lead only when it is unusual, significant or deserving of that emphasis:

> ~~At a press conference in Washington, D.C., today, Neil A. Schuster, spokesperson for the U.S. Bureau of Labor Statistics, announced that~~ , *U.S. Bureau of Labor Statistics officials said Friday* ~~last month~~ the cost of living rose 2.83 percent, a record high. *last month*

Originally, the lead devoted more space to the attribution than to the news. As revised, it emphasizes the news—the information the Bureau of Labor Statistics released. The attribution has been condensed and can be reported more fully in a later paragraph.

Minimizing the News

Chronological order rarely works in a news story. By definition, news is what just happened. The first events in a sequence rarely are the most newsworthy. Decide which facts are most interesting and important, and then write a lead that emphasizes them regardless of whether they occurred first, last or in the middle of a sequence of events.

Here are two leads. The first begins with actions taken at the start of a city council meeting. The second begins with an action likely to affect a large number of city residents. Which would attract a larger audience?

> The City Council approved the minutes from its last meeting, approved paying omnibus budget bills and examined a list of proposed ordinances.

> The City Council voted 6-1 Monday night to increase the city's police department budget by 15 percent to hire more officers and buy new weapons.

Look for a story's action or consequences. That's what the lead should emphasize. The second version of the following example stresses the effects of the accident:

> A 15-year-old boy learning to drive his family's new car struck a gasoline pump in a service station on Hall Road late Tuesday afternoon.

> A 15-year-old boy learning to drive created a fireball Tuesday. The family car he was driving struck a gasoline pump at a Hall Road service station, blocking traffic for three hours while firefighters extinguished the blaze.

Using Agenda Leads

An opening paragraph that places too much emphasis on the time and place at which a story occurred is called an "agenda lead." Although these leads are used to announce an upcoming event—public relations news releases use them to promote an organization's product or event—they should never appear in a news story about something that occurred the previous day. A lead should focus on the news, as the following revised lead does:

> ➤ *There's gold in the garbage society discards, the*
> ∧ ~~James Matthews,~~ president of ~~International Biotech Inc.,~~ a company that manufactures recycling and composting machinery~~,~~
> *said, staking his claim on the future of recycling*
> ∧ ~~was the keynote speaker at Monday night's opening ceremony of the Earth Preservation Society's annual conference at the Lyceum Center~~.

The revised lead focuses on what the speaker said, something the original lead failed to do.

Here is a lead that focuses on the time of a story:

> *won five of its seven games and placed second*
> ➤ ~~Last weekend~~ the women's volleyball team ∧ ~~participated~~ in the
> *last weekend*
> regional playoffs ∧.

Using Label Leads

"Label leads" mention a topic but fail to reveal what was said or done about it. Leads should report the substance of a story, not just its topic. A good lead does more than report that a group met, held a press conference or issued a report. It reveals what the group did at the meeting, what was said at the press conference or what was written in the report.

Label leads are easy to recognize and avoid because they use similar words and phrases, such as "was the subject of," "the main topic of discussion," "spoke about," "delivered a speech about" or "interviewed about." Here are two examples and how they might be improved:

> *An additional fee for business licenses is one way the*   *is considering*
> ^~~The~~ City Council ~~Tuesday night discussed ways of~~ ^regulating a new topless club ~~in the city~~.

> *College f*   *said*
> ^Faculty and staff ~~members and other experts~~ ^Thursday
> *they favor a new scholarship program as a way of recruiting*
> ^~~proposed strategies to recruit~~ more minority students.

Listing Details

Most lists are dull. If one must be used in a lead, place an explanation before it, never after it. The audience can more quickly grasp a list's meaning if an explanation precedes it. The following lead is improved by reversing the order:

> The company that made it, the store that sold it and the friend who lent it to him are being sued by a 24-year-old man whose spine was severed when a motorcycle overturned.

> A 24-year-old man whose spine was severed when a motorcycle overturned is suing the company that made the motorcycle, the store that sold it and the friend who lent it to him.

Stating the Obvious

As previously discussed, avoid stating the obvious or emphasizing routine procedures in leads. For a story about a crime, do not begin by reporting police "were called to the scene" or ambulances "rushed" the victims to a hospital "for treatment of their injuries." This problem is particularly common in sports news, where many leads have become clichés. For example, stories that say most coaches and players express optimism at the beginning of a season report the obvious: Both want to win most of their games.

The following lead is ineffective for the same reason:

> The Colonial Park school board has decided to spend the additional funds it will receive from the state.

Including the specifics of the decision improves the lead:

> The Colonial Park school board voted Monday night to rescind the 5 percent spending cut it approved last month after learning the district will receive more money from the state.

Reporting the Negative

When writing a lead, report what happened, not what failed to happen or what does not exist:

> ➤ Americans over the age of 65 say ⋀ *their greatest fears are poor health and poverty* ~~that crime is not their greatest fear~~, two sociologists reported Friday.

Exaggerating

Never exaggerate in a lead. If a story is weak, exaggeration is likely to make it weaker, not stronger. A simple summary of the facts can be more interesting (and shocking) than anything that might be contrived:

> A 78-year-old woman left $3.2 million to the Salvation Army and 2 cents to her son.

> A restaurant did not serve a dead rat in a loaf of bread to an out-of-town couple, a jury decided Tuesday.

Distorting the Story

Every lead must be truthful. Never sensational- ize, belittle or misrepresent. A lead must also set a story's tone—accurately revealing, for exam- ple, whether the story that follows will be serious or whimsical:

> The party went to the dogs early—as it should have.

> Parents who host parties for their children can understand the chill going up Susan Ulroy's spine. She was determined guests wouldn't be racing over her clean carpet- ing with their wet feet. "This could be a real free-for-all," she said.

> Even though only seven guests were invited, eight counting the host, that made 32 feet to worry about.

> This was a birthday party for Sandi, the Ulroys' dog.
> *(The Ann Arbor [Michigan] News)*

Following All the Rules

Reporters who use their imagination and try something different sometimes can report the facts more cleverly than the competition.

Edna Buchanan consistently made routine stories interesting. Here's a lead she wrote with some imagination. Notice the active verbs and description she uses:

Gary Robinson died hungry.

He wanted fried chicken, the three-piece box for $2.19. Drunk, loud and obnoxious, he pushed ahead of seven customers in line at a fast-food chicken outlet. The counter girl told him that his behavior was impolite. She calmed him down with sweet talk, and he agreed to step to the end of the line. His turn came just before closing time, just after the fried chicken ran out.

He punched the counter girl so hard her ears rang, and a security guard shot him—three times.

Forgetting Your Audience

While writing every lead, remember the audience. Leads must be clear and interesting to attract and keep people's attention. The following lead, until revised, fails both tests:

➤ Two ∧ ~~policy resolutions will come~~ before the Student Senate
this week ∧ .

proposals

would raise student parking and athletic fees by more than $100 a year

Is the original lead interesting? Why not? It emphasized the number of resolutions the student senate was scheduled to consider. Yet almost no one would care about the number of resolutions or, from the lead, would understand their significance: the fact that they would affect every student at the school.

Using the First Draft

Critically examine all leads and rewrite them as often as necessary. First drafts are rarely so well written that they cannot be improved. Even experienced professionals often rewrite their leads three or more times.

The Writing Coach

Oh Where, Oh Where Does the Time Element Go?

BY JOE HIGHT

You've just finished your lead and something is missing: the day. Oh, the dreaded time element. Where to place the day so it doesn't tarnish your fine lead or be criticized by your editor?

In his column "Writers Workshop," which formerly appeared in Editor & Publisher magazine, Jack Hart wrote, "Faulty time element placement produces much of the strange syntax that often taints newspaper writing. We regularly come up with oddities such as 'A federal judge Monday approved' or 'Secretary of State Warren Christopher threatened Monday. . . .'"

If you have problems, and most of us do, with the time element trap, here are six tips from Hart, the AP Stylebook and others:

1. The most natural place to put the day is immediately after the verb or the main clause. Thus, you follow the basic formula for writing a lead, especially in a hard news story (who, what, time, day or date and place):

   The robber was killed Friday at the convenience store.

2. Avoid placing the time element so it appears that it's the object of a transitive verb. If this occurs, use "on" before the time element.

   ➤ The city council postponed ^*on* Thursday a resolution. . . . (The original makes it seem that the council postponed Thursday.)

   ➤ Deputies arrested ^*on* Thursday a man wanted. . . .

3. Use "on" before the principal verb if it seems awkward after the verb or main clause.

   ➤ The embassy ^*on* Friday expelled several diplomats.

4. And use "on" to avoid an awkward juxtaposition of the day and a proper name.

   ➤ Police told Smith ^*on* Tuesday. . . . (The original makes it seem that the name of the person is Smith Tuesday.)

Please remember, however, that you do not use "on" if the time element would not confuse the reader:

The council meeting will be Wednesday.

5. Hart recommends breaking the tradition of always putting the day or time element at the beginning of the sentence. However, he adds that it's occasionally the best place, especially when considering the example he provided:

Richard "Joe" Mallon received the phone call this week he had dreaded for 19 years.

The day or time element can be used properly as a transitional expression, but probably should not be used in your lead.

6. Place your time element in a different sentence. Don't think that the time element must be in the lead, especially when you're writing a profile or issue, trend or feature story. In many cases, the time element can be effectively delayed for later paragraphs.

As always, the best advice is that you read your sentence out loud or to another person to ensure that the time element doesn't sound or seem awkward. This will ensure that your Mondays, Tuesdays and so on are in their proper place today.

Joe Hight has been editor of the Colorado Springs (Colorado) Gazette and the Oklahoman of Oklahoma City. He is now the owner and president of Best of Books, Inc.

The Reporter's Guide to Writing Leads

1. Be specific rather than vague and abstract.

2. Avoid stating the obvious or the negative.

3. Emphasize the story's most unusual or unexpected developments.

4. Emphasize the story's most interesting and important developments.

5. Emphasize the story's magnitude and its impact on its participants and the public.

6. Use complete sentences, the proper tense and all the necessary articles—"a," "an" and "the."

7. Be concise. If a lead exceeds three typed lines, examine it for wordiness, repetition or unnecessary details and rewrite it to eliminate the problems.

8. Avoid writing a label lead that reports the story's topic but not what was said or done about it.

9. Begin leads with the news—the main point of the story—not the attribution or the time and place the events occurred.

10. Use relatively simple sentences and avoid beginning leads with a long phrase or clause.

11. Use strong, active and descriptive verbs rather than passive ones.

12. Avoid using unfamiliar names. Any names that require lengthy identification should be reported in a later paragraph.

13. Attribute any quotation or statement of opinion appearing in the lead.

14. Localize the lead, and emphasize the latest developments, preferably what happened today or yesterday.

15. Eliminate statements of opinion, including one-word labels such as "interesting" and "alert."

16. Remember the audience. Write a lead that is clear, concise and interesting and that emphasizes the details most likely to affect and interest people.

17. Read the lead aloud to be certain that it is clear, concise and easy to understand.

Review Exercises

1. Evaluating Good and Bad Leads

Critically evaluate the following leads. Select the best ones and explain why they are effective; point out the flaws in the remaining leads. Finally, look for lessons—"do's and don'ts"—that you can apply to your own work.

1. A 24-year-old Greeley man was charged with multiple counts of first-degree murder and arson in the deaths of his wife and three children who died in an early morning fire in their home.

2. City Council has to return a grant it received last year to fix deteriorating road conditions on Main Street.

3. People are jumping into swimming pools and switching buttons to high on air conditioners as temperatures in the Midwest soared to record numbers over the past three days.

4. University administrators say they are considering imposing the largest tuition and fee increases in a decade because of state budget cuts.

5. A petition filed by Councilman William Bellmonte to force the City Council into a special session to reduce local property taxes was thrown out in court Monday after it was discovered that half the names listed on the petition were dead people.

6. An 85-year-old woman stepped off the curb and into the path of a moving car. She was struck by the car and tossed 50 feet into the air. She died instantly.

7. Ray's Mini-Mart at 2357 S. Alderman St. was the location of a burglary sometime Friday night.

8. Police Chief Barry Kopperud is concerned that crime is rising in the city.

9. This weekend will offer the best chance yet to see a brilliant performance of "My Fair Lady" at the Fairwood Community Theater, so reserve your tickets now.

10. Loans become a popular way to cut college costs.

11. The tree-lined campus is home to many wild and stray animals.

12. Two men suspected of burglarizing five churches, two homes and a pet store all in one night were captured Wednesday during another burglary attempt.

13. The union representing university secretaries and maintenance workers reached a tentative agreement Friday that will give members a 6.5 percent raise over three years.

14. Fingerprints on a candle led the FBI to a man accused of blowing up the building he worked in to hide the shooting deaths of the man's boss and three co-workers.

15. A teenage driver lost control of his car Wednesday night killing himself and a female passenger, while a 14-year-old friend who was riding in the back seat walked away with only scratches and bruises.

2. Writing Leads

Section I: Condensing Lengthy Leads

Condense each of these leads to no more than two typed lines, or about 20 words. Correct all errors.

1. Christina Shattuck, 43, and Dennis Shattuck, 45, and their three children, ages 7, 3 and 9 months, all of 532 3rd St., returned home from a shopping trip Saturday night and found their two-story frame house on fire and called firefighters, who responded to the scene within five minutes, but were unable to save the house and its contents, which were totally destroyed.

2. The local school board held a special meeting Tuesday night so Superintendent of Schools Greg Hubbard could address a group of angry parents who were demanding to know why they were never informed that a middle school student had brought a gun to school and may have been targeting their children during an incident on school grounds last Friday.

Section II: Using Proper Sentence Structure

Rewrite the following leads, using the normal word order: subject, verb, direct object. Avoid starting the leads with a long clause or phrase. You may want to divide some of the leads into several sentences or paragraphs. Correct all errors.

1. In an effort to curb what city officials are calling an epidemic of obesity among young people in the city, which mirrors national data on overall obesity of the population, your local city council voted 7-0 to offer free memberships at its meeting Monday night to local youth centers and health clubs in the city for children ages 8 to 15 whose parents do not have the financial wherewithal to purchase the memberships.

2. Despite the efforts of Karen Dees, 19, a student at your university who lives at 410 University Avenue, Apartment 52, and performed cardiopulmonary resuscitation for more than 20 minutes, she was not able to help sheriffs deputy William McGowen, 47, of 4224 N. 21st St., who died while directing traffic after being struck by lightning during an electrical storm.

Section III: Emphasizing the News

Rewrite the following leads, emphasizing the news, not the attribution. Limit the attributions to a few words and place them at the end of the leads. Correct all errors.

1. The National Institutes of Health in Washington, D.C., released a report today indicating that more than 90 percent of all heart attack victims have one or more classic risk factors: smoking, diabetes, high cholesterol and high blood pressure.

2. According to a police report issued Monday, accident investigators concluded that Stephanie Sessions, 16, daughter of Jeffrey D. and Michelle A. Sessions, of 9303 Vale Drive, had just gotten her drivers license two days before she was involved in an accident in which she rolled the Jeep Wrangler she was driving, injuring herself and two other passengers.

Section IV: Combining Multisentence Leads

Rewrite each of the following leads in a single sentence, correcting all errors.

1. Gary Hubard, superintendent of schools, announced a new program for your local school district. It is called the "Tattle-Tale Program." The program involves paying students to tell on classmates who bring guns or drugs to school or violate other school rules. The program is in response to an incident last month in which a high school student was caught carrying a loaded handgun on school property.

2. The Bureau of Justice Statistics of the U.S. Department of Justice released a report Monday on the number of people in the United States who have spent time in prison. Last year, about one in every 37 adult Americans was imprisoned or had been in prison at one time. The 5.6 million people who were either serving or had served time in prison represented 2.7 percent of the adult population of 210 million people, according to the report. The figures represent people who served time in federal, state and county prisons after being sentenced for a crime, not those temporarily held in jail.

Section V: Stressing the Unusual

Write only the lead for each of the following stories, correcting all errors.

1. The city is sweltering under a heat wave. Temperatures have hit 100 degrees-plus for the past week and humidity levels have hovered between 75 and 90 percent each day. Authorities have been cautioning people, especially the very young and the elderly to stay inside in air conditioning and avoid exerting themselves outside in the sun. City Health Department officials held a press conference this morning to announce that three people had died over the past two days because of the heat. All three were elderly people who lived in the downtown area. Two of the three were a married couple. The one victim was identified as Betsy Aaron, 86, of 410 Hillcrest Street, Apartment 302. Aaron was a retired teacher who had taught elementary school for more than 30 years. The other two victims were Jeffrey Ahsonn, 84, and his wife, Teresa Ahson, 79, both of 49 Groveland Avenue. Ahsonn was a retired mechanical engineer who had worked for the city for many years. Police and health department officials were alerted to the deaths in each case by relatives who discovered the bodies. When they entered the dwellings, police told officials that they found a pair of fans and an air conditioner in each dwelling. The fans and air conditioners had been delivered by city workers to disabled elderly people to help them

cope with the heat wave. But authorities found the fans and air conditioners still in their boxes. They had never been installed.

2. Destiny Schfini is a vice president with SunBank. Schifini is divorced and the mother of two children—a 10-year-old girl and an eight-year-old boy. The children visit her once a month. Schifinis son, Ronald, was visiting this weekend. Schfini is 36 years old and lives at 3260 Timber Ter. Ronald was injured in an accident Saturday afternoon around 2 p.m. The boy was struck by a train. Police said Schifini and her son were riding bikes along Fremont Avenue when the mother decided to take a shortcut across the railroad tracks that run along Fremont Avenue. The boy is on life support in Mercy Hospital and listed in critical condition. He was struck by a train. Witnesses said the mother saw the train coming and crossed anyway and encouraged her son to cross. The boys bike got caught on the tracks and as he tried to free it, the train struck him. Ronald was thrown through the air and sustained broken ribs, a broken pelvis and a bruised heart. Police charged Destiny Schifini with aggravated assault, reckless endangerment, endangering the welfare of a child and failure to obey a train signal. Police said they charged Schfini after they learned from witnesses that Schifini did not help the boy, but taunted him as the train approached.

3. Julius Povacz is a paramedic in your community who serves with the rescue squad in the fire department. The 34-year-old Povaz lives at 210 East King Avenue, Apartment 4. Eight years ago he was tested for human immunodeficiency virus, or HIV, the virus that causes AIDS, and told that the test was positive. Povacz never told his superiors that he had tested positive. A routine check of his medical records last month by fire department officials found the notation that the test was positive. Povacz was relieved of his duties. Povacz said at the time he may have been infected with the virus accidentally by coming in contact with an infected patient at the scene of an emergency. When he learned that he lost his job, Povaz said it was worse than learning that he had tested positive for HIV. Being a paramedic was all he ever wanted to do. He said for eight years he has feared

that his medical condition would be discovered or that he would develop AIDS and die. The state Department of Health computer system tracks HIV patients and periodically reviews cases. An official at the state Health Department informed Povacz and his superiors yesterday that Povacz is not and never was HIV positive. A second test that was performed eight years ago to confirm the first test indicated no presence of HIV, but the information was never placed in Povaczs medical records by his physician, Dr. Nadine Caspinwall, and Caspinwall never informed Povacz. Povacz is now fighting to get his job back.

4. The police department in your community are investigating a two-vehicle accident. The accident occurred at 5:38 p.m. Thursday during rush hour. The accident occurred at the busy intersection of Huron Avenue and Timber Trail Road. Police said a blue Toyota Camry driven by Cheryl Nicholls, 25, of 1287 Belgard Avenue, ran into the rear of a pickup truck driven by Ronald Dawkins, 44, of 1005 Stratmore Drive. Dawkins is a bricklayer. Nichols Toyota suffered severe damage, but she sustained only bruises and a laceration on her leg. Police said the car was a total loss. Police charged Nicholls with inattentive driving and operating a cell phone while driving. The cell phone law was passed last year by the state legislature and banned the operation of a cell phone while driving. Nicholls was talking to her car insurance company about an error on a car insurance bill when she struck the rear of Dawkins pickup truck.

5. A home at 2481 Santana Avenue was burglarized between the hours of 1 p.m. and 4 p.m. yesterday afternoon. The owner of the home is Dorothy R. Elam, a sixth-grade teacher at Madison Elementary School. She said no one was home at the time. Neighbors said they saw a truck parked in the driveway but thought some repairmen were working at the home. The total loss is estimated at in excess of $8,000. The items stolen from the home include a color television, a videocassette recorder, stereo, sewing machine, computer, 2 pistols and many small kitchen appliances. Also, a stamp collection valued at about $1,000, some clothes, silverware and lawn tools were taken. Roger A. Elam, Mrs. Elams husband, died 2 days ago.

The robbery occurred while she was attending his funeral at 2:30 p.m. yesterday at the Powell Funeral Chapel, 620 North Park Avenue. Elam died of cancer after a long illness.

Section VI: Localizing Your Lead

Write only the lead for each of the following stories, correcting errors if necessary. Emphasize the information that would have the greatest local interest.

1. The U.S. Department of Justice is calling identity theft the crime of the 21st century. Identity theft is the illegal appropriation of another persons personal information—Social Security card number, driver's license number, credit card numbers, etc.—and using them to drain bank accounts or go on a buying spree. Justice Department officials say it is the fastest-growing crime in the United States. Criminals can get access to peoples personal information by going through their trash or stealing their mail. The Federal Trade Commission estimated the dollar loss to businesses and individuals last year was in the billions. The number of victims nationally is running as high as 750,000 a year. The rate of identity theft complaints nationally is averaging 22 victims per 100,000 people. Justice Department officials say that is too high. But the rate of identity theft complaints in your city is 77 victims per 100,000 people. State Representative Constance P. Wei is sponsoring a bill that would establish a web site that would allow credit card holders to check to see if their numbers have been stolen. The bill also would increase the penalties for identity theft and raise the crime from a misdemeanor to a felony.

2. Your state's department of education announced that it is awarding more than 30 million dollars in federal grant money to 53 school districts throughout the state. The money is to be used to offset recent cutbacks in state funds given to school districts for educational programs and materials. Among the programs eligible for grant money are innovative programs to help identify and support at-risk youth who are not receiving the help they need. At-risk youth are more prone to failing in school and dropping out, becoming involved with drugs, becoming involved in crime or gang-related activity, and ending up in prison.

The states Commission on Crime and Delinquency identified your local school district as a leader in the effort to help at-risk youth with its Community Helping Hands program. The program identifies at-risk youth at an early age and then engages teachers, community members and other students to help at-risk youth through academic tutoring, social activities and counseling. The state Commission on Crime and Delinquency through the state department of education is providing $1.2 million to your school districts at-risk program. The funds will help support the programs operation for at least three years.

Section VII: Updating Your Lead

Write only the lead for each of the following stories, correcting errors if necessary.

1. Dorothy Heslin is the manager of the Mr. Grocer convenience store at 2015 North 11th Avenue. Heslinn is a 48-year-old single mother with three children. She is seen as a hero by some and a villain by others. Yesterday, two masked men carrying guns barged into the Mr. Grocer and demanded money. As she reached for the cash drawer, Heslinn pulled a .357-caliber Magnum pistol from beneath the counter and fired four shots, killing one robber and seriously wounding the second. Some in the community say it was justified because her life was in danger, but others say she used excessive force. Police today charged Heslinn with aggravated assault with a handgun, attempted murder, second-degree murder and failure to properly register a handgun.

2. There was a grinding head-on collision on Cheney Road yesterday. Two persons were killed: Rosemary Brennan, 27, and her infant daughter, Kelley, age 2, both of 1775 Nairn Dr. The driver of the second car involved in the accident, Anthony Murray, 17, of 1748 North 3 Street, was seriously injured, with multiple fractures. Police today announced that laboratory tests have confirmed the fact that Brennan was legally drunk at the time of the accident.

3. The Steak & Ale restaurant is a popular restaurant and lounge in your community. It is especially popular with college students. The restaurant is located at 1284 University Boulevard. Last year,

a group of students was celebrating at the restaurant after a football game. The five students became rowdy and were asked to leave by Sarah Kindstrom, a waitress at the Steak & Ale. The students left the restaurant, but one of them, James Ball, who was 20 at the time, of 1012 Cortez Avenue, Apartment 870, became separated from the group, wandered into the street and was struck by a car. He died at the scene. His parents sued the Steak & Ale for serving underage students alcohol and causing the death of their son. Monday the restaurants owners settled the suit for one million dollars.

3. Writing Basic News Leads

Write only a lead for each of the following stories. Correct all errors.

1. It was nearly a tragedy on Monday. Police said it is amazing no one was killed. A train struck a sport utility vehicle at a crossing on Michigan Avenue near the intersection with Wayne Boulevard in your city. Police said the accident occurred at 5:48 p.m. in the evening. Abraham and Estelle Cohen were the passengers in the 2010 Ford Explorer that was struck by the eastbound train. Abraham is 35 years old, and he was driving the vehicle. Estelle is 33 years old and is five months pregnant. The couple's daughter Emily, who is three years old, was a passenger in the back seat. No one was seriously injured. Abraham works for the city school system. He is assistant director of computer services. Estelle is a public relations representative for Evans Public Relations Group. Abraham, Estelle and their daughter live at 1903 Conway Rd. All three were taken to the local hospital for observation. Abraham suffered contusions on his ribs. Estelle received a small laceration on her forehead that required six stitches. Their daughter, Emily, suffered minor bruises to her right arm and face. Two ambulances were called to the scene to take the family to the hospital. Police said Mr. Cohen was driving west on Michigan Avenue when he came to the train crossing. The crossing does not have warning lights or an automated barrier gate. There are warning signs and a stop sign that require motorists to stop and look for trains before crossing the tracks. Police say Mr. Cohen failed to stop at the stop sign and drove into the path of the train. The train was traveling at approximately 15 to 20 miles per hour when it struck the car. Emily was riding in a child safety seat, which police said saved her life. Police said the vehicle suffered extensive damage and had to be towed from the scene.

2. For the past five years, researchers at the National Institutes of Health in Bethesda, Maryland, have been studying a sample of 4,000 adult males. The men range in age from 45 to 75. The research cost $1,500,000 and was paid for through the U.S. Department of Health and Human Services. The researchers announced the results today. The researchers have been studying the effects of meditation on men suffering with heart disease. Many of the men involved in the study either had suffered one or more heart attacks and/or had heart valve or heart bypass surgery. The study attempted to determine what effects meditation had on the heart for those suffering from heart disease. Researchers found that the men who were involved in a regular program of meditation lowered their stress and had fewer occurrences of repeat heart attacks or other problems associated with coronary heart disease. Dr. William Smithson, one of the researchers at the NIH who participated in the study, said: "Not only did we find that 75 percent of the men who meditated for an hour to an hour and a half at least three times a week lowered their blood pressure significantly during the period of the study, but we also found that their cholesterol and triglyceride levels dropped significantly. And even the numbers for the other 25% of the men in the study who participated in the meditation group showed some improvement. On the other hand, nearly 80 percent of those who did not participate in the meditation program saw an increase in their episodes of heart attacks, angina or chest pain, shortness of breath and other coronary symptoms. The link between the effects of stress on the heart and coronary heart disease are well known, but this study attempted to find a link between reducing stress levels and the effect on the heart." Researchers plan to release more information as they analyze the data. Researchers said that meditation alone would not help all heart

disease patients, but could be used in conjunction with a good diet and exercise.

3. People in the United States are concerned about the environment. Many are concerned about the waste that is generated by Americans each day and buried in landfills. The Environmental Policy Group, a non-partisan environmental research and lobbying organization based in Washington, D.C., released a report recently. According to the report, only about one-quarter of the country's paper, plastic, glass, aluminum and steel is recycled. That amount is only a slight increase from what it was 20 years ago. "This rate needs to be doubled or tripled in the next decade to have a positive impact on the environment. Steps must be taken to increase collection of recycled materials, increase public awareness, increase public participation, increase the development of new markets for recycled products and increase government support for recycling programs. Without these efforts, the planet's resources will be exhausted," the report said. Mayor Sabrina Datoli announced a new program at Tuesday nights city council meeting and council voted 6-1 to implement the new program. The new program will provide blue recycling bins throughout the city. Residents will be able to drop their recyclable items in any of the designated bins. In addition, the city will provide smaller blue recycling bins to keep in their homes for recyclable items. Residents will place the smaller household bins by the curb with their normal trash cans. The city will have special trucks that will pick up recyclable items on trash collection days. Datolli said residents will be able to use the larger recycling bins if they have a large quantity of items to recycle. Businesses also will be able to use the bins. Even if someone has only one item to place in a recycling container, it will be worth it, according to Datolli. "Too many times while I have been walking or driving around the city, I have seen someone finish drinking a bottle of water or soda and throw the plastic container in the trash because there is no convenient place to put the recyclable material. These public, recycling bins, placed in strategic places around the city, will address that problem," Datolli said. The program will cost around $280,000 initially to purchase and distribute the recycling containers and another $120,000 a year to gather and haul away the recycled items. City Council Member Roger Lo is opposed to the program because of the cost. He is in favor of turning the program over to a private contractor who would collect and sell recycled materials for a profit as a way to pay for the program.

4. It's another statistical study, one that surprised many sociologists around the country. The research was conducted by sociologists at the University of Florida. The $1.5 million study was funded through grants provided by the National Institute of Mental Health and the National Science Foundation. For years, sociologists thought that advanced education translated into greater marriage stability. Now, with new data from the study released Monday, researchers have discovered that marital disruption is greater among more highly educated women than any other group, except those who have not graduated from high school. The study found that many young women who do not graduate from high school cohabitate rather than get married. The sociologists who conducted the new study found some of the reasons why women with graduate degrees are more likely to divorce. The key factor seems to be timing. Women who married early, before they began graduate school, are more likely to have established traditional family roles which they find difficult to change. When the wife goes back to school and no longer wants to handle most of the housework, it causes resentment on the part of husbands. If the husband refuses to pitch in and do his share, it creates tension. Such unhappiness on both sides often leads to divorce. The study found that more than one-third of the women who began graduate school after they were married ended up separated or divorced. By comparison, only 15.6% of those who married after they had finished an advanced degree ended up divorced or separated. This group of women seemed more likely to find husbands supportive of their educational goals, according to the study.

5. It was a sad tragedy. There was a fire Saturday evening in your city. Firefighters said the fire broke out around 9:15 p.m. Ann Capiello, a

nineteen year old student at the local university, called 9-1-1 to report the fire. Firefighters arrived on the scene around 9:25. The fire occurred at the residence of Johnnie and Jacquelin Lewis, 1840 Maldren Avenue. Jonnie, is 29 years old and works as an inspector for Vallrath Industries. Jacquelin is 28 and is a stay-at-home mother who cares for their two children, Krista, age 5, and Jeremy, age 3. Jacquelin and Jonnie had gone out for the evening to go to dinner and a movie. They were celebrating their 10th wedding anniversary. Capiello was babysitting their two children. Capiello was watching television in the living room while the children were playing in Krista's bedroom. According to Tony Sullivan, the city's fire chief, the children apparently were playing with matches and attempting to light a candle. Capiello told Sullivan she smelled smoke and ran to the bedroom. She did not hear the smoke detectors go off. She heard the children crying and screaming for help, but she could not reach them because of the smoke and heat from the flames. She called 9-1-1 before returning to the bedroom to try to rescue the children. She suffered first-and second-degree burns on her hands, arms and face as she tried to get back into the bedroom. Firefighters were able to extinguish the blaze quickly, but not in time to save the children. They were found dead in a corner of the bedroom. Sullivan said the children most likely succumbed to the heat and smoke from the fire. Firefighters determined that the batteries in the smoke detectors were dead and were not working at the time of the fire. The fire caused an estimated $39,000 in fire, water and smoke damage to the house. Mr. and Mrs. Lewis discovered the tragedy when they arrived home around 10:30 p.m. to find firefighters and ambulances at their house.

6. Vernon Sindelair is the treasurer for your county. He has served as county treasurer for 31 years. He is responsible for overseeing the economic and financial business of the county. He is responsible for generating revenue through tax collection and paying the bills for the county. He appeared in the county's Court of Common Pleas Wednesday morning to plead guilty to charges of embezzlement. State police investigators and County Attorney Ronald McNally had been investigating Sindelair for more than a year before charging him three months ago with embezzling more than $1.7 million in tax receipts. Sindelair is 63 years old. He told investigators he embezzled the money to pay medical bills for his wife who died of cancer last year. MacNally said Sindelair faces up to 30 years in prison and fines of more than 1.5 million dollars. Judge Edward Kocembra delayed Sindelair's sentencing for two weeks until a sentencing report is completed. Sindelair resigned as county treasurer two weeks after he was charged with embezzlement by state and county officials.

7. A random survey of Americans was recently conducted by the United States Congressional Research Service. CRS staff members analyze current policies and present the impact of proposed policy alternatives to members of Congress. Pollsters asked a random cross-section of more than 2,000 American adults about their attitudes toward the nation's federal income tax, and the results are contained in a 12-page report. The survey was conducted because members of the House of Representatives are about to sponsor a bill to abolish the federal income tax and the Internal Revenue Service. More than 56 percent of those surveyed said the federal income tax is unfair and the system needs to be changed. A similar survey conducted 10 years ago found that most Americans expressed more dissatisfaction with their property taxes than with their federal income taxes. However, that trend seems to be reversed because the new survey revealed that only 38 percent of those surveyed were dissatisfied with their current property taxes. The survey, which did not reveal the identity of those surveyed, also found that nearly 30% of respondents admitted to cheating on their taxes at some point during the past five years. The characteristic most respondents used to describe their feelings toward the income tax was "unfair." Many said they favored a simplified flat tax rate or a national sales tax.

8. Workers from your state's Department Environmental Resources and rescue personnel from your city's fire department responded to an emergency around 1 p.m. Thursday. The emergency was at the office of Vallrath Plastics, 1620 Industrial

Boulevard. A large thermometer used on a display of the company's products broke loose from the display board and crashed to the floor. The thermometer contained mercury, which spread around the office. Fire Chief Tony Sullivan said the thermometer contained about two pounds of mercury. A special hazardous materials unit from the city's fire department responded to the scene to clean up the mercury. Workers from the Department of Environmental Resources responded with special monitors to make sure all the mercury was cleaned up and that no one in the office was contaminated with the substance. Exposure to mercury can cause birth defects and poisoning, Sullivan said. Wanda Albertson, 39, of 529 Adirondack Avenue, is the personnel director at Vallrath Plastics. She was in the office when the incident occurred. She told emergency workers that it sounded like a bomb going off when the thermometer crashed to the floor and that she saw what looked like little silver balls of metal rolling around on the floor.

9. Don Brame is an inmate in the state correctional facility in your state. Braem is a former city employee whose former address was 3402 Virginia Avenue. He is 32 years old. He was an inspector for your city's housing authority. He is serving an 8-year sentence for burglary. He was found guilty last year of breaking into people's homes and stealing jewelry, money and electronic devices such as cell phones and iPods. Two months ago he was charged with swindling dozens of women of thousands of dollars from his prison cell. Wednesday he pleaded guilty to the new charges against him and was sentenced to an additional 10 years in prison. Police officials said Barlow mailed letters to men who recently died. The letters were received by the men's widows. Brame told police he got the names of the men from the obituaries in the local newspaper. The letters were written as bills seeking payment for "services rendered." The amounts of the "bills" were usually less than 100 dollars. Most of the women who received the bogus bills paid them because they thought their dead husbands had incurred the debt before their deaths. Or the women may have been too upset at the time to give the bills much thought, said Detective Larry Chevez of the

city's police department. The scam was discovered when Chevez's mother received one of the letters and asked him about paying the bill shortly after Chevez's father died.

10. English teachers in your local school district are facing a dilemma. The local school board voted to ban the teaching of certain books in English classes. Milan Scott teaches 10th-grade English classes at Kennedy High School. One of the books he teaches in his English literature class is "The Adventures of Huckleberry Finn." The book was written by Mark Twain. Critics, including some parents, attended last Monday's school board meeting at 7 p.m. in the cafeteria of Kennedy High School and said that the book should be banned from all schools in the city because it is racist. School board member Jane Tribitt agreed with the critics and proposed a resolution asking the local school board to ban the book along with numerous other titles. The board voted 5–4 to ban the books. Many students and parents who attended the meeting were against the ban. Gary Hubbard is the superintendent of schools. Hubbard said the book still will be available to students in the schools' libraries. Teachers just will not be permitted to use the books in class or for reading assignments. Scott announced that he intends to ignore the ban and continue to assign the books as part of his literature classes. He said "The Adventures of Huckleberry Finn" is a depiction of society at the time it was written. Students can learn about that society by studying the historical setting of the book, the characters being depicted and the social context, including the prejudices that existed at the time depicted in the book. The book describes the adventures of runaway Huck Finn and a fugitive slave named Jim as they float on a raft down the Mississippi River. Hubard says Scott will face disciplinary action if he defies the ban.

11. A Kennedy High School soccer player died early Monday morning. Thomas Alvarez was 18 years of age. He is the son of Harold and Tina Alverez of 854 Maury Drive Apartment 11B. Police said he was speeding because he was late for school and lost control of his 2006 Ford Focus and collided with a tree in the 5000 block of Cypress Avenue. He was rushed to Memorial Hospital

with severe head injuries and later pronounced dead by County Coroner Devin White. The crash occurred around 7:15 a.m. He was pronounced dead at 8:30 a.m. Two friends who were riding in the car with Alvarez, James Foucault, 17, of 1452 Penham Avenue, and Margaret Hamill, 16, of 811 North Cortez Avenue, walked away from the accident with minor lacerations and contusions, police said. Fire Chief Tony Sullivan said emergency personnel had to cut Alvarez out of the car. He said Alvarez was not wearing a seatbelt. Maureen Verdugo, principal of Kennedy High School, said the school's crisis intervention team would be available to talk to students, teachers and staff who are mourning Alvarez's death.

12. Marc Johnson, a construction worker who lives at 2643 Pioneer Rd., was arrested last week and charged with speeding, drunken driving and vehicular manslaughter after the pickup truck he was driving struck and killed a 13-year-old boy and severely injured the boy's 41-year-old father while they were riding their bicycles in the 4000 block of Holbrook Drive. Johnson is 23 years of age. Johnson was pronounced dead at Memorial Hospital at 2:30 a.m. today. He was rushed to the hospital from the county jail. A corrections officer at the jail checks each cell in the jail every 30 minutes. At about 1:30 a.m. an officer saw Johnson lying in his bed. When the officer came by Johnson's cell at 2 a.m., he found Johnson hanging from a bar in his cell. He had torn strips of cloth from his shirt and fashioned a noose around his neck that he then attached to the bar. Corrections officers attempted to revive him before emergency personnel arrived, but were unsuccessful.

4. City, State and National Leads

Write only a lead for each of the following stories. The first set of stories involves events in your city; the second involves events in your state; and the third involves events in the nation. As you write the leads, correct the stories' spelling, style and vocabulary errors. Discuss your leads with your classmates.

City Beat

1. There was a shooting in your city last week. The incident occurred early Wednesday morning.

Barry Koperud, the chief of police for your city, said the shooting was senseless and was an execution-style killing of one of the citys police officers. Killed in the incident last week was Officer Allison Biagi, 26 years old, who lived at 2634 6th Street Apartment 906B. Biagi was a 4 year veteran of the police department. According to police reports, Biagi was sitting in her patrol car when a twenty-two year old white male approached her vehicle and fired eight shots through the driver side window. Bullets struck Biagi in the arm, neck and head, according to reports. She died at the scene. Police, with help of witnesses and video from a nearby bank's surveillance camera, later identified the shooting suspect as Ronald Collins, 20 years of age, of 2814 Ambassador Dr. Apartment 47D, a constuction worker for Wagnor Development Corporation. Police gave no motive for the shooting. Chief Kopperud announced this morning that Collin had surrendered to police. The Police Chief said that Collin walked into the newly remodeled and modern police headquarters at 9:03 a.m. this morning and calmly said, "I am the one you are looking for. I'm the one who shot the police officer." Collins did not resist officers as they arrested him and officers handcuffed him without incident.

2. Your city has a planetarium that was built in 1970, the year after American astronaut Neil Armstrong walked on the moon. The facility is located at 625 Park Place adjacent to Memorial Park, which has soccer fields, baseball and softball diamonds, a running track and public swimming pool. The land for the planetarium was donated by Jonathan Herwarthe, a local real estate developer, who also donated some of the money for its construction. The planetarium is supported through a trust fund established by Herwarthe in his will. However, the planetarium, which is enjoyed by many people in the city, is in need of repair. It needs a new projector, new seats, repairs to the roof, better handicapped access, as well as many other repairs and improvements. Jonathan Hurwarthes son, Gregory Hurwarthe, 56 years of age, and his wife, Ruth, of 410 Baltimore Avenue, told city council members that the repairs will cost $500 thousand. Mayor Sabrina Datolli told council members at Tuesday nights meeting that the city did not have

the money to fix the planetarium and would shut it down at the end of the year if repairs could not be made to bring the building in compliance with city building codes. Jonathan Herwarthe told council members at the meeting that he had been able to raise only $250,000 of the half million dollars needed. Thursday morning, the mayor announced that two local attorneys, James R. and Margaret Ungarient, of 7314 Byron Avenue, had pledged $100 thousand dollars to help repair the building and started a crowd-funding campaign to raise the other $150,000 needed. The planetarium is named The Jonathan Herwarthe Memorial Planetarium. "I always thought the planetarium was an asset to our young people," Datolli said. "It's there to help children study and learn about the universe. But the city just does not have the funds to make all these major repairs."

3. Mayor Sabrina Datoli and City Council members William Belmonte and Sandra Gandolf want the city to launch an investigation into a construction accident that killed a local man and injured another man last month. James Randolph, 39 years old, who lived at 654 Harrison Street, was the construction worker who was killed in the accident. The injured construction worker was Lynn R. Pryor, 28 years of age, who lived at 2634 Sixth Street Apartment 45. Both men were employed by Rittmann Engineering Company. According to a report by the police who investigated the accident, the two men were working on a stormwater drain project when the trench they were working in collapsed. Randolph was completely buried in the collapse and Pryor was buried up to his chest in dirt and rock. Passersby heard Pryor screaming for help and were able to dig him out. However, by the time rescuers reached Randolph and were able to dig him out, he had already expired. City Medical Examiner Dr. Marlene Stoudnaur pronounced Randolph dead at the scene. Stoudnour later conducted an autopsy and reported that the cause of death was suffocation. Datolli and Belmonte claim that Rittmann Engineering Company violated city, state and national safety standards, which led to the tragedy. Director of the Code Enforcement Board Todd Drolshagen told city officials he inspected the construction site 2 weeks before the accident

happened and ordered engineers at Rittmann to halt work on the drain project until the trench could be reinforced to make it safer. Drolshagen said the work never stopped and the safety measures were never implemented. The citys district attorney Ramon Hernandez filed papers in county court charging Rittmanns president Anthony Rittmann, 61 years of age, who lives at 9600 Holbrook Drive, with manslaughter and willful negligence in the death of Randolph. A Rittmann spokesman declined to comment on the charges.

State Beat

1. Last week, officials in your state announced the name of the winners of the state's weekly lottery. It was the largest lottery prize ever won in the state. The value of the winning ticket was 330 million dollars with a cash payout option of 208 million dollars. One of the winners is Ethel Shearer, 28 years of age, who lives at 408 Kasper Avenue Apartment 718. Shearer is a waitress at the Melody Lounge, which is located at 2790 Bolling Drive. Shearer bought her winning ticket at the Jiffy Foods convenience store when she was driving home from work early one morning. It was the first time she had ever won any money playing the states lottery. Shearer contacted officials at the state lottery office the day after the winning number was drawn and she checked her ticket to identify herself as one of the winners. The other winner was identified as Joel Fowler, who lives at 2006 Hillcrest Street. Fowler is a student at your school. He is an out of state student who transferred to your school last year. Fowler came forward with his winning ticket two days after Shearer identified herself as one of the winners of the top prize. It was the first time in the history of the state lottery that two winning tickets of the top prize have been sold in the same city. Fowler, however, will not be able to claim his winnings. State officials claim that Fowler purchased his ticket illegally. State law requires that players must be twenty-one years of age to purchase lottery tickets in the state. Fowler is only 19 years of age. Fowler is eligible to purchase lottery tickets in his home state because the eligible age to purchase tickets is 18. He told lottery officials he thought

the eligible age to buy tickets was the same for all states. Fowler bought his ticket at a Safeway Supermarket in the city and state lottery officials are investigating to determine if Safeway employees are checking identifications of ticket purchasers to see if they are of age to legally buy tickets.

2. A 13 year old girl wanted to know what happened to money that was earmarked for arts programs in public schools around the state. The girls name is Alyssa Allen. She is the daughter of Christopher and Julie Allen, who live at 1504 Lincoln Drive. Christopher is the director of the Center for the Arts in your city and Julie is a university professor. Julie teaches in the universitys art department. Alyssa filed a Right-To-Know request at the state capital to get information about the grant program that was approved by the state legislature three years ago but schools have never received any grant money. State officials are saying that Alyssa has no legal right to file the request because she is too young. State officials also said Alyssa will have to pay attorneys fees for placing a burden on the state and wasting officials time. Mr. and Mrs. Allyn are threatening to sue the state over the rejection of Alyssa's request.

3. James Rueben is a state center from the district that represents your city. Mr. Rueben, 54 years of age, who lives at 12494 Hillcrest Rd., received a letter from one of his constituents, Shirley Dawson, 59 years of age, who lives at 492 Melrose Avenue. Mrs. Dawson is a teacher at Colonial Elementary School. She is also a widow. Her husband, Steven, was killed in a car accident involving a drunk driver. Mrs. Dawson filed a negligence lawsuit against the driver of the vehicle that killed her husband. Mrs. Dawson was struggling financially after the death of her husband and after seeing an advertisement for a lawsuit loan program, in which a finance company would loan her money in advance of her settling the lawsuit against the driver involved in her husbands death. She borrowed $25,000 dollars, pledging to repay the sum when the suit was settled. The company she borrowed the money from was Sunset Legal Finance. When her lawsuit was settled for $500,000, Mrs. Dawson received a bill from Sunset Legal Finance for $265,000,

which company officials said represented interest and processing fees. Mr. Rueben claims that the loan program is abusive because it is not regulated by the state and takes advantage of people who are in financial trouble. Mr. Rueben wants to introduce a bill that would require lawsuit loan companies to be licensed and establish disclosure requirements, as well as cap the amount of interest and processing fees the companies can charge.

National Beat

1. Cellphones are outlawed in prisons across the United States. However, a recent government study found that in your state alone, prison officials confiscated more than nine thousand smartphones from inmates in federal and state prisons located in the state. The study estimated that the nine thousand devices were used to place 1,643,500 calls and text messages over a year. Congress recently passed a law making possession of a cellphone or a wireless device in a federal prison a felony, punishable by up to a year of extra sentencing. But the phones are still getting into the hands of prisoners who use the phones to connect to Facebook and play games. Some inmates, however, use the phones to stay in touch with gang members outside the prison walls and continue to conduct unlawful business, such as drug trafficking, according to the government study that was released Monday. The study stated that cellphones have been smuggled into prisons by guards, visitors and new prisoners entering the prison system. However, the study also stated that cellphones have been concealed inside footballs, tossed over prison walls, or launched from a device called a potato cannon, which shoots a projectile through a pipe. Federal legislators say that they are proposing a bill that would authorize federal and state prison officials to jam cellphone signals in federal and state prisons. Opponents of the proposal say the technology used to jam the signals in prison is not precise enough and could also jam the signals of residents living near the prisons.

2. According to government statistics, more than 300,000 American service members who served in Iraq and Afghanistan are suffering from Post Traumatic Stress Disorder or major

depression. Officials at the Veterans Administration say that fewer than 800 service members attempted suicide last year. Members of Congress are saying that the figures released by the Veterans Administration are wrong and amount to outright lies. A federal investigation into the Veterans Administration uncovered a string of emails that indicated that more than 1,000 veterans that the VA is caring for attempt suicide each month. That is more than 12,000 attempts last year. Federal investigators are saying that Veterans Administration officials are misleading Congress in regard to the number of suicide attempts to hide the strain the conflicts in Iraq and Afghanistan are having on the United States Department of Defense and the Veterans Administration. Members of Congress claim that the Veterans Administrations mental health programs are being overwhelmed and are seeking remedies. Some legislators are proposing providing funds so veterans can seek help through private mental health services in order to get the help they need to deal with their depression and Post Traumatic Stress Disorder. Congress is looking at providing as much as 50 million dollars to launch the program to pay for private mental health care.

3. Its another national study, this one of married men and women. It found that many married Americans admit keeping a major secret from their spouses, but most secrets have nothing to due with an affair or fantasy. Of those married men and women with a secret:

48% said they had not told their spouse the real price of something they bought.

About 40% of the wives and 30% of the husbands said they wish they could persuade their spouses to be less messy.

About a quarter of each sex said they cannot get their partners to lose weight.

About 20% of the nations marrieds have dreams or aspirations they haven't mentioned to a spouse, ranging from living somewhere else (50%) to getting a dog (8%).

16% of both men and women admitted that, at least once during their marriage, they wished they could wake up and not be married any more.

About 15% had not told their spouse about a failure at work.

About 15% had not told their spouse about a childs misbehavior.

14% kept quiet about being attracted to another person.

Only 9% of the respondents, equally split among men and women, said they had an extramarital affair that remains a secret.

The poll was conducted last month by the Centers for Disease Control, which interviewed by phone 700 husbands and 700 wives.

ALTERNATIVE LEADS

Two reporters from competing news organizations attend a city council meeting where the mayor, Sabrina Datolli, announces that the city faces a $6.7 million deficit. Datolli tells council members that a tax increase will be needed unless the city has a little luck. Specifically, tax revenues must exceed expectations, expenditures must stay within estimates, and health care costs and other employee benefits must remain reasonable.

Both journalists listen carefully and take copious notes, intent on capturing the sometimes contentious tone as city officials debate this fiscal dilemma. When the meeting ends, the reporters write their stories. But one piece will be more widely read than the other. One begins with the following lead:

> City officials Wednesday night debated the possibility of a tax increase to erase the city's $6.7 million deficit.

The other starts this way:

> City officials are going to need a pretty big rabbit's foot to keep the city's budget in the black.
>
> Mayor Sabrina Datolli told council during a budget meeting Wednesday night it will take a lot of luck to keep the city out of a financial hole next year.
>
> "If we're lucky, health care costs and our other insurances won't have a big increase. If we're lucky, our tax revenues will come in higher than expected," Datolli said. "If we're unlucky . . ."
>
> If the city is unlucky, it will be looking at a deficit of more than $6.7 million.

The first reporter began the story with a standard summary lead, covering the who, what, when, where, why and how (see Chapter 7). While there is nothing wrong with this method, sometimes a story begs for a more creative approach.

163

Photographs such as this one, taken during the annual No Pants Subway Ride, give reporters the opportunity to be creative when composing a lead. Writers often use unusual situations, stark contrasts or irony in their leads to grab and hold an audience.

The second writer began with an alternative, or "soft," lead—in this case, a multiparagraph lead. Journalists employ at least a dozen variations of soft leads, but most begin with a story's most interesting details, often an anecdote, description or question. These leads, which may run four or five paragraphs, are usually followed by a nut graph that states the story's central point and serves some of the same functions as the summary news lead.

Basic summary news leads are more common—and probably easier to write—than alternative leads. The former get right to the central point of the story in order to be concise, but the latter may linger over one aspect. Writing an alternative lead requires thought and imagination: the ability to recognize and convey an interesting idea uniquely. The reporter must paint a picture with words, with an attention to details that the summary lead cannot include because of its conciseness.

Alternative leads do not require an unusual story. In the following example, the first lead appears as a routine report about the first day of a smoking ban. The alternative lead captures the news better:

> **Summary Lead:** A new smoking ban took effect Monday at Baltimore Washington Medical Center that ends the use of parking lots and outdoor shelters by smokers.

> **Alternative Lead:** Terre King's Monday morning might have been rougher than just about anyone else's.

> Not only was it the first day in her 16 years at Baltimore Washington Medical Center that she couldn't light up, but her job required her to remind people at the entrance about the brand new no-smoking policy.
> *(The Maryland Gazette)*

Good reporters can write many kinds of leads, choosing an appropriate one for each story. This versatility allows them to avoid the trap of blindly following a particular formula in news writing. Although summary leads are effective for many stories, alternative leads allow journalists to stretch the boundaries of their creativity. However, appropriateness is important. The use of alternative leads depends on the publication and the self-imposed stylistic restraints of the writer.

When reporters finish a story, their editors expect it to be well written: clear, concise, accurate and interesting. If a story meets these criteria, editors are unlikely to object if its lead uses an alternative form. Nor are they likely to object to a summary lead that creatively and freshly captures the essence of a story.

Consider this example. When members of a Bronx street gang crashed a christening party, a fight broke out, someone fired shots, and a 10-year-old girl was killed. The New York Post, the Daily News and The New York Times all covered the incident. The first two papers used summary leads; the third used an alternative lead that linked the killing to the shooting of another girl in Brooklyn:

> A 10-year-old altar girl was killed by stray bullets outside her Bronx church yesterday after a gang of armed street thugs crashed a christening party and began arguing with guests.
> *(New York Post)*

> Little Malenny Mendez went to church to celebrate a new life, but instead she lost her own.
> *(New York Daily News)*

FROM THE NEWS

Summary and Alternative Leads

Here are more examples of standard summary leads and the alternative leads that lend freshness to the story:

Summary Lead	Alternative Lead
Police are investigating the theft of more than $17,000 in cash and checks from a Sunday night religious service in Franklin County.	The Lord giveth and the Lord taketh away, but He is not a suspect in the theft of $17,000 in checks and an undetermined amount of cash Sunday from the collection taken at the Cumberland Valley Steve Wingfield Encounter. *Hagerstown (Maryland) Herald-Mail*
A 21-year-old Hampden Township woman was shot and killed by her former boyfriend despite having a court-issued protection-from-abuse order, according to township police.	Trisha Edelman got a protection-from-abuse order, but she still died last week. Edelman was 21 and lived in Hamden Township. She was pregnant and had a 2-year-old daughter. Her former boyfriend, Adam Trump, 25, shot her in the stomach, then carried her body into his New Cumberland apartment, police said. When police found Trump on Wednesday morning, he was in bed with her body. Edelman had secured a PFA order in July after she told police Trump pulled a gun on her and tried to smother her. A PFA order is designed to protect domestic-violence victims from further abuse. Do they go far enough to protect victims? *Harrisburg (Pennsylvania) Patriot-News*
A Food and Drug Administration advisory panel last month recommended allowing doctors to use the Lap-Band, a less drastic form of weight-loss surgery, in somewhat thinner, but still obese patients, offering possible relief for millions struggling with their weight.	After years of trying—and failing—to lose weight with diet and exercise, Esther Eppler decided last summer she was ready to take a more extreme step: surgery. But Crozer Chester Medical Center gave Eppler, 46, of Boothwyn, some disappointing and ironic news. At 5 feet tall and 174 pounds, she wasn't fat enough. Her Body Mass Index (BMI) of 34 fell just short of what doctors and insurers usually require for weight-loss surgery. Eppler, who has high blood pressure and a family history of diabetes, now has reason to hope she may yet get the procedure. A Food and Drug Administration advisory panel last month recommended allowing doctors to use the Lap-Band, a less drastic form of weight-loss surgery, in somewhat thinner, but still obese patients. *The Philadelphia Inquirer*

Malenny Mendez, a 10-year-old girl from the Bronx, loved to strap on her in-line skates and smile at anyone who sauntered past her parents' grocery store. Katherine Crisantos, a 4-year-old girl from Brooklyn, loved the connotation of the word Friday, because it meant a trip with her big sister to Burger King for fries and soda.

Early yesterday morning, both girls, children of Mexican immigrants, were shot in the head less than an hour apart at parties given by friends and relatives.

(*The New York Times*)

Criticisms

During the 1940s, The Wall Street Journal became one of the first daily newspapers to use soft leads. Many others, including the Los Angeles Times, The Miami Herald and The Boston Globe, have since given their reporters more freedom to experiment with their writing, leading the dailies to become known as "writers' newspapers." Proponents of soft leads say whether the lead works is what matters, not the type. They disparage the traditional summaries as "suitcase leads," meaning that newspapers tried to jam too many details into leads, like a traveler trying to fit too many clothes into a suitcase. They also say summary leads are unnatural, deter reporters from writing good stories and eliminate the possibility of surprise, thus making all stories sound alike.

The more literary style of soft leads may help traditional print versions of newspapers compete for readers in an ever-changing media landscape. By using soft leads, newspapers can make their stories more interesting. Even as newspapers have moved into web-based news delivery, thereby increasing the immediacy of their content, alternative leads are still being employed to entice readers.

But not everyone embraces alternative leads. Critics call their use "Jell-O journalism." They complain that soft leads are inappropriate for most news stories: too arty, literary and pretentious. Furthermore, they are too long and fail to emphasize the news. If a story begins with several paragraphs of description or quotations, for example, its most important details may be buried in a later paragraph. Critics also complain that some reporters strain to write fine literature, and many lack the necessary ability.

The following example illustrates how poorly constructed alternative leads can confuse readers and make them impatient. You have to read more than 145 words before getting to the story's main point:

Eleanor Lago considers herself an intelligent, educated woman.

She's read the information provided her by the Grand Rapids Township Board. She's talked to friends and neighbors. And she intends to vote Tuesday in a special election that could determine the township's future.

"I just want to do what's best," says Lago.

Like many residents, though, she's not sure what that is.

An unusual battle is being fought in this smallest of Kent County townships, a raggedy-shaped 16 square miles set cheek to jowl against the cities of Grand Rapids, East Grand Rapids and Kentwood. The battle is not about zoning, the more typical flash point of local politics. Nor is it about leaf burning ordinances or other grass-roots laws in this suburb of nearly 11,000 people.

This battle is about what the community can do to keep from being nibbled to pieces by annexation.

Former Los Angeles Times sportswriter Jim Murray, who won the National Sports Media Association (NSMA)'s Sportswriter of the Year award 14 times, was known for leads such as "Mickey Charles Mantle was born with one foot in the Hall of Fame. Unfortunately, the other was in a brace" and "Excuse me while I wipe up the bloodstains and carry off the wounded. The Dodgers forgot to circle the wagons."

The writer's intention was good: describing an intelligent voter who is confused about an important issue. But the introduction would have been more effective if cut in half. The reporter could have eliminated some description, cut the clichés and avoided saying what the election was not about.

The remaining sections of this chapter describe and offer examples of the various alternative leads.

Types of Alternative Leads

"Buried" or "Delayed" Leads

A "buried," or "delayed," lead is the most common type of alternative lead. Typically, it begins with an interesting example or anecdote that sets a story's theme. Then a nut graph—perhaps the third or fourth paragraph—states the central point and provides a transition to the body, moving the story to the general issue or problem. Like a traditional lead, it summarizes the topic; it may also explain why the topic is important.

Here are two examples of buried leads. The first is by Walter R. Mears of The Associated Press, who takes a different approach to writing about a company filing for bankruptcy. The second is by Jeremy Roebuck of The Philadelphia Inquirer, who wrote about the sale of a dilapidated landmark wooden bridge.

> Washington (AP)—Time was, writing meant typewriting. Words like these—written on a television screen—were composed on the solid keyboard, banged noisily onto a piece of paper, XXXXd out when they weren't quite right, ripped out and scrapped when the paragraphs just didn't work.

> It's easier and faster with the computer, a reality that pushed Smith Corona Corp., the last big-name American typewriter manufacturer, into bankruptcy on Wednesday.

> Philadelphia—While his childhood friends spent their days on the sports fields, Mike Hart spent his digging through dumps.

> Trolling the detritus for old bottles and kerosene lamps, he found fascination in objects other people cast aside.

> Now 49 and head of his own historic building preservation firm, Hart, of Harleysville, plans to take home one of his greatest finds yet.

> He's getting the bridge no one wanted.

After giving more details about the bridge's history, the story reaches the central point in the ninth paragraph, which is the nut graph:

> But four years after the Pennsylvania Department of Transportation closed it to pedestrian and motorist traffic, citing concerns about its structural integrity, the township decided the bridge had to go.

PAINT OUT

Students: Pratt booting beloved recycled art store for dull chain

BY ALLEGRA HOBBS

Call it a brush off.

Pratt Institute is short-changing its students by booting a beloved store that sells recycled art materials off its Clinton Hill campus because it already has a contract with a national art-store chain, claim cash-strapped scholars of the art and architecture school.

"I'm paying for school on my own

campus by Nov. 1 — and Turn Up Art can't stay on as a regular business because the school already has a contract with Blick Art Material, giving it exclusive rights to sell art supplies on its grounds.

Pratt claims the store always had a set expiration date — participants in the incubator have to clear out by an agreed upon time in order to make

This alternative lead, from an article in the Brooklyn Courier, connects with the subject of the story.

The rest of the story addresses the struggles of government officials to come up with the money to remove the bridge, the attempt to sell it on an internet auction site, the agreement with Hart to remove the bridge and what he will eventually do with it.

A delayed lead can introduce a complex or abstract problem by showing how the problem affects a single individual—someone the audience may know or identify with. Or an anecdote can illustrate a problem and arouse interest in the topic.

Some buried leads surprise their public with an unusual twist. If a story is only three or four paragraphs long, journalists may save the twist for the last line. If a story is longer, they use the twist to lure readers to the nut graph, which then provides a transition to the following paragraphs.

Multiparagraph Leads

Other news writers think of a lead as a unit of thought. Their summary leads consist of two or three paragraphs that flow into each other as if they were one:

> Carlisle—It didn't take Mark Toigo and Jay Shettel long to realize they had bought an aerodynamic pile of junk.
>
> They had paid $75,000 to a West Coast aircraft broker who'd advertised the early 1950s Grumman Albatross amphibious plane on the Internet auction site eBay.
>
> It was a sight-unseen deal.
>
> Toigo of Shippensburg and Shettel of Carlisle didn't get a good look at the Albatross until they ventured to a Brazilian air force base outside Sao Paolo, where the venerable old bird was roosting. The Albatross was grimy, beaten-up, partially scavenged and anything but airworthy.
>
> "Right away, we named her 'Dirty Girl,'" Toigo said.
>
> Four years and about $500,000 worth of work later, Dirty Girl still needs a final face-lift, but she flies.
> > (The [Harrisburg, Pennsylvania] Patriot-News)

> The ATVs kicked up sprays of dirt, their riders waving American flags and protest signs as they rumbled along a disputed canyon trail that federal officials had closed to motorized vehicles.
>
> Their message Saturday was clear amid the dust: This was the latest challenge by citizens saying they are defending state and local rights against an increasingly arrogant federal government that's overstepped its role in small communities such as Blanding.
>
> The protagonist this time wasn't a private rancher like Cliven Bundy, who prevailed in a standoff with the Bureau of Land Management in Nevada. This protest was the brainchild of a public official, San Juan County Commissioner Phil Lyman, who contends that this town of 3,500 residents has tried hard to compromise with the bureau to reopen scenic Recapture Canyon to all-terrain vehicles.
> > (Los Angeles Times)

Quotation Leads

Reporters usually avoid using quotations in leads. Sources generally do not provide quotes that meet three criteria for leads: summarize the entire story (not just part of it), be brief and be self-explanatory. Some editors prohibit the use of quotation leads because they lack clarity and often are too long and complicated.

As with the use of any quotation in a story, the source's statement should be so effective the reporter cannot improve it. When used in the first line of a story, a quotation also must reveal the central point, as these two examples do:

> "I wanted to slam the plane into a mountain so I could die with my husband," said Betty Smith, whose husband died at its controls. But then she thought of her children on the ground.

> "Our children can't read, add or find countries on a map," the nation's teacher-of-the-year said at a congressional hearing Wednesday.

If a quotation is only sensational, it fails to satisfy the criteria for a lead. It may be suitable elsewhere in the story, however. Reporters have other ways to startle an audience or grab its attention. Remember that the lead provides the organization for the rest of the story. If the quotation fails to bring people into and set the stage for the story, it will confuse and discourage them. A long, complicated quotation, even within the body of a story, will raise unnecessary questions.

Quotations that begin with words needing identification or explanation—such as "he," "she," "we," "they," "it," "that" and "this"—should not be leads. The audience has no way of knowing to whom or what the words refer and, when the subject's identity is revealed, may have to reread the quotation to understand its meaning.

Consider the following example:

> "The water was rising so fast and the bank was so muddy and slippery I just didn't think I could get away from that torrent of water." That's how a Bremerton man described his ordeal just before rescue workers used a utility truck to pluck him out of a tree he had climbed to escape a flashflood during Monday night's thunderstorms.

Such leads can be rewritten with a brief introduction to enhance clarity:

> A Bremerton man who was rescued from a tree he had climbed to escape a flashflood Monday night said, "The water was so fast and the bank was so muddy and slippery I just didn't think I could get away from that torrent of water."

Question Leads

Questions can make effective leads. Some editors, though, prohibit this type because they believe news stories should answer questions, not ask them. Question leads also often run the risk of being clichés.

"I don't understand your question. Could you restate it as an answer?"

To be effective, question leads must be brief, simple, specific and provocative. The question should contain no more than a dozen words. Moreover, the audience should feel absolutely compelled to answer it. Avoid questions if people's responses may discourage them from continuing with the story, as in this example:

> Are you interested in nuclear physics?

A few might be interested in nuclear physics, but many would think the topic too complicated. This question lead also fails because someone can answer "yes" or "no," possibly ending his or her interest in the story.

A question should concern a controversial yet familiar issue that interests and affects an audience. Avoid abstract or complicated questions requiring a great deal of explanation. The following question is ineffective because it is too abstract, long and complicated. Furthermore, it fails to ask about issues that everyone is certain to care about:

> If you were on vacation miles from your house, and you thought the mechanics at a service station deliberately damaged your car, then demanded an exorbitant fee to repair it, would you be willing to file criminal charges against the mechanics and return to the area to testify at their trial?

The following questions also fail, but for different reasons. The first asks about an issue unlikely to concern most people. The second is unanswerable and flippant, treating a serious topic as a trivial one:

> Have you thought lately about going to prison?

> Someone was swindled today. Who'll be swindled tomorrow?

Here are two more effective question leads. Notice that each reporter immediately answers the questions.

> Fill out college application? Check.

> Take the SATs? Check.

> Have three or four college courses already under your belt?

> For students hoping to get accepted at higher-end colleges, taking a few Advanced Placement courses—accelerated high school classes that count for college credit depending on how students score on a standardized test—is no longer a nice add-on to college resumes. It's the norm.
> *(The [Harrisburg, Pennsylvania] Patriot-News)*

> Could this be the end of cereal aisle showdowns between parents and sweet-toothed tots? New reduced-sugar versions of popular children's breakfast cereals—everything from Froot Loops to Frosted Flakes—certainly sound promising, but consumers might want to hold off chiming in when Tony the Tiger says, "They're Gr-r-reat!"
> *(The Associated Press)*

Suspenseful Leads

Some reporters write leads to create suspense, arouse people's curiosity or raise a question in their minds. By hinting at some mysterious development explained in a later paragraph, this type of lead compels the audience to finish a story:

> It is the fire bell that signals the beginning of each firefighter's day.
>
> It is the same bell that summons firefighters to action.
>
> And it is the same bell that marks their last alarm.
> *(The [Palm Springs, California] Desert Sun)*

> It is difficult to run a successful business when you keep losing half of your work force year after year.
>
> Just ask James Griffe—or any other beekeeper.
> *(The [Harrisburg, Pennsylvania] Patriot News)*

The first story focuses on the deaths of several Palm Springs firefighters; the second reports on the economic devastation an insect parasite was causing for beekeepers.

Descriptive Leads

Other leads begin with descriptive details that paint a picture before moving gradually into the action. The description should be colorful and interesting so that it arouses the public's interest. It should also help summarize the story.

The following examples show the effectiveness of descriptive leads. Notice the use of concrete images and active verbs in the first one: "sirens wail," "lights strobe" and "vehicles speed." The second sets the scene and provides background details for a feature story about a couple with Parkinson's disease. The focus of the story is the doctor who treats them and the relationship his father had with Maurer's family as their doctor in Illinois many years ago.

> Sirens wail in the night. Emergency lights strobe red and blue through the windows as a Lincoln Navigator and Ford Crown Victoria rush through a red light in Northwest Washington, the cars ahead of them slowing, pulling to the curb. The big black vehicles speed past, straddling the solid yellow center lines, a mile or so from the White House.
>
> Are they outriders for the president? Is he headed this way?
>
> Is it the vice president? The king of Siam?
>
> It's Mayor Adrian M. Fenty. And he's late for a citizens meeting near Anacostia.
> *(The Washington Post)*

Serving the University of California, Los Angeles community since 1919

DAILY BRUIN
A Paper Trail

MONDAY, NOVEMBER 9, 2015   CHAPTER ONE IN A 3

A BRIDGET O'BRIEN FOUNDATION REPORT

EDITOR'S NOTE

While federal legislation on undocumented immigrants continues to stall, state policy continues to be a powerful predictor of the course of their lives. Depending on where they've settled, undocumented students in the United States can either be admitted to college with resident tuition and state aid, or they can be banned from public institutions entirely.

Reporter Natalie Delgadillo, opinion columnist Ryan Nelson and photojournalist Angie Wang spent 11 months piecing together the

full picture of what it means to be an undocumented student in the United States – from California, where policies are comparatively lenient, to Georgia, where students are subject to some of the harshest higher education policies in the country.

The Bridget O'Brien Scholarship Foundation has funded eight years of UCLA student journalism with global reach and local impact, including this project. To learn more about the scholarship, visit rememberingbridget.com.

CHAPTER ONE IN A THREE–PART SERIES: A PAPER TRAIL

STORIES   COLUMNS

Driving under the radar

For years, college women across the country have been going to off-campus parties through a kind of anonymous taxi system organized by fraternities to prevent drunk driving.

BY MARJORIE KIRK
news@kykernel.com

Anna Jones and Madeline Berlin rocked back and forth on their heels, glancing at their phones.

Just after 10 p.m. a car pulled up beside the freshmen at the corner of Hilltop and Woodland avenues, and idled with its hazards on.

The women peered through the windows, trying to make out the unknown driver.

The car had no sign or decal indicating that the driver belonged to a certified company or program. It was an unassuming vehicle, nothing that would stand out to a late night UK Police Department patrol.

Without a second thought, the girls got into the backseat behind a man they didn't know, trusting the system that their friends assured them was the proper way to get to an

A Police Chief's Concern

Jones and Berlin were participating in a kind of anonymous taxi service where strangers pick up college women and haul them to frat parties.

It's a system that fraternities have used for years as a way to prevent drunk driving, but the anonymous nature of the process has gone largely unscrutinized.

That's something UK Police Chief Joe Monroe wants to change.

When the Kernel brought this system to his attention earlier this year, his thoughts immediately turned to his daughter, and other women like her.

"If you've got one or two females who are getting into a car with an unknown male to go to an off-campus

These articles—from the college newspapers the Daily Bruin and the Kentucky Kernel, respectively—feature excellent descriptive leads.

Parkinson's disease worked on Goldie Maurer like a slow-moving robber, taking away things one at a time.

Baling hay. Birthing calves. Working the controls of a John Deere tractor.

Each lost activity seemed to pull Maurer further from what she was—a Midwestern-born farm girl, raised in the 1920s on a farm near tiny Lena, Ill.

The tremors and faulty sense of balance started 25 years ago, long after Maurer moved from Illinois to a farm in northern Dauphin County.

First, she surrendered garden chores, such as tending strawberry and potato plants. Then, she had to give up handling equipment, such as riding a snowmobile to far-flung parts of her farm in Washington Township.

It was the tremors, she said.

(The [Harrisburg, Pennsylvania] Patriot-News)

Shockers: Leads with a Twist

Reporters like "shockers": startling leads that immediately capture the public's attention. The following examples have an unusual twist that adds to their effectiveness:

Soon it will be spring again. The snow will melt, the dogwoods flower. Trumpets will blast, graves will open, and the Earth will begin a five-month descent to its fiery end.

Radio evangelist Harold Camping can hardly wait.

(The Philadelphia Inquirer)

Managua, Nicaragua—She had been raped. She was pregnant. And she was poor. And Rosa was 9. That gave her one more reason to want an abortion.

> (Los Angeles Times)

Ironic Leads

Closely related to shockers are leads that present a startling or ironic contrast. The use of striking details is likely to arouse curiosity:

For months, high school sophomore Sara Corbett of New Hartford, Conn., had begged her mother for permission to get her tongue pierced. On Aug. 7, 2004, Sara's mother, Robin DeBaise, relented and the two went to a nearby mall.

The next day, Sara, 16, was in severe pain. At her aunt's house, she found a couple of methadone pills—amounting to twice the recommended dosage—and took them. She passed out and was rushed to a hospital, where she died.

> (USA Today)

When union activist Oliver French goes on trial today on charges of killing two auto plant colleagues and wounding two others, he likely will be portrayed as the victim.

> (The Detroit News)

Direct-Address Leads

Reporters occasionally use a form of direct address, speaking directly to their audience:

If you think you're too smart to fall for an Internet scam, you're probably kidding yourself.

> (The [Harrisburg, Pennsylvania] Patriot News)

If you just spent another Valentine's Day alone and lonely, the state of Maryland can hook you up.

> (The Baltimore Sun)

Words Used in Unusual Ways

Journalists who are clever and have a good imagination (or a good grasp of literature), might use a common word or phrase in an uncommon way:

Sufferin' succotash—Sylvester had better stay home. A statewide vote in Wisconsin could pave the way for legally shooting stray cats there.

> (USA Today)

Perhaps it was God's joke on a newly ordained priest when the Rev. Jim Farnan, former class clown and no stranger to the detention room, was asked to speak with the occasional clone of his former self at Our Lady of Fatima School.

(The Pittsburgh Post-Gazette)

This style is difficult, because what seems funny or clever to one person may seem corny or silly to another. Also, the subjects may be too serious for such a light touch:

Oakland County Prosecutor Richard Thompson wants to be known by the criminals he keeps.

(The Detroit Free Press)

The story was about the high costs a prosecutor was creating for the county by refusing to plea bargain with criminals.

Other Unusual Leads

The following leads are effective but difficult to categorize. Notice their simplicity, brevity and clarity, as well as their emphasis on the interesting and unusual. The first lead introduces a story describing the effects of uncommonly cold weather on the economy. The second reports the death of actress Audrey Hepburn, who starred in the movie "My Fair Lady." The third introduces the man in charge of demolishing Three Rivers Stadium in Pittsburgh, Pennsylvania.

Washington—Jack Frost is nipping at our growth.

(The Wall Street Journal)

Audrey Hepburn was the fairest lady of them all.

(The Detroit News)

Circuses have ringmasters. Military boot camps have drill sergeants. The Three Rivers Stadium implosion has Greg Yesko, who's a bit of both.

(The Pittsburgh Post-Gazette)

The Reporter's Guide to Writing Alternative Leads

1. Be curious. Be observant. Be creative.

2. Make sure the alternative lead is appropriate for the story.

3. Understand that the "news" is still the most important aspect of the story—don't focus on writing a brilliant lead and then not apply the same rigor to the rest of the story.

4. Use alternative leads with the proper story structure.

5. Vary your use of alternative leads. Don't rely on just one or two types because your story leads will become predictable and your writing stilted.

6. Know that some alternative leads—quotation, question and direct-address leads—should be used sparingly. Don't overuse them or they lose their power.

7. Look for a "play" on words—using words in an unusual way—to catch the audience's attention.

8. Make sure that the alternative lead "fits" the story — do not use an ironic lead if there is no irony present in the story or a suspenseful lead if the story is merely about a routine government meeting in which there is nothing controversial or suspenseful. Do not try to "oversell" the story with an alternative lead.

9. When writing question leads, be sure to answer the question in the story, preferably near the question itself.

10. Paint a picture with words when using a descriptive lead to set the scene of the story. Use descriptive nouns and powerful, active verbs.

Review Exercises

1. Evaluating Alternative Leads

Critically evaluate the following leads, each of which uses one of the alternative forms discussed in this chapter. Select the best ones and explain why they succeed. Point out the flaws in the remaining leads. As you evaluate, look for lessons—"do's and don'ts"—that you can apply to your own work.

1. Are you ready for a big change?

2. "I saw the train coming at us and I knew it would never get stopped."

3. No shirt! No shoes! No service!

   Unfortunately, the 350-pound black bear that wandered into the city limits and pried open a window to break into the Oakhill Restaurant couldn't read. The bear was captured by state game commission officers after it had ransacked the restaurant's kitchen and helped itself to a variety of treats.

4. Amy Clauch sat beside the rough-hewn pine fence, her fingers rubbing the worn knuckles of the knots in the rope she held in her hand.

   The sweet scent of clover hay wafted on the light breeze that blew through the barn. She sucked in a deep breath and held it. The scent lingered. She wished it always would.

   The sun hung in the early morning cobalt blue sky like a spotlight in a theater, illuminating her, the actor on this stage. This is where she wanted to be—free from the confines of the four pale beige walls that surrounded her in clinical sterility for months.

   She tugged at her jeans. Her lips pursed. "You can do this," she whispered in prayer to herself. Clauch rocked the wheelchair to the left and reached for the stirrup hanging limply from the saddle. Pulling herself upright, she grimaced as she felt the braces tighten on her legs. The muscles in her arms clenched as she pulled herself into the saddle. The chestnut mare flinched at the load and Clauch grabbed the worn leather saddle horn to steady herself. Her smile stretched her cheeks to their limit. She was back where she belonged.

   It had been eight months since a riding accident left Clauch temporarily paralyzed from the waist down.

5. Too much work. Too many demands. Too many responsibilities. Not enough time.

   Stress is killing Americans, the American Medical Association said in a report released Monday.

6. Should high school students have to take a competency test before receiving their diplomas?

7. The state's motorcycle riders won the right today to have the wind in their hair and bugs in their teeth. The state Legislature passed a bill eliminating the state's helmet requirements for riders 18 and older.

8. How much would you pay for, say, a triple heart bypass? Or gall bladder surgery?

   As government officials struggle to rein in health care costs without sacrificing the quality of care, they find themselves confronted with the question of who should pay how much.

9. "If we can't solve the state budget crisis today, the students of tomorrow will suffer the consequences," school Superintendent Gary Hubbard said about the state's failure to pass a budget before the start of the school year.

10. The Freedonia County Fair begins today and if you want to catch all the action this week, you better get to the fairgrounds.

11. Billy Lee Anderson pushes the blond hair away from his blue eyes, exposing the dusting of freckles on his forehead.

    The 12-year-old sits in a chair that is a bit too adult for his small frame, his feet, clad in gleaming white athletic shoes, dangling several inches above the floor.

    There is an air of innocence surrounding the boy that will make it hard for any jury to believe that he could have set the fire that killed his parents and baby sister. But that is what prosecutors will attempt to do as Anderson's murder trial gets underway today.

12. You're driving down a tree-shaded city street when a child runs out from between two parked cars. Could you stop in time?

13. Thompsontown hit a grand slam over the weekend as all four of its Little League teams won their championship games.

14. When Jim and Suzanne Baker left the mall, they were loaded down with Christmas presents and laughing about the surprises they had in store for their children.

    Half an hour later, they were dead.

15. It actually was a dark and stormy night when Sharon Murphy sat down in front of her typewriter to start writing her first novel.

2. Writing Alternative Leads

Using techniques you studied in this chapter, write an alternative lead for each of the following stories. Correct any errors you find.

1. A group of ecologists and biologists at your university and other schools have come up with a unique idea. They want to transplant African wildlife to the Great Plains of North America. Julie Allen, 1504 Lincoln Drive, is an associate professor of biology at your university. She had this to say about the idea, "I think it would be wonderful to drive across the Great Plains and see lions and elephants and giraffes roaming the prairie." The idea was developed by more than 30 scientists as a way to perpetuate species that are slowly facing extinction because of declining habitat in Africa. The scientists say there is plenty of room left in the American West for these types of animals. Relocating the animals could help them increase their numbers. The plan is being criticized by ranchers, developers and other scientists, who say that it would be difficult to introduce animals to a place they had never lived. Ranchers, such as Jim Smithson, who lives in North Dakota and is vice president of the Western Stockman's Association, claims such a move would devastate the regions cattle industry. "How many steers or dairy cows can a pride of lions eat in a week?" Smithson said. Supporters of the idea say the animals they want to relocate would be held in large game parks or private reserves. They would not be allowed to roam free. Other critics say the transplanting of alien creatures could have devastating effects on native creatures. The animals being brought to places they have never lived could introduce new diseases or could destroy native wildlife. In addition, taking wildlife from Africa could hurt the tourist trade on that continent.

2. It was an intense situation for police Wednesday afternoon. It was an adventure for the six-month-old daughter of Michael and Ethel Perakiss of 876 Collins Street. Everything ended OK, police said. Megan Perakiss, the daughter of Michael and Ethel, was in the back seat of a 2006 Ford Explorer sport utility vehicle when it was carjacked by a man who had just held up the convenience store where Ethel had stopped to get gas. The robbery of the Quik Shoppe convenience store at 2752 Michigan Avenue occurred shortly after 2 p.m., according to Police Chief Barry Kopperud. Kopperud said the suspect walked into the store and waved a handgun in the face of Edwin C. Jimenez, manager of the store. He ordered Jimenez to empty the cash register into a cloth bag he threw on the counter and threatened to shoot him if he did not. The thief made off with an undetermined amount of money. Megan was unaware of what was going on. Police said Ethel pulled into the convenience store to get fuel and had just finished pumping the gas when the robber ran from the store and pushed her away from the vehicle. Reports of the carjacking sparked a massive, multi-agency search for Megan that at one point included nearly two dozen units from the city's police force. Ethel Perakiss left her keys in the ignition while she was filling the fuel tank. Police described the armed robbery and carjacking suspect as a 6 foot 1 inch tall white male in his early to mid-20s wearing a white T-shirt and long black pants. He had short, neatly cropped hair. "My baby's in the back seat," Perakiss shouted as the carjacker drove away. About 40 minutes after the ordeal began, Kopperuud said, police officers spotted the missing vehicle abandoned in the parking lot of a Chinese restaurant with Megan inside. The carjacker apparently had fled, leaving the vehicle unlocked and running with the air conditioner on. Police said they were shocked but pleased that the incident ended so quickly and without harm to the child.

3. It was just one of those days for Representative Constance P. Wei. Wei is the representative for the 86th District. Wei, who lives at 206 North Wabash Avenue, is a proponent of limited government. State representatives have been trying to

pass a ban on using cell phones while driving. Wei thinks it is an infringement on individual rights. "All this is is Big Brother telling you what to do," she said. Advocates of the ban say it is an issue of safety. They point to a recent accident in which five people were killed in a two-car accident. The driver who caused the accident was a 48-year-old man who was talking on his cell phone while trying to pass another car on a two-lane stretch of road. Witnesses said the man swerved into the path of the other car and the two vehicles collided head-on. Two of the five people killed were children. The state legislature has never backed a ban on cell phone use, but other states have instituted successful bans. Opponents of the ban, including Wei, claim the ban will not affect safety because forcing people to pull off the road and get out of their cars to talk on the phone could be more hazardous. In addition, opponents say that the state cannot ban all distractions drivers create, such as eating, reading or applying makeup while driving. Proponents of the ban want it to take affect in January of next year. Wei was on her cell phone Wednesday as she was driving home. She was talking to State representative Peter Mackey, 89th District, about postponing a vote on the bill banning cell phone use while driving when her Cadillac Sedan de Ville struck the rear of a car driven by Michael Jeffreys, 41, of 2781 Collins Ave. Jeffreys suffered minor injuries and was taken to Mercy Hospital. He was treated and released. Police said the accident occurred at 5:37 p.m. at the intersection of 29th Street and Melrose Avenue. Jeffreys was stopped at a traffic light. Wei did not see the red light or the cars stopped in front of her and rammed the rear of Jeffreys Toyota Camry. Police said the Camry suffered severe damage. Weis Cadillac sustained an estimated $8,000 in damage.

4. It's a unique idea. The National Association of School Boards said it had no record of any other district doing it or considering it. School board members and school administrators in your local school district are considering changing the school week to cut costs. The state announced that it does not have enough money to fund schools because of the slow economy and schools will have to cut their budgets. Superintendent of schools Gary Hubbard told school board members at Monday night's meeting that the district has cut all the fat out of the budget that it can. "We've cut out after-school programs and eliminated all but the essential teacher's aides positions," Hubbard said. "We've even raised the price of school lunches, but we are still coming up short." Hubbard and school board members are proposing to go to a four-day school week to help the district save money. The school day, which now runs from 8 a.m. to 2:30 p.m. would be lengthened by two hours, running from 8 a.m. to 4:30 p.m. to make up for the loss of one day during the week. Hubbard and the board say the district could save more then one million dollars in transportation, food service and janitorial costs. The board voted 7–0 in favor of the proposal.

5. Your city officials received a gift on Tuesday. Attorney Richard Cycler handed a check for over $2 million to Mayor Sabrina Datolli. The money will be used to build the Willie Hattaway Center in an annex of City Hall. Plans to develop the annex into a community center, senior citizens center, a historical exhibit hall and meeting and conference rooms had been postponed for several years because of a lack of funds to complete the project. The city had built the annex with money from a federal grant but could not raise enough money to complete the project. The building has been an empty shell for more than seven years. City officials were using the space to store boxes of old water bills and other papers. Willie Hattaway gave the money to the city in his will. Hattaway died last year. He was 98. He was a widower. His wife, Estelle, died 10 years ago. Everyone, including his neighbors, was surprised that Willie had that much money in the bank. Willie lived in a modest two-story, white clapboard house on Virginia Avenue for more than 60 years. Flowers surrounded the house. Hattaway loved to work in his garden and flower beds. He was particularly fond of roses and grew several assorted varieties. He had entered Sunnyview Retirement Home on Wisconsin Avenue last year, shortly after his 97th birthday. Neighbors said he could no longer take care of himself after he fell and broke his hip.

Neighbors said Hattaway drove a car that was 40 years old and never traveled very far from home. The car, a green Chevrolet Impala, is still parked in the garage. Hattaway did not want to sell the car even though he had not been driving since he was 90. He enjoyed sitting on his porch and talking to neighbors or giving neighborhood children treats of candy or fruit. He did not live extravagantly. "It just goes to show that you never really know your neighbors. Willie was such a wonderful, friendly gentleman. He was so generous with his time helping neighbors and playing with the neighborhood children. It doesn't surprise me that he would be so generous with his money, too," said a former neighbor Marilyn Boudinot, 41, of 4340 Virginia Ave. Hattaway and his wife had no children. He was a retired construction worker who had invested his money in the stock market for many years.

6. It was an unusually harsh sentence, according to some people. Sarah Zerwinn, 27, of 2021 Dyan Way, was sentenced yesterday by Circuit Court Judge JoAnn Keappler. Zerwinn was sentenced to 60 days in jail for failing to take her daughter to kindergarten. Or Zerwinn could go back to school. Public education is compulsory in the state, and school officials have been asking the courts for years to provide stiffer penalties for the parents of chronically truant children. School officials say that children who fall behind early because they do not attend school regularly have a harder time succeeding in the higher grades. Zerwins daughter, Jennifer, who is six years old, missed 111 out of 180 days of school last year and was late an additional 21 times. All of the absences were unexcused.

Jennifer told school officials that her mother often slept late and was not able to help Jennifer get ready for school. Several months ago, school officials declared Jennifer a habitual truant, and Zerwinn was ordered to appear in court. A judge ordered Zerwinn to make sure Jennifer attended school, but the absences continued. Zerwinn was taken back to court by school officials and Kaeppler found her in contempt of a court order to ensure she took her daughter to school. After pronouncing the sentence, Zerwinn was led away in handcuffs. Zerwinns attorney, Miguel Aceveda, asked the judge not to sentence his client to jail, but give her probation instead. Kaeppler said during the sentencing that Zerwinn could avoid jail time if she agreed to attend kindergarten with her daughter to make certain that she attended and got there on time. Zerwinn would have to attend the classes her daughter attends and participate in the activities here daughter does. "Perhaps you will learn something about the importance of your daughters education," Kaeppler said. Acevede told the court that Zerwinn works nights and is unable to wake up in time to get her daughter ready for and off to school. However, Kaeppler said that is no excuse for Zerwinns failure to provide an education for her daughter. Acevde told the judge he felt the judges sentence was too harsh because it would place an unreasonable burden on the defendant. Karen Bulnes, attorney for the school board who brought the case against Zerwinn, said, "I certainly think this sends a message that the courts are willing to take a strong stance against parents of chronically truant children. We are doing this for the good of the children."

9

THE BODY OF A NEWS STORY

The portion of a news story that follows the lead, called the "body," contains the information a reporter believes the public needs to know. This information can be presented in several styles: inverted pyramid, hourglass, focus or narrative. While no single technique works best for all people, all stories or all reporters, each requires thorough reporting, organization and effective presentation. Whatever story style a writer chooses, he or she must determine how best to convey information to the audience.

Think of writing a news story as driving a train along a track. The rails are the story's central point and give the story direction. The railroad ties—who, what, when, where, why and how—provide a foundation. The train's engine is the lead; it must be strong enough to pull the rest of the story, and its whistle must capture the public's attention. Each car that follows represents a paragraph containing information and providing structure; these "cars" can be arranged in whatever sequence—for example, from most important to least or chronologically—seems most effective. Cars filled with research, verification, multiple sources, quotes, anecdotes and descriptions strengthen the train. The amount of information needed to complete the story determines the number of cars. Holding the train cars together are couplings, which represent the transitions between paragraphs. Without strong transitions, the paragraphs disconnect from one another.

This chapter discusses the writing styles and techniques reporters often use to write effective bodies for their news stories.

The Inverted-Pyramid Style

Inverted-pyramid stories arrange the information in descending order of importance or newsworthiness. The lead states the most newsworthy, important or striking information and establishes the central point for the rest of the story. The second paragraph (and sometimes the third and fourth) provides details that amplify the lead. Subsequent paragraphs add less important details or introduce subordinate topics. Each paragraph presents additional information: names, descriptions, quotations, conflicting viewpoints, explanations and background data. Beginning reporters must learn this style because it helps them decide what is most important and what is least important. It also helps discover "holes" in their information—details that have not been collected and need to be found.

The primary advantage of the inverted pyramid is that it allows someone to leave a story after only one or two paragraphs yet still learn the newest, most newsworthy and most important facts. The inverted pyramid also ensures that all the facts are immediately understandable. Moreover, if a story is longer than the space or time available, editors can easily shorten it by deleting paragraphs from the end.

News consumers, whether in print or online, are skimmers. They glance at headlines and then check the lead to determine if the story interests them. The inverted-pyramid story structure gives an audience the important information at the beginning of the story. So even on a short subway ride, they can read stories that are important to them and learn what is going on in their community and the world.

The inverted-pyramid style also has several disadvantages:

- Because the lead summarizes facts that later paragraphs discuss in greater detail, some may be repeated in the body.
- A story that follows the inverted pyramid rarely contains any surprises; the lead immediately reveals the major facts.
- The inverted-pyramid style evolved when newspapers were the public's first source for breaking news; now radio, television, social media and the internet fill that role.
- Readers with less than a high school education cannot easily understand stories written in this style.
- The inverted pyramid locks reporters into a formula and discourages them from trying new styles.

Many writing coaches discourage using the inverted pyramid, saying it is overused, confusing and often irrelevant. Nevertheless, the style remains a common format for organizing news stories, partly because of its inherent advantages and partly because using it is a difficult habit to break. Daily deadline pressures in the age of the internet and social media also encourage its use because devising new styles requires additional time, critical thinking and, perhaps, more rewriting.

Organizing the Information

An inverted-pyramid story about a two-car collision that injured several people might contain a sequence of paragraphs similar to those outlined in Figure 9.1. Normally, reporters emphasize people: what they do and what happens to them.

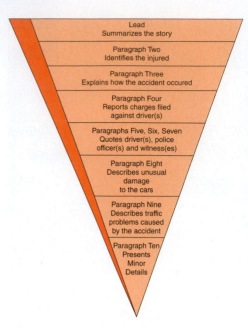

| Lead |
| Summarizes the story |
| Paragraph Two |
| Identifies the injured |
| Paragraph Three |
| Explains how the accident occured |
| Paragraph Four |
| Reports charges filed |
| against driver(s) |
| Paragraphs Five, Six, Seven |
| Quotes driver(s), police |
| officer(s) and witness(es) |
| Paragraph Eight |
| Describes unusual |
| damage |
| to the cars |
| Paragraph Nine |
| Describes traffic |
| problems caused |
| by the accident |
| Paragraph Ten |
| Presents |
| Minor |
| Details |

Figure 9.1   Inverted-Pyramid Style   The inverted-pyramid style of story writing has been a staple of news writing for decades.

Consequently, the injuries to the people would be described early in the story. Damage to the cars is less important and would be reported later; it might also be left out, unless it was unusual. Paragraph three would describe the accident itself—the recent action and main point of the story. Quotations add detail and color as well as a pleasing change of pace. The remaining paragraphs add less essential information and might be deleted if space or time was limited.

The exact organization varies depending on the story's unique facts and most newsworthy points. The second, third and, maybe, fourth paragraphs should provide details that develop and support the lead. The following inverted-pyramid stories are cohesive because the leads summarize their topics and the second and third paragraphs present their most important details. Neither story ends with a summary or conclusion; instead, the final paragraphs present the least important details.

LOTHIAN—A Glen Burnie man was in serious but stable condition yesterday, a day after he fell asleep at the wheel and collided with a box truck in south county.

David A. Calligan Jr., 19, was driving a 1998 Ford Explorer east on Route 258 near Brookswood Road just before 3 p.m. when he fell asleep and crossed the center line, county police said.

The Ford collided with a westbound GMC box truck, which overturned, trapping Calligan.

A county fire department spokesperson said it took 15 to 20 minutes for fire-fighters to free Calligan, who was flown by state police helicopter to the Maryland Shock Trauma Center in Baltimore.

The box truck driver, 29-year-old Ulise Trujillo-Hetteta of Waldorf, and passenger Raphael Ignot, 26, of Fort Washington, were not seriously hurt.

(The Maryland Gazette)

HARRISBURG—Pennsylvania was put on notice Thursday that it faces another credit downgrade and higher borrowing costs if it does not improve its deficit-ridden finances.

The sharply worded warning by Standard and Poor's that suggested state government is guilty of financial mismanagement came amid a six-day-old stalemate as lawmakers tussle over how to pay for a $32 billion spending package. They face a midnight Monday deadline for Democratic Gov. Tom Wolf to make a decision on the main appropriations bill on his desk.

Pennsylvania has struggled with an entrenched post-recession deficit, and credit downgrades in 2012 through 2014 have left it with among the nation's lowest credit ratings.

(The Associated Press)

In the first example, an editor could easily remove the last couple of paragraphs if necessary and still retain the essential information of the story. The second example contained a total of 14 paragraphs; the last four addressed the fact that negotiations among state legislators were ongoing. As you can see, these final paragraphs could easily be cut without affecting significant information presented at the beginning of the story.

Many of the facts reported in longer news stories are of approximately equal importance. These stories are more likely to resemble Figure 9.1. However, other stories are organized in the manner shown in Figure 9.2.

Immediately after the diagram's summary lead, section 1 presents several paragraphs that contain information of roughly equivalent importance. Those paragraphs may present some additional information about a single topic or several different but related subtopics. Section 2 may describe a somewhat less important aspect of the story. Section 3 presents more facts of about equal importance to one another but of less importance than those in section 2. Section 4 contains the least important details, perhaps routine procedures, background information or a reminder of related or similar incidents that occurred in the past.

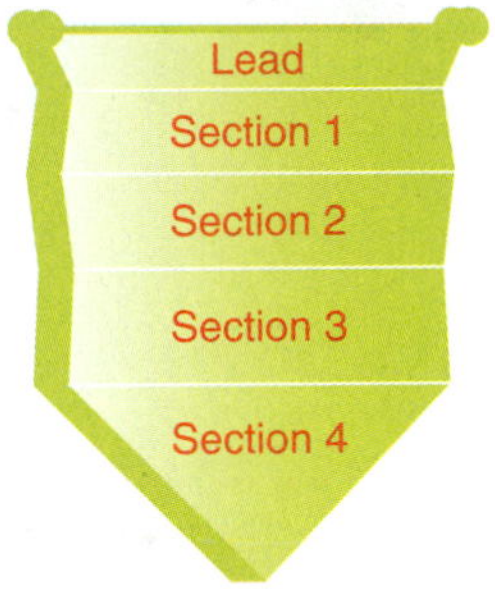

Editors at Franklin & Marshall College's The College Reporter work on the next edition of the school's online newspaper. The inverted-pyramid story structure allows editors to cut a story's length quickly and efficiently.

Figure 9.2   An Alternative Inverted-Pyramid Style   The inverted-pyramid style often resembles this shape rather than the typical pyramid.

Writing the Second Paragraph

The second paragraph in a news story is almost as important as the lead—and almost as difficult to write. Like the lead, the second paragraph should emphasize the news. In addition, it should provide a smooth, logical transition from the lead to the following paragraphs. When using the delayed-identification style of summary lead (discussed in Chapter 7), it is important to identify the story's source or subject in the second paragraph. Journalists must also use an effective transitional word or phrase to ensure that the audience understands the connection of the source or subject identified in the opening paragraph. Here is an example of a lead and second paragraph:

> An Indiana woman died early Monday morning in a fiery three-vehicle accident on the Pennsylvania Turnpike that closed the highway for more than six hours.
>
> The victim, Mary A. Burnett, 56, of Bloomington, lost control of her SUV, crossed the median and collided with an oncoming westbound tractor-trailer, according to Pennsylvania State Police.

Note that the words "The victim" are used as a transitional device to identify "Mary A. Burnett" as the "Indiana woman" used in the lead to avoid confusion.

Sometimes reporters fail to emphasize the news in a story's second paragraph. Other times they fail to provide smooth transitions. As a result, their stories seem dull or disorganized. The following pages discuss both of these problems and present some solutions.

AVOID LEAPFROGGING

Journalists often introduce an individual in their lead and begin their second paragraph with a name. However, many fail to say clearly that both refer to the same person. The audience is forced to guess. Most people usually guess right—but not always.

This problem is so common that it has a name: "leapfrogging." To avoid it, provide a one- or two-word transition from the lead to the name in the second paragraph:

> ALLENTOWN (AP)—A man rammed his car into his wife's car, then shot her in the arm and leg before bystanders tackled him, police said. Police expressed gratitude to the bystanders who helped bring *the man suspected of the attack,* Felipe M. Santos, 53, of Allentown into custody Monday.

CONTINUE WITH THE NEWS

After providing a smooth transition between the lead and the second paragraph, continue with information about the topic summarized in your lead. Some reporters shift to a different topic, a mistake certain to cause confusion:

> The mayor and City Council agreed Monday night to freeze wages and make city workers pay more for benefits in an effort to close a budget deficit that is now larger than officials expected. Mayor Sabrina Datolli, who has been a lifelong resident of the city, is in her fourth term as mayor. She has seen many ups and downs over her years as mayor, but hopes the city can overcome its problems.

This story seems to discuss two different topics. The lead summarizes a problem that confronts city officials everywhere: balancing budgets. The second paragraph shifts to the mayor's career and hopes. It fails even to mention the problem of balancing the budget. The following revision corrects the error:

> The mayor and City Council agreed Monday night to freeze wages and make city workers pay more for benefits in an effort to close a budget deficit that is now larger than officials expected. Mayor Sabrina Datolli said the wage freeze and other measures are needed to prevent layoffs of city employees, cuts in programs and more drastic fiscal surgery to balance the city's budget.

NAMES, NAMES: DULL, DULL

Reporters sometimes place too much emphasis on their sources' identities. As a result, their second paragraphs fail to convey any information of interest. Consider the following example:

> A highway engineer was killed Wednesday at an Interstate 95 construction site when a tractor-trailer owned by Shearson Trucking Inc. plowed through

a concrete barrier and struck him. A materials engineer, Riley Patterson of Independent Testing Laboratory Inc., was killed in the mishap. Jonathan Martin, a site manager for Baldini Construction Co., saw the accident happen.

The paragraph can be rewritten to emphasize the news—what the source said, saw or did, not who he is:

> A tractor-trailer plowed through a concrete barrier at an Interstate 95 construction site Monday, killing a highway engineer. The force of the crash pushed the concrete barrier into a piece of road equipment, crushing the engineer, Riley Patterson. Patterson had been using a core-drilling machine to bore a sample hole in the concrete roadbed when the accident occurred.
>
> He was pronounced dead at the scene. Jonathan Martin, a worker at the site, said he saw the truck crash through the barrier but could not warn Patterson because of the noise of the drilling machine.

BACKGROUND: TOO MUCH, TOO SOON

Avoid devoting the entire second paragraph to background information. The second paragraph in the following story is dull because it emphasizes routine, insignificant details:

> Local Red Cross officials expressed alarm Wednesday that blood supplies are dangerously low prior to the beginning of the long holiday weekend.
>
> Nancy Cross, executive director of the Broward County Chapter of the American Red Cross, said the Red Cross strives to maintain an adequate blood supply for emergency situations. "The role of the Red Cross since it was founded is to help people during times of need," she said.

The story shifts from the news—the lack of adequate blood supplies—to the organization's purpose. Yet that purpose has not changed since the Red Cross was established. Thus, the second paragraph says nothing new, nothing likely to retain interest in the story. Fortunately, the problem is easy to correct:

> Local Red Cross officials expressed alarm Wednesday that blood supplies are dangerously low heading into the long holiday weekend.
>
> Restocking those supplies will require a 50 percent increase in blood donations over the next three days, said Nancy Cross, executive director of the Broward County Chapter of the American Red Cross.
>
> "Holiday periods are often a problem because people are traveling or have other plans and don't think about the need for blood," Cross said. "But the holiday period is also a busy time for emergency rooms and trauma centers, which increases the demand for blood."

The revised second and third paragraphs describe the solution to the blood supply problem and explain the reasons for the issue—details central to the story, not minor or unnecessary ones.

Bruce DeSilva, formerly of AP, says that endings must tell people the story is over, nail the central point, and resonate. He says, "The very best endings . . . surprise you a little. There's a kind of twist to them that's unexpected."

Ending the Story

The term "kicker" can have two meanings: It can refer to an additional line set above the main head of a story that helps draw attention or to the ending of the story. Ending the story well is important because it helps to nail down the central point and can leave a lasting impression in people's minds. Sometimes the kicker, in the latter sense of the word, is just as important as the lead.

"Want to write well? Open with a punch, close with a kick." This advice from Matthew Stibbe, freelance journalist and CEO of Articulate and Turbine, serves journalists well. By default, many writers will use a dramatic quote to end the story. While this can be an effective kicker, there are other ways to end a story that rely on the reporter's skills of observation and creativity to tell the audience the story is over. Waiting until the end to use a dramatic quote can often diminish its power. It may be better to use an anecdote that ties into the story's lead, describe a scene as a wrap-up, or focus on a detail, such as a statistic, that is tied to the central point.

Here are the first couple of paragraphs from a story in the Philadelphia Inquirer about research that led to the discovery of freshwater mussels—which scientists had long thought extinct—in the Delaware River:

> If not for the heat of a summer day, one of the major biological finds in the Delaware River in recent years might not have occurred.
>
> It was June and researchers were scouring the banks and shallows of the river between Trenton and Philadelphia for evidence of freshwater mussels, important water-filtering organisms that are becoming increasingly hard to find in the region's streams.

The story continues to describe how one researcher, Danielle Kreeger, became hot sitting in her boat and decided to go for a swim; she discovered the mussels while snorkeling along the bottom of the river. Other subsequent paragraphs describe the scientists' reactions and explain the mussels' benefits to the ecology of the river. The last two paragraphs form the kicker, tying the story to the central point:

> If subsequent research shows that the newly discovered mussel beds are large enough, Kreeger and others think they just might be the ones responsible for cleaning up this stretch of the river.
>
> She hopes to be back out in the water come summer.

Notice that the second paragraph builds on the lead and adds detail to the central point it introduced. The last two paragraphs of the 45-paragraph story mention a detail about the mussels being the reason for the health of the river and the need to continue the research.

This story from the St. Louis Post-Dispatch reports on efforts to deal with financial problems at the city's science center:

> The St. Louis Science Center will slash $600,000 in expenses this year and hopes to cut $1.5 million more next year in an effort to tighten spending, Interim President Philip Needleman said Tuesday.
>
> The announcement comes one week after the science center's board of commissioners approved a restructuring plan that reduces the number of vice presidents to four from nine. The board also expanded its oversight of executive pay and six-figure spending.

The second paragraph adds a chronological detail to the board's actions that explains the central point of the rest of the story—the board's efforts to trim costs to make the center more efficient and able to maintain its programs. In the story, the writer addresses criticisms from the board and others that executive pay was too high. The story ends with a quote kicker from one of the board members:

> Another board member, real estate broker Jerome Glick, said during the meeting, "I think they got the message."

The following story from The New York Times about a decline in Brazil's oil production and the dire consequences for the country begins with a summary assessment of the problem and continues with details about the dilemma. The last paragraph, the kicker, invokes a warning of what the future holds for the country.

> RIO DE JANEIRO—Brazil's oil production is falling, casting doubt on what was supposed to be an oil bonanza. Imports of gasoline are rising rapidly, exposing the country to the whims of global energy markets. Even the nation's ethanol industry, once envied as a model of renewable energy, has had to import ethanol from the United States.
>
> Half a decade has passed since Brazilians celebrated the discovery of huge amounts of oil in deep-sea fields by the national oil company, Petrobras, triumphantly positioning the country to surge into the top ranks of global producers. But now another kind of energy shock is unfolding: the colossal company, long known for its might, is losing the race to keep up with the nation's growing energy demands.

The kicker of the 27-paragraph story ties into the central point and leaves the reader with a dire prediction:

> José Carlos Cosenza, a Petrobras executive, has warned that Brazil may need to import large amounts of fuel for almost another decade. Moreover, gasoline demand is expected to climb even higher as Brazilians buy more cars.

Complex Stories

Stories that contain several major subtopics may be too complex to summarize in a brief lead. The U.S. Supreme Court, when it is in session, may in one day take action in several cases. Two or three may be important, but most news outlets report them all in a single story to save space and time. Because reporters can mention only the one or two most significant actions in their leads, they often summarize the remaining ones in the second, and sometimes the third, paragraphs of their stories.

After summarizing all the major actions, reporters discuss each in more detail, starting with the most important. By mentioning the cases in their stories' opening paragraphs, journalists alert the audience to their entire contents. People interested in the second or third case immediately learn that it will be discussed later in the story. If the lead and following paragraphs mention only the most important action, people might mistakenly assume that the entire story concerns that one case. Many might stop reading before reaching the story's account of other cases that might be of greater interest to them.

The following story begins with the Supreme Court's newest action and, in subsequent paragraphs, summarizes others taken the same day:

> WASHINGTON—The Supreme Court Monday refused to overturn a ban on the private possession of machine guns. A National Rifle Association lawyer called it "the first ban on firearms possession by law-abiding citizens in American history."
>
> In a defeat for the NRA, the justices refused to hear a Georgia gun manufacturer's argument that the Second Amendment "right of the people to keep and bear arms" allows him to make or possess a fully automatic weapon.
>
> The Court also decided cases involving anti-abortion protests, the sanctuary movement, libel and local regulation.
>
> NRA lobbyist Jack Lenzi said his organization was "disappointed but not surprised." He said the federal ban is "an infringement on the rights" of about 100,000 Americans who collect automatic weapons.
>
> Gun control and law enforcement groups told the high court that the NRA's argument would permit private persons to have "bazookas, hand grenades, Stinger missiles and any other weapon of mass destruction. . . . The public safety implications of such a position are truly staggering."
>
> In other matters, the court:
> - Refused to lift limits on demonstrations by opponents of abortions at a Dayton, Ohio, abortion clinic and a ban on protests by the opponents at the homes of the clinic's staff and patients.
> - Left intact the criminal convictions of eight sanctuary movement members who helped Central American aliens smuggled into this country.
> - Heard arguments in a libel case in which a psychologist says a New Yorker magazine staff writer made up quotes attributed to him.
> - Agreed to decide whether communities may regulate the use of pesticides or whether such local regulations are pre-empted by federal law.

Journalists often use lists in news stories that involve several ideas, subtopics or examples. If all the ideas or examples are important, reporters may begin a news story by summarizing one or two main points, adding a brief transition and presenting the other ideas or examples in a simple, orderly list. They can discuss each point in greater detail later in the story. The initial summary may contain all the essential information about a topic; in that case, it need not be mentioned again.

Each item in a list must be in parallel form. If one item is an incomplete sentence that begins with a verb, the rest must have the same structure, as in the following example:

> The governor said he wants to raise the state's sales tax and to increase state spending on education.
>
> He told the National Education Association he would use the money to
>
> - Raise teachers' salaries.
> - Test new teachers to assess their competence.
> - Place more emphasis on English, science and math.
> - Reduce the number of students in each class.
> - Give schools more money to educate gifted students.

Reporters also use lists to summarize less important details placed at the end of news stories. Lists are particularly useful when the details are minor and concern several diverse topics that would be difficult to organize in any other manner. Some newspapers number each item in a list; others mark each item with a dash, bullet, asterisk, check mark or some other typographical symbol.

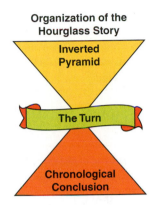

Figure 9.3 The Hourglass Style The hourglass style begins with a summary lead and inverted pyramid and then turns into a sequence of events.

The Hourglass Style

Roy Peter Clark, senior scholar at the Poynter Institute, found that the inverted pyramid often forced writers to tell their stories in unnatural ways. It also homogenized the news, making stories about bank robberies and congressional debates sound similar. At the same time, writers who experimented with narrative structures for their stories often lost sight of the news. The most important and newsworthy information might be buried so far down that frustrated audiences never found it. Clark offered the hourglass style (Figure 9.3) as one that combines the strengths of the inverted pyramid and the narrative format (discussed later in the chapter).

The hourglass story has three parts: an inverted pyramid top that summarizes the most newsworthy information, a turn (or pivot)

Journalists Adam Nossiter, Aurelien Breeden and Katrin Bennhold used the hourglass style for their story on the Paris terrorist attacks.

paragraph and a narrative. The inverted pyramid top, which may be only three to five paragraphs, gives the audience the most newsworthy information quickly. The narrative allows the writer to develop the story in depth, using the storytelling power of chronology. The key, Clark says, is the turn, which makes the transition between the two formats.

Here's an excerpt from a 15-paragraph Washington Post sports story illustrating the hourglass style:

The hourglass style of story can begin with a standard summary lead or an alternative lead, such as an ironic, suspenseful, shocker or question lead.

The Washington Capitals couldn't finish any of their scoring chances through the first 40 minutes against Carolina on Friday night and entered the third period trailing by one goal. One might think they had the Hurricanes right where they wanted them.

The beginning of the story is written in standard inverted-pyramid style. It continues for several more paragraphs, giving more detail about the Capitals' winning streak; the play of certain players in the game, especially Holtby and Carolina goalie Cam Ward; and the coaching that helped the Capitals win.

Third-period tallies by Alex Ovechkin and Matt Hendricks along with a 40-save outing by rookie goaltender Braden Holtby propelled the Capitals past the Hurricanes, 2-1, at Verizon Center, giving Washington its longest winning streak of the season at seven. Six of those wins, and nine of the team's last 20 wins overall, have been decided by one goal.

The close contests have become a calling card for the team that now finds itself with 88 points and a three-point lead over Boston for second place in the Eastern Conference.

(The story continues for another five paragraphs describing the game and win streak before reaching the transitional paragraph.)

Following the inverted pyramid that provides readers with basic facts regarding the story, the writer provides a turn to let the reader know that the story is changing direction.

Carolina's advantage wouldn't even last a minute into the third as Ovechkin, after a nice drop pass from Marcus Johannsson, let a wrister fly that beat Ward blocker side to tie the contest at 1 just 47 seconds into the final frame.

Although the Capitals showed more energy after tying the game, the Hurricanes continued to pepper Holtby with 16 shots in the third period. One shot that the Washington netminder wouldn't be required to stop, however, was a shot by Carolina's Tim Gleason in the waning seconds of a Hurricanes' power play. Hendricks made one of the Capitals' 26 blocks on Gleason's attempt and the puck jumped out to center ice, where Jason Arnott picked it up as he came out of the penalty box.

Arnott raced down the ice on a breakaway. Ward made a stellar stop on the initial shot but Hendricks, trailing his teammate, was able to send the rebound into the net to give Washington a 2-1 lead.

The second part of the story provides more complete facts in a sequential or chronological order. The story on the Capitals' game continued for several more paragraphs, sequentially listing the facts in the pivotal third period, and ended with a quote.

(The story continues for three more paragraphs before ending with a quote from then Coach Bruce Boudreau.)

"I think they carried the play to us. They were beating us to the puck. We made the plays in the third period that you had to make to win, that was it."

The first seven paragraphs tell the story in traditional inverted pyramid fashion, reporting the newsworthy facts that the Washington Capitals won the game and continued their winning streak. The eighth paragraph is the turn: It tells the reader how the momentum of the game shifted in the third period. The next paragraph (not included here) begins to sequentially tell the rest of the story in a more narrative style, using quotations, details and anecdotes to enhance the details.

The hourglass style will not work for all stories, as Clark admits. For stories that have no meaningful chronology, such as an account of a city council meeting in which topics are discussed in no particular order, the hourglass style is useless. But for stories about many newsworthy events—sports contests, criminal investigations, natural disasters and political campaigns—the hourglass can be an effective way of organizing information.

The Focus Style

The Wall Street Journal's front-page feature stories usually employ the focus style, which the newspaper has used for years. Many other newspapers and their reporters have adopted the focus style as well. Like the hourglass style, this method tries to incorporate storytelling techniques in news writing. But unlike the hourglass, the focus story begins with a lead that focuses on a specific individual, situation or anecdote and uses it to illustrate a larger problem.

The focus story has four parts. The first is the lead; unlike the lead for an inverted pyramid story, it may run three or more paragraphs. Also unlike the hard-news lead, the focus lead describes a person, place, situation or event that may not be newsworthy by itself but exemplifies a larger problem that is newsworthy.

The second part of the focus story is a nut graph—which can actually be two or three paragraphs—stating the central point of the story and how the lead illustrates that point. The third part is the body, which develops the central point in detail. The final part is a one-, two- or three-paragraph close kicker that concludes the story. The kicker usually relates to the person, place or situation described in the lead.

The following excerpt from a story in the Philadelphia Inquirer shows some elements of a focus story:

> Awake at 4 a.m., Rodney Walker dressed for a bitter-cold morning and scrambled to be first in line at Feast of Justice, the free food cupboard inside St. John's Evangelical Lutheran Church in the Lower Northeast.
>
> Exhausted by the stress of needing handouts to feed his family, the 57-year-old part-time security guard set his cell phone to chirp every hour so he wouldn't fall into a deep sleep in line. By the time the doors opened at 9 on a recent day, more than 150 unemployed, retired, or working-poor residents of the brick rowhouse neighborhoods near the church were assembled behind him, enveloped in clouds of frozen breath.
>
> To be sure, there are much poorer parts of Philadelphia. Average household income here is about $50,000. In Fairhill, Philadelphia's poorest section, about five miles southwest, average income is just under $18,000.

The focus style begins with a focus lead, an anecdote of one to several paragraphs that highlights someone involved in the story. That person's experiences are used to introduce the story.

The beginning of the story is often very descriptive in order to give a general impression of what the story is about and dramatically highlights the experiences of the person in the focus lead.

The nut graph of the story is used to create a transition from the focus lead into the body. The latter then adds details about the subject of the story.

But the Oxford Circle/Castor-Tacony/Wissinoming-Mayfair swath of the Lower Northeast, formerly one of the city's most stable sections, had the greatest increase in the percentage of people living in poverty over the last decade—up a whopping 110 percent since 1999, according to U.S. Census Bureau data released in December.

The first paragraphs of the story describe the focus, the plight of the poor in a section of Philadelphia. The writer introduces Rodney Walker and describes his life and his struggle to provide for his family. Several paragraphs into the story the writer then provides the nut graph—explaining in detail the story's central point, the growing level of poverty in Philadelphia. Following paragraphs expand on the nut graph, providing much more detail.

The body of the story continues for another 33 paragraphs, weaving Walker briefly into the story in some parts but mainly focusing on the causes of poverty in the city and what volunteer organizations are trying to do to help. In those paragraphs, the reporter also writes about the neighborhood's changing demographics, the work by city officials to address the problems and the lack of economic and employment opportunities in the area.

The last three paragraphs of the story provide the kicker—tying the end of the story back to the beginning and providing a sense of conclusion to the story:

Julie Zaebst, policy-center manager for the 10-year-old Greater Philadelphia Coalition Against Hunger, said the changes were particularly hard on longtime residents in proud neighborhoods.

"We are seeing more people unemployed over the long term, and the consequences of that on family finances. Primary breadwinners are forced to take jobs that just don't support their families at the level they need to. More and more folks who haven't sought [food cupboard] assistance in the past are needing it now," she said.

The kicker is used to conclude the story. It ties the body of the story back into the beginning and sometimes the person who was the subject of the focus lead.

"It's an explosion of need," she said, in an area still better off than much of the city.

The success of the focus story depends on the selection of the lead. Some beginners start their stories with interesting anecdotes or descriptions that have little or no connection to the central point. Without this connection, the audience is likely to be confused and frustrated.

The focus style also has flexibility. The body of the story can be developed in any number of ways. If the story has several subtopics, they can be arranged in descending order of importance. Or if the material lends itself to a narrative structure, the information can be arranged chronologically.

The Narrative Style

A narrative has two components: a story and a storyteller. A storyteller writes as a playwright or novelist would, depicting people interacting with other people and within their surroundings. To write in the narrative style, a reporter must find people who are crucial to the story and record their actions. This technique requires more than just interviewing sources, recording quotes and reporting numbers. It requires observation.

Observation does not mean reporters are free to interject their opinions into a story. Instead, journalists observe people, places and events important to a story and describe them in vivid detail. Through those particulars, the audience gets a better sense of what is occurring. But to paint a picture with words, reporters must be specific. Notice the difference between the following sentences:

> Students are angry about the board of trustees' decision.

> Students gathered in the administration building lobby waving signs protesting the board of trustees' decision.

The first sentence presents an opinion. Without using attribution it says the students are angry at the board's decision. The reader does not know whether the writer is reporting a fact or his or her opinion. The second sentence, however, shows the student's negative behavior in response to the board's decision.

The narrative approach allows reporters to be more creative. Reporters can describe the drama—even if it is not high drama—at a school board meeting, for example. What happened? What did they see? Were people shouting? Were people laughing? Did the participants exchange views? Journalists cannot answer these questions and others unless they take extensive notes.

Longtime writing coach Don Fry describes the style this way:

> Narrative writing requires narrative thinking, narrative reporting and narrative forms.

> Narrative thinking means seeing the world in terms of people doing things, not as piles of disparate facts. Actions connect to one another to create meaning, mostly based on human motives. The best journalistic storytellers let their curiosity lead them into stories, because they want to find out why real people do things.

A story written in narrative style can still lead with the news—the most important part of the story—but then quickly switch to using chronology, flashbacks, dialogue and other storytelling techniques. Or it can employ a strictly chronological organization, ending with the most recent (and perhaps most newsworthy) information. Generally, such stories have a beginning, middle and end, each of relatively equal importance. It is more difficult to cut the final paragraphs of narrative stories than those of stories written in the inverted-pyramid style.

The following story about railroading in Pennsylvania by Harrisburg Patriot-News writer Ford Turner illustrates the narrative style:

> The railroad engine looks like a sleeping blue-and-white giant, resting on the tracks in the half-light of a cloudy dawn.

Rolling Stone and other magazines, such as Esquire and The New Yorker, are well known for the narrative style of their articles.

It dwarfs John Rudy as he climbs aboard.

On the metal catwalk that clings to its side, Rudy swings open a door and leans into the dark interior cavity filled by the huge, silent motor.

In a moment, the 1,500-horsepower engine shudders to life. It puts out a wall of grinding, rumbling diesel sound, and throbs with energy as Rudy walks to the cab.

Another day on the railroad has begun.

The raw mechanical might of engines mesmerized Rudy 50 years ago, when he was a little boy growing up in Enola, across the street from one of the biggest railroad yards in the nation. That same might shaped his career in railroading, which has spanned 30 years.

It was the same way for generations of boys and men in central Pennsylvania, and particularly around Enola. A childhood fascination with smoke-belching engines, followed by a career in one of the region's formative industries, one where long hours and danger often were part of the job.

A key rail state

Rudy, 57, is an engineer for Norfolk Southern.

He still recalls his childhood days of watching, awestruck, the powerful engines and long lines of freight cars.

But railroading was ingrained in his family even before he was born. Two uncles, a grandfather and two great-grandfathers were career railroad men.

Their triumphs and frustrations mirrored the rise and decline of the industry and the Enola Yards, whose massive spread of tracks, trains and equipment remains a riveting image of the mid-state's blue collar history.

The yards formally opened in 1905 on 316 acres along the Susquehanna River, where more than 50 tracks ran side by side. Seven major freight routes converged there. Cars were sorted and assigned to trains bound for places such as Buffalo, Detroit, Chicago, and St. Louis.

The geography of the maturing nation made Harrisburg a natural transportation center. About 8,000 people worked on railroad jobs in and around Harrisburg—including the Enola Yards—in the industry's heyday from 1910 to 1930, according to mid-state rail historian Daniel Cupper.

The Enola Yards was fantastically busy. With all its tracks, nearly 9,700 railroad cars could be accommodated at one time, and it once handled 20,661 cars in a single day.

A dangerous job

Bill Rudy, John's uncle, still remembers the black snow.

That's what the feathery granules seemed like when they wafted down after being shot skyward by steam engines in the Enola Yards. Bill Rudy, now 81, grew up in West Fairview.

Seventy years ago, he and his grade school buddies loved the engines. They'd go out on a plank bridge above the Enola tracks just to be close to the blasts of smoke and steam.

The grimy fallout, though, wasn't popular with neighborhood women who were doing laundry. It would stick to clothes drying on clotheslines.

"They would have black stuff all over the clothes, and it would really make them mad," he said. Bill Rudy quit school in the ninth grade. It was the middle of the Depression. He worked for a plumber for a time, then went to work at 45 cents an hour for Pennsylvania Railroad, where his father had been a machinist. "It was a dangerous place," he said.

His father's stepfather had been scalded to death by steam from an engine.

At work, Bill Rudy once saw a brakeman get thrown into the air when two boxcars collided and land on the couplers between cars, breaking some ribs. He once saw a man near the tracks who had just lost a leg beneath a train. Another day, the side of a train car fell on a man in the Enola Yards' steel shop, killing him.

Bill Rudy kept working for "Pennsy" and its successors, though, and it became a career. He was a mechanic, and over his 40 years he repaired steam, electric and diesel engines.

He retired in 1980.

"It was rough," he said. "If I ever had my life to live over again, I'd hunt something different than the railroad . . . I did it because it was a living."

An industry in decline

The great hum of railroad activity that reached its zenith in central Pennsylvania during World War II began to decline soon afterward.

One factor was Pennsylvania Railroad's 1952 decision to spend $34 million upgrading the Conway Yard near Pittsburgh. After that, Conway became Pennsy's major east-west freight yard.

Another factor was heavy government regulation. For years, it sapped railroad profits while competition in the trucking industry benefited from government spending on highways.

As profits dried up, ownership changes occurred.

Pennsylvania Railroad, via a merger, became part of Penn Central. Then, bankrupt, Penn Central was wrapped into the government-supported Consolidated Rail Corp., or Conrail. Later, Norfolk Southern took over a portion of Conrail, including most of the former Pennsylvania Railroad.

A kid's fascination

As a kid growing up in Enola, John Rudy was just as fascinated by the Enola Yards as his uncle had been decades earlier.

He'd watch the engines blasting steam and smoke.

"I couldn't wait to see the dirt and the cinders come flying out . . . They made coal dirt so thick you could put your hand up and catch it," he said.

He and his buddies roamed about Enola. There were livestock pens, where pigs and cattle were fed during breaks in their journeys to slaughter houses, and John and his friends poked the animals with sticks just for something to do.

John became a tool and die maker. In 1972, at the age of 27, he was operating a Mobil service station in Lower Paxton Township, and having some success.

But he heard that the Penn Central Railroad had a job opening that might fit him. Because of damage caused by the [Hurricane] Agnes flood and a rash of retirements of men hired in the war year of 1941, the railroad needed people. John applied.

"I always wanted to be on the railroad," he said.

Full time, and then some

He makes $52,000 a year now. He has daytime, weekday hours, assigned to a "yard job" in York where he drives engines around a small Norfolk Southern yard, grabbing a car here and two cars there to put together trains.

In past years, he made even more money. But he worked 65, 75, or even 85 hours some weeks.

"Twenty-four hours a day, you are on call. Seven days a week," he said. ". . . The freight does have to move, and you have to be responsible enough to say, 'Yeah, I'll be there to do it.'"

The railroads, he said, had a penchant for hiring men whose fathers or uncles had been in the business because those men would know what they were getting into.

He said, "I would classify it as a hard, good life."

Notice how the writer has used quotations, dialogue and description to give readers a sense of working on the railroad and of each source's distinctive personality. The details easily bring images to the reader's mind. One can imagine the train's engine "shuddering to life," or the Rudys as youngsters "mesmerized by the smoke and steam." Notice, too, the length of the story. Stories using the narrative style tend to be longer, yet the rich detail and concrete imagery make them easier to read than many shorter, straight news stories.

Narrative style can be a refreshing change from the inverted pyramid, but it is not appropriate for all stories. Stories about breaking news events, speeches or most government meetings, for instance, often make more sense to readers when told in traditional inverted-pyramid fashion. Narrative touches, such as dialogue and colorful descriptions, can make any story more readable, however. Regardless of the occasion, the success of a narrative story depends on the depth of the reporting. A writer who has not attentively gathered details and quotations will have difficulty constructing a narrative story.

Using Transitions

Transitions help stories move from one fact to the next in a smooth, logical order. Recall from the train analogy we used at the beginning of the chapter that the transitions are the couplings that hold the cars together. Reporters introduce ideas by relating them to others reported earlier in a story. Often, the natural progression of thought, or sequence of facts and action, is adequate. Alternatively, journalists may repeat a key name or pronoun:

> Richard Nolles, editor of the Weekly Outlook, said the newspaper tries to report the truth even when its readers do not want to hear it.

> "A newspaper that reports only what its readers want to hear is dodging its moral obligations," Nolles said.

> In a speech Wednesday, Nolles added that many readers want to avoid unpleasant news, and threaten to cancel their subscriptions when he reports it.

> "But if a problem exists, they need to know about it so they can correct it," he said. "Ignorant citizens can't make wise decisions."

In the example, the repetition of the words "Nolles," "newspaper" and "readers" and the use of the pronouns "they" and "their" make it easier for readers to follow the progression of thought.

Other transitional devices include words that can indicate time, addition, causation, comparison or contrast. Word phrases, sentences and questions also can serve as transitional devices.

Explain the Unfamiliar

Reporters should avoid words that are not used in everyday conversation. When an unfamiliar word is necessary, journalists must immediately define it. Stories that fail to explain unfamiliar terms may annoy as well as puzzle the audience. A story about a 19-year-old Olympic skater who collapsed and died before a practice session at the University of Texas reported that she died of clinical terminal cardiac arrhythmia. The journalist placed the term in quotation marks but failed to define it. Many people would be interested in the death of an Olympic skater and would wonder why an apparently healthy young athlete had died, but the story failed to satisfy their curiosity because it failed to explain the medical term.

Instead of using an unfamiliar term and then defining it, journalists may use only the definition instead:

> She said the school will ∧ ~~have K–6 facilities~~.
> *accept children from kindergarten through the sixth grade*

Journalists can make even the most complicated stories understandable. For example, former (Tucson) Arizona Daily Star environmental reporter Jane Kay wrote about several wells in Arizona contaminated by trichloroethylene. The topic was complex, yet the stories were clear and dramatic. Kay explained that the chemical, also called "TCE," is an industrial degreaser that may cause cancer in humans:

> TCE is a tasteless, odorless, colorless—and very toxic—chemical. It is volatile, meaning that it evaporates quickly, much like common household cleaning fluids.
>
> Only a teaspoon of it poured into 250,000 gallons of water—about the amount used by five people in an entire year—would create a taint slightly beyond the 5 parts per billion suggested as a guideline for safety by the state Department of Health Services.

The wells contaminated by TCE were closed, and government officials assured people their drinking water was safe. But after hundreds of interviews, Kay discovered, "For 10 to 30 years, many South Side Tucson residents unknowingly got minute quantities of TCE almost every time they turned on the tap water." As many as 20,000 people "drank TCE at home, inhaled it in the shower and absorbed it through their skin when they washed the dishes." Apparently as a result of the TCE contamination, residents of Tucson's South Side suffered from an unusual number of serious illnesses, including cancer.

Large numbers also need explaining. For example, few people who read, watch or listen to stories about a city's or the country's budget and deficits would really comprehend the numbers. Reporters can help audiences understand large numbers by converting them into something related to everyday life.

For example, The Washington Post reported that an investment bank offered to pay $20.6 billion to take over RJR Nabisco Inc., a conglomerate that made Oreos, LifeSavers and Camel cigarettes. (The company has since split into R.J. Reynolds Tobacco Co. and Nabisco.) RJR Nabisco rejected the offer, saying it was not big enough. If $20.6 billion cannot buy a cookie company, what is it good for? A Post writer calculated it could, among other things, provide shoes for every American for a year, house two million criminals in prisons for a year, sponsor 80 million destitute children around the world for one year and cover the cost of every movie ticket bought in the United States in the previous four years.

When a sentence must explain several items in a list, the explanation should precede the list, not follow it. If the explanation follows the list, people might fail to grasp the relationship between the items or the significance of the list:

> ∧~~To~~ provide children with better nutrition, better health care and better educational opportunities ~~were the reasons the senator voted for the bill~~.
> *The senator said he voted for the bill to*

The Importance of Examples

Examples make stories more interesting, personalize them and help audience members understand them more easily. A story about a teenager who became an alcoholic and flunked out of college might include examples of the problems she experienced:

> She said school became unimportant, adding: "I can remember staying up all night before my public health final. When I took the test I was smashed. And if that wasn't bad enough, then I ran the entire 10 blocks back to my apartment so I could drink some more. Of course, I flunked public health."

Examples are especially important in stories about abstract issues. Sometimes numbers help put those issues into perspective. A story about the lives of people who drop out of college might include the percentage of students who drop out of college nationally, their reasons for dropping out and what they do afterward: join the military, get married, find a job. In addition to reporting the general trends, a good writer would illustrate the story by describing the lives of two or three dropouts—specific examples of the trend.

Reporters can clarify unfamiliar concepts by comparing them to familiar things. Many people struggle to understand business and finance, and stories of financial fraud can be extraordinarily complex. Paul Krugman, a columnist for The New York Times, used the following analogy to help readers understand how mutual fund managers and major investors were cheating ordinary investors:

> You're selling your house, and your real estate agent claims that he's representing your interests. But he sells the property at less than fair value to a friend, who resells it at a substantial profit, on which the agent receives a kickback. You complain to the county attorney. But he gets big campaign contributions from the agent, so he pays no attention. That, in essence, is the story of the growing mutual fund scandal.

The Use of Description

Descriptions, like quotations, make stories more interesting and help people visualize scenes. But many journalists are reluctant to use descriptive phrases; they summarize whatever they hear but are less likely to describe what they see, feel, taste and smell. For instance, a student who attended a speech by an expert in communications technology handed her instructor a story that said:

> The speaker, John Mollwitz, showed some examples of electronic newspapers and talked about how they fit into the newspaper industry.

The student failed to describe what the electronic newspapers looked like and how they "fit into the newspaper industry." She also neglected to mention that the crowd intermittently applauded Mollwitz, who has developed some profitable electronic newspapers.

When asked to write descriptions, most students rely too heavily on adverbs and adjectives. Nouns and verbs are more effective. They are also less redundant and less opinionated than adverbs and adjectives.

 HOT TIP

Three Ways to Explain the Unfamiliar

Here are three techniques journalists can use to define or explain unfamiliar terms:

1. Place a brief explanation in parentheses:

   The law would ban accessory structures (sheds, pool houses and unattached garages) in new subdivisions.

2. Place the explanation immediately after the unfamiliar name or term, setting it off with a colon, comma or dash:

   Amy and Ralph Hargis of Carlton Drive filed for bankruptcy under Chapter 13, which allows them to repay their creditors in monthly installments over a three-year period.

   About 800 foreign students at the university are on F-1 student visas—which means that they are allowed to stay in the United States only until they complete their degrees.

3. Place the explanation in the next sentence:

   The major banks raised their prime rate to 12.5 percent. The prime rate is the interest rate banks charge their best customers.

Beginning reporters sometimes resort to vague generalities when they try to write descriptions:

She spoke with authority.

She seemed to enjoy talking about her work.

Neither sentence is an actual description. The first fails to explain why the writer concluded that the woman spoke authoritatively. Moreover, what one observer interprets as speaking with authority might seem as overbearing arrogance to another. The second does not specifically describe either the speaker or what she said.

Reporters train themselves to observe and describe specific details, such as descriptions of people's voices, mannerisms, facial expressions, posture, gestures and surroundings. They may also include details about the height, weight, age, clothing, hair, glasses, jewelry and family of the people they write about. For example, a journalist might describe a man's hands by mentioning their size, calluses, nails, smoothness, wrinkles or veins. Avoid generalities and conclusions. In the following examples, the first sentence is vague, but the second is descriptive:

He is a large man.

He is 6 feet tall and weighs 210 pounds.

FROM THE NEWS

Describing the Aftermath of Hurricane Harvey

The following descriptive passage is an excerpt from Manny Fernandez's New York Times story on the destruction of Houston and surrounding areas of Texas by Hurricane Harvey:

ROCKPORT, Tex.—In the days since Hurricane Harvey slammed into his hometown, Colin McBurney has become his own first-responder—a 16-year-old in a backward baseball cap with bare feet, a pistol and a truck. He drove to the houses of his neighbors all weekend, checking on the people no one had heard from.

One friend made the kind of request people make in this bay town of nearly 11,000 whose spirit is equal parts fishing village, millionaire's retreat and working-class country—please get the horse.

Right before sunset Saturday, Mr. McBurney, still in bare feet and beach shorts, tied a piece of rope into a leash and waded into his friend's front yard. She had evacuated, but her horse, Stew, had wandered out of the stable

through the busted fence. Mr. McBurney walked past the blown-down barn, put the leash on Stew and led the horse back to the stable, a barefoot cowboy after the storm.

"We're just going to get through this together," said Mr. McBurney, a student at the storm-damaged Rockport-Fulton High School.

The most powerful hurricane to hit Texas in decades struck land here on Friday, damaging or destroying hundreds of homes, apartments, businesses, churches and government offices and killing at least one resident in a mobile-home fire. Rockport is a piece of rural Texas on the water, sandwiched between Copano Bay and Aransas Bay, and separated from the Gulf of Mexico by thin strips of islands. Not far from its palm-beach-lined waterfront, cattle graze. Not far from its multi-million-dollar mansions, there are trailer parks, water towers and homes with boats in the front and pigs in the back.

Or at least there were.

Butler looked as though he had dressed in a hurry.

Butler's shirt was buttoned halfway, his socks were mismatched, his shoelaces were untied and his hair was not brushed.

Descriptions help the audience see the situation or person through the eyes of the reporter. When describing people, however, journalists should not write anything about a woman that they would not write about a man in the same situation and vice versa. Do not note, "The woman had long slender legs" if you would not write in the same situation, "The man had long slender legs."

The Need to Be Fair

Regardless of how a story is organized, it must be balanced, fair and accurate. Reporters who write about a controversy should present every significant viewpoint fully and fairly. They must exercise particular care when their stories might harm another person's reputation. A reckless or irresponsible charge may destroy an innocent person's reputation, marriage or career.

If a story contains information critical of an individual, that person must have an opportunity to respond. It is not enough to get the person's response after a story has been published and report it in a later story because not everyone who read, watched or heard the original criticism will catch the second story. The New York Times has an unbreakable policy requiring that a person criticized in a news story have an immediate chance to respond. If the person cannot be reached, editors and reporters should consider holding the story. If the story cannot be held, it must describe the efforts made to reach the person and explain that those efforts will be renewed the next day.

When the subject of a negative story is unavailable or refuses to respond, that fact should be mentioned. A brief sentence such as one of the following three options might explain:

Repeated attempts to reach a company employee were unsuccessful.

A vice president at the company declined to comment about the charges.

Company officials did not return phone calls made by reporters.

The Final Step: Edit Your Story

After finishing a story, edit it ruthlessly. Novelist Kurt Vonnegut said, "If a sentence, no matter how excellent, does not illuminate your subject in some new and useful way, scratch it out." Vonnegut also urged writers to have mercy on their readers: "Our audience requires us to be sympathetic and patient teachers, ever willing to simplify and clarify—whereas we would rather soar high above the crowd singing like nightingales."

Good reporters will reread and edit their stories. Lazy ones immediately submit their stories to an editor, thinking their work needs no editing or expecting the editor to correct any mistakes. That attitude ignores the realities of today's newsrooms. Many news organizations have reduced staff, including copy editors. Increasingly, journalists are expected to edit their own copy, particularly if the story is one that will appear online almost immediately. Copy editors have less time nowadays to edit more stories, which increases the possibility that errors will be missed. In such cases, the reporters are the ones who suffer the embarrassment and bear the responsibility. If a poorly written story receives careful editing, the editor may decide it needs extensive changes, perhaps even total rewriting. When that happens, reporters often complain about the changes. Reporters who correct their own errors will develop reputations as good writers and earn better assignments, raises and promotions.

The Writing Coach

How to Find the Right Endings to Stories

BY JOE HIGHT

Reporters sometimes ask this question about their stories: How do you know when you have a good ending? Gary Provost, author of "100 Ways to Improve Your Writing," offers the advice I've heard the most:

> Look at the last sentence and ask yourself, "What does the reader lose if I cross it out?" If the answer is "Nothing" or "I don't know," then cross it out. Do the same thing with the next to last sentence, and so forth. When you get to the sentence that you must have, read it out loud. Is it a good closing sentence? Does it sound final? Is it pleasant to the ear? Does it leave the reader in the mood you intended? If so, you are done. If not, rewrite it so that it does. Then stop writing.

I suggest that you end with a quote or phrase that leaves an impression. Ask yourself, someone who sits near you or an editor if your ending solves a problem, stirs an emotion (for example, it takes the person back to a significant moment in his or her life) or makes a point about an issue. If it did, the ending is appropriate.

So strive for powerful endings, and, if you're an editor, don't automatically whack the ones with that power!

Joe Hight has been editor of the Colorado Springs (Colorado) Gazette and the Oklahoman of Oklahoma City. He is now the owner and president of Best of Books, Inc.

The Reporter's Guide to Writing News Stories

Use the following checklist to evaluate all your stories.

1. Place the most important details in your lead.

2. Throughout the story, emphasize the details most likely to interest and affect your audience.

3. Include details from your observations to create a picture your readers can visualize.

4. In the story's second paragraph, continue to discuss the topic initiated in your lead.

5. Do not leapfrog. If your lead mentions an individual, and your second paragraph begins with a name, provide a transition that makes it clear you mean the same person.

6. Make your sentences clear, concise and to the point. (Avoid passive verbs. Also, use the normal word order of subject, verb, direct object.)

7. Vary your sentence structure.

8. Avoid overloading your sentences.

9. If your story discusses several major subtopics, mention all the major subtopics in your story's opening paragraphs so your audience knows what to expect.

10. If you use a list, make sure each item is in parallel form.

11. Provide transitions to lead your readers from one sentence or paragraph to another smoothly and logically.

12. Make your transitional sentences specific; say something intriguing to sustain interest in the topic.

13. If you use a question as a transition, make it clear, short and simple.

14. Avoid generalities that have to be explained in a later sentence or paragraph. Be specific.

15. Resist the temptation to end your story with a summary, conclusion or opinion.

16. After finishing your story, critically edit and rewrite it.

Review Exercises

1. The Body of a News Story

Section I: Second Paragraphs

Second paragraphs are almost as important as leads. Like leads, second paragraphs must help arouse the public's interest in a topic. Critically evaluate the second paragraphs in the following stories. Judge which of the second paragraphs are most successful in providing a smooth transition from the lead; continuing to discuss the topic summarized in the lead; and emphasizing the news—details that are new, important and interesting. Give each second paragraph a grade from A to F.

1. A Pinkerton courier was robbed at gunpoint and fatally wounded on Tuesday while leaving Merchants Bank with the day's daily transaction records.

   Edwin James, 59, of 826 Bell Drive, was following standard bank procedures and carrying no money.

2. A 41-year-old teacher who fell and broke an ankle while stopping for a cup of coffee on her way to work sued a convenience store Monday.

   The teacher, Tina Alvarez, has worked at Washington Elementary School for 21 years.

3. Two young men are presumed dead after falling off a 30-foot rock formation into the Pacific Ocean at a California park Saturday.

   The men remain unidentified, and their bodies have not been recovered.

4. Police responding to a 911 call about a shooting at 10 p.m. Sunday discovered Ralph Beasley on Bennett Road with a gunshot wound to his head.

   County sheriff's deputies arrived at about the same time in response to a radio request for assistance. An ambulance was already at the scene, as were Fire Department paramedics.

5. A 32-year-old woman who said she smoked marijuana to ease the pain of a rare intestinal disease was charged Tuesday morning with possessing illegal drugs.

   Ruth Howland was stopped at the Municipal Airport after a K-9 dog singled out her suitcase. She and her husband, Terry, were returning from Mexico.

6. Three gunmen who entered a restaurant on Wilson Avenue at 10:30 p.m. Tuesday held four employees and 12 customers at gunpoint while taking more than $3,000 from several cash registers.

   Peggy Deacosti, the restaurant's hostess, was on duty when the robbery occurred.

7. Eileen Guion, 38, a food and beverage coordinator at Walt Disney World for 18 years, died at her home Tuesday of unknown causes.

   Although she was offered many other jobs at restaurants, she never accepted them. She once said, "I've loved working at Disney because I get to work with people from all over the world, and I think that is very neat."

8. Police are searching for a man who attacked a woman outside the Bayside Bar & Grill Thursday night. Terry Smythe, a bartender at the restaurant, said he heard a woman screaming outside the entrance at 9 p.m. Smythe darted to the foyer, where he saw the woman trapped in the entryway. Smythe said it was "kind of like a tug of war," with the assailant trying to pull the woman outside while waitresses tried to pull her inside.

Section II: Transitions

Critically evaluate the following transitions. Which would be most likely to entice you to continue reading the stories? Which provide a smooth, specific, informative and interesting introduction to the next idea? Give each transition a grade from A to F.

1. Other students said they would tell their teachers about cheaters because cheating is not fair to those who take the time to study.

2. But what should happen when a husband and wife disagree about having a baby?

3. A concerned citizen then addressed the commission about the fence.

4. Next, the Task Force presented its plan for preservation and renovation of the downtown.

5. In a flat, emotionless voice, Howard responded that he and Jackson stole a red Mustang convertible on the night of June 3, picked up the two 14-year-old girls and took them to the motel.

6. Gary Hubbard, superintendent of schools, then addressed his concerns about security in the city's schools.

7. Police Chief Barry Kopperud said his department is trying to combat juvenile crime by changing the way officers interact with children.

8. He then discussed prejudice as a problem that plagues society.

9. She also spoke about the different religious celebrations and rituals.

10. Parents who love, care for and respect their children don't raise delinquents, she said.

2. Pro Challenge: Writing Complete News Stories

Write complete news stories based on the following information. Select the story structure that best fits the information in the scenario. Where more than one story structure could be used, write a story using each and compare the results. Be thorough; use most of the information provided. Because much of the material is wordy, awkward and poorly organized, you will have to rewrite it extensively. Correct all errors in your rewrite.

When you finish, you can compare your work to a professional's. Experienced reporters have been asked to write stories for each set of facts, and their work appears in a manual available to your instructor.

1. Your county officials are running out of money. The need for services in the county has increased with the growing population. According to 2010 census data released by the United States Census Bureau, the county population increased more than 18 percent. Revenue for the county declined by more than 31%. The county is growing faster than its ability to generate revenue, county officials said. The county needs a new, larger jail, which could cost 30 million dollars to build. The county also needs to modernize and expand its courthouse, which could cost between $20,000,000 and $30,000,000 as well. The county also needs to expand and modernize its nursing home facilities and roads and bridges in the county are in need of repair. The county library system needs more money as well, according to officials. "The county has been growing so rapidly that it will be unable to supply these services without more revenue. The county needs more income to deal with the unprecedented growth it is experiencing," said Harold Alvarez, who is the county administrator. County commissioners want to increase revenue two ways. They want to institute an impact fee on all new construction—residential, commercial and industrial—in the county. They want to reassess all existing properties—residential, commercial and industrial—that are subject to property taxes. County officials say they want new residents, businesses and industry moving into the county to pay for some of the impact the growth is having on the county, but that current residents should share in the burden as well because they are getting benefits from the growth as well. Six months ago the county hired a consulting firm to investigate the situation. The consultants presented their report last week and county commissioners intend to vote on the recommendations at their meeting next Tuesday at 7 p.m. According to the recommendations, the impact fee to construct a single-family home in the county would be $3,500. Construction of a multi-unit dwelling consisting of three or more units, such as an apartment complex, would have an impact fee of one thousand dollars per unit. Current residential, business and industrial properties that are subject to county property taxes would be reassessed according to their market value. Many residential properties have not been reassessed for more than 20 years. The reassessment could raise property taxes more than 10 to 15 percent for some residents and five to 10 percent for some businesses. Developers object to the idea, saying the proposed fees would raise the price of a new home above the level that many new and current residents could afford. In addition, developers say the increased cost to do business in the county would cause business and industry to look to other counties in the state to locate their facilities. County commissioners plan to issue $500 million in bonds to finance the needed improvements for the county. The impact fee and the reassessment of existing property are expected to generate approximately $38,000,000 a year, which will be used to repay the bonds. County commissioners say their goal

is to keep pace with and perhaps get ahead of the unprecedented growth the county is experiencing. County officials say that without new revenue services that residents have come to expect will have to be curtailed. Roads and bridges will deteriorate. The library system will have to be shut down. The county nursing home facility would have to close because it will not meet state regulations.

2. Accidents occur in your city nearly everyday. One of the accidents listed in the police reports Tuesday morning was a hit-and-run accident. A pedestrian who was walking along the roadway in the 700 block of Meadow Creek Drive was killed. Police said the accident occurred around 11:20 p.m. Monday. The victim was identified as Vivian Hoffmann, who is 67 years of age and lives at 711 Meadow Creek Drive. Hoffman was a clerk at the Quik Shoppe convenience store located four blocks from her home on the corner of Meadow Creek Drive and Gladsen Boulevard. Hoffman was a widow whose husband Gary died five years ago. There were no witnesses to the accident but this morning, three days after the accident, police announced the arrest of a suspect in the case. The suspect is Todd Burnes, 27, of 1502 Matador Drive, Apartment 203. Police Chief Barry Kopperud made the announcement at a press conference this morning. "No one—not one of our officers, not even me—is above the law. Sadly, today, I have to take one of our own into custody because he failed to live up to our motto of to protect and to serve," Kopperude said. Burnes is a police patrol officer with your city's police department and has been with the police department for four years. Police charged Burnes with vehicular manslaughter, fleeing the scene of an accident, failure to report an accident, failure to render assistance and filing a false police report. Burnes was driving a tan unmarked police car when the accident occurred. Kopperud said the investigation is continuing and charges are pending against police detective Marlene Griffin, a 10-year veteran of the police department. Griffin is 32 years of age and lives at 3130 Joyce Drive. Griffin is facing charges of conspiracy, aiding and abetting a crime and filing a false police report. Griffin was the detective who was investigating

the hit-and-run accident that killed Hoffmann. According to the police report, Burnes was responding to a reported car accident and was driving west on Meadow Creek Drive when his police vehicle apparently struck Hoffmann as she walked along the road. There are no sidewalks or streetlights and the road is narrow along the wooded section of Meadow Creek Drive where the accident occurred. Burnes told investigators that he did not see the victim but heard a loud thump. He said he thought he hit a dog or deer or something but did not stop to check because he was hurrying to respond to the accident call. The morning after the accident news organizations reported the death of Hoffmann, Burnes noticed that the front right fender of his patrol car was damaged. He is dating Griffin and told her about the incident. Griffin told Burnes not to say anything until he heard from her. The two later took the patrol car to a secluded, abandoned building lot and drove toward a utility pole, sideswiping the passenger-side fender to hide the damage. She told Burnes to report that the damage occurred as he was responding to the accident, but that he did not think the car was damaged that badly until he checked it the following morning. Burnes filed a false report stating that he had lost control of his vehicle on the way to the accident scene and damaged the car. Police said a resident of the apartment complex where Burnes lives saw the detective and the officer the morning after the hit-and-run accident looking at the fender. The witness said she saw the officers leave and later Burnes returned, but there was more damage to the fender than she noticed before. The witness' report was handed over to the Internal Affairs Division of your city's police department and detectives began to question Burnes about the accident and his report. They found gray wool fibers stuck to the fender of the car. Hoffmann was wearing a gray wool coat at the time of her death. Griffin had reported to her superiors earlier that there were no suspects in the hit-and-run accident.

3. The demand for energy products is growing. Your state has seen a growth in the number of gas wells being drilled. Many of the wells being drilled use

a process called hydraulic fracturing or fracking. The process involves injecting millions of gallons of water, chemicals and sand deep into shale rock beds to fracture, or shatter, the rock and release methane gas that is trapped there. The problem is what to do with the wastewater byproduct of the drilling. The wastewater contains salts and heavy metals that are harmful to humans. Your state's Department of the Environment recently announced that it will conduct a study in an effort to determine the most effective way to dispose of the wastewater. Currently, gas drilling companies treat the wastewater to remove the most harmful byproducts in the wastewater and then dump the treated water into rivers and streams that are the source of drinking water for many residents of your state. State regulators and state legislators are trying to deal with the boom in gas drilling and tighten environmental regulations because of health concerns regarding the wastewater. State environmental officials say the brine that gushes from the wells as wastewater contains carcinogenic chemicals used by the gas drillers in the fracking process, as well as barium, radium and strontium. The wastewater brine is 10 times saltier than seawater and often contains bromides. Bromides can mix with the chlorine used to disinfect public drinking water to form trihalomethanes. High levels of trihalomethanes can cause an increased risk of cancer. State researchers want to determine whether it is better to treat the wastewater and discharge it into streams as is currently done or if the drilling companies should be forced to drill wells thousands of feet deep to dispose of the wastewater. In the past year, drilling companies have released more than 4.5 million gallons of treated wastewater into the state's rivers and streams. Jim Abbott is the director of public information for CleanEnergy Oil and Gas Company, a major driller. He said: "The wastewater from fracking has not caused any serious harm anywhere in the state. The water that is dumped into the state's rivers and streams is treated to remove many of the harmful chemicals and minerals, and it is safely diluted by the streams and rivers we dump it into. We wouldn't do anything that is harmful to the environment because we live in

that environment and our employees live in that environment, too. Treating the wastewater and dumping it into streams is the most cost effective and efficient way to dispose of it. If the state requires CleanEnergy and other gas drillers to dig wells that are thousands of feet deep to dispose of the wastewater, it is going to increase the cost of energy and cost jobs." CleanEnergy Oil and Gas Company is a subsidiary of APEC Corporation, which is a holding company that also is a major stockholder of News Media Company, the media organization that owns your newspaper, as well as the local television station. State Representative Constance P. Wei is spearheading the effort to create stronger regulation of the drilling process. Wei said: "We want to determine the best way to dispose of the wastewater in a safe and cost effective way. No one wants to drive the drilling companies out of business. But we want regulations, sensible regulations, that will set guidelines on how the wastewater should be disposed of and how dirty that wastewater can be when it is disposed of." The study by your state's Department of Energy is expected to cost $3.3 million and take 18 months to complete. Currently the Department of Energy is requiring daily testing of drinking water in cities and towns that get their drinking water from streams that are downstream from drilling wastewater treatment sites. According to Department of Environment records obtained by you, several communities in the state have reported rising levels of salts and heavy metals in their drinking water.

4. Yesterday happened to be "Take Our Daughters to Work Day," a special occasion observed by people all over the United States, including people in your local community as well as people nationwide. No one knows how many people participated nationally or locally, but from accounts you received at least several hundred local parents took the opportunity on this special day to take their daughters to work with them. The purpose of the occasion local sponsors and promoters say was to expose young girls to a variety of career opportunities, some traditionally not pursued by women. One of the persons locally who participated with his 14 year old daughter

was Joseph Murphy, who is 40 years old and lives at 114 Conway Road. Murphy is the director of research at Collins Industries, which specializes in making and selling health care products and medical equipment. Murphy and his daughter, Jennifer, arrived for work at 8 a.m., Murphy's normal starting time. Jennifer observed her dad at work much of the morning, talked to some co-workers, and ate lunch with her dad in the company cafeteria. "Its better than school lunches," Jennifer said. At 2 p.m., Joseph was called in to talk to the director of personnel, who told him he was being fired. Marilyn Quentin, the personnel director, told him that, because of financial problems, the company was eliminating a number of middle managers in the company and his position was one that was being eliminated, that the company no longer needed his services. A total of 8 mid-level managers were being let go effective immediately as a necessary cost cutting measure. Murphy was then escorted back to his office by security officers, given an hour to pack his office, then escorted from the building with his daughter, then in tears. Murphy had worked for the company since graduating from college 18 years ago. He started as a research assistant. He got two promotions during that period of time and eventually was appointed director of research, managing a staff of fourteen researchers and their assistants. The President of the company was called five times by you but has not yet returned your call. "It's not me I worry about," Murphy told you. "It's my daughter. It's not right. They shouldn't have fired me yesterday when I had my daughter there. I can't believe they couldn't have waited one damn day. It was too traumatic for Jennifer, seeing me treated like that, and I think we'll have to get help for her, professional help. It was just so unbelievable, so cruel, that they would do that with my daughter there." All company employees had been sent by the company's Office of Human Resources an email reminder that they were free and encouraged to bring their daughters to work with them for the day. The company will give Murphy three months severance pay and help finding a new job. "The timing of the dismissal of Mr. Murphy was

regrettable," said Quentin. The company has been laying off employees and restructuring itself after disclosing unexpected and mounting financial losses last Summer in the wake of the economic downturn that hit the nation. Murphy's wife, Kathleen, told you that she thinks the family should sue the company for the way the dismissal was handled.

5. Marilyn Picott is a judge in your city. She has served as a judge for eight years after a distinguished career as one of the areas most successful defense attorneys. As a judge, she has a reputation as being a tough, no-nonsense presider over trials. Attorneys who appear late are chastised. Her sentences are tough. She attended a party one night several weeks ago at a daughters home, celebrating the daughters engagement. On the way home, her BMW sport sedan rammed into the back of a Chevrolet Traverse stopped at a stop sign at the intersection of Hanson Road and Wendover Avenue. Police called to the scene cited Picot for failure to have her vehicle under control. Officers at the scene testified today that she appeared unhurt but belligerent and wobbly with the odor of alcohol they smelled emanating from her. They therefore proceeded to administer a roadside sobriety test, which she failed. Today she appeared in court for her trial, since she pleaded not guilty, on a charge of drunken driving, which lasted five hours. She was convicted after the officers testified, and Circuit Court Judge Edward Johnson sentenced her to serve one year on probation, pay $750 in fines and court costs and drive only on business for the duration of her probation. The jury in her case deliberated less than an hour. Prosecutors were hampered because Judge Johnson prohibited them from telling jurors that her blood alcohol content had been measured at 0.21 percent. He made that ruling after the defendant's attorney pointed out to the court that the machine used to measure such blood alcohol levels had not been properly maintained according to its manufacturer's specifications, or at least there were no records showing that it had been properly maintained although such records are supposed to be meticulously kept. Her defense attorney also throughout the trial attacked the credibility of the prosecution witnesses.

After her conviction her defense attorney said an appeal is very likely. As part of her sentence, Picot must attend a victim awareness program. Counselors determined she has no alcohol problem. Picot refused to take all but one field sobriety test, claiming that blindness in one eye would affect her ability to perform successfully. Prosecutors, however, showed a video of Picot during her arrest and called some of her answers slurred and argued that she seemed unable to walk straight or steadily and that she was loud and belligerent, telling her arresting officers that they were "making a big mistake" that they would soon regret. Her defense attorney tried to discredit the accident victims, Samuel and Lucinda Jones of 4851 Edmee Circle, who were in the Chevrolet Traverse when it was struck and who were both injured so they required hospitalization for treatment of their injuries, and who both testified that judge Picot seemed drunk in their opinion from what they saw, smelled, and observed, pointing out that a verdict against the judge would help the Joneses in their civil lawsuit against her, as they are suing her for thousands of dollars as compensation for their pain, suffering, loss of work, and damage to their vehicle in a separate civil suit. Her defense attorney also argued that people at the party said the judge drank only two drinks, both vodka, and that she seemed sober to them as she left.

6. It is a bizarre story. It is a sad story. It involves a wealthy couple in your city. Both were sick, very sick. Police notified by neighbors found their dead bodies this morning. They were in their car, a Cadillac Sedan de Ville, parked in the garage attached to their home at 976 Grand Avenue. The motor was still running and the couple apparently died from asphyxiation brought about by carbon monoxide poisoning. A friend, Sonia Meir, who lives two blocks away at 811 Moor Street who attends church with the couple, found them. Meyer told police that when she got up this morning to get her newspaper off the front porch, she found an envelope containing a letter taped to her front door. The letter was from the couple and asked her to notify the authorities. The note was apparently taped to the door sometime after Meyer went to bed around 11:30 p.m.

last night after watching the 11 p.m. local news cast on television. Also enclosed was a lengthy letter explaining the couple's actions. Samuel and Terest Pinckney had no family, no children, no known relatives still alive. Mrs. Pinkney had an older sister, but she died eight years ago. Their estate is estimated by their attorney to be worth about a total of $10 million, and their will states that they want to leave the entire amount to local charities. The attorney said that $1 million each goes to the Salvation Army, Boy Scouts, Girl Scouts and United Way, $5 million goes to their church, the Faith Assembly of God, and smaller amounts go to other charities in the city. The couple had been married 52 years. Samuel was 78 and his wife, Teresa, was age 79. Both were well educated with college bachelor's degrees, his in business and hers in home economics. In recent months, Samuel had been confined to a wheelchair after suffering a third stroke, which partially paralyzed the left side of his body and made it impossible for him to walk or even go to the bathroom by himself. His wife, Terese, suffered from rheumatoid arthritis and diabetes and was losing her vision so she could no longer read a book or newspaper or magazine. Meyer told you that Mrs. Pinckney was afraid that the state was going to take her driver's license away because of her health problems and she would no longer be able to get around. The Pinkneys needed 24-hour care and, after Samuel's third stroke, hired nurses to help care for them. "We have the means to afford the best doctors, hospitals and around-the-clock home care to the end of our lives, which could be years away, but neither of us wants that kind of life, confined to our house in constant pain," the Pickneys said in the note to Meyer. Identical notes were found in the car with their dead bodies and also on a kitchen table. "It would consume a substantial part of our money, which through our will and through the mission work of our church and other charities is destined to help many young people throughout the world who may one day be able to help many more. We have no immediate family or heirs. In a sense, this legacy represents the final purpose of our lives. It would be a poor use of money to spend it on care for our deteriorating bodies." The Pinckneys made their money through hard work. As a young couple, newly married, they established a bakery, Pinckney's Bakery, worked 12 to 14 hours a day 6 days a week, never on Sundays, gradually over a period of years expanded, eventually employing a total of 74 employees, selling their goods to restaurants and supermarkets throughout the city as well as to individuals who came to their shop at 1012 2nd Avenue where they continued to work, although only about 10 hours a day in their later years, until they retired at the age of 70 at which time they sold the bakery to their employees.

Brock Turner, a 20-year-old swimming champion and former Stanford University student, walked into a Santa Clara, California, courthouse to learn his fate. About two months earlier, he had been convicted of sexual assault, which under state law carries a maximum prison sentence of 14 years. Prosecutors said the circumstances of the assault warranted a stiff sentence. The victim, whom Turner met at a fraternity party but who was not a student, was intoxicated and unconscious during the incident, which occurred behind a trash bin. Witnesses discovered Turner, who was also drunk, lying on top of the partially clothed woman. Furthermore, the court had reports Turner had prior alcohol and drug violations.

But Judge Aaron Persky decided that a much lighter punishment would be appropriate. He sentenced Turner to six months in jail and three years' probation. Persky explained, "A prison sentence would have a severe impact on him. I think he will not be a danger to others." A probation officer had recommended a lenient sentence because Turner had been drunk at the time of the assault. Turner's father, Dan Turner, submitted a long plea for leniency that included this statement: "His life will never be the one that he dreamed about and worked so hard to achieve. That is a steep price to pay for 20 minutes of action out of his 20 plus years of life." This passage, or parts of it, appeared in many of the news stories about the sentencing. To some, it seemed to minimize the injuries inflicted on the victim. The New York Post considered the quotation one of the year's most memorable.

Quotations like the one from Dan Turner can illuminate issues, reveal emotions and heighten the public's understanding of events and the people involved in them. That is why reporters attach so much importance to getting and effectively using quotations.

"Words can be like X-rays if you use them properly—they'll go through anything. You read and you're pierced."

Aldous Huxley, writer

211

Stanford swimmer's dad argues 6-month sentence is too steep for '20 minutes of action'

POSTED 9:32 PM, JUNE 5, 2016, BY STEPHEN CANEY, UPDATED AT 09:44PM, JUNE 5, 2016

'You took away my worth': A sexual assault victim's powerful message to her Stanford attacker

Strong quotations reveal strong emotions, as these two headlines about the sentencing of Brock Turner demonstrate. The first focuses on the emotional reaction of Turner's father and the second on that of Turner's victim.

Quotations

Reporters can incorporate quotations into their stories in one of three ways: direct, indirect or partial. Direct quotations present a source's exact words and, consequently, are placed entirely in quotation marks. Indirect quotations lack quotation marks because reporters use their own words to summarize, or paraphrase, the source's remarks. Partial quotations directly quote key phrases and paraphrase the rest. See Table 10.1 for examples.

When to Use Direct Quotations

Reporters use direct quotations when their sources say something important or controversial or state their ideas in a colorful manner. The best quotations are often short and full of emotion. A story about a herpetologist included this quotation: "I've caught over 1,000 rattlesnakes in Nebraska and I've liked every one. I can't say the same for the people I've met." In 22 words, the writer captured and conveyed to the audience why this man enjoys his work and some insight into his personality.

Direct quotations are so much a part of news stories that reporters and editors may think a story is incomplete without them. But journalists who merely decorate their stories with quotations are not using them effectively. Jack Hart, former managing editor for staff training and development at Portland's The Oregonian, has identified several reasons for using direct quotations:

- To let the sources talk directly to the reader.
- To give the speaker's exact words when you cannot improve on them or match the speaker's wit, rhythm, color or emotion.
- To tie a controversial opinion to the source.
- To provide evidence for a statement.
- To reveal the speaker's character.

TABLE 10.1 Types of Quotations

Direct quotation	Ambrose said, "Journalism students should be dealing with ideas of a social, economic and political nature. There's too much of a trade-school atmosphere in journalism schools today. One spends too much time on minor technical and mechanical things, like learning how to write headlines."
Indirect quotation	Ambrose said journalism students should deal with ideas, not mechanical techniques.
Partial quotation	Ambrose criticized the "trade-school atmosphere" in journalism schools and said students should study ideas, not mechanical techniques.

Archbishop Desmond Tutu, recalling the days when he and others worked to end apartheid in South Africa, told of meeting a nun in California who said she prayed every day for him and for all opponents of segregation. "We're being prayed for in the woods in California at 2 in the morning. What chance does the apartheid government stand?" Tutu asked. His remark satisfies many of Hart's criteria.

The best stories combine quotations and paraphrases for a pleasing effect. Good reporters can usually summarize facts and major ideas more succinctly than their sources, but a story that has only a reporter's voice can be dull. In the following passage, the journalist's description and summary effectively sets up a direct quotation from the source:

> The most important thing women's basketball coach Vance Coleman carries in his briefcase is not a sketch of a new defensive scheme, a game plan for the upcoming opponent or even the phone number of a basketball colleague.
>
> It's a crumpled, yellowed piece of paper with a list full of scratches and redos. It's his list of five life goals. Coleman lists living a long and healthy life, playing the role of a good father and husband and earning a million dollars as his top three goals. The other two, he said, constantly change as he ages.
>
> But the point, Coleman said, is to always have them.
>
> "There is an equation I use that works on the basketball court, on the playing field, in business and in life," Coleman said, "and that is performance equals ability times motivation. You may have all the ability in the world, but with no motivation, you won't accomplish anything. Zero times anything is nothing.
>
> "No matter what you do in life, you have to have goals. And you have to stick to those goals."

Reporters often summarize a major point before offering a direct quotation. The quotation augments the summary with emotion, details or controversy, but it must provide new information. The following excerpt, from a story about a corporate executive's speech to college students, is an example of how a quotation can effectively support a point:

> Gather five people in your life who helped to shape your views, Johnson said. Whether it's a mentor, a parent, a preacher or a friend, he said, advisory board people can provide support and confidence.
>
> "My mom is part of my advisory board. As a person of color, it really wasn't popular to be nonwhite in my elementary school," he said. "My mom had to come to school every day because I was picked on. She'd say: 'Art, you are the best. Always remember that.' She instilled a sense of self-confidence in me that I still have today."

A quotation should not repeat, or echo, facts reported earlier in a story:

> Company officials said they are not worried about the upcoming audit.
>
> "We're not expecting anything to worry about," treasurer Peter VanNeffe said.

Quotations can emphasize a story's dramatic moments, which, because of their importance, should be described in detail and placed near the beginning of a story. Myeshia Johnson, the widow of La David Johnson, a U.S. soldier killed in an ambush while combating terrorists in Niger, said the way President Donald Trump spoke to her in a phone call angered her. "He (Trump) couldn't remember my husband's name. The only way he remembered my husband's name is because he told me he had my husband's report in front of him," she told reporters. That quotation appeared high in many of the news stories reporting on the incident and even in some of the headlines.

When to Use Indirect Quotations

Some sources are more quotable than others, but even colorful ones sometimes say dull things. Reporters may be tempted to use whatever quotations happen to be available, but a weak quotation is worse than none. If a quotation bores or confuses people, many will immediately stop reading, listening or watching. Compare Myeshia Johnson's quotation with these:

> "It's something that's pretty unique here," she said.

> "The positive response was tremendous," Wesely said.

Neither of these quotations is interesting; each should be paraphrased or omitted entirely.

Reporters use indirect quotations when their sources fail to state their ideas effectively. Indirect quotations allow them to rephrase a source's remarks and state them more clearly and concisely. Journalists can also emphasize the source's most significant comments and revise or eliminate ones that are unclear, irrelevant, libelous, pretentious or otherwise unprintable.

Here's a quotation from an FBI statement about a shootout in which an agent was killed. The quotation is wordy and dull; the paraphrase that follows it states the essential point more clearly:

> "Preliminarily, information suggests the agent may have been fatally wounded as a result of the accidental discharge of another agent's weapon during a dynamic arrest situation."

> An FBI statement said the agent might have been killed by a round fired by another agent during the shootout.

Reporters can never justify a weak quotation by responding, "But that's what my source said." They should use their interviewing skill and judgment to elicit and report quotations that are clear, concise, dramatic and interesting. Asking questions that encourage the source to elaborate on her or his ideas or reactions or provide examples or anecdotes often produces good quotations.

Avoid quotations—direct or indirect—that state the obvious or let sources praise themselves:

> "We really want to win this game," coach Riley said. (Does any coach want to lose?)

Lyons called her program a success. "We had a terrific crowd and a particularly good turnout," she said. (Would she be likely to say her program was a flop?)

Extracting material for an indirect quotation can be difficult, especially when the source is unclear or simply incoherent. President Trump's stream-of-consciousness style of speaking produces "word salad," or passages that jump from topic to topic with little logical connection. In one address during his presidential campaign, Trump covered several topics in 90 seconds:

Look, having nuclear—my uncle was a great professor and scientist and engineer, Dr. John Trump at MIT; good genes, very good genes, OK, very smart, the Wharton School of Finance, very good, very smart—you know, if you're a conservative Republican, if I were a liberal, if, like, OK, if I ran as a liberal Democrat, they would say I'm one of the smartest people anywhere in the world—it's true!—but when you're a conservative Republican they try—oh, do they do a number—that's why I always start off: Went to Wharton, was a good student, went there, went there, did this, built a fortune—you know I have to give my like credentials all the time, because we're a little disadvantaged—but you look at the nuclear deal, the thing that really bothers me—it would have been so easy, and it's not as important as these lives are (nuclear is powerful; my uncle explained that to me many, many years ago, the power and that was 35 years ago; he would explain the power of what's going to happen and he was right—who would have thought?), but when you look at what's going on with the four prisoners—now it used to be three, now it's four—but when it was three and even now, I would have said it's all in the messenger; fellas, and it is fellas because, you know, they don't, they haven't figured that the women are smarter right now than the men, so, you know, it's gonna take them about another 150 years—but the Persians are great negotiators, the Iranians are great negotiators, so, and they, they just killed, they just killed us.

Not only is this passage difficult to read, it is difficult to paraphrase what Trump was trying to communicate. This example is an extreme one, and any person who speaks extemporaneously is likely to utter jumbled sentences. The reporter's job is to clarify such sentences by asking the speaker to explain or rephrase his or her ideas.

When to Use Partial Quotations

Sometimes reporters try to get around the problem of weak or confusing quotations by directly quoting only a few words from a sentence. Most partial quotations, however, are awkward, wordy or unnecessary. Sentences that contain several partial quotations are particularly distracting. Usually, the quoted phrases can be turned into indirect constructions, with the quotation marks simply eliminated:

➤ He said the press barons "such as William Randolph Hearst"

created "an amazingly rich variety" of newspapers.

FROM THE NEWS

Defamatory Quotation Marks

Can sloppy use of punctuation make a sentence defamatory? A New York judge said yes.

New York police were investigating the murder of a business executive named Brenhouse. A story about the investigation in the New York Post contained these paragraphs:

> As police delved into his tangled business affairs, several women described as "associated" with Brenhouse were questioned at Hastings Police Headquarters.
>
> Among those questioned were Mrs. W.B. Wildstein who, with her husband, shared the second half of the two-family house in which Brenhouse lived.

Walter and Arlene Wildstein sued the Post, saying the quotation marks around "associated" implied she was having an extramarital affair with Brenhouse. The judge agreed, saying, "The use of quotation marks around the word 'associated' might be found by a jury to indicate that an inverted meaning was intended by the writer and so understood by the average reader of that newspaper in the community, and not its normal or customary meaning."

Journalists also should avoid using orphan quotes, which put quotation marks around an isolated word or two used in an ordinary way. The quotation marks imply the word or phrase is being used in an unusual, sarcastic or ironic way. Such implications are inappropriate for news stories. Similarly, there is no reason to place quotation marks around profanities, slang, clichés or grammatical errors:

➤ He complained that no one "understands" his problem.

➤ She said that having to watch her child die was worse than "hell" could possibly be.

Reporters may use partial quotations to attribute more clearly controversial, important or interesting phrases to a source:

Phil Donahue accused the television critic of "typing with razor blades."

The petition urged the City Council to ban the sale of Penthouse and Playboy magazines "for the sake of our wives and children."

When Sources Seek Quote Approval

Sources often ask that information be kept off the record or on background (the information can be used, but the source cannot be named or quoted in the story). Lately, they have been making a new demand: the opportunity to approve specific quotations that appear in the stories.

Officials in a range of federal agencies have made this demand, as have politicians. When Barack Obama ran for re-election, leaders of his campaign and that of Republican Mitt Romney routinely demanded the right to approve quotations as a condition for any interview. The campaign workers were not objecting to the accuracy of the quotations; they wanted to prevent the publication of statements their opponents might use against them.

News organizations pushed back. The New York Times, the National Journal, the Washington Examiner and some other publications prohibit their writers from allowing sources to approve quotations. Others urge their writers to resist such requests. Reporters confronting such a demand should know their organization's policy. Even if the organization does not forbid such agreements, they should carefully weigh the value of the information they expect to learn from the interview before agreeing. They should also remember that allowing sources to approve or edit quotations drains interview stories of their spontaneity and humanity. The result is a story that portrays the sources and the issues less accurately and completely.

Blending Quotations and Narrative

Every news story must have a central point, and everything in the story must relate to that point. The sources may have spoken about a number of topics, but only some of what they said may bear on the story's central point. Reporters must blend relevant quotations with the narrative to create a coherent, well-focused news story. This blending presents several problems and dilemmas for journalists.

Explaining Quotations

Sometimes reporters use a quotation and then realize the audience needs background information to understand it. In print journalism, they might insert explanatory material in parentheses or tack on the explanation after the attribution. Others might put a large block of background information high in the story, hoping it will give readers the information they need to understand the quotations and new facts reported elsewhere. Neither of these approaches works well.

Lazy writers insert explanatory material in parentheses within the quotation. When reporters pepper their sentences with inserted explanations, the stories become difficult to read. Each bit of parenthetical matter forces readers to pause and absorb additional information before moving on with the rest of the sentence. The occasional use of parentheses to insert brief clarifications may be acceptable, but reporters should paraphrase quotations that need several explanations. If reporters find themselves using parentheses repeatedly, they should consider reorganizing their stories. The following sentence can be rewritten to remove the parentheses:

> "When (head coach Tom) Whitman decides on his starter (at quarterback), the rest of them (the players) will quit squabbling," the athletic director said.

> The football players will quit squabbling when head coach Tom Whitman selects a starting quarterback, the athletic director said.

The next example includes an acceptable use of parentheses:

> Dr. Harold Termid, who performed the operation, said, "The technique dates back before the 20th century, when it was first used by the French to study ruminants (cud-chewing animals)."

Adding the explanatory information after the quotation or attribution is little better than using parentheses. Such backward constructions force readers to complete the sentence before they can figure out what the topic is. Here's an example:

> "We're mobilizing for an economic war with other cities and states," the mayor said of his plan for attracting new businesses to the city.

Instead of using this "said-of" construction, turn the sentence around and quote the speaker indirectly:

> The mayor said his plan for attracting new business amounted to mobilization for an economic war with other cities and states.

Beginning journalists sometimes think they must report their questions so that the audience can understand the source's answers. The news is in the answers, however, not in the questions. Using both is repetitive and dull:

> The president was asked whether he plans to seek a second term, and he responded that he would not announce his decision until winter.

Reporters usually omit the question. If the question provides important context, they incorporate it in the answer:

> The president said he would not announce his decision regarding a second term until winter.

Or

> In response to a question, the president said he would not announce his decision regarding a second term until winter.

To Change or Not to Change Quotations

A source may use words inappropriate for a news story; reporters may be tempted to alter these words to make the quotation usable. Whether writers should ever change a quotation is a matter of debate among journalists. Some accept making minor changes to correct grammatical errors or delete profanity. Most, however, say reporters should never change quotations.

The Associated Press Stylebook says, "Never alter quotations even to correct minor grammatical errors or word usage. Casual minor tongue slips may be removed by using ellipses but even that should be done with extreme caution." The guide also states that if a speaker's words are unclear, seek a clarification or don't use them. The New York Times follows a similar policy: "Readers should be able to assume that every word between quotation marks is what the speaker or writer said. . . . The Times does not 'clean up' quotations."

Some sources are well known for the way they misuse words or create confusing sentences. Cleaning up their quotations would rob stories about them of their color. For example, President George W. Bush is famous for his malapropisms, mispronunciations and fractured syntax. When during his first presidential campaign he mispronounced "subliminal" as "subliminable," many news reports noted the slip. Bush later joked about it by intentionally mispronouncing the word.

Using a source's exact words also eliminates questions about accuracy. Reporters who are uncertain about the source's exact words or who think a statement needs rewriting should use indirect rather than direct quotations. Doctoring a quotation could lead to a mistake that would injure the source's reputation and the journalist's career.

Even those who oppose altering quotations recognize a few instances where changes are necessary. A reporter should paraphrase a quotation if it is so ungrammatical that it becomes difficult to understand:

> "The council and the mayor is giving them corporations too much tax breaks so the load's not fair no more," Andrews said.

Paraphrasing makes the sentence much clearer:

> The council and the mayor have given so many tax breaks to corporations that the tax burden is no longer fairly shared, Andrews said.

Other situations involve the deletion of unnecessary words and profanities (discussed in the next section):

➤ He said, "~~Look, you know I think~~ Nuclear power is safe, absolutely safe."

Reporters may use an ellipsis—three periods—to show where they deleted a word or phrase. An ellipsis that appears at the end of a complete sentence should have four periods. Policies vary from news organization to news organization, and some journalists do not use ellipses in reporting ordinary interviews. Reporters are more likely to use them when quoting formal statements or documents.

Reporters are obliged to present a source's views as faithfully as possible; therefore, they must be certain that they are not removing important context when quoting a source. During his campaign for the Republican presidential nomination, U.S. Sen. Ted Cruz argued against Obama's plan to allow 10,000 refugees from Syria to enter the United States. Cruz said ISIS terrorists were likely to be among the refugees and, to support his view, said Obama's director of national intelligence, James Clapper, agreed with him:

> *There is a reason the director of national intelligence said among those refugees are no doubt a significant number of ISIS terrorists. It would be the height of foolishness to bring in tens of thousands of people including jihadists that are coming here to murder innocent Americans.*

In fact, Clapper said no such thing. He had described the situation in Syria as a major humanitarian crisis that western nations had to address. Then he added,

> *I don't, obviously, put it past the likes of ISIL to infiltrate operatives among these*

Tennis star Serena Williams (right) told Vogue some people may see her game face and think she's mean, whereas they are likely to think of Maria Sharapova as nicer. A British newspaper distorted the quotation and made it appear there was a feud between the two players.

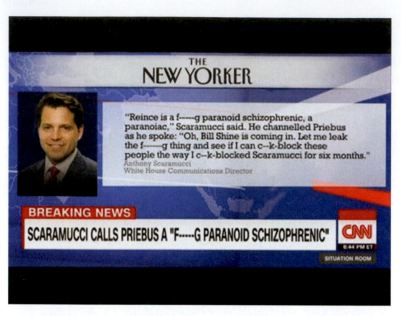

Anthony Scaramucci, who for a brief time was the White House communications director, gave a profanity-laced interview to Ryan Lizza of The New Yorker. The interview made big news, and news organizations had to decide whether to use any of the profanity and how much.

refugees. So that is a huge concern of ours. We do have a pretty aggressive program for those coming to this country, for screening their backgrounds. I'm not as uniformly confident about each European country that is going to be faced with welcoming or allowing refugees into their countries. So this is a huge issue for all kinds of reasons. The security implications are just one small part of it. The economic, the social impacts, are huge.

While Clapper admitted there were security concerns, he stopped far short of saying a significant number of the refugees admitted into the U.S. would be ISIS terrorists.

Deleting Profanities

Reporters usually omit profanities from quotations. Children read, view and listen to news, and some adults find four-letter words offensive. News organizations are becoming more candid, however, and some publish mild profanities that are essential to a story. Casual profanities—those used habitually and unnecessarily by many people—remain forbidden in most newsrooms:

➤ "~~Shit,~~ I wasn't going to try to stop that ~~damned~~ idiot," the witness testified. "He had a knife."

Print and broadcast journalists face a dilemma when a prominent official uses profanity in a public statement. What government officials say is important to the public they serve, but reporting quotations with profanity verbatim may offend many people. During his presidential campaign, Donald Trump often used profanity in his speeches. On one occasion, he said companies that do not like his tax plan can "go fuck themselves." Most news organizations omitted or disguised the profanity. In a video released late in the campaign, Trump talked about grabbing women "by the pussy." Many broadcast news organizations bleeped the last word and many publications avoided using it as well. Democrats responded to Trump in kind. Party Chairman Tom Perez described the Trump administration's proposed budget this way: "They call it a skinny budget, I call it a shitty budget." When CNN reported the story on its web site, it replaced the "i" in "shitty" in the headline with an asterisk, but used the full word in the body of the story.

Editorialization

Avoid unintentional editorials. If worded carelessly, partial quotations, and even the form of attribution used, can express an opinion:

➤ The mayor ~~made it clear that~~ *said* the city cannot afford to give its employees a raise.

The phrase "made it clear" implies that the mayor stated a fact in a convincing manner. Others might regard the statement that the city cannot afford pay raises for employees as an opinion or political posturing.

Connecticut State Police Lt. Paul Vance talks to the media about Sandy Hook Elementary School during a press conference in Newtown, Connecticut. Readers, viewers and listeners have more confidence in news stories when they know whom the information comes from.

Attribution

The Purpose of Attribution

Reporters are not economists or ecologists, detectives or diplomats. Nevertheless, they must write effectively about such things as unemployment, the effects of oil spills on the environment, the search for serial killers and the prospects for peace in the Middle East. To write these stories, reporters rely on experts and insiders for information and ideas. Attribution lets the readers know who the reporter's sources are. Ideally, all direct quotations, opinions, evaluations and secondhand statements of fact should be attributed to specific individuals. This information lets readers draw their own conclusions about the credibility of the story.

Reporters can attribute information to people, documents or publications but not to places or institutions. For example, reporters can quote a hospital official, but not a hospital:

➤   *A* ~~The~~ hospital *spokesperson* said the epidemic had ended.

➤   *The mayor of* Atlanta announced that all city offices would be closed Monday.

Statements That Require Attribution

Reporters need not attribute undisputed facts, such as that World War II ended in 1945, that Boston is in Massachusetts or that three people died in a given accident. Nor must they attribute things they witness. However, they must attribute facts that are not common knowledge, statements about controversial issues, statements of opinion and all direct and indirect quotations. An audience will interpret statements lacking attribution as the reporter's personal opinions rather than as the sources'. Two or three words of attribution are usually adequate:

➤   *Director Sally Malone said the* ~~The~~ Birthing Center is an alternative for pregnant women who prefer more personalized care.

Reporters must attribute statements that praise or condemn any person or organization. The audience should immediately recognize that a story reports what someone else said, not the journalist's or news organization's opinions:

➤   *The House Republican leader said* Congress has wasted time while the problem of unemployment has worsened.

> *The deputy said she was*
> *a*
> ∧Acting in self-defense, ∧~~the deputy~~ *when she* shot the teen three times in the chest.

Statements that imply carelessness, recklessness or culpable conduct can provoke lawsuits. Careful attribution, particularly if the statements come from official sources, reduces the risk of being sued.

Guidelines for the Placement and Frequency of Attribution

Attribution may be placed at the beginning or end of a sentence or at a natural break within it. However, it should never interrupt a thought:

> *I shall*
> ~~"I shall,"~~ Gen. MacArthur said, "∧return."

This form of attribution is acceptable:

> "Some men are killed in a war and some men are wounded," President Kennedy said, "and some men never leave the country. Life is unfair."

Attribution should appear as early as conveniently possible; readers, viewers and listeners should never have to guess who is speaking. Stories written for broadcast usually put the attribution at the beginning of the sentence. In print stories, the attribution should appear near the beginning of quotations of one long sentence or of two or more sentences. It should not be delayed until the end of the second or third sentence:

> "However close we sometimes seem to that dark and final abyss,∧"
> *the president said, "*
> ∧let no man of peace and freedom despair. For he does not stand alone. If we all can persevere, if we can in every land and office look beyond our shores and ambitions, then surely the age will dawn in which the strong are just and the weak secure and the peace pre-served,∧" ~~the president said.~~

For print stories, the attribution should come at the beginning of any quotation—even a short one—when there is a change of speakers. If reporters fail to provide transitions from one speaker to another, readers may not understand who is speaking, particularly when the statements are contradictory:

The newspaper's editor said he no longer will accept advertisements for X-rated movies. He explained: "These movies are worthless. They contribute nothing to society and offend our readers. They're depressing and pornographic."

"Newspapers have no right to pass judgment on matters of taste. If they do, they should also ban the advertisements for other products considered harmful: cigarettes, liquor and pollutants like automobiles," a theater owner responded.

These two paragraphs are confusing. Readers beginning the second paragraph might think the editor is contradicting himself. The writer can avoid the confusion by placing a brief transition at the beginning of the second paragraph, such as the following:

> However, a local theater owner responded, "Newspapers have no right. . . ."

Direct Quotations

A direct quotation should be attributed only once, regardless of the number of sentences it contains:

> ➤ "I'm opposed to any laws that prohibit the sale of pornography," the attorney said. "The restriction of pornography infringes on Americans' First Amendment rights," he said. "I like to picture myself as a good guy defending a sleazy thing," he concluded.

Even a direct quotation that continues for several paragraphs needs attribution only once.

Reporters must avoid "floating" quotations, direct quotations that lack clear attribution to a speaker. Careless writers sometimes name a source in one sentence and then deliver an unattributed quotation in the following sentence or paragraph. The reader must guess whether the quotation comes from the person just named or someone who will be identified later. The uncertainty halts the reader, and several such delays can cause him or her to put down the newspaper or magazine. Clear attribution makes the reader's work easier:

> ➤ Wendy Mitchell, a sociologist, said there is a trend toward vocationalism on college campuses.
>
> "Many students now demand from college not a chance to think," she said, "but a chance to become qualified for some job."

Partial Quotations

On the rare occasions when writers quote part of a sentence, they should separate it from complete sentences that also are being quoted. Combining partial and complete quotations sometimes causes confusing pronoun shifts, which can be avoided by either placing attribution between the partial quotation and the full-sentence quotation or paraphrasing the partial quotation:

> ➤ Ross said he expects to find a job "within a few weeks." He added, "And when I do get a job, the first thing I'm going to buy is a new car."

Or

> ➤ Ross said he expects to find a job "within a few weeks. "And when I do get a job, the first thing I'm going to buy is a new car," he added.

The original passage is confusing because of a shift in pronouns. The first sentence uses the third person, referring to Ross as "he." But in the second sentence, which is the full quotation, Ross refers to himself in the first person. Rewriting the partial quotation eliminates the confusion.

Indirect Quotations

Indirect quotations need more frequent attribution than do direct quotations. Every opinion or unverified fact in an indirect quotation must be attributed. In the following example, the first version is missing attributions; the revised version corrects the problem:

> The police chief insisted that the death penalty must be retained. The death penalty, harsh as it may seem, is designed to protect the lives and rights of law-abiding citizens. Without it, criminals' rights are overly protected. Because of the almost endless mechanisms of the appeal system, it is unlikely that an innocent person would be put to death.

> The police chief insisted that the death penalty must be retained. The death penalty might seem harsh, he said, but it is designed to protect the lives and rights of law-abiding citizens. Without it, criminals' rights are overly protected, he said. Because of the almost endless mechanisms of the appeal system, he said, it is unlikely that an innocent person would be put to death.

Often, every sentence of indirect quotation should have attribution, but writers should avoid inserting phrases that attribute a quotation twice, as in this example:

➤ ~~In making the announcement,~~ the fire chief said arsonists caused 20 percent of the blazes reported in the city last year.

Here are more examples of double attribution, each of which can be replaced by either "said" or "added":

made it clear that	said that he thinks that
further stated that	brought out the idea that
went on to say that	went on to say that in his opinion

With both direct and indirect quotations, writers strive to vary the location of the attribution. Writing becomes dull if every sentence begins "She said" or some variation. Moving the attribution keeps stories interesting. Often the most effective location for attribution is after the first natural pause in the sentence.

Word Choice in Attributing Statements

The verbs used to attribute statements must be accurate and impartial. For straight news stories, they also should be in the past tense. For feature stories, writers may use present tense attribution.

Some form of the verb "to say" best describes how sources speak. For variety, reporters sometimes use such verbs as "comment," "reply," "declare," "assert," "explain," "state," "continue," "point out," "note," "urge," "suggest" and "warn." Each has a more specific meaning than "say" and can be used only when that meaning accurately reflects how the source spoke. "Explain," for instance, means to make something comprehensible or less obscure. Unless the source was discussing a complicated or unclear topic, "explain" would not be an appropriate verb for attribution:

> The city council meeting will begin at 8 p.m., he explained.

This sentence states a fact that needs no explaining. The next sentence clarifies a point of law that may be confusing; therefore, "explained" is acceptable:

> She explained that tort law requires that the injurious consequences of a person's actions be foreseeable before that person can be held liable for damages.

Even worse than using an inappropriate verb for attribution is using no verb at all, as with "according to." Beginning reporters find it tempting to use this phrase, but they should remember that verbs always strengthen sentences.

Identifying Sources

Ideally, every source quoted should be fully identified so that what he or she says is on the record and can be quoted directly and attributed properly. The amount and nature of the identification depends on the type of story and the source's contribution.

For many basic news stories—crimes, fires, business actions or rallies by interest groups—the major sources are public officials, business executives or owners and officers of interest groups. The best way to identify these sources is by name, title and organization:

> The robbers left the store in a dark red 2011 Chevrolet Malibu, police Sgt. Maureen Fonoti said.

> "The purpose of this protest is to demand that the legislature repeal or revise the state's voter identification law," said Robert Watson, the executive director of Voters Unbound.

People being quoted because they witnessed newsworthy events or because their opinions have been sought through an informal poll should be identified by name, age (if the person is willing to reveal it) and address, if they live in the same city where the news is published, or hometown, if they live in another town. A person's occupation may also be relevant:

> Patricia Mulrooney, 39, of 1748 N. Third St. said she first saw the smoke about 3 p.m. and called the fire department.

> Wendell Morgan of Altoona, Kansas, said he had opposed the Affordable Care Act when it was before Congress. But Morgan, a 56-year-old hardware store owner, said he had changed his mind now that he can find an insurance policy that fits his budget.

People increasingly are concerned about their privacy. They may prefer that news organizations not use their home address in a story. In such cases, the reporter can identify people by their neighborhoods.

"In Washington, today, an unidentified source made an unattributable statement which under the agreed ground rules is not to be quoted."

Names alone fail to provide enough information about the sources for a story. Audiences want to know enough about each person quoted to form at least a general picture of who he or she is. This is especially important with people who are quoted in or are the subjects of feature stories or are the subjects of anecdotal leads.

Here are the first few paragraphs from a story about December as a popular time of the year for couples to get engaged:

> Carmen Nunziata loves this time of year.
>
> Every Thanksgiving, she puts up holiday decorations and listens to nothing but Christmas music until the beginning of January. Each room in her house has Christmas flair, even the bathroom, which has a Santa hat hanging from a towel rack.
>
> Grady Smith, her live-in boyfriend, knows how special the holidays are to Nunziata. He also loves the holiday season, and thought it would be the perfect time to propose.
>
> Nunziata and Smith are certainly not the only couple to become engaged during this holiday season. In fact, a trendy new label describes this time of year as "Engagement Season."

Who are Nunziata and Smith? What do they do? How old are they? Where do they live? The story provides none of these details. One might have a different reaction to it if Nunziata and Smith were retirees living in a center for senior citizens than if they were university students getting ready to graduate. A story that fails to identify sources fully is incomplete.

Occasionally, reporters use sources who want their identities concealed. They will speak only on background—sometimes called not-for-attribution—meaning the reporter can quote the source directly but cannot use his or her name. In this case, the journalist must describe the source using phrases such as "a law enforcement officer familiar with the investigation," "a source close to the president" or "a legislator who is participating in the negotiations."

Editors and producers dislike the use of unnamed sources because it diminishes the credibility of the news. Readers, viewers and listeners are skeptical of stories with unnamed sources, in part because of some well-known incidents in which reporters simply made up sources and quotations. Editors at The New York Times, which was the victim of a journalist who manufactured sources, tell their staff that anonymity for sources is a last resort.

If reporters want sources on the record, why do so many stories use anonymous sources? Sometimes sources want to remain anonymous for legitimate reasons. Corporate or government officials who want to blow the whistle on waste, fraud or other illegal or unethical conduct at their workplace may fear retaliation. Many have lost jobs or been demoted because they disclosed truths that made their supervisors uncomfortable.

🔥 HOT TIP

Guidelines for Using Anonymous Sources

On the rare occasions when justification exists for using anonymous sources, news executives tell their reporters to follow guidelines like these:

- Do not use anonymous sources without the approval of your supervising editor or news director.

- Be prepared to disclose the identities of anonymous sources to your editors or news directors and, possibly, to your news organization's lawyer.

- Use anonymous sources only if they provide facts that are essential to the story, not just interesting quotations or opinions. Be sure the source is appropriate for the story and that he or she is in a position to give authoritative information. Even then, information from anonymous sources should be verified.

- Be sure you understand the motives of the anonymous source, such as whether he or she is carrying a grudge or trying to puff a program or an agency. The motives help

Reporters on some beats have to rely on anonymous sources. Bill Hamilton, the New York Times' Washington editor, says people with knowledge about security issues almost never talk on the record. Obtaining information about the National Security Agency or the Central Intelligence Agency has become increasingly difficult as federal officials have tried to stop leaks. Some people who have spoken to reporters have been criminally prosecuted or threatened with prosecution under the Espionage Act. And reporters who cover national security issues have been subpoenaed to reveal their sources' identities. If they refuse to do so, they may be jailed for contempt of court.

you evaluate the reliability of the information.

- Identify sources as specifically as possible without revealing their identities so that the audience can judge their importance and reliability. For example, instead of attributing information to "an informed source" or "a key official," you might attribute it to "an elected city official." This tells readers, viewers or listeners the level of government in which the official works and alerts them to the fact that he or she may have political interests. Never include any misleading information about the identity of a source, even if your motive is to protect him or her.

- Explain in the story why the source does not want to be identified.

- Never allow an anonymous source to attack other individuals or groups. Anonymous attacks risk involving you and your employer in a libel suit and are inherently unfair to the person attacked.

The Writing Coach

Do You Use *Said* Enough?

BY JOE HIGHT

Can you *claim* too much in your stories? Or *explain*? Or *allege*?

It seems less experienced writers want to use every word except *said* when quoting a source in a story.

This can be especially dangerous in crime and courts stories when the verb "claimed" is used but a simple, impartial "said" would be better. Remember, "claimed" calls into question the truthfulness of what was said. It has a negative connotation, however unintended.

Here are a few other words of attribution that could have negative connotations: "acknowledged" (disclosed, perhaps under pressure); "admitted" (implies reluctance); "alleged" (charged or claimed without proof); "conceded" (can mean acknowledged grudgingly or hesitantly).

Then, in feature stories, words such as "explained" are often overused.

In short, stick to "said" or "wrote" as verbs of attribution.

Joe Hight has been editor of the Colorado Springs (Colorado) Gazette and the Oklahoman of Oklahoma City. He is now the owner and president of Best of Books, Inc.

The Reporter's Guide to Quotations and Attribution

Quotations

1. Use quotations sparingly to emphasize a point or change pace, not to tell the story or state facts.

2. Place only the exact words of the source within quotation marks.

3. Use quotations to serve a purpose, such as to reveal the source's character, describe or emphasize a point or present an opinion.

4. Include direct quotations that are clear, concise, relevant and effective.

5. Avoid awkward combinations of partial and direct quotations.

6. Report only the source's answers, not the questions you asked.

7. Eliminate orphan quotations and floating quotations.

8. Make sure the quotations do not repeat facts reported elsewhere in the story.

9. For a one-paragraph quotation that includes two or more sentences, place the quotation marks only at the beginning and end of the entire quotation, not at the beginning and end of each sentence.

10. Capitalize the first letter of all quotations that are full sentences but not of partial quotations.

11. Divide long quotations into shorter paragraphs; place open quotation marks at the beginning of each paragraph, but place close quotation marks at the end of only the final paragraph.

12. Use single quotation marks for quotations that appear within other quotations.

Attribution

1. Attribute all secondhand information, criticisms, statements about controversial issues, opinions and all direct and indirect quotations. (Do not attribute undisputed facts.)

2. Punctuate the attribution properly. Put a comma after an attribution that introduces a one-sentence direct quotation and a colon after an attribution that introduces two or more sentences of direct quotation.

3. Put the attribution at or near the beginning of a long quotation.

4. When including an attribution in the middle of a sentence, place it at a natural break rather than interrupt a thought.

5. Vary sentences and paragraphs so that all do not begin with attribution.

6. Place the attribution outside the quotation marks.

7. Attribute each direct quotation only once.

8. Attribute each separate statement of opinion in indirect quotations.

9. Attribute statements only to people, documents or publications, never to places or institutions.

10. Provide transitions between statements from different sources, particularly when a quotation from one source immediately follows a quotation from a different source.

11. Select the verb of attribution that most accurately describes the source's actual meaning and behavior.

12. Do not use such verbs as "hope," "feel," "believe," "think," "laugh," "cough" and "cry" for attribution.

13. Make the attribution as concise as possible.

Review Exercises

1. Improving Quotations and Attribution

Section I: Avoiding Double Attribution

Rewrite the following sentences, attributing them only once. Correct any other errors.

1. In a report issued Tuesday, the state Department of Environmental Quality said fertilizer runoff from farms was endangering fish populations in 12 percent of the state's rivers and streams.

2. In her speech to the members of the Home Builders Association, Carson added that the demand for new homes and apartments was expected to pick up in 18 months, she said.

3. Professor Heather Wong said the companies that benefitted the most from U.S. defense spending were concentrated in six states, according to her data.

Section II: Correcting Placement Errors

Correct the attribution placement in the following sentences. Correct any other errors.

1. No matter how famous a person has, she said, been, no one can win an election on fame alone.

2. The team should win, the coach said, every game this season.

3. Kopperud said, "Crime is down in this city for two reasons. First, the department has added 30 new patrol officers who have concentrated on high-crime areas. Second, unemployment is down, and the crime rate always declines when more people are working."

Section III: Condensing Wordy Attribution

The attributions in the following sentences are too wordy. How many words can you eliminate? Rewrite the attribution if necessary. Correct any other errors.

1. *Mayor Datoli announced to the council members at the start of her speech that* she will interview 10 candidates for the city comptroller job.

2. School board member Judy Lu *pointed out that in her opinion the district was spending* 20 percent too much on salaries.

3. *Judge Hall added that her experience shaped her belief that* short sentences for nonviolent offenders were more effective than long ones.

4. *Grauman went on to point out how surveys by several local professors demonstrated that* few people were willing to pay more taxes to have more paved roads.

5. Modern corporations waste too much of their investors' money on public relations, *Carson said as he began offering his analysis of the stock market in a speech to the Chamber of Commerce.*

6. Politicians must pay more attention to climate change, *he continued by insisting that listeners realize the need for immediate action*, or the country will face droughts and famine in the near future.

Section IV: Improving Attribution

Correct all the problems and errors in the following sentences.

1. Hendricks said, 'winning this case was the most satisfying of my career. It's saved the county's taxpayers $5 million.

2. Saul Bellow once said "a novel is balanced between a few true impressions and the multitude of false ones that make up most of what we call life.'

3. When Datolli was asked why she had rejected the Fire Department's request for three new fire trucks, she replied 'because we don't want to raise taxes this year."

4. The bank president said the "dollar" and the "euro" were the two currencies that were most likely to suffer because of the "economic policies" of China.

5. "All immigrant groups in the United States, said the FBI director, deserve the same level of respect and legal protection as citizens of this county.' he explained

6. The president spoke to the students telling them that. "The challenge of the next half century is whether we have the wisdom to use our wealth to enrich and elevate our national life.

7. "The basic tenet of black consciousness" said Steve Biko "is that the black man must reject all value

systems that seek to make him a foreigner in the country of his birth".

8. "For several years, winter has been bringing less and less snow." "Meanwhile, summers have been longer and hotter." Said Bonita Nichols, the director of the state Office of Agriculture.

9. 'The enemy of the market.' argued economist John Kenneth Galbraith. 'is not ideology but the engineer.

10. The $1 million shortfall in revenues for the city should be "easy to replace," Mayor Sharon Datolli said. "Although no one wants to pay more in taxes." She said. "The city should be able to cover the deficit with a small additional tax on cable television'.

11. The veteran of fighting in Iraq and Afghanistan praised the commanders and comrades of her military police battalion. "I've never worked with a more determined group of people". "The conditions were horrible and the enemy implacable". "If we hadn't held together, we all might have died".

12. Sure, I swipe credit card numbers sometimes." said the waiter who asked not to be named. "Its easy to just write down the numbers and then use them to order stuff over the Internet.' "I've done that several times and haven't been caught so far. "I think these people must not look at their credit-card statements." The waiter added.

13. "Too many pupils think school is dull or doesn't matter." 'They must be getting these ideas from their parents or siblings. And their coming to school with these attitudes at younger and younger ages, as young as 7 or 8, said the principal.

14. Chester Johnson, a teller, described what happened during the bank robbery. I was in my teller's cage when these three guys came in. They were all wearing raincoats, which was strange on a sunny day. But then they pulled out their guns. One had a shotgun I think and the others had pistols.

2. Using Quotes in News Stories

Write complete news stories based on the following information. Use some quotations in each story to emphasize its highlights, but do not use them to tell the entire story. Use the most interesting, important and revealing quotations, not just those that happen to appear first.

1. Carlos Vacante is a police officer who has worked 3 years for your city's police department. Last night he had an unusual experience. This is his story, as he told it to you in an interview today: "I remember his eyes. They were cold, the eyes of a killer. He was pointing a gun at me, and it fired. I smelled the gunpowder and waited for the pain. I thought I was dead. The whole thing had started at about 11 p.m. This man was suspected of stealing from parked cars, and I'd gotten his description by radio. Then I spotted him in a parking lot. This morning we learned he's wanted in the robbery and murder of a service station attendant in Tennessee. There's no doubt in my mind he wanted to kill me last night just because I stopped him. I was an object in his way. I'd gotten out of my car and called to him. He started turning around and I spotted a handgun in his waistband. As he drew the gun and fired, I leaned to the right and dropped to one knee. It was just a reflex that saved my life. When I heard the shot, I thought he hit me. I couldn't believe it was actually happening to me. I thought I was going to cash everything in. Then I was running—zig-zagging—behind some cars. He fired another shot, but my backup arrived, and he fled. Maybe 60 seconds had passed from the time I spotted him. Five minutes later, we found him at the back door to a house, trying to break in and hide. I ordered him to stop, and he put his hands up and said, 'You got me.' I still smell the gunpowder this morning. I thought I was dead."

2. The city's Ministerial Alliance spoke out today against the death penalty. A copy of a resolution it adopted will be sent to the governor and to every member of the state legislature. As its spokesman, the Rev. Stuart Adler declared: "None of us is soft on crime. There must be just punishment for those who commit violent crimes, but what we are saying is we stop short of taking another person's life. We object because several independent studies have concluded that the death penalty is no deterrent to crime, rather the violence of the death penalty only breeds more violence. Also, the method of sentencing people is inconsistent. There is a

great disparity between the victim being black or white. Defendants accused of killing black victims often are not sentenced to death, but when the victim is white, the death penalty is often imposed. People are frightened by the amount of violence in our society, and they've been sold a bill of goods. They've been told that the death penalty is a deterrent, and yet every major study disproves that reality. We're not getting at the deeper causes. We're a violent society, and getting more violent. Half the households in this city have guns, and it's inevitable some are going to use them. If we're really serious about stopping crime and violence, we have to recognize and correct its root causes: poverty, racial and sexual discrimination, broken homes and unloved children. Also drugs and alcohol. That's what's responsible for most crimes. And television. Studies show the average child in America witnesses, on television, 200,000 acts of violence by age 16. So we're against the death penalty. It's not going to solve our problems, and it's not fair, not fairly applied. It'll take time, but we intend to abolish it, and we'll persist. We're already beginning to stimulate discussion, and we expect that discussion to spread."

3. A rise in insurance rates is being blamed for a rise in hit-and-run motor vehicle accidents within the state. Richard Byrum, state insurance commissioner, discussed the problem during a press conference in his office today. He said, "The problem is serious. At first, we thought it was a police problem, but police in the state have asked my office to look into it. There has been a dramatic increase in hit-and-run accidents in the state, particularly in big cities where you find the higher insurance rates. I'm told that last year we had nearly 28,000 motor vehicle accidents in the state, and 4,500 were hit-and-run. People are taking chances driving without proper insurance coverage, or they're afraid of a premium increase if they have insurance and stop and report an accident. They seem to think, 'What the heck, no one saw it, and I won't get caught,' and they just bug out of there. If you look at the insurance rates in the state, it's practically impossible for some people to pay them, and as insurance rates go up, the rate of leaving the scene of an accident increases. Drivers with the worst records—those with several accidents and traffic citations—pay as much as $3,600 a year in insurance premiums, and they may pay even more than that if they are young or have a high-powered car. Even good drivers found at fault in an accident may find their rates going up several hundred dollars for the next three to five years. So leaving the scene of an accident is definitely tied to the economic situation, yet the insurance company people I've talked to say they can't do anything about it. It's just not realistic to expect them to lower their rates; they aren't making that much money. Right now, I'm not sure what we'll do about the situation. In the meantime, we can expect more hit-and-run accidents and more drivers going without any insurance coverage because of its high cost."

4. Michael Ernest Layoux, 22, is a clerk at a convenience store at 1284 East Forest Boulevard. He was robbed late yesterday. Here is his account of the incident: "First, you have to understand where the store is. It's located in a remote area in the northeast corner of town. There's nothing around that's open at night, so I'm all alone in the store. I started carrying a gun to work last year after I read where two clerks at another convenience store in the city were robbed and killed. Carrying a gun is against company policy, but I figured I had to protect myself. We're open 24 hours, and the store has a history of holdups, particularly at night when there aren't any customers in the store. But it never happened to me personally before. Just after 11, when the store was empty except for me last night, this guy walks in and asks for a pack of Winston cigarettes. I handed him a pack, and then he pulled a gun and says, 'You see what I got?' He had a pistol, and he held it low, level with his hip, so no one outside the store could look in and see it. Then he asked me for the money, and I gave it to him. We never have more than $30 in cash in the register. It's company policy. We put all the big bills we get into a floor safe we can't open. So he didn't get much, maybe $20. Then he motioned for me to move toward the cooler. We have a big cooler in the back for beer and soda and other stuff we have to keep cold. When he started shoving me toward the cooler I really got

scared. There's no lock on the cooler, so he couldn't lock me in while he was getting away. There's no reason for him to put me in the cooler; I could walk right out. The only thing I could figure was that he wanted to shoot me, and he wanted to do it in some place where no one could see what was happening. That's where the two other clerks were shot last year, in a cooler in their store. Since they were killed, I've kept a .25-caliber pistol under the counter, and when he motioned for me to get into the cooler I shot him. He'd started turning toward the cooler, and then he must have heard me cocking the pistol because he started jerking his head back around toward me. I shot him 3 times in the chest and side, but I didn't know right away that I hit him. He just ran out through the front door. He didn't even open it. He ran right through the glass. I called the police, and they found his body in a field about 200 yards away. He was dead, and now I've lost my job. But I wouldn't do it any different. The police talked to me for almost two hours, and they said it was OK, that I acted in self-defense. Then this morning, just after 8, I got a call at home from my district manager, and he said I'm fired because it's against company policy to have a gun in the store. It's a real shame, because I'm still a college student, and I need the job. I can attend classes during the day and then work at night at the store. I've been doing it for 4 years now, and I want to graduate in a couple more months. But I can understand the company's rules. Most people don't know how to handle guns. I do. I've been around them and using them all my life." Company officials refused to comment about the robbery or the firing. Ramone Hernandez, the district attorney, confirmed that his office considered the shooting self-defense and would not prosecute Layoux. Officer Alan Nega, who investigated the incident, said the body found in the field near the store was that of Robert A. Wiess, 2032 Turf Way, Apt. 388.

5. Lillian Shisenaunt is a pharmacist. She was elected president of your County Pharmacists Association at a meeting held last night. During an interview with you today, she talked about an issue of concern to pharmacists, one that the group talked about at the meeting, along with possible solutions. She said: "We find that we've got an awful lot of older people taking three or four or five different drugs all at once. If they think that's going to do them any good, they're fooling themselves. We find that, in many cases, the medicine—the dosage and the way it's taken—are all wrong. Patients, especially the elderly, sometimes get all their different drugs confused, and then they take two of one and none of the others. Even when the elderly take all the right pills, sometimes the different drugs nullify each other. Different doctors these people see give them prescriptions without knowing what else a patient is taking for some other problem. So some of these oldsters become real junkies, and they don't even know it. As they get older and have more problems, they take more and more medication. After a few years, their children think their minds are going because they're so heavily sedated all the time. But if they get a good doctor, or a good druggist, they probably can stop taking some of the medicines, and then they don't actually have all the problems people think they have. A lot of these older people aren't senile; they just take too many different drugs, and then it hits them like senility. Drug companies don't help. If you look at most drug companies, they test their products on healthy young adults, a 25-year-old, 180-pound male. Then the companies set a normal adult dosage based on the clinical tests with these young adults. But the things that determine how drugs affect you change with age, so what the drug companies set as a normal daily dosage doesn't always fit an older person with a number of conditions. If you look at studies of hospital emergency rooms, you'll find that people over 60 are admitted twice as often for adverse drug reactions as the young. Most people don't know that. They think about all the problems of the young, not the old. But most of the problems can be solved, and without too much effort. People should talk to a good pharmacist or physician. Unfortunately, we find that most people are scared of their doctors and don't ask them enough questions and don't understand what their pharmacists have to offer. Patients also should make a list of all their different medicines and dosages each time they go to a doctor

and tell him what they're taking. Then when they get a new prescription, they should write down the doctor's instructions, and they should get all their prescriptions from just one pharmacist so the pharmacist knows everything they're taking and can watch for any problems. If they ask, the pharmacist can color code their pill bottles so they can't be confused. But patients also have a responsibility for their own health care. Each morning, they should sort out all that day's pills ahead of time, and then they'd be less likely to make a mistake."

INTERVIEWING

Reporters rarely turn to Supreme Court justices for reactions to events on a football field. But during her 2016 interview with Justice Ruth Bader Ginsburg, Katie Couric asked the jurist about San Francisco '49ers quarterback Colin Kaepernick's refusal to stand during the national anthem as a protest against police killings of blacks. "I think it's dumb and disrespectful," Ginsburg said, while acknowledging Kaepernick and other athletes had a First Amendment right to express their beliefs.

> "I talk with people and notice things, and then I turn those things into a column for the most wonderful gift a storyteller can be given—an audience on the other end."
>
> *Bob Greene, columnist*

After Turing Pharmaceuticals acquired the drug Daraprim, which is used to treat patients with parasitic diseases and to prevent pneumonia in HIV/AIDS patients, company founder and then CEO Martin Shkreli raised the price of a pill from $13.50 to $750. The 5,000 percent increase angered many, but Shkreli responded: "To me the drug was woefully underpriced. It is not a question of 'Is this fair?' or 'What did you pay for it?' or 'When was it invented?' It should be more expensive in many ways."

Just six months into his presidency, Donald Trump undercut the position of Attorney General Jeff Sessions, who recused himself from decisions regarding the investigation into Russian involvement in the U.S. presidential election. "Sessions should have never recused himself, and if he was going to recuse himself, he should have told me before he took the job and I would have picked somebody else," the president said.

All three of these comments made news; some had an impact on government policies and national politics. Why did these three people say these things? Ginsburg later regretted her remark and apologized to Kaepernick, but neither Shkreli nor Trump backed down from their remarks, even though many found them shocking. Whatever the reason, the comments were made in response to questions asked by reporters. The Couric–Ginsburg interview appeared on Yahoo News. Shkreli was giving an interview to a Financial Times reporter, and Trump's remarks came in a 50-minute interview with reporters and editors for The New York Times.

Katie Couric (left) interviews Justice Ruth Bader Ginsburg. Along with her question about the NFL players' protest, Couric covered various topics, including the judge's recently deceased colleague, Anthony Scalia, Hillary Clinton and Donald Trump and his travel ban on Muslims.

Interviewing—asking questions, getting answers and asking more questions—is a basic tool of the journalist. For the experienced investigative reporter as well as the fresh-from-college police reporter, interviewing provides much of the fact, background and color for any news story. When used properly, interviewing can be an effective method of gathering information.

Preparing for the Interview

No matter what kind of story a reporter writes, it usually will require at least one interview. Successful interviews do not just happen; they are the product of thought and planning. An interview's purpose determines the length and required preparation. Often interviews are short and focused on gathering a few specific pieces of information. A journalist may ask a legislator a few questions about a bill's objective or provisions. Another may question a police officer to get details about a recent crime. On other occasions, reporters may ask one or two specific questions of many people to gather an unscientific sampling of public opinion. Some reporters specialize in writing profiles of famous or interesting people. They usually conduct long interviews—sometimes stretching over several days—with the subjects of their stories.

Reporters preparing to interview a source should ask themselves, "Why am I conducting this interview? What kind of story will I write from this information?" The answers to these questions will determine what they ask, the sources they seek and their conduct during the interview. The reasons for interviewing are as varied as the resulting stories, but most often journalists are seeking information for one of three story types: the news story, the feature story or the investigative story (see Table 11.1).

Reporters who cover a news story, such as a crime or a city council action, usually interview several individuals to gather all the relevant information. They may seek just a few facts or a brief reaction from each individual. Collectively, however, the material allows them to construct a complete narrative of a newsworthy event or explanation of an important issue.

Reporters writing feature stories, such as personality profiles, must gather additional information that will provide the color and detail the audience needs to better understand a person or a situation. Investigative reporters must dig deeper still to uncover actions and motives that their subjects may prefer to keep hidden (see Chapter 18).

Many experienced interviewers think of an interview as a conversation, but it is a conversation with a specific purpose: gathering information for an unseen audience of readers, viewers or listeners. To accomplish that purpose, interviewers must control the conversation, and they can do that only if they have properly

TABLE 11.1 Information Reporters Seek, by Story Type

Information Reporters Seek	Stories in Which the Information Is Used		
	News	**Feature**	**Investigative**
Facts and details, including dates, names, locations and costs	✓	✓	✓
Chronology showing the unfolding of events	✓	✓	✓
Relationships among the people, organizations or issues involved	✓	✓	✓
Context and perspective, including the significance of events or issues and their relationships to other issues	✓	✓	✓
Anecdotes that illuminate events or issues and make them more dramatic and understandable for readers or viewers	✓	✓	✓
The environment in which the subject lives or works		✓	✓
How the subject appears and dresses		✓	✓
The subject's mannerisms		✓	✓
Smells, sounds and textures associated with the subject's home or work		✓	✓
The subject's version of events and how it differs from that of other sources and records			✓
Explanations of contradictions between the subject's version of events and that of other sources or of contradictions within a subject's version			✓
The subject's replies to all charges and allegations the reporter may have heard from other sources during an investigation			✓

prepared. In the case of in-depth personality interviews or investigative interviews, the planning process might be long and complicated, but even with simpler interviews, it can involve several steps.

Selecting Interview Sources

Once reporters know an interview's purpose, they decide whom to interview. For a personality profile, they will interview the subject and his or her friends, enemies and co-workers. But when the story is about an issue or event, they may have to determine who has the necessary information.

Reporters working on stories that will be published days or weeks later can try to interview everyone who might have relevant information. They can ask each subject for the names of people who might contribute information and repeat the process until the list of potential sources has been exhausted. Journalists working on deadline must find the best possible sources quickly. They want sources who possess knowledge, expertise or insight relevant to the story. The subjects

Journalists speak with doctors following a press conference about the mass shooting at the Pulse nightclub in Orlando, Florida. In this interviewing situation, reporters are able to question several sources in one venue, but they have little time with each subject.

should be able to explain complicated matters in a clear and interesting manner. Sometimes the best available source is a document or record rather than a person. Reporters can save themselves and their interviewees time and trouble if they begin by searching for documents or public records that provide the factual background for a story.

When choosing interview subjects, reporters should never let any organization, governmental or private, make its public relations person the scapegoat. Tony Kovaleski, an investigative reporter for KMGH-Channel 7 in Denver, said the job of the reporter is to hold accountable the real decision maker, not the PR person.

HOW MANY SOURCES ARE ENOUGH?

Beginning reporters sometimes wonder how many sources they need for a story. The answer depends on at least four factors: deadline pressure, the expertise of the sources, the degree of controversy raised by a topic and the complexity of a topic.

When stories involve breaking news, which readers, viewers and listeners need as soon as possible, reporters lack the time to search widely for sources and information. They must construct a story from the materials readily available. Still, they should get as complete an account of the event and include as many points of view as possible. If a journalist cannot interview a key source before the deadline, the story should say so clearly.

If sources possess broad expertise in a topic, three or four might be enough. If interviewees have more limited experience, reporters might need to speak to dozens. Academic and government economists, for instance, may have extensive knowledge about the economy of a city or region, while individual business owners may know what is happening only in their particular business.

The degree of controversy also affects the number of sources. If a topic is not controversial—the cause of polio, for example—one source may be sufficient. If the topic is the likelihood of developing cures for diabetes or Alzheimer's disease from fetal stem cells, about which experts disagree, a reporter must include all reasonable points of view in the story.

Finally, the more complex the story, the more sources the reporter will need. A story about a particular crime committed by a particular teenager may need only a few sources. A story about the causes of teenage crime in general would require talking to dozens of sources from such fields as law enforcement, criminology, psychology and social work.

However many sources reporters talk to, they must evaluate each one by asking, "What is the basis of the source's knowledge?" "How credible or reliable is the source?" When a subject makes an assertion, ask him or her, "How do you know that?" Determining the credibility and reliability of the source requires asking about his or her credentials and cross-checking information from one source with that from others. The process is not simple or easy, but it is essential for producing sound, accurate news stories.

Researching Sources and Topics

Lawrence Grobel, a journalist who has interviewed scores of famous and important people and has written about interviewing, says the successful interviewer must be well informed. That means reading books and articles by or about the person the reporter will interview, researching a company's annual reports and reviewing public documents. When Grobel prepared for an interview with mystery and western novelist Elmore Leonard, he read 14 of the author's books. Sportscaster Jeanne Zelasko was once assigned to cover the Daytona 500, but she knew nothing about NASCAR—in the two weeks she had to prepare for the assignment, she read every book she could find about the sport in a local bookstore. Pat Stith, a former investigative reporter for The Raleigh (North Carolina) News & Observer, says the goal is to know more about the small portion of the subject's job the reporter is interested in than the subject knows.

Journalists who have thoroughly researched a person or topic before an interview will

- Have fresher, more interesting questions for the interview subject.
- Not waste time asking about already established facts.
- Not embarrass themselves by appearing ignorant.
- Be prepared to recognize newsworthy statements the subject makes and ask intelligent follow-up questions.
- Be prepared to spot inconsistencies and evasions in a source's responses.
- Discover additional sources.
- Encourage sources to speak more freely, because they are more likely to trust knowledgeable reporters.

Preparing Questions for the Interview

Good questions elicit interesting quotations and details. Constructing good questions begins when reporters select a unifying central point for their story. With this point in mind, interviewers can decide whom they should interview and what questions they should ask. Say a journalist is planning a profile of a local bank executive who has won several marathons. The central point for the story may be that long-distance running enhances the bank executive's personal and professional life. That idea suggests certain questions to ask the executive and his or her friends and family. If the reporter is investigating the bank's treatment of minorities, however, he or she may still want to interview the same executive, but the central point will be different. It may be how the bank's lending practices affect minorities who want to buy homes or start businesses.

🔥 HOT TIP

Steps in Preparing for an Interview

1. Define the purpose. Is this a news, feature or investigative interview? What information is necessary for the story?

2. Decide whom to interview. Sometimes the choices are obvious; other times the reporter may have to research who the best sources are.

3. Assess the character of the interviewee. This may be crucial for feature and investigative interviews where the reporter will have to shape the interview strategy to the interviewee's character.

4. Identify the areas of inquiry. What topics will the interview focus on? What questions will yield the information necessary to write about those topics?

5. Anticipate possible answers to questions. Reporters often can predict an interviewee's answers from their advance research. On the basis of those predictions, they can plan the interview and prepare possible follow-up questions.

FROM THE NEWS

Preparation Helped FBI Interrogate Al-Qaida Suspects

Ali Soufan—a former FBI agent, native of Lebanon and Arabic speaker—was one of the lead interrogators of al-Qaida suspects following the 9/11 attacks. Al-Qaida operatives had been coached to appear to cooperate with investigators by answering questions without offering any new information. Nevertheless, Soufan was able to get valuable information from the suspects he questioned, without using torture—or enhanced interrogation techniques, as it was euphemistically called by some U.S. officials.

The key to a successful interrogation, Soufan explained in his book "The Black Banners," is thorough preparation. He and other FBI interrogators studied al-Qaida extensively and learned as much as they could about the background of each person they questioned. "You have to convince the detainee that you know all about him, and that any lie will be easily uncovered," Soufan wrote. "To do this, you plan the interrogation around what you know."

Journalists rarely will encounter interview subjects as reluctant to cooperate or as well trained in techniques for deflecting questions as al-Qaida operatives. But the principle of thorough preparation still applies. The reporter who has prepared thoroughly for an interview will know when interviewees are being deceptive, trying to spin a topic to make themselves look good or providing newsworthy information.

Sometimes, a journalist may find it helpful in an interview to feign ignorance. While this tactic may be useful in certain cases, being ignorant never helps the journalist.

Once reporters have selected a central point and have researched the topic, they write their questions in advance. They need not write out full questions. Often it is enough to jot down a word or phrase to remind themselves what to ask.

Reporters craft questions to elicit as much information as possible. This means asking open-ended rather than closed-ended questions. The latter can be answered with a yes or no: "Will the state's new tax lid hurt schools?" If journalists want more information, they have to ask follow-up questions. An open-ended question would be, "What will be the effect of the state's new tax lid on schools?" The question requires the source to provide an analysis of the problem.

John Sawatsky, an investigative reporter renowned for his interviewing skill, advises journalists to ask short, neutral questions that begin with "what," "how" and "why" and to a lesser extent "who," "when" and "where." Questions structured as Sawatsky suggests encourage interviewees to tell their stories and reveal their feelings. Questions like "Are you angry?" or "Were you scared?" are not only close-ended but also imply that the interviewer has a preconceived notion about how the subject should have acted or felt. The source might not want to tell his or her story to a reporter who appears to have already decided what happened.

When interviewees have a story to tell, such as how they survived a plane crash or what happened during a bank robbery, reporters should simply let them talk. Something like "Tell me what happened to you" might be enough to encourage people to tell their story as they remember it. As interviewees talk, journalists should listen carefully. They might think of questions as the subject tells the story, but they should not interrupt. They should wait until the interviewee has finished and then ask any specific follow-up questions.

For feature interviews or personality profiles, some reporters have questions they often use to gain insight into the subject. Here are some examples:

● What do you read?
● Who are your heroes?
● What goals do you have?
● What is a typical day like for you?
● What are your weaknesses or drawbacks?
● How do you compensate for your weaknesses?
● What caused the most significant change in your life?
● How did you cope with that change?

When news sources generalize or give vague answers, reporters ask for anecdotes and examples that support the generalizations or clarify ambiguous responses. Reporters can use the anecdotes, examples and quotations to make their stories more colorful, interesting and understandable. Here are examples of questions crafted to elicit anecdotes and quotations:

● What crime was the most difficult for you to solve in your career as a detective?
● How has the state's new science curriculum changed the way you teach?
● What do you fear the most when you perform before a live audience?
● What steps will you take to prepare your business for the city's sales tax increase?
● How did you overcome your fears following your accident?

Reporters should ask for clarification when they do not understand things sources say. Sometimes that means asking questions that might appear naive or silly, but journalists should not fear asking them. Those who assume they understand what a source said or who fail to ask a critical question out of fear of appearing ignorant could make serious and embarrassing mistakes when they write their stories.

Conducting the Interview

Selecting a Location

The prospect of being interviewed creates anxiety for some people, making it harder for them to answer questions. Reporters can reduce the unease by conducting interviews in sources' homes or offices, where they feel more comfortable. Additionally, reporters can learn more about a subject by being in his or her environment. Eric Nalder, former senior enterprise reporter for Hearst Newspapers, advises reporters to survey the person's office or home, looking for clues and details. The photos people display on their walls, the clutter on their desks or the items on their refrigerator doors all give insights about their lives or suggest questions to ask them.

No matter where reporters interview people, they always look for details that will reveal information about the subject. They look for body language, facial expressions, manner of dress, tone of voice and anything else that reveals the source's character. Louisa Thomas' profile of Australian tennis star Nick Kyrgios for The New Yorker included a brief conversation between the two after he had lost a match in a French tournament. Notice how Thomas incorporates description of Kyrgios' dress and appearance:

> Half an hour after the match, I was waiting for the elevator in the lobby of my hotel, when I heard Kyrgios request a new room key. He was still in his kit: black shorts, a magenta Nike top, shoes smeared with ochre clay. His beard was trimmed tight along his jawline, his dark hair shaved on the sides of his head and sculpted on top like a flame.
>
> He stared at his phone as he shuffled to the elevator. As he stepped inside, he looked up. We had met the previous day, and he sounded surprisingly cheerful as he greeted me. "Sorry about the match," I said.
>
> He gave a quick, harsh laugh, and then his voice lightened. "It's all right. It's not a big deal," he said.
>
> He stepped out of the elevator, and I watched the doors close behind his slumped shoulders. There are message-board threads dedicated to Kyrgios's posture, with dozens of comments debating whether the curvature of his upper back requires surgery, interferes with his hormone circulation, or is a faker's lazy pose.

Some places are poor locations for interviews. For example, people unfamiliar with newsrooms may find their noise and chaotic pace intimidating. Lunch appointments also have drawbacks. The idea of a leisurely interview over a meal sounds pleasant, but crowd noise and interruptions from servers interfere with the conversation. Also, reporters or their news organizations should pay for lunch to avoid any appearance that they can be influenced by a generous source. Thus, the practice of interviewing people at a restaurant can become expensive. Whatever the location, a journalist should always arrive early, keep the interview within the agreed-on time and dress appropriately, usually in business clothes.

As shown in the documentary "Citizenfour," Glenn Greenwald (right) interviews Edward Snowden about the NSA documents he leaked to the public. The interview took place in a Hong Kong hotel room, not for Snowden's comfort but to protect him from extradition to the United States.

Organizing the Questions

Reporters should start an interview with a clear statement of its purpose, if that's not already understood. For brief news interviews, they usually try to get right to the main questions. Longer interviews often begin with a few minutes of small talk to put a source at ease.

Once the serious questioning begins, reporters should take charge of the conversation, decide what questions to ask, keep the interview on track and make sure the source answers every question fully. If a subject wanders or tries to evade questions, journalists bring the conversation back to the central topic and politely but firmly ask him or her to respond to the questions.

Questions should be grouped by topic. A reporter who is planning to profile a candidate for mayor, for example, may want to cover the person's education, work history, family life, community service, political experience and campaign platform. For each of these topics, the reporter might have four or five questions. Journalists try to organize the topics, making it easy for the interviewee to move from one to the next. Chronological organization and reverse chronological order are two methods used. For a reporter interviewing a scientist about the effects of global warming, chronology is meaningless; it would make more sense to use a different organization, such as moving from effects on oceans and ocean life to effects on land animals and finally to effects on humans. In still other situations, the reporter might let the topics come up on their own and simply make sure that the interviewee covers all essential points.

Reporters organize the questions they ask as well as the topics they want to cover. One approach—sometimes called the funnel—starts with a general question and moves to progressively more specific ones (see Figure 11.1). The reverse funnel starts with questions about specifics and moves to more general matters.

Journalists start interviews with some noncontroversial comments or soft questions that will break the ice. Even a polite question about the weather can start the conversation. Once the interviewee becomes comfortable talking, the reporter asks more difficult questions. The most embarrassing or difficult questions are held for the end. By then, the subject should be more at ease. Moreover, if a source refuses to answer embarrassing questions and abruptly ends the interview, the reporter will have already obtained most of the information needed for the story.

Experienced interviewers prepare so thoroughly before an interview that they encounter few surprises, but occasionally an interview yields unexpected information. If the information is newsworthy, reporters abandon their original plans and pursue the new angles. "Morning Joe" hosts Joe Scarborough and Mika Brzezinski were wrapping up an interview with Michael Avenatti, attorney for Stephanie Clifford (better known as Stormy Daniels) who claimed to have had a sexual encounter with President Donald Trump, when Brzezinski asked Avenatti if Clifford had been threatened to keep silent about the incident. Avenatti's statement that she had been threatened surprised them and became the most newsworthy disclosure of the interview.

At the end of an interview, reporters should always ask sources if they have anything to add. Sometimes the most newsworthy information emerges in their response. Journalists should ask for the names of other people to interview or for documents that might provide additional information or verification. They also should determine the best time to call sources if they have follow-up questions. Finally, they should thank subjects for granting the interview.

HOT TIP

Interview Traps to Avoid

Reporters have an infinite number of approaches they can take to conducting an interview, but they should avoid some traps:

- Don't make statements; just ask questions: Questions will elicit the subject's opinions and ideas, but statements might lead the subject to suspect the journalist is biased and will not report the interview fairly.

- Don't ask double-barreled questions, which might have more than one correct answer: An interviewer asked Bill Clinton, when he first ran for president, "Was Gennifer Flowers your lover for 12 years?" Clinton answered, "That allegation is false." But which part was false? Splitting the question into two might have yielded a better answer.

- Don't use loaded words in questions: "Mayor Datolli, will your budget scheme save the city from bankruptcy?" A "scheme" may seem disreputable. A more neutral term would be "plan."

- Don't ask questions that suggest what you think the answer should be: Asking "Was the robber carrying a shotgun?" implies that you think the robber did so. An uncertain interviewee might be tempted to confirm that suspicion, even if it is wrong.

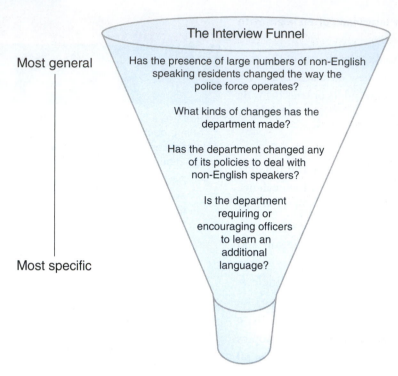

Most general

Most specific

The Interview Funnel

Has the presence of large numbers of non-English speaking residents changed the way the police force operates?

What kinds of changes has the department made?

Has the department changed any of its policies to deal with non-English speakers?

Is the department requiring or encouraging officers to learn an additional language?

Figure 11.1   The Interview Funnel   The funnel style of organization places the broadest—or most general—questions at the top and the most specific at the bottom. The reverse funnel approach moves from most specific to the most general. The approach a reporter uses depends on the situation, topic and source.

Dealing with Reluctant Sources and Asking Tough Questions

Most sources cooperate with reporters because they welcome the opportunity to tell their side of a story. Some, however, dislike talking to journalists or are hostile. They may fear a topic is too difficult for reporters to understand; they may have been embarrassed by reporters in earlier interviews; or they may suspect the resulting story will portray them in a bad light.

Reporters first try to learn why the source is hesitant to speak to them. They may then be able to overcome the specific objection. In some cases, sources fear the interview will turn into an interrogation. Journalists might ease this anxiety by showing empathy. Grobel has said, "To be a good interviewer, you have to become a chameleon, changing the colors of your personality to fit the mood of the person you are interviewing." Good interviewers convey the feeling they are more interested in sources than in themselves.

When sources fear their words will be distorted or misunderstood, reporters can demonstrate their knowledge of the topic and background by asking intelligent questions or pointing to other stories they have written on the topic. The interviewees may then be willing to fill in the gaps. Explaining the purpose of the interview and the story also can help convince sources that reporters are knowledgeable and trustworthy.

Some sources worry the story will cause them to lose their jobs or money or even to face criminal prosecution. Reporters can soothe these fears by explaining that the interview is an opportunity for subjects to put their side of a story before the public and that failure to do so will make them look worse.

Interviewers have a variety of tactics for getting reluctant sources to talk. If an interviewee is unresponsive, reporters may switch topics, trying to find something that will get him or her to talk. In some instances, journalists can build rapport with sources by expressing admiration (if it is genuine) for something the person did or said. Or they might draw on their background to establish a connection with a reluctant source. If the interviewee is a college president, the reporter might mention that his or her father was a college professor (if that is true).

Many interviews—whether done for feature or investigative stories—require reporters to ask tough questions that the source might find embarrassing or potentially harmful. Failure to ask the questions, however, means an interview will be incomplete and lack news value. Asking difficult questions is easier when reporters maintain their neutrality. If interviewees believe reporters are just asking questions and not expressing opinions, they answer tough questions more willingly.

Reporters can enhance their appearance of neutrality by asking questions in ways that distance them from the opinions the questions may imply. They can, for example,

- Attribute the question or point of view implied in the question to a third party or to public opinion generally. For example, "Chancellor Smith, some faculty members have said you attach more importance to intercollegiate athletics than to academics. What is your response?"
- Sugar-coat questions. Asking a person, "Is there anything about your marriage that you now regret?" is easier than asking, "Did you abuse your spouse?"
- Ask interviewees to explain their previous statements or actions or give their versions of controversial events.
- Ask interviewees to talk about others. Once they begin, it often is easier to shift the interview to their own ideas and actions.
- Ask interviewees for the names of people who support or criticize them. Then ask them to guess what their critics are most likely to say about them. Nalder says this tactic often elicits information and tips for additional interviews.

No matter what approach reporters use, they must be persistent. If sources refuse to talk, hang up the phone or slam the door, reporters should go back the next day or next week and try again.

Sources pressed to talk about sensitive topics sometimes try to evade the question or even lie. When subjects avoid an issue or give fuzzy answers, reporters can restate the question, forcing them to be more forthcoming. Reporters can also simply remain silent, which tells sources their answer is insufficient and pushes them to elaborate. In some cases, journalists might want to confront sources directly about evasive answers, saying they will note evasions in the story.

Reporters who have done their homework will often know when a source is lying. Nalder lets interviewees he suspects are lying spin out their tales. He interrupts them only to ask for elaboration or more detail. Once he has the source's entire story, he can begin to use the facts he has already gathered to pick the story apart and get that person to tell the truth.

Although he probably was not aware of it, Soufan's interrogation method, described earlier in this chapter, follows Nalder's techniques for dealing with sources who lie. In his book mentioned earlier, Soufan says the questioning never began with big or intimidating questions like "Did you meet Osama bin Laden?" Instead, the FBI agents focused on getting details with questions like these:

- Why did you go to Afghanistan?
- How did you travel there?
- How was the trip funded?

Award-winning journalist Eric Nalder, former chief investigative reporter for the Seattle Post-Intelligencer, offers various tips for interviewing reluctant sources in his article "Loosening Lips: The Art of the Interview."

FROM THE NEWS

An Interview with Bill Cosby

Sometimes a source will simply refuse to answer the hard question, as happened when National Public Radio's Scott Simon interviewed Bill and Camille Cosby for Weekend Edition. Simon was interviewing the Cosbys because they had contributed to an art exhibit. But shortly before the interview, The Washington Post published a column by Barbara Bowman, who said Cosby had sexually assaulted her several times in 1985. Simon felt obliged to ask Cosby about it. Here is their exchange:

SCOTT SIMON: This question gives me no pleasure, Mr. Cosby, but there have been serious allegations raised about you in recent days.

BILL COSBY: [SILENCE]

SIMON: You're shaking your head no. I'm in the news business. I have to ask the question. Do you have any response to those charges?

COSBY: [SILENCE]

SIMON: Shaking your head no. There are people who love you who might like to hear from you about this. I want to give you the chance.

COSBY: [SILENCE]

SIMON: All right. Camille and Bill Cosby. They have lent 62 pieces from their collection of African and African-American art to create an exhibit called *Conversations: African and African American Artworks in Dialogue*. It's now on display at the Smithsonian National Museum of African Art through early 2016. Thank you both.

- Who picked you up at the airport?
- Where did you stay in Afghanistan?
- Whom did you meet?

By focusing on the small details, the FBI investigators made it hard for the al-Qaida operatives to maintain a cover story. Inconsistencies in the details exposed lies and revealed areas where the interrogators could focus their efforts.

Reporters should never try to bully hostile sources or try to deceive them about the purpose of an interview. Information obtained from a source who has been intimidated may be unreliable. People who have been led to believe an interview will be about one topic when the reporters want information about something else will feel unprepared to respond fully and accurately.

Special Situations

TELEPHONE INTERVIEWS

Telephone calls save reporters enormous amounts of time. Some sources are more comfortable talking without someone watching them; others consider it a welcome break in the day. But telephone interviews have disadvantages, too. They must be brief and superficial. Sources usually have other work, and long telephone conversations may bore or annoy them. Particularly frustrating for reporters is playing phone tag with a source while on deadline.

Telephone calls are an unsatisfactory means of conducting in-depth interviews about controversial or complex issues and personalities. Cultivating sources is difficult if they are known only by telephone. Getting a source to discuss embarrassing or personal matters requires a rapport best established face to face.

EMAIL INTERVIEWS

Email offers another way of interviewing sources. Reporters use this method to contact hard-to-reach or reluctant sources. Even people who travel a lot check their email. Sources who dodge phone calls or hesitate to return voice mails may answer a journalist's email. A reporter trying to contact several sources for similar information can use email to send the same message to each of them.

Email interviews have some advantages over telephone interviews. Besides being more convenient for some sources, the format also affords them an opportunity to develop their thoughts in detail, which means reporters get more thorough answers to their questions. Email also provides a written record of the interviews, lessening the chance for misquotation.

However, journalists relying on email interviews are deprived of their sources' facial expressions, vocal inflections and body language, all of which can help reporters understand their sources better. Also, the email response is less spontaneous. The offhand comments sources make in person or telephone interviews give reporters additional insights that they can follow up on quickly. Finally, reporters conducting email interviews recognize the possibility that the person responding is not the one they want to contact. For example, a business executive might have a PR person draft an answer to a journalist's email.

ONLINE INTERVIEWS

Reporters can use their computers to interview subjects, using programs like Skype or Zoom. Because the programs use the computer's video capabilities, reporters and subjects can see as well as hear each other. And the responses the journalist gets are more spontaneous than those obtained through an email interview. Some of the programs for online video allow one or both parties to record the conversation, creating a permanent record of what was said.

Online interviews, however, are essentially high-tech telephone interviews, so subjects are just as likely to get bored. If the subject is at work or at home, he or she may have to deal with distractions. And if one party or the other has a poor internet connection, the interview may become difficult or impossible to carry out.

INTERVIEWING FOR BROADCAST

Reporters interviewing sources for radio or television experience problems print reporters don't face. Terry Gross, host of the NPR program "Fresh Air" and one of the best interviewers in the business, told American Journalism Review, "For most print journalists the interview is the raw material for the piece, along with everything else the reporter has seen and heard in researching the story. For me the interview is the piece." Gross arranges her questions so that the answers produce a narrative, not just a series of disconnected answers.

Television reporters need to plan their interviews in advance with the technicians who will be operating the cameras and sound equipment, especially if the interview needs to be shot quickly for broadcast that day or if the source does

---

🔥 HOT TIP

Telephone and Email Etiquette

For telephone interviews, reporters should

- Identify themselves and their news organizations clearly at the start of the conversation.

- Never pose as someone other than a reporter.

- Ask permission to record the interview digitally or on tape.

For email interviews, reporters should

- Use a salutation (such as "Dear Mrs. Ramirez,").

- Identify themselves and the news organization they represent.

- Usually review the background of an event or issue before they ask their questions.

- Tell sources their deadline and thank them for their time and expertise.

- Never write in all capital letters, which some regard as shouting.

- Never use acronyms, such as "BTW" ("by the way"), because not everyone understands them.

Terry Gross interviews musician Questlove for a live "Fresh Air" recording at the Penn Museum in 2016.

not want to appear on camera. They also should show the interview subject doing more than talking. Where possible, television journalists ask the subject to demonstrate an activity or respond to a video or another source.

Taking Notes

Skilled interviewers take copious notes, writing down much more information than they can possibly use. Unless reporters take detailed notes, they will forget much of what is said. They might not recognize the importance of a piece of information until well after the interview—or several interviews—when they are writing their stories. Recording as much as possible decreases the chances for errors or omissions. Reporters can easily ignore notes that later prove to be unimportant or irrelevant, but filling gaps left by poor note taking is more difficult.

Most reporters develop their own shortcuts for taking notes. They leave out some words, abbreviate others, or jot down names, numbers, good quotations and key ideas. When sources speak too rapidly, interviewers can ask them to slow down or repeat important statements. Note taking makes some sources nervous. Journalists should explain that the notes will help them write more accurate and thorough stories.

After completing interviews, reporters review their notes immediately, while everything is fresh in their minds. They may want to fill gaps in their information or be certain they understand everything a source said. Journalists often write their stories as soon as possible after their interviews. The longer they wait, the more likely they are to forget some facts or distort others.

Recording Interviews

Using a digital or a tape recorder frees reporters to concentrate on the questions they want to ask and sources' responses. Recorders also provide verbatim and permanent records, so interviewers make fewer factual errors. When reporters play the recording, they often find important statements they failed to notice during the interviews.

Recorders also have drawbacks. After recording a one-hour interview, reporters may have to replay it at least once before writing the story. They may also have difficulty locating important facts or quotations. By comparison, they may need a minute or less to find a fact or a quotation in their handwritten notes.

Even reporters who record major interviews usually augment recordings with written notes.

Reporter Vanessa Schledier Bild interviews Major Aryeh Shaliker, a spokesman for the Israeli army, near Ashkelon, Israel.

They can consult their notes to write the stories and use the recordings to verify important facts and quotations. If a recorder has a counter, reporters can use it to note the location of important or interesting quotations.

Although recorders are commonplace, some sources still refuse to be recorded. Recorders are small enough that reporters can easily hide them in their pockets or handbags, but taping a conversation without the other party's consent is sometimes illegal. As noted in Chapter 5, in most states, one may record a conversation with the consent of only one party. In the case of an interview, the consenting party would be the person doing the taping. Eleven states require the consent of all parties in most or all circumstances. Even where it is legal, taping a conversation without the other party's consent raises ethical questions. Undisclosed recording seems manipulative and invasive. Audiences may consider any information reporters obtain in this manner tainted.

Final Thoughts

Interviewing is an art form that requires practice. Journalists who are most successful at interviewing have done it for years and have developed insights into their sources and into their own strengths and weaknesses in relating to other people. Gross says, "My theory of interviewing is that whatever you have, use it. If you are confused, use that. If you have raw curiosity, use that. If you have experience, use that. If you have a lot of research, use that. But figure out what it is you have and make it work for you." Student journalists often lack the experience and the maturity to know what they have and how to make it work for them. Their initial attempts at interviewing may disappoint them. Young reporters should not become discouraged, however. With time and persistence, they can become excellent interviewers.

Writing the Interview Story

Writing a story based on an in-depth interview, such as a personality profile, is little different from writing any other news story. Most interview stories begin with a summary lead that presents the story's central point. The following paragraphs include the highlights. Reporters may use an alternative lead, such as an anecdote or description that introduces a nut graph containing the central point.

The body of the story usually is organized by topic, with facts and quotations presented in the order of their importance, not the order in which the source provided them. Reporters must be sure that they keep every direct and indirect quotation in its proper context. A well-written interview story will not string together quotations from the sources but use them for emphasis and impact. Journalists also usually limit background information to a minimum and incorporate it where it is most necessary and helpful for explaining a source's remarks.

An alternative form for writing an interview story is the question-and-answer format. Few reporters use it, however, because it requires too much space and makes it difficult for the audience to grasp a story's highlights quickly. The Q-and-A structure works best with celebrity interviews, self-help stories and sidebars for main stories. Q-and-A stories are never verbatim transcripts of interviews, even though the format creates that impression. The interviews are usually heavily edited to eliminate boring and irrelevant passages.

Guest Columnist

Interviewing Three People about a Deadly Accident

BY DON STACOM

Celebrating one of the last summer nights of school vacation in Connecticut, four teenagers hung out at a friend's pool party and then sped home on a dark, two-lane road in a Subaru WRX.

Police estimate the driver was doing 100 to 140 when he lost control on a curve. The WRX slid sideways, demolished a Taurus in the other lane and then slammed roof-first into a utility pole. Everyone in the WRX was killed.

For news reporters across the state, this was another "reckless teenage drivers" story. They happen a lot.

Covering them can be as depressing as a funeral, and every bit as predictable: It starts with a splashy story, follows with profiles of the dead teens, and then shifts to the memorial services, the weeping friends, the grieving relatives.

And that's about it. The news moves on.

Every so often, though, there's a chance to report something much deeper. At these times, the reporter's work becomes as challenging, emotionally draining—and as rewarding—as any job that exists. You get to do something that genuinely makes a difference.

With the WRX case, it began with thinking about all the people who were hurt: Literally hundreds of teenagers showed up at the crash scene to stare and cry. And there were, of course, the four devastated families.

Beyond that were the overlooked victims: the innocent people in the Taurus who sustained crippling injuries, and the emergency crews who saw carnage that battered their psyches.

They all suffered in very different ways, but they also shared an agonizing frustration at how needless this tragedy was. They desperately wanted to put some meaning to their pain.

All of that provided the structure for a story showing how one bad decision could crumple many, many lives. The plan was simple, though not easy: Months after the crash, three people would tell exactly how they experienced that night of horror. The father of one of the dead girls, the first cop on the scene and the front-seat passenger in the Taurus would relive what they went through.

That was the theory. But how do you make that actually happen? Step one is the research; a reporter who already knows the fundamental facts will have much more credibility when approaching these people to talk. To do that, reporters for the Hartford Courant reviewed the police reports, read obituaries and Facebook memorials and revisited the scene.

Next came building rapport with the dad, the cop and the woman from the Taurus. This story hinged on their cooperation; a reporter must develop their trust that the story won't be tawdry or exploitative. At the same time, the reporter gently talked them through what the interviews will be like—letting them know ahead of time that these conversations would bring up the worst of the painful stuff. This was the time to invite them to decline; if they're committed, they'll persevere.

Pre-interview preparations are crucial here. To build intelligent questions, first imagine a bit of what they saw and felt. Imagine being the first police officer at such devastation; this brings the interview questions "Whom do you go to first?" and "How does your mind even process all of this?" For the woman from the Taurus, you ask about her memory of the moments before the impact—and those right afterward, too. Has she made peace with being the entirely innocent victim of such a horrific crash?

Through the interview, the reporter had to stay alert for what's fresh and what's powerful, for the sights and sounds and feelings that these people recall. And most importantly, the end of the talk was time to softly, genuinely thank each person for putting themselves through that again. After that came the job of organizing and writing a story that would make it worthwhile.

Don Stacom is a reporter for The Hartford Courant in Connecticut.

The Reporter's Guide to Interviewing

1. Determine whether the story will be a news story, a feature or an investigative story.

2. For all types of stories, interview to get facts, details, chronologies, context and anecdotes.

3. For feature stories, capture the source's environment, appearance and mannerisms.

4. For investigative stories, get the source's version of events, explanations of contradictions and replies to charges.

5. Identify the best available sources who can provide the necessary information for the story.

6. In deciding how many sources to interview, keep in mind deadlines, the expertise of the sources, the degree of controversy regarding the issue and the complexity of the issue.

7. Research people and issues as thoroughly as possible before conducting any interviews.

8. Select questions that will address the central point of the planned story.

9. Use questions that will encourage interviewees to talk—then let them talk with as few interruptions as possible.

10. Interview sources in places where they will be comfortable, not newsrooms or restaurants.

11. Organize questions by topic and raise topics in an order that will make it easy for sources to move from one to the next.

12. If a source is reluctant to talk or is hostile, find out why and try to address the concern.

13. Maintain neutrality when asking tough questions. Sources are more likely to answer tough questions from neutral interviewers than from those who seem to be advocates for a point of view.

14. Telephone interviews save time, but they are unsatisfactory for long, in-depth interviews.

15. Email is an effective way of interviewing some sources, but the interviewer is deprived of information about the source's demeanor and personality.

16. Remember that a broadcast interview is the story and not just raw material for a story.

17. Take thorough notes during the interview, making sure to write down names, dates, numbers and good quotations.

18. Recorders provide a verbatim permanent record, but they are sometimes clumsy to use.

Review Exercises

1. Class Projects

1. List 10 interviewing tips provided by other sources.

2. Interview an expert on interviewing, body language or nonverbal communication, perhaps someone in your school's psychology or speech department, and report on the information's usefulness to journalists. You might also invite the expert to speak to your class.

3. Interview government officials who frequently deal with reporters. Ask what they like and dislike about the interviews and how they handle the questions (to avoid echo) and the reporters conducting the interviews.

4. Ask several government officials which local reporters are the best interviewers, and then interview those reporters about their interviewing techniques. You might invite one to speak to your class.

5. Ask every student in your class to write one paragraph about the three most newsworthy experiences in his or her life. Select the students with the most interesting events and have your entire class interview them, one by one, and write news stories about their experiences.

2. Interview with a Retired FBI Agent

Write a news story based on the following interview with Edward Vargas. He was born in your city 62 years ago, and graduated from your university 40 years ago with a degree in sociology. For the last 35 years, he has been an FBI agent, much of it working undercover. He retired from the bureau earlier this year after being recognized as one of its top agents. He lives in the Cleveland area, but he is on campus to receive an award as a distinguished alumnus. Vargas has agreed to be interviewed for a story you're writing for the school newspaper. Here are the notes of your interview. Statements in quotation marks are the words of Vargas; all other material is a paraphrase.

Came to the university when he was recruited by Coach Bill Sandman to play football. Was recruited by several other major universities, but chose this university because of Sandman.

"When I came here to visit, I talked with Sandman. He took me to lunch and then to a basketball game that night. And we hit it off pretty well. Recruiting wasn't the big deal it is nowadays. It was all pretty informal. I really loved the school spirit here, so it just seemed natural to come here."

Was lineman. Weighed 250 pounds, height 6'2".

"At 250, I was big for that day. It wasn't like today where you have linemen who are 300, 320 or even 340. I don't see how any one that big can move, but they do, and they're faster than I was when I played."

Majored in sociology because it didn't require too many hours, could take lots of other courses. Also, really loved professor Ed Mitchell's criminology class. "That's where I got my first taste of law enforcement. I didn't think about it as a career until several years later, but Mitchell's class really set my imagination on fire."

Jobs were scarce when he graduated. Tried to find some entry-level job in a business or corporation. But everyone wanted either business administration grads or people with experience.

"I even took the test for a federal government job, but I didn't do well enough to get ahead of those guys who had been in the military. They kind of went to the head of the line, so to speak."

Only job available was working in a meat packing plant. His ability to speak Spanish was key. Many meat workers were Spanish speakers even then. Helped him move up to foreman after about a year.

Also played for a semi-pro football team for three years.

"Man, that was tough. I thought college ball was physical, but some of those semi-pro guys were suicidal. And you were playing with second rate equipment. Hell, you even had to buy your own helmet. Actually, they took it out of your pay, so the first half of my first season I was paying off the helmet."

After a little more than 3 yrs at the meat packing plant, got a call from a local FBI agent asking if there were any Spanish-speaking college grads at the plant. FBI needed Spanish-speaking agents. Vargas couldn't think of any other than himself. Wasn't sure he was interested.

"But then I got another call from the agent and he said, 'Why don't you give it a try?' So I figured, what the hell, I'll take a shot at it and I bombed completely."

After that he got a job at the university supervising maintenance crews, but the agent called again. That was about the time he married Ellen, his sweetheart from college.

"I wasn't sure it was worth trying to take the test again, but this guy was persuasive. I flew back to Washington to take this test I was sure I would fail, so I really didn't care. That attitude must have worked because I aced the thing."

Less than a month later, he was sent to the FBI training center at Quantico, Va. Split his time for next 17 weeks between Quantico and Washington.

After training sent with Ellen to El Paso, Texas. First job was trailing a KGB agent from Soviet Union who was getting information from someone on the Ft. Bliss Army base. Had to trail agent w/o being seen and get enough photos and information on his travels through Texas, Mexico and Cuba that he would be worthless to KGB as an agent. The plan worked. KGB realized its agent was known. Stopped using him or gathering information from Ft. Bliss. "I don't know who on the base was giving out information or whether it was intentional or simply carelessness. That end was handled by someone else, but I think they did get that leak plugged."

While Vargas working on this assignment, Ellen gave birth to their first child, a son named Edgar.

He next went to Denver where he was assigned to help with the investigation of a group of militant Chicanos.

"I was only one of 45 Mexican Americans employed by the FBI at this time. So we received a lot of assignments dealing with Mexican gangs and drug dealing."

First assignment over quickly. The gang was suspected of making bombs. Were being tailed while delivering bombs to others in gang.

"These guys were real amateurs, though. They didn't know how to handle the explosives, and they blew themselves up, all except one guy who had left the car to buy some beer from a liquor store. He was pretty shaken when he came out and saw what happened. But we picked him up and he spilled all the details when we questioned him."

Next assignment was undercover doing sting operation on robbers and burglars in the Denver area. This was first of several undercover assignments.

Vargas and team set up a sting operation in Denver. He posed as a fence for stolen goods. Guys with stolen property came to him to unload it. "They didn't know they were selling their booty to a federal agent. Nor did they know they were being photographed, videotaped and audio taped throughout the whole process. So it was easy to go back and arrest all of them."

Worked that for more than 2 1/2 years. Made many arrests. Still holds the record for sting arrests in the state of Colorado.

From Denver he was sent to Miami. Family had grown to two children with birth of daughter, Daniella.

In Miami, his first target was gangs of Haitian revolutionaries. Jean-Claude Duvalier was the ruthless dictator of Haiti. Had the nickname Baby Doc. But U.S. State Dept. saw Duvalier as a bulwark against spread of Communism in Caribbean and Central America.

"Knowing what I knew about conditions in Haiti, I kind of hated to bring some of these guys in. If I'd been a Haitian, I probably would have been trying to get rid of Baby Doc Duvalier myself. But I don't set policy."

Helped round up most of the revolutionaries, about 20; rest fled U.S.

Much of rest of career was focused on drugs. "95 percent of all cocaine that comes into the United States moves through Miami. That was true then and it's still true now."

His assignment was working on air transport of illegal drugs. He used impounded planes to make contact with dealers, to buy and sell drugs and build cases for arrest of dealers.

"Some of the deals I worked on involved 150 to 300 kilos of cocaine. When you consider that one key of cocaine at that time sold for $2,500 on the streets, well, you can see a lot of money was involved."

Most of the information FBI used came from former dealers or couriers who were in trouble with one or another of the South American drug cartels.

"Once you got crossways with one of the drug cartels, you needed to find some protection, and the FBI could offer that. It was from sources like these that we learned that most of the drugs coming into the U.S. were being smuggled in small, single-engine planes that could carry about 150 keys."

Vargas offered tips for students interested in career in FBI.

"You should never do drugs, not even once. The FBI will find out and most likely you won't get the job. Also, you should learn a foreign language, and today, it would be best to learn Russian or Chinese as these are the new drug traffickers and violent gangs entering the world market."

Vargas now retired. Living in Cleveland area with wife. Children grown and in college, one at Ohio State and one at Penn State.

3. Interviews with Spelling Champions

Next week the State Spelling Bee will be held in your community. The winner of the competition will go to the National Spelling Bee, which is held in Washington, D.C. You have found the names of five people who won your state's spelling bee in past years and you want to write a story about them, their recollections of the event, how it affected their lives and what word they misspelled. Your notes from the five interviews follow. The material in quotation marks is direct quotation from the subject and may be quoted directly. All other material is paraphrased. Use this information to write your story.

Wendy L. Shavers of Cotter Creek
Born Wendy Langston. Won state Spelling Bee 35 years ago. Was 14 at the time. Went to school in the same town where she lives now.

Misspelled "turnstile." Had excuse. At the time there was a chain of department stores in the area called Turn Style. Remembered seeing the name on the store and in newspaper advertisements for the store. So when she was given that word to spell, she spelled it the same as the department store chain. Now she thinks about it all the time.

"Every time I walk through a turnstile, I think about that. I had gotten so many harder words right, and I go out on 'turnstile.'"

Finished 20th at the national bee. Came home and was a successful student at Cotter Creek H.S. Graduated 3rd in her class and won a scholarship to a state university. Scholarship didn't pay for everything she needed. And she met Cole Shavers. Fell in love and married him. He was two years older and had graduated. Wendy dropped out to help him start a business, but Cole died 7 years later in a car accident. The business—a hardware store—failed. Had a 4 yr. old son to raise, so she took a job as a truck driver.

"There were damn few women driving over-the-road trucks when I started. And the other guys were not friendly to me. And the long stretches away from home were hard. But the money was so good, I was determined to stick it out. I'm lucky my mom and sister lived in town so they could keep an eye on Jimmy as he was growing up."

Never remarried.
Still loves words.
"I'm addicted to crossword puzzles. I'll do them in almost any newspaper, except the New York Times. I only do that when I'm brave."

Todd Drolshagen, 2604 Alabama Av
Competed in the bee 22 years ago at 13 yrs old. In 8th grade at North Middle Sch.

Prepping for bee taught good study habits. Helped later in H.S. and college. Graduated at top of class from North H.S. and went to Stanford University.

"It shaped the study habits for the rest of my life. It helped me develop a tolerance for really diligent, repetitive study that I used in high school and college."

Bee also helped him bond with his mom, Daniella Drolshagen—died 3 yrs ago. Spent 2 evenings every week with his mother studying for the bee.

"It really brought us closer together. A teenage boy doesn't have a lot in common with his mother, but those memories are something I'll never forget."

Was nervous from start at nationals. Didn't recognize the first word he was asked to spell—paronymous.

"I swear, the guy who read that word mispronounced it or I didn't hear it or something. I thought almost every vowel in the word was an a. So I spelled it p-a-r-a-n-a-m-o-u-s. And that's how I ended my spelling career."

Studied public affairs at Stanford and returned to work in city government. Is now director of the City Code Enforcement Board. Has held the job for 8 yrs.

Paronymous—derived from the same root; a cognate.

Tonya Livermore, Chicago
Won the state spelling bee 18 years ago. Was in 8th grade at Kennedy Middle Sch.

"I loved the atmosphere at the nationals. Everywhere we went we were treated like royalty. We got attention from the media, from politicians, from almost

everyone. That's what sparked my interest in performing, that's what made me want to be on stage."

After H.S., went to Northwestern University to study music. She specializes in religious music and broadway show tunes. Did some acting in Chicago and New York. Eight yrs ago returned to Chicago, got teaching certificate. Now teaches music to middle and elementary school children in Chicago. Also performs occasionally in community theater productions, esp in the summers.

"The spelling bee was a great experience. It gave me a lot of confidence and opened up a lot of different people and opportunities."

The word she misspelled was "pelisse."

"I had no idea what it meant. The judge said it was a long cloak or outer robe. I certainly didn't know how to spell it. I don't remember what spelling I gave it, but I know I was way off."

Clara Warneky, 428 N. Wilkes Rd.
Won the state bee 28 years ago. Was 13 yrs old and in 7th grade at Colonial Middle.

Of the 108 in the national bee, she finished roughly in the middle of the pack. The word she missed was "acetone." Knew what it was because father was a painter and had used it as a solvent. Had seen containers of it. But botched the spelling of it.

"I was deeply disappointed by that. I knew how to spell that word. But I guess I just got nervous or overconfident or whatever. Anyway, that's how I was eliminated."

"The trip to D.C. did reinforce my love of words, though. I wasn't so disappointed that I didn't continue reading and studying. I still love to read. I read almost everything I can get my hands on. My big love is biographies. I finished a biography of F.D.R. last week, and I'm working on a book on Rachel Carson now."

"I'd love to be a writer. That's always been and still is my dream. With work and family, I don't have time for it now. Maybe in a few years I'll be able to sit down and try to write something of my own."

Thinks she inherited her passion. Mother, grandmother and brother were all ace spellers and all voracious readers.

Works as a manager for Hertz car rental. Has held job for 15 years.

Her oldest daughter, Karen, 15, seems to share interest in words and writing. But she may not be interested in competing in spelling bees.

"I told my husband I had to see if she has the gift. My other two children are younger, so I don't know if they're going to have it too. I'll have to see later if they have the gift and the desire."

Colin Castilango, Eureka, Calif.
Placed 18th in the National Spelling Bee 48 years ago. Was a 7th grader at North Middle—then called North Jr. High.

Won $50 because of 18th place finish. Disappointed because his grandmother had promised him $100 if he won. "That was a lot of money then. Now, you can spend $100 in the time it takes to sneeze."

After H.S. went to the state university and graduated cum laude with a degree in teaching. Took a job teaching English to H.S. students in San Jose, Calif. Taught for about 35 years and spent last few years as district coordinator for teaching literature in H.S. Retired 3 yrs ago.

Still loves words and considers them magical.

"I dream about words. I dream about pronouncing them, spelling them and teaching them. I just love words."

Continues to teach, but now teaching English to refugees in Eureka area. Taught a woman from Guatemala how to read. After reading her first book the woman "thrust her hands into the air to thank God and then gave me a big hug."

"Getting gifts like those makes it easy to go to work."

Tries to keep his income below the level at which he must pay federal income tax. "I don't want a penny of my money going for these wars in Iraq and Afghanistan. They're stupid and wasteful. When I saw on TV one of my last students had been killed in Iraq, I just broke down in tears. Why do we have to do this?"

Misspelled "plebiscite" to lose the national contest.

"I spelled it p-l-e-b-e-s-c-i-t-e. Too many e's and not enough i's. I didn't even know what it meant. Now, I know what it means and why it's important."

FEATURE STORIES

> "In the English language, it all comes down to this: Twenty-six letters, when combined correctly, can create magic. Twenty-six letters form the foundation of a free, informed society."
>
> *John Grogan, journalist, non-fiction writer and author of Marley and Me*

Feature stories are everywhere—in magazines and newspapers, on radio, TV and podcasts and online. They can be an emotional story about an illegal immigrant's escape from death while crossing the sea, an adventure story about traveling in a submarine or an informative story about holiday celebrations in various countries.

Audiences like feature stories, also called "human-interest" stories, because they say something about life. Features are soft news because they exclude the news element of immediacy found in hard news stories.

Journalists borrow techniques from short stories, often using descriptions, sensory details, quotations, anecdotes and even personification. They might use characterization, scene setting, plot structure and other novelistic elements to dramatize a story's theme and to add more details. Yet feature stories are journalism, not fiction or creative writing. Everything is factual; nothing is made up. After all, fact can be stranger than fiction. Features are fair and balanced, based on verifiable information. They also are objective—they are not essays or editorials.

Finding Story Ideas and Gathering Information

Almost everything one sees or does has a story behind it—journalists just have to open their eyes and ears. Feature writers find ideas by being curious and observant. News stories may provide spin-off topics for features. A story on a restaurant that closed because it failed inspections may prompt a sidebar on federal cleanliness standards. A report on Trump's wall between Mexico and the United States may generate stories on types of walls, the labor required to build them, farmers and ranchers affected by the wall and more. A general news story about a hurricane may spark human-interest stories about the reactions of victims, heroism in crises and other "people" angles that bring natural disasters into sharper focus.

The concept of universal needs can also help journalists find stories and attract large audiences—one of the major news elements. Universal needs are those that all human beings have in common: food, clothing, shelter, love, health, approval, belonging, self-esteem, job satisfaction, entertainment and more. Audiences are interested in ways to satisfy those needs. For example, the intersection of health and children might be a story on how the acid in soft drinks corrodes tooth enamel. Sources could be dentists (authorities), parents (affected individuals) and prosthodontists (those who make dentures for children). Visuals might include corroded teeth, dentures for children, people interviewed and an animated timeline of corrosion. Table 12.1 presents a universal needs chart; completing such a chart can help reporters think of ideas for stories.

After selecting an interesting topic, journalists narrow it down to a central point that emphasizes, perhaps, a single person, situation or episode. If they fail to identify a central point, their stories become long and disorganized. This leaves audiences confused, and they will quit the story because the point is lost.

Journalists personally visit and observe the places they write about, and they interview people in their customary surroundings. They also research the story's background to ask good questions when interviewing sources and to provide context when writing. Reporters use all their senses; record how people move, speak and dress; and use descriptive verbs instead of adjectives and adverbs. They give audience members a reason to care about the subject.

For the lead of his article "New Leash on Life: Group Finds Old Pets New Homes," Mike Householder described his observations from his visit to a unique

Using courtroom testimony and details of the case to construct a moving narrative of a woman who survived a brutal attack, The Stranger's Eli Sanders earned a Pulitzer for feature writing.

TABLE 12.1 Universal Needs

	Food	Shelter	Love	Health	Education	Self-Esteem
Babies	Breast milk and formulas		Parental instincts	Premature births		Importance of smiles
Children	Socializing; the use of candy as a reward	Homeless numbers		Soft drinks and teeth	Watching TV	
Students	Fast food	Dorms vs. apartments	Leaving for college	Free medical clinics	Home-schooling	Peer pressure
Young Adults	Obesity		Suicides after breakups	STDs		
Adults	Meal kit delivery services			Insurance fees		Unemployment
Parents	Restaurant costs	Housing costs		Sleep and being a new parent	Incomes	In the workplace
Elderly	Ordering online: grocery store deliveries	Marriage		Social Security		Stereotyping

animal rescue facility. The story described the circumstances and successful placement of older pets into new homes:

> A 15-year-old cat. A 14-year-old dog with a mouthful of bad teeth, a wart on his head and a kidney infection. Even a 17-year-old parakeet named Bubba.
>
> Tyson's Place Animal Rescue helps old pets find new homes.

While gathering the information for feature stories, journalists consult several sources, perhaps a half-dozen or more, to obtain a well-rounded account. They gather two or three times as much information as they can use in the story, then discard all but the most telling details. Gathering a lot of information is essential to helping the reporter understand more about the issue or event.

Parts of Feature Stories

Journalists are creative in writing human-interest stories. Skilled writers use different techniques for the lead, body and ending, depending on the type of feature. Great feature stories capture people's attention and carry them along like a flowing river. Before they know it, they have reached the end.

The Lead of a Feature Story

The only requirement for the lead of a feature story is that it interests people, making them want to stay with the story to learn more. The story can start with either a summary lead or a type of alternative lead (described in Chapters 7 and 8, respectively).

One cannot help but admire the flowing prose in the lead of "Nation Marks Lives Lost and Hopeful Signs of Healing," a story written to commemorate Sept. 11. The anniversary narrative by Robert McFadden and his colleagues appeared in The New York Times:

> Once more the leaden bells tolled in mourning, loved ones recited the names of the dead at ground zero, and a wounded but resilient America paused yesterday to remember the calamitous day when terrorist explosions rumbled like summer thunder and people fell from the sky.

This lead rises to the solemn occasion it represents. It is an emotional, heavy and poetic lead that embodies great sorrow and history. It causes people to pause and reflect, which is the intended effect. Not all stories can carry this type of lead. Yet, no matter what kind writers choose for a feature story, they try to make it as unique as possible.

Dick Thien, a founding editor of USA Today, advised that some leads—such as questions, figures of speech and shockers—generally sound trite and should be used sparingly. His list of cliché leads to avoid is available on the Society of Professional Journalists' website.

The Body of a Feature Story

Like the lead, the body of a feature story takes many forms. The inverted-pyramid style may be appropriate for some features and chronological order for others.

Regardless of the form or style chosen, every feature is coherent. All the facts fit together smoothly and logically. Transitions, which are usually brief, guide the audience from one segment of the story to the next and clearly reveal the relationship between those segments. They might ask a question, announce shifts in time or place or link ideas by repeating key words or phrases.

Journalists write concisely and never waste their audience's time. Features emphasize lively details—the action—and they provide an occasional change of pace. James L. Edwards III of the Lansing State Journal varied his sentence length to emphasize the tension felt by a local golfer in an important game:

> Nathan Clark knew the pressure was on. (7-word lead.)

> By the time the former Mason High School and Michigan State golfer . . .

The 45-word sentence that made up the second paragraph established the golfer's connection to the community and identified the tournament and his main competitor.

> The 54-year-old Matthiesen . . .

The 35 words in the third paragraph, composed of two sentences of 19 and 16 words, described Clark's competitor. The graph ended with:

> And Clark knew he would have to refrain from any serious missteps to have a chance.

> He did just that. (4 words)

The next paragraph described who won the tournament (40 words), followed by a narrative about the tournament and quotes from the winner.

A good journalist uses quotes sparingly. Instead, he or she might use several paragraphs of narrative, followed by some quotations to explain an idea, then some description and finally more quotations or narrative.

Journalists use observation to illustrate character and personality. Instead of summarizing that a student was timid, they describe how the person acted or what he or she did: sat quietly in the back corner of the room; listened, but never talked in class; or blushed and stammered when (correctly) answering questions.

Successful feature writers use elements such as characterization, setting, plot and subplot, conflict, time, dialogue and narrative. They plan the beginning, middle and end. They reveal the character of the people they write about with quotations and descriptions of mannerisms, body language, appearance, dress, age, preferences, prejudices, use of personal space and a host of other traits.

The setting reveals the subject's character and provides context for the audience to understand the subject. Geography and family may influence physical and mental traits, determine life span and impact ways of earning a living. Journalists tell where a subject grew up, what the person's surroundings are now and how these factors

THE MORNING CALL

Being young and transgender

Bethlehem teens seek treatment in Philadelphia after finding few resources in the Lehigh Valley.

BY SAM KENNEDY
OF THE MORNING CALL

This story shares the experience of Sebastian Montiel and Sasha Rivera—two transgender teenagers. The article includes a sidebar with a glossary of terms and ends with resources for transgender youths.

contribute to who he or she is. Such touches of description sprinkled throughout a story show what the subject is like.

The plot often describes the obstacles that lie between the subjects and their goals. The resolution of conflict presents the theme of most human-interest stories. The main variations are the clashes between humans and nature, humans and their inner self, and humans and humans. As journalists ask people about events in their lives, plots naturally emerge. Often a subplot materializes, a secondary line of action that runs in counterpoint to the main action and either helps or hinders the person's progress. If journalists listen and identify plot and subplot elements as the subject tells the story, a natural order appears.

Time is handled in a variety of ways. To organize some types of features, journalists use a dramatic episode in the present as an opener, then flash back to the beginning of the story and bring it forward in chronological order. Reporters can foreshadow the future or build in a series of flashbacks arranged in the order of occurrence.

Feature stories need dialogue. Journalists use quotes to show temperament, personality, plot, events, time, customs or continuity. They are careful to select only the best, most revealing quotes, and use them sparingly. For example, a former running back for the San Diego Chargers, LaDainian Tomlinson, was recently inducted into the Pro Football Hall of Fame. Associated Press (AP) journalist Barry Wilner chose two short paragraphs from Tomlinson's induction speech about "Team America" to show why he received standing ovations from the audience during his passionate talk about Americans working together:

> "Football is a microcosm of American," Tomlinson said. "All races, religions and creeds, living, playing, competing side by side. When you're part of a team, you understand your teammates—their strengths and weaknesses—and work together toward the same goal, to win a championship.

> "Let's not choose [in America] to be against one another. Let's choose to be for one another. . . . I pray we dedicate ourselves to being the best team we can be, working and living together, representing the highest ideals of mankind. Leading the way for all nations to follow."

Whereas journalists use dialogue for impact, their narrative weaves the story together. Wilner wrote the following narrative to lead his story: "As he so often did in the field, LaDainian Tomlinson stole the show." Narrative introduces, summarizes, arranges, creates flow and transitions and links one idea to the next. Narratives are often unobtrusive and subtle, helping to guide the flow of the story.

The Ending of a Feature Story

A feature has a satisfying conclusion, perhaps an anecdote, quote, key word or phrase repeated in some surprising or meaningful way.

Journalists avoid ending a feature story with a summary. These endings are too likely to state the obvious or to be repetitive, flat or boring. For example, a story about children on an unusual field trip would not end with a summary sentence such as "And they all had a good time."

Some endings come back around to the beginning. For example, the body of Householder's story on Tyson's Place Animal Rescue (see pp. 257–258 earlier in this chapter) uses Bosco, the "14-year-old rat terrier with the lousy choppers" to show how the shelter cares for the health of animals. The story ends with a quote that lets readers know the older dog is now in a good home:

> Eventually, Jen Wilson and her husband, Frank, came forward for Bosco, giving him a new home in Grand Rapids, where the now-15-year-old is rarely seen without his little tail wagging behind him.
>
> "We adore this dog. We love him," Jen Wilson said. "I started it with: 'Let's just give this dog a loving home throughout the last of his life, love him through his golden years and not get too attached.'
>
> "Well, that definitely didn't happen."

After finishing a feature, a professional is likely to edit and rewrite the narrative many times. He or she will also angle the feature for a particular audience, publication or news program, emphasizing the story's relevance and importance to it.

Types of Feature Stories

Feature stories come in a wide variety. The following sections describe a few of the most common types.

Profiles or Personality Features

Profiles describe interesting people—individuals who may have overcome a disability, had a unique hobby, pursued an unusual career or became famous because of their colorful personalities. Profiles reveal the person's character. They make audiences feel as if they know the person. Profiles do more than list achievements or dates, minutiae that no one remembers anyway.

To gather the necessary information, feature writers observe their subjects at work; visit them at home; and interview their friends, relatives and business associates. Completed profiles quote and describe the subjects. The best profiles are so revealing that readers, listeners and viewers feel as though they have actually talked to the person. Here's a shortened version of Sarah Lyall's profile of Daniel Tammet. Published in The New York Times, the full story describes his childhood troubles that stemmed from Asperger's syndrome and his ability to cope with ordinary daily routines because of the love of his family.

saving the last dance

story by juliana keeping
photos by bryan terry

For almost two decades, renowned dancer Shannon Primeau has been transforming the lives of young people at her Oklahoma City dance studio, where the highlight of the year is the annual spring recital.

Like NewsOK on Fac[
NewsOK

The Oklahoman staff writer Juliana Keeping won a national feature writing award for her four-part series about a dance teacher struggling with cancer while organizing an anticipated dance recital. Keeping discovered the former Flamenco expert transformed the lives of her young pupils. The story and a podcast with the writer are available on the newspaper's website.

Bullied by other children and bewildered by ordinary life, Daniel Tammet spent his early years burrowed deep inside the world of numbers. They were his companions and his solace, living, breathing things that enveloped him with their shapes and textures and colors.

> *Conflict (news element) with others and within himself.*
> *Surprises! Numbers can be similar to people.*

He still loves them and needs them; he can still do extraordinary things with them, like perform complicated calculations instantly in his head, far beyond the capacity of an ordinary calculator. But Mr. Tammet, who at the age of 25 received a diagnosis of Asperger's syndrome, a high-functioning form of autism, has made a difficult and self-conscious journey out of his own mind.

> *Unusual (another news element).*
>
> *Reason for the story—overcoming struggles.*

"I live in two countries, one of the mind and one of the body, one of numbers and one of people," he said recently. Slight and soft-spoken, dressed in a T-shirt and casual combat-style pants, he sat cross-legged in his living room and sipped a cup of tea, one of several he drinks at set times each day.

> *Direct quote to follow up prior sentence.*
> *Journalist's personal observations from interviewing the subject in his home.*

Not so long ago, even a conversation like this one would have been prohibitively difficult for Mr. Tammet, now 28. As he describes in his newly published memoir, "Born on a Blue Day: Inside the Extraordinary Mind of an Autistic Savant," he has willed himself to learn what to do. Offer a visitor a drink; look her in the eye; don't stand in someone else's space. These are all conscious decisions.

> *Draws in the audience—they are privy to the conversation in the room.*
>
> *Examples to support prior sentence.*

Mr. Tammet's book is an elegant account of how his condition has informed his life, a rare first-person insight into a mysterious and confounding disorder. He is unusual not just because of his lucid writing style and his ability to analyze his own thoughts and behavior, but also because he is one of fewer than 100 "prodigious savants"—autistic or otherwise mentally impaired people with spectacular, almost preternatural skills—in the world, according to Dr. Darold Treffert, a researcher of savant syndrome.

> *Unusual.*
>
> *Authority.*

He wears his gift lightly, casually. When he gets nervous, he said, he sometimes reverts to a coping strategy he employed as a child: he multiplies two over and over again, each result emitting in his head bright silvery sparks until he is enveloped by fireworks of them. He demonstrated, reciting the numbers to himself, and in a moment had reached 1,048,276—2 to the 20th power. He speaks 10 languages, including Lithuanian, Icelandic and Esperanto and has invented his own language, Manti. In 2004, he raised money for an epilepsy charity by memorizing and publicly reciting the number pi to 22,514 digits— a new European record. In addition to Asperger's, he has the rare gift of synesthesia, which allows him to see numbers as having shapes, colors and textures; he also assigns them personalities. His unusual mind has been studied repeatedly by researchers in Britain and the United States.

> *Observation.*
>
> *Journalist verifies, asking subject to demonstrate what he says he does.*
>
> *Example of being a "savant" (unusual) to educate audiences.*
>
> *More examples of being a "savant" (unusual) to educate audiences.*
>
> *Prominence.*

Mr. Tammet sees himself as an ambassador and advocate for people with autism.

> *Use of present tense to show this is happening now.*

"Autistic people do fall in love," he said. "They do have joy; they do have sorrow; they do experience ups and downs like everyone else. We may not have the same ability to manage those emotions as others have, but they're there, and sometimes our experience of them is far more intense than the experience of other people."

> *Direct quote to support prior sentence. Also, audiences identify with joy, sorrow, ups and downs.*

But he is not an easy person to live with, Mr. Tammet said. He is discomfited by disturbances like a suddenly ringing telephone, a last-minute change of plans or a friend's unexpected visit. When he gets upset, he paces in circles. He splashes water on his face exactly five times each morning, and cannot leave the house without first counting the items of clothing he is wearing.

> *A contrast to the prior sentiment.*

> *Examples to support discomfiture.*

Historical Features

Historical features commemorate important events, such as the Boston Tea Party, the Civil War or the Great Depression. The 100th anniversary of the beginning of World War I inspired a number of historical features. Stories on 9/11 memorialize the tragedy every year. News organizations also note the anniversaries of the births and deaths of famous people with feature stories.

Current events can inspire historical features. If a tornado, flood or earthquake strikes the city, news organizations will likely present stories about earlier disasters. Stories of this type might also describe famous landmarks, pioneers and philosophies; improvements in educational, entertainment, medical and transportation facilities; and changes in an area's racial composition, housing patterns, food, industries, growth, religions and wealth.

In observance of Black History Month, Matt Miller of the Lansing State Journal researched and wrote a story commemorating the 25th anniversary of a black student sit-in at Michigan State University.

The first students arrived at Michigan State University's Administration Building at 4:31 p.m. Dozens more came in behind them. They brought books and blankets and waited in near silence for almost an hour.

> *Chronological order to describe events.*

> *Unusual (news element) draws in audience, who doesn't know what is happening yet.*

Jeffrey Robinson, head of the campus NAACP chapter and son of a prominent Detroit minister, broke it.

> *Contrast.*

"The Administration building is supposed to close at 5:30 p.m.," he said, "but we're going to stay."

> *Direct quote to support prior sentence. Audience now knows this is a flashback.*

It was 1989, the 9th of May, a Tuesday, the culmination of discontent. No single incident sparked the protest. Over the winter, black students had first asked and then demanded that the university do more to address racism on campus and the academic success of black students. They felt they'd been brushed off, that the people in power weren't listening.

> *Explanation for the event.*

"There was this yearning, this desire for us to make a statement and have that statement heard and responded to by the administration," said Robinson, who is now the principal of Paul Robeson Malcolm X Academy in Detroit.

> *Direct quote to support prior sentence.*

> *Flash forward to the present. (Great to have found original subject!)*

The Reckoning

by PAMELA COLLOFF

Fifty years ago, when Claire Wilson was eighteen, she was critically wounded during the 1966 University of Texas Tower shooting—the first massacre of its kind. How does the path of a bullet change a life?

Pamela Colloff, a national award-winning journalist and former executive editor at Texas Monthly, includes interviews, photographs, police reports and video in her story on how being a victim of the 1966 University of Texas Tower shooting changed Claire Wilson's life. Colloff also weaves in information about more recent school shootings.

The full story continues with descriptions of the peaceful protest, sit-ins at other universities, interviews with those same students who are now alumni, and the sentiment of black students today. Visual communication components include a timeline of events that led to the demonstration and photos of the sit-in and rallies that occurred for eight days.

Adventure Features

Adventure features describe unusual and exciting experiences—perhaps the story of someone who fought in a war, survived an airplane crash, climbed a mountain, sailed around the world or experienced another country. Many writers begin with the action, the story's most interesting and dramatic moments, and use quotations and descriptions.

Karin Stanton of the AP wrote her adventure in first and second person to draw in her readers. She used description to enable readers to imagine standing on the edge of a volcano:

> *Prominence of "world's most." Present tense, use of second person to put audience with the journalist, who personally visited and observed the volcano.*

When the world's most active volcano begins belching molten rock into the ocean, you've got to see it.

> *Journalist uses powers of observation to describe what she sees and hears and the second person to bring the audience with her.*

Thick, heavy clouds of steam cover the entire shoreline, and each new lava flow adds to the island's land mass—an additional 550 acres at last count. Sounds are whipped away by the wind, but when the wind dies momentarily, you can hear the lava snapping and popping—a reminder that land is being created, right at your feet.

> *The phrase "gaggle of volcano-watchers" better than "tourists."*

A gaggle of volcano-watchers stood within eyebrow-singeing range of an oozing-sizzling, foot-wide finger of lava flowing from Kilauea to the sea. A wider glob moved at a snail's pace to the edge of a cliff and toppled off. The glowing frost grayed as it cooled. The wind was scorching and relentless.

Stanton tucked in other information as the story continued, including the history of Kilauea, Big Island, and the Hawaii Volcanoes National Park. Readers also learn tips on the best way to experience the volcano.

Seasonal Features

Editors and news directors often assign feature stories about seasons and holidays: Christmas, Easter, Hanukkah, Ramadan, the Fourth of July and Martin Luther King Day. Journalists find new angles to make them interesting. Stories about international holidays, such as this one from AP, also are informative and entertaining. The journalist continued his story by tracing the traditional rituals for celebrating the holiday.

The Arctic's natural beauty lies at the center of this historical feature by Nellie Huang.

Taiwan's leader marked the first day of the Chinese Lunar New Year on Thursday by giving out 15,000 envelopes stuffed with cash to people in his hometown.

> *Unusual (news element).*

President Chen Shuibian handed out a comparable $5.80 in every envelope, totaling about $87,000 in the southern farm village of Kauntien. He ran out of envelopes before he got to the end of a line that stretched out about two miles.

> *Translates currency to dollars so audience can identify and have context.*
>
> *Helps audience imagine the line.*

People traditionally begin lining up at dawn to get an envelope, which they believe brings them good luck.

> *Answers "why" the people line up.*

People of all ages lined up and patiently shuffled past the sheds, machine shops and traditional low-slung farmhouses with tile roofs in Kauntien. There were mothers clutching babies sucking on milk bottles, elderly men dressed in pinstriped suits and teenagers in sweatshirts and baseball caps. All were celebrating the new Year of the Ram.

> *Verbs and description from personal observation.*
>
> *Description of the "people in his hometown" from the lead.*

Explanatory Features

Explanatory features (also called "local situation" or "interpretive" features or "sidebars") often are the result of other news stories or accompany them. In these, journalists provide more detailed descriptions or explanations of organizations, activities, trends or ideas in the news.

Explanatory features might localize national events or personalize an issue or event. After news stories describe the federal health care reform law, an explanatory feature might highlight how it will affect individuals from different socioeconomic levels or with diverse health issues. An editor might couple a story about a family that won a lottery with a feature on how others who won are doing today.

How-to-Do-It Features

This type of feature tells audiences how to accomplish a psychological or physical task, such as keeping emotions in check at the office or communicating better with roommates. Stories might focus on strengthening a marriage or overcoming shyness. They can explain how to find a reputable tattooist or how to live on a shoestring budget while in college.

Journalists gather preliminary information from several sources, including books, magazines and online articles. They also interview experts and get tips from people who have done what their stories describe. In addition, good reporters try to observe or participate in the procedure. For instance, they might watch a pet masseuse to better understand the topic.

Journalists divide the task into simple, clear, easy-to-follow steps. They tell the public what materials the procedure requires and what it will cost in money and time. They often include a chart or end such stories with a list or summary of the process. Stories might range from how to make glasses to watch the solar eclipse to how to tie a tie to how to use silverware properly.

Kate Nolan of the Gannett News Service wrote a story on teen sleep deficit. It described a Scottsdale, Arizona, teen whose schoolwork, athletics and job were

Executive pastry chef Jason Etzkin puts one of 2,100 gingerbread bricks onto a holiday season gingerbread house in the lobby of the Fairmont Hotel in San Francisco. Holiday traditions and activities often provide ideas for timely feature stories.

keeping him up until 1:30 a.m. almost every night. He finally became so tired he slept for a week. The syndicated story included tips on how to recognize a problem and suggestions for solving it. In one newspaper, the layout included sidebars and charts on the recommended hours of sleep at different stages of life, statistics on sleep-deprived teenagers' problems at school and advice on helping teenagers get their nine hours of needed sleep.

Occupation or Hobby Features

Journalists might prepare feature stories about occupations that are dangerous (mining) or hobbies that are highly specialized (rock climbing). Or they could report on a job many people think is boring (being a server at a restaurant) and turn it into something exciting (meeting celebrities while working on the job). An AP journalist discovered a worker who found her job as a short-order cook rewarding:

> *Journalist personal observation to watch the subject at work in the diner's kitchen.*

Twenty-nine-year-old Jordyn James is going through a lot of eggs this morning.

"Eggs are the easiest to do," James said, barely looking up from the yellow batter on the stovetop to glance at the seven tickets dangling in front of her. "With eggs, you can do a lot of things at one time. I can work on about six orders simultaneously."

> *Unusual (news element). Draws in audience to read further to find out why.*

James cracks one after another, and carton after carton is tossed out. Her hands are working at lightning speed, turning the eggs into scrambled, over easy, Benedict and poached.

> *Present tense used to make the audience feel as if they are also watching James.*

"You know, I've done a lot of other things with my time . . ." James pauses to place a basket of hash browns on the counter, ". . . but there wasn't anything that makes me as happy as this."

Collectors and crafts enthusiasts often make good subjects for feature stories because they are passionately involved and often eccentric, quotable and entertaining. Strange or trendy hobbies and interests, such as noodling, duct tape art and taphophilia (a love of funerals, graves and cemeteries), also make good topics because they tend to involve colorful characters.

Behind-the-Scenes Features

Behind-the-scenes features convey a sense of immediacy, allowing the audience to see, feel, taste, touch, smell and understand the "backstage" work that goes into an event. Journalists look for people who perform jobs out of the public eye but essential to many citizens. They interview sources, visit them on location and use the source's own words to tell the story. They also include details they observe, such as atmosphere, working conditions, physical appearance of people and their workspace, specialized terms and conversations between workers.

A story about a dairy farm and the milking process became more exciting when readers were enticed by a headline to "Meet Ellie," the matriarch cow of the farm. RJ Wolcott wrote a 19-paragraph profile about Ellie, describing her age ("The 11-and-a-half-year-old Holstein is two years older than the next eldest cow on the farm"), personality ("not a troublemaker") and appearance to readers ("Her dark-colored eyes shined bright as she hung her head below a nearby guard rail"). As readers followed Ellie through her day, they also learned about the inner workings of a dairy farm and the milking process. "Ellie contributed 28 pounds of milk during her time at the milking parlor . . . The 15-minute process involves . . . Over her lifetime, Ellie has given more than 240,000 pounds of milk, which becomes . . . Once the milking is done, . . ." Readers also learn interesting tidbits about the calves, the bulls, the naming process and when they could visit the farm.

For his feature story on the Foo Fighters, Barry Nicolson spent three days with the band as it prepared for the 2017 Glastonbury Festival.

Participatory Features

Participatory features give another kind of inside view, this time through the senses of a journalist who is actually experiencing an event or situation. Reporters might immerse themselves totally into the world of a police officer on patrol or a chimney sweep on the job. They arrange such experiences with the person they are shadowing or that person's supervisor, making it clear that they are journalists and will write a story about the experience that will appear in the media.

Whereas news stories are usually written in the third person, with the journalist as a neutral observer or outsider, feature stories can be written in the first person, addressing audience members directly. For example, Casey Jones and her fiancé decided to start their marriage by dispensing with television. Her participatory feature described the year they spent in a TV-free home. She organized the year into subheads: The Plan, The Beginning, The Adjusting, The Verdict. She ended with the following sentence: "For now, as peculiar as it may seem, this TV-free experience is giving us a priceless gift: the ability to kick off our marriage with a solid foundation of communication."

Other Types of Feature Stories

Successful journalists find the human interest on all reporting beats and topics—politics, medicine, sports, business, technology, education, medical and science. Reporters find individuals affected by the status quo or by change. They look for emotion. The narratives may portray typical conditions or unique aberrations to common systems, but they all include a human element. Journalists gather facts from documents, experts and individuals affected by a situation to give a story context and to present it on a personal level. They might talk to family and friends of individuals who are subjects for the story. They use quotes, allowing subjects to tell about their experiences and feelings. Journalists go to the scene of the story—a person's home or a place of business, for example. They observe the details found in the physical surroundings and in people's mannerisms and body language. Other elements such as smell, sounds, taste or texture make the story more interesting and realistic, drawing the reader into the narrative.

The Reporter's Guide to Features

1. Select a topic likely to interest a large number of readers. Often a spin-off from a major news story or event can be such a topic.

2. Profiles or personality features reveal the character of the person who is the subject.

3. Historical features may be pegged to anniversaries, describe famous leaders or landmarks or illuminate trends.

4. Adventure features describe what happened to people who had unusual experiences, such as climbing a mountain or surviving a plane crash.

5. Seasonal features are tied to holidays, annual events or changes in the weather.

6. Explanatory features might illuminate new scientific discoveries or describe how people are coping with the aftermath of a disaster.

7. How-to-do-it features tell readers or viewers how to make something, accomplish some goal or solve a problem.

8. Hobby or occupation features describe what people with unusual hobbies or in interesting jobs do.

9. Behind-the-scenes features take readers or viewers backstage, describing what is involved in making a public event happen.

10. Participatory features often involve the journalists in the actions they are describing.

11. Feature stories are more likely to use alternative leads—ones that describe a scene or tell an anecdote—than they are to use a summary lead.

12. Features can use an inverted pyramid form but often they develop chronologically or use flashbacks or foreshadowing.

13. The ending of a feature story does not summarize the story, but it should use some scene, quotation or anecdote that brings it to a conclusion. Often the ending harkens back to the lead.

Review Exercises

1. Generating Ideas with Grids

1. The following grid lists items associated with Christmas in various countries. To generate story ideas, fill in the blanks and then identify three different types of people to interview.

	Observance	History	Date	Gifts	Decorations	Food	Songs	Other Traditions
Netherlands			December 5			Stollen Christmas cake		Sinterklass
United States	Birth of Jesus			Santa Claus	Lights	Turkey and ham		Santa Claus, mistletoe
Australia			December 25		Presents and stockings	Cold foods and gold nuggets		Christmas bushes
England		Year 336, Roman Emperor Constantine				Roast beef and plum pudding		Christmas crackers, Yule log
China	Holy Birth Festival (Sheng Dan Jieh)				Lanterns, red paper chains and pagodas			
Ethiopia	Christ's birth (Ganna)		January 7			Fasting		White clothes

2. Prepare a version of a students' universal needs chart, using the example in the chapter as a guide. Write some universal needs across the top of the chart (e.g., finances, technology, food, time, health) and list different facets of college down the left side (e.g., classes, dorms, apartments).

3. What are some current concerns in your hometown (e.g., finances, embezzling, street conditions, court cases, festival locations)? Create a grid that includes the problems across the top and those affected by them down the left side. Fill the grid with story ideas.

4. States have worries similar to and different from each other. List issues in your state across the top of the grid (for example, gender identification, voting laws, gun control, state fairs and industry). List those who might be affected down the left side. Or list the 50 states and find out how each one deals with the same concern. Fill the grid with story ideas.

5. List across the top of the grid some current national issues (e.g., click bait and fake news, media literacy, military spending, civil war monuments, health care, illegal immigrants, social security, foreign aids. List ethnicities, cultures, religions and genders down the left side. As you fill in the grid spaces on how different ethnicities might be affected, you might also make comparisons.

6. Identify some global discussions (e.g., North Korea, climate change, agriculture and food, population, tourism, violence, drugs) across the top of the grid and various countries down the left side. Your intersection spaces might produce story ideas on how these global issues affect various countries.

7. You can also downsize the topics in a grid. For example, if a local university experiences a dramatic decrease in enrollment, how do the different areas associated with the decline (e.g., student population, housing, university employees, state funding, reputation) affect the university (e.g., budget, jobs, dorms, classrooms, cafeterias) or the community (e.g., businesses such as apartment owners, grocery stores, health clinics)?

2. Finding Ideas and Selecting a Topic

1. Politicians on the campaign trail make promises to their constituents. They espouse a particular political platform that makes up their beliefs and goals for when they are elected. Compare an elected official's platform goals to actual accomplishments and use the results to create a story idea. Elected officials may range from student body president to the mayor to the governor to the president.

2. Al Tompkins of the Poynter Institute offers 50 story ideas that can trigger other interesting topics: https://www.poynter.org/news/holiday-bonus-50-stories-you-can-do. Choose three ideas that interest you most and explain why.

3. Delve into the Census Bureau website to ignite your imagination on story ideas. Its "special topics" areas and its "press releases" site offer history and statistics on many subjects. Compare national and your state stats with those of your local community. Click on the Newsroom menu to find Facts for Features and Stats for Stories: http://www.census.gov/.

4. Explore posts on social media, such as Twitter, Facebook and blogs. What issues are people discussing? What seems to be uppermost on their minds?

5. Find a list of the top 10 searches for the day or week. Create a story idea for three of the items on the list.

6. Listen and observe to find a feature topic. Ride a city bus to the end of the line; sit in the student union or in a cafeteria. Based on what you see and hear, make a list of potential feature topics.

7. Survey students to get a story idea. Stand in the lobby of the student union or administration building or other popular places on campus and ask students about their major concerns. For instance, they might be troubled by NFL players being arrested for domestic abuse, North Korea's nuclear program, problems at their dorm, dating or student government. Qualify or narrow your questions to get informative responses.

8. Pair up with another student. Write for 10 minutes, completely free and uncensored, about one or more of the following topics: my pet peeves; things I am curious about; favorite places in my hometown; my biggest problem in school. Read each other's papers and discuss how you could conduct research and interviews to make a story from an idea one of you generated.

9. With your partner, list college experiences, such as advice to first-year students, what you wish you'd known when you first came to college, good experiences, bad experiences, medical facilities, friends and living arrangements. Which ones would generate the most interest for a school newspaper? How would you conduct research and whom would you interview? What type of research is needed for context?

10. Observe your surroundings as you walk to class. Make a list of 10 potential story ideas, such as dangerous traffic circles, bicycle safety, students who talk or text on cellphones while walking to class or places to eat on campus.

11. People in every region, city and school have experienced interesting events. Some students get ideas for stories by reading newspapers that publish "On This Date in History" columns, by interviewing the historians of clubs or by visiting the community or state historical society. A good feature writer will learn more about those events, perhaps by consulting historical documents or by interviewing people who witnessed or participated in them.

12. Scan newspaper notices, chamber of commerce websites or news websites for community hobby club meetings, senior citizens' activities, church and school events and speeches on unusual topics. Develop a story idea based on your findings.

13. Ask other people what they do to relax. Read classified ads and seek out people with a unique

occupation or hobby. Develop a story idea based on your findings.

14. Look for the human interest in stories of promotions, new businesses, the local economy and even the election of club officers. Find a human-interest angle by highlighting one person or aspect of local commerce. Consider, for example, fad businesses such as singing messengers and diaper delivery services; online dating sites, computer software merchants and shopping services for elder citizens that respond to new needs in society; and old, established firms, perhaps focusing on the personality of a founder or dynamic leader.

15. Think about health and medical story ideas. Everyone is interested in mental, emotional and physical health stories, and subjects abound: the cost of being sick, new treatments for illnesses, pregnancy, child rearing, andropause and menopause, death and the grief process, steroid use, sports and concussions, support groups, workshops for patients with a chronic disease, volunteer programs, new medical equipment and ethical issues surrounding medical advances. You can gather facts from medical experts, people with a particular condition, relatives and friends. Use the latest published research or go to the local hospital to discover any recent services.

3. Ideas for Campus Features

Here are 20 ideas for feature stories that you can write about your campus. Interview some students affected by the issues as well as authoritative sources. You need to identify the purpose of the story in order to write it well.

1. Identify college trends happening nationally. Make a local comparison, using the people and data from your campus.

2. Tuition is increasing nationally because state support and enrollments are declining. Are there other reasons? What is the situation on your campus? How are students paying for their college education?

3. More campuses offer classes online and hybrid courses. How do students compare these educational experiences to campus classes?

4. Do more students today than 10 years ago work to support themselves? What are the numbers of students who work full or part time? Do they work on campus or elsewhere? How hard is it to find a job on campus?

5. Is the number of international students increasing on your campus? Compare your local statistics to national levels. Why do international students choose to attend undergraduate or graduate programs in the United States? Do international enrollments affect domestic acceptances?

6. What does your campus do to assimilate international students into the student body? Are international students comfortable on campus while pursuing a degree from your campus and in your city?

7. Some research says that reading a printed textbook and handwriting notes on paper (compared to using a computer to read a digital textbook and take notes in class) is better for learning and retention of information. What does the data indicate, and what do students and faculty think?

8. Most students do not get the amount of sleep they need. What is the average number of sleep hours for students on your campus, and how does this affect them?

9. Students often experience stress while completing a college education. Is there a different type of stress associated with undergraduate, master's or doctoral students?

10. Many campus counseling centers are overwhelmed, and students often have to wait several weeks for their first appointment. What are the most common reasons that students visit these facilities, and how are the counseling centers responding to student needs?

11. Does your campus have a university ombudsman? If so, what are the most frequent problems he or she hears?

12. Many colleges and universities have study abroad programs, where faculty members take students to another country to study a topic for credit in a particular class. What are the most popular programs? Why are they so popular? Are there programs in warring countries, and, if so, what safety provisions are made? You should get some quotes from students who have participated in these programs.

13. Plagiarism and fabrication seem to be increasing on campuses nationally. What is the situation on your campus? Compare it to national figures. What are the punishments for cheating?

14. Write about a successful teacher, coach or another interesting personality on your campus. Interview other students, friends, relatives and colleagues so you have enough information for a well-rounded portrait of the person.

15. Find a campus club that helps people, such as Alcoholics Anonymous or Gamblers Anonymous. Interview club members about their problem and how it affects their lives.

16. What excuses do your faculty members hear most often from students who miss classes, assignments and tests or simply do poorly in a class?

17. Do students on your campus ever complain about faculty members they have difficulty understanding, especially ones from other countries? How serious is the problem, what's being done to correct it and how successful is the effort? Also, why does your college employ faculty members with language problems?

18. Write about the problems and perceptions of students with physical challenges. Are all buildings accessible? You might look specifically at the problems of students who are blind or use wheelchairs.

19. Write a historical feature that describes your college's establishment and early years.

20. What, if any, are the advantages to being an athlete (or an honors student) at your institution? Do athletes meet the same entrance and graduation requirements as other students? Do they have special courses or degree plans, tutors, housing, food or financial aid?

4. Information for Features

Write a feature story based on the following set of information regarding missing people. Assume the data is correct. Revise writing errors and stereotypes.

You won't believe the numbers involved. They're astonishingly high. Its typical of the situation in each and every one of the nations 50 states. Last year alone in just your one state alone a total number of 57,152

men, women, and children were reported at one time or another to be "missing." A total of 48,384 of the missing individuals sooner or later reappeared or were found or otherwise recovered. But nearly 9,000 remain missing, and that seems to be a typical number for a years total annual figures for your one state. Some of the missing people each year are kids—assumingly runaways. Others are people with Alzheimers—supposedly old people who wander some distance away from their homes. There are deadbeat dads, too. There are people trying to run away from their debts. There are always young men and women running away with lovers with whom they are deeply and idealistically, and perhaps unrealistically, in love. And there are each year a few, but very few, bona fide crime victims: people apparently kidnapped or robbed or murdered, with their bodies hidden, perhaps burned or buried or tossed into some deep body of water somewhere and thus hidden.

Police estimate that the true crime victims total no more than 75 in number and perhaps as few as 40 or 50. Sgt. Manuel Cortez of your citys police dept. said a woman may disappear, and everyone—friends, co-workers, relatives, everyone—swears that she was a totally reliable person and happy and stable, so everyone believes she's a victim of foul play. 5 years later she may call her parents to say she's now happily married and has three kids, a new job, and a new name, and ran off 5 years ago because she was in love with someone her parents didn't like, or didn't like pressures at home or work or just wanted to try someplace new, or hated a boyfriend or her husband at the time who, unknown to all others, perhaps drank or beat her or abused her both physically and mentally.

"I've worked around missing persons for the past 10 years, and it's rare to find someone after more than a year," Cortez said. "We find a lot of people disappear because they've got troubles, want to leave them behind and start over again. A lot of people think about it, and some do more than think about it. Normally its more men than women, except among juveniles. Among juveniles, runaway girls outnumber boys 3 to 1. Kids, particularly those 11 to 17, flee in droves." Another authority, Psychology Prof. Alan Christopher, says, "Most adults will stick around and handle their problems, but a lot of kids think its easier to run away. Or they just don't think. They see some place on social media, and it looks good, so they try to go there."

Nationwide, 450,700 youngsters were reported to have fled their homes and juvenile facilities and all sorts of other places they were supposed to be living last year and another 127,100 were "thrown away," meaning their parents or guardians or whoever in the world was caring for them would not let them come back, according to statistics compiled by the U.S. Justice Dept.

Three-fourths of the missing persons in your state last year were runaway juveniles. Nearly 6,500 have not yet been found or located.

Sabrina Diaz, a 14 yr. old, is an example, now residing at 1987 Holcrofte Ave. in your city. "My parents got divorced" she told you after you promised not to use her last name. "I hated my stepfather. He's a jerk. He got drunk and hit my Mom and expected us to wait on him like we were his slaves or something. "So, uh, I met this guy on Snapchat—'cause you only have to be 13 to use it—who was moving to New York, and sent him a picture of me. We talked and then met. He didn't want to take me, said I was too young, but I, uh, got him to change his mind. So, uh, like I was there two years, then got caught shoplifting and prostituting and the cops somehow they came up with my real name and

my mom came and got me. She's dropped the jerk, so it's better now, just the two of us, and so we can, uh, talk and stuff."

Another example is Jason Abare, who is a 31 year old man currently residing in your county jail on charges of nonsupport. At the time of his divorce from his wife, Anne, of 9 years, he was ordered to pay alimony and child support for his four kids, a total of $940 a month. Ann currently resides at 855 Tichnor Way. "I wasn't going to give her a penny, not with the hell that woman put me through," he said. He left the state. "It was easy, real easy," he told you during a jailhouse interview today. "I'm in construction, a carpenter, and good, so I can pick up a job almost anywhere and kinda drifted around. If I liked where I was I'd stay a couple months, even a year. Other times I just stayed a week or two until I got my first payday then skipped town. I figured no one could ever find me that way. I got caught last month, charged with drunken driving and didn't have a drivers license anymore so they checked my prints and found out who I really was. Then they searched social media and found my old Facebook postings and returned me here. Bad luck, that's what it was, just bad luck."

WRITING FOR BROADCAST NEWS

At the time of writing this chapter, things in America are tense. The president is trying to dismantle Obamacare; hurricanes are flooding cities along the coastline and fires are raging across California; and a single mass shooting is one too many.

People want regular updates on these events because they depend on Obamacare, have family homes teetering on the brink of disaster or worry about safety. During the day they check their news apps, listen to news on the radio or podcasts, or read their RSS (really simple syndication) news feeds while working on their computer. When they get home from school or work they often pick up the remote to watch the news, either from their local station or a 24-hour news network.

Radio, TV and podcast news informs audiences in ways different from print media. Text-based news provides detailed information structured to be read, using the eyes. Audio news is written for the listener's ears, hearing only spoken words and environmental sounds that are combined to create a story. Video news is for viewers tuning in with their eyes and ears. Unlike print or audio consumers, TV viewers do not have to draw on their imaginations because they see exactly what happens as the journalist covers the event. Reporters convey important information with aural and visual elements, creating stories in real time (live) or delayed broadcast, satellite or cable.

This chapter introduces ways to think about broadcast news style and focuses on the basics of broadcast news writing. "Broadcast" is used here because it is a generally accepted term for news written for radio, TV or podcasts, although more precise terms might be "audio news" and "video news."

The Broadcast News Story

Although writing styles vary among media, good news judgment and the types of news stories chosen are similar. The best audio and visual stories typically resemble the best stories for print. They involve the audience. Compelling themes and writing draw people into a story, encouraging them to connect to the issue.

Similar to print reporters, broadcast journalists identify a newsworthy angle for a story and then thoroughly research the issues and events to tell the story accurately. They home in on a central point, conduct background research on their sources, ask important questions and employ good interviewing skills to obtain interesting quotes because this part of the process is recorded.

All reporters write well and spell correctly so their work is easy to understand. Broadcast copy must be error-free so that announcers can read it easily. It must be written smoothly because audiences have only one chance to hear it, unless the story is published online. And it must be written well because sometimes the transcript of the story appears online.

Pam Oliver covers the National Basketball Association (NBA) and the National Football League (NFL) for Fox Sports. She graduated with a degree in journalism, began her career as a news reporter and also worked for ESPN. She was named Outstanding Woman in Journalism by Ebony magazine.

Whereas print journalists think about the readability of their story, broadcast reporters also consider how audiences hear or see the story. Other differences between print and broadcast center on the structure and style of stories. The following is an example of how the same event is presented in each form. For a list of the differences between them, see Table 13.1.

Broadcast News Copy	Print News Copy
Escaped Convict	Escaped Convict
Shannon Ha	Shannon Ha
11-15-18	11-15-18
Police are looking for an Austin woman this afternoon.	A woman from Austin escaped yesterday from the Travis County Courthouse after being convicted of assault and battery charges from last May.
Maria Lopez fled the Travis County Courthouse moments after being convicted of assault and battery.	Maria Lopez hit a guard after her trial ended at 3 p.m. and ran out of the courthouse, according to Darnel Rodriguez, a county assistant prosecutor.
Assistant prosecutor Darnel Rodriguez says Lopez hit a guard, and ran for freedom at three o'clock.	"We consider Lopez to be armed and dangerous," said Sheriff Lyle McNeil.
The woman is 28-years-old and was wearing jeans, a white short-sleeved shirt and red tennis shoes.	Lopez, 28, was last seen wearing jeans, a white short-sleeved shirt and red tennis shoes.
Sheriff Lyle McNeil says Lopez is armed and dangerous.	###
###	

TABLE 13.1   Differences Between the Escaped Convict Broadcast and Print Stories

Broadcast	Print
The lead focuses on one fact.	The lead is a summary of who, what, where, when and why.
The next sentence answers why.	The bridge answers how from an authority.
Verbs are in present tense.	Verbs are in past tense.
Attribution begins sentences (who said what).	Attribution follows statement (what, said who).
Listeners cannot hear quote marks.	Direct quotes signal authority.

Leads

As the previous example shows, the summary lead of a broadcast story is shorter than that of a print story. When read aloud, print sentences are often long and difficult to follow, which frustrates listeners. Broadcast leads give one or two important facts and ease the audience into the rest of the story.

The best leads capture attention by connecting the news to audience's lives. People care more about stories that are relevant to them or their situations. For example, Iowa has many corn farmers, who all care about corn market prices. Other people might disregard a story on the topic because they think it does not involve them. A good lead convinces them otherwise. Even if they are not farmers, almost everyone will encounter the domino effect of market prices when they shop for fresh, frozen or canned sweet corn or for meat from animals that eat feed corn. Consumers also may feel the effect because of the crop's other competitive uses, such as corn pellets, corn ethanol and high-fructose corn syrup, the major sweetener in most processed foods and beverages in the United States.

Consider the following two leads regarding corn prices. The second lead also includes the body of the story:

> It is expected that corn market prices will increase as the drought continues throughout the Midwestern states.
>
> ###
>
> Thanks to the abnormally long dry weather in the Midwest, your grocery bill is likely to go up this year.
>
> The drought has wasted thousands of acres in top corn-farming states. Iowa, Nebraska, Illinois and Minnesota—the four states that farm most of our corn—have been hit especially hard.
>
> What does this mean to you? Well, the price of gum, soft drinks, cereals and hundreds of other products that use corn sweetener will increase because of the higher demand for the corn that survives the heat.
>
> ###

Although the lead focuses on one or two points, it also withholds much important information until later because people usually do not hear the first two or three words of a story. They mentally tune in after they hear or see something that interests them.

Broadcast journalists rewrite leads quickly throughout the day to update audiences waiting to hear the latest news about an ongoing story. When broadcast stories are rewritten, they focus on a new angle to update or localize the story.

Four common types of leads are the hard, soft, throwaway and umbrella. Each is written to intrigue and interest listeners or viewers and provides a transition to the rest of the story.

The Hard Lead

Hard leads give important information immediately. Some audience members want to hear the most meaningful details first. However, some broadcasters believe that the significant facts are gone before audiences realize they need to "tune in" to what is being said. Here is an example of a hard lead, followed by the remainder of the story:

> Car bombs have killed at least 23 people this morning in an Iraqi [i-RAK-ee] holy city.
>
> Two bombs exploded in a crowd of Shiite [SHEE-eye-t] pilgrims ending a 40-day religious mourning period in Karbala [kar-BAH-lah]. Similar bombings have killed about 160 people during the past week. This has raised concern about the abilities of Iraqi [i-RAK-ee] forces to take over their own security in the face of a full U.S. military pull-out.
>
> ###

Notice that this copy contains the pronunciation of certain words. Including this information makes it easier for the announcer to read them and avoids mistakes.

The Soft Lead

The soft lead tells a broadcast audience that something important is coming up and invites them to continue with the story. Soft leads, like soft news stories, feature some information before getting to the hard news. This lead usually reveals why the upcoming information is important or how it affects people:

> As we near the April 1 tax deadline, you might want to know that the Internal Revenue Service has a new phone app that offers tax tips.

During Facebook's initial public offering, CNBC provided frequent updates on the stock trades, keeping audiences informed.

The story continues:

> The I-R-S's new app helps you with filing instructions and notifies you when your refund hits the bank. . . .

###

The Throwaway Lead

The throwaway lead intrigues listeners or viewers and makes them focus on the story. The second sentence begins the real lead. A story would make sense without the throwaway—but, without it, the story might not attract attention:

> Finally, it's beginning to feel a lot like Christmas.
>
> After more than a week of unseasonably warm weather across our state, cold temperatures are back. Light snow is possible today in the Texas Panhandle and in other parts of the state. Today's highs are expected to reach about 40 degrees.

###

The Umbrella Lead

The umbrella lead summarizes or ties together two or more loosely related news stories before delving into each separately. In other words, it describes the relationship between the stories:

> The bitter cold snap outside is thought to be the cause of two separate deaths in the city this morning.

Here is the rest of the story:

> Police say an 82-year-old woman who apparently fell on the ice outside of her home in Bunker Hill Township died of hypothermia this morning. Alva Saint Clare slipped on her sidewalk sometime during the night, broke her hip and froze as temperatures dipped in the single digits.
>
> About three hours later and a few miles away, neighbors found Joshua Johnson frozen to death in his truck in his driveway. Police are unsure why Johnson, who was 57-years-old, was sleeping in the vehicle on a night when temperatures dropped below zero.

###

The Body of a Story

The body of broadcast news stories usually is one of two types, depending on the story being reported. Broadcast hard news stories follow the pyramid formula, in which the one or two most important facts come first, followed by more information (Figure 13.1). The lead does not tell the whole story. And, because stories

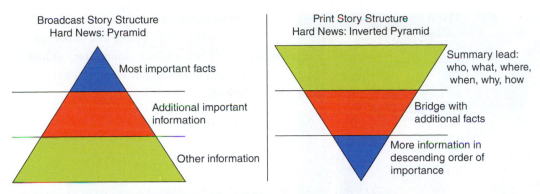

Broadcast Story Structure
Hard News: Pyramid

Most important facts

Additional important information

Other information

Print Story Structure
Hard News: Inverted Pyramid

Summary lead: who, what, where, when, why, how

Bridge with additional facts

More information in descending order of importance

Figure 13.1   Structures for Broadcast and Print News   Hard broadcast stories often have the reverse structure of hard print stories.

and newscasts are timed before they are aired, journalists can write a complete story, using as many facts as needed, without fearing that the ending sentence or paragraph will be edited out at the last moment.

Soft news stories follow more of a wineglass structure (Figure 13.2). The single most important or emotional information is placed toward the top of the story to catch the audience's attention. It is followed by several pieces of information important to understanding the issue or event, usually in the form of expert sources. The story then closes with a single memorable ending or summary, sometimes a lesson learned from the main subject.

Overall, broadcast stories keep to the point with shorter sentences and fewer facts than those used in print stories. Every sentence of a story is important because when someone leaves it, he or she is usually leaving the newscast. Also, listeners and viewers generally cannot digest a lot of information all at once and cannot review it, so broadcast stories are short. Stories are tight, with every word tied to the central point. Although the most important information comes early, what follows is important, too.

Whatever the structure, the facts of any broadcast story are usually presented in one of two ways: descending order of importance or chronological order with a narrative format. For descending order, the broadcast journalist figures out the most significant piece of information, which normally goes in the story's lead. Then the journalist decides what else the audience wants to know; this information makes up the body of the story. Although a story may contain several pieces of information, their order tends to be dictated by the facts given in the lead. If the lead reports that a man attacked his ex-wife and her husband, as the next example does, people will want to know who the victims are and where, how and why they were attacked. They also will want to know about the suspect and what police are doing about the case:

> Police are looking for a man who posed as a salesperson this afternoon and used a hammer to attack a Roseville couple.
>
> Janna and Dylan Banner are in stable condition at Community Hospital after Marten Keller repeatedly hit the couple and forced his way into their home.

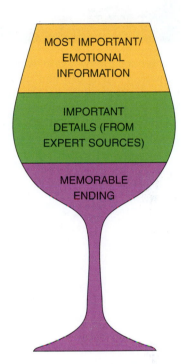

MOST IMPORTANT/ EMOTIONAL INFORMATION

IMPORTANT DETAILS (FROM EXPERT SOURCES)

MEMORABLE ENDING

Figure 13.2   The Wineglass Story Structure   Most soft broadcast stories use the wineglass structure.

Reporter and Emmy Award–winner Jackie Nespral anchors the 5 p.m., 5:30 p.m., 6 p.m. and 11 p.m. newscasts for WTVJ-TV in Miami. She has a degree in journalism and has worked at Univision, Television Marti, CNN and the Today Show.

By the time police responded to a neighbor's 9-1-1 call, Keller had already fled in his car, a 2015 black Honda Civic. Janna Banner had a restraining order on Keller, who is her ex-husband.

Keller is six-feet-tall, and was last seen wearing a light blue suit.

In the chronological type of broadcast news story, the climax—the most significant part—is the lead. Then, the journalist relates the details in the order of their occurrence, not the order in which he or she learned each fact:

A Roseville couple was hospitalized this afternoon after being repeatedly attacked by the woman's ex-husband.

Authorities say Marten Keller knocked on the Banners' door at noon, posing as an evangelist. When Dylan Banner tried to shut his door, Keller became violent, repeatedly hitting Banner with a hammer while forcing his way into the house. Keller then attacked Janna Banner when she tried to help her husband.

Keller had disappeared in a 2015 black Honda Civic by the time neighbors called police, who arrived about five minutes later.

An ambulance took the Banners to Community Hospital where they are in stable condition.

Police are looking for Keller, who is six-feet-tall and was wearing a light blue suit at the time of the attack.

Updating Broadcast News Stories

Many radio and television stations have several newscasts throughout the day. Different new stories replace old ones. In addition, stations keep the public updated on developments to older stories. Thus, the same story may be a topic throughout the day, but freshened with new angles, additional interviews or more recent information. The lead sentence and body of the story never stay exactly the same in successive newscasts. Here are three updated leads for the story on the Banners:

1. A Roseville man accused of attacking his ex-wife and her husband has been arrested in Houston (Or, Police have arrested a Roseville man. . . .)
2. Police say a man who attacked his ex-wife and her husband was trying to regain custody of his son.
3. A woman and her husband are out of the hospital this afternoon after her ex-husband attacked them with a hammer.

Guidelines for Copy Preparation

The format and aesthetics of broadcast news copy are important because too many marks can distract an announcer and, consequently, detract from the story. If an announcer gets confused, the audience surely will be.

Formatting Copy

Many instructors require their students to submit printed copy of their stories. And announcers often practice with printed news copy. Television announcers usually read the final version from a teleprompter, but might have printed stories or stories on an iPad nearby for emergencies. Radio announcers use printed stories, monitors or iPads or other types of tablets to read the news. The tablets have software that allows announcers to add hand-drawn symbols to personalize the copy, which can remind them to slow down their tempo, emphasize certain words or group certain words together in a phrase.

Broadcast news copy preparation may differ from station to station, but it is similar to print in many ways, such as including the slug in the top left corner and double-spacing the lines of the story for readability or for adding copy-editing symbols. Copy can be in all uppercase or all lowercase letters. Sentences and paragraphs begin and end on the same page so audiences do not hear the ruffling of pages, which might obscure the announcer's words in the middle of a story. Sometimes an announcer discovers that a page is missing or is in the wrong order. If sentences and paragraphs are kept together on one page, the story will sound coherent; the announcer will not scramble for something to say while he or she looks for the rest of the sentence or story. Using a symbol (###) at the end lets the announcer know that the story is finished.

Editing Copy

Broadcast reporters never use newspaper copy-editing symbols because they are too difficult for an announcer to interpret quickly while reading on air. To edit a word, simply black it out and rewrite it in the space above it. If the copy requires a lot of editing, type a new copy. The fewer editing marks, the fewer times an announcer hesitates or stumbles while reading.

Timing Copy

Margins are often set at 60, with an average of 10 words to a line. Depending on how fast one reads, three lines of copy take about 10 seconds. For most announcers, nine lines of copy are about 30 seconds and 18 full lines equal one minute of reading time. The timing of the story in seconds (for example, ":30") and the number of lines are written in the top right corner of the copy page. Some journalists prefer to note only the number of lines. And some announcers circle the timing, as well as the slug and end mark, to indicate that that it is not to be read on air.

Reviewing Copy

A journalist or announcer reads all copy aloud to become familiar with what has been prepared for the newscast. If the reader stumbles, the story must be revised.

Ira Glass narrates and produces "This American Life," a long-running radio and podcast documentary series that was also on Showtime.

While reading each story, the announcer confirms that his or her reading time matches the average number of lines per minute. One reason announcers use printed copy is so they can make notes to personalize their reading style. The announcer marks the copy for word emphases or difficult pronunciations, for example.

Story Length

The time allotted for the story usually indicates story importance. Broadcast stories can run from 10 seconds in a radio newscast or audio podcast to five minutes for a TV or video story. If the story is not visually or aurally interesting, it should run less than a minute. If the story warrants special attention, it could run from one to three minutes. If the story rambles, however, journalists eliminate details that detract from its focus. The type of news outlet—commercial or public—can also affect the story length.

Story Script

Journalists write their script after they have reviewed their audio and video bites captured in the field or from any syndicated news clips. Journalists use natural sound and visuals gathered at the scene so listeners can experience the story. The strength of broadcast stories is that they can trigger senses that cannot be experienced through other media.

Effective broadcast writing matches words to pictures and sounds. Journalists are careful to avoid words that repeat what the audience member already is hearing or seeing on the screen.

Television scripts also require captions, such as the name and title of the people being interviewed. This information must be spelled correctly on the script.

Three examples of broadcast news scripts appear in the "From the News" box, starting on page 283. These are actual news stories in their original formats. Scott Pohl, a 25-year radio news veteran of WKAR, an NPR affiliate, wrote the first two stories. Robert Gould, who has been in the TV news business for about 20 years, wrote the third.

Using Audio

Planning to record audio requires several decisions: whom to record; where to record; what natural, or environmental, sound is needed; and what music, if any, is appropriate to use. When determining to include the recording into a story, journalists have more choices to make: where to insert the audio clip into the story and how long it should be. The story could include brief statements from someone explaining, emphasizing or dramatizing a point. Or the audio could be a long interview that tells almost the entire story.

FROM THE NEWS

Examples of News Readers

1. EXAMPLE OF A RADIO NEWS READER
The announcer reads this story directly from news copy. It has no other sound.

QURAN BURNING UPDATE
DATE
POHL

East Lansing police say a person surrendered today in connection with the recent desecration of a copy of the Quran [ker AN] at the Islamic Center.

A 10-thousand-dollar reward was recently offered for tips on the case, but none of the money was paid out. Police say the individual is cooperating with investigators, and they have determined it was an isolated incident.

Officials expect to conclude their investigation early next week, and the case will then be sent to the Ingham County Prosecutor.

The burned Quran [ker AN] was found Saturday at the entrance to the Islamic [is LAM ic] Center of East Lansing.

\#\#\#

2. EXAMPLE OF A RADIO NEWS READER WITH SOUND ON TAPE
This reader contains a sound bite. The SOT (sound on tape) from an interview is labeled and timed "(SOT: 0:14)."

STATE OF THE CITY
DATE
POHL

Lansing Mayor Virg Bernero [burr NARROW] will deliver his annual State of the City address tonight.

Mayor Bernero [burr NARROW] isn't expected to talk about the city of Lansing's looming 15-million-dollar budget deficit, as many people had hoped. He will wait to discuss the city budget at a press conference next week, instead.

Mayoral representative Randy Hannon says Bernero [burr NARROW] will talk about recent progress in the face of economic challenges, and the prospects for the year ahead.

(SOT: 0:14) "Things like GM's upcoming investment in the Lansing Grand River plant to create 600 new jobs, the long-awaited opening of the Accident Fund's new headquarters on our riverfront, and the fact that the Lansing region is leading the state's economic recovery."

The speech will be delivered from the former Knapp's [NAP's] department store building downtown. The Eyde [EYE-d] Company is working on a 30-million-dollar plan to renovate the building.

This will be Bernero's [burr NARROW's] sixth State of the City address. It's set to begin at 7 p-m. The speech will be televised by W-I-L-X-T-V.

\#\#\#

3. EXAMPLE OF TV NEWS VOICE-OVER WITH SOT
In this story, the viewer sees and hears the anchor read the introduction, then hears the anchor's voice over a visual (voice-over, VO), then hears and sees event participant Janie Mitchell talking about her experience (SOT) with a total running time of 12 seconds (TRT:12). The camera goes back to the anchor reading the ending of the story (tag line). The time of each tape is noted within the story.

MASON NEW ART MUSEUM
DATE
GOULD

Anchor Intro/lead:
AFTER 2-YEARS AND 16-MILLION-DOLLARS LATER, ART LOVERS ACROSS THE AREA FINALLY CAN CELEBRATE THE OPENING OF THE NEW MASON ART MUSEUM.

Take VO: (:25)
MAYOR JONAS CARTER AND THE MUSEUM'S CHIEF DONOR, ALANA LEE, CUT THE RIBBON THIS MORNING . . . THE FIRST VISITORS THEN GOT A V-I-P TOUR OF THE NEW FACILITY.

HIGHLIGHTS OF THE MUSEUM INCLUDE 20TH CENTURY PAINTINGS, INTERACTIVE EXHIBITS AND A SCULPTURE GALLERY.

THOSE ON THE TOUR SAY THE NEW MUSEUM IS A CROWN JEWEL FOR THE CITY.

Take SOT: (Janie Mitchell-TRT:12)
This place is amazing. We loved every bit of it and our kids were fascinated with the interactive exhibits. This is a great thing for the area. We can't wait to come back and really explore it further.

Anchor Tag:
MUSEUM OFFICIALS EXPECT HUGE CROWDS THIS WEEKEND. THEY SUGGEST YOU ARRIVE EARLY SO THAT YOU HAVE A CHANCE TO SEE THE MANY EXHIBITS. THE NEW MUSEUM WILL BE OPEN BOTH SATURDAY AND SUNDAY, FROM 9 A-M to 7 P-M.

\#\#\#

The New York Times produces "The Daily," a 20-minute podcast that focuses on a single story per episode. It features audio clips from interviews and discussions between the host and other journalists. Through this format, audiences gain a better perspective of a news story and also feel a more personal connection to the journalists by hearing their voices. Many news organizations produce podcasts to enhance digital multimedia packages and give audiences an additional way to understand and connect with a story.

In addition to being an important form and element of news stories and podcasts, audio may also accompany news photo slideshows. As a series of pictures is displayed, the audio recording—or VO—of an announcer or narrator explaining the images can be heard. Sometimes, natural sound accompanies the slideshow.

Using Video

Journalists have the same considerations for video as for audio: it is used as a tool to better explain or illustrate a story. In planning for video in a story, journalists decide if it will be a short clip of a source or subject, a several-minute analysis highlighting several people or VO analysis of a scene from b-roll video. Many news documentaries use multiple long interviews interspersed as narratives over video scenes or photographs and music to give viewers a sense of place.

For a short TV news story or video podcast on a property tax increase, reporters consider whom to record. Government officials would explain why they think the increase is needed and how the additional revenue will be spent. Business leaders and local residents would respond about how the proposed tax increase affects their businesses and personal income. B-roll might add context to the video story. It could be a city council meeting in which the proposal is debated or images of the community affected by an increase, such as storefronts in a downtown area or homes in a local subdivision. The reporter also may include video of the places that are to benefit from the increased tax revenue, such as local schools or road construction. (For more on using audio and visual elements, see Chapter 14.)

Sources for Broadcast News

Broadcast journalists get their news from the same sources print or online journalists use. However, instead of writing down what a source has said, broadcast reporters record the interviews for portions to be played on the air. This change in voice—the use of sound bites—enables the audience to feel close to the people involved in the news and to hear their exact words. Although personal interviews are best, broadcasters sometimes record telephone interviews with the source's permission. Common sources for broadcast news include news services or news feeds, people, newspapers, news releases from public relations agencies and internet resources, all of which are attributed.

News Services

News services have written, audio and video stories on their websites for subscribing stations to use. "News feeds" is the term for audio or video stories that journalists can integrate into their newscasts. At designated times of the day, forthcoming story topics and lengths are listed by the news service, and the news feeds are transmitted to subscribing stations. Journalists can record any stories they want, then simply add the opening and closing.

Newspapers, Online News and Broadcast News Sources

Reporters scan local newspapers, broadcast competitors or other news outlets for news of important events to make sure their station has covered them. They can report on these events by focusing on different angles. On the rare occasions that journalists use information from their competition, they rewrite the story in broadcast style for newscasts and credit the source.

Public Relations News Releases

Public relations (PR) practitioners who represent governments and businesses flood news organizations with print and video news releases (VNRs) announcing events or happenings (see Chapter 19). Journalists can also go online to press release sites such as prnewswire.com. News releases are quite helpful on slow news days. Reporters look to them for ideas or additional information about changes within the community, updates on local companies or to localize a story happening elsewhere. Ideally, the release is regarded as a news tip, to be followed up with research and interviews that incorporate opposing viewpoints. Rarely are news releases objective; they always favor the PR company's client.

People

Many good news tips come from people who contact the station about an event that has just happened or is about to happen. Some stations encourage tips by advertising a telephone number to call or text or an email address. Following up on tips with in-depth questions and research can uncover more sources and interesting stories. In addition, interviewing people about one subject can lead to tips and ideas on other subjects.

Broadcast Interviews

Interviewing for broadcast requires the reporter to behave differently from one who interviews for print because the audio or video footage is recording all sounds. Broadcast journalists minimize their movements so that the microphone does not pick up unnecessary and distracting noise. They also respond nonverbally—with nods—to their subjects during the interview so that their voices will not be recorded. Facial expressions in an interview should be minimal because they can be misinterpreted as agreement with everything the source is saying. Nods should indicate that the source's words are being heard.

Lester Holt, center, interviews U.S. Army Sgt. 1st Class Todd Straw of Davenport, Iowa, as part of NBC's "The Today Show" from Kabul. Holt began his career as a disc jockey while in college. He anchors "NBC Nightly News" and "Dateline NBC."

Journalists select sound bites that convey the heart of the story. Reporters ask open-ended questions to encourage discussion during an interview. Then, they write a script around the chosen sound bites that most represent the issue or event. Most sound bites are six to 20 seconds long. The text of the script lets the audience know that a sound bite is coming up, but it does not repeat what the subject will say on tape.

Writing the Broadcast Story

Broadcast journalists adhere to a combination of Associated Press (AP) general rules and a broadcast presentation style. Many networks and stations have their own style guides. The procedures given in the following sections point out the major differences between AP and broadcast writing styles, but are by no means exhaustive.

No matter what style they use, broadcast journalists think in terms of time because newscasts fit into a standard time frame. Newscasts begin and end on the minute, considering introductions and closings, commercials or public service announcements (PSAs) and transitions from story to story. Thus, journalists must total the length of all their stories to fit the allotted time. In terms of presentation, they write for both the audience and the announcer.

Writing for the Audience

Broadcasters structure stories for audiences who multitask. They might be driving a car while listening to the radio or a podcast or eating dinner while watching TV. Thus, as emphasized throughout this chapter and book, a news story must capture and retain audience members' attention throughout their day and in concert with their habits.

Here are some general guidelines for broadcast news writing:

- **Adopt a conversational, informal and relaxed style.** Write the way you would talk to a friend. Sometimes this style includes using contractions, incomplete sentences and first- and second-person pronouns (e.g., I, me, us, we, you) to establish a rapport with listeners. Yet, one should keep the conversation more formal and respectful than too casual.
- **Write short, declarative sentences that are to the point and limited to one idea.** People cannot listen to a long sentence and always associate the end with the beginning. Sentences in broadcast style often have fewer than 15 words, and none should have more than 25 words. They are simple sentences in the active voice, keeping the subject, verb and object together—and in that order. Long sentences should be divided into shorter ones, as in this example:

  A park, or some people might call it a farm or facility, is being planned by several developers, who they themselves are not farmers but plan to rent acreage to others, will be ready on the east side with irrigation and other necessities that would make it one of the largest places to growing marijuana plants, sometimes termed "weed" or older folks called it "marijane" and they are still a controversy for our city.

  The following revision is clearer:

  A proposed two-hundred-acre medical marijuana park on the east of town will be the second-largest in the country.

- **Use present-tense verbs to emphasize recentness.** People turn to radio and TV news for quick updates to breaking stories. Examples include "says," not "said"; "is searching," not "searched." If the present tense does not work, try the present perfect tense:

  Two scientists have found a potential cure for hepatitis C.

- **If past tense is used, include the time element immediately after the main verb** to tell listeners how recent the information is:

  Senator Deb Schmidt announced this morning that she will not run for public office again.

- **Use round numbers.** It is difficult for someone to remember the exact figure of 2,898. It is easier to remember "almost three-thousand."
- **Give numbers meaning.** What does it mean to a resident that "the school board approved a 64-million-dollar bond proposal to taxpayers"? Sound overwhelming? Saying that "for a person with a 100-thousand-dollar house, it would equal about 140 dollars a year" gives listeners and viewers a personal context and clearer understanding.
- **Shorten long titles.** Long titles can be confusing and use up most of the time allotted to a story. Use one- to two-word titles. For example, "Andrea Dove is a lottery advocate with the North American Association of State and Provincial Lotteries" could be shortened to "lottery advocate Andrea Dove."
- **Never put a name first in a story.** People might miss it. Also, the individual's name is usually less important than the actual focus of the story. Delay the name until the story has captured the audience's attention, or at least until the second sentence of the script:

  The uncle of the two missing boys says he is praying for their safe return. The last time Charles Hastings saw his two nephews was near the family's lake cabin this morning.

- **Omit a person's middle initial**, unless it is commonly recognized as part of that person's name. Broadcast writing uses a conversational style, and speakers rarely refer to others by their initials in conversation.
- **Place the description, age or identification before a person's name.** Newspaper style, with description often placed after the name, is not conversational:

  Meredith Hinojosa [eenoh HO sah], 13, a Friendswood Middle School student, has won the national championship spelling bee.

  In broadcast the style, the sentence would be revised to

  A Friendswood youth is being celebrated this afternoon in Washington, D-C.

- **Leave out ages and addresses if they are unimportant to the story.** However, writers might need to include general information to differentiate people with similar names, especially in stories reporting arrests or allegations of criminal conduct.
- **Place the attribution before what is said.** The broadcast formula "who said what" is the opposite of newspaper style "what, said who." Journalists prepare

the audience for the quotation or paraphrase coming next, to allow them to concentrate on what is being said:

> County Circuit Judge Horacio Diddi [hor RAY shee oh DEE dee] says that his colleague engaged in disruptive behavior while presiding over cases last week.

● **Avoid direct quotes.** People cannot hear quotation marks, so broadcast journalists paraphrase what someone said. If a direct quote is necessary, use special language to make it clear, as in these examples:

> And quoting directly here, "...

> As she put it, "...

> In his own words, "...

● **Avoid homonyms.** Words that sound alike but have different meanings and spellings can confuse listeners. ("The gambler cashed/cached his chips before going to his room.") Audience members might miss the rest of the story if they spend time wrestling with a confusing sentence.

● **Avoid too many pronouns.** It is often difficult to figure out who is being referred to in a particular sentence:

> Rasheeda Longman and Sung-Mi Lee were in the canoe when it tipped over. She is credited for saving her friend, who doesn't know how to swim.

● **Use descriptive language, but sparingly.** Some words help a listener to better visualize an event (e.g., "hurled" instead of "threw"). However, too much description can take away from the rest of the story. The audio or video that accompanies stories can provide the description.

Writing for Your Announcer

Broadcast copy is "announcer-friendly." At some stations, the writer is the announcer, but at many others, writers and announcers are different people. Therefore, a broadcast journalist writes stories that can be delivered aloud by someone else.

Here are common writing tips broadcast writers use to make announcing easier:

● **Add phonetic spelling.** To mispronounce a name on the air is a journalistic sin. Announcers often need the name of a place or person spelled out phonetically, directly after the word. The Voice of America has a pronunciation guide online for words that are in the national and international news.

> Juanita Diaz [Wha-NEE-ta DEE-ahz] has placed first in the Rifle Association's annual sharpshooters contest.

Sometimes, the same spelling is pronounced differently in different regions of the United States. Thus, "Charlotte" can be [SHAR-lot] in North Carolina or [shar-LOT] in Michigan.

- **Hyphenate words that go together in a group.** Announcers will then avoid taking a breath between these words, saying them as a group:

   A 15-year-old boy from Arkansas has won the national fishing contest.

   The 18-52 volume of "Uncle Tom's Cabin" is a first edition.

- **Spell out numbers one through eleven.** Spell out eleven because it might be confused with two letter l's. For example, an announcer might pause when reading "11 llamas" instead of "eleven llamas."

- **Use a combination of numerals and words for large numbers and generalize.** An example is "40-thousand." Also, the numeral 6,500 is written as six-thousand-500 or as 65-hundred. Announcers might stumble at the numeral "$10,110,011," but can glide along more easily when reading (and rounding) "about ten-million-dollars."

- **Use words instead of abbreviations.** Spell out rather than abbreviate titles, state names, months of the year, measurements and other words so that an announcer can easily recognize and pronounce them without guessing their meaning. The following are examples:

   Saint or Street, not St.

   Association, not Assn.

   miles-per-hour, not m.p.h.

- **Spell out figures, signs and symbols.** And never use a period for a decimal. Try to round numbers or use fractions instead of decimals, as shown here:

   70-percent, not 70%

   500-dollars, not $500

   three-and-a half-million or three-point-five-million, not 3.5 million

- **Hyphenate some numbers and some abbreviations on second reference.** Hyphens let an announcer know that the letters are to be read individually, not as a word:

   C-N-N News

   Triple-A Insurance

   Acronyms, such as Navy SEAL and OSHA [OH shuh], are written without hyphens because they are pronounced the way they are spelled.

- **Use hyphens for numbers to be read individually.** Numbers in phone numbers and addresses are usually read individually.

   That telephone number is 5-2-7-0-0-6-6.

   His apartment number is 21-85.

- **Avoid alliterations or tongue twisters.** These word combinations might trip up an announcer. Also avoid words in a series that have several snaking "S" sounds or popping "Ps." They don't translate well into a microphone, which magnifies these sounds.

- **Limit punctuation because it functions as a brake.** Use only periods, commas and ellipses. While reading the script, a comma denotes a slight pause, a period represents a little longer pause and an ellipsis (. . .) means that the announcer should take a much longer pause. However, in print, an ellipsis means that there is an omission of words. All other punctuation is unnecessary in broadcast because the audience cannot see it.

- **Never split a word between lines, nor a sentence or a paragraph between pages of copy.** The announcer needs to read smoothly and not have to look for extended endings on other pages. Furthermore, the story will sound less confusing if a thought (paragraph) is completed even though the rest of the story happens to be on another page that might be missing.

Being a Broadcast Journalist

To many students, broadcast journalism looks glamorous. It is fun, but it requires hard work. For example, radio and TV stations have several daily newscasts. News outlets produce several podcasts daily. And public radio stations, such as NPR affiliates, host news talk shows and news documentaries and schedule longer news programs with more stories than do commercial radio stations. Many local and national radio and television news channels, such as MSNBC, Al Jazeera and Fox Business Network, run news stories 24 hours a day on cable and satellite and feature live stream and news podcasts.

Broadcast reporters obtain news tips from various sources, call people to verify information or interview and record sources at the scene, analyze what was recorded, write the news, read it aloud, personalize the copy, and edit it for broadcast and again for online. Reporters have several daily deadlines, so they learn to connect to sources quickly while covering the issue accurately, efficiently and ethically. Radio and television require reporters to be physically at the location to cover the story, rather than gathering information via phone. Those who can become proficient at conveying the heart of a story in a few words should do well in this area of journalism. With enough practice, writing stories quickly and well can become a habit.

The Reporter's Guide to Broadcast News Writing Style

1. Write in a conversational style for the listener.

2. Make your copy announcer-friendly for quick, easy reading.

3. Use the present tense.

4. Construct simple sentences in subject, verb, object order.

5. Focus on one important news element when framing your story.

6. Do not start a story with a person's name or important information; capture your listener's attention first and save important information for when the listener has mentally tuned in.

7. Use numbers sparingly, round them and give them meaning.

8. Write out titles, numbers and symbols.

9. Keep sentences short, about 15 words or fewer. Details are added through the use of audio and visuals.

10. Place a person's title before his or her name. Attribute before what is said (who says what).

Review Exercises

1. Identifying Broadcast Style

The following are correctly written broadcast leads. Explain how they differ stylistically from leads written for digital and print newspapers. Think about time, verb tense, titles, personal identification, amount of information and a conversational mode.

1. Another actress has stepped forward to accuse Hollywood producer Harvey Weinstein [WINE stine] of sexual harassment. Lena Headley [LEE na HEAD ly], the star of H-B-O's television show called Game of Thrones, tweeted today about her encounter with Weinstein [WINE stine] when she met him at the Venice [VEN iss] Film Festival a few years ago.

2. People are in shock over the Las Vegas shooter who killed almost 60 people and left 500 wounded.

3. Brace yourself for another scorcher. Temperatures are expected to hit 95-degrees today, the hottest it has been on this day in history since 19-0-7.

4. There's a new sheriff in town. Wanda Clarke has won the city's election for mayor with one-thousand votes over incumbent Asa Mullingsworth.

5. A Northwest University football player has been charged today with driving with a suspended license. This is the seventh driving violation for running back Stephen Marshal, and could mean up to one year in jail if convicted.

6. A Harrisburg woman was killed at about 8:30 this morning when her pickup truck hit a curb and struck a utility pole on Seagull Street.

7. A seven-year-old girl is credited with saving a man's life near Tulsa, Oklahoma.

8. A city council member wants to put an end to motorists' text messaging while driving within the city limits.

9. Good news for many workers. Minimum wage is expected to increase eight-percent in five months. Minimum-wage workers currently earn seven-dollars an hour.

10. The U-S has begun extradition procedures against the political leader of an Islamic militant group.

11. Prosecutors want more time to build a case against a city official accused of illegal trading.

12. After encountering barriers to raising money to pay for a new stadium, officials say construction finally is expected to begin next year.

13. Medicare officials say that a new auditing system will hold insurers more accountable.

14. About 40 members of the Texas Air National Guard returned to Dallas today after serving a year in Kuwait [Koo WAIT].

15. Government offices are closed in honor of Columbus Day.

2. Identifying Different Broadcast Leads

The following broadcast leads (the first sentence) and the subsequent paragraphs are written correctly. Identify the style of each lead: hard, soft, throwaway or umbrella.

1. You hear a ring, and reach for your cell phone to find out that it actually is not ringing.

    Stanford University researchers are calling this state of panic . . . "ringxiety." Researcher David Hill says people feel as though the phone is another limb of their body. The cell phone has become people's connection to their friends, family and colleagues. The ring of the phone acts as a reassuring mechanism to let them know that they are not isolated from other people.

2. A Friendswood teenager is the center of attention today at the governor's mansion.

    Sixteen-year-old Gordon Elliott has received the state's Good Citizenship Award for saving two children from drowning in Grand River last fall.

3. Smoke still fills the air over western Colorado.

    A wildfire that injured 30 firefighters and threatened homes has already burned 12-thousand acres. High temperatures and strong winds make the job harder for the 15-hundred firefighters who continue working around the clock.

4. Police are looking into the possibility of a connection among 20 recent dognappings in the area.

Parson's Animal Shelter Director John Ertos says he has received 12 inquiries about lost dogs since yesterday. Most of these dogs were in fenced-in back yards or on leashes.

In nearby Colleyville, police officer Annie Bearclaw says the station has logged eight calls reporting missing dogs within two days.

5. The chair of the House Ways and Means Committee says she wants to abolish our current tax structure.

   Texas Republican Rachael Morgan set that as her goal today as she opened hearings on our tax system.

6. You can be 25-thousand-dollars richer if you tip police with information that helps solve a homicide case.

   Metropolitan Police Chief Stone Willow says that people who provide information that leads to a conviction stand to receive ten-thousand-dollars more than they did last year.

7. More than 165 passengers are safe, after a seven-47 jetliner made an emergency landing at the Minneapolis Metro Airport today.

   Airport director Jean Richards says shortly after takeoff, a door blew open in the luggage compartment. The plane then dumped its fuel and returned to the airport.

8. When faced with the choice of paper or plastic, environmentally conscious grocery shoppers should choose neither.

   It is more environmentally beneficial to instead purchase reusable quality bags or carts to take with you to the grocery store according to the Washington Post. Plastic bags are not biodegradable, and paper cannot degrade because of a lack of water and light available at most landfills.

9. The use of lethal injection in death penalty cases has been put on hold in Missouri and Delaware.

   Critics claim that the method is unconstitutional and inhumane because it causes unnecessary pain.

10. Even the South is no escape from cold weather this week.

    According to the National Weather Service, temperatures in parts of Arizona will reach an icy 20 degrees over the next two days.

3. Broadcast Style and Format

The following are groups of facts, written for hard news text stories. Turn these stories into radio readers, using correct broadcast style and story format. Time each one for 30 seconds. Remember to use phonetic spelling when necessary, use a conversational tone, spell out large numbers and correct any errors. Think about putting the attribution first and shortening the description of someone's title.

Your instructor might ask you to use the same group of facts to write one or more of the following: radio stories with an SOT, TV stories that include a VO or TV stories with SOT.

1. Millions of protestors in Egypt celebrated the news that President Hosni Mubarak had abruptly resigned. Mubarak's resignation today brought to an end 18 days of largely nonviolent protests. The Egyptian army has taken charge of running the country until free elections can be held. The Head of the Constitutional Council has joined the military council in leading the country in the interim. Mohamed ElBaradei, the leading figure in the opposition to Mubarak, expected elections would be held in about one year. Mubarak, 82 and a former air force commander, left without comment for his home in Sharm el Sheik. His departure ended nearly 60 years of rule by a secular dictatorship.

2. A St. Peter's Catholic High School student in your city who police said had a handgun in his locker is being treated at a psychiatric hospital and could face charges in juvenile court when he is released. Sherlock County sheriff's deputies were called to the school Oct. 13th, after a student told the principal that the boy had a gun in his locker. The school went on lockdown for about an hour. The boy was taken into custody, and his parents were called, officials said. Sherlock County Prosecutor Meredith McDougall said that her office is waiting for results of psychiatric tests and for the boy to be released from the hospital. She did not know when that might happen. McDougall would not say if she has decided to bring charges against the boy.

3. In an update to No. 2, apparently the gun was loaded with two bullets. According to a note in the boy's locker, one bullet was intended for his girlfriend and the other for himself. It is unclear as

to whether the boy told a friend about the gun or whether the friend saw the gun in the locker.

4. In another update to No. 2, Sherlock County Prosecutor Meredith McDougall said that they boy might be tried as an adult because the evidence looks as if it could be premeditated murder.

5. A woman was mortally wounded when a car struck her as she was crossing Main St. yesterday. Apparently, Estrella Sanchez, who was 60, slipped and fell on some ice in the intersection of Main and Mountain Streets, according to police reports, as she was on her way to a church rummage sale at the First Presbyterian Church of your city. Due to the icy conditions of the weather, the car lost control as it rounded the corner at too high of a speed, according to a passenger in the car, the driver's sister, named Tina Concorde, who was not injured and neither was the driver. and it could not stop. There were no other passengers. The car was a 2002 black Honda Civic that the driver Eric LaFey had just bought secondhand. The victim was pronounced dead on arrival at St. Mercy Hospital.

6. Shabazz Daas, 19, of the 400 block of Turnball St., was charged Friday in your city with 11 felonies and 5 misdemeanors in connection with a series of home burglaries this month, mostly in the Beauregard neighborhood. From Sept. 9–17th, Daas, sometimes with others, broke into or attempted to break into 7 homes in the 1200 block of Elm St., the 1200 block of James Ave., the 2600 block of Downhill Lanes, the 4200 block of Johnson Blvd., the 1600 block of Quaker St., and the 300 block of McDonald Avenue, according to police. Daas admitted to police he stole electronics and guns and some other items, and sold some of them. He is on probation for burglary and has a prior conviction for robbery, according to court documents.

4. Story Ideas and Format

1. Choose several stories—one hard news, one soft news or feature—from today's newspaper (online or print) to rewrite in broadcast style as a radio news reader (all text format). Time each one for 30 seconds. Remember to use phonetic spelling when necessary, use a conversational tone and spell out large numbers. Think about putting the attribution first and shortening the description of someone's title.

2. Pretend that you are at the scene, covering the story you wrote in No. 1. Rewrite and format the radio story as if you were including a short sound bite.

3. Imagine that you are at the scene, covering the story you wrote in No. 1. Rewrite and format a TV news story, using a short video clip.

4. Choose a hard news story from today's newspaper (online or print). Rewrite it as two radio stories, the first story with facts appearing in chronological order and the second one with facts in order of descending importance.

5. Practice using broadcast style and radio reader format by rewriting the exercises for leads and stories in Chapters 7, 8 and 9.

VISUAL JOURNALISM

mages have the power to convey information. From the cave drawings at Lascaux, France, to the paintings of the Battle of Waterloo to photographs of the Great Depression, the Vietnam War and terrorist attacks, audiences find compelling and dramatic images in newspapers and magazines and on television and websites. While drawing and painting were the means of conveying visual messages for centuries, the development of photography, motion pictures and television introduced a sense of realism that the earlier formats lacked—with a painting, for example, an artist can make the subject more appealing or dramatic than it actually is. Paintings also require an exclusive artistic talent that many individuals do not possess, but photography became the art form of the masses.

Today, the internet and social media host millions of images taken by professional photographers and videographers with years of training and experience as well as by ordinary people with little or no training. In addition, these media are able to capture events as they happen and transmit that information quickly to an audience, making it an ideal tool for news organizations.

The Roots of Visual Journalism

Written communication has always been a visual medium. In ancient times, information was passed by word of mouth. People performed scenes that represented an event, but it was hard to maintain the accuracy of the message because different actors told the story. As writing systems were invented, stories were carved into clay, stone or wood tablets. With the development of writing on paper by the Chinese and Egyptians, information became truly transportable and permanent; the printing press, invented in the 13th century, allowed information to be accurately reproduced and made available to a wider audience. The introduction of images—hand-drawn engravings at first, then photographs—made print media visual.

Frenchman Louis Daguerre is credited as the father of modern photography for his invention of the daguerreotype, the first commercially viable photographic system, in 1839. While its novelty made it spectacularly successful, other technological advances in the science of "picture-taking" soon overshadowed it, such as those by George Eastman, the founder of Kodak, bringing the world of photography and visual communication to the masses in the late 19th century. Photographers such as Matthew Brady and Alexander Gardner, whose images of the American Civil War in the 1860s brought the reality of war to the attention of Americans, helped transform photography from a scientific curiosity to a tool for visual journalism.

Initially, engravers had to make copies of photographs to print them on paper, which sometimes altered or eliminated details from the original. When the half-tone process was developed in the late 1870s, newspapers and magazines were able to reproduce photos more easily and thus included more with their stories. However, it was not until the early decades of the 20th century that modern photojournalism, the telling of stories with pictures, was born.

French inventor Louis Daguerre is credited as the father of modern photography with his creation of the daguerreotype.

A number of people were involved in the development of photojournalism. Erich Salomon, who worked for the German pictorial magazine Berliner Illustrirte Zeitung, was in the vanguard of the field when, in 1928, he began taking candid photographs of world leaders. Eight years later, Henry Luce purchased Life magazine, a humor and general interest publication, and turned it into a newsweekly with a focus on photojournalism. Henri Cartier-Bresson, a French photographer whose emphasis on "street photography" led him to be credited as the father of modern photojournalism, shot numerous assignments for Life. From the 1930s through the 1960s, it and other

A sample of four daguerreotypes, c. 1840s, by W. Vogel of St. Louis, Missouri.

magazines, such as Look, created the "window on the world" that served audiences until the widespread adoption of television assumed that role.

As photography developed, inventors strove to use the new medium to produce "moving pictures." Thomas Edison invented the first motion picture camera in 1891, which was improved upon by the French brothers Auguste and Louis Lumière. When the modern motion picture industry was born in 1895, audiences flocked to storefront "movie houses" to watch moving images of everyday life, some that lasted only several minutes. The debut of director D.W. Griffith's "Birth of a Nation" in 1915 ushered in the modern era of film in America. This feature-length silent film, which was three hours and 10 minutes long, introduced new filmmaking techniques, such as panoramic long shots and panning camera shots, and included an orchestral musical score to be played simultaneously. The sound era of film began in 1927 with the release of "The Jazz Singer," a film that featured actor Al Jolson singing to the audience. Two years later, the talking picture, or "talkie," had taken over the movie industry.

The concept of transmitting moving pictures, or television, was established in the 1870s. Like many ideas, it took decades and inventors in several countries to develop the required technology. In 1888, Heinrich Hertz, a German physicist, discovered radio waves; 11 years later, Italian inventor Guglielmo Marconi, who based his pioneering work on long-distance radio transmission on Hertz's findings, was sending radio signals nearly 10 miles over open water. By 1901, he was sending signals across the Atlantic Ocean.

Marconi's radio could send only signals, but improvements led to the transmission of voices and music. Other inventors explored the possibility of sending and receiving images on the same radio waves that carried sound. The first transmission—using a still image of letters of the alphabet—occurred in 1909. It was not until 1926 that Scottish inventor John Baird, using an electromechanical device, successfully demonstrated the first transmission of a moving image: a human face. The picture was very crude compared to today's standards, but it had a tremendous impact on the distribution of images.

In 1936, the British Broadcasting Corporation (BBC) began transmitting the first public television service from London. The company originally used Baird's electromechanical system, but it was soon replaced by an all-electronic system employing a cathode ray tube (CRT), which would be the dominant means of transmitting and receiving television signals until the digital age. The concept of this technology was established in 1908, but it was not successfully employed until the late 1920s and early 1930s. American inventor Philo Farnsworth was instrumental in developing an all-electronic television system. The system he helped develop began regularly scheduled broadcasts to the public in 1939, when the National Broadcasting Company (NBC) transmitted the opening of the New York World's Fair. Many people attending the fair

Scottish television pioneer John Logie Baird, seen here, invented the original television model. It includes a rapidly revolving disc with lenses that the object being recorded reflects through; a slotted disc that also spins quickly and breaks the light down further; and a light-sensitive cell that receives many flashes consisting of minute squares of the image and generates electrical impulses transmitted to the receiving apparatus.

In the first news event covered by television, David Sarnoff, founder of RCA, dedicates the company's pavilion at the 1939 World's Fair.

were seeing television for the first time, and it was not long before the new technology began spreading throughout the country. By the late 1950s, television had become the major means by which Americans received news and entertainment.

Technologically, film—a flexible, permanent material for capturing images for photography and television—was the prevailing medium used by journalists from the late 1880s until the digital revolution of the 1990s. The invention of videotape in the 1950s made capturing and editing images for television much easier than working with film clips during newscasts. Attempts to develop digital imagery began in the mid-1970s, but it was not until the 1990s that the process of digitizing and storing images became commercially viable. By the beginning of the 21st century, digital had supplanted film as the preferred means of capturing and distributing images to audiences.

Visual Journalism Today

With the introduction of the personal computer, followed by software applications for word processing, publication design, photography and video, the ability to create visual content for the media exploded. What artists, page designers and production people once did by hand could now be done on a computer in less time and with fewer people. Electronic pagination allowed newspapers and magazines to design pages and send them directly to production, eliminating several steps in the process. Digital production made it easier to create and incorporate elements such as pictures, illustrations and infographics on the pages, making them even more visual.

The digital revolution hit photography as advances in the quality of digital cameras began to rival film. News organizations adopted the former because images could be captured, edited and put into production faster and more cheaply than processing film and making prints. Digital photography also eliminated the need for expensive and environmentally harmful chemical processing facilities. And when the internet arrived, it opened a visual platform that became a showcase for photography and video. Now, an hour of video is loaded onto YouTube every second and more than four billion videos are viewed every day. Over 300 million photos are added to Facebook every day. More than five billion photographs were uploaded to Instagram within four years of its launch.

The internet and social media play an increasingly important role in the dissemination of visual content, including news. Recall from Chapter 1 that more and more Americans get at least some of their news online. In today's world of digital journalism, visual elements are easy to record and distribute and have become integral to every story package (see Figure 14.1 for an example). Increasingly, people are getting their

Jonathan Bachman of Reuters took this photograph of Ieshia Evans being arrested during protests in Baton Rouge, Louisiana, after a black man was shot by police. The photo went viral and Bachman was a Pulitzer Prize finalist.

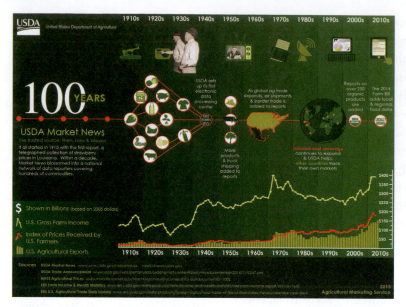

Figure 14.1 Compelling infographics are now important tools for delivering news.

news and information from digital sources, and much of the content they access includes photography and video.

Ethics of Visual Journalism

As the digital age of photography and video began to evolve, it opened a Pandora's box of ethical concerns. A major issue for media analysts is the manipulation of digital imagery. There have been some rather embarrassing moments involving major media organizations allowing photo editors or photojournalists to change images. AdWeek magazine featured a photograph of actress Kerry Washington that had been manipulated in Photoshop to change the bone structure of her face and the color of her skin. Actress and singer Zendaya posted on social media side-by-side images of the real photo and the manipulated one that Modeliste magazine published, showing how photo editors had slimmed her torso and hips and altered her skin tone. In one of the historically more infamous examples, Time magazine digitally altered the police mug shot of O.J. Simpson to make him look more sinister after he had been accused of killing Nicole Brown Simpson and Ron Goldman. Unfortunately for Time, Newsweek magazine ran the same photo—not manipulated—on its cover the same week. Audiences could compare the two images side by side in newsstands across America.

Whether they use film or digital, photojournalists have always had the ability to manipulate photographs and video. They can distort the scene by choosing whom and what to photograph and how to compose the shot. They can alter the image through cropping and other production processes. These changes can influence the message presented. Although it often takes a trained eye to see what has been manipulated, the willful elimination or digital alteration of elements in a photograph or video crosses an ethical line that has cost photojournalists their jobs and news organizations their credibility. When it comes to news, what readers and viewers see must reflect reality. The National Press Photographers Association (NPPA), a professional organization for photojournalists, states: "Accuracy in our work and integrity in our relationships with the public we serve are essential qualities for all photojournalists."

The question is, "What can and cannot be changed?" Editing images to improve quality is permissible. For example, correcting exposure problems, eliminating unwanted background elements or emphasizing the subject usually has been allowed. If a photographer wants to remove "red eye" in a head-and-shoulder image, it is easy to do in a software program such as Photoshop. Such improvements, however, do not alter the message or the reality of the scene recorded. In some cases, photographers may take multiple shots of a scene at different exposures, then combine them to get the best exposure possible. Again, the reality of the scene has not been altered. The photographer is trying only to provide the sharpest and best-exposed image. If something intrudes on the edge of the photograph—such as a pole, sign or other distracting element—the photographer can crop it out without affecting the reality of the image.

Changing the content of an image crosses the ethical boundary. However, there are times that, for artistic or illustrative reasons, a page designer or photo editor needs to manipulate an image. Doing so is unethical only if the public is not informed that the photo has been altered. An image always should be labeled as an illustration or composite so people know and understand that what they are seeing does not represent reality. In a well-known example, Newsweek ran a cover photo of Martha Stewart upon her release from prison, looking thinner and younger than usual; the magazine had put her head on a model's body and digitally altered her face. Officials at Newsweek responded to criticism by saying that the photo was never meant to represent reality and was only an illustration of what Stewart might look like when she was released. Editors had put a small credit line on the contents page, indicating that the photograph was a fake, but the image looked real; therefore, people could mistake it for an actual photograph of Stewart. The disclaimer should have been placed where readers could see it easily. Intentional or not, falsifying reality is unethical and undermines the media's credibility.

Newsweek magazine had its ethical judgment questioned when it ran this digitally manipulated cover photograph of Martha Stewart.

The Digital News Package

Beginning reporters need to be multi-skilled and able to gather information in a variety of ways for dissemination on a variety of platforms. Creating news packages for digital media goes beyond writing and editing a story. Journalists working with digital media need to not only be comfortable with the written word but also be able to think about the other elements that enrich the web news environment—photography, video and audio.

Remember that visual elements should add value to the story, not merely repeat information that is already there. The images should create a richer story that will draw people to the website and keep them coming back.

Capturing Photographs

The web is changing the role played by photographs in journalism, sometimes making them seem less important than videos. Part of the reason perhaps lies in the nature of website design and how pictures are viewed online. While photographs have a central role in the design of a newspaper page, they may not be the main element of a website. The photos may be small and require readers to click on them to enlarge—or even see—them. However, photography on the web remains a powerful tool that can attract readers and help tell a story. The key is learning how to incorporate photos in the story and then planning what and how many are needed.

Photographs can dramatize or emphasize specific parts of a story, or they can tell the entire story. Life magazine was famous for its photo stories that featured numerous images surrounded by brief explanatory text. Newspapers occasionally ran photo stories; however, they did not have as much space to devote to photographs as Life did. Newspapers might include two or three photos with a story, if warranted. Stories of historic importance, such as the 9/11 attacks, would use numerous photographs to help tell the story.

6. Editing should maintain the integrity of the photographic images' content and context. Do not manipulate images or add or alter sound in any way that can mislead viewers or misrepresent subjects.

7. Do not pay sources or subjects or reward them materially for information or participation.

8. Do not accept gifts, favors or compensation from those who might seek to influence coverage.

9. Do not intentionally sabotage the efforts of other journalists.

Ideally, visual journalists should:

10. Strive to ensure that the public's business is conducted in public. Defend the rights of access for all journalists.

11. Think proactively, as a student of psychology, sociology, politics and art, to develop a unique vision and presentation. Work with a voracious appetite for current events and contemporary visual media.

12. Strive for total and unrestricted access to subjects, recommend alternatives to shallow or rushed opportunities, seek a diversity of viewpoints, and work to show unpopular or unnoticed points of view.

13. Avoid political, civic and business involvements or other employment that compromise or give the appearance of compromising one's own journalistic independence.

14. Strive to be unobtrusive and humble in dealing with subjects.

15. Respect the integrity of the photographic moment.

16. Strive by example and influence to maintain the spirit and high standards expressed in this code. When confronted with situations in which the proper action is not clear, seek the counsel of those who exhibit the highest standards of the profession. Visual journalists should continuously study their craft and the ethics that guide it.

Source: https://nppa.org/code-ethics

Websites have unlimited space compared to newspapers and unlimited time compared to television news programs. Newspaper websites can include numerous photographs with a story. The images do not have to be laid out on a page as they would be in the print edition, but could be "stacked" one behind another—the reader simply clicks on the series to "flip" through them. Thumbnail images can also be lined up beside or below the story or under the main photograph, and the reader can click on and view them in a larger format. Finally, a series of photographs can be arranged in a slideshow accompanied by narration and music and hyperlinked to the story. The reader can click on the link to see the images appear automatically in a timed sequence and hear the narrator tell the story.

An important aspect to remember when shooting digital photos for print or online use is the resolution, or the number of pixels, in the image. Photographs displayed on a website are set at 72 pixels per inch (ppi) to match the calibration of computer monitors. Saving an image at a higher resolution makes the file larger, which means longer download times for readers. Even with today's high-speed internet connections, the reader will "turn the electronic page" and move to another area of the website or to another site if a large file takes too long to download.

While photographs for websites display at 72 ppi, those printed in newspapers or magazines need higher resolution to appear sharp and clear when printed. Newspapers normally require resolutions of around 200 ppi because of the lower quality of newsprint. Magazines usually require 300 ppi because of the high-quality, coated paper used in printing, which allows the pictures to "pop" off the page.

When planning to shoot photos, one of the first things to consider is where the photographs will be used—online only, print only or both. Digital cameras can be set to shoot in small, medium or large image quality, which basically corresponds to the ppi of an image and the amount of space it takes up on a memory card. Photographers can pack more images on a memory card by shooting in the small format, which is suitable for pictures that will appear only online. Because reproduction quality is limited, the camera controls should be set to medium or large for photos that will appear in print. In these formats, the resolution will be high enough for the photos to print on paper. Journalists can then "shrink" the images with compression software for use on a website.

To get the best results when shooting photographs, keep the following points in mind:

Focus: Most digital cameras feature automatic focusing (autofocus) to ensure that the subject appears clear and sharp. However, if the photographer points the lens at the wrong spot, such as just to the side of the subject, the camera may focus on the background instead. When taking photos of a person against a busy background, focus on his or her face.

Steady the camera: Keep the camera as still as possible; any movement can blur the image.

Move around: Instead of shooting the photo straight on, look for a different angle or viewpoint. Shooting from a slight angle is better than shooting from

Neither photo is a successful visual element: the one on the left is out of focus, and the one on the right contains a merger (the plant seems to be growing out of the sleeping woman's head).

straight on because it creates depth. Shooting from a high or low viewpoint adds drama to a photo.

Take tight shots: Close-ups and medium shots are the best in most cases for telling the story. A combination of medium and panoramic shots can be used when including more than one photograph. Panoramic shots are used to set the scene.

Shoot action: Static photographs are boring. The key to a good photograph is to capture action at its peak. Whether shooting a sports event or a speaker at a presentation, take pictures of people in motion.

Avoid mergers and intrusions: Look at the subject carefully to make sure nothing is protruding into the photo or out of the subject's head or body that interferes with the image. A signpost or tree branch that appears to jut out of a person's head can create an unwanted intrusion with sometimes comical results.

Digital photographs can be downloaded to a computer and edited with software such as Adobe Photoshop, Corel AfterShot Pro, Apple's iPhoto or free online editing programs such as PicMonkey, Picasa, Pixlr, Nik Collection or SumoPaint, which offer basic and advanced photo editing tools. Here are some basic steps for this process:

Do not edit the original photo: Always edit a copy of the photograph rather than the original. Save the original image in case you need to use it again.

Crop the photo: Cropping a photo simply means cutting out unwanted background. This step can make a photo more dramatic and improve its composition. However, a photo should not be cropped so tight that it alters the meaning.

Size the image: Depending on the resolution at which the photo was taken, it will probably be too large to put online or in print. If it is going to be used online, it can be resized as a small, low-resolution image. If it is going to be printed in a magazine or newspaper, it will have to be a large, high-resolution image. The physical size of the photo is determined by the amount of space provided on the website, measured in pixels, or on the page, measured in picas or inches.

Set the resolution and file type: The resolution should be set while the image is being resized. Photos for display on websites are usually saved as JPEGs (joint photographic experts group), which allows the files to be smaller and thus load faster on a website. Photos that will be published on paper are usually saved as TIFFs (tagged image file format), which are much larger files. Since JPEG is a compression format, you will lose a bit of quality each time you edit and save the image. If you are going to publish the image online and in print, save a copy of the original file as a TIFF and edit it instead of working from a JPEG. You can always change the resolution to 72 ppi and save it as a JPEG later.

Adjust exposure: Photo editing software provides tools to improve the image quality of a photograph by altering the brightness and contrast, both generally and for specific areas. You will need to adjust the exposure if you plan to use the image both online and in print. What seems normally exposed on a computer monitor may look very dark when printed because the reproduction process applies ink on paper rather than appearing on a brightly backlit computer display. An image that is to be printed often needs to be lighted as much as 20–30 percent for it to be properly exposed in a newspaper or magazine.

Capturing Video

Many reporters, from small to large news organizations, carry compact, handheld digital video recorders to capture images to be viewed on a computer monitor or a mobile device. NPR has developed a major presence in digital media with its website, which includes written stories and commentaries, blogs, video stories, photographs and numerous audio segments. NPR is a radio network, after all, but its website shows the depth and richness digital media offer audiences.

With the advent of digital video technology, anyone—with patience and practice—can create digital video. Gone are the days of using small but bulky 8 or 16 mm film cameras to make grainy home movies that took time and effort to produce and edit and required a projector and screen to view. Many of the current recorders have overcome these limitations with standard or high-definition digital recording that is captured on internal hard drives or compact flash storage devices and downloaded to and edited on a computer. One has only to look at the growth of YouTube to see the impact that video has had in regard to digital media.

But reporters must decide how to use video and how much to use with the story. Digital journalists typically shoot much more video than they will need. There are three possible approaches to video story content: breaking-news, highlight, and full documentary-style. Each one varies in content, time and presentation. There is no rule for how long a video segment in a web story package should run—it often depends on the subject and length of the story and the quality of the video available.

BREAKING-NEWS VIDEO

Breaking news is difficult to plan for because reporters do not know in advance what the story will be. They have to react to the situation as it develops, but they can have an idea of what video they need to shoot. For example, if they are covering a fire that is still burning, they will shoot the scene, capturing images of the burning building and the firefighters working to extinguish the blaze. This material will serve as background video, or b-roll. The story's main footage will be video reactions of witnesses and fire officials. Breaking-news video that accompanies a story may be from two to three minutes long.

Videographer Lindsay Pierce shoots footage of Brutus, a Rottweiler who lost his feet to frostbite when he was a puppy and was later outfitted with four prosthetic legs.

HIGHLIGHT VIDEO

Highlight videos are short clips—sometimes no more than 15 or 20 seconds—that can be used to explain complex elements or emphasize dramatic moments of a story. Sometimes, only one person is interviewed in the video; other times, several people may offer comments. The clips can be assembled into a video story of one to three minutes long.

Many reporters use a highlight video in the same way as a breaking-news one, interspersing short segments of action with comments from sources. These short clips accompany the written story to dramatize the action and place the audience at the scene. One of the differences between the two forms is that reporters have time to plan for the highlight video. They can determine what footage they want to shoot and who may be the best source to capture on video.

DOCUMENTARY-STYLE VIDEO

This type of video content is the longest of the three, often five or more minutes in length. A New York Times' web video about the disappearance of 796 Irish children who had been placed in homes for unwed mothers over several decades was more than 11 minutes long. The video featured interviews with the amateur historian who uncovered the story and several adults who had been children in the homes, along with video footage of the location of the demolished home and what it looks like now, diagrams of the location, video of government officials and voice-overs by a reporter narrating the story. The documentary-style video is the most complex of video story formats and needs the most planning to be successful.

Creating Good Video

The key to creating good video for the web is to plan the shots around the story you are writing. Reporters usually have an idea of what video clips they need to capture, whether it is just a short series of comments from the person being interviewed interspersed with action and scenic shots or a longer documentary-style piece. However, even when journalists plan for the video they need, they must be flexible enough to change their plans as the facts demand. Part of that is thinking through the series of shots, which has to be logical, smoothly flowing and dynamic.

Static videos—such as those where the camera remains stationary and the scene never leaves the action or the subject's face—are boring, even if action takes place during an interview. Good videos combine a variety of shots: close-ups, or tight shots; medium shots; and distant, or wide-angle shots. A tight shot of the subject becoming emotional is more dramatic than a medium shot. Yet if there is action, a medium shot is needed so the viewer can make sense of the scene. A wide-angle shot places the scene in context. Changes from shot to shot, called jump-cuts, take practice to make the transitions smooth. Video editing software, such as Apple's iMovie and Final Cut Pro or Adobe Premiere, provide tools to make jump-cuts that flow seamlessly from one scene to the next.

Care must be taken when going from one shot to the next. Nearly every digital video recorder has a zoom function that allows the videographer to go from one shot to another without having to move. Yet zooming in and out can create problems with focus as well as with the appearance of the video. The same problems arise with panning, or following the action with the camera. When recording a video story, it is best to stop recording, adjust the video recorder for the next shot and continue from shot to shot until done. Use the zoom function as sparingly as possible. The different shots can be pieced together during editing.

With longer video interviews, reporters sometimes become a part of the video by recording themselves or their voices as they ask questions. In this case, journalists should work from a script and rehearse the questions to avoid stumbling over them during the interview. Of course, the reporter needs flexibility to follow the interview where it leads, but having prepared questions ensures things will flow smoothly. Long pauses during an interview that is being recorded can lead to awkward jump-cuts.

While brief highlight videos may need only titles, credits and an introduction, longer videos may also need voice-overs, or narration, to introduce new segments or new subjects being interviewed, as well as background music. Adding voice-overs to a video can be done in the editing process and is usually best accomplished by first writing a script, as was discussed in Chapter 13. Reporters often rehearse the script and warm up their throats by reading a few lines before they begin recording the narration. When reading, they try to talk in a normal, conversational tone that is not rushed or overly dramatic. Pace is important in narration, as is inflection. The former should not be so fast that the narrator runs out of breath, and the latter—the rhythm or pattern of speech—should not be monotone or too up and down.

Capturing Audio

Just as technology has simplified the process of recording video, so has it simplified gathering, editing and distributing audio. The New York Times and other news organizations sometimes include short audio clips on their websites to dramatize, emphasize or explain something in a story.

Reporters may record an entire interview and then edit the audio for the parts that will make a good presentation. Or they may prepare a series of questions to ask a source specifically for the audio clip. They may also want to add narration to put the clip into context, along with environmental, or natural, sound. To ensure variation in natural sound, they should record 10- to 15-second segments from different places and times; doing so also provides options during editing. If a reporter is interviewing a contractor at a construction site, for example, he or she may gather several seconds of machinery and other construction noise to play in the background during a voice-over. The narration may include an introduction at the beginning of the clip and the questions posed to the source before his or her responses.

An audio clip that accompanies an online story may not need any context beyond the accompanying text and visual elements. But if the clip is downloaded, the narrator will have to provide the story's background in an introduction. If the audio story includes the voice of more than one source, the narrator will have to introduce each new segment and identify each person. Audio stories can be just about any length, whether they accompany the story on the news organization's website or are posted as podcasts.

Interviews can be recorded face-to-face or over the telephone. As stated in Chapter 11, location is one of the most important considerations for in-person interviews. In the preceding example, the reporter would need to find a quiet place to conduct the interview and gather natural sound later. Background construction noise could drown out the speaker or force him or her to shout over the noise. If the noise ends, the person may still be shouting a response. An office or home is a good location, but avoid restaurants, coffee shops or anywhere with a lot of crowd or background noise.

If the audio is going to be used for a lengthy podcast, reporters usually prepare the subject. As with a written interview, they tell the person what the story will be about, how long the interview will last and where and when the podcast will be available. Journalists sometimes send a few questions to sources prior to the interview so that they have an opportunity to prepare answers. This practice is especially helpful when interviewing sources about complex topics. Sometimes reporters do not start recording at the start of the interview but talk to the subject to help relax him or her before turning on the recorder and beginning the real interview. The key to successful podcast interviews is to keep the tone conversational and natural sounding as though the listener is in the room with you.

When a reporter finishes recording material for a story, the editing process begins. Most digital audio recording devices can be connected to a computer with a USB cable and the audio files then downloaded for editing. A number of free software programs, such as Audacity, are available for both PCs and Macintosh computers.

Most of these programs offer time track marks so that interview quotes can be flagged at minute/second marks and can be easily found when compiling the final audio story.

The first step in editing is to cut poor or unnecessary segments. Remove long pauses in which there is no sound, the "ums" and "ahs" that sources sometimes utter, verbal gaffes and any small talk at the start or end of the interview. People

BuzzFeed employees use software to edit video and audio stories for the website.

sometimes do not realize they are still being recorded at the end of the interview and say something inappropriate or irrelevant.

Next, voice-overs, music clips and natural sound can be added. Several techniques can be used to flow from one audio segment to another, such as fades and segues. There are also a number of helpful guides and online resources that offer detailed assistance in editing audio effectively for podcasting and audio highlights.

Required Technology

Reporters writing for the web need a wider array of tools than those who write only for print. Nevertheless, most of the technology is easy to learn and available at a reasonable cost. Even journalists new to digital media can create video and audio segments using a medium-priced video recorder and Apple's iMovie or Adobe's Premiere Elements digital video editing software. However, mastering the skills takes time, patience and practice.

Digital Video Recorder

More and more cameras are able to shoot video clips. For shooting longer, more involved video stories and highlights, however, it is best to use a digital video recorder. Professional video cameras and recorders used for television and documentary films cost thousands of dollars, but amateur standard and high-definition digital video recorders cost from around $200 to $1,200 and take good quality video for display on a website or mobile device.

Digital Camera

While smartphones are becoming more popular for point-and-shoot photographs and will perform adequately in an emergency, professional photographers still favor the image quality of a standard digital camera. There are hundreds to choose from at varying levels of complexity, quality and cost. Inexpensive point-and-shoot digital cameras have limited zoom range, flash power and ability to capture high-speed action, which makes such cameras less than ideal. The full-function point-and-shoot looks similar to digital single-lens reflex (DSLR) cameras but is a bit more compact. The difference is that the former has a fixed lens while the latter has an interchangeable lens system so that different focal length lenses, such as normal or telephoto, can be used. Cameras can range in price from $250 to $600 for a full-function point-and-shoot and from $600 to several thousand for a DSLR.

Many beginning photographers often question whether an 18-megapixel camera is better than a 10- or 12-megapixel in terms of image quality. "Megapixel" refers more to the file and print size than it does to overall sharpness of the image. The sharpness is controlled more by the photographer, the quality of the lens and the type and quality of sensor the digital camera uses to capture the image. A three-megapixel camera will produce an excellent 5×7-inch image at 300 ppi and a good quality 8×10-inch image at 200 ppi. A 12-megapixel camera will produce an excellent 10×15-inch print at 300 ppi and a good quality 14×21-inch image at 200 ppi. The questions to ask are: How big does the image need to be? Where will it be displayed? The answers will determine the size of the file.

Digital Audio Recorder

Miniature digital audio recorders can capture high-quality stereo sound at a very affordable price. Key things to consider when buying this device are recording quality, ease of use, battery life, computer compatibility for transferring files and external inputs for headphones and a microphone. Good digital audio recorders range from $100 to $200. High-quality recorders can cost as much as $500.

The Reporter's Guide to Visual Journalism

Photographs

1. Create a list of photo opportunities for the story.
2. If posting online, decide how photos will be displayed on the website—as a series of photos or an audio slideshow.
3. Select image quality—small, medium or large—at which you want to capture images.
4. Make sure the subject is in focus.
5. Keep the camera steady.
6. Look for the best angle or viewpoint to shoot photos.
7. Take tight shots to dramatize and emphasize the subject.
8. Shoot action as often as possible to make photos more interesting.
9. Avoid background mergers.
10. Crop and size the photo when editing.
11. Set resolution at 72 ppi for the web and adjust the exposure when editing.

Video

1. Determine how much video you want to or can use for the story.
2. Shoot close-up, medium and wide-angle shots.
3. Limit panning and zooming to prevent blurring video.
4. Edit the video to remove poor quality scenes; piece together different segments of video to tell the story.
5. Add voice-overs during editing to explain a scene or introduce a new source.

Audio

1. Decide whether you will use just clips of an audio interview or the entire interview as an audio story.
2. Decide whether the interview will be face-to-face or over the telephone; be sure to inform a source on the telephone that he or she is being recorded.
3. When interviewing face-to-face, pick a quiet spot for the interview to avoid intrusive background noise.
4. Record natural sound to use for background in the audio clip or story.

Review Exercises

1. Photojournalism Project

Select a photo or photos of a news event, controversial issue or feature story (e.g., the aftermath of a natural disaster, a fire or vehicle accident, or a demonstration) from a newspaper, news magazine or news website. Choose an image that depicts the event or controversy, not a mug shot of someone involved. Analyze the photo(s) you selected by answering the following questions:

- What do you see?
- What story is the photographer trying to tell?
- What message is he or she sending? Is the photograph conveying it successfully? Why or why not?

- Does it dramatize, emphasize or help summarize the story? Give details to explain your answer.
- Why do you think the photographer chose that particular scene to capture and explain the story? Why do you think the photo editor and editor selected the photo or photos for publication?

2. Video Journalism Project

Select a video embedded in a news story or one that stands alone. As with Exercise 1, choose something connected to a news event, a controversial issue or a feature story. Analyze the video by applying the questions from the previous exercise.

APPLYING THE SKILLS OF JOURNALISM

SPEECHES AND MEETINGS

15

From the moment Donald Trump announced his candidacy for the Republican presidential nomination until his election 16 months later, news organizations struggled over how to cover him and his campaign. Trump's promise to build a wall along the U.S.-Mexico border, his attacks on the characters of fellow candidates such as Ted Cruz and Carly Fiorina, his denigration of John McCain's war record and many other statements broke nearly every custom of political campaigning. At the same time, Trump said—and repeated—things that were demonstrably untrue, such as his insistence that he had seen thousands of Muslim Americans cheering as the World Trade Center buildings collapsed on 9/11 and that African-American communities were in the worst shape they had ever been. News executives wondered how they should cover such an unconventional campaign, and reporters grappled with how to let readers know that much of what Trump said was false without calling him a liar.

> "Today's public figures can no longer write their own speeches or books, and there is some evidence that they can't read them either."
>
> *Gore Vidal, author*

One assignment that seemed to be straightforward was Trump's inaugural address. Covering speeches is a staple of journalism. What knowledgeable and important people say about current events is news, and journalists make that information available to members of the public who may not be able to attend the speech or listen to or read all of it. The reporter's job is to present in concise and clear form the essence of the speaker's message and some sense of what those who attended the event experienced.

Equally important, and equally common as assignments, are the meetings of local governments or of civic groups concerned about public issues. The actions taken at these meetings often directly affect how people in a community live.

Reporters assigned to cover speeches or meetings usually write two kinds of stories: an advance story and a follow story. The former alerts people to a soon-to-happen event, and the latter describes that event for those who were unable to attend it in person.

Advance Stories

News organizations usually publish advance stories the day a speech or meeting is announced or shortly thereafter. As a reminder to their audiences, they may publish a second advance story a day or two before the event. For an important speech or meeting, the initial announcement is often followed by additional advance stories about the purpose, participants and location of the event and about opportunities to attend.

For events of unusual importance, news organizations may run several advance stories. For example, Trump's inauguration received extensive coverage beforehand. The date of the inauguration was known well in advance; it's set by the 20th Amendment to the Constitution. News organizations, nevertheless, had a wealth of material for stories leading up to the event. The New York Times reported that Trump would take the oath of office on the same Bible used in the inaugurations of Abraham Lincoln and Barack Obama. Another story reported that the inaugural luncheon would include lobster and shrimp for the first course and beef with chocolate and juniper juice and potatoes gratin for the second. Yet another story reported the times and locations of the Inauguration Day events, such as the Trump family's private prayer service, the swearing-in ceremony and the inaugural parade. What the new president would say in his speech, however, was still a matter of speculation.

The leads for advance stories should emphasize what is important and unusual, not just the fact that someone has scheduled a speech or meeting. Often, leads mention celebrities who will be involved or the topics that will be discussed. The rest of the story, usually no more than two or three paragraphs, might elaborate on the speaker or the topic or the most important items on the meeting's agenda. The date, time and location of the event should also be included. The story should mention whether there is a charge for attending or whether the event is open to the general public. Some news organizations will not publish advance stories about closed events.

Because of time limitations, broadcasters usually carry advance stories for only the most important speeches and meetings. Newspapers run more advance stories but, to save space, may publish them in roundups or digests (often called "Community Calendars") that list all the newsworthy events for the coming week.

Nikki Haley, U.S. ambassador to the United Nations, speaks during an emergency meeting of the U.N. Security Council, after North Korea tested an intercontinental ballistic missile earlier in the week. Her speech was covered by many news organizations, both in the United States and around the world.

Covering the Speech or Meeting

Speeches and meetings quickly become routine assignments for most reporters. Covering them effectively, however, requires perfecting some basic reporting skills: advance preparation, sound news judgment, accuracy, an ear for interesting quotations and an eye for compelling details.

Journalists may cover speeches about topics they are unfamiliar with or meetings about complicated issues. Meetings of some government agencies can be particularly confusing. In larger communities, a city council might vote on issues without discussing them at its regular meeting because all the discussion occurred earlier in committee meetings. Unless reporters are familiar with the committee action, they might misunderstand the full council's decision or fail to recognize newsworthy developments.

Preparation helps reporters cover speeches and meetings. Journalists usually try to learn as much as possible about the participants and issues before a speech or meeting. As a first step, they might go to their news organization's library and research the topic, the speaker or the group.

Reporters who cover meetings should learn all the participants' names beforehand to identify the people who are speaking or making decisions. To understand everything that is said, they should also learn as much as possible about every item on the agenda. Journalists can get agendas before many meetings and research the issues that will be discussed.

In some cases, an agenda provides more than just a list of topics. It may be a small packet with supporting information on each item coming before the board or council. For instance, if a school board is considering a pay increase for substitute teachers, the agenda packet might include the superintendent's rationale for the increase, projections of its impact on the budget and comparisons with the pay substitutes earn in nearby districts. Even if the published agenda lists only the topics to be considered, additional documents and information presented to board and council members are public records under most state laws, and reporters can get copies simply by asking and paying for them.

Sometimes, unexpected or confusing issues arise during a meeting. Journalists prepare for those situations by arranging to see the leading participants to ask follow-up questions after a meeting adjourns.

Reporters who cover speeches often try to talk to a speaker so they can clarify issues or get additional information. Groups that sponsor speeches will sometimes accommodate journalists by scheduling press conferences with speakers before or after the speech. If no formal press conference is arranged, they may ask to see speakers for a few minutes immediately after their appearances. Reporters also like to get advance copies of speeches when possible. Instead of having to take notes, they can follow the printed text and simply record any departures from the prepared remarks.

Follow Stories

Published after a speech or meeting, follow stories report on the event in detail. Therefore, they are longer than advance stories and harder to write.

HOT TIP

Common Steps for Covering Speeches or Meetings

- Reporters arrive early and find seats that will allow them to hear and see as much as possible. Those who arrive late may have to sit in the back of the meeting room and struggle to hear what is said or see who is speaking.

- Reporters introduce themselves to speakers, if possible, or the participants in the meeting, if they have never covered the group before. They may also ask a few quick questions or arrange to talk with speakers or meeting participants later.

- Reporters take detailed notes. Thorough notes will help them recall and understand what was said or done and reconstruct it for their audience.

- As they listen to a speech or meeting, reporters try to think of groups or individuals who might have different points of view or who might be affected by any actions taken. They will try to speak to these individuals or groups later so they can provide the public with as complete a news story as possible.

Like any story, a speech or meeting story needs a central point. But the fragmented nature of most meetings and some speeches makes identifying that point difficult. An expert on economic development in rural areas might deliver a speech on the obstacles such areas face in attracting new businesses and the resources for overcoming them. Should the central point be the obstacles or the resources? Or should it cover both and, therefore, be vague and difficult to understand? In a single meeting, a school board might adopt a set of achievement standards for district pupils, announce a major expansion of the district's soccer facilities and hear a report on why construction of a new high school has been delayed. All are important but unrelated issues. How can a writer work all three into a single coherent news story?

A reporter's decision on a central point depends on his or her news judgment about what is most important and interesting to the audience. As a result, journalists may differ in their approaches to a complicated story. For example, different news organizations emphasized different themes from President Trump's inauguration speech. Several stressed the dark picture Trump painted of the nation's condition. The Guardian said he offered a "bleak portrayal of a nation under siege." Similarly, The New York Times said that the new president "vowed [to] shatter the established order and reverse a national decline that he called 'this American carnage.'" The Los Angeles Times also reported that Trump described "a bleak version of a country marked by 'rusted-out factories scattered like tombstones.'" The Associated Press took a different approach, saying Trump promised "to empower America's 'forgotten men and women.'" Bloomberg News said, "Donald Trump began his presidency with a combative, populist address aimed squarely at his aggrieved supporters, making little effort to reach beyond his political base or reassure foreign leaders."

Some news organizations, such as Vox.com, did not simply report the speech but also annotated it with commentary and supplementary information. At one point Trump said: "Politicians prospered, but the jobs left and the factories closed. The establishment protected itself, but not the citizens of our country. Their victories have not been your victories. Their triumphs have not been your triumphs and while they celebrated in our nation's capital, there was little to celebrate for struggling families all across our land." Vox.com staffer Matthew Yglesias inserted this commentary: "This line clearly speaks to how many people feel, but in reality there are more people employed in the United States in January 2017 than at any previous time in American history, and inflation-adjusted wages are higher than they have ever been."

National Public Radio (NPR) also published an annotated transcript of the inaugural speech. Trump said:

> *Mothers and children trapped in poverty in our inner cities, rusted out factories scattered like tombstones across the landscape of our nation, an education system flush with cash but which leaves our young and beautiful students deprived of all knowledge. And the crime, and the gangs, and the drugs that have stolen too many lives and robbed our country of so much unrealized potential. This American carnage stops right here and stops right now.*

In his annotations, Eric Westervelt noted that the money for public schools comes largely from local and state taxes and only about 10 percent from the federal government. Overall, spending on public education in many states had declined since 2008. He also noted that while test scores in math for U.S. children had declined relative to the math scores for children from other counties, reading and science scores were stable. On the issue of crime, Westervelt said violent crime rates had been trending downward for many years, although a few cities were experiencing spikes in homicide rates.

Stories about the speech included not only the president's words but also the public's reaction. The Washington Post quoted presidential historian Douglas Brinkley: "It was a nativist and at times jingoistic speech. People around the world will be frightened that we are really going to hunker in on them, creating a Fortress America. This is American nationalism on steroids." Democratic Sen. Sherrod Brown of Ohio told The New York Times: "I was pretty shocked by how dark it was. I love this country, and I don't understand how a president of the United States that loves his country could paint a picture of its failures." On the other hand, the Los Angeles Times spoke to Trump supporter Pam Lazarites of Dayton, Ohio, who had traveled to Washington with her husband to see the inauguration. "It sounded like someone was speaking to us—finally," the 61-year-old said. "I'm tired of hearing about the establishment—the government, the politicians."

News stories also reported on the ambiance of the inauguration, including the size of the crowd. The Associated Press said, "At the inauguration, the crowd that spread out before Trump on the National Mall was notably smaller than at past inaugurals, reflecting both the divisiveness of last year's campaign and the unpopularity of the incoming president compared to modern predecessors." Other news reports made similar comparisons, and some published side-by-side photos of the National Mall during Barack Obama's 2009 inauguration and during Trump's, showing much of it empty for the latter ceremony.

The reporting on the crowd size became a matter of controversy the day after the inauguration, when Trump's then-press secretary, Sean Spicer, accused the news media of intentionally manipulating the photos so as to minimize the support Trump had. News organizations responded that Spicer's claims about the inauguration crowd were demonstrably false.

Organizing Speech or Meeting Stories

Reporters usually must select one idea or issue from a speech or meeting as the central point for the story. If an event involves several important topics, they generally focus on the most newsworthy in the lead and summarize the others in the next two or three paragraphs. Journalists then develop each topic in detail, starting with

Displaying photos of Trump's inauguration, Sean Spicer speaks to the press about what he considered inaccurate and unfair coverage of the event.

the most important. If the opening paragraphs mention only one topic, the audience will think the story discusses nothing else if other topics are not mentioned early in the story. If the topic in the lead fails to interest people, they may stop paying attention.

Some beginners report events in the order in which they occurred, as if the sequence were somehow important to the audience. Meeting agendas rarely reflect the importance of the topics discussed. Major issues may be taken up early or late, but readers, viewers or listeners should not have to endure descriptions of minor actions before learning about important ones. Although speeches usually have a more logical order, speakers tend to put their most important points at the middle or end.

Reporters write most follow stories in the inverted-pyramid style, presenting information in the order of its importance (see Chapter 9). They can move statements around; for example, they may begin with a statement made at the end of a one-hour speech or meeting, then shift to a topic discussed midway through the event. If topics brought up early are unimportant, reporters may not mention them at all.

When writing a follow story, journalists should never simply report that a speaker or group "discussed" or "considered" another topic, even if it is a minor one. If a topic is important enough to mention, give the audience meaningful information about it. As specifically as possible, summarize the discussion or action. The original sentence in the following example is vague; the second sentence is more specific:

> Finally, Commissioner Cycler expressed concern about the Senior Citizens Center on Eisenhower Drive.

> Finally, Commissioner Cycler said several people have called her to complain that the staff at the Senior Citizens Center on Eisenhower Drive is arrogant and unhelpful.

Another factor to keep in mind when organizing speech or meeting stories is attribution. When a writer fails to vary the location of the attribution, the story can seem dull and repetitious. If reporters see the following pattern or something like it in their finished stories, they need to rewrite:

- City Manager Faith An-Pong began by discussing the problems that recycling is creating for the city.
- Next, An-Pong said . . .
- Turning to a third topic, An-Pong said . . .
- She then went on to add that . . .
- Continuing, An-Pong said . . .
- In conclusion, she added . . .

Writing Effective Leads

Inexperienced reporters often err by writing overly broad leads that contain no news. These leads may say that a speaker "discussed" a topic or "voiced an opinion" or that a group "considered" or "dealt with" an issue. Consider the following examples:

The president of the Chamber of Commerce discussed the dangers of higher taxes in a speech Tuesday night.

The City Council considered the problems of billboards and panhandlers in an eight-hour meeting Monday.

Neither lead contains any news. The advance stories for these events would already have included the topic of the chamber president's speech and the agenda for the city council meeting. The news is what was said or done about these issues, as these revised leads illustrate:

If the city continues to raise property taxes, major businesses will leave town, throwing thousands of people out of work, the president of the Chamber of Commerce warned Tuesday night.

The City Council voted to ban most billboards and to restrict panhandling to about two dozen zones downtown during a meeting that lasted eight hours Monday.

Usually, leads for follow stories emphasize the most newsworthy information to emerge from a speech or meeting. Often that is the speaker's main point or the most important action taken or issue discussed at a meeting. Sometimes, other aspects are more newsworthy:

Follow Story Lead (Emphasis on Main Point): The world needs an immediate reduction in the burning of fossil fuel to head off potentially disastrous effects from global warming, a prominent American scientist warned Sunday in Vancouver.

James Hansen, head of NASA's Goddard Institute for Space Studies and an iconic figure among climate researchers, said "even the skeptical scientists now agree" that Earth is undergoing a warming trend.

(Vancouver, British Columbia, Sun)

The scientist referred to here is James Hansen, who is well known in climate science circles for his research on global climate change and his advocacy for cutting the emissions of carbon dioxide and other greenhouse gases. But Hansen lacks the name recognition of prominent politicians, like Al Gore, or celebrities, like Leonardo DiCaprio. Thus, the substance of the message is more important and more meaningful than the fact the message is coming from James Hansen. At other times, who said something is more important than what was said:

Follow Story Lead (Emphasis on Speaker): In his first speech since being sworn in as attorney general, Jeff Sessions tied a recent increase in violent crime to a lack of respect for police officers, vowing that his Justice Department would be more supportive of local departments and "not diminish their effectiveness."

Sessions spoke Tuesday in worried tones about the uptick in violence in a number of major cities, warning that he believed this was not "a one-time blip" but rather "the beginning of a trend." He then suggested that the increase was linked to changing perceptions of law enforcement after years of protests nationwide against how police officers use deadly force.

(The Washington Post)

Some law enforcement officials argued the Black Lives Matter movement and other critics of police were making officers reluctant to use force, even when it was necessary, which may allow crime to flourish. But when the new U.S. attorney general makes the same point, it is newsworthy not only because of Sessions' prominence but also because it signals a change in federal policy.

Sometimes, the most important news is made not in the speech or the meeting but in reaction to it:

> **Follow Story Lead (Emphasis on Reaction):** BERKELEY, Calif. — A speech by the divisive right-wing writer Milo Yiannopoulos at the University of California, Berkeley, was canceled on Wednesday night after demonstrators set fires and threw objects at buildings to protest his appearance.
>
> *(The New York Times)*

Audiences usually respond politely to speakers, even if they disagree with the views expressed. A completely different response faced Milo Yiannopoulos, then an editor at Breitbart News. Yiannopoulos, whom the Berkeley College Republicans had invited to speak, had been banned from Twitter for inciting trolls to attack actor-comedian Leslie Jones. He is also famous for his denunciations of political correctness, which have sometimes devolved into racially charged attacks. Opponents' response to his speech was notable not only for its violence but also for the criticism it evoked. Many conservatives cited the incident as an example of left-wing censorship.

Yet another approach to the follow story uses a lead that might be an anecdote from the speech, a description that sets a scene or a bit of dialogue from a meeting to introduce a nut graph that states the central point:

> **Follow Story Lead (Anecdotal):** When President Barack Obama visits his home in Chicago, he often peruses a stack of newspapers from before the 2008 election. Obama says he likes to look at what he said during the campaign and compare it with what he has accomplished in office.
>
> "Lord knows I've made mistakes in this job," Obama said in a speech Monday at the presentation of the Toner Prize for political reporting, "and there are areas where I've fallen short, but something I'm really proud of is the fact that, if you go back and see what I said in 2007 and you see what I did, they match up."
>
> A major reason the two match up, Obama said, is the work of political journalists like the late Robin Toner of The New York Times, for whom the prize is named. Knowing that journalists were recording what he said and would challenge him if he promised too much forced him to check his facts and be realistic, the president said.
>
> The task of holding politicians to account and checking their statements and promises is even more important now, Obama said, in a presidential campaign that seems untethered to fact and reasoned analysis.

Police carry a man into a building during a protest over a scheduled speech by Milo Yiannopoulos at the University of California, Berkeley.

FROM THE NEWS

Speech Story

Here's a speech story that illustrates how a description of a dramatic part of the speech can make an effective lead.

Internet Brings Pornography to Children,
Researcher Says

"I sit down as a 14-year-old and type in a few words and let the mouse roam where the mouse will roam," said Edward Donnerstein as he started to demonstrate what's available on the internet.

And roam the mouse did.

Donnerstein, a professor of communication and dean of the division of social science at the University of California at Santa Barbara, typed the words "free porn" into the computer search engine he was using. The program responded with a list of dozens of websites offering pornographic images.

Donnerstein clicked on a few of the links as his audience of university students and faculty watched, and he brought to the screen still and moving pictures of naked women and men, vaginas, erect penises and couples having intercourse. And then he moved on to the rough stuff.

From sites that specialized in bondage and sadomasochism, Donnerstein opened photographs of women tied up and tortured. One image showed a naked woman with what appeared to be cigarette burns covering her breasts, belly and thighs.

"That's a 14-year-old not being asked age, not paying a cent and getting some pretty violent things," Donnerstein said.

Sex, violence, hate-group messages, bomb-building instructions and promotions for tobacco and alcohol are just some of the culturally nonconformist messages children have access to over the internet, Donnerstein said Monday during a lecture on children and the internet at the student union. And the most frequently mentioned solutions to the problem—government regulation, blocking software, ratings systems and safe sites for children—have weaknesses. The lecture was part of a lecture series on media and children sponsored by the university's Family Research and Policy Initiative.

Some parents may decide the best solution is to keep children off the internet altogether, but Donnerstein said that was wrong.

"The solution is not to pull the plug. In fact, it's just the opposite," he said. Children need to be online to access valuable educational information, Donnerstein said, adding that he cannot imagine writing a scholarly paper without using the web. And internet access is likely to become more important, he said, as people conduct online more and more of their daily business, from trading stocks to seeking medical advice.

Children have embraced the internet, Donnerstein said, but parents have little knowledge or understanding of what their children are doing.

Of children between 9 and 17, Donnerstein said, 79 percent say they are online daily and prefer using their computers to television or the telephone. And 44 percent of those children say they have found X-rated material; 25 percent say they have seen hate-group sites; and 14 percent have seen bomb-building instructions.

By comparison, parents are ignorant of computers, the internet and what their children are doing with them, he said. The internet is the first mass medium, Donnerstein said, where children and parents are at opposite ends in terms of their use and knowledge of the medium. Most parents, he said, don't know what sites their children visit, don't have rules for using the internet and haven't installed blocking software, even if they own it, because it's too complicated for them.

Every new medium—movies, radio, television—has raised concerns among parents about how it will affect children, but the internet is different, Donnerstein said. The sex and violence in the movies and on television, even cable, are benign compared to what is on the internet, he said.

"The internet is whatever you want. Things that have no other media correlation are available," Donnerstein said. Also, the interactive nature of the internet may heighten any arousal the user experiences. Theoretically, he said, the effects of the internet may be much stronger than those of older media.

Parents are justified in worrying about what effects exposure to internet sex and violence may have on their children, he said, but the most frequently mentioned solutions have shortcomings.

Government regulation won't work, he said, in part because of the First Amendment, which allows government to prohibit only messages that meet the stringent legal definition for obscenity or that are child pornography.

(continued)

Speech Story *(continued)*

Even if the First Amendment allowed greater regulation of the internet, it would not stop access to sex and violence. Many of the most salacious sites, Donnerstein said, are based overseas, beyond the reach of U.S. law.

Ratings systems suffer a similar defect. They rely on the content providers to rate content as to its level of sex and violence, Donnerstein said. The systems are voluntary and would not bind content providers from other countries.

Parents can buy computer programs that block access to certain websites. But Donnerstein said studies of these programs show that sometimes they fail to block pornographic sites. Other times, he said, they may block access to valuable information, such as sites that deal with breast cancer or AIDS.

Websites specifically designed for children can provide a safe environment. National Geographic Kids, Kidsreads and How Stuff Works are examples of sites that allow children to see educational materials but not pornography, violence and hate. Such sites are not likely to satisfy older children, he said.

The best approach, Donnerstein said, may be for parents to learn more about the internet and what their children are doing with it. Parents can teach their children "critical viewing," he said, in which the children and parents view websites together and discuss what they see.

Children are aware of computer technologies and will make use of them, Donnerstein said; parents need to teach children how to use those technologies productively and safely.

Quotations can hook readers with a colorful phrase, but they rarely make good summary leads. As a rule, writers should use a quotation in the lead only if it accurately and succinctly states the most newsworthy point of the meeting or speech. In practice, few quotations will satisfy that standard. Quotations can be effectively used in anecdotal or delayed leads, which offer an opportunity to grab an audience with a bit of narrative or description but must clearly lead into and support the nut graph.

Writing Transitions

Transitions shift a story from one idea to another. A good transition will connect the ideas and arouse the audience's interest in the topic being introduced.

Transitions should be brief. The repetition of a key word, phrase or idea can serve as a transition to a related topic or can shift the story to a new time or place. If the new topic is markedly different, a transitional sentence or question might be necessary. The transition should not, however, simply report that a speaker or group "turned to another topic." Instead, it should function as a secondary lead, summarizing the new topic by giving its most interesting and important details. In the next examples, a weak transition is rewritten to include specific information:

> The board also considered two other topics.
>
> The board also considered—and rejected—proposals to increase students' health and athletic fees.

> Hunt then discussed the problem of auto insurance.
>
> Hunt then warned that the cost of auto insurance rose 9.6 percent last year and is expected to rise 12 percent this year.

Remember Your Audience

Reporters should write with their audience in mind, clarifying issues so that people can understand how events will affect them and their neighborhood, city or state. Sometimes journalists forget this rule and try to please the people they are writing about instead of the people they are writing for. One news report of a city council meeting began by saying three employees received awards for their 25 years of service. Placing the awards in the lead probably pleased the city officials, but few people would care. The public was likely to have a greater interest in a topic presented later: plans for the city government to help people with low incomes buy their own homes.

Reporters also need to clarify jargon, especially the bureaucratic language used at government meetings, so that readers, viewers, and listeners can understand the stories. A story reported that a county commission had imposed "stricter signage requirements" for adult bookstores, theaters and clubs. Instead of repeating such jargon, journalists should give specific details. In this case, the commissioners limited the size and location of outdoor signs advertising adult entertainment businesses.

Check Facts

Reporters have an obligation to go beyond what is said or done at the speech or meeting to check facts, find opposing points of view and get additional information and comments. People say things in speeches that may not be true or may be largely opinion. And because a speech represents the views of only the speaker, a journalist who does nothing more than report the speaker's words may be presenting a one-sided and inaccurate view of a topic.

Two websites devoted to checking the factual claims of officials, politicians and opinion leaders are PolitiFact.com and FactCheck.org. Donald Trump and Hillary Clinton kept both fact-checking organizations busy during their presidential campaigns. At one point, Trump claimed:

> Wikileaks also shows how (Clinton campaign chairman) John Podesta rigged the polls by oversampling Democrats, a voter suppression technique. And that's happening to me all the time. When the polls are even, when they leave them alone and do them properly, I'm leading. But you see these polls, where they're polling Democrats—"how's Trump doing" "oh he's down"—they're polling Democrats!

Trump was complaining about public polls showing he trailed Clinton, but the Podesta emails described internal polls. Moreover, the oversampling did not mean the polls were ignoring Republican voters; oversampling certain demographic groups is a polling technique that ensures there are enough group members in the sample to allow pollsters to draw reliable conclusions about how they will likely vote. Trump's claim was so false that PolitiFact ranked it as "pants on fire," its worst rating.

A major issue for Clinton's campaign was her use of a private email server during her time as secretary of state. FactCheck compared some of her statements

PolitiFact's Truth-O-Meter includes the following rankings of political claims: true, mostly true, half true, mostly false, false and pants on fire.

about her emails with the facts uncovered by an FBI investigation of the matter and found some contradictions. Clinton had claimed, for instance, that some emails had been deleted from the server before a congressional committee had subpoenaed them; in fact, they had been deleted after the subpoena was issued. Clinton also said everyone in government knew she was using a private email server, but emails sent through that server did not display her address and only 13 people knew what it was.

Websites like PolitiFact and FactCheck help reporters spot and correct errors in speeches because often the distortions spoken by one politician will be repeated by others. Checking facts about state or local issues may require journalists to invest some of their own time in research. Still, much of the information for checking facts is already on the websites of state and local governments. The web has made the process of holding politicians and public officials accountable much easier than it was decades ago.

Reporters must be especially diligent about double-checking personal attacks in order to avoid libel suits. If a defamatory personal attack is made at a speech or meeting that is not an official government proceeding, a person who is attacked may sue both the speaker and any news organizations that report the statement. The fact that news organizations accurately quoted a speaker is not a defense. Even if a personal attack is not defamatory or is made in an official government meeting—and therefore cannot be the basis for a libel suit—the journalist still has an ethical obligation to check facts, get opposing points of view and give people who have been attacked a chance to respond.

Adding Color

Report What You Hear

Quotations, direct and indirect, help the writer describe debates that occur in a public meeting. The public needs to know why certain actions were taken or why elected representatives voted a certain way. Simply recording votes and actions will not give citizens the information they need to make informed judgments. They also need to know the competing points of view.

An effort to train Lincoln, Nebraska, public school teachers to use gender-inclusive terms in the classroom provoked an angry response from many residents. At a 2.5-hour meeting, school board members heard from both opponents and proponents of the program:

> Courtney Criswell, the mother of three Lincoln Public Schools students, said the materials shared with teachers on gender inclusiveness have broken a trust with middle school parents, who are being held hostage and forced to decide what to do when such materials are used.
>
> "We cannot strip away one part of a child's identity to build another one up," she said. "Make no mistake, that is exactly what these materials

promote. It creates unnecessary confusion for the majority of students."

Diane Walkowiak, the parent of a transgender child, took some speakers to task and said teachers must be informed about issues of gender identity to reach all students.

"You are telling me my son is immoral," she said, and not worth the staff time needed to learn about the issues he faces. "You may not agree, you may firmly believe in a binary gender, but please accept that staff needs to be informed about this issue and many other issues because education is not just reading, writing and arithmetic. It is so much more. I believe that God is so much greater than all of us and made us in so many different ways, perhaps to test our compassion and love for others."

Portland residents speak to their City Council during a meeting about rent control proposals.

Describe What You See

Vivid descriptions of participants, audiences and settings add drama to speech and meeting stories. The descriptions can appear anywhere. The following example shows how vivid description can enliven a meeting story:

> A public hearing on an ordinance that would limit the number of animals allowed in homes drew a standing-room-only crowd to a County Commission meeting Thursday.
>
> Some of the spectators wore T-shirts inscribed with pictures of their pets, primarily cats and dogs.

The Writing Coach

The Expectations of Public Officials toward Journalists

BY JOE HIGHT

Despite their watchdog roles, U.S. journalists have two commonalities with public officials in that they want to preserve our democracy, especially the rights granted by the Constitution and First Amendment. They also want people to see them as credible, responsible and honest.

After more than 30 years as a journalist, I've concluded these commonalities should guide public officials as they consider how to treat reporters and editors—even in crises.

So, in dealing with journalists, a public official should expect the following:

- Reporters will be skeptical about what you are saying. They are trained that way—trained that our Constitution gives them the right to report on and question the motives of people who serve the public. And accept that good reporters are skeptical of anyone in authority, including their own supervisors. So wouldn't they be skeptical of you?

- More reporters will cover high-profile events—ones that involve many people, force closings of public attractions or sites, are tragic or are unusual. And accept that inquiries about these events may come from local, state and national media.

- Journalists will push for open meetings of public officials and pursue public records with the tenacity of a pit bull. And accept that these meetings should be open, and that public records deserve scrutiny.

- You will receive more scrutiny as you are named or elected to higher offices or gain public acclaim. My father said, "You have to pay the fiddler if you want to dance." That goes for journalists as well as public officials. As you go higher in public office, accept that you have to support your speculative comments with facts and that you'll be seen unfavorably if you say, "No comment"—the worst comment of all.

- You will be criticized if you make decisions that go against the norm. Thomas Jefferson did. Abraham Lincoln did. John F. Kennedy did. So why shouldn't you? Accept that criticism with grace, diplomacy and reasons for your decisions.

- You will be vilified if you vilify the press or fail to respond to their questions. Be ready to accept the consequences of your anti-press sentiments.

- You'll need to provide accurate and up-to-date information to journalists. And accept that you must be proactive in getting your message and accurate information to reporters and editors. This works especially well at local and state levels. Nationally, you can be proactive by providing accurate information through websites or materials pertinent to your cause.

- After a major event you must serve in an explanatory role to several or many journalists. Realize that your role—and perhaps other credible sources—will help bolster your positions.

- You must be consistent with journalists, even in the mass frenzy after a disaster. That means providing them with consistent information as soon as possible and explaining why they'll have to wait. U.S. General Al Gray was correct in saying: "Don't finesse. Get the facts before the American people."

- The truly objective journalist may not exist. However, you can know that credible journalists must strive to be fair, ethical and clear to readers, viewers or listeners. And, most of all, accurate.

- Other views, even ones considered radical, may be presented in the aftermath of an event. Journalists are not doing this to spite you but to be fair to all sides. Accept, however, that editorial pages are different from news pages and may present views different or critical of yours.

If you're consistent, credible, honest and open, you can expect that the public will listen to you more than others. And you'll be accepted more favorably in history.

Joe Hight has been editor of the Colorado Springs (Colorado) Gazette and The Oklahoman of Oklahoma City. He is now the owner and president of Best of Books, Inc.

The Reporter's Guide to Reporting Speeches and Meetings

Advance Stories

1. Report what speech or meeting will happen, when and where it will happen and who will be involved.

2. Keep advance stories short—normally three or four paragraphs.

Covering the Speech or Meeting

1. Get background information on the group or speaker, including a copy of the agenda or the speech, if it's available.

2. Learn the names of all participants.

3. Find out if there will be an opportunity to interview the speaker or the participants before or after the event.

4. Arrive early and find a seat where you can see and hear as much as possible.

5. Introduce yourself to the speaker or the participants in the meeting if they do not know you.

6. Take detailed notes, making sure you record colorful quotations, information about the setting of the event and the responses of the participants and observers.

7. Identify and seek responses from people who may be affected by what happens or who may have views or interests different from those expressed at the speech or meeting.

Follow Stories

1. Identify the issue or decision that is most likely to interest your audience and make that your central point. If other important issues or decisions arose in the speech or meeting, be sure to mention them early.

2. Focus the lead on specific actions or statements to keep it from being overly broad.

3. Organize the story in inverted-pyramid fashion, not according to the order in which statements were made or topics considered.

4. Vary the location of the attribution in direct and indirect quotations so that the story does not become monotonous.

5. Provide transitions from one topic to another.

6. Avoid generalities and eliminate or explain jargon or technical terms.

7. Check controversial facts and give any person or group who has been attacked in the speech or meeting an opportunity to respond.

8. Include color in speech and meeting stories by providing direct quotations and descriptions of speakers, participants, settings and audience responses.

Review Exercises

1. Evaluating Speech and Meeting Leads

Critically evaluate the following speech and meeting story leads, giving each a grade from A to F. Then discuss the leads with your instructor and classmates.

1. The County Commission voted unanimously Tuesday against raising the county tourism tax by one cent to pay for a new baseball stadium.

2. A spokesperson for Citizens Against Crime warned parents Wednesday night about violent crime and its impact on families in the city.

3. By a vote of 5-4, the City Council rejected on Monday night a proposal to build an apartment complex near Reed Road and State Road 419.

4. A heated debate took place at the City Council meeting Thursday night over the need for police dogs.

5. Fifty percent of the drug abusers entering treatment centers go back to using drugs within a year, Mimi Sota told an audience here Monday.

6. In a speech Monday, reporter Samuel Swaugger talked to journalism students about his past as a journalist and his experiences with the two largest newspapers in the state.

7. During a speech to the American Legion last night, former Marine Lt. Col. Oliver North discussed his work in the Reagan White House.

8. County commissioners heard testimony from more than 20 people Tuesday morning on plans to license and regulate snowmobiles.

9. The County Commission reviewed a resolution Wednesday to create a committee that will identify conservation and recreation lands within the county.

10. Blasting opponents of the plan, Mayor Sabrina Datoli last night defended a proposal to establish a police review board.

11. Traveling by airplane has never been more dangerous, Ramon Madea charged in a fiery speech Sunday night.

12. The City Council voted unanimously Monday to change the zoning along three streets from residential to commercial.

13. The business before the School Board flowed smoothly Tuesday night as the board proceeded through the agenda.

14. The county commissioners continued to struggle with the issue of protecting the water quality in Butler Lake at their meeting Monday. They eventually denied a petition to build a new boat ramp on the lake.

15. The County Commission unanimously passed an ordinance that makes it illegal for anyone to possess an open container of alcohol in a vehicle. A previous law made it illegal to drive while drunk, but legal to drink while driving.

2. Writing Advance and Follow Stories

Write separate advance and follow stories about each of the following speeches. Because the speeches are reprinted verbatim, you may quote them directly. Correct the stories' grammatical and spelling errors, including all possessives. You may want to discuss with classmates the problem of handling speakers' errors in grammar and syntax and statements that seem sexist.

1. Americans' Work

Information for advance story:

Leslee D'Ausilio will speak this forthcoming Saturday night to the Chamber of Commerce at the organizations annual meeting. The affair will start with an open bar at 6:30, dinner at 7:30, and the speech to begin promptly at 8:30 PM, all in the spacious Grand Ballroom of the Downtown Hilton Hotel. Cost for the dinner and speech: $39.00 for members and their guests, $49.00 for nonmembers.

Tickets are conveniently available at the Chamber of Commerce office until Noon Saturday. The speaker, a famous celebrity and frequent TV guest commentator, is the author of 3 best-selling books, all about American workers, their jobs, their characteristics, their problems. She received her B.A. and M.A. from the University of Wisconsin in Madison Wisconsin where for both degrees she majored in Sociology, and Ph.D. from Harvard where she majored in Management with a speciality in Labor Relations. She currently teaches at Harvard, serves as a consultant for the UAW-CIO, and was Assistant Secretary of Labor in the Clinton administration. Her announced topic will be "Today's Workers, Workweeks, and Productivity."

Speech for follow story:

Today, the U.S. ranks Number One in the world in productivity per worker. That has both advantages and disadvantages for workers, their families, and employers.

On the upside, American families are enjoying more prosperity, but not due solely to rising wages. More family members are working, especially among Black and Hispanic families. During the last 10 years, the average middle-class familys income rose 9.2% after inflation, but the typical familys wage-earners had to spend 6.8 percent more time at work to reap it. Without increased earnings from wives, the average middle-class familys income would have risen only 3.6%. The share of married women working full-time rose from 41 to 46%. Plus, the average workers work-week has risen from about 38 hours for full-time workers to slightly more than 41 hours a week. Executives, on average, work 47 hours a week.

On the downside, workers complain they're working harder and that they're having difficulty balancing their jobs and personal lives. American workers seemed to be squeezed during both booms and busts. In expansions, companies keep giving their workers more work, and in recessions companies downsize. Then, with fewer employees, those that remain have to work longer and harder to get everything done. So its not surprising that American workers are sometimes frustrated. Forty-one percent feel they do not have enough time to accomplish all their tasks each day.

Its a complex issue, and there're also other culprits. One is technology. More than ever before, technological advances keep people tethered to their office by cell phone and computer. Think about it! It doesn't matter where you go: to a movie, a nice restaurant, or even a golf course or your church. People carry telephones everywhere and, while some calls are social, many are business.

There's also the American psyche and culture. Much of the increase in time spent at work is voluntary. Workers want to earn more and to move up economically. They're eager to make a good impression: to impress their boss and co-workers. Also, work is important to them, sometimes the most important

thing in their lives. Many are ambitious, even obsessed, with getting ahead. Increasingly, then, some Americans work even on holidays and are forgoing vacations and time with their families and friends.

During the past decade, Americans added nearly a full week to their work year, working on average 1,978 hours last year. That's up 36 hours almost a full week from ten years ago. That means Americans who are employed spent nearly 49 weeks a year on the job. As a result, they worked longer than all other industrial nations last year. Americans work 100 more hours (2 weeks per year) than Japanese workers. They work 250 hours (about 6 weeks) more per year than British workers, and 500 hours (12 weeks) more per year than German workers.

Why? Among the reasons for the differences are the fact that Europeans typically take 4 to 6 weeks of vacation each year while Americans take only 2 to 3 weeks. Also, while American employers offer or require lots of overtime, the French government has reduced that countrys official workweek to 35 hours. That's because the unemployment rate in France is high, and the government wants to pressure companies to hire more workers.

Clearly, all these trends, whether good or bad, have contributed to our countrys outstanding economic performance, which translates into more income for employees and more profits for employers. So, no one can deny that Americans are working harder, and I don't like that, but I don't see the situation as all bad. Our economy is booming. There are good jobs for most workers, and incomes are going up along with our productivity.

2. College Athletics

Information for advance story:

Erik Nieves, your schools Athletic Director for the past twenty-four years, has previously announced his retirement, effective at the end of next month. Before then, he's planning a farewell speech and today he told you it will be "a candid discussion about some serious problems in athletics, primarily college athletics." Its all free this coming Saturday night at the annual meeting of members of your schools Athletic Boosters Club. The speech is being held in the beautiful Grand Ballroom of your Student Union with only Booster Club members and their guests invited. Each member of the club donates $500 or more annually to your schools Athletic Foundation. Bronze Key Club members donate $1000 or more, Silver Key Club members $5000 or more, and Gold Key Club members $10000 or more. There's an open bar at 6:30, dinner at 7:30, and the speech at 9:00pm, with good fellowship for all. "Its my farewell address to the club," Nieves said. (Press kits will be available, with free seating available to the press. No radio or TV tapings or broadcasts of any type will be permitted, all such rights being exclusively retained by the Athletic Boosters Club.)

Speech for follow story:

As I look around this room, I see many familiar faces: good people, generous people who've been friends and supporters for as long as I've been here. Now, all of you know I'm retiring at the end of next month. I'm 64, and its time. What you don't know is that I've decided to devote the time I have left to increasing public aware-ness of a serious problem for our athletes and athletic programs. I'll continue with that effort after I retire. What I'm going to say isn't going to be popular, but its something I feel I have to say, something eating my heart out. The fact is, its no longer fun to play college football; its become a fatiguing grind. Its a full-time job, a year-around job, and that's true of every college football program across the country.

The insanity has to stop. Coaches demand more, colleges demand more. Alumni demand more, so college football has turned into a 12-month-a-year job that never ends. We've got fall games and winter workouts. There's spring practice, and there're summer conditioning drills. So our players work and work and work during the season. Then, when the season ends, they work even more. They push harder and stay longer, and it doesn't matter what time of the day or what month of the year.

You've got wonderful young players some still teenagers literally working themselves to death, dying so you can have a winning season. Eleven college football players died in the past 12 months year, and its a tragedy we have to stop.

Heatstroke is a part of the problem, especially during those damned summer drills. Heatstroke can cause your body temperature to soar to 108 degrees, cause a heart attack, and induce a coma. On col-lege teams its hard to help people 50 to 100 pounds sometimes even 150 pounds above the ideal weight for their height. With people who are so overweight, often deliberately, you're going to have problems. We tell our players on a hot day he should drink 16 to 20 ounces of fluid and then continue to drink every 15 minutes whether he's thirsty or not. You can't depend on your thirst mechanism. The center of the brain doesn't click on and tell you that you're thirsty until a long time after all your fluids are gone. If you're a coach, whether in high school or college, and your kids aren't getting water every 15 or 20 minutes, you shouldn't be coaching.

"Actually, heat stroke is one of the easier problems we deal with. Some of our players have pre-existing conditions we don't know about. We require players to have physical exams before letting them play. Still, right here in our state, we had a freshman die after a series of early-morning agility drills. He was just 19, 6 feet 4, and 230 pounds, with no history of heart problems. When he reported to campus doctors detected no heart abnormalities during his physical exam. That non-detection is no surprise. Many cardiol-ogists say arrhythmia can be difficult to find.

Cardiac arrhythmia is an irregular heartbeat. The heartbeat is not constantly out of kilter, so the problem is not likely to be detected even in an athlete undergo-ing a yearly physical. But at some point under exertion, the heart is pushed beyond its limits, and there's no way of knowing when or why it will happen. There are a number of causes for this problem, including defects in the heart structure. People are born with these defects but often show no outward signs of the problems. Including high school teams and all sports, about 100 to 200 young athletes die each year from the condition.

Now, some of this is the coaches fault and some the fans fault. Coaches work their players too hard. They work themselves too hard. And players give every last drop of their time, energy and effort. They sacrifice way too much for far too little. They have tremendous pride and ambition, and they all want to be drafted into the professionals, so they push themselves through heat and pain.

To solve the problems, our coaches at every level need more sports medicine knowledge. We don't have a system of coaching certification in this country. In other countries, especially Europe, you have to have ex-pertise and take courses and pass tests. In this country

I could be an accountant who never took a course in first aid, and so long as I can win football games, it doesn't matter.

Other things are just common sense. If you're a coach, you take your team out at 7:00 in the morning or 5:00 or 6:00 in the evening. On hot days, you don't work outside at noon. Somehow, we also have to cut back on off-season drills. They take way too much of our athletes time, so an awful lot of these young men never graduate. There's just no time left for their studies.

We also need better physicals. That will cost several hundred dollars for every player every year but should be a priority, and schools can afford it.

Plus, fans put way too much pressure on their coaches, forcing coaches to put more pressure on their players. You see it in every game, high school, college, and professional. You see coaches send too many injured players back into games before they're ready. We've also got fans who like to brag their teams linemen average 250 or 300 pounds. That's not healthy for young men to gain an extra 50 or 100 pounds. I'd rather have fans brag about how many of our athletes graduate. To get this awful pressure off coaches, give them tenure just like you give faculty members. No coach should be fired after just one or two losing seasons.

Now all this isn't going to happen soon, and it can't happen at just one or two schools. It has to be a national effort. Football is a game. Enjoy the game whether your team wins or loses. A few more victories aren't worth risking a players life.

3. The Police and the Press

Information for advance story:

Barry Kopperud is scheduled to speak to the local chapter of the Society of Professional Journalists Monday of next week. The club meets for dinner the second Monday of every month at the Blackhawk Hotel. Both the dinner and the speech are open to the public.

The dinners are $17.50 per person. Those wishing to hear the speech only may attend free. The evening begins with a social hour and cash bar at 6 p.m. Dinner starts at 6:30 p.m., and Kopperuds speech will begin at 7:30 p.m. Anyone wishing to attend the dinner must make reservations in advance by calling LeeAnn Verkler at the university.

Kopperud is the chief of police, and he will speak about issues regarding press coverage of crime and the police.

Speech for follow story:

Good evening, ladies and gentlemen. I've met most of you before. A couple of you I've seen just within the last hour. I'm glad we have this opportunity to talk under conditions that are more pleasant than when we usually meet.

The police beat is among the most active beats for any reporter. I've noticed that a good share of the content of the news broadcasts and the newspaper comes from the police.

This heavy reliance by the media on the police probably accounts for a situation police and news people have observed in many towns and cities. There is a symbiotic, co-dependent, love-hate relationship between cops and reporters that develops about everywhere.

Obviously, reporters rely on the police to provide information about some of the most important and dramatic events of the day. But police need reporters to get out information on the things they want to promote. Police understand that people read and watch news stories about crime. One of the first places people turn to when they get their daily paper is the police blotter. Although the police department has had generally good relations with the press, there are some common problems—points of friction, you might call them—that arise from time to time. One of these points of friction involves the release of information through unofficial channels.

The police department has lots of information, some of it secret that it doesn't want released to the public. A classic example is information relevant to a homicide, such as autopsy information and details about the scene of the crime. Why do we want to keep this information secret? Because doing so helps us investigate the crime. A few years ago we had a homicide in which a man was bludgeoned to death with a tire iron. The killer then doused the body with gasoline and tried to set it afire. The body was in a wooded area and not discovered for several weeks. We got a lot of tips about that murder. We also had a couple of people show up trying to confess. Because we withheld the details about the crime scene and cause of death, we were able to distinguish the real culprit from the cranks and the real sources from the phony ones. Because the details were never published in the media, we could trace leads back to the one person with first-hand knowledge—a person who is now serving a life sentence. But those details are exactly the kind of thing reporters most want.

One of the banes of my existence is that there are people in the police department who like to release that kind of information. Maybe these leaks are intentional—from disgruntled officers—or maybe the leaks are unintentional, where an officer tells a friend who tells a reporter. Either way, reporters will call us back asking for confirmation of these leaks, but the police department will never confirm or deny anything.

That brings me to some ethical questions. Both police and reporters deal with ethical issues. Sometimes we err and release information that we shouldn't. Sometimes we wonder why you folks in the media publish what you do. I just want to share with you some recent incidents that raise ethical issues and ask you to consider them.

A few weeks ago, a police dog bit its handler's daughter. The dog was retired from service but had been living with its handler. As a result of the incident the girl needed stitches. Somehow a TV reporter got onto the story and wanted to do an on-camera interview with someone from the department. We refused. The reporter suggested it was because the story would embarrass the department or suggest irresponsibility or create problems with the city council. But none of those was correct. We refused because the dog had been put down, and the little girl didn't know that. She was fond of the dog, and the dog had meant a lot to her. Her mom and dad asked that the story not be released, and we agreed.

In another recent case, we had an accidental death of a graduate student in a university dorm. The man had suffocated to death, and the newspaper reported—correctly—that he had died while practicing autoerotic asphyxiation. I read that article and thought, "How crass!" Imagine how that must have made that students mother and father feel. I'd like to think that reporters would take that kind of thing into account before they publish a story. Sometimes the feelings of the family outweigh the publics need to know.

The case that for me presented the most searing ethical problem was the Wendy Ray case. You all remember that Wendy was a university student who was abducted from just outside her parents apartment one night, repeatedly raped, tortured and then murdered.

For weeks she was just missing, and no one knew where she was. We got our first break in the case when we arrested a couple of men for burglarizing an electronics store. After we had charged them, Donald Hendricks, the assistant county attorney, called and said one of them, Scott Reed, wanted to cut a deal: He'd tell us about Wendys murder if we promised not to seek the death penalty for him. Reed told us where to find Wendys body.

At this point, I went to Bill and Liz Ray, Wendys parents, and told them we had remains and believed them to be Wendys, pending a dental match. I also told them that we knew a lot more about how she had died and that I would tell them as much as they wanted to know when they wanted to know it. They understood that I meant there were grisly details about Wendys death. A few hours later, we had a positive dental match, but before I could get back to Wendy's parents, one of the radio stations had aired a news story with all the gory details. I can't tell you how devastated the Rays were. I think it was not a good way for the family to learn those details.

I guess the moral of these stories is a simple one: People really are affected by news stories. I hope reporters have enough humanity not to get caught up in the competitive practices of the business and realize how they may hurt others. I understand some people may reach different decisions about how to handle these ethical issues. I have no problem with someone who disagrees with me. I have a real problem, however, with reporters who won't consider other points of view.

3. Summarizing Speeches

1. U.S. Withdrawal from the Paris Agreement on Climate Change

Using the background information and the official transcript provided, write a story summarizing President Trump's announcement that the United States will withdraw from the Paris Agreement on climate change.

Background on the Paris Agreement
The Paris Agreement was negotiated in December 2015 within the United Nations Framework Convention on

Climate Change (UNFCCC). It was signed by 195 countries and ratified by 148. Only Syria and Nicaragua did not sign the agreement.

The agreement's goal is first to hold the increase "in the global average temperature to well below 2 degrees C above pre-industrial levels and to pursue efforts to limit the temperature increase to 1.5 degrees C above pre-industrial levels." Temperatures in the first half of 2016 were already about 1.3 degrees C above 1880 levels, when records first were kept. The agreement also calls on signatories to do the following:

- increase "the ability to adapt to the adverse impacts of climate change and foster climate resilience and low greenhouse gas emissions development, in a manner that does not threaten food production"
- make "finance flows consistent with a pathway towards low greenhouse gas emissions and climate-resilient development"
- aim to reach "global peaking of greenhouse gas emissions as soon as possible"

Under the agreement, each country determines the steps it will take to mitigate climate change. Countries are urged to be ambitious in their goals, and they are supposed to report them every five years to the UNFCCC secretariat. Each new set of goals should be more ambitious than the previous set. Nothing compels any country to abide by its own targets or achieve them by a specific date, although the UNFCCC will report on how much success countries have had in meeting their objectives. This practice has been called a "name and shame" or a "name and encourage" system of enforcement. The agreement also calls for a Global Stocktake in 2018, to assess how much countries have accomplished toward achieving their nationally determined contributions to carbon-emission reduction. That will be followed by further evaluations every five years, the first being in 2023.

The participating developed countries said they would contribute $100 billion to finance initiatives to mitigate climate change by 2020 and spend an additional $100 billion a year. In 2016, the Obama administration issued a grant of $500 million to the Green Climate Fund, the first of the $3 billion it had committed to financing the agreement. By June 2017, the fund had received $10 billion, mostly from developed countries, but some from developing countries such as Mexico, Indonesia and Vietnam.

A country may withdraw from the agreement three years after it goes into effect in that country, with a one-year waiting period until the departure becomes effective. Therefore, the earliest the United States can fully withdraw from the agreement is November 4, 2020.

President Trump's Speech
White House Rose Garden, 3:32 p.m. Eastern Time
THE PRESIDENT: Thank you very much. (Applause.) Thank you. I would like to begin by addressing the terrorist attack in Manila. We're closely monitoring the situation, and I will continue to give updates if anything happens during this period of time. But it is really very sad as to what's going on throughout the world with terror. Our thoughts and our prayers are with all of those affected.

Before we discuss the Paris Accord, I'd like to begin with an update on our tremendous—absolutely tremendous—economic progress since Election Day on November 8th. The economy is starting to come back, and very, very rapidly. We've added $3.3 trillion in stock market value to our economy, and more than a million private sector jobs.

I have just returned from a trip overseas where we concluded nearly $350 billion of military and economic development for the United States, creating hundreds of thousands of jobs. It was a very, very successful trip, believe me. (Applause.) Thank you. Thank you.

In my meetings at the G7, we have taken historic steps to demand fair and reciprocal trade that gives Americans a level playing field against other nations. We're also working very hard for peace in the Middle East, and perhaps even peace between the Israelis and the Palestinians. Our attacks on terrorism are greatly stepped up—and you see that, you see it all over—from the previous administration, including getting many other countries to make major contributions to the fight against terror. Big, big contributions are being made by countries that weren't doing so much in the form of contribution.

One by one, we are keeping the promises I made to the American people during my campaign for President whether it's cutting job-killing regulations; appointing and confirming a tremendous Supreme Court justice; putting in place tough new ethics rules; achieving a record reduction in illegal immigration on our southern border; or bringing jobs, plants, and factories back into the United States at numbers which no one until this point thought even possible. And believe me, we've just begun. The fruits of our labor will be seen very shortly even more so.

On these issues and so many more, we're following through on our commitments. And I don't want anything to get in our way. I am fighting every day for the great people of this country. Therefore, in order to fulfill my solemn duty to protect America and its citizens, the United States will withdraw from the Paris Climate Accord—(applause)—thank you, thank you—but begin negotiations to reenter either the Paris Accord or a really entirely new transaction on terms that are fair to the United States, its businesses, its workers, its people, its taxpayers. So we're getting out. But we will start to negotiate, and we will see if we can make a deal that's fair. And if we can, that's great. And if we can't, that's fine. (Applause.)

As President, I can put no other consideration before the wellbeing of American citizens. The Paris Climate Accord is simply the latest example of Washington entering into an agreement that disadvantages the United States to the exclusive benefit of other countries, leaving American workers—who I love—and taxpayers to absorb the cost in terms of lost jobs, lower wages, shuttered factories, and vastly diminished economic production.

Thus, as of today, the United States will cease all implementation of the non-binding Paris Accord and the draconian financial and economic burdens the agreement imposes on our country. This includes ending the implementation of the nationally determined contribution and, very importantly, the Green Climate Fund which is costing the United States a vast fortune.

Compliance with the terms of the Paris Accord and the onerous energy restrictions it has placed on the United States could cost America as much as 2.7 million lost jobs by 2025 according to the National Economic Research Associates. This includes 440,000 fewer manufacturing jobs—not what we need—believe me, this is not what we need—including automobile jobs, and the further decimation of vital American industries on which countless communities rely. They rely for so much, and we would be giving them so little.

According to this same study, by 2040, compliance with the commitments put into place by the previous administration would cut production for the following sectors: paper down 12 percent; cement down 23 percent; iron and steel down 38 percent; coal—and

I happen to love the coal miners—down 86 percent; natural gas down 31 percent. The cost to the economy at this time would be close to $3 trillion in lost GDP and 6.5 million industrial jobs, while households would have $7,000 less income and, in many cases, much worse than that.

Not only does this deal subject our citizens to harsh economic restrictions, it fails to live up to our environmental ideals. As someone who cares deeply about the environment, which I do, I cannot in good conscience support a deal that punishes the United States—which is what it does—the world's leader in environmental protection, while imposing no meaningful obligations on the world's leading polluters.

For example, under the agreement, China will be able to increase these emissions by a staggering number of years—13. They can do whatever they want for 13 years. Not us. India makes its participation contingent on receiving billions and billions and billions of dollars in foreign aid from developed countries. There are many other examples. But the bottom line is that the Paris Accord is very unfair, at the highest level, to the United States.

Further, while the current agreement effectively blocks the development of clean coal in America—which it does, and the mines are starting to open up. We're having a big opening in two weeks. Pennsylvania, Ohio, West Virginia, so many places. A big opening of a brand-new mine. It's unheard of. For many, many years, that hasn't happened. They asked me if I'd go. I'm going to try.

China will be allowed to build hundreds of additional coal plants. So we can't build the plants, but they can, according to this agreement. India will be allowed to double its coal production by 2020. Think of it: India can double their coal production. We're supposed to get rid of ours. Even Europe is allowed to continue construction of coal plants.

In short, the agreement doesn't eliminate coal jobs, it just transfers those jobs out of America and the United States, and ships them to foreign countries.

This agreement is less about the climate and more about other countries gaining a financial advantage over the United States. The rest of the world applauded when we signed the Paris Agreement—they went wild; they were so happy—for the simple reason that it put our country, the United States of America, which we all love, at a very, very big economic disadvantage. A cynic would say the obvious reason for economic competitors and their wish to see us remain in the agreement is so that we continue to suffer this self-inflicted major economic wound. We would find it very hard to compete with other countries from other parts of the world.

We have among the most abundant energy reserves on the planet, sufficient to lift millions of America's poorest workers out of poverty. Yet, under this agreement, we are effectively putting these reserves under lock and key, taking away the great wealth of our nation—it's great wealth, it's phenomenal wealth; not so long ago, we had no idea we had such wealth—and leaving millions and millions of families trapped in poverty and joblessness.

The agreement is a massive redistribution of United States wealth to other countries. At 1 percent growth, renewable sources of energy can meet some of our domestic demand, but at 3 or 4 percent growth, which I expect, we need all forms of available American energy, or our country—(applause)—will be at grave risk of brownouts and blackouts, our businesses will come to a halt in many cases, and the American family will suffer the consequences in the form of lost jobs and a very diminished quality of life.

Even if the Paris Agreement were implemented in full, with total compliance from all nations, it is estimated it would only produce a two-tenths of one degree—think of that; this much—Celsius reduction in global temperature by the year 2100. Tiny, tiny amount. In fact, 14 days of carbon emissions from China alone would wipe out the gains from America—and this is an incredible statistic—would totally wipe out the gains from America's expected reductions in the year 2030, after we have had to spend billions and billions of dollars, lost jobs, closed factories, and suffered much higher energy costs for our businesses and for our homes.

As the Wall Street Journal wrote this morning: "The reality is that withdrawing is in America's economic interest and won't matter much to the climate." The United States, under the Trump administration, will continue to be the cleanest and most environmentally friendly country on Earth. We'll be the cleanest. We're going to have the cleanest air. We're going to have the cleanest water. We will be environmentally friendly, but we're not going to put our businesses out of work and we're not going to lose our jobs. We're going to grow; we're going to grow rapidly. (Applause.)

And I think you just read—it just came out minutes ago, the small business report—small businesses as of just now are booming, hiring people. One of the best reports they've seen in many years.

I'm willing to immediately work with Democratic leaders to either negotiate our way back into Paris, under the terms that are fair to the United States and its workers, or to negotiate a new deal that protects our country and its taxpayers. (Applause.)

So if the obstructionists want to get together with me, let's make them non-obstructionists. We will all sit down, and we will get back into the deal. And we'll make it good, and we won't be closing up our factories, and we won't be losing our jobs. And we'll sit down with the Democrats and all of the people that represent either the Paris Accord or something that we can do that's much better than the Paris Accord. And I think the people of our country will be thrilled, and I think then the people of the world will be thrilled. But until we do that, we're out of the agreement.

I will work to ensure that America remains the world's leader on environmental issues, but under a framework that is fair and where the burdens and responsibilities are equally shared among the many nations all around the world.

No responsible leader can put the workers—and the people—of their country at this debilitating and tremendous disadvantage. The fact that the Paris deal hamstrings the United States, while empowering some of the world's top polluting countries, should dispel any doubt as to the real reason why foreign lobbyists wish to keep our magnificent country tied up and bound down by this agreement: It's to give their country an economic edge over the United States. That's not going to happen while I'm President. I'm sorry. (Applause.)

My job as President is to do everything within my power to give America a level playing field and to create the economic, regulatory and tax structures that make America the most prosperous and productive country on Earth, and with the highest standard of living and the highest standard of environmental protection.

Our tax bill is moving along in Congress, and I believe it's doing very well. I think a lot of people will be very pleasantly surprised. The Republicans are working very, very hard. We'd love to have support from the Democrats, but we may have to go it alone. But it's going very well.

The Paris Agreement handicaps the United States economy in order to win praise from the very foreign capitals and global activists that have long sought to gain wealth at our country's expense. They don't put America first. I do, and I always will. (Applause.)

The same nations asking us to stay in the agreement are the countries that have collectively cost America trillions of dollars through tough trade practices and, in many cases, lax contributions to our critical military alliance. You see what's happening. It's pretty obvious to those that want to keep an open mind.

At what point does America get demeaned? At what point do they start laughing at us as a country? We want fair treatment for its citizens, and we want fair treatment for our taxpayers. We don't want other leaders and other countries laughing at us anymore. And they won't be. They won't be.

I was elected to represent the citizens of Pittsburgh, not Paris. (Applause.) I promised I would exit or renegotiate any deal which fails to serve America's interests. Many trade deals will soon be under renegotiation. Very rarely do we have a deal that works for this country, but they'll soon be under renegotiation. The process has begun from day one. But now we're down to business.

Beyond the severe energy restrictions inflicted by the Paris Accord, it includes yet another scheme to redistribute wealth out of the United States through the so-called Green Climate Fund—nice name—which calls for developed countries to send $100 billion to developing countries all on top of America's existing and massive foreign aid payments. So we're going to be paying billions and billions and billions of dollars, and we're already way ahead of anybody else. Many of the other countries haven't spent anything, and many of them will never pay one dime.

The Green Fund would likely obligate the United States to commit potentially tens of billions of dollars of which the United States has already handed over $1 billion—nobody else is even close; most of them haven't even paid anything—including funds raided out of America's budget for the war against terrorism. That's where they came. Believe me, they didn't come from me. They came just before I came into office. Not good. And not good the way they took the money.

In 2015, the United Nation's departing top climate officials reportedly described the $100 billion per year as "peanuts," and stated that "the $100 billion is the tail that wags the dog." In 2015, the Green Climate Fund's executive director reportedly stated that estimated funding needed would increase to $450 billion per year after 2020. And nobody even knows where the money is going to. Nobody has been able to say, where is it going to?

Of course, the world's top polluters have no affirmative obligations under the Green Fund, which we terminated. America is $20 trillion in debt. Cash-strapped cities cannot hire enough police officers or fix vital infrastructure. Millions of our citizens are out of work. And yet, under the Paris Accord, billions of dollars that ought to be invested right here in America will be sent to the very countries that have taken our factories and our jobs away from us. So think of that.

There are serious legal and constitutional issues as well. Foreign leaders in Europe, Asia, and across the world should not have more to say with respect to the U.S. economy than our own citizens and their elected representatives. Thus, our withdrawal from the agreement represents a reassertion of America's sovereignty. (Applause.) Our Constitution is unique among all the nations of the world, and it is my highest obligation and greatest honor to protect it. And I will.

Staying in the agreement could also pose serious obstacles for the United States as we begin the process of unlocking the restrictions on America's abundant energy reserves, which we have started very strongly. It would once have been unthinkable that an international agreement could prevent the United States from conducting its own domestic economic affairs, but this is the new reality we face if we do not leave the agreement or if we do not negotiate a far better deal.

The risks grow as historically these agreements only tend to become more and more ambitious over time. In other words, the Paris framework is a starting point—as bad as it is—not an end point. And exiting the agreement protects the United States from future intrusions on the United States' sovereignty and massive future legal liability. Believe me, we have massive legal liability if we stay in.

As President, I have one obligation, and that obligation is to the American people. The Paris Accord would undermine our economy, hamstring our workers, weaken our sovereignty, impose unacceptable legal risks, and put us at a permanent disadvantage to the other countries of the world. It is time to exit the Paris Accord—(applause)—and time to pursue a new deal that protects the environment, our companies, our citizens, and our country.

It is time to put Youngstown, Ohio, Detroit, Michigan, and Pittsburgh, Pennsylvania—along with many, many other locations within our great country—before Paris, France. It is time to make America great again. (Applause.) Thank you. Thank you. Thank you very much.

2. School Board Meeting

Assume that your school board held its monthly meeting at 7:30 p.m. yesterday. Write a news story that summarizes the comments and decisions made at this meeting. Correct all errors.

The school board opened its meeting by honoring seven retiring teachers: Shirley Dawsun, Carmen Foucault, Nina Paynich, Kenneth Satava, Nancy Lee Scott, Lonnie McEwen, and Harley Sawyer. Paynich worked as a teacher 44 years, longer than any of the others. Each teacher was given a framed "Certificate of Appreciation" and a good round of applause.

The school board then turned to the budget for next year. The budget totals $618.7 million, up 5% from this year. It includes $9.3 million for a new elementary school to be built on West Madison Ave. It will be completed and opened in two years. The budget also includes a 4.5% raise for teachers and a 6% raise for administrators. Also, the salary of the superintendent of schools was raised by $10,000, to $137,000 a year. The vote was unanimous: 9-0.

The school board then discussed the topic of remedial summer classes. Board member Umberto Vacante proposed eliminating them to save an estimated $2.1 million. "They're just too expensive, especially when you consider we serve only about 900 students each summer. A lot of them are students who flunked their regular classes. Often, if they attend the summer classes, they don't have to repeat a grade. If we're going to spend that kind of money, I think we should use it to help and reward our most talented students. They're the ones we ignore. We could offer special programs for them." Supt. Greg Hubbard responded, "Some of these summer students have learning disabilities and emotional problems, and they really need the help. This would hurt them terribly. Without it, they might never graduate." The board then voted 7-2 to keep the classes one more year, but to ask its staff for a study of the matter.

During a one-hour hearing that followed, about 100 people, many loud and angry, debated the issue of creationism vs. evolution. "We've seen your biology books," said parent Claire Sawyer. "I don't want my children using them. They never mention the theory of creationism." Another parent, Harley Euon of 410 East Third Street, responded: "Evolution isn't a theory. Its proven fact. Creationism is a religious idea, not even a scientific theory. People here are trying to force schools to teach our children their religion." A third parent, Roy E. Cross of 101 Charow Lane, agreed, adding: "People can teach creationism in their homes and churches. Its not the schools job." After listening to the debate, the board voted 6-3 to continue using the present textbooks, but to encourage parents to discuss the matter with their children and to provide in their individual homes the religious training they deem most appropriate for their families.

Finally, last on its agenda, the board unanimously adopted a resolution praising the school systems ADDITIONS: adult volunteers who contribute their spare time to help and assist their neighborhood schools. Last year, Supt. Greg Hubbard reported, there was a total of 897 ADDITIONS, and they put in a total of 38,288 hours of volunteer time.

3. City Council Meeting

Assume that your city council held a meeting at 8 p.m. yesterday. Write a news story that summarizes the comments and decisions made at this meeting. Correct all errors.

Background

For 10 years, the First United Methodist Church at 680 Garland Avenue has provided a shelter for the homeless, allowing them to sleep in the basement of its fellowship hall every night and feeding them both breakfast and dinner. The church can house 180 people each night and relies on a staff of more than 200 volunteers. In recent years, they've been overwhelmed, and the church, by itself, is unable to continue to afford to shoulder the entire burden. It has asked for help: for donations and for more room, especially in winter, for the homeless to sleep. Civic leaders have formed the Coalition for the Homeless, Inc., a nonprofit organization, and hope to build a new shelter. The coalition has asked the city to donate a site, valued at $500,000. Coalition leaders said they will then raise the

$1.5 million needed to construct the shelter. The coalition leaders say they will also operate the shelter, relying on volunteers; a small, full-time professional staff; and donations from concerned citizens.

First Speaker

Ida Levine, president of the Coalition for the Homeless, Inc.:

"As you, uh, know, what we're trying to do here is raise $1.5 million to build the shelter. We're approaching everyone that might be able to help and, so far, have collected about $200,000 and have pledges of another $318,000, and thats just the beginning, in two months. So we're certain that if you provide the land, we'll be able to, uh, come up with all the money for this thing. The site we have in mind is the old fire station on Garland Avenue. The building is so old that its worthless, and we'd tear it down, but its an ideal location for our purposes."

Second Speaker

Lt. Luis Rafelson:

"I'm here officially, representing the police department, to say that we're all for this. It costs the taxpayers about $350,000 a year to arrest homeless people for violating city ordinances like trespassing on private property and sleeping at night in parks and such. During the average month last year we arrested 300 homeless people, sometimes more. It takes about 2 hours to arrest a person and do all the booking and paperwork, while taking five minutes to transport them to a shelter. So you're wasting police time, time we could be spending on more important things. So if the city spends $500,000 on this deal, it'll save that much in a year, maybe more."

Third Speaker

Banker Irvin Porej:

"The people who stay in shelters are just like you and me. The difference is that we have a place to go. They're good people for the most part, just down on their luck. This would provide a temporary shelter for them, help them get back on their feet. Until now, we've had churches doing this, and the Salvation Army has a shelter, too, but we should put an end to the church shelters. Its not fair to them because the churches are burdened by a problem that everyone should be helping with, and the problem is getting too big for them to handle."

Fourth Speaker

Council member Sandra Bandolf:

"We have to address this problem. It's not going to go away. And with this solution, it really won't cost the city anything. No one's asking us for money or anything, only for a piece of land that's been lying unused for years."

Fifth Speaker

Council member William Belmonte:

"I suppose I'm going to be the only one who votes against this. Why should taxpayers suddenly start paying for this, people who work hard for their money and are struggling these days to support their families? And what happens if the coalition doesn't raise all the money it needs for the shelter, what happens then? What happens if they breach the agreement? Then we'll be left holding the bag, expected to pay for this damn thing and to support it for years. That'll add a whole new bureaucracy to the city, and where'll the money come from then?"

Sixth Speaker

Trina Guzman, president of the Downtown Merchants' Assn.:

"The members of my association are strongly opposed to this. We agree that the city needs a shelter, that we have an obligation to help the people who are really homeless and needy, but not on Garland Avenue. That's just a block from downtown, and we've been having trouble with these people for years. Some of them need help, have all sorts of problems like alcoholism and mental illness that no one here's talking about. Remember too that these people aren't allowed to stay in the shelters during the day. Theoretically, they're supposed to go out and work, or at least look for work. What some of them do is hang around Main Street, panhandling and annoying people and using our parking lots and alleys for toilets. We've got customers who tell us they won't come downtown any more because they're afraid of being approached and asked for money and being mugged or something. Let's feed these people and help them, but put them out somewhere where they can't hurt anyone."

Outcome

The council voted 6-1 to donate the land. Belmonte cast the single vote against the proposal.

BRIGHTS, FOLLOW-UPS, ROUNDUPS, SIDEBARS AND OBITUARIES

16

Tell a new reporter to write a speech or a meeting story and he or she will immediately understand what is required. However, someone who has never worked in a newsroom might scratch his or her head when asked to write a bright, follow-up, roundup, sidebar or obituary. Yet all are common assignments for beginning reporters.

> "I do not apologize for the effort of anybody in the news business to be entertaining, if the motive is to instruct and to teach and to elevate rather than to debase."
>
> *Max Frankel, newspaper editor*

Brights

Brights are short, humorous stories that often have surprise endings. Some are written in the inverted-pyramid style: After a summary lead, the story reports the remaining details in descending order of importance. Others have unexpected or bizarre twists, and reporters might try to surprise the audience by withholding them until the story's final paragraphs. Brights that have surprise endings are called "suspended-interest stories." These stories often begin with facts likely to interest people and end with facts that are the most newsworthy or put the rest of the story in a new and surprising light.

Here are two versions of the same story. The first uses a summary lead that puts the unusual facts of the story at the beginning. The second also uses a summary lead, but it withholds the most unusual facts until the end, giving the story an unusual and amusing twist.

Version 1

Two armed men robbed the owner of a local pizzeria at gun point Tuesday night and took off with a bag full of dough—pizza dough, Police Chief Barry Kopperud said Wednesday morning.

Two men have been arrested in connection with the crime: Frederick

Version 2

Police arrested two men shortly before midnight Tuesday on suspicion of robbing the manager of a local pizza parlor at gun point.

The two in custody are Frederick C. Taylor, 25, of 4828 N. Vine St. and Grady Smith, 22, of 8213 Peach St. Police Chief Barry Kopperud told

C. Taylor, 25, of 4828 N. Vine St. and Grady Smith, 22, of 8213 Peach St.

The robbers, both of whom wore masks, confronted Y.Y. Cho, the manager of Giovanni's Pizza Parlor on North Wisconsin Avenue, as he was leaving the store, shortly after 11:30 p.m.

One of the robbers pointed a gun at Cho and demanded that he give them the bag he was carrying. Cho did so, and the robbers fled, Kopperud told reporters at his daily briefing. Cho told police he thought the robbers must have believed the bag contained the night's receipts, but all it held was five pounds of pizza dough he was taking to the Giovanni's parlor on Hazel Street.

Kopperud said Cho immediately called police and gave a description of the car the robbers used to escape. The car was spotted by Larry Chevez, a police detective who was on patrol in the vicinity, about 11:45 p.m. Chevez saw a bag in the back seat of the car, which turned out to contain pizza dough.

"If Mr. Cho had not had the presence of mind to call the police immediately and to get a description of the car, the robbers might not have been caught," Kopperud said.

Taylor and Smith were formally charged with armed robbery at an arraignment Wednesday afternoon.

reporters Wednesday morning that two masked men confronted Y.Y. Cho, the manager of Giovanni's Pizza Parlor on North Wisconsin Avenue, a little before 11:30 p.m. They demanded that Cho give them the bag he was carrying. He did so and the pair of robbers fled.

Cho immediately called the police department, Kopperud said, and gave a description of the car the robbers were using.

"If Mr. Cho had not had the presence of mind to call the police immediately and to get a description of the car, the robbers might not have been caught," Kopperud said.

The description of the vehicle was relayed to officers on patrol. Detective Larry Chevez saw a vehicle matching Cho's description and pulled it over at 11:45. Chevez saw a bag in the back seat of the car similar to the bag that had been taken from Cho.

When police opened the bag, it was found to contain exactly what Cho said had been stolen from him: five pounds of pizza dough. Cho had been taking the dough to the Giovanni's Pizza Parlor on Hazel Street. He told police the robbers must have thought the bag contained the evening's receipts.

Taylor and Smith were formally charged with armed robbery at an arraignment Wednesday afternoon.

Editors and news directors search for humorous stories and display the best ones prominently in their newspapers and news broadcasts. Brights entertain people, arouse their emotions and provide relief from the seriousness of the world's problems. When media in Los Angeles carried a story about a man who ran out on his blind dates, leaving them with the restaurant bills, it was picked up around the country. Thefts are common, and no one wants to be the victim of a crime, but the unusual nature of this incident—and the relatively minor harm it caused— made the story precisely the kind that editors and producers like to cover.

The "serial dine-and-dasher" story illustrates another aspect of brights: Reporters must be careful not to make fun of the ill fortune others experience. One account quoted a victim who said the thief left her with a $163 bill at a pricey steakhouse, where he ordered "a ton of food." Another journalist noted that the alleged perpetrator had a minor criminal record. The story might have its lighter side, but reporters knew it had to be told tastefully and with respect for the victims' feelings.

Animals are a favorite topic for brights. Since the 1940s, the presentation of a National Thanksgiving Turkey to the U.S. president has been part of the holiday celebration. And every year, news organizations carry brief humorous stories about the turkeys, which are pardoned from winding up as dinner the next day. Other animal stories can bring a tear to a person's eye and generate a big reaction. For instance, dogs have often been used in wars and veterans often want to adopt them. A group of veterans and animal activists took five such dogs to Washington for a briefing called "Military Dogs Take the Hill" in 2014. While reporters wrote lightly about the event—with one referring to "dog days on Capitol Hill"—the widely covered stunt led to a law requiring that such military dogs be brought home. One journalist wrote approvingly of dogs who "paw-tect" the country.

An American soldier pets Paris, a military working dog, during a security patrol in Farah province, Afghanistan. The relationship between people and animals is a common subject for brights.

Some brights draw their humor from the stupid things even smart people might do. One example is the arrest of an 18-year-old for drunken driving. New York City police officers handcuffed him and put him in their squad car; he climbed into the front seat and took the vehicle on a 13-mile joyride.

Follow-Ups

Major stories rarely begin and end in a single day, and news organizations prepare a fresh article or package each time a new development arises. These stories are known as follow-ups, or "second-day" or "developing" stories. Coverage of trials, legislative sessions, political campaigns or flights to the moon might appear in the media every day for weeks. Major events, like the devastation Hurricane Maria caused Puerto Rico or the restrictions the Trump administration placed on immigration, remain top news stories for weeks or months. Follow-up stories for such events might describe efforts to rescue or treat victims, government actions to help individuals and businesses, disruptions to the national or local economy and increased security or regulation to prevent similar events in the future. Although the follow-up is tied to a past event, its lead always emphasizes the latest developments. Follow-ups might summarize previous events, but that information is presented as concisely as possible and placed later in the story.

On March 4, 2017, President Trump accused former President Barack Obama of tapping his phones at Trump Tower shortly before the election. In a series of tweets, Trump called his predecessor a "bad (or sick) guy" and claimed that Obama "had my 'wires tapped.'" While Trump offered no proof and did not identify the source of his information, he compared the supposed tapping to "Nixon/Watergate" and "McCarthyism." These tweets triggered weeks of news coverage, calls for investigations by Congress and the FBI, reviews of records and an international incident with Britain, as well as an awkward press conference with the German head of state.

For weeks after Trump's wiretapping claim, The New York Times and other media carried multiple daily follow-ups on the truth or falsity of the claim and its many ripple effects. Each story emphasized the day's newest and most important developments, and, because the wiretapping claim was so significant, new developments abounded:

March 4—Trump issued his initial tweet with the wiretap claim saying, "How low has President Obama gone to tap (sic) my phones during the very sacred election process. This is Nixon/Watergate. Bad (or sick) guy!"

March 5—FBI Director James Comey asked the Justice Department to reject Trump's allegation. Comey said it was "highly false" and required correction. In a separate story, Times reporters Peter Baker and Maggie Haberman traced the wiretap allegation to a remark by conservative radio talk-show host Mark Levin.

March 13—White House Press Secretary Sean Spicer tried to clarify Trump's allegation. Spicer said Trump was alleging he had been targeted with a variety of surveillance techniques and not necessarily wiretapping specifically.

March 15—Republicans on the House Intelligence Committee complained about the lack of evidence to support Trump's claim he had been subject to surveillance during the campaign. Committee Chairman Devin Nunes, R-Calif., said he did not believe Trump Tower had been wiretapped.

March 17—During an awkward meeting with German Chancellor Angela Merkel, Trump suggested the two shared one thing in common: Both had been wiretapped by President Obama.

March 22—Congressman Devin Nunes said he had reason to believe Trump and his campaign aides may have been inadvertently swept up in surveillance by U.S. intelligence agencies, even though they had not been specifically targeted.

The wiretapping allegations remained in the news for several months, often entangled with other issues involving the Trump presidency. Even with stories of less scope and significance than a president allegedly ordering surveillance on a presidential candidate, each new event prompts a follow-up, and each follow-up recapitulates earlier stories.

Sometimes viewers and readers grow weary of the repetition and believe the news media do it only to sensationalize stories. People who were unhappy with the amount of coverage given to the murder

Trump's wiretapping claims were the subject of several follow-ups months after his original tweets, especially when former FBI Director James Comey rebuked the idea during his testimony before the Senate Intelligence Committee in June 2017.

trials of O.J. Simpson and Casey Anthony often expressed such views. Yet news organizations cover trials, wars and disasters so intensely because large numbers of readers, viewers and listeners are interested. Americans were so enthralled with the Simpson trial that audiences for the nightly network news broadcasts declined as much as 10 percent because people were watching the trial live on cable channels.

Follow-ups have become more common as news organizations devote resources to making sure important stories are followed to their conclusions. Media critics sometimes complain that journalists, like firefighters, race from one major story to the next, devoting most of their attention to momentary crises. These critics claim that, as one crisis subsides, reporters move on to a newer one. The older crisis often has disappeared from the news before all the questions have been answered. To address this complaint, news organizations regularly return to important stories and report on what has happened since they dropped out of the headlines.

Roundups

To save space or time, news organizations summarize several different but related events in roundup stories. For instance, instead of publishing separate stories about each traffic death that occurs in a given weekend, newspapers and broadcast stations often summarize several fatal accidents in a single story. News organizations often report all the weekend crimes, fires, drownings, graduation ceremonies or football games in roundup stories.

Another type of roundup deals with a single event but incorporates facts from several sources. Reporters might interview half a dozen people to obtain more information about a single topic, to verify the accuracy of facts they have obtained elsewhere or to obtain new perspectives. For example, if a city's mayor resigns unexpectedly, reporters might ask her why she resigned, what she plans to do after she leaves office, what she considers her major accomplishments and what problems will confront her successor. They might then ask other city officials to comment on the mayor's performance and resignation, ask the city clerk how the next mayor will be selected, and interview leading contenders for the job. All this information could be included in a single roundup story.

The lead for a roundup emphasizes the most important or unique developments and ties all the facts together by stressing their common denominator, as in the following example from the Associated Press reporting on Easter happenings around the Middle East:

> JERUSALEM (AP)—Christians celebrated Easter on Sunday across the Middle East, where many are struggling to maintain their embattled communities in the face of war, religious violence and discrimination.

The story included details on how Christians flocked to services at a Jerusalem church on the site where they believe Jesus Christ was crucified, as well as accounts of how Egypt's Coptic Christians were marking a somber week after terrorists killed dozens of worshippers at churches in two cities. The story also reported on how some Iraqi Christians were marking the holiday in displacement camps, having fled ISIS and military operations to clear the group out of Mosul, and on how Pakistani Christians celebrated amid high security after a major attack was foiled.

Several news podcasts present brief coverage of the most important events of the day. For example, NPR News Now produces five-minute episodes; the podcast is updated hourly and highlights breaking news.

After the lead, roundups usually organize facts and quotations by topic, starting with the most newsworthy accident, crime, fire or drowning and moving on to the second, third and fourth most important. Some beginning reporters make the mistake of organizing their material by source. For example, they might start a crime roundup with all the information they got from the police chief and then all the information they got from the prosecuting attorney. Stories organized in this way are disjointed and repetitious. Each source is likely to mention the same events, and comments about a particular event will be scattered throughout the story.

Sidebars

Sidebars are separate stories that describe developments related to a major event. Sometimes, news organizations use them to break long, complicated stories into shorter, more easily understood ones. Other times, sidebars report information of secondary importance. They give readers additional information about the main topic, usually from a different source or perspective. They also provide background information, explain a topic's importance or describe the scene, emphasizing its color and mood.

After the video of David Dao being removed from a United Airlines flight was released, The Wall Street Journal published a story, exploring why the carrier behaved as it did, on the first page of its Business & Finance section. The page also included a sidebar about the lawyer representing Dao, called "Media-Savvy Lawyer Fights United." This article explained how Chicago attorney Tom Demetrio had long fought airlines and other large organizations on behalf of aggrieved plaintiffs. A second sidebar, "United's Investor Call to Garner Attention," reported that United would release its first-quarter earnings on the day these stories appeared and previewed important topics CEO Oscar Munoz might touch on in a telephone briefing with stock-market analysts on the following day.

News organizations also use sidebars to report on local angles to national stories. Such was the case for many news organizations in June 2015, when the U.S. Supreme Court declared that the federal Defense of Marriage Act was unconstitutional. The court's decisions did not require states to recognize gay marriages or overturn any state laws or state constitutional provisions banning gay marriage. In its coverage of the story, The Atlanta Journal and Constitution published a sidebar discussing the decision's likely impact on people in Georgia, one of a number of states that had prohibited gay marriage. The story said the ruling would change little for most Georgians. Those most affected would be gay military and civilian federal government employees, who became eligible for more than 1,000 tax, Social Security and retirement benefits already offered to straight couples. Georgia gay couples who were not federal employees would probably remain ineligible for the benefits, legal experts told the reporter, because the federal government follows the law of the states in deciding eligibility.

In addition to the main story, The Detroit News ran a front-page sidebar on Brian Huff, a veteran Detroit police officer who was killed in the line of duty.

A Chicago Tribune sidebar examined the decision in light of efforts to push through the state legislature a bill that would allow same-sex marriage and recognize those performed in other states. Proponents had hoped the bill would pass, but the sponsor decided against seeking a vote, fearing it would be defeated. The Tribune reported that these supporters hoped the court's ruling would reignite enthusiasm. And it did: A few months later, the bill passed.

Sidebars are usually briefer than the main news stories and are placed next to them in a newspaper or just after them in a newscast. If, for some reason, the sidebars must run on a different page or later in a program, editors or producers will tell the audience where or when the related stories will appear. Because some people read or view only the sidebars, most briefly summarize the main stories even when the two stories are close together.

Obituaries

Obituaries—descriptions of people's lives and notices of their deaths—traditionally have been among the most popular features of newspapers. Relatives scrutinize obituaries, townspeople inspect them and others who have moved away peruse them on their hometown paper's website.

Newspapers used to have reporters write an obituary for every local resident who died. They also carried obituaries for out-of-town celebrities and prominent political figures. Some smaller news organizations may still follow this practice, but it is largely a thing of the past at medium to large ones. Now it is more common that the funeral home or the family writes the obituary, in which case the latter pays for its publication. If a person is unusually famous, newspapers will publish a feature obituary written by a staff reporter and publish it at no charge. Charging for obits gives everyone the opportunity to have an obit in the newspaper. In addition, when family members write obits, the printed record is precisely as they want. A criticism of paid obituaries, however, is that newspapers lose their ability to check them for accuracy and completeness.

In a recent front-page feature, headlined "Haze the Dead! More Obit Writers Tell It Like It Was—Warts and All," The Wall Street Journal reported that family members increasingly offer "frank, humorous assessments of the departed." Citing several examples, the piece noted: "Most obituaries remain more solemn, but funeral directors have noted an increase in those that are a bit playful— tributes acknowledging that people tend to be mixed bags and that few are candidates for sainthood. Obituaries published by U.S. newspapers or websites over the past few years describe deceased relatives as 'cantankerous,' 'grouchy,' 'demanding old fart,' 'sore loser' and 'pain in the butt.'"

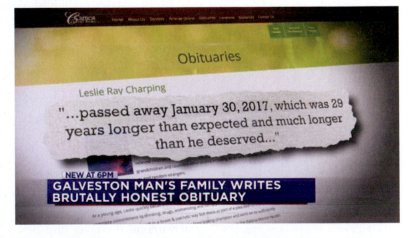

Obituary databases have become a popular part of online newspapers. Some publications, such as the Richmond (Virginia) Times-Dispatch, offer death notices, archives, a search engine and notices by email. Visitors can also write in a "guest book" for friends and family.

Many news outlets reported on this honest obituary—the posting on the funeral home's website went viral and crashed the site.

Newspapers publish three types of death reports: death or funeral notices, biographical obituaries and feature obituaries. Death or funeral notices are prepared by the funeral home and placed in the newspaper for a fee. In a short paragraph, they include only basic information—name, age, city of residence, date of death and funeral home. Some might include cause of death, the deceased's profession and time and place of the funeral.

Biographical obituaries include more details about the person, such as lists of accomplishments and survivors. The central point of the biographical obituary is the life of the deceased and what made it unusual or interesting. Well-written obituaries capture people's personalities and convey their unique attributes and experiences. Increasingly, these reports are written by either family members or funeral directors and, like death notices, run in newspapers for a fee. Regardless of who writes them, biographical obituaries appear on a page set aside for this type of notice.

Feature obituaries are full stories on the news pages and cover noteworthy individuals whose names are familiar to most readers. These stories cover events in the person's life and the circumstances surrounding his or her death. The feature obituary is much like the biographical obituary but is usually longer and more detailed.

Writing the Biographical Obituary

In some respects, a biographical obituary resembles a feature profile—it describes a person's life and work. Thus, reporters write obituaries as they would news stories about living people. Although journalists might be reluctant to question grieving relatives and friends, they soon discover most family members are willing to talk about the deceased.

A biographical obituary usually contains the following information, in the same approximate order:

1. Identification (full name, age, address).
2. Unique, outstanding or major attribute.
3. Time and place of death.
4. Cause or circumstance of death.
5. Major accomplishments.
6. Chronology of early life (place and date of birth, moves, education).
7. Place and date of marriage.
8. Occupation and employment history.
9. Honors, awards and offices held.
10. Additional interests and accomplishments.
11. Memberships in churches, clubs and other civic groups.
12. Military service.
13. Surviving relatives (spouse, children, grandchildren, etc.).
14. Religious services (location, officiating clergy, pallbearers).
15. Other burial and funeral arrangements.

Funeral directors give newspapers much of this information. Some have the families fill out forms provided by the newspapers and immediately deliver the completed forms to the papers. Just before their daily deadlines, reporters may call the funeral homes to be certain they have not missed any obituaries. Journalists gather more facts about the person by going to their newspaper's library and reading previous stories published about him or her or by calling the person's family, friends and business associates. Most people cooperate with reporters; they accept the requests for information as part of the routine that occurs at the time of death. Also, people want their friends' and relatives' obituaries to be accurate, thorough and well written.

After journalists have gathered the details they need, they begin the obituary by establishing the central point: the unique, most important or most interesting aspect of the person's life or some outstanding fact about that person, such as a major accomplishment. The lead also includes the person's name and identification.

In the following examples, the original leads contain dull, routine facts: the people's ages, addresses and causes of death. These facts make dull leads. The revisions contain more specific and interesting facts about the people who died and their accomplishments. Other good leads might describe a person's goals, hobbies, philosophy or personality.

> Arizona D. Markham of North 13th Street died when a car hit her while she was jogging two miles from her home Saturday. She was 42.

> Arizona D. Markham, who never missed a trip in 23 years to gamble at the Kentucky Derby, died Saturday at the age of 42.

> Michael J. Jacobs, 68, of Eastwood, died Wednesday at his home surrounded by family and friends.

> Michael J. Jacobs, an award-winning fisherman and avid sportsman who was 68 years old, died Wednesday.

An obituary's second and third paragraphs should immediately develop the central point stated in the lead. For example, if the lead reports the deceased was an electrician who also won ballroom dancing contests, these paragraphs should describe that person's work and hobby.

Midwest Medical Examiner's Office
14341 Rhinestone Street NW, Ramsey, MN 55303
Phone: 763-323-6400 • Fax: 763-323-6479

A. Quinn Strobl M.D. Chief Medical Examiner

Anne Bracey M.D. • Michael Madsen M.D.

Press Release

As of June 2, 2016, the Midwest Medical Examiner's Office has completed its death investigation of Prince Rogers Nelson. The Midwest Medical Examiner's Office hereby releases all public data relating to this death investigation as specifically defined in Minnesota Statute, Section 13.83, subd. 2. This public data includes the manner and cause of death. Under Minnesota law, all other medical examiner data is considered private or nonpublic data. The Medical Examiner's Office is unable to make any further comments about its death investigation of Prince Nelson.

The Carver County Sheriff's Office continues its investigation.

MIDWEST MEDICAL EXAMINER'S OFFICE
14341 Rhinestone St NW, Ramsey, MN 55303

Release of Public Data   MN Statute 13.83   Subd 2

Deceased: Prince Rogers Nelson   DOB 06/07/1958   DOD: 04/21/2016
Address: 7801 Audubon Road   Age: 57   Sex: Male
City: Chanhassen   State: MN   Zip: 55317   Name of spouse: NA
Marital status: ☐ Never married ☒ Divorced ☐ Widowed ☐ Married ☐ Separated
Occupation: Artist   Business: Music
Citizenship: U.S.A.   Race: Black/African American   Served in armed forces of United States: No

Decedent's place of birth: Minneapolis, MN
Father's name: John J. Nelson   Birth name: ---   Birthplace: unk
Mother's name: Mattie D. Nelson   Birth name: Shaw   Birthplace: unk
Type of disposition: Cremation   Date of burial: unk
Burial place name & location: unk
Funeral home: Cremation Society of Minnesota   Funeral director: Kevin J. Waterston

Place of death: Residence   Hospital: na
Date of injury: unknown   Place of injury: Residence
Death at work? No   Address of injury: Residence
How injury occurred: The decedent self-administered fentanyl

Height: 63 inches   Weight: 112   Hair color: Black   Eye color: Brown   Complexion: Light   Build: Petite
Identifying marks: na
Scars & amputations: Scar, left hip; scar, right lower leg
Description of decedent's clothing: black cap, black shirt, grey undershirt, black pants, black boxer briefs, black socks

Autopsy performed: Yes
MANNER: ☐ Natural ☒ Accident ☐ Homicide ☐ Suicide ☐ Undetermined
Cause: 1: Fentanyl toxicity
2: na
3: na
4: na
Other significant conditions: na

Signed by Medical Examiner's Office: _____

x A. Quinn Strobl, MD, Medical Examiner   ___ Anne H. Bracey, MD, Assistant ME   ___ Michael S. Madsen, MD, Assistant ME

Documents such as this press release regarding Prince's death can provide information for an obituary.

This feature obituary focuses on Camacho's work, family and her talent for dancing; it includes quotes from her employer, grandsons and daughter. The piece also provides details on the history of the restaurant and its upcoming 50th anniversary.

Inexperienced journalists mistakenly shift too quickly to chronological order and, in their second paragraph, report the earliest and least interesting details of the person's life: dates of birth, graduation from high school or marriage. Instead, if time and space are available, reporters should include anecdotes about the person's life and recollections of friends and relatives, as well as other biographical highlights.

Some newspapers try to report the cause of every death because it is often newsworthy information. Others do not because that information is difficult to obtain. Family members and funeral directors might be reluctant to announce a cause of death. Some causes, such as suicide or drug overdose, have social stigmas attached to them. In such cases, news organizations may report the death, including the cause, in a short story separate from the obituary, carefully attributing the cause of death to some authority, usually the coroner.

After describing the deceased person's life, the obituary lists survivors. Usually, the list includes only the immediate family, beginning with the name of the person's spouse and followed by the names of parents, brothers and sisters, and children. Other survivors—more distant relatives and nonrelatives— may be included if they played an important role in the person's life.

Normally, the times and places for the religious services and burial appear near the end of an obituary. The information should be as specific as possible so that mourners will know when they can call on the person's family, and when and where they can attend the funeral and burial.

Writing the Feature Obituary

Obituaries for national celebrities emphasize different types of information from that in obituaries for other people. Newspapers almost always report the cause of death when a celebrity dies. Politicians, athletes and entertainers have lived their lives before the public, and the public usually wants to know what caused their death. When the celebrity's family tries to withhold this detail—for instance, when the celebrity dies of a drug overdose—reporters will work to uncover it.

Because few readers are likely to know a national celebrity personally or to attend the funeral and burial, the obituary might not mention those services. Instead, it will emphasize the celebrity's personality and accomplishments. Sometimes, journalists repeat what the person had said on earlier occasions to show his or her character. Sometimes the person's personality will come through in quotes from family and friends.

Here are the first two paragraphs from The New York Times' obituary for Vitaly I. Churkin, a prominent Russian diplomat:

> UNITED NATIONS—Vitaly I. Churkin, the Russian ambassador to the United Nations, who represented his country through times of domestic tumult and rising tensions with the West, died on Monday morning while at work in Manhattan. He would have turned 65 on Tuesday.
>
> The Russian government said he died suddenly but did not specify a cause. The New York City police said there were no indications of foul play.

While discussing how Churkin's death came at a difficult time in U.S.-Russian relations, much of the obituary described Churkin's background, style and personality. The account told of how Churkin had been a child actor and had starred in two biopics about Soviet leader Vladimir Lenin. Saying he was widely considered a "masterly diplomat," the piece noted that he "could be caustic and wry in equal measure, especially in exchanges with his American counterparts." It also referred to a sharp exchange between the deceased and Samantha Power, a former U.S. ambassador to the U.N., in which he accused her of acting like Mother Teresa.

Obituaries for celebrities report both the good and the bad about the person's life. Obituaries for Washington Post publisher Katharine Meyer Graham reported on the obstacles she overcame in her personal life as she built one of the world's most important media companies. Newsweek said, "Katharine Meyer grew up in a kind of chilly grandeur. She was surrounded by governesses and private tutors, but once had to make an appointment to see her mother. Agnes Meyer was a self-dramatist who fed her own ego by trampling on her daughter's." The Orlando Sentinel reported that her father invited her husband, Philip, to become publisher at 31 and later gave him the newspaper. "Eugene Meyer also arranged for him to hold more stock in the company than his daughter because, he explained to her, 'no man should be in the position of working for his wife.'" U.S. News & World Report reported, "Manic-depressive illness turned Phil into an erratic, abusive husband who played upon his wife's insecurities. Taunting her before friends with the nickname 'Porky,' he briefly abandoned her for another woman."

The Reporter's Guide to Writing Brights, Follow-Ups, Roundups, Sidebars and Obituaries

Brights

1. Choose either an inverted-pyramid style or a suspended-interest style for the story.

2. If you use a suspended-interest approach, write a lead that will intrigue readers without revealing the story's bizarre or amusing twist.

Follow-Ups

1. Write a follow-up each time something newsworthy develops in a continuing story.

2. Stress the new developments in the lead and body of the story.

3. Summarize the important background and earlier developments.

Roundups

1. Emphasize the most important or unique incident or development in the lead.

2. Explain in the lead what is common to all the incidents reported in the roundup.

3. Organize facts and quotations by topic, not by source.

Sidebars

1. Focus the lead on background, color, mood or some other aspect of the story not emphasized in the lead to the main story.

2. Summarize the news event described in the main story.

Obituaries

1. Gather basic information about the individual's life: name, age, occupation, area of residence, activities (hobbies and organizational memberships), honors and awards, survivors and funeral arrangements.

2. Find the unique trait or ability of the individual that makes him or her stand out from all other individuals and that can be expanded into another paragraph or two.

3. Paint a picture of this person, using character traits and personality and, perhaps, physical characteristics.

4. Gather quotes from family and friends. Quote something the deceased had said, if it reflects his or her personality.

5. Consider the good and not-so-good. No one is perfect, and it is often people's quirks that make them human or give them character.

6. Add some historical context to give readers a better feel for what it was like to grow up or live as this person did.

7. Remember that the obituary is about a life, not a death.

Review Exercises

1. Brights

Use the following information to write brights. Write some with a summary lead and others with a surprise ending. Correct all errors of spelling, punctuation, grammar and style.

1. Squirrels

University officials are blaming squirrels for a rash of problems students, teachers and staff members have been experiencing with their cars. One person whose car has been damaged by squirrels is Oliver Brooks, an associate professor of English, 5402 Andover Dr. One of the headlights in his van went out a few weeks ago. He replaced it, but it still didn't work. When he opened the hood, however, he was surprised to find a squirrels nest. "There was a big squirrels nest in the corner where the light wires were," he said. Brookes spent $184 to get the wiring replaced. Linda Kasparov, university dietitian, 9301 Lake St., had a similar experience. She was driving home one night when the headlights, speedometer and oil-pressure gauge on her new sedan all quit working. She pulled into a service station and asked the attendant what was wrong. She said, "The attendant put up the hood and then jumped back exclaiming, 'My God, what have you got in there!'" She said there was a nest made of sticks, string and plastic bags. One of the bags started moving, and when the attendant pulled it out, he discovered three baby squirrels. The squirrels had chewed through every wire in the engine compartment except two. The repair bill for Kasparov was $425. Laura Ruffenboch, a wildlife professor at the university, said the insulation on many electrical wires is made from a soybean derivative, and the squirrels may find that attractive. She also said it was unusual for squirrels to make nests in cars that are used regularly.

2. Misdirected Love

Joseph R. DeLoy told the judge today that he's in love. DeLoy, 26, said he loves a 29-year-old woman, Patty McFerren. DeLoy met McFerren while they were both shopping at a supermarket in the city. DeLoy asked McFerren for a date. McFerren refused. "But she was wonderful, and I could tell she really liked me, so I called her," DeLoy said. In fact, DeLoy tried to call Mc-Ferren more than 200 times, sometimes in the middle of the night. However, it wasn't really her number that he called. By mistake, he got the wrong number and called Patrick McFerren instead. The two McFerrens are unrelated and do not know each other. Patrick informed DeLoy that he was dialing the wrong number. DeLoy said he didn't believe him and continued to call. "I was hoping that she'd answer," DeLoy said in court today. Patrick began screening his calls and finally called the police, who told DeLoy to stop making the calls, but no charges were filed against him. The calls continued, so Patrick sued, accusing DeLoy of intentional infliction of emotional distress and invasion of privacy. The calls were a costly mistake for DeLoy. In court today, DeLoys attorney explained that his client was acting "on his heart and hormones, not his head." A jury of 5 men and 7 women decided that his calls were worth $25 each—for a total of $5,000. The jury ordered DeLoy to pay that sum—$5,000—to Patrick. "I'm satisfied," Patrick said.

3. Underage Driver

Charles Todd Snyder was charged with drunk driving following a traffic accident in your city one week ago. He was also charged with driving without a drivers license in his possession. He was scheduled to appear in court at 9 a.m. this morning. He failed to appear in court. As a consequence, Judge Edward Kocembra ordered police to go to Snyders home and to haul Snyder into court. Police went to the address Snyder had given officers at the time of the accident: 711 Broadway Avenue. The police returned to the court at approximately 10:15 a.m. and appeared before Judge Kosembra with Snyder. Snyder was in his mothers arms. He is a 13-month-old child, and his mother insisted that he drinks only milk and that the only vehicle he ever drives is a stroller. So the judge apologized for the inconvenience and told the officers to give Snyder and his mother a ride back to their home. Snyder, apparently frightened by the unfamiliar surroundings and people, cried. Police said that whoever was stopped had falsely given the arresting officers Snyders name and address when he signed the drunken driving ticket and the ticket for driving without a drivers license in his possession. They told the judge that they have no idea who that person might be.

4. Truck Theft

There was a motor vehicle theft which occurred in the city at some time in the middle of last night. The vehicle was taken from a building located at 7720 Avonwood Dr. The building was unlocked at the time, and 12 occupants sleeping in an upstairs room said they heard nothing unusual. They were all in bed by midnight and the first got up at 6 a.m., discovering the theft at that time. Police describe the missing vehicle as a bright canary-yellow fire truck, marked with the name of the city fire department. The custom-made truck cost a total of $192,000 and was delivered to the city just three months ago. Firemen said it had a full tank of gas, about 50 gallons. However, it gets only 1.5 miles to the gallon. It contained enough clothing and equipment for six firemen, a dozen oxygen tanks, 1,000 feet of hose, four ladders (each up to 60 feet tall) plus miscellaneous other equipment. The people sleeping upstairs were all firemen and the building was a fire station. The firemen suspect that someone opened the stations main door, then either pushed or towed the truck silently outside and started its engine some distance away from the building. It is the first time in its history that the city fire department has reported that one of its trucks has been stolen. It was not insured. The keys are always left in the truck to reduce the response time when firemen receive a call for help.

5. Burglar's Escape

Marilyn and Ralph Kubick returned to their home at 1456 North Third Street last night and found a surprise. There was a woman in their house, a stranger they did not recognize, and she was going through the desk in Marylin's home office. The stranger was wearing dark blue jeans and a black hooded sweatshirt with the hood over her head. Mrs. Kubick uses the desk mostly for her writing, but she told you later when you interviewed her, "I keep some extra cash in the top left drawer for emergencies. This woman found it and was stuffing it in a bag when we found her. The bag—it was one of the pillow cases from our bed—already had some stuff in it. Later, we found she had already grabbed all of my jewelry and Ralph's coin collection." Marilyn said as soon as they saw the burglar, Ralph shouted, "Call the cops!" and Marilyn ran to the kitchen phone to call. Ralph said he moved around the left side of the desk hoping to trap the burglar in the office and keep her there until police arrived. "She was sure nimble, though. She juked like an NFL running back and got past me. I grabbed the back of her sweatshirt as she slipped by me. She dropped the bag of loot, but I had a fistful of her clothes and I didn't intend to let go. She

was strong, though, and she spun around and twisted and wiggled until she had worked her way out of her sweatshirt, blouse and brassiere. Then she ran out through the front door. I was so astonished I just stood there for a half minute or so. By the time I went to the door to see where she went, she was gone." Officer George Ruis, the police officer who responded to the Kubic's call, said a neighbor reported seeing a person wearing no shirt get into a Toyota that was about 10 years old and drive away rapidly. The neighbor was not sure whether the topless person was a male or female. Ruiz said the Kubics described the burglar as Caucasian, about five and a half feet tall, weighing about 120 lbs. She had light brown hair that was pulled into a bun at the back of her head. She also had a small tattoo on her right shoulder blade of a spider or a crab.

2. Follow-Ups

Write a story summarizing the initial set of facts and then the lead for a follow-up about the later developments. Your instructor might ask you to write a complete news story about each day's developments. Correct all errors.

Yesterday

Two boys were playing in Nichols Lake in Lakeside Park in your town. They were wading along the shore of the lake at about 12 noon at a point where the bottom drops off steeply. The two boys were Randy Stockdale, age 9, son of George and Lillian Stockdale, 472 Bolling Dr., and Edward McGorwan, age 10, son of Karen McGorwann, 4320 Elsie Drive, Apt. Six. Edward waded too far from shore, lost his footing and was unable to get back to shore. He and Randy started to yell for help. A man whose name has not been released by police heard their screams and ran to the lake to help. James Kirkman, a cab driver who was taking his lunch break in the park, heard the screams, too. He radioed his dispatcher who called 911. Kirk-man said later that the unidentified man waded out as far as he could and tried to reach out to Edward, but the boy had drifted too far from shore. "When the boy went under and didn't come back up for air, this guy dove under to find him. But he didn't come back up, either," Kirkman said. Police Officers Kevin Barlow and Eddie Linn arrived on the scene at 12:18. Barlow immediately stripped to his shorts and started diving into the lake to find the victims. After several dives, he came back up with Edward McGorwan, who was unconscious. Linn tried to resuscitate the boy, but he was still unconscious when he was taken by ambulance to the Regional Medical Center. Barlow continued to search for the unidentified man for another 20 minutes until Dorothy Heslin, a scuba diver who assists the police on a volunteer basis, arrived. She pulled him from the water about 1:15 p.m. Wayne Svendson, a paramedic, tried to resuscitate the man. Svendson said the water was unusually cold and hypothermia had set it, which was indicated by the fact the mans skin had started to turn blue. The man was taken to the Regional Medical Center. Dr. Catrina Lowrie, a physician at the Medical Center, said the man was pronounced dead when he arrived. She also said that Edward McGorwan was in critical condition. Officer Barlow also was treated at Regional Medical Center for minor shock caused by the long period of time he spent in the water looking for the victims. He was released that afternoon.

Today

This morning, the police department released the name of the man who died trying to save Edward McGorwann from Nichols Lake. His name is William McDowell and he is an unemployed housepainter. He was 30 years old and he had lived at 1429 Highland Dr. Police Chief Barry Koperud said, "McDowell risked his life without hesitation to try to save someone in trouble. He was a real hero." Also this morning, Dr. Lowrie at the Regional Medical Center announced that Edward McGorwann had died. "He spent the night on a respirator, but his condition did not improve. This morning, at his mothers request, we took Edward off the respirator. He died less than half an hour later." McDowells sister lives in your town. Her name is Janice Carson and she lives at 2197 Marcel Av. She said her brother had dropped out of Colonial High School one year before graduating and joined the navy. He spent six years in the navy, and after he left he held a succession of jobs, including electronics technician, cook, construction worker and painter. She said he always enjoyed his jobs but was too restless to stay at one for more than a couple of years. "I guess some people would call him a drifter, but to me he was a free spirit. He loved people but he didn't want to be tied down with a house and a mortgage and all of that. There were only two things he never learned how to do. He couldn't hold a job for more than two years and he could never say no to anyone who needed help," she said with tears in her eyes.

3. Roundups—Multiple Events

Write a single news story that summarizes all three events described. Correct all errors.

Crime 1

Daniel G. Silverbach, 42, is a police officer. He has 17 years on the police force. Police spokeswoman, Officer Sarah Howard, gave the following account of events: On Thursday night, he was off duty and not in uniform and was visiting a friend in an apartment complex at 1010 Eastview Rd. Silverbach was emerging from one of the apartments when he was approached by two men. This was about 8:30 p.m. One of the two men pulled a knife from underneath his jacket and came toward Silverbach in what he called a threatening manner. Silverbach pulled his service pistol and shot the man with the knife. Two men are being held in jail in connection with the incident. One is Wesly Barlow, 23, of 977 4th St. Apt. 2. The other is James Randolf, 24, of 645 Harrison St. Both have been charged with assault with a deadly weapon and attempted armed robbery. Barlow was treated at Mercy Hospital for a gunshot wound to the right shoulder. He remains there in good condition. Randolf is in custody at the county jail.

Crime 2

Go-Go Galore is a strip club on Aloma Ave. According to police spokesman Sarah Howard, officers were called to the club at 9:53 p.m. Thursday night. The caller reported a shooting at the club. Detective Marlyne Griffin and Officers Allison Biaggi and Alan Nego responded to the call and arrive at about 10:07. The officers found one person and two wounded. One of the wounded was a topless dancer at the club. One of the patrons of the club was being held by several of its other customers, all of whom identified him as the shooter. The officers took John R Williams of 814 Hardin Ave into custody. The district attorney is determining what charges, if any, to bring against Williams. Det. Griffin said the story from the club's patrons and employees was that Williams got into an argument with Tony DeWitt of 2230 Cortez Ave Apt 828 over one of the dancers, Diana Nyer of 550 Oak Park Way, Apt 264. Nyer was talking with Williams when DeWitt tried to enter the conversation. Williams told DeWitt to leave, but he refused. The argument became heated and Williams pulled out a pistol and shot and killed DeWitte. Nyer ran toward the door. Williams told her to come back. When she refused, he pointed the pistol in her direction and said, "Then you're next." Before Williams could fire, one of the club's doormen, Robert A. Wiess of 2032 Turf Way Apt 338, stepped between Williams and Nyer. Williams fired and the bullet hit Wiess in the right arm and Nyer in the left. Several other patrons of the club grabbed Williams, took his pistol from him and held him until police arrived. Wiess and Nyer were treated for gunshot wounds at Mercy Hospial. DeWitt was pronounced dead at the scene.

Crime 3

On Monday, police discovered the body of Rhonda Harmon of 816 Westwinds Dr Apt. 8, in a black suitcase tossed in a trash dumpster. On Thursday morning, police announced they had arrested a suspect in the homicide. The suspect is Alan Macco of 503 29th St. Police Chief Barry Kopperud announced the arrest. Kopperud said, "This arrest is due in no small part to the surveillance cameras that were installed throughout the downtown area a year and a half ago. Video from those cameras showed a man wheeling the suitcase down South Street. Neighbors of Macco's called the police department to say they thought Macco was the man pulling the suitcase." Although Harmon, 29, worked as a waitress at a local restaurant, police said she had a record of arrests for prostitution. "We think she may have been turning a trick for her killer and something went wrong, something happened to make the john angry," Kopperud said. The autopsy report listed the cause of Harmon's death as strangulation. The report also said there was evidence she had been struck on the head with a blunt object. Harmon was arraigned Thursday afternoon on a charge of second degree murder. As he was being led from the courtroom where he was arraigned, a reporter asked if he was sorry about Harmon's death. Macco replied, "Yes," but said nothing else. Neighbors of Macco's said he used to brag about bringing women to hotel rooms and robbing them of their credit cards.

4. Sidebars

Use the following information to write two separate stories, first a news story reporting the Senate's action and then a sidebar based on the interview with the sheriff. Correct all errors.

Main Story

The state Senate today approved a bill overwhelmingly. The bill has already been approved by the house and now goes to the Governor, who has indicated that she will sign it. The bill was passed almost unanimously by angry lawmakers who want inmates housed in jails throughout the state to help pay the costs of their room and board. There were only 2 votes against the measure in the senate and none against it in the house. The bill will go into effect next January 1st. It will require persons housed in a jail within the state to reveal their incomes and, if they can afford it, to pay the entire cost of their room and board behind bars, or whatever share of the cost they can reasonably afford. The bill requires the State Department of Offender Rehabilitation to draw up guidelines on how prisoners will disclose their finances and how much they will be required to pay. The department will consider a number of relevant variables, such as whether a prisoner must support a family and devote all his or her income to that family. The idea for the bill arose a number of months ago when lawmakers touring a state prison were told that some inmates received Government benefits (mostly Social Security and veterans' benefits). The lawmakers were told that some of the prisoners opened bank accounts in the prisons and that the money they received piled up so they had thousands of dollars accumulated in the accounts when they were released. A subsequent survey requested by legislative leaders found 19,000 inmates in the state and that, of that total, 356 received government payments of some type. The same survey found that the inmates had a total of $8.1 million in inmate accounts at state prisons. Prison officials cautioned that the prisoners may have more money deposited in banks outside the prison system and that it would be difficult to locate those accounts. To enforce the new bill, lawmakers stipulated that prisoners who refuse to disclose their finances cannot be released early on parole. Officials have not yet determined how much each prisoner will be charged. Lawmakers also noted that some inmates may have other assets, such as farms, homes, automobiles, and stocks and bonds, and that those prisoners can also be expected to help defray their prison expenses.

Sidebar

Gus DiCesare is the county sheriff. He has held that position for 11 years. To retain the position, he must run for re-election every four years. As sheriff, DiCesare is in charge of the county jail, which has a capacity of 120 inmates, mostly men but also a few women. Criminals sentenced to terms of less than one year in prison usually are sentenced to the county facility rather than to a state prison. Despite its capacity of 120 persons, the county jail usually holds 140 to 150 persons—20 or 30 more than its rated capacity. When interviewed today about the legislatures approval of the bill in question, DiCesare said: "Hey, I think its a great idea. Some of these prisoners got more money than I'll ever have. When we pick them up, they're driving fancy cars, living in big homes and carrying a thick wad of money. Not most of them, but there're always a few in here, mostly drug dealers. We sentence them to jail as punishment, but it punishes honest taxpayers who pay to keep them in here—pay for this building, their food, clothes, jailers and all the rest. A couple of years ago, we calculated that it cost about $75 to keep one prisoner here one day. Hell, if they can afford it, prisoners should help pay for it all; that could be part of their punishment. I'll bet our costs are up to nearly $110 a day apiece now, and they're still rising. It'd help me too. I've got a damned hard problem trying to run this place on the budget the county gives me. With a little more money, I could improve the food, come up with more recreational facilities and maybe even try to rehabilitate a few prisoners—bring in some teachers and counselors and that type of thing. Now, all I really do is keep them locked behind bars all day, and that's not going to rehabilitate anyone."

5. Writing Obituaries

Using the information provided, write an obituary for each individual described. Correct all errors.

1. Obituary Notice Form: Terrence C. Austin

Full Name of Deceased Terrence C. Austin **Age** 81

Address 418 Cottage Hill Rd.

Date and Cause of Death Died late last Sunday of cancer of the throat

Place of Death Mercy Hospital

Time and Date of Funeral 4 p.m. Friday afternoon so his entire family have time to travel here for the funeral.

Place of Funeral St. Mark African Methodist Episcopal church

Place of Burial All Saints Cemetery with a reception afterwards at the family home.

Officiating Cleric The Rev. James J. Burnes

Place of Birth Chicago

Places and Length of Residences Mr. Austin moved here as an infant with his family and lived in the city all his entire life except three years service in the marines during the Korean War.

Occupation Retired. Former chef at Deacosta's Restaurant

Did Deceased Ever Hold Public Office (When and What)? None

Name, Address of Surviving Spouse Wife Anna Austin, 418 Cottage Hill Rd.

Maiden Name (if Married Woman)

Marriage, When and to Whom Married to his widow the former Anna L. Davis 56 years

Names, Addresses of Surviving Children Three sons. Walter J. Austin and Terrence L. Austin both of Atlanta. Also James K. Austin of Chicago. Two daughters who live locally, Heather Kocembra of 388 31st St. and Betty Sawyer of 2032 Turf Way Apt. 512.

Names, Addresses of Surviving Brothers and Sisters Brothers Edward John Austin of Chicago and Robert Wesley Austin of Montreal in Canada.

Number of Grandchildren (Great, etc.) 14 grandchildren, 27 great grandchildren and 2 great great grandchildren.

Names, Addresses of Parents (if Living) Mother Lulu T. Austin died 10 years ago and his father Frank died 27 years ago.

Other Information Mr. Austin was a retired chef for Deacosta's Restaurant for more than 25 years. He was also a member of the New Day Singers male chorus and a member of St. Mark African Methodist Episcopal church. After retiring from the restaurant he and his wife catered for weddings and other social gatherings. He learned to cook as a child from his mother, and was further trained as a cook in the Marines but then was moved to rifleman, winning two purple hearts and a bronze star during service in Korea. After returning home he got a job in a restaurant kitchen and learned more via on-the-job training. In recent years he never tired of playing with his grandchildren and great grandchildren. He said he missed spending as much time with his own children as he wanted since he often went to work at 11 a.m. or 12 noon and didn't get back home until after midnight.

Reporter's Additional Notes—Interviews with Friends, Relatives and Co-workers:

His wife said, "He worked hard cooking all week at work and then relaxed by cooking at home, but he refused to do the dishes which was fine with us. Until he retired his job didn't often allow him to be with the family for the holidays. Those were the times he worked 12 hours a day preparing other people's feasts. Since he retired he just loved singing at church. But he smoked those damn Camels, 2 or more packs a day, and that's what killed him, caused his cancer. I wanted him to stop but he was hooked, really hooked on 'em ever since Korea."

His son Walter said, "Dad loved to cook, and he loved working with people. During the holidays and family gatherings he'd cook up a storm. As soon as we stepped in the door we'd smell the hams, turkeys, greens, and baked pies. He liked Deacosta's because they let him use his imagination to create new dishes and they gave him a big bonus every Christmas. He always went right out and spent every penny of it on toys for us kids and things for the house and Mom, which made Christmas a really happy time for our family."

Peggy Deacosta said, "His specialty was creating dishes filled with edible colors and designs using fresh fruits and vegetables. Plus desserts, he made the best desserts in town."

2. Obituary Notice Form: Anne "Kitty" Capiello

Full Name of Deceased Anne "Kitty" Capiello

Age Twenty

Address 8210 University Boulevard, Apartment 311

Date and Cause of Death Police say apparent suicide via overdose of prescription drugs

Place of Death Corpse found at 7:40 a.m. this morning on a bench in Riverside Park.

Time and Date of Funeral Not yet scheduled. Body awaiting autopsy. Coroners report on cause of death is due in a few days.

Place of Funeral University Chapel

Place of Burial Body to be cremated/no burial

Officiating Cleric Campus ministry/The Reverend and Professor Mildred Berg

Place of Birth Mercy Hospital in this city

Places and Length of Residences A life-long resident of the city.

Occupation College student currently in her 2nd year of study, major in pre-med.

Did Deceased Ever Hold Public Office (When and What)? no

Name, Address of Surviving Spouse Parents said she was committed to her boyfriend, Jorge Alberto Coto. The two shared a college apartment.

Maiden Name (if Married Woman)

Marriage, When and to Whom Never married

Names, Addresses of Surviving Children Gave up her only child for adoption 3 years ago, a baby girl.

Names, Addresses of Surviving Brothers and Sisters A brother, Burt, age 17, and a younger sister, Amy, age 15, both still living with their mother and stepfather.

Number of Grandchildren (Great, etc.) None

Names, Addresses of Parents (if Living) Mother Sara Knoechel and stepfather Alvin Knoechel; father and stepmother Otto and Sandra Capiello.

Other Information An honors student at Kennedy high school in this city and on the deans list at your college with a 3.92 GPA (only 1 B and all her other grades As) during her first completed semesters of college. The winner of several scholarships. Enrolled in your colleges Honors Program. Not a member of a sorority or any church. Secretary of the Pre-Med Club. To help pay her college expenses she worked part time, twenty hrs. a week, as a clerk in the Student Health Center.

Reporter's Additional Notes—Interviews with Friends, Relatives and Co-workers:

Friend Thomas Alvarez said, "She was a top student, got As in everything. She was very giving, caring, and I think that's why she wanted a career in medicine. She was a smart, beautiful person, but never very secure. She'd do anything for you and never ask anything in return."

Sue DaRoza, another friend, said, "At first she wanted to major in engineering, then switched to pre-med, but wasn't always certain if she wanted to be a nurse or a doctor. She loved kids and wanted to help them, kids with special needs. I think she really wanted to be a doctor, but her family couldn't afford to send her to med school, and she didn't want to be a burden."

Friend Patricia Richards said, "Ann was very serious, very competitive, always pushing herself, trying to do better, to be Number One. We've been friends since elementary school. She was 14 when her parents got divorced, and that really hurt her. I'd gone through the same thing and we were always talking about it, trying to understand it. She wanted to marry Jorge but he said he wanted to wait until they finished college, and then they started having problems a couple months ago, and she caught him with someone else. They'd been going together since high school, and it was hard, so hard for her."

PUBLIC AFFAIRS REPORTING

During the 1970s, New York City's Times Square was jammed with sex businesses, some of which were involved in prostitution. In an attempt to clean up the area, the City Council passed a nuisance abatement law that allowed police to shut down businesses engaged in illegal activities. Between 1977 and 1983, police closed more than 100 sex businesses. Gradually, however, the use of the law expanded to include residences and to curb other illegal activities, such as gambling, drugs and underage drinking. Thus a law that had been used only a few times against non-sex-related businesses in the 1980s was used in more than 1,000 cases in 2013, most involving allegations of drug activity.

One person targeted was Jameelah El-Shabazz, a 43-year-old mother of five. Police raided her Bronx apartment on an anonymous tip that her son was selling PCP. Police found only a small amount of marijuana and 45 cups containing a white powder they suspected was cocaine. They arrested El-Shabazz, her sister and her son. The three spent weeks in Rikers Island jail before tests showed that the substance was not cocaine but crushed egg shells, which El-Shabazz used in a spiritual ritual. The prisoners were released and the charges dropped. But just weeks later, police returned to El-Shabazz's apartment with an eviction order issued under the nuisance abatement law. As in many such cases, a court issued the order in a secret hearing in which only police participated; the targets had no opportunity to object or respond, and the law did not require that they be convicted of a crime.

The New York Daily News and ProPublica, a nonprofit investigative news organization, reviewed 516 instances of the New York Police Department's nuisance abatement actions against homes and apartments. In 297 cases, residents were forced to abandon their homes or surrender their leases. In half of those

"Power can be very addictive, and it can be corrosive. And it's important for the media to call to account people who abuse their power, whether it be here or elsewhere."

George W. Bush, U.S. president

"I have a running war with the media. They are among the most dishonest human beings on earth. . . ."

Donald J. Trump, U.S. president

The Daily News' Sarah Ryley, Robert Moore, Jim Rich and Arthur Browne celebrate winning the Pulitzer Prize for investigating nuisance abatement actions against New York residences.

incidents, the people evicted were never charged with a crime. In addition, the vast majority targeted were minorities. The investigation earned the news organizations a Pulitzer Prize for their investigation and spurred the New York City Council to pass a series of bills restricting the use of the nuisance abatement law against residences. Among other things, the reforms require judges to hear both sides before issuing eviction orders and prohibit the use of eviction in cases based solely on evidence from confidential sources or of drug possession only.

The work of the Daily News and ProPublica exemplifies why news organizations have First Amendment protection: They function as a watchdog, bringing attention to instances where government has acted improperly or has failed to act to protect the public. While news serves people in many ways, reporting on public affairs is the core function of the news business. Much public affairs reporting focuses on the federal government—the president, Congress, and federal courts—but the actions of state and local governments affect more people day to day than do actions of the federal government. Many journalists begin their careers covering local government.

Crime and Accidents

The first assignment many newspaper reporters have is the police beat. Beginning television or radio journalists might have more varied assignments, but covering crimes and accidents will be a major part of their jobs as well.

Not all police reporters are beginners; some have covered the beat for many years. Nevertheless, it is an excellent training ground. Police reporters quickly learn their community, both geographically and sociologically. They develop their sense for what is newsworthy and their appreciation for accuracy. They also develop sources who will serve them for many years, no matter what beats they cover.

The work of police reporters varies with the size and type of community they cover. In a small community, even a minor theft might be newsworthy. In big cities, where two or three homicides a day are common, only the most bloody, most unusual crimes receive detailed coverage. Police reporters also cover the activities of the department, including community service projects, promotions, retirements and internal investigations. They might cover traffic accidents, but usually only the most noteworthy ones.

A lot of the information for these stories is available at police headquarters or the precinct stations. Thus reporters might be able to write their stories without ever leaving headquarters or the newsroom. But experienced journalists know that they must go to the scenes of crimes and accidents to be able to report on them vividly.

Police Sources

Reporters and law enforcement officers often are leery of one another, which sometimes deters thorough reporting. Journalists must work to overcome the suspicion and distrust of the police because they need information from such sources to write their stories. The first step to gaining officers' confidence is to spend as many hours as possible at police headquarters and precinct stations. Reporters should chat with officers about their work and their professional concerns. They also should try to get permission to ride along in patrol cars. Those who do will see how officers spend their time and will learn what their lives are like. The best way journalists build trust with the police is to prove their professionalism by reporting on police matters accurately and thoroughly and by treating sources fairly.

A reporter interviews a Boston police officer. To have a successful professional relationship, each party must gain the other's trust.

How well police officers cooperate with reporters depends on the public records laws of each state and on the traditions and culture of each community. In some communities, either the police department has a policy of openness and cooperation with news reporters or state open records laws compel disclosure of much information. Elsewhere, police routinely may withhold as much information as possible, particularly where open records laws are weak or ambiguous. Most states allow police to withhold investigative records. Some states permit the withholding of almost any kind of investigative record, even if it is not part of a criminal investigation. Others say police can withhold only the records of active criminal investigations; once the investigation is complete, the records become public.

Even if a police department's public information officer provides information readily, reporters still need to talk to the officers who investigated the crime or accident. Edna Buchanan, a former police reporter for The Miami Herald, says reporters need details to make their stories complete. Public information officers, who rarely visit crime scenes, cannot furnish those specifics. Only the officers who were present know what a reporter needs.

Reporters find the information they need when they develop good work habits. This means following a regular pattern for checking sources, such as police reports, jail records, the medical examiner's office and the department's public information officer. Other helpful sources journalists should cultivate are police union leaders, prosecutors, defense attorneys and bail bond agents.

Key Police Documents

Along with human sources, public documents enable reporters to put together stories that inform citizens and public officials about how their law enforcement agencies operate. Journalists should learn how to use the following records, available from police departments, courts and other agencies:

- The police blotter is a record of all calls for assistance received by the police. It usually tells where and when an event occurred and, possibly, whether someone was arrested and charged. The blotter best serves as a lead to other sources.

- Incident reports give a more complete description of events, including the nature of the crime, its location and time; the name of the victim; what property was stolen or damaged; and the name of the investigating officer. Other information might be available, depending on the law of the state. Some states withhold information about witnesses and victims; others suppress the investigating officer's narrative of the crime.

- Affidavits for arrest and search warrants can provide detailed information about investigations and help reporters understand what police are doing and why. Officers usually have to get a warrant from a magistrate before they can arrest a suspect or legally search private property. They get warrants by filing affidavits—identifying the suspect they want to arrest or the place they want to search and the items they are searching for—with a court. The warrants also provide more details about the suspects and their alleged crimes than police might be willing to divulge directly to reporters. Affidavits and warrants usually become public records once the arrest or search is complete; they and related documents can be found in district or circuit court files, not at the police station.

- Jail booking records indicate when a person was taken into custody and when that person was released.

- Autopsy reports are completed by coroners in cases involving violent or unexplained deaths. These documents describe the cause and manner of death. The cause of death is the medical reason the person died, such as gunshot wound to the heart or poisoning. The manner of death refers to the circumstances under which the person died: accident, suicide or homicide. Some states withhold autopsy reports from the public.

- Medical examiner's reports may be separate from the autopsy, and they often include information about the crime scene, witnesses and next of kin that might not be in the police incident report.

- Arrest reports describe a person who has been arrested and the offense, name the officers involved, list the witnesses and, eventually, give the outcome of the case.

- Criminal history records disclose a person's previous arrests and convictions. The information is public in some states; others limit access to it. Disclosing that a suspect has a criminal record can turn public opinion against that person and make it harder for him or her to receive a fair trial. Journalists should use such information carefully and only after weighing the risks and benefits.

- Police misconduct investigation records reveal how a department has handled allegations that officers have broken the law or violated department regulations. In some states, these documents are confidential personnel records; other states open them to the public.

- Accident reports describe motor vehicle accidents and identify the time and place of the accident, drivers involved, passengers, injuries and property damages. The reports usually describe how the accident occurred as reconstructed by the investigating officer.

One example of using public documents is a series by Leila Atassi and Rachel Dissell, reporters at the Cleveland Plain Dealer. When Cleveland police tried to serve an arrest warrant on Anthony Sowell, they discovered 11 bodies hidden or buried in his home and backyard. This finding led to another revelation: In an earlier incident, a woman had reported being attacked by Sowell, but police had not considered her story credible. The two journalists decided to examine how police in the city and other Cuyahoga County communities handled sexual assault reports.

Atassi and Dissell, who described their work in the IRE Journal, began their investigation by collecting data on sexual assaults in Cuyahoga County. They compiled police reports, prosecutors' reviews of cases and court dispositions. From that data, the journalists learned that police often improperly cleared sexual assault cases. National standards and Cleveland Police Department policies required identifying suspects, but police failed to do so in 52 instances. They also discovered that many reports of sexual assaults were misclassified as "miscellaneous" or "departmental information." And they learned that the police had failed to record which rape kits had been tested for DNA and which had not. Atassi and Dissell's stories led to the institution of a countywide standard for handling sexual assault cases.

A sexual assault evidence collection kit.

Police departments also keep records on how they spend money, and reporters can use them to examine police performance. A story for The Chicago Reporter by Jonah Newman examined 655 misconduct lawsuits filed against the Chicago Police Department between 2012 and 2015. While half of the cases were won by the city or dismissed, the other half resulted in jury awards or settlement payments to the plaintiffs. These cases cost the city $215 million plus another $53 million paid to outside law firms. The cost of the awards and settlements exceeded the city's budget for such expenses by about $50 million a year. The city borrowed money to pay for the lawsuits, increasing its already high debt load. Newman also found that the police department was not using the cases to identify and correct police practices that led to the lawsuits, a practice common in many other U.S. cities.

Respecting Victims

Because crime stories arouse strong emotional responses, they tempt news organizations to over-report them. The intensive coverage can distort the public's understanding of the accused, interfere with the work of police and the courts and traumatize the victims and their relatives. The killing of 20 children and six adults at the Sandy Hook Elementary School in Newtown, Connecticut, was a major news story that deserved extensive coverage. But as the people of Newtown faced the one-year anniversary of the killings, they feared the arrival of a wave of reporters, television cameras and satellite trucks. Citizens pleaded with reporters to stay away: "Give us

Approximately a year after the Sandy Hook tragedy, victims' relatives gave a press conference about the formation of MySandyHookFamily. org, a website that allows the families to honor their loved ones.

FROM THE NEWS

Police Use of Lethal Force

The following incidents were widely covered by the media and set off a national debate about the use of lethal force by police, especially against minorities.

- Darren Wilson, a 28-year-old white police officer in Ferguson, Missouri, was responding to a call about a robbery in progress when he spotted one of the suspects, Michael Brown. Wilson stopped the 18-year-old black man; their two-minute encounter ended when the officer fired several shots at Brown, killing him. Although both a Missouri grand jury and a Department of Justice inquiry found no basis for prosecuting Wilson, the death of Michael Brown set off several days of civil unrest in Ferguson.

- In Baltimore, 25-year-old Freddie Gray died of spinal cord injuries while in police custody. Police arrested Gray on suspicion he was involved in illegal activities and possession of an illegal switch blade. The arresting officers placed him in a police van to take him to the station. How and when he suffered his injuries is a matter of dispute, but shortly after he arrived at the police station, he was taken to a hospital in a coma. He died a week after the arrest. Six officers were charged with manslaughter in connection with Gray's death. Three of the officers went to trial; one case ended in a mistrial and two officers were acquitted. The state dropped the charges against the remaining three. The city paid Gray's family $6.4 million to settle a wrongful death suit.

- In North Charleston, South Carolina, Officer Michael Slager fired eight shots at Walter Scott, hitting him five times and killing him. Slager said he feared for his life when Scott, who had been stopped because his car had a broken tail light, had tried to take his Taser. A bystander's cell phone video showed the Taser had dropped to the ground and Scott was running away when the officer started shooting. A state jury failed to reach a verdict on murder charges filed against Slager, but he later pleaded guilty to federal charges of violating Scott's civil rights.

- In Chicago, Officer Jason Van Dyke was charged with murder in the shooting death of 17-year-old Laquan McDonald. Van Dyke claimed he feared for his life when he shot McDonald 16 times, but dashboard camera video seemed to show the victim walking away as the officer opened fire. Three other police officers have been charged with conspiracy to obstruct justice for giving misleading statements about how McDonald was behaving at the time of the shooting.

These and other incidents led reporters and social scientists to ask questions: Has police violence against minority members increased? Are police more likely to harm or kill black people than white? Is the apparent surge in the use of lethal force against minorities just an illusion created by the media attention?

Roland G. Fryer Jr., a Harvard economist, looked at 10 years of data on police arrests and use of force from 10 major cities. He found that although police are more likely to stop and arrest and to use non-lethal force against black people, there was little difference in the rates at which police shot black and white suspects. But ProPublica looked at two years of federal data on 1,217 fatal shootings by police and concluded that black males between 15 and 19 years were killed at a rate of 31.17 per million while whites of the same age were killed at a rate of only 1.47 per million.

The two studies used different methodologies, which partly explains the different results. The major obstacle to figuring out exactly what is happening, however, is a lack of systematically collected data. The FBI collects data on justifiable homicides by police, but that count relies on information voluntarily provided by local law enforcement agencies, and experts believe it greatly understates the number of shootings. The FBI does not ask for data on how often police shoot civilians, on shootings that are not justifiable or on police-involved shootings by the race of the victim.

Partly in response to the news coverage, the U.S. Department of Justice will start collecting data on all "arrest-related" deaths, whether by shooting, physical force, Tasers or certain vehicular collisions. Until more reliable data are available, reporters and news organizations should refrain from drawing any conclusions about trends in police-involved shootings.

some space. Give us the opportunity to recover together as a community," Patricia Llodra, the Newtown first selectman, told the Bergen (New Jersey) Record. Many news organizations complied with the town's request: CNN, NBC and CBS all kept their camera crews away. But others, including the Associated Press, argued they had an obligation to inform the public about how Newtown was coping. They sent reporters, but promised to be respectful of the community's wishes.

Writing the Crime or Accident Story

Most crime stories have summary leads that identify the central point immediately. Usually, that point is the aspect of the crime that makes it newsworthy—deaths, money taken or some unusual or ironic twist to an incident. The stories should describe the specific crimes involved, not just the legal charges, which often fail to reveal exactly what happened. Moreover, because they are expressed in general terms, the same legal charges could be repeated in thousands of stories:

> ➤ Three people arrested in a church parking lot Sunday morning were
>   *siphoning gasoline from a car*
> charged with ∧ ~~petty larceny~~.

As instructed in Chapter 3, never report a suspect's race or religion unless it is clearly relevant to the story. In the past (and sometimes even today) journalists mentioned the race only of suspects and criminals who were minorities. Race is relevant, however, in the description of a suspect who is at large.

If police have identified a suspect in a crime, reporters must be careful not to imply that he or she committed the offense. Until the person has been tried and convicted or pleaded guilty, he or she should be presumed innocent. To avoid implying guilt, news organizations say a suspect has been "arrested in connection with" a crime instead of "arrested for" one. Police or prosecutors may allege the suspect robbed a store, beat up a witness or murdered someone, but the story should make it clear that those are accusations from law enforcement officers, not facts.

Reporters should strive to include the following information in crime stories or in follow-up stories as the details become available:

- Any deaths or injuries. When they occur, they are often the most important facts and should appear early in the story.
- The nature and value of any property stolen or damaged.
- As complete an identification of the suspect as possible: full name (including middle initial), age, address and occupation. Complete identification prevents the audience from confusing the suspect with someone else with a similar name, which can lead to libel suits.
- Identification of victims and witnesses. To protect them, some news organizations will not publish their addresses. News organizations also routinely withhold the names of victims of sex crimes.
- Whether weapons were used in the commission of the crime and, if so, what types.
- The exact charges filed against the suspect.
- A narrative of the crime and arrest of the suspect.

Accident stories resemble crime stories in many of their elements. The central point of an accident story usually is deaths or injuries, property damage or unusual circumstances. The body of the story may include the recollections of the people involved in the accident or of other witnesses and the observations of the investigating officer. If people were injured in the accident and taken to hospitals, journalists try to get reports on their conditions.

Reporters covering accidents should avoid saying that one party or another was responsible. If police officers state in an accident report that one driver's conduct led to the accident or issue a ticket to a driver, the information should be included in the story. But such statements should be treated as allegations by the police and not assumed to be fact. The people involved in the accident may have a different view, and the differences may have to be resolved in court.

WORDS AND PHRASES TO AVOID

Never say a crime was committed by an "unidentified" person. Criminals rarely announce their identities, and most crimes are never solved. Thus, most criminals are never "identified." Similarly, if police do not know a criminal's identity, the story cannot report that the police are looking for "a suspect." Police have a suspect only if they have good reason to believe a particular person committed the crime.

Reporters also should avoid using the phrase "person of interest." Terms like "suspect," "target" and "material witness" have specific legal meanings; "person of interest" does not. Law enforcement agents sometimes use the phrase as a synonym for "suspect." When used that way, it encourages audiences to think of a person as guilty long before he or she has been formally accused of a crime, let alone tried by a jury. Finally, journalists do not say that a person "received" injuries (see Figure 17.1). People "receive" gifts but normally "suffer" injuries.

Local Government

When dangerously high levels of lead were found in the drinking water in Flint, Michigan, news organizations around the country covered the story. Excessive lead levels can damage brains, kidneys, bone marrow and other organs. But Flint is not the only city with this water problem, as WALA-TV Fox10 News of Mobile, Alabama, discovered. Reporter Kati Weis used records from the state's Department of Environmental Management to determine that eight water districts in two counties along the Gulf Coast reported lead levels exceeding the legal limits. Among the eight was the

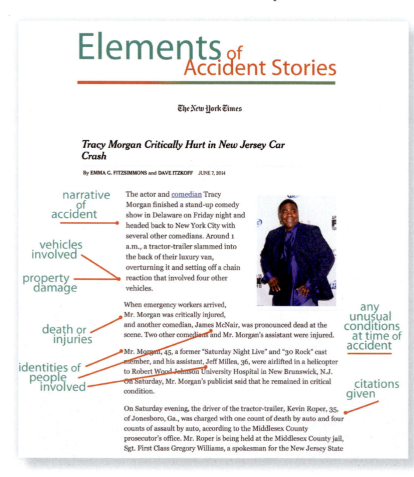

Figure 17.1   Elements of Accident Stories   This article includes the important details of the accident.

area's largest district, the Mobile Area Water and Sewer System. The station also conducted tests on water from area homes and public drinking fountains. While some homes had dangerously high levels, the fountains were below the legal limit.

State law requires water systems to check the water of homes most vulnerable to high lead levels, usually ones built before 1980. But Weis found that in some instances, systems were unable to comply because they lacked the information required to identify the relevant homes. Weis also investigated lead levels in area schools, but state law does not require school districts to test for lead. Fox10's reporting prompted the state Department of Education to announce that it would help local districts test the water in schools.

Americans expect their drinking water to be safe and their taxes to be spent wisely. If ill-conceived laws or poor government administration diminishes the quality of public services, readers, viewers and listeners expect news organizations to tell them about it. They also want to know how well local governments are doing their jobs and how efficiently tax money is being spent.

City and County Governments

City governments provide residents with a wide range of services: police and fire protection, sewage treatment, water, street construction and maintenance and parks and recreation services. Some cities also include trash pickup and disposal, public transportation and electricity or natural gas. Others operate hospitals or control the local school system. They also adopt ordinances regulating such things as local speed limits, zoning and the use of outdoor signs by businesses.

County governments usually have more limited powers. They collect taxes levied by all governments in the county. They may assess the value of all property and hear appeals from citizens who believe those assessments are too high. County governments are repositories for records of births, deaths, marriages, real estate transactions and motor vehicle registrations. They also supervise elections and handle voter registration in many states.

LOCAL BUDGETS AND TAXES

Reporters covering city or county government write about such issues as the awarding of contracts for construction or major equipment purchases, the creation of fire protection districts, the progress of urban redevelopment projects and the regulation of adult movie theaters. An important annual story is the budget, which determines how much money a local government will have to collect from taxpayers and how it will spend that money for the coming year. It is the blueprint by which a local government works.

City budgets are set by the council or commission, county budgets by the commissioners. Usually department heads or officeholders submit budget requests for the coming year.

Ahren Menard (left) and Adam Batist check mineral rights records at the Fairfield, Illinois, county clerk's office.

Calculating a city's property tax levy

	$19,000,000	Projected spending
—	$8,000,000	Income from other sources
=	$11,000,000	Amount from property taxes
÷	$875,000,000	Assessed valuation of city
=	.01257	Tax rate
X	100	
=	1.257 cents	Tax per $1 assessed value of taxable property

Explaining the tax levy

	$119,000	Median home value Assume it is assessed at 100 percent of market value.
X	.01257	Tax rate
=	$1,495.83	Property taxes due on median-priced home

Figure 17.2   Property Tax   This chart illustrates how a local government might calculate its property tax rate and how a reporter might explain the process in terms the public can readily understand.

The council or commission reviews the requests and makes the changes it considers prudent. Some states have statutory limits on spending increases; others have been forcing local governments to roll back taxes and spending. Such restrictions force the council or commission to make difficult budget choices.

To help meet budgetary needs, local governments get some money from federal and state governments, sales taxes, local income taxes, user fees and other miscellaneous sources. But taxes on personal and real property provide the bulk of local revenue in most communities (see Figure 17.2). Personal property includes such things as automobiles, boats, stocks and bonds. Real property is land and buildings.

The annual budget is a news story in itself, but it can also be the starting point for other important and interesting stories about local government. For instance, how much is the city or county spending on fire protection? Is the spending concentrated in certain neighborhoods? Martin Stolz, a reporter for the Cleveland Plain Dealer, wanted to know whether Cleveland and Cuyahoga County had more fire stations than it needed. Stolz's colleague Thomas Gaumer used mapping software to show the locations of all 103 fire stations and to draw a one-mile radius circle around each. The resulting map showed some areas where fire stations were densely clustered and other parts that appeared to have gaps.

CITY AND COUNTY SOURCES

Covering city hall or the county courthouse requires establishing a routine for visiting the various offices and departments and taking the time to get to know each officeholder or department chief. Reporters also should cultivate contacts among office workers, such as assistants, staff members and secretaries. Department staff can steer journalists to information for a story and help them find important documents.

Some local officials fear press coverage or want to control information released to the press. When they do talk, they often speak in jargon and technical terms: "ad valorem taxes," "capital outlays," "tax-increment financing," "percolation ponds," "rapid infiltration basins," "secured and unsecured debts," "tax increment financing" and "tangible personal property." If a legal or technical word is essential to a story, the reporter should define it. Otherwise, those terms should be replaced with simpler and more familiar ones.

City hall and county courthouse reporters also need to be familiar with public records. Not every document held by government is a public record, but a wide range of information is available in city halls and county courthouses (see Table 17.1 for a list of examples). Jonathan Austin, the editor and publisher of the Yancey County News, a weekly published from 2011 to 2014 in Burnsville, North Carolina, was curious about the pawn shop business. The state requires pawn shop

TABLE 17.1 Local Government Documents

City or County

Purchase orders (paid and not paid) show what products or services were obtained from what vendors at what prices.

Payroll records tell not only how much each employee was paid but also deductions, time records, sick leave, vacations and other absences.

Expense records may show which public officials are traveling, where they are going and how much they are spending.

Telephone records, including cellphone records, for top officials may show who is trying to influence government decisions.

Bids and bid specifications are the government agency's description of what it wants to buy or build and are sent to all contractors or vendors that might want to submit bids.

Contracts between a government and vendors for goods or services can show who is getting paid, how much and for what. Sometimes government agencies can award contracts without taking bids, but the contracts should always be public.

Licenses are issued by cities for various kinds of businesses (liquor stores and food markets), occupations (private detectives and security guards), pets and many other things.

Inspection reports from fire departments, building inspectors and health inspectors can reveal information about fire, safety and health dangers.

Zoning records include maps, reports, petitions and case files pertaining to planning and zoning actions and are usually public.

Campaign contributions and financial statements show where city officials got the money they needed to run for office and how they spent it. In some states, officials also must disclose the sources of their income and where they have their money invested.

Resumes tell where public officials were educated, where they have worked in the past and what they've done.

County Only

Tax-assessment records reveal the owner, legal description and assessed value of the land and buildings for each piece of property in a community. The records usually are cross-indexed so they can be accessed in a number of ways.

Motor vehicle registration records show who owns what vehicles, their value and the taxes paid on them. In some states, counties keep tax records on motor vehicles; in others, the state keeps all motor vehicle and driver's license records. Much of this information is no longer public because of a law Congress passed to protect privacy.

Deeds indicate who owns a piece of property, who sold it and when the transaction occurred. These are usually found in the register of deeds office.

owners to record each transaction and keeps the information at county courthouses, where it is available to law enforcement officers. Austin's inspection of some of these records revealed that a person with the same name as a sheriff's deputy—Tom Farmer—had pawned guns. Austin then used the state open records law to get a copy of the inventory list of firearms owned by the sheriff's office. The serial numbers on some of those weapons matched the numbers on the pawned ones. Farmer was eventually charged with a felony but pleaded guilty to a misdemeanor and was placed on probation.

For generations, local governments kept their records on paper. Now those records are stored on computers. This transfer has created both problems and opportunities for reporters. Most states consider records public whether they are in electronic or paper form. However, states differ on whether journalists and citizens are able to get copies of records in electronic form. The difference is important because reporters can analyze data that are available in electronic form in ways that would be impossible with paper documents.

School Districts

More local tax money flows into public schools than into any other area of government, and parents want to know the schools their children attend are effective and safe. For these reasons, public interest in news about schools is high, but digging out stories requires patience and time from reporters.

One measure of a school system's effectiveness is its graduation rate, so Minnesota Public Radio (MPR) looked at the numbers in its state, how those rates varied for different ethnic groups and how they compared with those of other states. The results were disappointing. Overall about 82 percent of Minnesota public school students graduate in four years, which is close to the national average. But that figure hides some dramatic ethnic disparities. For Native Americans, Asian-Americans, African-Americans and Hispanics, graduation rates in Minnesota are at or near the worst in the United States. African-American students had a graduation rate of 62 percent, the third lowest among states, and the rate for Hispanics was 63.2 percent, the worst in the country.

A number of factors affect graduation rates, including whether students are native English speakers and whether they are poor. Minnesota has higher levels of immigrant students and poor students than many other states. But MPR found another factor that helped explained the schools' poor performance: state spending for non-classroom student support. Reporters working on the story learned that the key predictors for graduation are attendance, behavior and course performance—the ABCs of high school graduation—and that counselors, social workers and other support staff are best able to track these measures and help students at risk of failing.

MPR reported that Minnesota had been spending about as much as most other states on these services until the early 2000s, when then-Gov. Tim Pawlenty campaigned for reducing such spending as an austerity measure. Local school districts got the message and complied. Now the state spends about 2.6 percent of its education money on non-classroom support, or less than half of the national average of 5.5 percent.

MPR's reporting on this issue is the kind of journalism that can help the public evaluate the performance of an essential area of local government.

Many news organizations prepare report cards for local school districts. Journalists have discovered that they must do more than simply report scores on standardized tests and compare the results from different schools and districts. Test scores vary depending on such things as the percentages of pupils who have one or more parents with a college degree, who qualify for free or reduced-price lunches, who enter or leave school during the year and who speak a native language other than English. Accumulating all of the data for a school report card and analyzing it correctly can take months, but the work can pay off in a story or series that many people will read, listen to or watch.

SCHOOL SOURCES AND DOCUMENTS

Education reporters should remember that the sources who are highest placed and most often quoted could have the least knowledge of what is happening in classrooms. Boards of education often concentrate on financial and administrative matters and pay less attention

Graduation coach Jon Zentner, a construction lawyer, volunteers with AchieveMpls at Minneapolis' Henry High School once or twice a month. The program helps students stay on top of their schoolwork and graduate on time, as well as gain confidence and develop life skills.

to curriculum issues. The superintendent of schools has day-to-day authority to direct the district and carry out policies set by the board. Superintendents generally deal willingly with reporters, but their contact with classrooms might be limited. In large districts, a number of assistant superintendents and program administrators report to the superintendent. They may have information about specific areas such as elementary education, art education, nutrition and foreign-language instruction. Principals and teachers know the most about what is happening in classrooms, yet they may be among the least accessible sources. Some of the best sources could be next door—or at the next desk. Neighbors, friends and colleagues who have school-age children could have a wealth of ideas or anecdotes for fleshing out stories.

School districts keep records on many of the things that happen in their buildings and the people who work in them (see Table 17.2). Reporters can put those records to good use. Students at Pittsburg High School in Pittsburg, Kansas, did just that when they investigated the background of Amy Robertson, the school's new principal. While working on a profile of Robertson, they quickly discovered that some of the experiences and education she claimed on her resume did not check out. For example, she claimed she had earned a bachelor of fine arts degree from the University of Tulsa, but the student journalists found the university does not award such a degree. Robertson also said she had a master's and a doctoral degree from Corllins University. Although Corllins has a website, it lists no physical address, and the university has been the subject of a number of consumer complaints.

A few days after the students ran their story in The Booster Redux, the school's newspaper, Robertson resigned from the $93,000-a-year job. Destry Brown, the Pittsburg superintendent of schools, praised the students' work: "I

TABLE 17.2   Examples of School Records Open to the Public

Laws and policies should be a starting point for any story about or investigation of a school. Until reporters know how a school or a program is supposed to run, they cannot evaluate how well it is running.

Budget and financial records show the district's priorities, and a comparison of budgets over several years can show how those priorities have shifted.

Bills and warrants show how a district actually spent its money.

Federal grant documents reveal what administrators said the money would be used for. Reporters can compare those proposals with vouchers showing how the money was actually spent.

Salary information for administrators and teachers is public record in most states. What constitutes a person's salary may vary—some states, like North Carolina, exclude bonuses and benefits. Mississippi holds that a public employee's net salary is closed, and Florida closes payroll deduction records. Many states, such as Hawaii, make only salary ranges or salary scales available. In still other states, disclosure of salary information may be subject to a balancing of the public's interest in disclosure against the employee's interest in privacy.

Employment contracts for school superintendents and principals are public record in many states. The contracts reveal what perks the administrator is getting in addition to a salary—travel expenses, automobile allowances and club memberships are some possibilities.

Accreditation reports, state audits and other assessment records can indicate how well a school district is performing. For accreditation, schools prepare a self-study report. A visiting team uses the self-study to guide its on-site investigation of the school and then issues a final report. Schools also prepare a variety of reports for state education officials, covering curriculum, personnel, students and district finances. The reports, which might include recommendations for upgrading school facilities, curriculum or personnel, can give reporters criteria for evaluating school performance over time.

Food service records may contain analyses of menus and receipts and expenditures for school lunch programs.

Transportation records may include inspection reports and service records on buses and reports of accidents, even minor ones.

By researching Amy Robertson's background, student reporters of The Booster Redux exposed inconsistencies in the principal's claims.

believe strongly in our kids' questioning things and not believing things just because an adult told them," he said to The New York Times.

Many school records, however, are closed to the public. Educational documents on specific students are closed by state and federal laws. Directory information on a student—name, age, address, major areas of study and height and weight (for athletes)—is usually available unless he or she objects to its release. Personnel records for district employees and supervisors may be confidential, depending on the law of the state.

Journalists cannot rely on records alone, however, to inform the public about schools and the education system. They have to observe what happens in classrooms. Schools are semipublic places, but administrators try to control access to school buildings to protect students and prevent disruptions. Reporters who want to cover classroom activities should arrange their visits in advance with the teacher and the principal and possibly with the superintendent as well.

Courts

A handful of trials and their outcomes attract national media attention. George Zimmerman's second-degree murder trial for the shooting death of 17-year-old Trayvon Martin evolved into a national story because of the races of the two people involved and because it shined a spotlight on Florida's Stand-Your-Ground law. Casey Anthony was prosecuted on a charge of having murdered her daughter, Caylee, and then dumping the body in a wooded area. Scott Peterson, a fertilizer salesman from California, was accused of having murdered his pregnant wife, Laci. Zimmerman was acquitted on all charges; Anthony was acquitted on the murder charge but convicted of giving false evidence to police. Scott Peterson, however, was convicted of murder and sentenced to death.

From sensational trials and television dramas, Americans acquire misconceptions about legal procedures. People might think criminal prosecutions depend heavily on scientific evidence, such as DNA tests. In fact, police and prosecutors on tight budgets often skimp on laboratory tests and rely on confessions to build their cases. People also might think criminal cases always result in trials that last weeks or even months, but most criminal cases are settled by plea bargains and never go to trial. When there is a trial, it usually lasts less than a week. Newsworthy cases might make people think lawyers engage in courtroom theatrics and make inflammatory statements to reporters. Generally, attorneys behave courteously toward one another and are restrained in what they say to the media. Some have a policy of never talking to reporters.

Even if most trials lack ballyhoo, they still can make interesting and important news stories. Crimes disrupt the community and challenge its moral order. The nation was shocked when a young white supremacist, Dylann Roof, killed nine African-Americans during a church prayer service in Charleston, South Carolina. Readers, viewers and listeners want to know that people like Roof who commit crimes are arrested, prosecuted and punished. As U.S. Chief Justice Warren Burger noted, the ability to see how the justice system handles crime has a cathartic effect on the public.

Citizens also want to know that law enforcement officers, prosecutors, defense attorneys and judges are doing their jobs. In most instances, the justice system works well, but a number of innocent people have gone to prison. Reporters who cover the courts must remain vigilant and skeptical of what police, prosecutors and judges do. In 1986, Christine Morton was found bludgeoned to death in her bedroom in the Austin, Texas, area home she shared with her husband and 3-year-old son. Police almost immediately suspected Christine's husband, Michael. During the trial, his defense attorneys suspected the prosecutor, Ken Anderson, was withholding evidence, but Anderson assured the court he had given the defense team all of the materials it was entitled to examine. Morton, who maintained his innocence throughout, was convicted and sentenced to life

Michael Morton speaks to the media during the 2013 case that determined if prosecutorial misconduct led to his wrongful conviction.

in prison. Eventually, he won the right to have DNA tests performed on evidence in the case; the results showed that he had not committed the murder. By the time he was freed, he had spent almost 25 years in prison.

As they fought for DNA tests, Morton's attorneys also sought and obtained information from the prosecutor's files. Those records showed that Anderson had withheld important evidence that might have convinced Morton's jury he was innocent. The concealed evidence included these facts: the Mortons' son had been in the house at the time of the murder and said the killer had not been his father; neighbors said a man had parked a green van near the Mortons' house on the day of the murder; and someone had tried to use Christine Morton's credit card, which had been stolen, at a store in San Antonio.

The Morton case inspired the Texas Legislature to pass a law expanding the right of criminal defendants to access evidence in prosecutors' files. Anderson, who had become a district judge by the time Morton was released, was prosecuted for failing to disclose evidence. He resigned his judgeship and reached a deal in which he agreed to serve nine days in jail and surrender his law license. In the meantime, Mark Alan Norwood, whose DNA linked him to the murder, was convicted of the crime.

Since 1989 more than 2,000 people, some of them sentenced to death, have been exonerated, often on the basis of DNA evidence, of the crimes for which they had been convicted. But DNA is irrelevant or unavailable in many cases; thus, the number of wrongful convictions might be quite large. A study supervised by a University of Michigan law professor concluded that more than 28,000 people may have been wrongfully convicted over a 15-year period. Reporters are not detectives or crime scene investigators, but they can keep their minds open about the evidence compiled by police and prosecutors and be willing to listen to defendants as well as victims.

General Information about the Court System

Criminal cases begin when the state charges someone with violating a criminal statute. Courts also hear civil cases, in which one individual sues another in matters such as divorce, contracts, personal injury and antitrust. Civil cases rarely attract as much press as criminal cases, but they may change more lives. For example, news organizations paid close attention to the arrest and prosecution of Justin Bieber on charges that he had been racing his yellow Lamborghini on the streets of Miami Beach while under the influence of alcohol, marijuana and prescription drugs. In contrast, a lawsuit brought by a coalition of doctors, researchers and patients against a company that had discovered and patented genes associated with higher rates of hereditary breast and ovarian cancer received a good deal less news coverage. The latter case, however, resulted in a U.S. Supreme Court decision that naturally occurring genes cannot be patented, a ruling that may lower the cost of genetic testing but also discourage companies from investing in some genetic research. Both consequences will affect many more people more directly than the outcome of Bieber's prosecution.

Court systems vary from state to state, but the general outlines are similar. Like the federal system, most have trial courts in which cases are initially heard, intermediate appellate courts and a highest appellate court.

The steps in a criminal court case resemble those for civil cases, but there are distinctions that might affect news coverage. Also, court procedures may differ from one state to another or between federal and state courts. Reporters who cover courts regularly should spend some time with local judges, prosecutors and defense attorneys to learn the state procedures. Bar and press associations in many states have collaborated to produce handbooks for journalists. These handbooks can be valuable resources as reporters follow court cases, both criminal and civil. The following sections summarize some of the major phases in criminal and civil cases and issues they present for news coverage.

Criminal Cases

PRETRIAL STAGES

Court action in a criminal case usually begins when a complaint is filed against the defendant. This stage happens at the initial appearance, when the defendant is brought before a judge in a magistrate or county court and informed of the charges. Misdemeanors can be settled at this level. If the case is a felony, the judge sets bail and a date for a preliminary hearing.

The purpose of the preliminary hearing is to persuade a judge that the state has enough evidence against the defendant to merit a full trial. The judge can decide to free the defendant or have him or her bound over for trial. Preliminary hearings usually are open to the press and public. About half the states use preliminary hearings in place of grand jury action. State use of grand juries is often limited to investigating public corruption or some similar task. In the federal system, however, no person can be tried for a felony unless he or she has been indicted by a grand jury. If a grand jury finds probable cause to believe the defendant committed a crime, it will vote a bill of indictment, or a "true bill." Grand juries also may issue presentments, which give the results of their investigations.

Grand jury proceedings are closed to the press and public, but reporters can sit outside grand jury rooms and watch who goes in to testify. Although witnesses can talk about their testimony freely, grand jurors and attorneys are sworn to secrecy. Anyone who violates that oath risks being charged with contempt of court. Journalists who publish stories based on grand jury leaks may be subpoenaed to testify about their sources; if they refuse, they may be held in contempt.

Once defendants have been charged, either by a grand jury indictment or by an "information" filed by a prosecutor, they are arraigned in the trial court. They enter their pleas, and trial dates are set. Because a defendant has a constitutional right to a speedy trial, the proceedings usually begin within two or three months of the arrest. Before the trial begins, each side must disclose to the other all witnesses and exhibits. At any time, the defense and the prosecution may reach a plea agreement, which usually requires the defendant to plead guilty to a lesser charge or to some of the charges if others are dropped.

As mentioned earlier in this chapter, reporters must remind themselves and their readers, viewers and listeners that people who are charged with crimes are not always guilty.

TRIAL

The trial begins with the selection of the jurors (except in a bench trial, which is heard by the judge alone). Prospective jurors are asked whether they have a connection to the case or any of the people involved. Any who do can be dismissed. Attorneys for each side also have a limited number of opportunities to dismiss prospective jurors without giving a reason. Lawyers use these peremptory challenges to exclude prospective jurors who they believe will view their clients unfavorably.

Jury selection, like the rest of the trial, is almost always open to the public and the press, although the court may protect the jurors' identities in highly publicized cases. The prospective jurors may be referred to by number rather than by name. In this way overly eager reporters and people with opinions about the case cannot speak to a juror by telephone or in person.

Courts always hear testimony in public, unless some overriding interest justifies closing the courtroom. Such an interest might be protecting a child from the emotional trauma of testifying in public about a sexual assault. Documents introduced as evidence become court records and also are open to the public. Here, too, the court might limit access in certain cases. For example, the court may prohibit public access to or copying of photographs, audiotapes or videotapes containing salacious or gory material.

The central point of a story about court proceedings should emphasize the most important testimony or ruling of the day. Mistakenly, beginners often emphasize a witness's identity or topic of testimony instead of what was said. Leads usually do not say whether a witness testified for the state or defense; that can be reported later. The news—the witness's most telling remarks—is more important.

The trial ends when the jury delivers its verdict. Jurors deliberate in private, but journalists try to talk to them after the trial to find out what evidence and arguments they found most persuasive and how they evaluated the witnesses, attorneys and defendant. Occasionally judges try to protect jurors either by reminding them they have no obligation to speak to reporters or by ordering reporters not to approach them. The latter approach raises First Amendment problems.

POST-TRIAL

If the trial ends in an acquittal, the reporter will want to interview the defendant, defense attorney, prosecutor, jurors and witnesses for a post-trial wrap-up. If the defendant is convicted, the next major step is sentencing. Congress and state legislatures have restricted judges' discretion in imposing sentences. Nevertheless, judges still can impose sentences within fairly broad ranges, depending on the crime.

Convicts usually undergo a series of examinations by psychologists and penologists to determine the appropriate sentence. These officials' recommendations are contained in pre-sentence evaluations. The severity of the sentence depends partly on these reports and partly on such factors as mitigating or aggravating circumstances associated with the crime.

Prosecutors cannot appeal an acquittal, but defendants always have the right to appeal a conviction. To succeed on appeal, defendants must show that the trial court made some grave error of law that warrants reversing the conviction and ordering a new trial. Although appeals rarely succeed, the process can go on for years, particularly in cases involving a death sentence. It might also take a case through several state and federal courts.

Civil Cases

PRETRIAL

A civil case begins when one party files a complaint in court against another party. The person filing the complaint is the plaintiff, and the other party is the defendant. The complaint, which is a public document, states the factual and legal basis for the lawsuit and tells the court the plaintiff's desired remedy. Usually, he or she wants money to compensate for injuries, lost wages, lost property or misfortunes arising from the defendant's conduct. However, he or she might seek a court order prohibiting the defendant from doing something or requiring the defendant to do something. This is called "equitable relief." Plaintiffs ask for both kinds of remedies in some cases.

Reporters should be skeptical of the money demanded in lawsuits. Plaintiffs can demand any amount they want, even though it might be obviously exorbitant. To attract news coverage, some lawyers encourage clients to demand millions of dollars as compensation for minor injuries. The plaintiffs normally settle for much less. News stories, therefore, generally should not emphasize the amount demanded.

The complaint presents only the plaintiffs' charges; defendants are likely to deny them, and a judge or jury may decide (months or even years later) that they are unfounded. Thus, a news story should indicate clearly that the charges are the plaintiffs' allegations, not accepted facts. For example:

➤ ~~Because of the accident,~~ Samuelson ∧ *'s lawsuit says he* will require medical care for the rest of his life.

Defendants who cannot persuade the court to dismiss the complaint must file answers, which set forth their version of the facts and interpretation of the law. Like complaints, the defendant's answers are public records. Whenever possible, the news story should include this response to the charges. If it is not in the case file, reporters should interview the defendant or his or her attorney. The following example and revision illustrate the inclusion of a defendant's response. They also illustrate the need to condense, simplify and attribute the claims in a plaintiff's lawsuit. Consider the following example; the second version is more concise than the first.

> He was caused to slip, trip and fall as a direct result of the negligence and carelessness of the store because of a liquid on the ground. This fall injured his neck, head, body, limbs and nervous system and caused him to be unable to lead a normal life and to lose his normal wages for a prolonged period of time.
>
> The suit charges that he slipped and fell on a wet sidewalk outside the store, dislocating his shoulder and tearing several ligaments.
>
> The store's manager responded, "He was running to get out of the rain and slipped and fell on the wet pavement."

As the case goes forward, both sides engage in the discovery process, during which they take sworn statements from witnesses and the opposing parties. They seek documents and other evidence from each other. The discovery process happens outside of court, and the press and public have no right of access to it. Exchanged information remains confidential unless it is filed with the court. Even then, the side producing the information can ask that the court seal material that is highly personal or that might disclose trade or business secrets.

In some jurisdictions, the practice of sealing the records in court cases has become almost routine. However, doing so deprives the public and even government agencies of information about problems and about how the courts function. The Boston Globe won a Pulitzer Prize for its stories about Catholic priests sexually abusing children in the city, but it was able to report on the problem only after persuading courts to unseal documents in scores of lawsuits. Some states have tried to limit the sealing of court records, either through legislation or through changes in court rules.

TRIAL

A civil trial proceeds much as a criminal one, and it is usually open to the press and public. The trial may be heard by a judge, who decides the case alone, or by a jury. Some states use juries that have fewer than 12 members to hear civil cases.

A civil trial, like a criminal one, can end at any time if the two sides reach an agreement. In fact, civil proceedings are more likely to conclude in this manner. Judges encourage settlements, preferably before the trial. The parties to the case usually keep secret the terms of any agreement. Sometimes a settlement must have court approval and thus may become public record.

POST-TRIAL

If the parties do not reach a settlement, the trial ends with the verdict. Losing parties may ask the judge to set aside the jury's verdict and render one in their favor (called a judgment as a matter of law) or ask for a new trial. Neither request is granted frequently. More commonly, the losing party appeals the verdict to a higher court. Again, the loser must argue that the trial court committed a legal error serious enough to warrant a reversal of the verdict or a new trial. Appeals rarely succeed.

Guest Columnist

Developing Sources on the Police Beat

BY ANDREW J. NELSON

The police beat is the most fascinating beat in any news organization. It has it all: Jealousy. Death. Drama. Political shenanigans. Reporters who have never spent at least part of their careers covering public safety are missing out.

Sourcing the police beat is much like sourcing any other beat. You figure out who the key people are, and you get to know them. And you just don't do that on deadline. You seek people out well before you need something from them.

Let's assume you have just been hired as a cops reporter. What do you do?

First of all, talk to your predecessor. With any luck, he or she is still working for your organization. Ask that person to tell you who the key people are. If your predecessor has moved to a different news organization and is unreachable, you may have to figure it out for yourself.

Once you figure out who the key people are, go out and meet them—lunch, coffee, a sit-down in their office.

Generally, the first people you need to get to know will be the police chief and his or her principal deputies. Plus the precinct commanders if the city is big enough. It goes without saying if your department has a dedicated information officer, you need to get to know that person, too. But he or she certainly should not be your only source— more on that in a moment.

If you work for a larger publication and begin, as many do, as the night cops reporter, getting to know the chief may not be as important as getting to know the night duty commander, the night patrol director or the night supervisor of detectives. All communities and news organizations are a bit different.

When you meet your top sources, show an interest in them and their work. Share a bit of yourself that won't be objectionable to the person you are trying to turn into a source.

Be genuine. Don't try to be something you are not or mislead someone about what your goals are. By the same token, you should legitimately be curious about the person who is your source and their work. If you are not, you are probably on the wrong beat. If you are not curious about anything at all, you shouldn't be in journalism.

Some police officers will be suspicious about any overtures on your part. The best thing to do is to tell yourself, and them, that we are going to be seeing a lot of each other and it is in our best interest and that of the public for us to get to know each other a little.

Do not give anyone the false impression that you are their department's public relations agent. You aren't.

In your stories, try to speak to the police officer who caught the mugger or solved the homicide. Often departments prefer you speak to a senior officer or the public information officer, and sometimes you are going to have to settle for that. But it is much better to speak to the street cop directly. The information is usually more accurate, it leads to more dramatic stories, and it helps police officers who do good things get their due.

When dealing with police, be punctual. Police culture tends to emphasize punctuality.

But it is not enough to get the police to like and respect you. With them you are getting only one side of the story. Sourcing only the cops is like sourcing only one side of a political race.

Every police department has its critics. Get to know them. They could be:

- A criminal justice professor at a local university.
- A criminal defense attorney.
- A civil rights organization.

Other people you should try to source:

- Retired officers.
- Low-level officers and detectives, even if you have to agree never to quote them by name.

Good practices to perform upon assuming the cops reporter role:

- Ask for a tour of the police station, the jail, places like that.
- Go on a ride-along. Get a feel for what it's like to be on patrol.

- Visit the early shift briefings (sometimes called "lineup") and introduce yourself to the police.

All this could take several months, and it is a never-ending process. But you really have to kick it into gear your first few months on the job.

Andrew J. Nelson is a staff writer for the Omaha (Nebraska) World-Herald.

Guest Columnist

Journalists Deliver the Information the Public Needs

BY DON STACOM

Fire damages a major factory, and suddenly a lot of jobs are on the line. Everyone is wondering whether the owners will rebuild.

Health inspectors accuse a tattoo parlor of using filthy equipment. Are the charges true, or just a way to shut down an unpopular business?

In the middle of the year, the community college reports it's running out of money and needs an emergency tuition increase next semester. Students, parents and faculty are all asking the same thing: What went wrong?

Situations like those come up every day in small farm towns, big cities and every type of community in between. Those situations are at the heart of journalism. People want somebody to tell them what's going on, somebody to make sense of events in this ever-more-complex world.

That somebody is usually a professional journalist.

Even as the journalism industry undergoes crises of finance and identity, the market for professionally reported news is still extraordinary. Perhaps "citizen journalism" will someday live up to its hype, but for now, the heavy lifting in the news field is still being performed by professionals.

Whether on the air, in print or online, the professionals carry the responsibility of finding out what's going on—and then telling everyone else. So often now, forums and workshops about the future of journalism can't get past debates about platforms and delivery modes, and seem to forget the very basics of why people bother listening, reading or viewing the news. The core reason is the *information*—and that's where traditional journalists still do work that nobody else does.

Who else will phone the mayor to ask why local roads are still rutted with potholes even after last spring's big tax increase? Who else gets to press the detective commander for answers about the wave of armed holdups downtown? Who else will use freedom of information laws to get copies of the high school's phone bills and then scrutinize them to see whether teachers are making long personal calls on the taxpayers' bill? Who else confronts the executive at a plant closing, asking about the company's guarantee just a year ago that it wasn't going anywhere?

On a day-to-day basis, that work simply isn't done by anyone else. Take away the journalists, and nobody will ask the questions, spot the patterns or challenge the spin doctors. It's a wildly imperfect profession that often falls short of "good" and never reaches "perfect," but it remains one of the few fields where an individual stands a good chance of making a difference in the community.

Don Stacom is a reporter for the Hartford Courant in Connecticut.

The Reporter's Guide to Public Affairs Reporting

Crimes and Accidents

1. Spend time at the police station and talk to officers; try to learn their concerns.

2. Get as much information as possible from the investigating officers, witnesses, victims and suspects.

3. Learn what records are available at the police station and what information they do and do not contain.

4. When writing crime stories, avoid implying that a suspect is guilty.

5. Avoid referring to a suspect's race or religion unless it is clearly relevant to the story.

Local Government

1. Learn how your local governments are organized, what their powers and limitations are and how the various governmental units interact.

2. Study the budgets of local government units, and learn how governments raise their money.

3. Develop a routine for visiting the local government offices on your beat, and become familiar with the people who work in those offices.

4. Learn what public records are kept in each office and how to use them.

5. Go beyond covering school board meetings; visit schools and talk to principals, teachers, parents and students.

Courts

1. Remember that the state files criminal charges against people suspected of violating criminal laws, whereas civil cases are usually between private parties.

2. Learn how state courts are organized, what the various courts are called and what kinds of cases they hear.

3. Learn how court records are kept and how to find the records on any particular case.

4. Do not imply that a defendant in a criminal case is guilty; only the judge or jury can make that decision.

5. Be skeptical of allegations and damage claims that appear in civil complaints; they present only one side of the story.

6. Be alert to the possibility that a plea bargain or a settlement will end a case before or during a trial.

Review Exercises

Many of the documents available to a public affairs reporter—lawsuits and police reports, for example—provide all the information needed for minor stories. Examples of such documents are reprinted in the following exercises. Write a news story about each document. Unless the instructions say otherwise, assume that the police reports have been prepared by officers who investigated incidents in your community, and that all other legal documents have been filed in your city hall, county courthouse or federal building.

Most of the exercises use genuine copies of actual government documents. Even the most unusual police reports are based on actual cases.

1. 911 Emergency: A Child's Heroism

Laura Burke, the 6-year-old daughter of Lynn and Randy Burke of 412 Wilson Avenue, placed the following call to a 911 dispatcher in your city today. Police arrested a neighbor, Andrew Caspinwall of 416 Wilson Avenue, and charged him with raping Mrs. Burke. Bail has been set at $250,000, and Caspinwall, 24, is being held in the county jail.

DISPATCHER: 911 em ergency. Hello?

GIRL: My mommy needs help.

DISPATCHER: What's wrong?

GIRL: Somebody's hurting my mommy.

DISPATCHER: Where do you live?

GIRL: At home with my mommy and daddy.

DISPATCHER: No, uh, that's not what I mean. Can you tell me where your house is, your address?

GIRL: Wilson Avenue.

DISPATCHER: Do you know the address, the number?

GIRL: Hurry. My mommy's crying.

DISPATCHER: No, honey, do you know your address?

GIRL, CRYING: I gotta think. It's, uh, it's, uh, 4 something, I'm not sure. 412. 412.

DISPATCHER: OK. I'll send help.

GIRL, CRYING: Hurry.

DISPATCHER: What's your name?

GIRL: Laura. Laura Anne Burke.

DISPATCHER: Can you tell me what's wrong, who's hurting your mother?

GIRL: A man. He came in the back door and hit my mommy.

DISPATCHER: Where are you now?

GIRL: Upstairs.

DISPATCHER: Does the man know you're there?

GIRL: No. I'm hiding.

DISPATCHER: Where are you hiding?

GIRL: In my mommy and daddy's room. Under the bed.

DISPATCHER: Can you lock the door?

GIRL: I don't know. Maybe.

DISPATCHER: Don't hang up. Just put the phone down and go lock the door. Then come back, talk to me some more.

GIRL: My mommy. What'll happen to my mommy?

DISPATCHER: We've got three police cars coming. They'll be there in a minute. Now go lock the door, and don't let anyone in until I tell you. OK?

GIRL: I guess so.

DISPATCHER: Hello? Hello? Laura, are you there?

GIRL: I locked the door.

DISPATCHER: How old are you, Laura?

GIRL: Six.

DISPATCHER: You're doing a good job, Laura. You have to be brave now to help your mommy. Tell me, is the man armed?

GIRL: What's that mean?

DISPATCHER: Does he have a gun?

GIRL: No. A knife.

DISPATCHER: OK, a knife. Is the man still there, Laura?

GIRL, SOBBING: I don't know. I'm afraid. Will he hurt me, too?

DISPATCHER: No one will hurt you, Laura. Be brave. The police are outside now. They'll be coming into your house. You may hear some noise,

	but that's OK. Stay in the bedroom, and don't let anyone in, OK?
GIRL:	OK.
DISPATCHER:	Your daddy's coming, too. We've found your daddy.
GIRL:	Soon?
DISPATCHER:	The police say they're in your house. They're helping your mommy now. They've found your mommy, and they're

going to take her to a doctor, a hospital.

GIRL:	The man?
DISPATCHER:	He's been caught, arrested. It's OK. It's safe to go downstairs now. There are people there to help you. They want to talk to you, Laura. Can you unlock your door and go downstairs? Laura? Hello? Are you there? Laura? Hello? Laura?

2. Complaint Report

SHERIFF'S OFFICE

COMPLAINT REPORT

ZONE ___1___ UNIT _5, 3, 9, & 14_   CASE NO. _K51-1020C_

GRID ___One___   PAGE ___One___ OF ___One___   OTHER AGCY CASE NO. ___None___

MESSAGE NUMBER ___31847P___   DATE ___Today___ (MONTH / DAY / YR)

TIME RECEIVED _01:22_   TIME DISPATCHED _01:22_   TIME ARRIVED _01:30_   TIME IN-SERVICE _03:12_   WEATHER _NA_

NATURE OF CASE _Armed Robbery_   CHANGED TO ____   F.S.S. ___ FEL. ___ MISD. ___

LOCATION OF OCCURRENCE (INCL. NAME OF BUSINESS/SCHOOL) _Jiffy Foods, 4010 Holbrook Dr._

VICTIM: _Terry DaRoza_ (LAST / FIRST / MIDDLE)   AGE _34_ R/S ___ MO. DAY YR (DOB)

HOME ADDRESS _410 University Boulevard #80_   PHONE _823-4771_

CITY _Yes/Local_   STATE ___ ZIP ___

BUSINESS ADDRESS _4010 Holbrook Dr._   PHONE _823-0333_

CITY _Yes/local_   STATE ___ ZIP ___

REPORTER ☐ WITNESS ☐ _See below_   PHONE ___

CITY ___ STATE ___ ZIP ___

PROPERTY MISSING/STOLEN

QUAN	ITEM	DESCRIPTION - SERIAL NO. - MFG NO. - ETC	EST. VALUES STOLEN	RECOVERED
		Cash register contained approx $80 but nothing was actually stolen		

■ MISSING ■ SUSPECT ■ ARRESTED ■ WITNESS ■ OTHER

NAME _Suspect #1: Keel, Timothy_ (LAST / FIRST / MIDDLE)   AGE _19_ R/S ___ MO. DAY YR (DOB)

ADDRESS _1413 Griese Dr._   PHONE _823-3411_

CITY _Yes/local_   STATE ___ ZIP ___

BUSINESS OR SCHOOL ADDRESS _Plaza Barber Shop_   _2140 West Av._

HEIGHT _5' 4"_ WEIGHT _120_ HAIR _Black_ EYES _Black_ COMPLEXION _Pocked_ OCCUPATION _Barber_

CLOTHING, ETC., _Blue plaid shirt, tan pants, dark blue jacket, Braves baseball cap_

VEHICLE INVOLVED

☒ USED   ☐ STOLEN   ☒ TOWED   ☐ DAMAGED   ☐ BURGLARIZED   ☐ WRECKER   ☐ OTHER ___

YEAR _'94_ MAKE _Toyota_ MODEL _Celica_ BODY STYLE _2-door_ COLOR _Brown_ DEALER ___

LICENSE TAG NO. ___ STATE ___ YEAR EXPIRES ___ I.D. OR VIN NO. ___

REMARKS ___

ENTERED FCIC/NCIC ☐ YES ☐ NO   BOLO ☐ YES ☐ NO   MESSAGE NO. ___

NARRATIVE: The complainant is currently employed full-time as a clerk at Jiffy Foods, a convenience store open 24 hrs. DaRoza states 2 men entered said premises approx. 01:15 today. DaRoza was cleaning a popcorn machine when the 2 asked to use the toilet. DaRoza walked behind the counter to get the key and was followed by Keel who then pulled a knife. DaRoza was recently injured in a construction job, with one leg still in a cast, and uses a cane. DaRoza adds he swung the cane as hard as he could into the arrestee's face, hitting him repeatedly. Paramedics say Keel's nose and jaw and other facial bones are broken. Suspect #1 fell to the floor and suspect #2 then tried grabbing the cane from DaRoza, who proceeded to turn it on him. While suspect #2 fled, DaRoza got help from an entering customer, Stuart Adler, 1847 Oakland Boulevard, who helped tie suspect #1 with their belts until we arrived. Keel is charged with armed robbery and resisting a merchant. DaRoza said he was not injured. He is 6' 4" tall and weighs about 260 pds and works at the store while recuperating from injuries received in a construction job accident.

DISPOSITION: ___

FURTHER POLICE ACTION TAKEN ☐ YES ☒ NO   REFERRED TO _Robbery Division_

REPORTING OFFICER'S NAME (PRINT) _S. Cullinan_   I.D. NO. (INITIAL) ___   APPROVED BY _D. Aneja_

3. Traffic Accident Report

An explanation of the numerical codes used in the following report can be found on the companion website. You may assume you obtained the additional information provided from interviews with the identified sources. Passages in quotation marks may be used as direct quotations.

Additional Information: Statements

Ruth Herwarthe, witness: "The car seemed to come over the hill just this side of 44th Street and for a moment it seemed to be airborne. Then when it hit ground, that's when it seemed to go out of control. In a flash it was over the curb and then it hit my tree so hard I thought it was going to knock it over. Two of the kids in the car were hurt pretty bad. I think the girl hit the windshield with her head. Her face was all bloody and she wasn't moving. One of the boys was hurt bad enough he couldn't walk. The other boy—I don't know if he was the driver—seemed just fine."

Barry Kopperud, police chief: "Nicole Ping was in the back seat and was not wearing a seat belt. The force of the impact propelled her into the windshield, which she struck head first. She was not responsive at the scene of the accident and was taken to Sacred Heart Hospital at 3:45 p.m. She was pronounced dead about an hour later. The driver, Anthony Gould, was also taken to the hospital. I understand he's been released but did receive serious injuries. Gould wasn't wearing a seat belt or shoulder harness, but his airbag did deploy. The third person in the car was Kevin Shadgott. He was the only person wearing a seat belt. Gould had his license revoked two months ago after two previous incidents of negligent and reckless driving. Neither of those incidents resulted in injuries, but one did involve his losing control of the vehicle, leaving the roadway and striking a mailbox."

Additional Information about Nicole Ping

Nicole Ping was a sophomore at Colonial High School. Sara Shepard, the daughter of Frank and Helen Shepard and a close friend of Nicole's said, "I just started screaming when I heard Nicole had died. I can't believe she's gone. We both loved music and science and math. We helped each other and cared for each other. Now she won't be there anymore."

Jeanette Weinstein, a teacher at Colonial, said Nicole was a 4.0 student and was especially strong in mathematics. "She was so bright that there was no topic she could not master. She was just one of the best," Weinstein said.

Louis Ping, Nicole's father, said, "For Nicole's mother and me, the light of our lives has just gone out. The shock and emptiness are beyond words right now. I don't understand what has happened or why it has happened. I just know that life will never be the same."

STATE TRAFFIC ACCIDENT REPORT FORM

TIME & LOCATION

DATE OF ACCIDENT: MO. May	DAY: 14	YEAR: 2016	DAY OF WEEK: Thursday	TIME OF DAY: 3:25 p.m.

COUNTY: Langford   CITY OR TOWN: This city   ACCIDENT REPORT NUMBER: 16-00376

ROAD ON WHICH ACCIDENT OCCURRED: Baltimore Av.   EXIT RAMP ☐ ENTRANCE E ☐   AT INTERSECTIN WITH: ☐ _____   INFLUENCED BY INTERSECTION: _____

IF ACCIDENT WAS OUTSIDE CITY, INDICATE DISTANCE FROM NEAREST CITY OR TOWN: _____   ☐ FEET ☐ MILES   ☐ N ☐ S ☐ E ☐ W   OF: _____

IF NOT AT INTERSECTION, ACCIDENT WAS: 25   ☒ FEET ☐ MILES   ☐ N ☐ S ☐ E ☒ W   OF: 45th Street

DO NOT WRITE IN ABOVE SPACE

TYPE MOTOR VEHICLE ACCIDENT

OVERTURNING	PARKED MV	RAILWAY TRAIN	MV IN TRANSPORT	OTHER NONCOLLISION	MV IN OTHER ROADWAY
ANIMAL	PEDESTRIAN	PEDAL CYCLIST	FIXED OBJECT X	OTHER OBJECT	HIT AND RUN	NONCONTACT

TOTAL NO. VEHICLES INVOLVED

VEHICLE 1

YEAR	MAKE	TYPE	LICENSE PLATE	STATE	YEAR	VIN
2013	Chrysler	sedan	357 AJK	This	2016	1C96KD248DW268946

AREAS OF VEHICLE DAMAGE: 01   DAMAGE ESTIMATE: 5   AMOUNT (approx.): $17,000   SAFETY EQUIP.: 05   VEHICLE REMOVED BY: Trendway Towing

NAME OF INSURANCE CO.: Consolidated Insurance of No. Am.   POLICY NUMBER: KYS-3479-6600021

OWNER (Type or print full name): Savila & Darlene Gould   ADDRESS: 4178 N. 11th Av.   CITY and STATE/Zip Code: This city

DRIVER (Exactly as on driver's license): Anthony K. Gould   ADDRESS: 4178 N. 11th Av.   CITY and STATE/Zip Code: This city

OCCUPATION	Driver's License Type		DRIVER'S LICENSE NUMBER	STATE	DOB (mo/day/yr)	RACE	SEX	Safety E.	Eject.	Injury
student		N/A	none	This	05/02/99	C	M	05	01	02

OCCUPANTS	Name	ADDRESS	AGE	RACE	SEX	Safety E.	Eject.	Injury
Front Right	Kevin Shadgott	8471 Chestnut Dr.	17	C	M	05	01	05
Rear Left								
Rear Right	Nicole Ping	348 Conroy Rd.	16	C	F	01	01	01

VEHICLE 2

YEAR	MAKE	TYPE	LICENSE PLATE	STATE	YEAR	VIN

AREAS OF VEHICLE DAMAGE: _____   DAMAGE ESTIMATE: _____   AMOUNT (approx.): _____   SAFETY EQUIPMENT: _____   VEHICLE REMOVED BY: _____

NAME OF INSURANCE CO.: _____   POLICY NUMBER: _____

OWNER (Type or print full name): _____   ADDRESS: _____   CITY and STATE/Zip Code: _____

DRIVER (Exactly as on driver's license): _____   ADDRESS: _____   CITY and STATE/Zip Code: _____

OCCUPATION	Driver's License Type	DRIVER'S LICENSE NUMBER	STATE	DOB (mo/day/yr)	RACE	SEX	Safety E.	Eject.	Injury

OCCUPANTS	Name	ADDRESS	AGE	RACE	SEX	Safety E.	Eject.	Injury
Front Right								
Rear Left								
Rear Right								

PROPERTY DAMAGE-Other than vehicles: tree, mailbox   AMOUNT: $650   OWNER-Name: Ruth Herwarthe   ADDRESS-Number and Street: 4410 Baltimore Av   CITY and STATE/Zip Code: This city

INVESTIGATOR-Name and rank (Signature): Ofc. Julius Tiller Julius Tiller   BADGE NO.: 468   DEPARTMENT: Middletown P.D.   DATE OF REPORT: 4/14/16

DIAGRAM WHAT HAPPENED–(Number each vehicle and show direction by arrows)

INDICATE NORTH WITH ARROW

← To 44th St.   ← Baltimore →   To 45th St →

= gouges
= utility pole
= mail box
= tree

Driveway

4410 Baltimore Av

POINT OF IMPACT

	V1	V2	
	☐	☐	Front
	☐	☐	Right front
	☐	☐	Left front
	☐	☐	Right side
	☐	☐	Left side
	☐	☐	Rear
	☐	☐	Right rear
	☐	☐	Left rear

DESCRIBE WHAT HAPPENED–(Refer to vehicles by number)

V1 was traveling eastbound on Baltimore at high rate of speech. After cresting a hill east of 44th V1 bottomed out. V1 then left the roadway striking the south curb of Baltimore before proceeding eastbound through yard of 4410 Baltimore, striking mailbox and tree. Witness Herwarth observed V1 eastbound on Baltimore accelerating rapidly, squealing its tires and revving its engine before V1 lost control and left roadway.

WHAT VEHICLES WERE DOING BEFORE ACCIDENT

VEHICLE No. 1 was traveling ☐☐☒☐ On Baltimore Av. at 70 MPH

VEHICLE No. 2 was traveling ☐☐☐☐ On ___ at ___ MPH

N S E W

Vehicle 1 2: ☒☐ Going straight ahead ☐☐ Making right turn ☐☐ Slowing or stopping ☐☐ Stopped or parked
☐☐ Overtaking ☐☐ Making left turn ☐☐ Changing lanes ☐☐ Other (Explain above)

WHAT PEDESTRIAN WAS DOING BEFORE ACCIDENT

☐ Along   Color of Clothing ☐☐ Light Dark

PEDESTRIAN was going ☐☐☐☐ ☐ Across or into
N S E W

☐ Crossing at intersection ☐ Stepped into path of vehicle ☐ Getting on or off Vehicle ☐ Playing in roadway
☐ Crossing not at intersection ☐ Standing in roadway ☐ Hitching on Vehicle ☐ Other roadway
☐ Walking in roadway–with traffic ☐ Standing in safety zone ☐ Pushing or working on Vehicle ☐ Not in roadway
☐ Walking in roadway–against traffic ☐ Lying or sitting on roadway ☐ Other working in roadway ☐ Other (explain above)

DRIVERS AND VEHICLES

		VEHICLE 1	VEHICLE 2
PHYSICAL EFFECTS (Drivers)		01	
VEHICLE DEFECTS		01	
CONTRI-BUTING		04	09
CIRCUM-STANCES			e

ACCIDENT Characteristics

LIGHTING CONDITION	01	ROAD DEFECTS	01	TRAFFICWAY CHARACTER	02	CLASS OF TRAFFICWAYS	01
WEATHER	01	TRAFFIC CONTROL	01	TRAFFICWAY LANES	02	TYPE TRAFFICWAY	01
ROAD SURFACE	02	TRAFFIC LOCATION	03	VISION OBSCURED	01		

WITNESSES other than occupants
NAME Ruth Herwarth ADDRESS–Number and street 4410 Baltimore Av City and State/ZIP Code This city

FIRST AID GIVEN BY Bryan Best ☐ Doctor or nurse ☒ Cert. First Aider ☐ Cert. First Aider (Police) ☐ Other (Explain)

CHEMICAL TEST: TEST RESULTS: Neg.
Driver No. 1 ☒ ☐
Driver No. 2 ☐ ☐

INJURED TAKE TO: Sacred Heart Hosp BY ☒ Priv. Ambulance ☐ Other (Explain) ☐ Gov't Ambulance

ARREST NAME Anthony K. Gould CHARGE manslaughter Citation No. AO-16-17355
NAME CHARGE Citation No.

PHOTOGRAPHS TAKEN ☒ ☐ Yes No

DATE AND TIME NOTIFIED OF ACCIDENT April 14, 2016 TIME ARRIVED AT SCENE 3:34 p.m. WAS INVESTIGATION MADE AT SCENE (If not, where) yes IS INVESTIGATION COMPLETE (If not, why) yes

4. Injury Reports

For this exercise, your instructor might ask that you
write about only one of the reports.

Submitting Agency	Police Dept.				Victim's Name (last - first - middle) Alvarez, Thomas J.		Comp. No. 87B-1241-GL	
Description of Victim	Sex M	Descent Hispanic	Age 20	Height 6'	Location of Occurrence Tom's Pizza		Dist. 4	Type
Weight 160	Hair Brown	Eyes Brown	Build M	Complexion Clear	Date & Time Occurred 11 PM yesterday night		Date & Time Reported to P.D. 11:07 PM yesterday night	
Identifying Marks and Characteristics					Type of Premises (loc. of victim) Carry-out pizza restaurant		Cause of Injury (instr. or means) Pistol	
None visible at scene					Reason (Acc.-ill health, etc.) Robbery/shooting		Extent of Injury (Minor or Serious) Fatal	
Clothing & Jewelry Worn					Remove To (address) County morgue		Removed By Coroners office	
Restaurant uniform of tan pants & shirt & cap					Investigative Division or Unit Notified & Person(s) Contacted Homicide			
					INJURY REPORT		UCR	

CODE	R - Person Reporting		D - Person Discovering		W - Witness			
	Victim's Occupation College student/part-time worker		Resident Address City 854 Maury Rd., Apt. 11B		Res. Phone 823-8892	x	Bus. Phone 823-5455	x
W/R	Name Anne Capiello		8210 University Blvd., #311		823 4117		None	
W	Andrew Caspenwall		416 Wilson Avenue		823-4417		823-5455	

(1) Reconstruct the circumstances surrounding the injury. (2) Describe physical evidence, location found, & give disposition.

The deceased, a pizza clerk, was shot fatally at about 11pm in a failed robbery attempt.
A lone gunman entered the premises and faked that he wanted a pizza. When asked what he
wanted on it suspect #1 said "I really want all your money". The clerk appeared to reach
beneath the counter and suspect #1 then shot him although we found no alarm or weapon the
clerk might have reached for, but our suspect claims that's what triggered the shooting.
The suspect then ran behind the counter and tried to open the register, even throwing it
to the floor but didn't know how to open it and then emptied his gun into it, 5 or 6 shots.
He proceeded to run outside to a waiting vehicle described by 2 eyewitnesses as an old
Ford mustang white in color. It was driven by another white male, and a deliveryman
arriving at this time chased the perpetrators vehicle. In the area of Pauley Park the
perps fired several shots at deliveryman Caspenwall who was not hit. Said getaway vehicle
attempted to make a left turn onto Parkvue Av. but was speeding too fast and flipped on its
side. Suspect #1 William McDowell, 1429 Highland Dr., was found dazed inside but otherwise
unhurt and was identified as the shooter. We are continuing to look for suspect #2. Witness
#1 (Capiello) identified herself as the victims girlfriend. She was present when the
shooting occurred, and the gunman may not have seen her as she was studying in a back
corner of the kitchen. McDowell said he has no job and admits to having a crack problem
and that he went in to rob the place for money. He's charged with murder.

If additional space is required use reverse side.

Supervisor Approving Sgt. A. Wei	Emp. No.	Interviewing Officer(s) Detective J. Noonan	Emp. No.	Person Reporting Injury (signature) *Anne Capiello*

602 - 07 - 23A   **INJURY REPORT**

Submitting Agency	Police Dept.				Victim's Name (last - first - middle)		Comp. No.

Submitting Agency Police Dept.

Description of Victim	Sex	Descent	Age	Height
	M	AA	8	4' 1"

Weight	Hair	Eyes	Build	Complexion
70	Black	Black	Medium	Clear

Identifying Marks and Characteristics

Chipped front tooth.

Small scar on lower left leg.

Clothing & Jewelry Worn

T-shirt, bluejeans,

white sneakers.

Victim's Name (last - first - middle) Curtis, Derek Andrew **Comp. No.** 87B-1336K

Location of Occurrence 663 Harding Av. **Dist.** 2 **Type**

Date & Time Occurred About 4PM yesterday **Date & Time Reported to P.D.** 6:52 PM

Type of Premises (loc. of victim) Family home **Cause of Injury (instr. or means)** Fall into freezer

Reason (Acc.-ill health, etc.) Accident **Extent of Injury (Minor or Serious)** Fatal

Remove To (address) Mercy hospital **Removed By** Paramedics

Investigative Division or Unit Notified & Person(s) Contacted

None. No further action required

INJURY REPORT **UCR**

CODE R - Person Reporting   D - Person Discovering   W - Witness

	Name / Victim's Occupation	Residence Address	City	Res. Phone	x	Bus. Phone	x
	Child	663 Harding Av.	Yes	823-8019			
R	Sara Curtis	663 Harding Av.	Yes	823-8019		823-6400	
D	Danny Jones, grandfather	1152 Arlington	Yes	823-1097		823-4110	

---

(1) Reconstruct the circumstances surrounding the injury. (2) Describe physical evidence, location found, & give disposition.

The deceased was located in a box-type freezer in the garage area at his home. He apparently fell in while trying to reach some popsicles. There was a small tool chest and some other boxes piled in front of the freezer that he apparently used as steps. It now appears that the deceased crawled high enough to open the lid and tumbled in. The lid closed on him & latched. We were dispatched to the scene in answer to a call of a missing child. The victims mother Sara Curtis said the boy disappeared at about 4pm after returning from school. He'd asked for one of the popsicles and she said she told him to eat some fruit instead. Neighbors aided in the search and at 8:30pm we instituted a full scale search of the neighborhood using dogs, the dept. helicopter, and more than twenty officers. The boy was recovered during a 3rd search of the premises by a grandfather at 11:10pm. Paramedics already on the scene said the boy, who was age 8, had no heartbeat and a body temperature of only 70. Icicles had formed on his body and he apparently spent approximately around 7 hours trapped inside the freezer. Hospital personnel said they managed to get the boys heart beating and returned his body temperature to normal while on life support but he never regained consciousness and died shortly after 1am today. When we opened the lid and let it go it did fall back in place and latch itself each time. A box of popsicles was open and its contents scattered over the bottom of the freezer, which was only about 1/3 full of food.

If additional space is required use reverse side.

Supervisor Approving	Emp. No.	Interviewing Officer(s)	Emp. No.	Person Reporting Injury (signature)
Sgt. T. Dow		M. Hennigen		*Sara Curtis*

602 - 07 - 23A   INJURY REPORT

5. Fire/Incident Reports

For this exercise, your instructor might ask that you
write about only one of the reports.

FIRE/INCIDENT REPORT

Date of incident: _____Today_____ Time call received: _____01:34_____ Time of arrival on scene: _____01:38_____

Time of return to station: _____08:12_____ Total time at scene: _6 hr., 34 min._ Response time: _____4 min._____

Address of location: _____2048 Main Street_____ Type of premises: _____218 seat restaurant_____

Name of owner: _____Mr./Mrs. Michael Deacosti_____ Telephone: _____823-0666_____

Nature of call: _____ 911 __X__ Phone _____ Box _____ Police _____ Other _____ Alarms sounded: 1 ② 3 4 5

Units dispatched: __4__ Pumper __2__ Ladder __1__ Rescue _____ Chemical __X__ District Chief _____ Other _____

Injuries: __X__ Yes _____ No _____ Fatalities: _____ Yes __X__ No

Commanding officer's narrative: First call came by phone from a passing motorist at 01:34 today regarding a fire at Deacosti's Restaurant. The structure was already fully involved when the 1st units arrived on the scene with flames having broken through the roof and shooting some twenty to thirty ft. up into the air. Heavy black smoke was pouring from the structure and flames flaring out the front door. We got 4 men inside via a west side window and a second alarm was immediately sounded. Upon arrival the District Chief ordered everyone outside for safety reasons.

The original building is old, having been opened somewhere around 1940 and was a wooden structure, remodeled and expanded several times. Fire was between and behind the current walls and difficult to reach and extinguish. Two tower trucks and 4 pumpers with deck guns doused all the flames by approx. 02:30. Two pumpers remained at the scene until approx. 08:00 when power company and other crews began coming to the scene in case any flames were re-ignited. Fire apparently started in the back NE corner of the restaurant, in either the kitchen or possibly an adjacent office area, possibly due to electrical problems, after the 11:00 closing hour. Private investigators from the insurance company are helping in the inquiry and an electrical engineer will inspect the damages later today. This may be a slow investigation because of extensive damage to the building which was totally and completely destroyed. There were no sprinklers. If it was constructed or remodeled today current codes would require the restaurant to have a sprinkler system. It would have been a whole different story if there were sprinklers. Sprinklers possibly could have saved the building.

2 firefighters were injured. FF John Charlton was taken to Mercy Hospital for treatment of smoke inhalation and released this a.m. FF Al Moravchek received 2nd and 3rd degree burns to his face, hands, and neck and is reported to be in satisfactory condition at the same hospital where he remains, having suffered said injuries during an explosion within the kitchen area at about 02:08 that sent a ball of flames up into his overhead ladder. No estimate of damage is likely to be available for several days. The premises were insured for $1.2 million.

Alarm system on premises: _____ Yes __X__ No   Alarm system activated: _____ Yes _____ No

Sprinkler system on premises: _____ Yes __X__ No   Sprinkler system activated: _____ Yes _____ No

Premises insured: __X__ Yes _____ No   Insurer notified: __X__ Yes _____ No

Recommended followup:
_____ None _____ Arson Squad __X__ Fire Marshal _____ Inspection Division _____ Prevention Division

Commanding officer's name: _____Lieut. Ron Sheppard_____ Signature _____*Ron Sheppard*_____

FIRE/INCIDENT REPORT

Date of incident: ___Yesterday___   Time call received: ___16:48___   Time of arrival on scene: ___16:52___

Time of return to station: ___17:57___   Total time at scene: __1 hr., 5 min.__ Response time: ___4 min.___

Address of location: ___West end of Liberty Av.___   Type of premises: ___Pond/undeveloped field___

Name of owner: ___Wagnor Development Corporation___   Telephone: ___823-3404___

Nature of call: _X_ 911 _X_ Phone _____ Box _____ Police _____ Other   Alarms sounded: ① 2 3 4 5

Units dispatched: _1_ Pumper _1_ Ladder _2_ Rescue _____ Chemical _X_ District Chief _____ Other

Injuries: _____ Yes _X_ No _____ Fatalities: _X_ Yes _____ No

Commanding officer's narrative: The victim has been positively identified as a boy, age eleven, by the name of James Roger Lo, son of Joan and Roger Lo, home residence at 1993 Collins Av. The deceased was a student at Lincoln Elementary School. Witnesses at the scene said the deceased and 3 other neighborhood boys were digging a tunnel in the side of a hill overlooking a pond at the West end of Liberty Av. and it collapsed. One boy ran for help while the others began trying to dig him out. The one boy's mother dialed 911, then ran directly to the scene with neighbors. When we arrived about twenty adults from the neighborhood and passing motorists were at the scene, digging mostly with their hands and few shovels. We took over the work and got the boys head exposed about ten minutes into the rescue but before medics could begin resuscitation efforts another collapse occurred. Victim was freed at 17:24, taken to the Regional Medical Center, and pronounced dead there by doctors from an extensive lack of oxygen. The collapse occurred about 16:40.
　Neighbors and witnesses at the scene were angry, expressing that they had told the property owner on numerous occasions and written him that the area was dangerous and that they needed a good fence around the entire pond area so none of the neighborhood children would drown in it, as it was apparently a popular play area for them. The survivors said they were building a fort and while the deceased was in it the walls caved in. When we arrived the boy had been buried about 12 minutes and completely covered. We found his body six feet from where the opening had been. It was basically a crawl-type cave, and getting the boy out was difficult because dirt (the sides and roof) kept collapsing back on us, and we had to be careful not to hit and further injure the victim without equipment. For that reason we were unable to use any heavy equipment. To expedite the rescue we tore sections from a fence at a residence at 8397 Liberty Av., using it as makeshift shoring in an effort to hold back the sand and dirt continuing to cave in on our men removing the interior dirt. The homeowner should be contacted as they may file a claim or have to be compensated for fence repairs.

Alarm system on premises: _NA_ Yes _____ No   Alarm system activated: _____ Yes _____ No

Sprinkler system on premises: _NA_ Yes _____ No   Sprinkler system activated: _____ Yes _____ No

Premises insured: _____ Yes _____ No   Insurer notified: _____ Yes _____ No
　　　　Unknown

Recommended followup:
_____ None _____ Arson Squad _____ Fire Marshal _____ Inspection Division _____ Prevention Division
Notify City Attorney of fence and Zoning Board of possible hazard for children

Commanding officer's name: ___Lt. Steven Chenn___   Signature ___Steven Chenn___

6. Court Documents

In the Circuit Court of
The 9th Judicial Circuit
in and for (your) County
Division: Civil

THADDEUS DOWDELL   Case No.: 1-78-1440
and LAURA DOWDELL,
individually and as next friends
and parents of JAMES
DOWDELL, a minor,   *Plaintiffs*,
vs.
MARVIN FERRELL,
GREG HUBBARD
and (YOUR CITY'S)
SCHOOL DISTRICT, *Defendants*.

COMPLAINT

COME NOW the Plaintiffs, THADDEUS DOWDELL and LAURA DOWDELL, individually and as next friends and parents of JAMES DOWDELL, a minor, by and through their undersigned counsel, and sue the Defendants, MARVIN FERRELL, GREG HUBBARD, AND (YOUR CITY'S) SCHOOL DISTRICT, jointly and severally, for damages and allege:

1. That this is an action for damages of $500,000, exclusive of interest, costs and further demands.

2. That at all times material to this cause, JAMES DOWDELL was and is the minor son of THADDEUS DOWDELL and LAURA DOWDELL, residing together with them in a family relationship as residents of this county.

3. That at all times material to this cause, the Defendant MARVIN FERRELL held and now holds the position of Principal of Kennedy High School, and that the Defendant GREG HUBBARD held and now holds the position of School Superintendent.

4. That the minor JAMES DOWDELL is and has been a student in Kennedy High School for the past three years and has been told that he will graduate from that school on or about the First Day of next June.

5. That the minor, JAMES DOWDELL, of this date, can barely read or do simple arithmetic and obviously has not learned enough to be graduated from high school or to function successfully in a society as complex as ours.

6. That the problem is not the fault of the minor JAMES DOWDELL, who, according to tests administered by guidance counselors at the high school, enjoys a normal IQ of 94.

7. That the failure of the minor JAMES DOWDELL to master the skills expected of high school students is the fault of the Defendants, MARVIN FERRELL, GREG HUBBARD, and (YOUR CITY'S) SCHOOL DISTRICT, that said defendants failed to employ competent teachers, to maintain discipline, to provide remedial help, and to provide an atmosphere in which learning might take place.

WHEREFORE, the Plaintiffs, THADDEUS DOWDELL and LAURA DOWDELL, individually and as next friends and parents of JAMES DOWDELL, a minor, sue the Defendants MARVIN FERRELL, GREG HUBBARD and (YOUR CITY'S) SCHOOL DISTRICT, jointly and severally, for compensatory damages in the amount of $500,000, exclusive of interest and costs.

FURTHER, the Plaintiffs demand that the minor JAMES DOWDELL be retained in Kennedy High School until he masters the skills expected of a high school graduate.

FURTHER, the Plaintiffs demand trial by jury of all issues triable as of right by a jury.

PILOTO and HERNDON, Attorneys

1048 Westmore Drive

Attorneys for Plaintiffs

BY: Kenneth T. Piloto

KENNETH T. PILOTO

7. House Bill 371

Assume that the vote on the bill reprinted here and the subsequent Senate debate both happened today. You may quote the senators' remarks directly. Assume also that your state's House of Representatives has already passed the bill by a vote of 101 to 23. In the text of the bill, the crossed-out passages will be deleted from the current law, and underlined passages will be added to it.

H.B. 371

An Act relating to crimes and offenses.

Section 1. Section 28-105, Revised Statutes, is amended to read:

28-105. (1) For purposes of the Criminal Code and any statute passed by the Legislature after the date of passage of the code, felonies are divided into eight classes which are distinguished from one another by the following penalties which are authorized upon conviction:

Class I felony	Death
Class IA felony	Life imprisonment
Class IB felony	Maximum—life imprisonment
	~~Minimum—ten years imprisonment~~
	<u>Minimum—twenty years imprisonment</u>
Class IC felony	Maximum—fifty years imprisonment
	Mandatory minimum—five years imprisonment
Class ID felony	Maximum—fifty years imprisonment
	Mandatory minimum—three years imprisonment
Class II felony	Maximum—fifty years imprisonment
	Minimum—one year imprisonment
Class III felony	Maximum—twenty years imprisonment
	Minimum—one year imprisonment
Class IV felony	Maximum—five years imprisonment
	Minimum—none

(2) <u>A person convicted of a felony for which a mandatory minimum sentence is prescribed shall not be eligible for probation.</u>

Section 2. Section 28-1205, Revised Statutes, is amended to read:

28-1205 (1) Any person who uses a firearm, a knife, brass or iron knuckles, or any other deadly weapon to commit any felony which may be prosecuted in a court of this state, or ~~any person~~ who unlawfully possesses a firearm, a knife, brass or iron knuckles, or any other deadly weapon during the commission of any felony which may be prosecuted in a court of this state commits the offense of using ~~firearms~~ <u>a deadly weapon</u> to commit a felony.

(2) <u>(a)</u> Use of ~~firearms~~ <u>a deadly weapon other than a firearm</u> to commit a felony is a Class III felony<u>.</u>

(b) <u>Use of a deadly weapon which is a firearm to commit a felony is a Class II felony.</u>

Section 3. Section 28-1206, Revised Statutes, is amended to read:

28-1206. (1) Any person who possesses any firearm ~~with a barrel less than eighteen inches in length~~ or brass or iron knuckles who has previously been convicted of a felony or who is a fugitive from justice commits the offense of possession of ~~firearms~~ <u>a deadly weapon</u> by a felon or a fugitive from justice.

(2) <u>(a)</u> Possession of ~~firearms~~ <u>a deadly weapon other than a firearm</u> by a <u>felon or a</u> fugitive from justice ~~or a felon~~ is a Class IV felony.

(b) <u>Possession of a deadly weapon which is a firearm by a felon or a fugitive from justice is a Class III felony.</u>

Section 4. Section 29-2221, Revised Statutes, is amended to read:

29-2221. (1) Whoever has been twice convicted of a crime, sentenced, and committed to prison, in this or any other state or by the United States or once in this state and once at least in any other state or by the United States, for terms of not less than one year each shall, upon conviction of a felony committed in this state, be deemed a habitual criminal and shall be punished by imprisonment in a Department of Correctional Services adult correctional facility for a ~~term of not less than ten nor~~ <u>mandatory minimum term of ten years and a maximum term of not</u> more than sixty years, except that:

(2) If the felony committed is manslaughter, armed robbery, rape, arson or kidnapping, as those terms are defined in the Criminal Code, or vehicular homicide while under the influence of alcohol, and at least one of the habitual criminal's prior felony convictions was for such a violation or a violation of a similar statute in another state or in the United States, the mandatory minimum term shall be twenty-five years and the maximum term not more than sixty years.

Section 5. Section 29-2262, Revised Statutes, is amended to read:

29-2262. (1) When a court sentences an offender to probation, it shall attach such reasonable conditions as it deems necessary or likely to insure that the offender will lead a law-abiding life. <u>No offender shall be</u>

sentenced to probation if he or she is deemed to be a habitual criminal pursuant to section 29-2221.

Section 6. Section 29-2525, Revised Statutes, is amended to read:

29-2525. (1) In cases where the punishment is capital, no notice of appeal shall be required and within the time prescribed by section 25-1931 for the commencement of appeals, the clerk of the district court in which the conviction was had shall notify the court reporter who shall prepare a bill of exceptions as in other cases. The Clerk of the Supreme Court shall, upon receipt of the transcript, docket the case. The Supreme Court shall expedite the rendering of its opinion on any appeal, giving the matter priority over civil and non-capital matters.

Section 7. The following shall be added to the Criminal Code of the Revised Statutes:

(1) A person commits the offense of assault on an officer using a motor vehicle if he or she intentionally and knowingly causes bodily injury to a peace officer or employee of the Department of Correctional Services (a) by using a motor vehicle to run over or to strike such officer or employee or (b) by using a motor vehicle to collide with such officer's or employee's motor vehicle, while such officer or employee is engaged in the performance of his or her duties.

(2) Assault on an officer using a motor vehicle shall be a Class IV felony.

Excerpts of Final Debate in the Senate

Sen. Dan Twoshoes, D-Henderson: "If a farmer finds a weasel in his henhouse, he shoots it. I wish we could do the same with some of the two-legged weasels. But at least we can lock them up and keep them away from decent people. That's what this bill will do. It increases the prison sentence for criminals who use deadly weapons—especially guns—in the commission of crimes and it increases the penalties on felons and fugitives who possess deadly weapons. This bill will keep criminals off our streets by preventing judges from placing criminals on probation when this legislature has imposed a mandatory minimum sentence. And most importantly, this

bill sets a mandatory minimum sentence for habitual criminals who commit serious crimes."

Sen. Sally Ong, R-Wakarusa: "I agree with Sen. Twoshoes that we need to keep habitual criminals off our streets, and if it were not for one provision, I could support this bill. I speak of the inclusion of vehicular homicide while under the influence of alcohol as one of those offenses requiring a 25-year mandatory minimum sentence. I understand the pain felt by those who lose a loved one in an accident caused by a drunken driver. That's how my brother died five years ago. But the people who drive while drunk need help, not a 25-year prison sentence."

Sen. John Percy, D-(Your city), and chairman of the Judiciary Committee: "I want to address Sen. Ong's concerns about the vehicular homicide provision. The Judiciary Committee debated this provision extensively, and we heard testimony from many people in law enforcement and social work. It was clear to us that a person who abuses alcohol and then drives an automobile is aware that she or he is behaving recklessly. If a habitual criminal engages in such reckless behavior and causes a fatal injury, then that should be treated as an extremely serious crime."

Sen. William Antonucci, R-(Your city): "We're fooling ourselves if we think that this bill will have any impact on crime in this state. Criminals don't think they'll be caught when they rob or kill, so increasing the penalties means nothing to them. What we'll be doing is wasting money warehousing criminals for years and years. The more people we jam into our prisons, the more we are going to have to pay to operate the prisons—even if we let the prisons become pigsties. We would do better to hire more police, prosecutors and judges. We will deter more crime by increasing the chances that crooks will be caught and prosecuted than by increasing the sentences for the few who now are prosecuted."

After debate, the Senate voted 40-12 in favor of the bill. The bill now goes to the governor, Laura Riley, who must sign it before it can become law. Her press secretary says the governor supports the bill and intends to sign it.

INTRODUCTION TO INVESTIGATIVE REPORTING

18

One function of this country's news organizations is that of watchdog. Investigative reporting has been a part of American journalism almost since the beginning of the modern newspaper industry in the 1830s. Holding government and corporate officials accountable for their actions has been the hallmark of investigative reporting, and many stories have led to major changes in laws and regulations for the benefit of citizens. Names such as Ida M. Tarbell, Nellie Bly, Lincoln Steffens, Ida B. Wells, Edward R. Murrow, Carl Bernstein and Bob Woodward became synonymous with investigative reporting.

"Given the multiple crises we are living through, investigative journalism is all the more important."

Arianna Huffington, cofounder and former editor-in-chief of HuffPost

The roots of investigative reporting can be found in both fiction and nonfiction. For instance, Upton Sinclair's "The Jungle," a novel that exposed Chicago's meatpacking industry, spurred passage of the Pure Food and Drug Act of 1906. "Silent Spring," Rachel Carson's nonfiction account of pesticide misuse, helped launch the modern environmental movement. Sinclair and Carson are just two of many writers who pursued stories of political or social injustice.

Newspapers have a long tradition of investigating scandals in and out of government. In the 1870s, stories in The New York Times detailed how William M. Tweed—a politician who controlled New York City's Democratic political machine—bilked millions of dollars from taxpayers. It is estimated that he and his associates stole more than $200 million (in 1870 dollars) to run his illegal political patronage operation. The newspaper's pursuit of Tweed ended when he was arrested and sentenced to jail.

In the early 1970s, Bob Woodward and Carl Bernstein of The Washington Post investigated a burglary of the Democratic National Committee headquarters, located in the Watergate office complex in Washington, D.C. Their investigation uncovered efforts by the Committee for the Re-Election of the President to sabotage the Democratic Party's presidential campaign, which led to the discovery that then-President Richard Nixon had sanctioned attempts to cover up the secret program of "dirty tricks" and the involvement of administration officials in

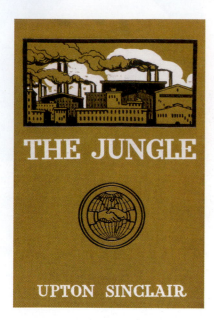

"The Jungle" recounts Upton Sinclair's experience working incognito in the meatpacking plants of the Chicago stockyards.

the break-in. The Watergate stories eventually hastened the resignation of Nixon, the first American president to ever step down.

Today, newspapers, television investigative documentaries, websites, blogs and social media all illuminate malfeasance and corruption by politicians and government officials. Social media played a pivotal role in the "Arab Spring," which saw a number of Muslim countries overthrow their dictatorial governments. Some governments, such as Turkey's, have tried to restrict or stifle the use of social media because of their ability to spread unfiltered information to millions of people.

Investigative reporting is a form of hard news. As defined in Chapter 2—and as the previous examples show—this type of news includes timely coverage of topics involving government meetings or actions, politics, crime, fires, accidents, speeches, labor disputes and so forth. It digs deeply into an issue that has major implications for the community a news organization serves. In this chapter, we will discuss the elements of investigative reporting and the ethical problems that arise.

What Is Investigative Reporting?

News reporting can be reactive or proactive. For example, something happens—a natural disaster (such as an earthquake), a plane crash, political upheaval or war—and news organizations react to it, providing coverage in newspapers and on websites, social media, radio and television. They publish stories about the who, what, when, where, why and how. In some cases, they investigate the how and why of the event more deeply to help people make sense of the circumstances or issues involved.

For example, most stories on the Russian takeover and annexation of the Crimean Peninsula from Ukraine included historical context of the conflict between the two countries, noting that the former Soviet Union had ceded Crimea, which had been part of Russia, to Ukraine in the 1950s. When the Soviet Union dissolved in the 1990s and Ukraine gained its independence, ownership of the peninsula, which had a large Russian population, became an issue because of Russian military installations based there. As events unfolded, the public learned of the historical, social, political and economic issues underlying the events and could thus better understand the situation.

News organizations followed a similar pattern of reactive reporting during the partial closure of the George Washington Bridge, which runs from Manhattan in New York to Fort Lee in New Jersey. This closure embroiled then-New Jersey Gov. Chris Christie and members of his administration in a supposed scheme to punish political enemies. Coverage of the event led to investigative reports on Christie's style of governing and political patronage in his office.

An investigative story is not always tied to an event. A reporter is given a tip or hears a rumor, such as Edward Snowden's revelations about the National Security Agency (NSA), or observes something that he or she questions and begins to search for answers. In such cases, the journalist is being proactive in his or her approach to the story. Whether it is government or corporate corruption, faulty products, unsafe workplaces, shoddy construction, or medical, environmental or social issues, reporters often take weeks, months or years to gather information and write the stories. Investigative reports frequently require in-depth and exhaustive research because the consequences of being wrong can be damaging. News organizations' and subjects' reputations and credibility can be ruined if the information in the story is not accurate and verified. Inaccuracies can also lead to libel suits.

Because of the work involved, an investigative report cannot follow the usual daily deadlines of other news stories. A news organization also has to commit resources for the story to be successful. And while it is not always popular, investigative reporting is often supported by the public when it is done well and reveals something that can have a major impact on people's lives now and in the future. The Boston Globe's investigation into sexual abuse in the Roman Catholic Church prompted a number of official investigations and ended in the prosecution and conviction of some former priests for their actions. It also brought attention to a worldwide problem and encouraged victims to come forward with their stories.

An important part of investigative journalism is the reporters themselves. While some claim that many investigative pieces are sensational accounts published or broadcast to hike ratings and circulation numbers, investigative reporters believe in the importance of what they do. They are concerned with seeking fairness and the truth and with helping those who lack the power to correct something that is wrong. Some journalists fail in their attempt to do investigative stories because their reporting is shallow and sometimes sensationalistic, but those with experience know that they need to spend many hours digging for information and chasing leads. They know that their stories must include everything an audience needs to know to make sense of the story and its impact.

Drug firms poured 780M painkillers into WV amid rise of overdoses

Eric Eyre, Staff Writer   December 17, 2016

Kay Mullins (left) and Tiffany Vincent, the mother and daughter of Mary Kathryn Mullins, pose for a portrait in the dining room of the house they both currently live in and where Mary passed away from a drug overdose on December 23, 2015. Over the years, Kay has helped raise her granddaughter Tiffany, who has also battled drug addiction, and her great-granddaughters, Kylie and Madyson.
Sam Owens | Gazette-Mail

Follow the pills and you'll find the overdose deaths.

The trail of painkillers leads to West Virginia's southern coalfields, to places like Kermit, population 392. There, out-of-state drug companies shipped nearly 9 million highly addictive — and potentially lethal — hydrocodone pills over two years to a single pharmacy in the Mingo County town.

Rural and poor, Mingo County has the fourth-highest prescription opioid death rate of any county in the United States.

The trail also weaves through Wyoming County, where shipments of OxyContin have doubled, and the county's overdose death rate leads the nation. One mom-and-pop pharmacy in Oceana received 600 times as many oxycodone pills as the Rite Aid drugstore just eight blocks away.

In six years, drug wholesalers showered the state with 780 million hydrocodone and oxycodone pills, while 1,728 West Virginians fatally overdosed on those two painkillers, a Sunday Gazette-Mail investigation found.

Eric Eyre of the Charleston Gazette-Mail in Charleston, West Virginia, won the Pulitzer Prize for his expose of the opioid crisis in economically depressed West Virginia counties that have the highest overdose death rates in the country.

Whom and What to Investigate

Just about any topic can be developed into an investigative story. While the supply of ideas may seem endless, investigative reporters know the limitations they face regarding available resources. Large news organizations have more resources than smaller ones and can often allow a journalist the time to conduct the extensive research needed to complete an investigative story. Reporters at smaller news organizations may have to continue their usual beats or general assignments while they work on an investigative piece. However, they can still pitch investigative story ideas to their editors. If the story is a major one that could raise the organization's prestige and credibility, an editor may give the reporter as much support as possible.

Founded in 1997, the International Consortium of Investigative Journalists (ICIJ) consists of over 200 journalists in 70 countries working together on investigative stories. Examples of topics covered by the group include secret corporate tax structures, war contracts in Iraq and Afghanistan, the climate change lobby and tobacco smuggling.

The same news values that apply to standard reporting—timeliness, impact, prominence, proximity, singularity, conflict—are relevant for investigative stories. However, impact is of utmost importance. If the story will have an effect on a majority of people in the community, a news organization may be more inclined to provide the needed resources for an investigative piece. For example, a story that a building inspector has been taking bribes to ignore unsafe construction practices will have more impact than a story about construction defects in a single apartment house.

If you want to become an investigative reporter, look at your beat and determine where possible stories exist. Make notes at meetings about possible story ideas to pursue. Stay in touch with the community and follow up on tips and rumors. You never know when one will lead to a really good story.

Developing an Investigative Story

Investigative reporters Donald L. Barlett and James B. Steele (who were mentioned in Chapter 7) note that journalists who want to develop investigative pieces need to create a "documents state of mind." Like Barlett and Steele, beginning investigative reporters need to research their stories thoroughly, gathering documents and conducting interviews. All of this information needs to be organized, such as in a database or filed by organization and topic, to make the information easy to find and analyze as the story develops.

The internet and online databases have made it easier for reporters to find documents and statistics. But reporters still must know what information they need for their stories. Then they have to analyze it to spot trends or discrepancies between what sources tell them and what documents or statistics indicate. Crowdsourcing, also discussed later in this chapter, can be an important tool in developing an investigative story. Reporters can reach out through social media, probing for information and leads. This method can also help reporters develop sources—both human and document—for an investigative piece.

The Story Idea

Ideas for investigative stories can come from many sources, but some are standard and developed by investigative journalists over many years.

TIPS AND RUMORS

Sometimes a tip can come from someone in the community who has observed something or a disgruntled employee who has insider information on his or her organization. Whatever the case, the reporter must verify the tipster's information to determine its credibility; doing so may mean digging into available documents or contacting some reliable sources. No investigative reporter should charge into a story without checking the information first.

TAPPING COLLEAGUES AND REGULAR SOURCES

Beat reporters cultivate sources as a way to cover their beats efficiently. They know that anyone—from the mayor to the assistant to the maintenance worker—can be a source of information. At smaller news organizations, these journalists can develop story ideas from their sources. Investigative reporters at larger news organizations can also tap into the beat reporter's network of sources to generate ideas.

FOLLOWING UP ON BREAKING NEWS OR OTHER STORIES

Investigative reporters need to read a lot and watch and listen to television news programs. They must to be able to analyze a story to identify missing information. General assignment and beat reporters often lack the time to follow up on a story; the investigative journalist may develop an idea that expands on the why or how of the event. The investigative reporter might read or hear something that piques his or her curiosity and leads to a story. Therefore, he or she needs to stay connected with the community and the world beyond it.

FOLLOWING BLOGS AND SOCIAL MEDIA

Staying connected in today's media landscape means being connected to online media. Investigative journalists should be consistent readers of blogs—both independent ones and those sponsored by news organizations—and should be connected to Facebook and Twitter, as well as other forms of social media. When US Airways pilot Chesley "Sully" Sullenberger safely performed an emergency landing on the Hudson River after his plane hit a flock of geese, a witness tweeted about the incident well before mainstream media started reporting the story. Several other onlookers posted the first pictures of passengers evacuating the plane. An investigative reporter might follow up on that story with one on flight safety and how well prepared airline pilots are to deal with such emergencies.

As discussed later in the chapter, it is essential for today's reporters to use the internet and social media as idea-generating tools and a means to develop sources. The interactive capability of social media allows the investigative journalist to build a community of followers who can be sources as well as readers or viewers.

One way reporters can find followers is by writing a blog. Blogging began in the late 1990s and continues to grow as a tool for mainstream news media as well as citizen journalists. The format allows reporters to focus on something they are interested in or comment on the beat they cover. It also gives them an opportunity to develop a personal identity and connect with an interested audience. Some newspaper bloggers are not reporters: They simply launched blogs—using free, easy-to-use platforms such as WordPress, Tumblr or Blogger—about topics that interested them. Anyone can create a blog on any subject and build an audience. They just need an ability to write, a nose for news and the dedication to update the blog regularly. Journalists who formerly worked at news organizations and citizen journalists have launched blogs to cover community news, filling in gaps left by large mainstream news organizations.

There are five key elements to keep in mind when creating and posting to a blog: planning, frequency, structure, links and interactivity.

Planning

The most important part of developing a blog is the planning. The first thing one needs to determine is the blog's purpose and content; without a goal, the blog may be unfocused and unable to attract an audience. Another important aspect is coming up with a name. A blog's name is the first thing that will attract readers; therefore, it should reflect what the blog covers. For example, The New York Times' blogs include "The New Old Age," which focuses on the elderly and the adult children who care for them; "Bits," which provides news and analysis on the technology industry; and "Well Family," which concentrates on parenting and child health. The name should not be so obscure that only a few people will understand its intended meaning. However, it has to be creative enough to attract readers.

Customizing the blog's appearance is the next step. Beginning bloggers do not need an in-depth knowledge of HTML or other sophisticated website creation skills. Many free blog platforms provide basic and simple customization tools to help beginners get started. Text for headers and pictures or other graphic elements can be added to make it more personal.

Another part of the planning process is organizing the topic or topics that the blog will cover. If the blog is about one topic, is it big enough to allow not just frequent posts, but also a variety of subtopics so posts do not become repetitive? A blog about a classic car, such as the Ford Mustang or Chevrolet Corvette, focuses on just one vehicle, but the long history of and fan interest in those particular cars means posts would probably not become repetitive anytime soon. If readers sense that the same material is constantly being covered, the blog is bound to lose its audience.

Subjects covered in posts can be random or follow a general theme, but they should not go "off-topic" too often. Yet they can evolve over time. Often, audiences identify with the blog's author and continue to follow him or her, even if the blog subject changes. David Pogue is a good example. His technology blog and column in The New York Times were so popular that his audience followed him when he left the organization. The move gave him the freedom to explore other topics he could not while at the Times.

If the blog covers multiple topics within a general framework, such as the environment, the writer can organize posts around the various subject areas. This is helpful if the blog is updated many times a week or several times a day. For example, a blog that focuses on news, opinion and information regarding the environment could be organized into categories that cover state and federal government legislation and its impact, state and federal government agencies and their regulations, the latest scientific research, initiatives by business and industry and initiatives by environmental groups and ordinary citizens. Organizing the broad range of topics into various categories makes it easier for the writer to find the information he or she wants to pass on to readers.

When it comes time to write the blog, planning is still an essential part of the process. A blog post, like any traditional news story, needs a central point. Identifying it in the planning stage will keep the writer focused on the topic. Blogs, by their very nature, give readers more information or a different perspective on a subject of interest, an event or an issue. It is often advantageous to start with an outline of the post so thoughts about the topic can be arranged in logical order.

Frequency

To keep readers returning, blog experts such as Mark Briggs, author of "Journalism Next," advise that a blog should be updated daily or even several times a day. Many news organization blogs follow this rule, depending on breaking news or the blog's topic.

However, as Briggs notes, "there is no hard or fast rule" regarding frequency of posting. It may depend on the topic or on the resources the blog author has available, but the more often the blog is updated, the more quickly it can build a loyal audience. Building an audience is important to building the author's "brand," as Pogue did with his technology blog.

If the blog cannot be updated daily, new material should be posted at least two to three times a week. The blogger should try to be consistent with the updates, selecting days of the week when new posts will appear and ensuring that they arrive on time so readers can log on for the latest information. If bloggers are updating only a few times a week, they might tease the audience with tweets to whet their appetite or promote a particular story.

Structure

Blogs, like news stories, need to be clear, concise, and written in the active voice. They need headlines that describe the topic of the post and include keywords so that search engines can find the article. They also need a lead that summarizes the topic and a body that adds detail to that lead. Blogs often have a conclusion at the end of the post or pose a question seeking reader comment.

Bloggers sometimes add photographs, video and audio clips to their blogs. A post by Pogue about a new electric bicycle included a video of the inventor and Pogue riding the bike. The short video helped readers see and understand the uniqueness of the invention better than Pogue could have by merely describing the bicycle.

If adding video to a blog, keep it short—one to two minutes. A blog can always link to longer videos hosted by the news organization's website or another website.

Links

Blog readers are as interested in the functionality of the blog as they are in the writing or the topic. Functionality can be added to any blog by including widgets (some blog platforms call them gadgets), such as a link to the pages of the blog, a calendar of blog posts and a blogroll, which provides links to other blogs on the same or related topics. Links also can take readers to Facebook, Twitter and RSS feeds. The more functionality a blog offers the audience, the more value readers will see in it.

Links provide connections to news and information that expand on a blog's topic. Blogs are shorter than news stories so they can be read quickly. Linking to other blogs and articles on news or organization websites enables the writer to keep the blog concise.

Interactivity

A great advantage of digital media is their ability to connect writers and readers. Print publications have letters to the editor, but they are limited by available space. Also, letters might not appear in print for days or even weeks. Some newspapers attempted to make reporters more accessible by adding their email addresses at the end of stories and encouraging readers to share their thoughts. While that was an improvement, it still fell short of the almost instantaneous ability to respond that exists in today's digital world.

Web-based news sites provide abundant opportunities for reporters to interact with readers and vice versa. Readers can comment on a story as soon as they finish reading. The ease with which they can interact with the news organization adds to the richness of the information available. Readers can point reporters to new sources of information or give them ideas for stories. News organizations can learn more about the community they serve and what issues are important to readers.

The interactivity of digital media has led to a process called crowdsourcing, in which a collective community contributes to the flow of information. Wikipedia is the collaborative effort of thousands of people posting entries to enhance the information available on the site. Reporters use crowdsourcing to gather information about the community or beat they cover, as it provides more "eyes and ears" within the area. Journalists benefit by getting more information, feedback on stories they have written and tips for stories or issues they might miss otherwise.

The most successful blogs offer a high level of interactivity for readers. The blog can allow readers to comment, to share the post with others, to print the blog or link to other blogs. Blogging gives reporters the opportunity to develop a relationship with readers. By allowing readers to respond to posts, adding their thoughts and opinions on a topic to the mix of information, reporters are allowing readers to be a part of the information system rather than passive receivers of news and opinion.

Microblogging

Microblogging is the process of composing and publishing brief messages. This content can be delivered through text messaging, instant messaging, email or posting to the web. Currently, Twitter is the most popular form of microblogging. Launched in 2006, the website began as a way for people to connect with one another. Postings resembled an electronic diary—people might write about something they were involved in, their favorite restaurant, a movie they had just seen or thoughts about an issue or event. However, it did not take long for news organizations to realize they could use the medium to connect with audiences and promote stories.

One advantage of microblogging is the speed at which information can be gathered and disseminated. People at the scene of a news story, even if they are not reporters working for a traditional news organization, can send tweets to their followers, as well as anyone who is searching the site for posts on a particular subject. Journalists working on breaking news stories can alert readers to the latest information and reach many more people more quickly than ever before. Even when working on a traditional story, reporters can use Twitter and other such services to promote the story to readers, letting them know what is coming in the next day's newspaper or appearing on the news organization's website.

When writing a microblog, it is important to remember that content is limited to 140 or 280 characters. Conciseness and clarity are essential. Reporters usually do not simply repeat the lead of their story; they may get only half the lead written before they run out of characters, and ending a post in midsentence can confuse readers. It is better to select key phrases or key words that will pique readers' attention and then provide the link to the rest of the story or blog.

Reporters use Twitter to stay in touch with sources, editors and other reporters as well as to update people on news stories. Some journalists use microblogging to verify information with sources and develop story ideas. The key is to build a network of followers that can help gather and disseminate information.

California Watch reporter Corey Johnson and his colleagues spent 19 months researching and writing their three-part series investigating the risk public schools face as a result of the state's failure to enforce its law on earthquake safety.

OBSERVATION

The community a person works and lives in can be a source of ideas, but he or she needs to know that community. Is it blue-collar with a lot of industry? Or is it white-collar with mostly technology or financial organizations and perhaps a major college or university? What stories can an investigative reporter generate from these areas? The simple question to ask is, "What isn't being covered or written about in the daily routine of newsgathering?" Making a list of things that are not being covered in depth can lead to potential investigative stories.

In communities with many big industries, stories about labor unions, environmental issues, tax deals for companies moving to the area or kickbacks and cronyism involving local officials can be investigated. A massive spill from a coal ash dump that flooded the Dan River in North Carolina with toxic chemicals led to an investigation of Duke Energy, the largest electric company in the United States. Reporters looked into the history of the organization's compliance with state and federal environmental regulations as well as the connections that Gov. Pat McCrory, who had worked for Duke for 28 years before entering politics, had with the company.

Possible story ideas for white-collar communities include medical facilities and health organizations, banking practices, savings and loans, insurance companies or educational institutions. The (Staunton, Virginia) News Leader published a series of stories about local pharmacies and pharmacists that violated state regulations. The series also investigated how the Board of Pharmacy notifies the public about such infractions, finding that many local residents did not know that their pharmacist was on probation. In one case, a local pharmacist had committed more than 40 violations over 27 years, but had never been suspended.

Resources

Once they develop a story idea and pitch it to their editor, investigative reporters must determine what resources are needed and accessible. Can reliable human sources be developed for the story? Are records or documents available? If the files are highly technical, are there expert sources who can help analyze and interpret them? Can the reporter or the news organization commit the time and money required to complete an investigative story successfully? Can one reporter handle the research and writing or does the size of the investigation require a team?

Knowing what resources are needed and available helps the news organization and the investigative reporter decide the scope of the story. Determining where and how to get documents and the possible cost to obtain them is part of that process. Are the documents available locally or will the journalist have to travel to another location to access them? Will he or she have to travel around the state or the country to track down possible sources?

Planning the Story

Planning is critical when working on an investigative piece. Once an idea has been identified, it is important to develop the central point of the story, which will help the writer maintain the focus of the piece throughout. Investigative stories are often longer than standard hard news stories and are sometimes broken into a multi-part series. The central point has to drive the story from beginning to end even if the story is published or broadcast over several days.

Creating a schematic similar to the story tree (see Chapter 7) can identify necessary sources and documents and establish a timeline for research and writing. The story tree also can help organize information as the investigation evolves. Interviews or other information from a source can be coded, dated and stored under the source's name or code name.

Initial research is part of the planning process and is as necessary as the in-depth research needed to complete the story. The reporter needs to understand everything he or she possibly can about the subject of the investigation, and initial research can provide that information. The material collected in this discovery phase of research can be filed and used later with the story if needed. If a journalist is investigating an individual, what is the person's personal and professional background? Is the information about the person complete and accurate? If a company or organization is the subject, what is its history? What is the organization's structure? Who owns and operates it, and are there any subsidiaries or connections to other companies? What is the organization's culture and reputation? Knowing as much as possible about the person or the organization at this stage can help guide the rest of the research and the story.

Gathering Documents

Exhaustive, in-depth research is vital to publishing a good investigative piece. And it is the first step in the process, before conducting extensive interviews with the human sources involved in the story.

Reporters and their editors do not want to waste valuable time chasing a trail of documents that contribute nothing to the investigation. Some documents and records may be public; others, such as personal bank statements and medical records, are private information. Some may be held by local, state or federal government agencies and require the filing of a Freedom of Information Act (FOIA) request, which can sometimes delay the research. Investigative reporters know when this step is necessary and how to file the request. They also know which government agencies store the various documents they will need—whether it is the clerk of courts, the election commission, the recorder of deeds or the county tax assessor. On the federal level, it might be the Securities and Exchange Commission (SEC) or the Environmental Protection Agency (EPA).

Table 18.1 provides just a short list of the types of documents that can be accessed, depending on federal or state regulations. Note that there are two types of public records—operational and disclosure. Operational documents, which are readily available for public inspection, involve the expenditure of public (tax) money. Government agencies, school districts and other public offices must keep records showing how their spending provides services. Disclosure documents contain personal information about a citizen. They are completed when someone buys property, applies to practice law or medicine, or licenses a dog. The information can be made public under certain conditions.

Investigative reporters must know and understand the public records laws of the state in which they work. They do not have to be lawyers, but they have to know the terminology used to access documents. Journalists first need to learn whether the information they want is held by a federal, state, or local government agency. In the case of federal groups, they will have to file a FOIA request to acquire documents or use the U.S. Government in the Sunshine Act to get access to

TABLE 18.1 Types of Documents Used in Investigative Research

Published Information	● Biographies: personal and professional information on government or corporate figures ● Stories in trade magazines: background information about a government or organization ● News releases: public relations efforts by government agencies or organizations ● Published scientific articles
Public Records	**Operational Documents** ● Minutes of meetings ● Budgets and budget negotiations ● Contracts ● Payrolls ● Elections **Disclosure Documents** ● Licenses ● Lawsuits ● Inspection reports ● Political contributions ● Filings with the SEC
Private Papers	● Personal letters ● Bank statements ● School papers ● Medical records ● Legislative voting records ● Annual financial reports ● Emails, text messages, Twitter communications ● Audio and video recordings of public hearings ● Video surveillance recordings at government buildings

meetings. If it's a state or local department, reporters must use the state's public records law or public meetings law.

The federal government and many states have tried to make it easier for citizens to get information. Often, you just have to ask or write a short letter requesting the material. But the laws have their complexities. Records available under federal law may not be available under some state laws, and state laws vary greatly as to what records and meetings are open to the public. The Reporters Committee for Freedom of the Press website (rcfp.org) contains details about the U.S. Freedom of Information Act, as well as the public records and meetings laws of all 50 states and the District of Columbia. The website can help reporters know what records and meetings are open under the relevant laws and how to go about requesting copies of documents.

Developing Sources

Researching documents can provide only so much information. Investigative reporters have to develop human sources to tell the entire story. When Woodward and Bernstein were investigating the Watergate scandal, they were aided by an inside source codenamed "Deep Throat." This source—who turned out to be Mark Felt, then associate director of the FBI—provided the journalists with invaluable information as they pursued the story that would ultimately bring down Nixon's administration. Shortly before his death in 2008, Felt revealed his identity, telling reporters that he became a source because he was upset that the then-president was trying to use the FBI as a political tool and to obstruct justice.

Determining a source's motivation for providing information to the press is sometimes difficult. Whistleblowers may have altruistic motives driven by a desire to correct an existing problem that they cannot correct within their organization. Some whistleblowers are less noble and provide information because they want to gain publicity or they have a grudge against an organization or officials in it. It is important that reporters try to determine a source's motives and verify the accuracy and credibility of the material provided before publishing their stories. They also must evaluate the reliability of the information. A source with firsthand knowledge of a situation or event is more useful than one who has only second- or thirdhand details.

Reporters should place the person being investigated or who leads the organization under investigation at the top of their source list, but they must determine when and how to interview him or her. Interviews will be most fruitful after the journalist has spoken with all other sources and reviewed all relevant documents. Remember, every effort must be made to allow those involved to tell their side of the story. Further, reporters cannot assume that the subject of the investigation will not talk to them.

Newspapers report on then-President Obama's commuting of Chelsea Manning's prison sentence. Manning, a former soldier, had been sentenced to 35 years for releasing classified or sensitive military documents to WikiLeaks.

Locating sources, especially those no longer involved with the agency, organization or company, can be a problem. Reporters can use the internet and online directories, printed telephone or city directories or workplace directories. As mentioned earlier, social networking is another means of locating sources.

The Investigative Interview

When sources have been identified, the difficult part—interviewing—begins. Interviewing sources for background information may be less challenging than confronting the subject of the investigation.

Unprepared reporters risk losing the source early in the interview. Therefore, as with gathering information and developing sources, the investigative journalist needs to know beforehand what he or she needs from the source during the interview. That knowledge helps focus the interview and the questions. Investigative report-

Mississippi State Auditor's Office special agent Chris Lott (right) and Harrison County Sheriff's Deputy Allan Cramer watch as Department of Marine Resources (DMR) records are delivered to the Harrison County courthouse in Gulfport. The records are the subject of a long-running public records dispute between the Sun Herald newspaper, which said the records belonged to the public, and the DMR and Auditor's Office, which argued the records should remain sealed. An appeals court overturned a lower court's decision to make the records public, denying the newspaper access to them.

ers have to be good interviewers, able to analyze a situation quickly and react accordingly. They should not be intimidated by threats if a subject becomes belligerent, especially if he or she feels threatened by the line of questioning.

When searching documents, reporters look for discrepancies in a person's biographic material or the company's history or financial records. They prepare questions about the inconsistencies and work them into the interview without sounding accusatory. They pose the questions as though they are trying to understand or clarify information. Journalists who ask, "Why did you lie on your resume?" without first indicating that they are attempting to understand information they found can quickly end an interview.

Some critics of investigative journalism cite reporters' desires to sensationalize a story with a "gotcha" or "ambush" interview. Critics contend that this practice is unethical because it puts the source on the spot and can make him or her appear guilty in the court of public opinion even before the facts are known. This device should be a last resort when all other attempts to contact a source have failed. Along with making every effort to seek an interview with a source, reporters should also give him or her adequate time to respond to allegations. Approaching a source a couple of days before a story will be published or broadcast may not give the source enough time to gather information for a response. Good investigative stories are detailed and balanced, giving all sides the opportunity to address the issues.

Because an investigative story can take weeks or months to compile, reporters try to stay connected to sources and give them progress updates, especially if a source is a whistleblower who may want to prepare for any repercussions. In addition, keeping in touch with the source opens the door for him or her to provide additional or updated information as the story develops.

Writing the Investigative Story

When the research is complete and the interviews have been conducted, it is time to write the story. Although reporters may begin sketching out their stories or putting together an outline earlier, they should save the bulk of the writing until all the research and interviews are done. That way, they will not miss important information and will keep the story flowing rationally from beginning to end.

It is best to work from an outline to maintain a logical order to all the facts that will appear in the story. Some reporters lay out the story from the beginning of the research to the end, placing documents and interviews together in chronological order. They may not write the story in that sequence, but the chronology helps them organize massive amounts of information and spot trends or links between sources and documents.

Investigative stories are often filled with a lot of facts and statistics. They can involve multiple sources and direction changes throughout the narrative. Keep in mind, however, that the audience wants to learn about people. The people involved in the story are often the most compelling part. Don't hide them under an avalanche of information. Connect the readers, viewers and listeners to the people in the story—the victims and the antagonists. Explain how the issue under investigation will affect people's lives. It will help to make the story more interesting.

Just as with any news story, the investigative reporter needs a powerful lead to open the story and grab the audience's attention. Some stories work best with a direct summary news lead or a shocking or ironic lead that piques the public's interest. Sometimes, investigative journalists will write their stories in the focus style. They will begin with a focus lead, or anecdotal narrative highlighting an individual involved, and use that person's experiences to introduce the piece before laying out the central point in a nut graph later in the story. Whichever lead is used, however, the writer should not oversell or hype the story. Good writing that tells a compelling story will attract people's attention and keep them involved.

The body of the investigative story should not get bogged down in long lists of statistics that bury the subjects of the story or confuse the audience. Make numbers come alive by interpreting them through examples. When a Malaysian jetliner disappeared over the Indian Ocean, a story in USA Today said one of the search areas was 198,000 square miles in size, but did not give a point of comparison. If the story had noted that the search site was bigger than the states of Oregon and Wyoming combined, readers would have had a sense of the searchers' difficult task.

To keep the audience's attention throughout the body of the story, keep the controversy at the forefront. Writers remember what piqued their interest or outraged them enough to pursue the story. That should be part of the central point. Investigative stories revolve around conflict, and conflict moves the story along.

Investigative reporters plan the ending of the story as well as the lead. Some will write the ending of the story first and use it to formulate the lead. The ending can provide the "aha" moment for the audience when the writer has tied up the various strings of the story. Whether the reporter uses a tieback to the lead or a dramatic conclusion to the story, knowing how it will end provides him or her with a basic blueprint of how to structure the rest of the story. The ending should leave the audience thinking about the story and pondering its implications, but the ending should not editorialize. Let people draw their own conclusions.

Investigative reporters also need to plan visual elements for their stories. Photographs, illustrations and infographics can more easily explain complex statistical information than a long narrative. Some information is best presented as text, but other details are more clearly presented in a graph, chart, illustration or infographic. Graphics have to stand on their own and be visually appealing; however, they should not simply parrot information that is in the story.

Finally, when investigative reporters finish writing the story, they edit it carefully—not just for grammar or style errors, but also for weak areas or holes that need more detail for clarity and accuracy. The final editing process should include extensive fact checking. Some writers will do line-by-line fact checking before a story is published. Accuracy is key to investigative reporting. A story containing errors will lose credibility very quickly. As we pointed out earlier in the chapter, the reporter and his or her news organization will lose credibility as well and open themselves to possible legal action.

Using Technology in Investigative Reporting

Using Computers to Get Answers

Investigative reporters sometimes have to analyze thousands of documents to spot trends or find important information. Computer-assisted reporting (CAR) has made that process much easier. For example, reporters rely heavily on the internet to gather information and to communicate with sources and other reporters.

Perhaps the most sophisticated use of computers in news reporting, however, is to analyze information in electronic databases that reporters have compiled on their own or obtained from government agencies. These databases contain vast amounts of information, and analyzing them without computers would take months. Reporters who are skilled in working with these programs, as well as spreadsheets and statistical tools, can analyze data such as budgets, reports, surveys and polls quickly and thoroughly.

Databases are nothing new. A common example is a city directory—an alphabetical listing of people and businesses (see Appendix A). But because the data are in a paper format, analysis is challenging. For instance, it would be difficult to calculate what percentage of the people listed owned their homes instead of renting. Once the data are in electronic form, a database management program can quickly make that calculation.

CAR projects can compare databases from a variety of sources, but government and public record databases are often key sources. The Atlanta (Georgia) Journal-Constitution filed an open records request to access information about graduation rates in the state. The search and subsequent story found that state education officials were inflating the number of students graduating from high schools across the state and underreporting the number of high school dropouts by more than half.

Other news organizations have used CAR to obtain stories about agriculture, business, child welfare, crime, discrimination, education, the environment, health care, highway safety and the justice system, to name some general areas. The opportunities are endless. And the stories often attract readers, viewers and listeners.

The booming market of data-centric journalism allows people to understand who is interacting with a story and informs future coverage. The local blog Homicide Watch D.C. has earned praise for helping solve unreported murders.

With continuing advances in computer technology and its use by news organizations, even small papers are using CAR to give their readers more in-depth information on issues. News editors and station managers require more CAR skills of the reporters they hire. Students who graduate with some basic computer skills in using spreadsheet software (such as Quattro Pro and Excel) and relational databases (such as FoxPro, Paradox, dBase and Access) will move to the front of the line in the job market. It also will be important for students to prove they can apply that knowledge to real stories. Journalists must learn to see the possibilities, develop story ideas and write stories that use these skills.

CAR does not replace good old-fashioned reporting skills. Computers do not interview sources, and they are only as good as the information that goes into them. They are merely another tool used by reporters to provide information to the public.

Using Social Media

When social media first came to the attention of the public at the beginning of the 21st century, it was more of a curiosity than a journalistic tool. People used it to connect with friends and family members. Messages were mostly personal notes about, for example, a movie they had seen, a restaurant they liked or a vacation they took. However, around 2007, journalists began to explore the use of social media as a means to connect with their audience.

The explosion in the use of social media has changed the face of many news organizations, making them more interactive and more accessible to their audiences. It has also given news organizations more sources for information, more eyes to look for wrongdoing and more people to scan documents. Social media are thus making investigative journalists more efficient and more effective.

Investigative reporters using social media sites can build a community of readers who are familiar with their bylines. Journalists can tap into that community when seeking information or trying to identify sources. A simple tweet can expand into several queries from the network, even from people who may not regularly follow the reporter.

Building a social media community can take time, but it can be an effective tool in developing story ideas and gathering information. News organizations often tweet their followers to ask if they have information or know something about a topic. As the 50th anniversary of the New York World's Fair was nearing, The New York Times tweeted its readers to locate people who had participated in or attended the event. Investigative reporters can use the same technique.

A major element is knowing which stories will benefit from crowdsourcing and which will not. If secrecy is a priority, it may be best to conduct the investigation without using social media. But if the story is one that can benefit from public assistance in research—an investigation into an internet banking scam, for example—tapping into social media resources can locate people who may have relevant information. People affected by the scam could relate their personal experiences, thereby adding a human-interest element to the story.

Using Statistics

Much of the information that reporters gather comes in the form of statistics. Statistics appear almost daily in news stories concerning budgets, taxes, census data, sports, politics, profits, dividends and annual reports. Other pieces based largely on statistics report rates of crime, productivity, energy consumption, unemployment and inflation. Journalists must learn to present statistics to the public in a form that is interesting and understandable.

Reporters who write stories based on statistics translate as many numbers as possible into words, which an audience can understand more easily. Writers also try to analyze the statistics, explaining their significance instead of simply reporting the numbers. Explaining the statistics requires looking for and emphasizing major trends, record highs and lows, the unusual and the unexpected.

Numbers by themselves lack context, and using percentages without a framework can be meaningless and misleading. The FBI reported that in one year there were 143 murders in Washington, D.C., which has a population of approximately 600,000. If 215 murders were committed the following year, reporters could write that the murder rate had risen 50 percent. On the other hand, if a crime reporter in Green Bay, Wisconsin, used a percentage figure to report an increase in that city's murder rate, it would be mostly meaningless. In the same year Washington had 143 murders, Green Bay had only one. If there were two the next year, the increase would be 100 percent. Comparing percentages suggests that violence is increasing more rapidly in the latter city. Journalists need to explain the numbers with helpful comparisons.

Emphasizing the story's human interest is another way to explain statistics. The following example gives numbers only in a routine and dull series:

> The fire department's annual report states that last year it responded to the following numbers and types of calls: bomb threats, 60; electrical fires, 201; false alarms, 459; first aid, 1,783; mattress fires, 59; burned pots left on stove, 78; rescues, 18; washdowns, usually of leaking gasoline at the scene of automobile accidents, 227; and water salvage, 46.

The revision includes a human element from a person who received first aid from the fire department. Another version could have examined the false alarms in greater detail. Did they come from a certain area of the city? Was anyone caught and prosecuted for setting off those false alarms? Where were the bomb threats? Was anyone injured?

> When Sarah Kindstrom needed help, the fire department responded. Kindstrom's heart attack last week was one of 5,024 calls the department

answered last year. First aid requests were the most common, according to the department's annual report, which was released today.

The five leading types of calls included, in order of frequency: first aid, 1,783; false alarms, 459; washdowns, usually of leaking gasoline at the scene of automobile accidents, 227; electrical fires, 201; and burned pots left on stoves, 78.

Other types included: bomb threats, 60; mattress fires, 59; water salvage, 46; and rescues, 18.

Stories that rely too heavily on numbers can be deadly for an audience, who might perceive them as boring and hard to understand. The reporter's job is to make the numbers interesting so readers, listeners and viewers will stay with the story until the end. The unusual nature of statistical information and its impact on people are what make the story interesting.

Reporters describing election results include more than who won and the number of votes that each candidate received. They search for additional highlights: Did incumbents win or lose? Was any bloc of voters (such as ethnic groups, women or conservatives) decisively for one candidate or another? Were there noticeable differences in precincts or voting districts from previous elections? Did any candidates win by unusually large or small margins? Answering those kinds of questions can make election stories more interesting.

Journalists who include statistics in their stories try to present them as simply as possible. They avoid a series of paragraphs that contain nothing but statistics. Instead, they use transitions, explanations and narrative to break up strings of numbers and clarify the information. Reporters also avoid the temptation to editorialize about statistical information. Readers, listeners or viewers might not agree with a writer's characterization of a budget increase as "big" or "huge." Although one person might think a 2 percent increase in a $1 billion budget is small, another might think that adding $20 million to the budget is a great deal.

Ethical Issues in Investigative Reporting

Newly licensed physicians pledge to "first, do no harm" when they take the Hippocratic oath. By its very nature, investigative journalism seeks to "cure" a problem. Every story leads to consequences for the reporter, the news organization, the sources and the subject. Even when the story is accurate and complete, some people may feel that the media sensationalize a story. Sometimes—whether through careless reporting or unethical behavior—an investigative piece can harm the reporter, the news organization or the subject of the story. Therefore, journalists need to know, understand and be able to justify their actions and the consequences to their audience.

A famous example is ABC's exposé of the Food Lion grocery store chain's handling of meat, dairy and other products. The story prompted a major discussion on the ethical and legal issues of investigative reporting, especially the secret video recording of subjects on private property. Two ABC News producers got jobs at Food Lion stores in North Carolina and South Carolina. Their applications falsified information regarding their employment histories, educational backgrounds and references. They worked at the stores for only a couple of weeks and used hidden video cameras to record employees at the stores treating, wrapping and handling meat as well as discussing meat department practices. The resulting segment, which aired on "Primetime Live," alleged that Food Lion required employees to engage in unsafe and unhealthy or illegal practices. After the story aired, the chain closed a number of stores.

According to Reporters Committee for Freedom of the Press, Food Lion sued ABC in North Carolina's federal court. The lawsuit did not attack the content of the story but the means the network used to gather the information. The supermarket chain alleged fraud, breach of the duty of loyalty, trespass and unfair trade practices under North Carolina law. The jury found ABC liable and awarded Food Lion $1,400 in compensatory damages, $5.5 million in punitive damages for fraud and $2 in damages for breach of loyalty and trespass. The court later reduced the punitive damages to $315,000.

Both parties appealed the judgment, and a federal appeals court later rejected the fraud claim, eliminating the punitive damages judgment but upholding the $2 award for trespass. The court said the producers had a right to be in the store because they had been hired by Food Lion to work there. However, the company had never given them permission to record other employees in non-public areas of the store. The decision demonstrated that the First Amendment does not protect journalists who trespass or commit other torts to gather news.

The Food Lion case raised ethical issues as well. Critics of ABC's use of hidden cameras questioned the use of deceptive practices to gather information about a subject or an organization. Supporters of the network said that journalists are sometimes justified in using deceptive means to expose wrongdoing that can harm people.

Is deception ever justified? The earliest days of "yellow" journalism and "muckraking" saw competing newspapers and magazines send their reporters to investigate numerous government agencies and corporate entities to increase circulation. In the late 1880s, Elizabeth Jane Cochran, better known by her pen name Nellie Bly, became famous for investigating inhumane conditions at a women's insane asylum in New York by feigning insanity and having herself committed. After spending 10 days in the asylum, she was released at the request of her employer, Joseph Pulitzer's New York World. Bly's reporting led to reforms at the asylum and more funds to care for the mentally disabled. Some would say that Bly's deception was necessary to get the story.

In 1900, Ida Tarbell, who worked for McClure's Magazine, began working on an investigative report of the Standard Oil Co. Employing modern methods of investigative journalism, Tarbell gathered documents pertaining to the company's business practices from all over the country and began to analyze them. She interviewed current and former executives and employees, government officials, executives at competing companies and legal experts. When the stories detailing the practices of Standard Oil and its founder, John D. Rockefeller, began to appear in McClure's in 1902, they galvanized public opinion and led to regulatory action that broke up Rockefeller's monopoly of the oil industry.

Many would say that Tarbell's hard work and attention to detail accomplished the same goal as the deception employed by Nellie Bly. Who is right? It often comes down to an ethical decision on the part of news organizations. Ethics deals with the gray areas that the law cannot answer—the areas between right and wrong. For some news organizations, deception can never be justified. For others, deception may be a last resort, employed when every attempt to document wrongdoing by traditional reporting has failed.

What about when the story involves the private lives of public figures? What questions should reporters ask themselves before pursuing the story? If a politician is having an extramarital affair, should it be covered in the news? Although rumors that former North Carolina senator and vice presidential and presidential candidate John Edwards was having an affair with campaign aide Rielle Hunter were reported initially only in supermarket tabloids, mainstream news organizations eventually reported the allegations. Edwards confirmed the affair and that the couple had a child. In South Carolina, news organizations became curious about then-Gov. Mark Sanford when he went missing for several days. Sanford's staff told the media that the governor was hiking the Appalachian Trail, but he was visiting his mistress in Argentina. Edwards' extramarital affair ended his political career, but Sanford was later elected to Congress. Is there a difference between the two stories? Both men were having extramarital affairs, and both affairs were consensual. Some would say the ethical position is to report the behavior only when it might compromise the official's job performance or affect society in a major way.

Investigative reporters are bound by the same ethical guidelines as beat and general assignment reporters. Chapter 6 discussed the Society of Professional Journalists' (SPJ) code of ethics. While SPJ has no power to enforce these guidelines, investigative reporters and their colleagues in the newsroom are bound by the organizational rules and policies of the news organization that employs them. It is best to raise possible ethical problems regarding investigative stories with senior editors and producers. Reporters should make sure their supervisors are aware of what they are doing to pursue the story.

Guest Columnist

Developing Investigative Story Ideas

BY PAULA LAVIGNE

When I'm trying to generate story ideas for television or for online, I have a few goals in mind. I want stories that reveal something new or make people think of something in a different way.

The key is to be counterintuitive. The reaction I'm going for is, "Huh, I didn't realize that," or "You've got to be kidding me."

I do a lot of work with data, because I have a background in computer-assisted reporting, and that kind of work lets you make connections and present findings that are unique and that get beyond anecdotal stories that don't really break the surface.

The story ESPN's "Outside the Lines" did in 2010 on sports stadium food safety is a good example. Local media had done plenty of stories about restaurants, concession stands, and so forth, that received bad ratings from health department inspectors. That wasn't new. But what we really wanted to do was see how bad it was across the board and to draw some comparisons. (People love rankings and ratings, whether it's a story for sports, business or lifestyles.)

We requested—using state and provincial public access laws—records of health department inspection reports for all stadium food outlets at professional sports stadiums and arenas in the United States and Canada. Compiling those results allowed us to say how much at risk people were overall and show which venues were the best and worst. Combing through the records also revealed some fascinating—and disgusting—examples, like this one, to punch up the story with sometimes gory and gross details:

> Mold in ice machines at six stands at Miller Park in Milwaukee. A cockroach crawling over a soda dispenser in a private club at Mellon Arena in Pittsburgh. Food service workers repeatedly ignoring orders to wash their hands at a stand at Detroit's Ford Field. . . . At 30 of the venues (28 percent), more than half of the concession stands or restaurants had been cited for at least one "critical" or "major" health violation. Such violations pose a risk for foodborne illnesses that can make someone sick, or, in extreme cases, become fatal.—ESPN.com

Another key to generating good stories is to know a great idea when it comes across your desk, and that can take some research. "Outside the Lines" got a tip a few years ago from a viewer who had seen a story we did that broached the topic of gambling among college athletes. His message on our tip line was, in essence, if we thought that was bad, we should see the gambling around little league football in South Florida.

That tip actually prompted a series of stories that led to a criminal investigation and arrests for illegal gambling, and earned the network a number of awards, including a part in ESPN's first ever duPont Award from Columbia University in December 2013.

But when I first started looking into it, I wasn't sure whether it was even worth a phone call. (And the tip was anonymous.) I looked online and through some of our newswire services to see if any stories about this had been done before. I didn't find anything. That could have deterred me, but it actually made me more interested in this because I thought perhaps we were on to something new, a scandal that no one else had reported.

Through a series of phone calls to sources in South Florida—and finally tracking down the original tipster—we had a handle on what was going on. Then it was a matter of catching the behavior in action, which meant going to several games just to see what was going on.

Producer Greg Amante and I did a great deal of shoe-leather investigating before we actually started reporting the story—by which I mean putting interviews to tape, shooting footage, and getting reaction.

I bring this up because I think it's important to realize the value of really exploring an idea, developing it and putting it in context before you start to compile it into a story. So much of the media environment today is knee-jerk reaction, in-and-out reporting of rumor or surface-level treatment of an incident. And when that happens, really good ideas don't get the treatment and the opportunity to blossom into the really great stories that they can become.

Paula Lavigne is a reporter for ESPN's enterprise unit. Her stories appear on "Outside the Lines," "SportsCenter" and ESPN.com.

The Reporter's Guide to Investigative Reporting

Investigative Reporting

1. Use a variety of methods to develop story ideas.

2. Follow blogs, websites and social media to connect to readers.

3. Determine what resources are available to conduct an investigative story.

4. Use a story tree to determine the required sources and documents.

5. Know how and where to get pertinent documents for the story.

6. Prepare for the investigative interview by studying the issue, the organization or the source so you can ask knowledgeable questions.

7. When writing the story, keep the controversy and the people involved in the forefront.

8. Make the ending of the story as important as the lead.

9. Use social media to gather and verify information as well as reach out to readers.

10. Follow best practices, and be ethical in your reporting.

Using Statistics

1. Verify the accuracy of statistical information.

2. Make sure the story's central point reflects the most important or unusual aspects of the statistical information.

3. Present statistical information in a concise and understandable way.

4. Look for links between statistics that might make the story more interesting.

5. Do not editorialize about statistical information. Let the numbers speak for themselves, and let people make their own judgments.

Review Exercises

1. Investigative Reporting

1. You hear a rumor that the recycling program at your college is not following state and local guidelines. A member of the college maintenance staff and a student who has worked with the maintenance department claim that, instead of recycling plastic, aluminum and other metals, glass and paper as required by law, your college allegedly has been carting recyclables to the local landfill. The staff member and student claim that the college administration is not recycling because it costs too much and would require the college to hire more staff to handle the recycling program. You decide to investigate their claims.

   How would you approach the story? Where would you begin? What information would you need to gather? What sources—primary and secondary—would you pursue? Are there primary and secondary off-campus sources you would need to include in the story? What ethical boundaries would you have to consider? In previous chapters, you were introduced to concepts of digital and visual journalism. How would you employ those concepts in creating a web and social media package for this story? What visual elements, still photography or video, would you need to gather for the story?

2. A classmate approaches you because she knows that you work for the student media. She is on the field hockey team, and she tells you that the graduation rate for student-athletes at your college has dropped significantly in the past three years. Budget concerns at the institution resulted in the elimination of all staff in the student-athlete support services office five years ago. What sources—primary and secondary—would you need for the story? What kinds of data would you need to gather to support the facts in the story?

   As in Exercise 1, think of digital and visual journalistic elements that you would employ in creating a package for the web and social media. What sources would you interview on video or for audio clips? What b-roll would you record? What still photography might you include? How could you use crowdsourcing through social media to gather information for this story? Finally, thinking ethically, what implications or consequences might arise for the college from the publication of the story? How do you defend your decision to pursue and publish the story?

19

JOURNALISM AND PUBLIC RELATIONS

Both journalists and public relations (PR) practitioners research and write stories for the public. The journalist writes stories to provide an objective account of current events and issues. The PR practitioner writes news releases (also called press releases) that promote a client, in the hopes of getting stories published in news media or circulated on social media.

PR people usually have degrees in journalism or a public relations specialization. A survey of the Public Relations Society of America's members found that professionals consider a news reporting course more important for PR majors than any PR course. A journalism class teaches students such things as news judgment, news writing style, media audiences and the importance of deadlines. In addition, many companies hire former journalists to handle PR because they have writing skills essential to the job; they can also translate complicated information into clear, readable stories and understand journalists' definitions of news. The more newsworthy the story and the closer it is to journalistic style, the more likely it will appear in a news publication or broadcast.

While PR practitioners need journalists to be interested in their stories, journalists need PR people for information and story ideas. The best practitioners know their client or organization well, locate information quickly for journalists and arrange interviews with experts and top executives. PR practitioners use these skills to build trust and a working relationship with reporters.

This chapter describes the PR practitioner's job, with a focus on writing news releases for the media and working with journalists.

What Is PR?

Public relations is planned and continuous communication designed to promote an organization and its image, products or services to the public. Practitioners write news releases, create visual communication (photos and information graphics, for example), produce video news releases (VNRs), orchestrate viral campaigns online, monitor social media, research markets and evaluate the success of publicity, all to improve their client's image.

The overall objective of this field is to promote the client and get its name into the news without paying for advertising. Some releases indirectly promote a client. Green Valley, a company that specializes in skin care products with natural ingredients, published a news release stating that other companies' personal care items still use chemicals banned by the U.S. F.D.A. The release quoted the company's chief executive officer (CEO), thereby promoting Green Valley.

PR practitioners work in independent agencies with several clients or in a corporation's communications department, representing only that company. Practitioners might be generalists or might specialize in a particular area, such as speech writing for public officials or risk or crisis communication. Risk communication involves preventative planning for any potential problems that might occur and having an action strategy if they do. Chemical companies need risk communication plans in case their products leak and affect a community. Automotive companies need to know how to react if their manufactured parts cause deaths or injuries and are recalled. Presidential candidates have a victory and a concession speech prepared, which covers either outcome.

Crisis communication is after-the-fact (i.e., when a problem has arisen), when PR must smooth things over between the company and the public. For example, United Airlines needed crisis communication when a video of security personnel forcibly removing David Dao from his seat went viral. The company needed this type of PR again when the public was outraged by its CEO's initial statements, which supported the employees and seemed to blame Dao. After the company lost about $1 billion in stock, the CEO finally issued a third statement that addressed the problem and apologized.

No matter where one works or the area of expertise, PR success depends on excellent writing and visual communication skills acceptable to the news media.

PR Agencies

Some practitioners work in a PR agency, representing companies or other organizations either throughout the year or for special events, such as a store opening, an anniversary celebration or an election campaign. Those in agencies handle several accounts simultaneously. Agencies may be as small as a one-person consultant contracted to write and edit a company's print and online communications, which could include news releases, newsletters, brochures, blogs, tweets,

News releases are a large part of public relations. The Bank of England stores its releases on the company website to allow easy access for journalists and the public.

John Guilfoil was recently named Crisis Manager of the Year by PR News. He manages more than 150 clients, including police and fire departments, in six states.

social media posts, RSS newswires, websites, webcasts and videos. Or an agency can be large, with many specialists in a global network of offices. International conglomerates usually hire agencies to handle their public relations needs in different countries and cultures.

Corporate, Nonprofit and Government PR

PR people may work within a company (e.g., Lego), a nonprofit organization (American Red Cross) or a government agency (U.S. Department of Agriculture) or for a celebrity (Rihanna). In these settings, they communicate with two groups: an internal audience of officers and employees; and an external audience of consumers, investors and the general public. Practitioners may handle internal or external communications, or both, depending on the size of the organization. In addition, they might specialize in event planning or risk or crisis communication.

INTERNAL COMMUNICATIONS

Practitioners handling internal communications work to keep a company's employees informed about the organization. They ensure that all staff, whether in the same building or in a remote branch office, think of themselves as part of the company.

For example, supervisors for Harley-Davidson in the Milwaukee, Wisconsin, headquarters want their employees, whether they work in a production plant in Missouri or stores in Singapore or England, to understand how they contribute to the company's success. The PR practitioner creates lines of communication between supervisors and employees to make the latter aware of their roles in and contributions to the company's operations. Through the company website, newsletter and annual report, the PR person informs staff of activities at headquarters, as well as at other plants or offices. He or she helps employees understand changes in policies, government regulations or business practices that will affect them, such as the opening of a plant or the launching of a new health care plan.

Some practitioners write features about employees and their role in the company. Others publish photographs and brief biographies of new employees in a company newsletter or news release or online article. Still others stage company-wide competitions or host awards banquets for all personnel. They might do the following to promote employees who won awards: Interview and quote the chief executive officer (CEO) praising the staff member and then write about it for a newsletter story, take photos of the CEO shaking hands with the award winner for a press release, or write a speech for the CEO to read at the awards banquet. In many ways, the PR staff coordinates the performances of others and the way they are perceived in the company and by the media.

EXTERNAL COMMUNICATIONS

PR practitioners promote a positive image of an organization by identifying different segments of the public and researching the best ways to reach them.

Those publics may be investors, customers, business associates, suppliers, government officials, industry advocates, community activists or opinion leaders. Practitioners may also want to enhance the employees' image of the organization.

To influence opinions or project a positive image, most practitioners write news releases and features and send them to the media. Other tools and skills include developing press kits that contain information about the company; setting up speakers' bureaus; staging events; filming news clips; writing public service announcements; holding meetings; and designing posters, brochures and pamphlets. Many of these and other public relations tools also appear in video form and online. Practitioners tweet and blog constantly and search print and online publications for mentions of their clients' names to assess if their promotion campaigns are successful.

Reporters collect press releases before a U.S. Federal Reserve news conference in Washington, D.C.

Working with News Media

Public relations practitioners use various media to get information about their client to the public. They determine which media outlets will best serve their purposes. They also know the writing styles, deadlines and other procedures of each target medium. A news release has a better chance of being picked up by the media if it is newsworthy, well written and adheres to the organization's style guidelines. News releases sent electronically to online and print news organizations are written in AP style. Releases for radio are written in broadcast style and format for the announcers to easily read them over the air. VNRs are produced so they can be inserted directly into a TV newscast.

To make their promotional efforts effective, practitioners also learn whom to contact. They identify the proper news departments and the people in charge before sending out a release. "Shotgunning" a release—sending it to multiple departments in a news organization—wastes time and money. For example, most editors will delete a press release about a promotion, but a business editor might report it in a weekly column or section devoted to the topic. Similarly, most editors would discard a release about a church's Christmas program, but a religion editor might mention it in a roundup about holiday activities. By sending news releases to the right editor, practitioners increase the likelihood of the story being used and decrease the chance of harming their reputations by wasting an editor's time.

Reporters might follow up on an idea presented in a news release, but interview their own sources, write their own stories and present their own angles. Thus, releases are a way to get news into the media and help journalists stay informed about their community. The most common types of press releases are advance stories, event stories, features and discoveries and results.

Advance Stories

Practitioners write announcements whenever their company or client sponsors an upcoming activity or event. Advance stories often use an agenda lead, telling news organizations or readers what the event is, where it will be, whom it is for and whether those who want to attend will have to pay or register.

The advance release may also include some background information explaining the event's importance or why the public should attend. For example, a movie theater might send a news release that it will mark the anniversary of the Battle of Dunkirk (May 26–June 4, 1940) by showing the movie "Dunkirk" and honoring a World War II veteran who lives in the community.

Event Stories

A PR person sometimes writes about an event as though it already happened and the news media is reporting on it. For example, a release about the grand opening of a new hotel might include events surrounding the opening and quotes from the hotel owner and hotel guests—just as the practitioner hopes the occasion will go. This type of release serves two main purposes: It lets reporters know what will occur at the event, in case they want to cover it, and it helps the story get published quickly after the event.

Journalists rarely publish these releases verbatim. If the release is newsworthy, they attend the event to verify the activities occurred as planned. Nothing is more embarrassing than publishing a story only to find out later that the event did not happen.

Practitioners also give reporters copies of speeches before they are delivered. This practice enables reporters to quote the speakers accurately. Nonetheless, journalists attend the speeches because speakers may change some of their comments at the last moment.

Features

Practitioners often write feature stories as news releases, and some may interest a national audience. Feature releases deal with subjects as varied as health, science, personal finance, home repair and auto care. A well-written feature appears as an informative story rather than a publicity piece. It includes the client or organization as the sponsor of an event or quotes the person or company as an authority or source for the article.

A religious organization, for example, might issue a feature release about a member who has just completed a mission abroad. The story might describe something unique about the people who were helped or the work that was done. Journalists might use this as a story idea and interview the member to prepare their own story, using some information from the release as background. Even if the release is never published verbatim, it will have served its purpose if it has attracted reporters' attention.

Discoveries and Results

Universities, hospitals, corporations and research institutions want the public to know about their discoveries and the results of their work. Such announcements highlight and enhance an organization's reputation and make people aware of new advances in science and technology.

A news release from the National Federation of the Blind announced the development of an automobile that could be driven by a person who is blind. The release described the car, the people responsible for creating it, the team of university students and engineers who developed the vehicle and the significance of the discovery for blind people and their families.

The Parts of a Press Release

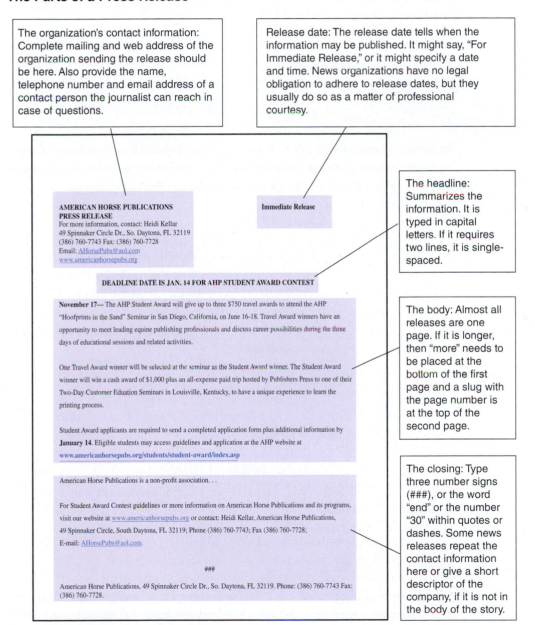

The organization's contact information: Complete mailing and web address of the organization sending the release should be here. Also provide the name, telephone number and email address of a contact person the journalist can reach in case of questions.

Release date: The release date tells when the information may be published. It might say, "For Immediate Release," or it might specify a date and time. News organizations have no legal obligation to adhere to release dates, but they usually do so as a matter of professional courtesy.

The headline: Summarizes the information. It is typed in capital letters. If it requires two lines, it is single-spaced.

The body: Almost all releases are one page. If it is longer, then "more" needs to be placed at the bottom of the first page and a slug with the page number is at the top of the second page.

The closing: Type three number signs (###), or the word "end" or the number "30" within quotes or dashes. Some news releases repeat the contact information here or give a short descriptor of the company, if it is not in the body of the story.

Figure 19.1   The Parts of a Press Release This example shows the information that most press releases contain and the typical arrangement.

Tips for Effective News Releases

Journalists use press releases when they are newsworthy and are well written. They should also include important information the public can use, have local angles and be timely. Here are some ways to make news releases successful.

List a Contact and a Follow-Up Person

Reporters might want to follow up a news release to verify information or ask a question. Thus, an effective release lists the contact information (name, email address, telephone number) of someone at the organization—usually the PR person who wrote the release—who is familiar with the subject.

Send the Release on Time

Timing is important. A news release received too close to deadline is less likely to be published or broadcast because editors have little or no time to verify information or get answers to questions. One sent too early will likely be forgotten.

Use Journalism's Five W's

Reporters appreciate PR practitioners who understand their definitions of news and write stories that could have an impact on the public. The best releases are so good that it is difficult to distinguish them from the final news stories.

Write Well

Similar to a journalist, a PR writer synthesizes sometimes difficult-to-understand information from different sources into something that is clear and useful to the public. A news release is written so readers with varying education levels can understand it. Language is concise and simple; grammar and spelling are perfect; sentences average about 20 words and are in active voice; and paragraphs are short and get to the point immediately.

Localize Information

News releases often omit how the information affects people in a community. Too often, practitioners think of localization as only geographic, such as a particular town or community. Localizing also can mean reflecting a psychological closeness. A press release from the Men's Fertility Center during Men's Health Month (June) may remind people that computers and cellphones can affect male fertility. This type of localization means it has the potential to affect the community of men who use digital devices, wherever they live.

Provide Visuals

Visuals, such as photographs or information graphics, catch the eye of readers, draw them into the story and illustrate major points. PR practitioners think about what visuals might be relevant to a release. Can a photograph help illustrate what the next eclipse will look like for an announcement of the opening of a new planetarium? Can an infographic help the audience grasp the trend of medical marijuana use over time for a release of a bill to allow medical marijuana clinics in the community? Thinking visually can help practitioners get their releases accepted by editors. But don't overwhelm them with visuals. If the news release is digital and for the public, an audio or video podcast, photos or animated graphic might help.

Provide Links

Most organizations or corporations have websites that provide additional information on the topic addressed in the release. Links to statistical information or other data may help answer reporters' questions. In addition, links to trade or professional associations can supply expert sources for a story, if journalists want to follow up. Effective releases have adequate details and the means for reporters to get additional information.

From the Journalist's Perspective: Working with Press Releases

News media are besieged by individuals and organizations seeking free publicity. Metropolitan news organizations receive thousands of releases each week, and smaller ones receive hundreds.

Reporters handle news releases as they would any other type of story—and they follow up for verification. Their first task is to identify a central point. If there isn't one, they discard it. If a central point is there, they find the relevant information and scrap the rest. They also use the central point to identify what information is missing.

Some editors do not read all the news releases they receive. They throw away those they recognize as coming from sources that regularly submit trivial information. Editors also discard releases from companies outside of the area because they hold little interest to people in the community. In some instances, however, the release may be an idea for a local story.

Editors rarely use news releases as submitted—nor do they simply repackage a press release. They know the same releases are sent to many news organizations and they want their story to be different. Some editors use releases primarily as a source of ideas and assign reporters to confirm the accuracy of the information, interview people named in the release, gather more information and write a story. The published story should be very different from the one presented in the release.

When journalists use any information from a news release, they attribute it properly. For example, if they use a quote from a company representative from a news release, they reference the release to indicate that they did not personally interview the source—someone else did the work and the writing. Taking the credit for another's person's work is wrong, sloppy and lazy. In a Poynter Institute survey, a majority of journalists responded that it is acceptable to use passages from press releases, but only if the release is attributed.

Wired fired blogger and author Jonah Lehrer as a result of press-release plagiarism, other plagiarism and recycling of his older work, among other issues. He also resigned from The New Yorker after it was discovered that he had fabricated quotes for one of his books. An investigator of Lehrer's work said he had a "reckless disregard for the truth."

The No. 1 Problem: Lack of Newsworthiness

Journalists prefer press releases that satisfy their definitions of news. They look for topics that are new, local, interesting, unusual, relevant and important to their audience. They also look for information likely to affect hundreds or thousands of people. Action is more newsworthy than opinions, and a genuine or spontaneous event is more newsworthy than a contrived one.

Limited Interest

News organizations reject releases similar to the following because the topics interest few people—except, of course, members of the organizations they mention:

> Brown & Brown Motor Company announced the launch of their charitable giving initiative, Brown Motors 4 Charity. The president said that 100 percent of the employees agreed to donate a portion of their paycheck in May to a charity of their choice.

This example would also interest few people outside of the company:

> Hotel New York announces the appointment of Julianna Santos as Senior Vice President of Retail. She is known for her good taste and her vast business experience well prepares her for overseeing the growing number of affluent stores located within Hotel New York.

Contrived Events

Editors would discard the following news release because it announces a contrived event:

> The Red Cross has joined with the blood bank community in proclaiming January as National Volunteer Blood Donor Month and is urging everyone who is healthy to donate blood to help others.

This release states the obvious. Certainly, the Red Cross would urge "everyone who is healthy to donate blood to help others." Also, every month of the year is dedicated to dozens of causes. For example, May is Arthritis Month, National High Blood Pressure Month, National Foot Health Month, Better Speech and Hearing Month, National Tavern Month and American Bike Month.

Here is another example of contrived newsworthiness for free publicity. The headline and lead make the purpose hard to decipher:

> **Headline:** NBA Hall of Famer Shaquille O'Neal Takes on The Cordish Companies' Chairman David Cordish in Epic Free-Throw Competition at Live! Casino & Hotel

> **Lead:** In a real life "David vs Goliath" battle at Live! Casino & Hotel, NBA Hall of Famer and 4-time NBA Champion Shaquille O'Neal took on David Cordish, Chairman of The Cordish Companies, in a head to head free-throw competition.

After a quote from the chairman and a bit more description, it is noted that the event was part of a promotion for the casino. Then, a dominant portion of the release describes the casino; the last line states the hotel is owned by an affiliation of The Cordish Companies. Two paragraphs about the organization conclude the release. (Aha! Now we understand the release is really about publicity for the company, not the event.)

Rewriting for Newsworthiness

Writers of news releases sometimes are more interested in pleasing their bosses than in satisfying the media and informing the public. They inappropriately begin their releases with the CEO's name. Or they might begin with the organization's name and information about the company before focusing on the news aspect of the release. The following is a poorly written news release:

> Rep. Wayne Smith, R-Mo., is leading the fight to push the Federal Trade Commission to combat predatory and exorbitant interest rates charged by the nation's banks and credit card companies.
>
> Smith is sponsoring legislation in Congress to cap interest rates that can reach as high as 24 percent on some credit cards. In addition, Smith says banks and credit card companies continue to send out credit card solicitation offers to people who already are weighed down by a mountain of debt.
>
> "These solicitations go out to everyone, but young people and seniors are among the most affected by these practices because they can get into debt quickly and never get the balances paid off," Smith said. "The payments are so low on many of these cards that the only thing that gets paid if there is a balance due each month is the interest."
>
> Smith said many people carry huge amounts of credit card debt because the high interest rates add so much to the balance each month.

A journalist might rewrite it this way:

> Congress is considering legislation to lower the interest rates that banks and credit card companies charge consumers.
>
> The legislation, sponsored by Rep. Wayne Smith, R-Mo., will seek to have the Federal Trade Commission investigate lending institutions accused of charging consumers exorbitant interest rates on their credit cards or practicing predatory soliciting to get consumers' business.

Other news releases are editorials that philosophize or praise a client rather than report information beneficial to the public. Journalists do not editorialize in a news story. Thus, a release submitted by a county's dairy association announcing National Dairy Milk Week and praising the flavor and health benefits of milk is unlikely to be used.

Rewriting for Wordiness

Many news releases bury the most important information among a lot of words:

> The National Coalition on Television Violence (NCTV) has just released its most recent monitoring results of prime-time network programs. TV programs that try to portray violence as exciting and fun entertainment are positioned

Deputy Editor of Audubon Magazine Jennifer Bogo said many news releases to the science magazine are sexist. They also don't check her name and assume she is a man. The releases can be offensive: "There is a press release in my spam box right now that says 'Rein in Your Girly Thoughts.'"

to lead the new Fall programs. Violence is portrayed at the rate of about seven violent acts per hour, with new programs taking three of the top four violent spots.

A journalist gets to the point of the news immediately:

Prime-time network programs contain about seven acts of violence every hour, and this fall's new programs are among the most violent, according to the National Coalition on Television Violence.

Quotes from authorities are important to include in news releases, but only if they have something to say. Otherwise, they can merely add to the wordiness of a release:

"Consequences of long-term usage of this chemical are very real, yet its functional purpose is questionable," stated Dr. Mi Na Park.

This quote is more informative:

"The chemical has limited benefits and unknown long-term effects," said Mi Na Park, a scientist with the U.S. Food and Drug Administration (FDA).

The No. 2 Problem: Lack of Objectivity

The purpose of public relations and news releases is to promote awareness about a client. Unfortunately, many have no news value and are similar to advertisements. They contain laudatory adverbs and adjectives, not facts.

Advertisements

The worst news releases are blatant advertisements, obviously written to help sell an image, product or service. Most journalists would reject the following news release for that reason.

Nothing says romance like an intimate getaway to a beautiful sugar-white sand beach, an evening of dancing, champagne toasts, culinary delights and spectacular sunsets. With several love-themed packages, the Baycliff Sandy Beach Golf Resort & Spa—located on the beaches of Northwest Florida—is giving couples the opportunity to experience the ultimate romantic escape this February.

Eliminating Laudatory Adjectives and Puffery

Journalists eliminate laudatory adjectives when rewriting news releases. Terms such as "world famous," the "best" or the "greatest" are subjective and difficult to verify. No news story—or release—should call a program "wonderful," "successful," "timely" or "informative." Similarly, nothing should be called "interesting" or "important." Everyone might not agree on how great something is. If a speaker is "famous," the public already will know the person and will not have to be told of his or her fame.

How many words of puffery can you identify in the press release below?

Jason Taylor is a well-known expert and extremely talented speaker on the subject of handling conflict. His six-step program on conflict resolution has been touted as the best program ever to help ordinary people deal with the huge conflicts that can arise in their lives and rob them of the quality of life they so richly deserve.

Taylor will be presenting a two-hour seminar about his program beginning at 7 p.m. Thursday, Sept. 9, in the Fellowship Hall of First Presbyterian Church, 1387 Downing Ave. The title of the program is "Managing Conflict in Your Life." It's free for everyone.

A journalist eliminates the laudatory adjectives and writes the facts:

Jason Taylor, an expert in conflict resolution, will lead a seminar on resolving conflict, at 7 p.m. Sept. 9, in the Fellowship Hall of First Presbyterian Church, 1387 Downing Ave. The public is invited at no charge.

Telling the Public What to Do

Instead of reporting news, some releases urge people to donate their time and money, buy new products, attend events or join organizations:

Tickets for the inspirational benefit concert are available to the public from the Performing Arts Center by calling 422-4896 or going on the website, for $15 each. Seating will not be reserved, so the public is urged to arrive early to hear this most important message on the subject of mental health care.

Journalists delete editorial comments or rewrite them in a more factual manner. For example, a reporter might summarize a story and, in the final paragraph, tell readers how they can respond, but not say that they should. Here is a revised version of the previous example:

Tickets for the benefit concert on mental health cost $15 and can be obtained at the Performing Arts Center by calling 422-4896 or going online to www.performingarts.org.

Other Problems with News Releases

Stating the Obvious

Public relations writers who lack journalism training often write releases that state the obvious:

Today, the state fire marshal's office emphasized the importance of having working smoke detectors in homes and businesses as a way to save lives.

Parents are worried more than ever about the amount of violence in our society.

These are not news. A fire marshal is expected to encourage the use of smoke detectors to save lives. That is a routine part of the official's job, not news. Similarly, violence has always been a problem; generations of parents have worried about it.

Absence of Solid Facts

Some sentences contain generalities, platitudes and self-praise, but not facts. By rewriting news releases, journalists eliminate sentences that praise a seminar's "array of speakers" or the "excitement" of a theatrical performance.

Such gush often appears in direct quotations, but that never justifies its use. If a quotation lacks substance, journalists will discard it:

> "We're very excited about the opening of the new store," said Betty McKinney, president. "The store represents a new direction for us and extends our commitment to provide customers with the highest quality products at the lowest possible prices."

These platitudes and generalities sound familiar because they are used so often. For example, the following news releases, from different companies, use similar language to describe new employees:

> We are fortunate to have a woman with Russell's reputation and background as a member of the team. Her knowledge and experience will be invaluable as we broaden our sales and marketing base.

> We were impressed with Belmonte's accomplishments and his professionalism. We're extremely pleased with our good fortune in having him join us.

One-Sided Stories

Almost all news releases are biased to benefit the client, and the client's opinions sometimes are presented as fact. Thus, journalists investigate the other sides of the story that were left out—and they localize the story. They also check the facts in a release to avoid serious errors.

The Reporter's Guide to Public Relations

Checklist for PR Practitioners

Does the News Release Provide the Proper Information?

1. A contact person, telephone number and email address?
2. The address of the public relations agency or department?
3. The client and a website?
4. A release date, indicating an appropriate publication date? (Normally, news releases are written in advance of an event.)
5. Links for more information?

Is the News Release Written in Journalistic Style?

1. Does the opening paragraph, or lead, of the release focus on the who, what, when, where and why of the story?
2. Does it have a short headline summarizing the release?
3. Does the text conform to AP style, especially in the handling of addresses, employee titles, dates and time elements?
4. Is it localized?
5. Is puffery eliminated?

Checklist for Journalists Handling News Releases

Does the News Release Have News Value?

1. What is the central point of the release?
2. Is it newsworthy?
3. Does it involve an issue likely to interest or affect many members of the community or only a few, such as the members of the organization distributing the news release?
4. Does it involve a genuine rather than a contrived event, such as a proclamation, groundbreaking or ribbon cutting?
5. Does it have unnecessary words and puffery?

Does the News Release Need Rewriting?

1. Does the lead emphasize the news, or is it buried in a later paragraph?
2. Does it begin by stating the obvious?
3. Does it begin with an unnecessary name?
4. Does the story need to be localized?
5. Is the release clear and concise?
6. Does the release contain only information necessary to develop its central point fully?
7. Is the release comprehensive enough to develop the central point?
8. Does the release contain any clichés, jargon or generalities? Even if they appear in direct quotations, eliminate them.
9. Whom does the news release benefit, the public or its source?
10. Is the release objective, or does it include puffery, self-promotion or unsubstantiated claims?
11. Does it unnecessarily urge the public to act (on the client's behalf)?
12. Does the news release present every side of a controversial issue? Most releases are not balanced, so the journalist has some work to do.

Review Exercises

1. Deciding What Is News

Review some recent news releases at prnewswire.com/news-releases and complete the following tasks.

1. List five news releases that are well written for news media. Explain why you chose them.

2. List five releases that are terrible, and explain why.

3. List 10 story ideas that originated from the news releases you read and explain why they would make good stories. How can you localize the story? Some releases may give you more than one idea.

2. Reviewing News Releases

The following are actual news releases. For each one, pretend to be the editor who received it. Ask yourself the following questions: Is the topic newsworthy, and why or why not? Where can the writing be improved? The first release includes jargon, questionable word choice, and sentence length and organization issues, among other challenges. The second includes misspelling of the company name (!), an incorrect cliché, run-on sentences, pronoun (dis) agreements, misplacement of "only," different topics in one paragraph, a sentence ending with a preposition, a "that" and "which" issue, combination of first and third person, wordiness, a sentence missing a verb, inconsistent use of "and" and "or," and other problems that you might identify.

PRESS RELEASE:

LipoScience Announces Data Presented at the 2013 American Diabetes Association Meeting

Sun Jun 23, 2013 5:30pm BST

* Reuters is not responsible for the content in this press release.

0 COMMENTS

QUOTES

LipoScience Inc
LPDX.O
$2.90
▲ +0.04   ▲ +1.40%
08/28/2014

PR Newswire

RALEIGH, N.C., June 23, 2013

LipoScience Announces Data Presented at the 2013 American Diabetes Association Meeting

Data Presentation Demonstrates Value of Lipoprotein Measurement in Identifying Insulin-Resistant Patients at Increased Risk of Developing Type 2 Diabetes

RALEIGH, N.C., June 23, 2013 /PRNewswire/ -- LipoScience, Inc. (NASDAQ: LPDX), a diagnostic company pioneering a new field of personalized nuclear magnetic resonance (NMR) diagnostics to advance the quality of patient care in cardiovascular, metabolic and other diseases, today announced the presentation of data at the 73rd Scientific Sessions of the American Diabetes Association (ADA) from June 21-25 in Chicago, Ill.

During a poster presented Sunday, June 23 at 11:30 a.m. CT, researchers from Duke University Medical Center demonstrate that the novel Lipoprotein Insulin Resistance score (LP-IR), which was developed by LipoScience, is a potentially clinically useful and convenient index of insulin resistance.

Dizzi Globile Taking Online Communication to Another Level Releasing 'CU'

Dizzi Globile recently released CU, a unique and one of its kind secure communication system.

NEWS PROVIDED BY

Dizzi Globile Pty Ltd

Aug 04, 2017, 14:15 ET

MELBOURNE, Australia, Aug. 4, 2017 /PRNewswire/– There is a new communication tool that is giving users more control over their private information. YapApp (Subsidiary of Dizzi Globile Pty Ltd) has developed and now officially launched their latest application,

CU, the next generation of communication providing high definition audio and video calls. CU is unique as it does not require any sign-up or sign-in, meaning you can chat with friends, colleagues or family without giving up any of your personal information such as email or phone numbers.

To get chatting, CU only requires a picture. Dizzy Globile saw that there was a gap in the social communication app market – knowing that many people don't like giving up email addresses or phone numbers which can be potentially used by developers for marketing purposes. CU uses QR codes – allowing the user to only share their unique QR code with whom they wish to connect with. You can be friends and connect with people you have actually met.

Salient Features of CU:
NO FEES: Without any hidden costs, CU uses your phone's Internet connection (4G/3G/ 2G/EDGE or Wi-Fi, as available) to let you message and call your friends and family, there won't be any need to pay for messaging or calling. There are no subscription fees to use CU.

HD VIDEO CALLS: No extra charges apply. Use your internet connection to connect with your contacts.

GROUP CHATS: Now you can also enjoy Group Chats with the people you select with CU.

CU WEB: You can also send and receive messages right from your computer's browser.

ALWAYS LOGGED IN: You don't miss any messages as you are always logged in with CU. No confusion of being logged in or logged out.

NO PERSONAL INFO REQUIRED: You don't need to input your personal information of any sort. CU provides completely private and secure communication.
Need more information? Users can find full details about CU here: www.getcuapp.com.

About CU (A Product Of Dizzi Globile Pty Ltd.)
Launched in 2017, CU developed by YapApp India Private Limited and is launched as a secure communication app. Its main objective is to provide a secure method of communicating with family, friends and people you just met without actually giving out or sharing any personal information to anyone.

Related Images
image1.png
image2.jpg
image3.png

Related Links
Google Playstore
iTunes App Store

Related Video
http://www.youtube.com/watch?v=psM6JAATCa8

SOURCE Dizzi Globile Pty Ltd
Related Links
http://www.getcuapp.com

3. Eliminating Puffery

Rewrite the following sentences and paragraphs to make them more objective. Correct any errors of style, spelling and grammar. Also, decide if the content is a necessary news story for the public.

1. As a proponent of innovative hiring practices, the companys president has worked diligently to hire older workers, disabled workers and the homeless.

2. The outrageously funny british farce, RUN FOR YOUR WIFE!, will romp across the Lake Street Players stage may 25-27 and may 31-june 2. It will be a fun-filled evening for the whole entire family, with each hilarious performance starting promptly at 8 p.m. in the evening. Hurry to get tickets now before we run out!!

3. In a move that shows how decisive she can be, the chancellor of the state system of higher education today appointed a very, very highly qualified search committee comprised of 14 distinguished members of the academic community to find a replacement for retiring board of trustees president Harold Walters. The chancellor charged the committee with the task of finding a replacement who could match Walters magnificent dedication toward education in the state.

4. Oak Ridge Homes is proud to announce the opening of its newest and most spectacular subdivision—Oak Crest. These unparalleled luxury four- and five-bedroom homes with spectacular views of Paradise Valley offer some of the latest in-home conveniences new-home buyers will surely want in their new homes. Built on 1/4-acre lots and beginning at $350,000, the quality of these new luxury homes has to be seen to be believed. Open houses are being scheduled by six of the areas finest and most prestigious real estate firms that have been selected to list homes in the Oak Crest subdivision.

5. Emerson is dedicated and committed to his work as president of the board of directors and while serving in that capacity has distinguished himself admirably as a proven leader. Other executives can't hold a candle to his unmatched drive to make Emerson Industries an unrivaled leader in precision manufacturing processes. During Emersons visionary leadership, production and sales of the companys products have increased a spectacular 37 percent for the year so far.

4. Editing a News Release: What's Important?

The following news release is much too long. Edit the release for publication by eliminating unnecessary information and correcting any errors in AP style and possessives.

News Release

Renowned Civil War historian Jonathan Wade will present the life and career of Gen. Robert E. Lee during the "Days of Destiny" celebration July 1-3 at the John Adams Memorial Public Library, 351 Bedford Sreet. Wade will give an insightful discussion on Lee's military career and his private life at 7 p.m. each night of the celebration in the Great Hall of the library.

The public is invited to attend the free presentation of "Meet General and Mr. Lee," which is being sponsored by the United States Endowment for the Humanities and the library's Humanities Council.

Wade, a former U.S. State Department Foreign Service Officer and current assistant professor of history at William and Mary College, is an expert in Civil War history, research and preservation. He specializes in the life and career of General Lee, serves on the advisory board of the new Civil War and Underground Railroad Museum of Philadelphia and is founder of the "Civil War Roundtable" at William and Mary. The roundtable provides an opportunity for scholars, graduate students and history buffs to gather and discuss the historical period that had a profound effect on the United States.

Wade has been studying General Lee and the Civil War era for nearly 30 years and is recognized as one of the foremost researchers on the subject. He has written seven books and many articles on the Civil War including a biography of General Lee. He has appeared in several historical shows for public television, lending his expertise and dramatic voice to the documentaries in which he has appeared.

The three-night presentation is a program sponsored by the library's Humanities Council that is supported in part by the Federal Library Services and Technology Act, which is administered by the state Public Library System, a consortium of public libraries throughout the state. Since 1986, the council has provided resources that empower local groups to help their communities explore history, literature, the arts and ideas that shape the human experience.

The "Days of Destiny" programs explore important and dramatic periods in American history to help members of the community learn about and understand pivotal historic moments and how those moments shaped people's lives today. The "Days of Destiny" features speakers, historical re-enactors, hands-on participation events for adults and children as well as period food and arts and crafts. The celebration culminates on July Fourth with a fun-filled day of period music, food and games topped off with a fireworks display at 9 p.m.

For more information about Wade's presentation and other events of the "Days of Destiny," contact the library at 555-1212 or email daysofdestiny@gmail.com.

5. Writing News Releases

The following information is from actual news releases. Write a release from each set of details. Remember to use AP style. Eliminate or keep as much information as you think is necessary to create an effective release, and add phrases and transitions to make it acceptable to editors. List yourself as the contact person for each sponsor, decide on the release date and write a headline.

1. The following information is being released by your county's Board of Elections.

    Anyone who wishes to vote in the upcoming municipal primary must be registered to vote.

    The deadline to register to vote in the primary election is April 16 and all applications must be postmarked by that date.

    Voter registration applications can be obtained by calling the Voter Registration Office at 555-1212 or by emailing a request to voter@county.gov.

    The form cannot be submitted online. It must be downloaded, printed, completed and mailed to the County Voter Registration Office, 157 W. Washington St. (your city or town).

    The registration forms are free of charge.

    The application must indicate any change in name, address or party affiliation.

    Absentee ballot applications also are available.

    Absentee ballot applications are available for persons who will not be able to go to the polls because of absence from their municipality, illness or physical disability.

    Absentee ballot applications are available by calling 555-1212.

    Absentee ballot applications must be received by May 8.

    All absentee ballots must be returned to the county courthouse by 5 p.m. May 11.

    Excepting for absentee voters who have a disability, all absentee ballots must be delivered in person or through the United States Postal Service. Absentee ballots delivered by any other means for absentee voters who do not have a disability will not be accepted or counted by the County Board of Elections.

2. The following results were released by your state's Department of Health and Human Services.

    A report was presented today at the American Diabetes Association's 67th Annual Scientific Sessions.

    The report indicated that an 8-year partnership among the Centers for Disease Control and Prevention (CDC), your state's Department of Health and Human Services, your County Human Services Department, and many facets of the community resulted in a significant change in behavior related to diabetes prevention and care, and reduced the expected rate of increase in the prevalence of Type 2 diabetes in your county.

    Nearly 21 million Americans have diabetes, a group of serious diseases characterized by high blood glucose levels that result from defects in the body's ability to produce and/or use insulin. Diabetes can lead to severely debilitating or fatal complications, such as heart disease, blindness, kidney disease, and amputations. It is the sixth leading cause of death in the U.S.

Type 2 diabetes involves insulin resistance—the body's inability to properly use its own insulin. It used to occur mainly in adults who were overweight and ages 40 and older. Now, as more children and adolescents in the United States become overweight and inactive, Type 2 diabetes is occurring more often in young people. African Americans, Hispanic/Latino Americans, American Indians, and some other ethnic groups are at particularly high risk for Type 2 diabetes and its complications.

The prevention program is called Project DIRECT, which stands for Diabetes Interventions Reaching and Educating Communities Together.

"Project DIRECT has been a successful program of outreach, health promotion, and diabetes care, in which the community participated in developing the interventions from the outset," said Walter Ames, MD, PhD, a Medical Epidemiologist at the CDC and Project Officer of Project DIRECT, in a recent interview. Ames added that the rate of increase in the prevalence of diabetes was markedly lower in the county compared to a comparable county, 80 miles away.

The program involved three key areas:

- *Outreach*—A major media campaign was launched with talk show appearances, cooking segments on TV shows, and newspaper ads. Other events included outreach to educators and church leaders to encourage them to talk about diabetes prevention and diabetes screenings conducted in schools, churches, and at civic and fraternal group meetings.

- *Health Promotion*—A "Ready, Set, Walk" program trained lay exercise leaders who then promoted self-paced walking programs based in schools, churches, community centers, YMCAs, senior centers, and other spaces where people naturally congregate, to encourage walking at least 30 minutes a day. School- and church-based nutrition programs worked with their cooks to help them reduce the fat content in lunches served at their facilities, and worked with officials to bring in health messages and professionals to help improve the health of members of their organizations, such as through cooking classes and health fairs on diabetes.

- *Diabetes Care*—Workshops were held for physicians, nurses, physician assistants, nutritionists, and health educators on the American Diabetes Association guidelines for management and diagnosis of diabetes with the goal of improving the quality of care of the disease. Workshops were given to people with diabetes on basic self-management to help them control their blood glucose and prevent complications.

Pre- and post-intervention surveys were conducted in each county six years ago and again last year using randomly selected samples of the population aged 18 to 75. The 2,311 pre- and 3,083 post-intervention participants were interviewed and had health examinations, including a fasting blood glucose test.

The prevalence of Type 2 diabetes in your county increased from 10.5% four years ago to 16.7% last year. The prevalence of Type 2 diabetes in the other county tested increased from 9.3% four years ago to 18.6% last year.

The American Diabetes Association is the nation's leading voluntary health organization supporting diabetes research, information and advocacy. Founded in 1940, the Association has offices in every region of the country, providing services to hundreds of communities. For more information, please call the American Diabetes Association at 1-800-555-1212 or visit http://www.diabetes.org. Information from both these sources is available in English and Spanish.

3. The following program is sponsored by your county's Women In Need (WIN) Victim Services.

Women In Need (WIN) is in need of help from members of communities across the county.

The prevention of any crime begins with awareness and the commitment and resolve to get involved.

The work of preventing sexual violence is a work that must become the commitment of everyone in every community in the county.

One in four girls and one in six boys will become the victim of sexual abuse before their 18th birthday. This kind of violence has a devastating effect on both its victims and their families.

This month is Sexual Assault Awareness Month and WIN Victim Services is encouraging the community to take action against this silent crime.

There are many ways to take action against sexual violence, but often sexual violence is a crime not often talked about openly. Campaigns against bullying and for respecting others can impact the amount of sexual violence occurring in communities throughout the county. Ways that can work to make a difference include:

- Families should talk openly in regard to age appropriate discussions about healthy sexuality and the importance of loving and respectful relationships.
- Educators should be encouraged to teach non-violent conflict resolution skills and promote anti-bullying values.
- Employers should be encouraged to enforce policies against sexual harassment.
- Young people can learn to value everyone's uniqueness and begin to recognize positive relationships and reach out to at-risk peers. They can learn leadership skills and show respect, modeling these behaviors as positive ones to their peers.
- Community groups can invite WIN into their meetings to learn how they can identify and support a victim of violence.
- Creating change starts with each individual family. Parents can teach their children well when they teach them to respect others.

6. Rewriting News Releases

The following is based on an actual news release. Style errors were inserted, and the locations and names were changed. Your instructor might ask you to write only the lead or to rewrite the entire story. Use the name of your community as the source, correct any style errors and use correct indentations, spacing and format.

New Survey! Recession Brings Greater Commitment to Stay Married

NEW YORK, TODAY'S DATE—A new survey reports that 38%of couples considering divorce or separation have now put off those plans due to the recession. StayMarriedUSA (www.staymarriedhelpUSA.org) — Feb 7 to 14 — releases "The Great Recession and Marriage", new research from the National Marriage Project at University of Virginia. StayMarried USA is a new initiative as part of a decade-old international marriage week movement in 12 countries during the week leading up to Valentine's Day (www.StayMarried-International.com) and has built a new clearinghouse of hundreds of events nationwide to help people strengthen their marriages. Although these opportunities are available annually throughout the year, we are making a big push especially during this particular week.

"Furthermore, 29% of all couples studied say that the Recession has deepened their commitment to their marriage, 58% say it had no effect, and 13% say it has not deepened their commitment," reports Brad Hershey, director of the StayMarriedUSA new survey about marriage and the economy. For full report, go to www.StayMarriedUSA.org/survey

"We want to get the message out that marriage is beneficial for both personal and national economic stability and for raising more well-adjusted children," says Shauna DeLong, CEO of StayMarriedUSA. "Marriage breakdown costs taxpayers at least 112 billion dollars a year. Forty % of all American babies are now born outside of marriage. We have an alarming drop in the marriage rate from 79% of all adults married in 1970 to 57% today. Combined with our 50% divorce rate, family breakdown is costly to the nation," says DeLong, citing earlier research from the Institute for American Values. "In these days of economic hardship, policy leaders and individual Americans need to get serious about our efforts to strengthen marriage."

"Marriage pays," says StayMarriedHelpUSA executive director MacKenzie Wheeler. "Research shows that marriage makes people happier, live longer, and build more economic security. Children with married parents perform better in school; have less trouble with the law, less teen pregnancy and fewer issues with addiction."

"Most folks don't know where to go to get the help they need," said Wheeler. "We've created a new clearinghouse of hundreds of marriage classes and conferences all around the country to help couples strengthen their own marriage, or to help others." Locate an event near you at www.StayMarriedUSA.org.

SOURCE: StayMarriedUSA
RELATED LINKS:
http://www.StayMarriedInternational

CITY DIRECTORY

Like other city directories, this directory lists only the names of adults (people 18 and older) who live in your community. The directory does not list children under the age of 18 or adults who live in other cities. Also, city directories (like telephone books) are published only once a year. Thus, they might not list people who moved to your community within the past year.

When it conflicts with information presented in the exercises, always assume that the information in this directory is correct and that the exercises are mistaken. You will be expected to correct the exercises' errors. If a name in an exercise is not listed in the directory, assume that the name is used correctly.

As you check the names of people involved in news stories, also check their addresses and occupations, as they might also be erroneous. Sources often make errors while supplying that information to police and other authorities. Also, a person's identity may add to a story's newsworthiness. You will find, for example, that some of the people involved in stories are prominent government officials.

Finally, assume that the people listed as university professors teach at your school.

SECTION I: DIRECTORY OF CITY OFFICIALS

Belmonte, William. Member, City Council

Brennan, Rosemary. Director, City Library

Cycler, Alice. Member, City Council

Datolli, Sabrina. Mayor

DeBecker, David. Member, School Board

Drolshagen, Todd. Director, Code Enforcement Board

Farci, Allen. City Attorney

Ferguson, Tony. City Treasurer

Gandolf, Sandra. Member, City Council

Graham, Cathleen, M.D. Director, City Health Department

Hernandez, Ramon. District Attorney

Hubbard, Gary. Superintendent of Schools

Kopperud, Barry. Police Chief

Lieber, Mimi. Member, School Board

Lo, Roger. Member, City Council

Lu, Judie. Member, School Board

Maceda, Diana. Member, School Board

Nemechek, Anna. Member, School Board

Nyad, Carole. Member, City Council

Nyez, Jose. Member, School Board

Onn, Tom. Director, City Housing Authority

Plambeck, Emil. Superintendent, City Park Commission

Ramirez, Luis. Member, City Council

Stoudnaur, Marlene, M.D. Medical Examiner

Sullivan, Tony. Fire Chief
Tribitt, Jane. Member, School Board
Tuschak, Joseph. Member, City Council

Vacante, Umberto. Member, School Board

SECTION II: DIRECTORY OF COUNTY OFFICIALS

Alvarez, Harold. County Administrator
Chenn, Anne. Member, County Commission
Dawkins, Kerwin. Director, Public Works
Dawkins, Valerie. Member, County Commission
DiCesari, Gus. Sheriff
Ellis, Faith. Member, County Commission
Gardez, Jose. Member, County Commission
Grauman, Roland. Member, County Commission

Hedricks, Donald. Assistant County Attorney
Laybourne, Raymond. Member, County Commission
McNally, Ronald. County Attorney
Morsberger, Diedre. Supervisor of Elections
Shenuski, Anita. Member, County Commission
Sindelair, Vernon. County Treasurer
Smith, Ronald. County Clerk
Wehr, Helen. Assistant County Attorney

SECTION III: JUDGES

Municipal Court

Hall, Marci	Kocembra, Edward

Circuit Court

Johnson, Edwin	Ostreicher, Marlene
Kaeppler, JoAnn	Pfaff, Randall
Levine, Bryce R.	Picott, Marilyn
McGregor, Samuel	Stricklan, Julian

SECTION IV: ABBREVIATIONS

acct	accountant	brklyr	bricklayer	cty	county
admn	administration	bros	brothers	custd	custodian
adv	advertising	capt	captain	dent	dental/dentist
agcy	agency	carp	carpenter	dep	deputy
agt	agent	cash	cashier	dept	department
appr	apprentice	cc	community college	det	detective
apt	apartment	ch	church	dir	director
archt	architect	chem	chemist	dispr	dispatcher
asmbl	assembler	chiro	chiropractor	dist	district
assn	association	cir	circle/circuit	dr	drive/driver
asst	assistant	clk	clerk	drgc	drug abuse counselor
athom	at home	clns	cleaners	econ	economist
attnd	attendant	co	company	ele	elementary
atty	attorney	colm	council member	electn	electrician
aud	auditor	com	commissioner	emer	emergency
av	avenue	const	construction	emp	employee
bd	board	cpl	corporal	eng	engineer
bkpr	bookkeeper	crs	cruise consultant	est	estate
bldr	builder	ct	court	exec	executive
blvd	boulevard	ctr	center	facty	factory

fed	federal	ofc	office	sen	senator
ff	firefighter	ofer	officer	serv	service
formn	foreman	opr	operator	sgt	sergeant
gdnr	gardener	optn	optician	slsp	salesperson
govt	government	pcpl	principal	slsr	sales representative
h	homeowner	pers	personnel	soc	social
hairdrsr	hairdresser	pharm	pharmacist	sq	square
hosp	hospital	photog	photographer	sr	senior
hwy	highway	phys	physician	st	street
inc	incorporated	pl	place	stat	station
ins	insurance	plmb	plumber	studt	student
insp	inspector	pntr	painter	supm	supermarket
jr	junior	po	post office	supt	superintendent
jtr	janitor	polof	police officer	supvr	supervisor
jwlr	jeweler	pres	president	tech	technician
la	lane	prof	professor	techr	teacher
lab	laborer	pst	postal	tel	telephone
librn	librarian	pub	public	ter	terrace
lt	lieutenant	r	resident/roomer	treas	treasurer
lwyr	lawyer	rd	road	univ	university
mach	machinist	recpt	receptionist	USA	U.S. Army
mech	mechanic	rel	relations	USAF	U.S. Air Force
med	medical	rep	representative	USM	U.S. Marines
mfg	manufacturing	repr	repairer	USN	U.S. Navy
mgr	manager	rept	reporter	vet	veterinarian
min	minister	restr	restaurant	vp	vice president
mkt	market	retd	retired	watr	waiter
mstr	master	Rev	reverend	watrs	waitress
mtce	maintenance	sav	savings	wdr	welder
muncp	municipal	sch	school	wid	widow
mus	musician	sec	secretary	widr	widower
nat	national	secy	security	wkr	worker

SECTION V: SAMPLE ENTRIES

<u>Hurley</u> <u>Carl J & Mary;</u> <u>printer</u> <u>Weisz Printing Co</u> & <u>ofc sec</u> <u>Roosevelt Ele Sch</u>
   1   2   3   4   5   6

<u>h</u>   <u>140 Kings Point Dr</u>
7   8

<u>Hurley Ralph</u>   <u>studt</u>   <u>r</u>   <u>140 Kings Point Dr</u>
    9   10   11   12

1 = Family name

2 = Names of spouses in alphabetical order

3 = First listed spouse's occupation

4 = First spouse's employer

5 = Second listed spouse's occupation

6 = Second spouse's employer

7 = Homeowner

8 = Home address

9 = Name of roomer or renter 18 years of age or older

10 = Roomer/renter's occupation

11 = Resident or roomer

12 = Address

SECTION VI: ENTRIES

Aaron Betsy retd r 410 Hillcrest St Apt 302

Abare Ann recpt Chavez Bros Chevrolet h 855 Tichnor Way

Abbondanzio Anthony & Deborah brklyr Wagnor Bros & athom h 473 Geele Av

Abbondanzio Denise pub rel rep Haile Associates r 3218 Holbrook Av Apt 832

Acevede Esther & Louis both retd h 8484 Highland Dr

Acevede Miguel atty h 812 Bell Av

Adams Jenna & Donald mgr Wendy's Old Fashion Hamburgers & pst wkr h 1943 Hope Ter

Adcock George & Lydia mgr Blackhawk Hotel & soc wkr Catholic Social Services h 141 N Cortez Av

Adler Sandra & Stuard athom & min Ch of Christ r 1847 Oakland Blvd

Adles Dora & John athom & rep Bach & Co h 1218 S 23rd St

Ahl Thomas C facty wkr Vallrath Plastics r 2634 6th St Apt 382

Ahrons Tommy managing editor The Daily Courier h 1097 Leeway Dr

Ahsonn Jeffrey R & Teresa both retd h 49 Groveland Av

Albertson Wanda pers dir Vallrath Plastics h 529 Adirondack Av

Alicea Carlos city emp h 2930 Leisure Dr

Allen Christopher univ prof Pierce CC h 1810 Collins Av

Allen James D & Margie mach opr Collins Industries & atty h 28 Rio Grande Rd

Allen Michael mech Allison Ford r 410 Hillcrest St Apt 82

Allersen Alice & Thomas athom & acct Mercy Hosp h 418 Meridan Av

Allyn Christopher & Julie dir Center for Arts & univ prof h 1504 Lincoln Dr

Alvarez Harold & Tina cty administrator & techr Washington Ele Sch r 854 Maury Rd Apt 11B

Alvarez Jose cpl state hwy patrol h 1982 Elmwood Dr

Alvarez Thomas studt r 854 Maury Rd Apt 11B

Amanpor Effie & Elton athom & technical writer Wirtz Electronics h 823 E Pierce Av

Ames Robert & Emily asst mgr University Bookstore & sec Cypress Av Med clinic h 2380 Wendover Av

Anchall Mildred dir Sunnyview Retirement Home r 2202 8th Av Apt 382

Andrews Ira auto mech Allison Ford h 561 Tichnor Way

Andrews Paula wid aud Blackhawk Hotel h 4030 New Orleans Av

Aneesa Ahmad univ prof h 1184 3rd Av

Aneja David & Tracy sgt sheriff's dept & carp h 488 Tulip Dr

Ansell Herman clk Blackhawk Hotel r 2814 Ambassador Dr Apt 61

Antonucci William plmb Rittman Engineering Co r 107 Hillside Dr Apt B

Arico James K pntr Kalina Painting & Decorating r 9950 Turf Way Apt 703C

Austin Anna & Terrance C chef & athom h 481 Cottage Hill Rd

Baille Maggy wdr Halstini Mfg h 810 N Ontario Av

Baliet Karen & Thomas adv exec Bailet & Associates & pres Republican Bldrs h 1440 Walters Av

Ball James studt r 1012 Cortez Av Apt 870

Barber Herbert & Irene vp Denny's Restr Group & athom h 2440 College Dr

Barlow Janet & Raymond hairdrsr Lynn's Styling & dir United Way h 2868 Moor St

Barlow Janie & Wesley r 977 4th St Apt 2

Barlow Kevin polof r 3363 Andover Dr

Barlow Robert A mech Allison Ford r 112 Hope Cir

Barsch Margaret & Michael athom & sgt police dept h 2489 Hazel La

Barton Eileen owner/mgr Barton Sch of Dance h 1012 Treasure Dr

Basa Shannon optn r 6718 Fox Creek Dr Apt 1010

Baugh Marcia state consumer advocate h 350 Meridan Av

Bealle Denise univ prof h 1018 Cortez Av

Beasley Ralph pntr Kalina Painting & Decorating r 810 Howard St

Beaumont Edward & Hazel pst wkr & athom h 7240 N Ontario Av

Beaumont Roger studt r 7240 N Ontario Av

Becker Maurine & Ricky athom & publisher The Daily Courier h 1521 Cole Rd

Belcuor Christine & Paul watrs Holiday House Restr & librn h 497 Fern Creek Dr

Belmonte Lucy & William mus & city colm & archt Belmonte & Associates h 177 Andover Dr

Berg Mildred univ prof h 984 Elmwood Dr

Best Bryan para Sacred Heart Hosp r 4320 Michigan Av

Biagi Allison polof r 2634 6th St Apt 906B

Biegel Franklin custd Filko Furniture r 782 12th Av

Blackfoot Jason & Veronica Dawn archt & atty h 2045 Wendover Av

Blake Amanda C & Carl P nurse & electn r 3314 Santana Blvd

Blanchfield Elaine owner/mgr Elaine's Jewelry r 780 Cole Rd Apt 282

Bledsoe Edward & Rosalie photog The Daily Courier & athom h 833 Meridan Av

Blohm Kevin cook North Point Inn r 5604 Woodland St

Bolanker Timothy studt r 854 Murray Rd Apt 107B

Boudinot Marilyn sec Westinghouse Corp r 4340 Virginia Av

Boyette Willis A jtr Barton Sch of Dance r 2121 Biarritz Dr

Boyssie Betty & Lee bkpr Allstate Ins & polof h 1407 3rd Av

Brame Don city emp h 3402 Virginia Av

Brayton Wayne studt r 410 University Av Apt 279

Brennan Rosemary dir City Library h 1775 Nair Dr

Brooks Oliver & Sunni univ prof & technical writer Halstini Mfg h 5402 Andover Dr

Brown Howard slsp Prudential Ins Co h 2745 Collins Av

Bulnes Karen atty sch board h 43 Princeton Pl

Burke Lynn & Randy athom & capt USA h 412 Wilson Av

Burmeister Abraham & Esther pres First Nat Bank & athom h 4439 Harding Av

Burmester Herman A & Sally const wkr Rittman Eng Co & athom h 1412 S 23rd St

Burnes James J min St. Mark African Methodist Episcopal Church r 3155 Marcel Av

Burnes Todd polof r 1502 Matador Dr Apt 203

Burnes Tyrone min United Methodist Ch r 8430 Wilson Av

Butler Irene & Max athom & courier First Nat Bank r 444 Jamestown Dr

Cain Fred & Irma mus & athom r 427 Hidden La

Cantrell Michael pres/mgr Mr. Muscles r 410 South St

Capiello Ann studt r 8210 University Blvd Apt 311

Capiello Otto A & Sandra J photog & wdr Rittman Industries h 47 Rio Grande Rd

Carey John priest St. John Vianney Catholic Ch r 2020 Oak Ridge Rd

Carey Myron univ prof h 641 N Highland Dr

Carigg Craig & Susan min Allen Chapel AME Ch & athom h 453 Twisting Pine Cir

Carigg James R studt r 453 Twisting Pine Cir

Carson Frank & Janice serv formn Allison Ford & athom h 2197 Marcel Av

Carter Deborah counselor Lovell Psychiatric Assn r 550 Oak Parkway Apt 821

Caruna Alyce min Howell Presbyterian Ch h 423 Charrow La

Carvel Reba techr Colonial Ele Sch r 1883 Hope Ter

Casio David & Gretta atty & athom r 711 N 31st St Apt 220

Caspinwall Andrew r 416 Wilson Av

Caspinwall Nadine phys h 416 Wilson Av

Cessarini Maxine & Richard M univ prof & phys r 4184 Cypress Av

Charton John city ff r 3158 Virginia Av

Cheesbro Marylin asst pub defender r 1010 Eastview Rd Apt 3

Cheng Beverly exec dir State Restr Assn h 643 Wymore Rd

Chenn Anne & Steven cty com & lt fire dept r 91 Melrose Av

Chevez Larry det police dept h 4747 Collins Rd

Chmielewski Albert nurse Mercy Hosp r 2814 Ambassador Dr Apt 82

Cho Jaclyn & Yung Yee techr Colonial High Sch mgr Giovanni's Pizza Parlor r 2032 Turf Way Apt 202

Christopher Alan univ prof h 4850 Elm Dr

Chuey Karen & William J slsp Allison Ford & clk police dept r 5710 Michigan Av

Cisneroes Andrew & Lillian min Redeemer Lutheran Ch & athom r 818 Bell Av

Claire Richard & Wanda dir state Dept of Corrections & athom h 12142 Decatur Rd

Clauch Amy clk Annie's Auto Parts r 2418 Seasons Ct Apt B

Clayton Amy univ pres r 820 Twisting Pine Cir

Cohen Abraham & Estelle asst dir computer serv city sch system & pub rel rep Evans Pub Rel Group r 1903 Conway Rd

Collin Ronald const wkr Wagnor Development Corp r 2814 Ambassador Dr Apt 47D

Colson Jonathan studt r 7240 N Ontario Av

Conaho Henry & Jeanne supvr sales ERA Realty & pres Lake CC h 820 Hope Ter

Correia Bobby & Dawn supvr Delta Airlines & athom h 9542 Holbrook Dr

Cortez Manuel & Nina polof & bkpr North Point Inn r 1242 Alton Rd

Cosby Minnie agt Watson Realty r 487 Jamestown Dr

Coto Jorge Alberto studt r 8210 University Blvd Apt 311

Courhesne Adolph & Gloria mech Fridley Volkswagen & athom h 1186 N Highland Av

Cowles Stephen jtr VFW Post 40 h 8217 Cypress Av

Cross Andrea & Lee chiro & city acct h 2 Virginia Av

Cross Dina & Raymond athom & pst wkr r 101 Charow La

Cruz Jena atty r 48 DeLaney Av

Cullinan Charles A & Susan both sheriff's dep r 848 Rio Grande Rd

Curtis Sarah sr vp SunBank r 663 Harding Av

Cycler Alice & Richard city colm & atty r 7842 Toucan Dr

Daigel Annette hairdrsr Anne's Beauty Salon r 431 E Central Blvd

DaRoza Sue & Terry studt & clk Jiffy Food Store r 410 University Av Apt 80

Datolli Roger & Sabrina retd & mayor r 845 Conway Rd

Dawkins Agnes & Kerwin athom & dir cty Dept of Pub Works r 2203 Coble Dr

Dawkins Ronald & Valerie bklyr & cty com r 1005 Stratmore Dr

Dawson Shirley wid techr Colonial Ele Sch h 492 Melrose Av

Deacosti Amy studt r 3254 Virginia Av

Deacosti Michael & Peggy pres Deacosti's Restr & hostess h 3254 Virginia Av

Deboare Ann & Jack R dir emp rel Rittmann Industries & mgr Lucky's Supm r 1415 Idaho Av

DeCastro Wilma teacher Kennedy High Sch h 3277 Pine Av

Dees Karen studt r 410 University Av Apt 52

DeLoy Joseph R phys r 280 Lancaster Rd Apt 110

Desaur Roland studt r 700 Classics St

DeVitini Brenda & Ronald asst min Redeemer Lutheran Ch & mach Rittman Industries r 313 Coble Dr

DeWitt Tony studt r 2230 Cortez Av Apt 828

Deyo Ashley & Ralph graphic designer & dent r 2814 Ambassador Dr Apt 7

DeZinno Marc & Nancy asmbl Vallrath Industries & athom h 205 Rockingham Ct

Diaz Diane & Richard author & nurse St. Nicholas Hosp h 1978 Holcroft Av

Diaz Enrique & Lisa atty & pst wkr r 3224 Mt Semonar Av

Diaz Juanita watrs Pancake House r 408 Kasper Av Apt 322

DiCesari Gus & Henrietta cty sheriff & athom h 980 Atlantic Av

Dillan Martha atty Westinghouse Corp h 702 S Kirkmann Av

DiLorrento Anthony univ prof h 666 Texas Av

Dolmovich Sandra M clk Dayton-Hudson h 714 N 23rd St

Dow Tammy sgt police dept r 2208 17th Av

Dowdell Laura & Thaddeus clk & jwlr Dowdell Jewelry h 620 Lexon Av

Doyle Cynthia & Wayne techr Colonial Ele Sch & pres National Homebuilders Assn h 428 Wilson Av

Drolshagen Illse & Todd athom & dir City Code Enforcement Board h 2406 Alabama Av

Dwyer Margaret studt r 2047 Princeton Av Apt 405

Dysart Tony & Wendy athom & attnd Sunnyview Retirement Home r 724 Aloma Av Apt 24F

Edwards Traci psychiatrist h 3303 Lake Dr

Einhorn Doris & Robert athom & univ phys h 8320 Meadowdale Rd

Eisen Priscilla phys r 1118 Bumby Av Apt 204

Ellam Dorothy R & Roger A techr Madison Ele Sch & landscape contractor r 2481 Santana Blvd

Ellerbe Robert widr pres Ellerbe's Boats h 3213 Hidalgo Dr

Emory Jonathan & Lori eng & athom h 849 Groveland Av

Eulon Harley & Martha jtr St. Nicholas Hosp & athom h 410 E 3rd St

Evans Mark & Trish W cty soc wkr & owner/mgr Evans Pub Rel Group h 4232 Stewart Av

Evans Nikki & Timothy loan ofer First Fed Sav & Loan & mgr Allstate Ins r 806 Apple La

Fairbairn Sean owner Advance Investments h 5235 Robinhood Dr

Farci Allen widr atty h 818 Texas Av

Favata Celia J wid h 9930 Bumby Av

Ferguson Marcia & Tony vet & city treas h 96 West Av

Ferrell Fannie & Melvin atty & pcpl Kennedy High Sch h 2384 West Av

Firmett Rene J serv stat attnd Bert's Shell Stat r 4474 Colyer Rd

Flavel Vernon J dir Becker Express h 827 Pigeon Rd

Forlenza Henry custd Kmart r 4620 Alabama Av Apt 22

Forsythe Scott cpl sheriff's dept h 1414 S 14th Av

Foucault Carmen wid techr Aloma Ele Sch h 1452 Penham Av

Foucault James studt r 1452 Penham Av

Fowler Barbara K & Fritz polof & owner Fowler Allstate h 88 Eastbrook Av

Fowler Joel studt r 2006 Hillcrest St

Franklin Allen sgt USA r 840 Apollo Dr Apt 322

Friedmann Leo asst dist atty r 2814 Ambassador Dr Apt C2

Fusner Charles tech h Peachtree Dr

Gable Frances & Jay athom & truck dr Becker Express h 1701 Woodcrest Dr

Gandolf Sandra wid city colm h 8 Hillcrest Av

Gant Diana univ prof h 810 Village La

Gardepe Ellen serv mgr Derek Chevrolet h 210 Lake Dr

Garland Charlotte & Chester athom & city health insp h 2008 N 21st St

Garner Cheryl & David athom & emp City Recreation Dept r 2814 Ambassador Dr Apt 88

Gianangeli David gdnr r 48 Stempel Apt 53D

Giangelli Marlene P pres Pestfree Inc h 214 Lake Dr

Gill Todd watr Fred's Steakhouse r 410 University Av Apt 279

Goetz Beryl dent & writer h 1010 McLeod Rd

Golay Evelyn & Thomas cash & ownr/ mgr Tom's Liquors h 1203 Texas Av

Goree Linda exec dir city Girl Scout Council r 2202 8th Av Apt 302

Gould Darlene & Savilla athom & slsp Anchor Realty Co h 4178 N 11th Av

Graham Cathleen & Ross R dir City Health Dept & phys h 710 Harding Av

Grauman Alice & Samuel athom & min First Covenant Ch r 610 Eisen Av

Grauman Roland & Tina cty com & asst supt for pub education r 3417 Charnow La

Green Joey atty h 604 Michigan Av

Greenhouse Irwin & Trina administrator Mercy Hosp & athom h 9575 Holbrook Dr

Griffin Marlene det police dept h 3130 Joyce Dr

Guarino Anne chiro r 4100 Conway Rd Apt 611

Guarino Belva retd r 84 Lakeland Av

Guarino Gerhard chiro h 1813 Texas Av

Guarino Tony A techr Colonial High Sch h 6139 Eastland Dr

Guerin Anita & Ronald E athom & city ff r 1045 Eastvue Rd

Guitterman Daniel bartender Jim's Lounge r 550 Oak Park Way Apt 7

Gulas Gail & William J studt & phys h 3405 Virginia Av

Guyer Joseph & Rita artist & athom h 4043 S 28th St

Guzmann Trina mgr Sports Unlimited r 2032 Turf Way Apt 230

Haile Jeffrey polof r 2634 6th St Apt 847

Hall Marci muncp ct judge h 34 Magee Ct

Halso Beverly & Jeff pres Haslo Pub Rel & vet r 879 Tichnor Way

Hamill Kimberly mgr Albertson's supm h 811 N Cortez Av

Hamill Margaret studt r 811 N Cortez Av

Hammar Margaret J secy ofer Macy's Dept Store h 1181 6th St

Hana Edward & Jena min Unity Ch of Christianity & athom h 134 Eisen Av

Hana Kyle cust Unity Ch of Christianity r 134 Eisen Av

Hanson Lydia atty r 880 6th St

Hanson Myron widr retd h 880 6th St

Harmon Rhonda watrs Red Lobster r 816 Westwinds Dr Apt 8

Harnish Cheryl & David supvr sales Cargell Corp & state sen h 288 Hillcrest St

Harris Jerry R & Jewel asst mgr House of Pancakes & athom h 2245 Broadway Av

Haselfe Jennifer & Richard athom & pres Haselfe Development Corp h 554 Beloit Av

Haserott Mildred wid ticket agt Greyhound Lines r 411 Wisconsin Av

Haskell Thomas widr lt fire dept h 2482 Elmwood Dr

Hattaway Willie widr retd r 411 Wisconsin Av

Hedricks Donald asst city atty r 4320 Elsie Dr Apt 884

Hermann Andrew J & Jennifer acct & teller First Nat Bank h 1888 Hope Ter

Hernandez Ramon dist atty h 84 Lake Cir

Herndon Joyce atty h 310 Mill Av

Herrin Raymond W univ prof h 410 Park Av

Herwarthe Gregory L & Ruth pres Knight Realty & asst mgr Harrington & Co Investments h 4410 Baltimore Av

Heslinn Allison & Burt clk Kmart & slsr Prudential Bache h 8197 Locke Av

Heslinn Dorothy L mgr Mr. Grocer r 8197 Locke Av

Higginbotham Gladdies Anne mgr Secy Fed Bank h 1886 Hope Ter

Hilten Randall J & Virginia lt fire dept & athom h 915 Baxter Dr

Hoequist Thomas owner/pres The Jewelry Shoppe h 2418 Collins Av

Hoffmann Vivian wid clk Quik Shoppe h 711 Meadow Creek Dr

Hoffsinger Nora wid retd r 411 Wisconsin Av

Holland George & Tanaka dr Greyhound Lines & athom h 4368 Normandy Dr

Holland Keith studt r 410 University Av Apt 11

Holland Maryanne adv exec Wilson Associates h 947 Greenbrier Dr

Holman Evelyn & Leonard athom & phys h 4366 Normandy Dr

Holten Liz owner Holten Doughnuts h 9512 Forest Grove

Holtzclaw Norma J wid slsp ERA Realty h 739 West Av

Horan Roger sheriff's dep r 118 Hillside Dr Apt C3

Howard Sarah polof h 812 Bell Av

Howe Lynn studt r 410 University Av Apt 318

Howland Ruth & Terry owner Blackhawk Hotel & secy ofer Memorial Hospital h 1808 Gladsen Blvd

Hubbard Gary & Peggy supt of city schs & athom h 384 Hilcrest St

Hyde Marie & Roger asst supt of city schs & slsp Ross Chevrolet h 1381 Lakeview Dr

Iacobi Neil atty r 6214 Maldren Av

Innis Alvin & Sarah lt police dept & athom h 1305 Atlantic Blvd

Jabil Stephen dr Becker Express r 800 Crestbrook Loop Apt 314

Jacbos Martha mgr Mom's Donuts r 1889 32nd St

Jaco Milan & Robyn dir Blood Bank & athom h 2202 S 8th St

Jacobs Bill & Carol sgt police dept & dispr Yellow Cab h 2481 Lakeside La

James Edwin cour Pinkerton Security Ser r 1010 Eastview Rd Apt 12

Jamison Peter J & Stephanie R phys & phys/surg Sacred Heart Hosp h 6004 Beech St

Janviere Jeanne techr Colonial Ele Sch r 1883 Hope Ter

Jeffreys Michael dir Humane Society h 2781 Collins Av

Jimenez Edwin C mgr Quik Shoppe r 3611 31st St

Joanakatt Cathy asst dir We Care h 2442 Collins Av

Johnson Edwin & Susan cir ct judge & athom h 148 West Av

Johnson Karen asst supt of city schs h 2344 S 11th St

Johnson Marc const wkr r 2643 Pioneer Rd

Johnson Mary bkpr Vallrath Plastics h 6181 Collins Rd

Jones Danny & Margaret min Metro Life Ch & athom h 1152 Darlington Av

Jones James dr City Cab Co r 977 4th St. Apt 10

Jones Lucinda & Samuel athom & lt USM h 4851 Edmee Cir

Jones Robyn & Sean med tech Mercy Hosp & capt USN h 4216 Winford Cir

Kaeppler JoAnn cir ct judge h 2192 West Av

Kaeppler Lori & Ronald athom & sgt USM h 9540 Holbrook Dr

Kalani Andrew mgr Kalani Bros Bakery h 2481 Kaley Way

Kalani Charles pres Kalani Bros Bakery h 2481 Kaley Way

Kasandra Kelli retd r 9847 Eastbrook La

Kasparov Linda univ dietitian r 9103 Lake St

Keegan Patrick Jr fed atty h 505 Walnut Dr

Keel Sally & Timothy asmbl Cargell Corp & barber Plaza Barber Shop h 1413 Griesi Dr

Kehole Marvin mtce wkr Cargell Corp r 182 W Broadway Av

Kernan Russell mach Vallrath Industries r 168 Lake St

Kindstrom Sarah watrs Steak & Ale h 4828 N Vine St

Kirkmann James dr Yellow Cab r 816 Westwinds Dr Apt 202

Knapp Erik A cook Frisch's Restr r 2314 N 11th St

Knoechel Alvin & Sara plmb & slsr The Daily Courier h 1112 E Lisa La

Kocembra Edward & Heather muncp ct judge & athom h 388 31st St

Koche Ellen Jane atty Neighborhood Law Ofc h 4214 Azalea Ct

Kopez Frank & Lisa city mech & athom h 1067 Eastland Av

Kopp Suzanne wid retd r 4200 S 11th St Quality Trailer Ct

Kopperud Barry widr chief of police h 458 Kaley Way

Kostyn Elizabeth & Ralph E athom & asst supt for ele education city schs h 284 Erie Av

Krueger Melody & William athom & pres Aladdin Paints h 48 Michigan Av

Kubic Marilyn & Ralph both techrs North High Sch h 1452 N 3rd St

Kunze Lauren & Robert athom & mach Vallrath Industries r 94 Jamestown Dr Apt 318

LaCette Cecil serv stat attnd r 2814 Ambassador Dr Apt 61

Lasiter Harriet & James athom & techr Roosevelt Ele Sch h 374 Walnut Dr

Layous Michael E studt r 212 N Wisconsin Av

LeClair George cir ct judge h 501 Mont Clair Blvd

Lee Fred owner/cook Kona Village h 1181 24th St

Leforge Ted dent h 537 Peterson Pl

Leidigh Floyd & Rose const wkr Rittman Engineering Co. & athom h 1812 Dickins Av

Levine Bryce & Trina cir ct judge & athom h 8521 Shady Glen Dr

Levine Ida mgr Mr. Waterbeds r 8521 Shady Glen Dr

Lewis Jacquelin & Jonnie watrs Holiday House & insptr Vallrath Industries h 1840 Maldren Av

Linn Eddy & Marie sgt police dept & athom h 6287 Airport Blvd

Linn Ronald studt r 6287 Airport Blvd

Lo Joan & Roger athom & city colm h 1993 Collins Av

Logass Jeffrey econ Larco Corp h 81 Venetian Way

Lowdes Enrico & Sandra dir Regional Medical Ctr & athom h 77 Maldren Av

Lowrie Catrina phys Regional Medical Ctr r 118 Hillside Dr Apt 74

Lowrie Cynthia studt r 118 Hillside Dr Apt 74

Lozando Marie clinical dir Mercy Hosp r 234 E Markham Dr Apt 4

Lucas Frank cpl hwy patrol h 2417 Country Club Dr

Lydin Charles R mgr LaCorte Printing Co h 888 Melrose Av

Macbos Martha dir of nursing Mercy Hosp h 1889 32nd St

Macco Alan mus r 503 29th St

Madea Ramon exec dir Bon Voyage Travel Agcy r 118 Hillside Dr Apt 606

Mahew Arthur mgr Fische's Bowling Alley h 1918 Pacific Rd

Majorce Albert & Monica archt & athom h 2882 Ambassador Dr

Marcheese Harvey O & Joyce min & organist Faith Baptist Ch h 1481 Cole Rd

Mariston Saundra watrs Freddy's Inn h 822 Kentucky Av

Matros Margo univ prof r 410 University Av Apt 818

McCartney Mildred wrk Holten Doughnuts h 1212 Alexandrea St

McCauley Melvin & Veronica truck dr Becker Express & athom h 540 Osceola Blvd

McDonald Herbert J & Rosalie owner/ mgr Tastee Popcorn & athom h 1842 Hazel La

McDowell William pntr r 1429 Highland Dr

McEwen Lonnie & Victoria techr Washington Jr High Sch & athom h 1024 Nancy Cir

McFarland Charlotte nursing supvr Sand Lake Hosp h 1090 Timberline Trail

McFerren Patrick J widr U.S. postmaster h 1227 Baldwin Dr

McFerren Patti const wkr Rittmann Engineering Co r 816 Westwinds Dr Apt 3

McGorwann Karen cc prof r 4320 Elsie Dr Apt 6

McGowen Bill & Rosalind const wkr Rittmann Engineering Co & maid Hyatt Hotel h 4842 S Conway Rd

McGowin William sheriff's dep h 4224 N 21st St

McGrath Sunni jtr Washington Ele Sch h 109 19th St

McGregor Carol & Samuel mgr trainee Albertson's Supm & cir ct judge h 1501 Southwest Ct

McIntry Eugene & Irene pres McIntry Realty & athom h 2552 Post Road

Meir Sharon pers dir Vallrath Industries r 810 Kalani St Apt 2

Mejian Colette pcpl Risser Ele Sch h 415 Ivanhoe Blvd

Merrit Jacob & June eng WTMC-TV & athom h 301 Wymore Rd

Meserole Alexander & Teresa owner Deerfield Country Club Restaurant

& adv slsr The Daily Courier h 5293 Mandar Dr

Meyer Robert & Sonia sgt USAF & credit mgr Sears h 811 Moor St

Miehee Margaret & Richard athom & asst U.S. postmaster h 1190 Euclid Av

Millan Timothy cook Grande Hotel r 1112 Huron Av

Miller Sharon optn LensCrafters h 2827 Norwell Av

Minh Stephen retd r 410 Hillcrest St Apt 842

Moravchek Albert & Dorothy city ff & clk police dept h 4187 N 14th St

Moronesi Donna slsr Adler Real Estate h 623 N 5th St

Morrell Cathy & Wayne athom & mgr Bon Voyage Travel Agency h 382 Arlington Cir

Morsberger Diedre city supvr elections h 898 Hemlock Dr

Muldaur Eddy studt r 660 S Conway Rd

Murhana Thomas lab Cargell Corp r 40 W Hillier Av

Murphy Joseph & Kathleen dir research Collins Industries & athom h 114 Conway Rd

Murray Blair & Patricia mgr Beneficial Finance & athom h 1748 N 3rd St

Murray Harold & Marty atty & curriculum resource techr h 1801 Hillcrest St

Neely Myron A det police dept h 1048 Jennings Rd

Nego Alan polof r 1840 Wymore Rd Apt 10

Nemnich Harland & Helen electr & retd h 1331 Mt Vernon Blvd

Nicholls Cheryl fed emp h 1287 Belgard Av

Nieves Erik & Krystal univ athletic dir & hairdrsr h 2894 Ambassador Dr

Noffsinger Nora wid retd r 411 Wisconsin Av

Noonan Jack widr det police dept h 5928 Jody Way

Nouse Sharon pilot Aerial Promotions Inc r 4740 Valley View La

Novogreski Harry R & Melba mach
Keller Plastics & athom h 2891
Morris Av

Nunez Carolynn & Roger athom &
eng Kelle-Baldwin Corp h 2820
Norwell Av

Nunziata Carmen h 1410 1st Av

Nyad Carol city colm h 850 Sutter
Loop

Nyer Diana studt r 550 Oak Park Way
Apt 264

Nyer JoAnne sec Washington Ele Sch
r 550 Oak Park Way Apt 264

O'Hara Allison city sec r 4729 Texas Av

Oldaker George polof r 2117 Wisconsin
Av Apt 488

Oldaker Thomas polof r 2117
Wisconsin Av Apt 488

Oliver Franklin R & Jeanette exec Gill
Assoc Inc Pub Rel & athom h 1121
Elm Blvd

Onn Esther & Tom C athom & dir
City Housing Authority h 3869
Jefferson Av

Ortiz Lynn & Randy athom & brklyr
HomeRite Builders r 816
Westwinds Dr Apt 78

Ortson Martha & Thomas J athom
& vp Secy First Bank h 810
N 14th St

Ostreicher Marlene wid cir ct judge
h 449 Ferncreek Cir

Paddock Cynthia & Thomas C credit
mgr Belks Dept Store & mach
Cargell Corp h 1736 Hinkley Rd

Palomino Molly & Ralph R athom &
vp Genesco Inc h 374 Douglas Rd

Parkinson Marie studt r 857 Murray
Rd Apt 204A

Patterson Michelle electn r 1012
Cortez Av Apt 915

Patzell Bruce & MaryAnne carp &
athom h 915 Bishop Dr

Patzell Larry studt r 915 Bishop Dr

Paynick Nina & Stanley techr
Washington Ele Sch & owner
Paynick's Carpets h 901 2nd St

Peerson Marc univ prof h 4851
Edmee Cir

Perakiss Ethel & Michael athom &
atty h 876 Collins Av

Percy John atty h 1037 2nd St

Perez Jason const wkr Wagoner
Development Corp r 2414 Skan Ct

Perez Joseph & Vicki city emp & lt
police dept h 2414 Skan Ct

Petchski Pearl asst cash Morrison's
Cafeteria r 411 Wisconsin Av

Peters Frederick & Rene C pharm
Kmart & pres Humane Society h
484 Sugar Ridge Ct

Peterson Sara wid h 1671 Drexel Av

Pfaff Randall cir ct judge h 2134 Oak
Ridge Rd

Phillips Teresa M clk The Jewelry
Shoppe r 800 Crestbrook Loop
Apt 228

Picardo Marie nurse r 510 Concord
St Apt 48

Picott James & Katherine slsp Allison
Ford & dent asst h 640 Lake Dr

Picott Marilyn cir ct judge h 901
2nd St

Piloto Claire & Kenneth T interior
decorator & atty Piloto & Herndon
h 1472 Bayview Rd

Pinccus Jennifer atty Piloto &
Herndon r 2021 Dyan Way Unit 2

Pinckney Samuel & Terest retd &
athom h 976 Grand Av

Pinero Jim Timmons dvlpr Pinero
Developers h 2411 Windsong Dr

Ping Dorothy & Louis athom & plumb
Lou's Plumbing h 348 Conroy Rd

Plambeck Dolly & Emil athom & supt
City Park Com h 6391 Norris Av

Porej Irvin vp for loans First Fed Sav
& Loan h 112 Anzio St

Povacz Julius city paramedic r 210 E
King Av Apt 4

Proppes Richard E asst mgr Safeway
Supm h 1012 2nd St

Pryor Lynne R const wkr Rittmann
Engineering Co r 2634 6th St Apt 45

Rafelsin Louis lt police dept h 934 Old
Tree Rd

Ramirez Harriet & Luis dent asst &
city colm h 982 Euclid Av

Randolph James const wkr Rittmann Engineering Co r 654 Harrison St

Ray Elizabeth & William David both retd r 550 Oak Park Way Apt 157

Reeves Charlton E & Polly state health ofer & athom h 658 Lennox Av

Reimer Maurice & Mildred acct & athom h 2529 Barbados Av

Richards Patricia r 42 Tusca Trail

Richardson Inez & Thomas E athom & polof h 5421 Jennings Rd

Richbourg Bud & Kathleen owner/mgr Buddy's Lounge & athom h 1014 Turkey Hollow

Richter Robyn Anne retd h 42 Tusca Trail

Riggs Gladies Ann wid retd r 1080 Harvard Rd Apt 4

Rivera Hector phys Medi-First Clinic r 800 Crestbrook Loop Apt 38

Rivera Maxwell tech h 11 Calico Ct

Robbitzsch John W psychiatrist h 1014 Bear Creek Cir

Roehl Cecil & Esther polof & athom h 1228 Euclid Av

Romaine Gerri & Nickolas H athom & wdr h 2876 Post Av

Romansaik Michael const wkr Wagnor Development Corp r 118 Hillside Dr Apt 8

Rudnike Harold & Martha athom & sales mgr Vallrath Industries h 4825 N Vine St

Rue Alexander studt r 8420 University Blvd Apt 218

Rueben James & Elizabeth state sen & atty h 12494 Hillcrest Rd

Ruffenbach Laura univ prof h 6741 Waxwing La

Ruiz George & Lila polof & athom h 263 9th St

Ruiz Guillermo & Harriet asst city med examiner & dir pub affairs Regional Med Ctr h 4718 Bell Av

Rybinski Kim owner Kim's Pets r 2634 6th St Apt 710

Salcido Martha & Tony athom & city ff h 10 Exeter Ct

Saleeby Claire & John athom & lt colonel USA h 626 N 3rd St

Saleeby Henry widr retd r 84 Sunnyvale Rd

Saleeby Olivida & Wesley both retd h 1916 Elizabeth La

Salvatore Hector R & Juanita M atty & athom h 1716 Forest Ridge Rd

Sanchez Gumersinda hairdrsr Lillian's Beauty Salon h 173 Burgasse Rd

Satava Kenneth widr techr Kennedy High Sch h 2204 Marcel Av

Saterwaitte Benjamin widr retd h 307 E King Blvd

Sawyer Betty & Harley athom & techr Kennedy High Sch r 2032 Turf Way Apt 512

Sawyer Claire min Christian Redeemer Ch h 7400 Southland Blvd

Schifini Destiny vp SunBank h 3620 Timber Ter

Schipper Michele studt r 4100 Conway Rd Apt 814

Schweitzer Ralph city building insp r 816 Westwinds Dr Apt 160

Scott Kerry & Nancy slsp Kohlerware & athom h 4189 Hazel St

Scott Milan & Nancy techr Kennedy High Sch & techr Wilson Ele Sch h 20 Magee Ct

Sessions Jeffrey D & Michelle A emer rm phys/dir emer servs Sacred Heart Hosp & athom h 9303 Vale Dr

Shadgott Carol & Frank D athom & phys h 8472 Chestnut Dr

Sharp Lynita L clk Jiffy Foods r 5836 Bolling Dr

Shattuck Christina & Dennis A mgr Perkins Restr & emp city garage h 532 3rd St

Shearer Ethel cocktail watrs Melody Lounge r 408 Kasper Av Apt 718

Shenuski Anita & Frederic cty com & dis mgr IRS h 1230 Embree Cir

Shepard Frank & Helen techr & rept The Daily Courier h 107 Eastbrook Av

Shepard Linn Marie studt r 854 Murray Rd Apt 107B

Sheppard Ronald lt fire dept r 2024 Vincent Rd Apt 1020

Shisenauntt Arthur & Lillian secy consultant & pharm Walgreen h 1243 Washington Av

Shoemaker JoAnn techr Colonial High Sch r 6139 Eastland Dr

Silverbach Daniel G & Jill polof & athom h 3166 Wayne Av

Simmons Karen dist dir Greenpeace r 708 E Lisa La

Simmons Rachel & Wayne athom & slsp Prudential Ins h 708 E Lisa La

Sindelair Elaine & Vernon athom & cty treas h 4164 Mandar Dr

Skinner Dorothy & Roger clk typist Lawson Bros & polof h 2080 Washington Av

Skurow Melvin widr carp h 4138 Hennessy Ct

Slater Carolyn & David athom & chiro h 8443 Turkey Hollow

Smith Grady r 8213 Peach St

Smith Linda M & Ronald studt & city clk h 1814 N 3rd St

Smitkins Marlene & Myron athom & mach Kohlarware h 417 Huron Av

Smythe Asa A & Carol city emp & athom h 4280 Timber Trail

Smythe Terry bartender Bayside Bar & Grill r 4280 Timber Trail

Snow Dale & Terri athom & nurse Mercy Hosp h 4381 Hazel St

Snowdin Elizabeth clk state employ-ment ofc h 952 Kasper Av

Snyder Christina dir pub rel Mercy Hosp h 711 Broadway Av

Sodergreen Karl & Lillian phys & athom h 788 Timber Trail

Sota Mimi dir Drug Abuse Unit Mercy Hosp h 655 Brickell Dr

Stevens Julie Ann mus h 624 N 3rd St

Stockdale George & Lillian capt USM & athom h 472 Bolling Dr

Stoudnaur John & Marlene mgr Rexall Drugs & city med examiner h 1350 41st St

Stovall Iris wid mgr Quikke Clns h 7204 Southland Blvd

Straitten Karen & Walter athom & city building insptr r 4450 Richmond Rd

Stricklan Julian cir ct judge h 4268 Wayne Av

Sulenti Allen D studt r 800 Crestbrook Loop Apt 1010

Sullivan Tony widr fire chief h 863 Benchwood Ct

Svec Wallace A mech Allison Ford r 4320 Elsie Dr Apt 1

Svendson Lillian & Wayne athom & city paramedic h 814 Washington Av

Swaugger Charlotte & Samuel cc prof & rept The Daily Courier h 4987 Huron Dr

Sweers Daniel & Karen fed emp & det police dept h 108 Eastbrook Av

Tai Wendy housekeeper Hilton Hotel r 84 Chestnut Dr

Talbertsen Sarah A artist h 3214 Riverview Dr

Taylor Frederic C r 4828 N Vine St

Taylor Marsha L mgr McDonald's h 2012 Lincoln Av

Temple Roger polof r 2032 Turf Way Apt 818

Thistell Dirk & Mildred R eng Rittmann Industries & counselor Roosevelt High Sch h 528 Kennedy Blvd

Thomas Joseph techr Kennedy High Sch r 2848 Santa Av Apt 2

Thompsen Yvonne studt r 1012 University Av Apt 812

Tifton Albert & Marsha capt fire dept & athom r 2814 Ambassador Dr Apt 417

Tijoriwalli Cathy owner Cathy's Sandwiches r 1320 Embree Cir

Tiller Ida & Julius athom & polof h 539 Sheridan Blvd

Tilman Marion & Randall C athom & city health insptr h 818 N 41st St

Tontenote Eldred L & Lisa mech Ace AutoBody & athom r 2634 6th St Apt 17

Totmann Gloria & Marvin dent asst & secy guard Brinks h 1818 4th St

Tribitt Jane mgr Colonial Apts r 1040 Colonial Way Apt 101

Tuschak Arlene & Joseph master electn & city colm h 2094 Byron Av

Ungarient James R & Margaret both attys The Law Office h 7314 Byron Av

Uosis Bobbie & Michael both retd h 4772 E Harrison Av

Vacante Mary & Umberto athom & technical writer Lockheed Martin h 3202 Joyce St

Vacanti Carlos & Carol polof & athom h 4910 Magee Ct

Valderama Lynn dir secy JC Penney h 1020 Lincoln Av

Valesquez George & Paula archt/ owner Valesquez Design Group & atty univ bd of trustees h 5405 Conway Rd

Van Atti Joseph & Trina city ff & athom h 960 Stratmore Dr

Van Den Shuck Margaret pub serv rep Allstate Ins h 7663 Robinhood Dr

VanPelt Audrey W & James min First United Methodist Ch & serv mgr Lane Toyota h 420 N Wilkes Rd

Vasquez Guillermo & Miranda dir State Dept of Corrections & athom h 2801 Norwell Av

Veit Helel Lynn min First Covenant Ch h 184 Nelson Av

Verdugo Maureen pcpl Kennedy High Sch r 816 Westwinds Dr Apt 482

Verkler LeeAnn univ prof r 800 Crestbrook Loop Apt 10A

Vernell Cathy S dr Yellow Cab r 1010 Vermont Av

Vorholt Andrew A owner/mgr Hallmark Cards h 10 E Lake Rd

Wagnor Kristine & Timothy Sr athom & owner/mgr Tim's Coffee Shop h 418 N Wilkes Rd

Ward Frances & Jon H athom & sgt/ recruiter USA r 3113 DeLaney Av

Ward Lonnie D mtce wkr Colonial Apts r 2814 Ambassador Dr Apt 22

Warniky Clara & Wayne mgr Hertz Rent A Car & polof h 428 N Wilkes Rd

Washington Bruce R atty David Casio & Associates r 1104 Esplada Av Apt 19

Waundry James R & Lisa mgr 2-Hour Clns & athom h 5310 Stratmore Dr

Weber Nancy techr Washington Ele Sch h 44 E Princeton St

Wehr Helen asst cty atty h 1298 Vermont Av

Wei Albert sgt police dept h 964 Jody Way

Wei Constance P & Donald S state rep & atty h 206 N Wabash Av

Weinstein Jeanette techr Colonial High Sch h 6139 Eastland Dr

Weiskoph Herman asst min John Calvin Presbyterian Ch h 4817 Twin Lakes Blvd

Wentilla Lorrie & Reid R athom & pres Keele-Baldwin Corp h 640 Clayton Av

West Billy L asst min John Calvin Presbyterian Ch h 452 Central Blvd

Whidden Bonnie sec cty fair h 2913 Oak La

White Katherine mgr Blackhawk Hotel h 4218 Bell Av

Whitlock Randall vp Wagnor Development Corp h 504 Sutter Loop

Wiess Robert A wkr Belks Moving & Storage r 2032 Turf Way Apt 338

Wilke Alan & Tracie state dir National Federation of Independent Business & techr North Mid Sch h 818 Woodland Dr

Wilke James & Laura sgt police dept & sheriff's dep h 2420 Highland Av

Willging Judy & Jurgen athom & owner/mgr Choice Video Rentals h 2204 S 8th St

Willging Marty & Tessie dir YMCA & athom h 1808 Gadsden Blvd

Williams Jon R tech K107 Radio r 814 Harding Av

Williams Patricia J retd h 1338 Biarritz Dr

Williams Phyllis nurse Lovell Psychiatric Assn r 1220 Jasper Av Apt 56

Williams Thomas & Mary Lee emp Parson's Funeral Home & athom h 2338 Vermont Av

Wong Phyllis & Steven I mgr Sears & athom h 441 S 28th St

Woods Amy dir State Federation of Independent Businesses h 640 Sherwood Dr

Wymann Barbara & Paul athom & mech Layne Toyota h 2020 Lorry La

Yamer Frank studt r 118 Hillside Dr Apt 1020

Yapenco Nancy & Thomas athom & writer h 4941 Pine St

Younge Rachel techr Kennedy High Sch r 3361 Bolling Dr

Zarrinfair Lois retd r 411 Wisconsin Av

Zerwinn Sarah h 2021 Dyan Way

Zito Allen & Linda archt Zito Associates & marketing dir Blood Bank h 818 Jamestown Dr

Zito Nancy & Robert athom & pharm Kmart h 328 Winford Cir

Zozulla Wesley polof h 5219 Ranch Rd

Zumbaddo Carlos mgr cty fair h 1902 White Av

SUMMARY OF AP STYLE

Based on the Associated Press Stylebook and Briefing on Media Law

This appendix summarizes some of the most commonly used rules in The Associated Press Stylebook and Briefing on Media Law. Section and subsection numbers have been added. Most newspapers in the United States—both dailies and weeklies—follow the rules recommended here.

Complete copies of The Associated Press Stylebook and Briefing on Media Law can be ordered from most bookstores.

SECTION 1: ABBREVIATIONS

1.1 COMPANY. The words *company, companies, corporation, incorporated, limited* and *brothers* (*Co., Cos., Corp., Inc., Ltd.* or *Bros.*) should be abbreviated and capitalized when used after the name of a corporate entity. *The board hired him to run Ford Motor Co.* Do not use commas before any of these abbreviations. When the words are used by themselves, do not capitalize or abbreviate: *He joined the company last summer.*

FOR BROADCAST: Use informal constructions of *company* and related words rather than formal company names (*Ford, GM, Apple, McDonald's*) whenever possible. Do not abbreviate *company* or other words that are part of a corporate entity's name and use commas before *limited* and *incorporated* (*Texas Instruments, Incorporated, . . .*).

1.2 DEGREES. Avoid abbreviations for academic degrees in most cases. Instead, use a phrase that identifies the person's degree and academic specialty: *Jane Austin, who has a doctorate in sociology, spoke at the conference.* Because it indicates possession, use an apostrophe in *bachelor's degree, master's degree (or a master's),* or *doctor's degree.* When identifying many individuals by degree on first reference, use abbreviations such as *B.A., M.A., LL.D.* and *Ph.D.* because the preferred form would make the sentence cumbersome.

1.3 DO NOT ABBREVIATE. The words *assistant, association, attorney, building, district, government, president, professor, superintendent* or the days of the week should not be abbreviated in news stories, nor should the ampersand (&) be used in place of *and*.

1.4 INITIALS. Some organizations and government agencies, such as *CIA, FBI, NASA, NBC, YMCA* are so familiar to readers that they may be identified by their initials on first reference. Use the full names of less familiar organizations or agencies on first reference. If the initials would be recognizable to most readers, they may be used on second reference. Generally, do not use periods with initials unless a more specific rule requires them.

FOR BROADCAST: Unless the organization is well known to the public, avoid using initials to refer to organizations. Use hyphens to separate letters that should be read individually (*F-B-I, C-I-A*). Do not put hyphens between letters of initials that are read as a word (*NASA*).

1.5 JUNIOR/SENIOR. *Junior* and *senior* should be abbreviated and capitalized after someone's name: *Martin Luther King Jr.* (omit the comma).

FOR BROADCAST: Spell out *junior* or *senior*: *Martin Luther King Junior* (no comma).

1.6 MPG/MPH. The abbreviations *mpg* (miles per gallon) and *mph* (miles per hour) are acceptable on all references. Neither abbreviation uses periods.

FOR BROADCAST: Do not abbreviate either. Use *miles-per-hour* or *miles-an-hour* or *miles-per-gallon*. Hyphenate the phrases.

1.7 STATES. Spell out the names of states when used in the body of a story whether they stand alone or follow the name of a city or county. Place commas before and after the state name unless it is the last word in the sentence. *The flight originated in Wichita, Kansas, and landed in Columbus, Ohio.* The following 30 city names may be used without the name of the state:

Atlanta	Milwaukee
Baltimore	Minneapolis
Boston	New Orleans
Chicago	New York
Cincinnati	Oklahoma City
Cleveland	Philadelphia
Dallas	Phoenix
Denver	Pittsburgh
Detroit	St. Louis
Honolulu	Salt Lake City
Houston	San Antonio
Indianapolis	San Diego
Las Vegas	San Francisco
Los Angeles	Seattle
Miami	Washington

State names should be abbreviated only when they are used in datelines, tabular matter and short forms for a public official's party affiliation: *Sen. Barbara Boxer, D-Calif.* Use the following abbreviations for states: *Ala., Ariz., Ark., Calif., Colo., Conn., Del., Fla., Ga., Ill., Ind., Kan., Ky., La., Md., Mass., Mich., Minn., Miss., Mo., Mont., Neb., Nev., N.H., N.J.,*

N.M., N.Y., N.C., N.D., Okla., Ore., Pa., R.I., S.C., S.D., Tenn., Vt., Va., Wash., W.Va., Wis. and *Wyo.* Eight state names are never abbreviated: *Alaska, Hawaii, Idaho, Iowa, Maine, Ohio, Texas* and *Utah.* Do not use U.S. Postal Service abbreviations for states, such as *PA, CA, NY,* etc.

FOR BROADCAST: Do not abbreviate state names in the body of a story or a dateline. Always put a comma between the names of the city and the state and after the name of the state, unless that is the last word in the sentence.

1.8 **TITLES.** The following titles should be abbreviated when used before a full name both inside and outside direct quotations: *Dr., Gov., Lt. Gov., Rep., the Rev., Sen.* and certain military titles such as *Pfc., Cpl., Sgt., 1st Lt., Capt., Maj., Lt. Col., Col., Gen., Cmdr.* and *Adm.* These titles are capitalized when abbreviated before a full name, but lowercase and spelled out when standing alone: *Gen. Adam Smith . . . , The general . . .* On second reference, use only the last name: *Smith said . . .* These rules also apply to military-style titles for firefighters or police officers. Do not use courtesy titles—*Mr., Mrs., Ms.*—except in direct quotations or when necessary to distinguish between two people with the same last name, such as a married couple.

FOR BROADCAST: Abbreviate *Mr., Mrs., Ms.* and *Dr.* when used before a name. Spell out any other titles.

1.9 **U.N./U.S.** *U.N.* and *U.S.* are acceptable as a noun or adjective for *United Nations* and *United States,* respectively (no space between initials). Omit the periods when used in headlines (*UN, US*).

FOR BROADCAST: *U-N* is acceptable in all references for *United Nations* and may be used as either a noun or an adjective. Spell out *United States* as a noun. Use *U-S* as an adjective before a noun.

SECTION 2: ADDRESSES

2.1 **ADDRESSES.** Always use figures for an address number, including numbers less than 10: *321 W. Main St.; 8 Strawberry Circle.*

FOR BROADCAST: Use addresses only when they are specifically relevant to the story. Spell out *one* through *eleven.* Use numerals for *12* and higher. Hyphenate numbers read as two-digit groups: *17-43 Willow Avenue.*

2.2 **DIRECTIONS.** Compass points used to indicate directional ends of a street or quadrants of a city in a numbered address should be abbreviated: *671 W. King St.; 38 S. 42nd St.; 600 33rd St. N.W.* If the address number is omitted, spell out both the compass point and street: *West King Street; 33rd Street Northwest.*

FOR BROADCAST: Spell out directional terms: *Six-71 West King Street; 600 33rd Street Northwest.*

2.3 **STREETS.** Spell out and capitalize *First* through *Ninth* when used as street names; use figures with two letters for *10th* and above: *101 Eighth Ave.; 2055 21st St.* Abbreviate *Ave., Blvd.* and *St.* only when used with a numbered address: *1600 Pennsylvania Ave.* Spell out and capitalize *Avenue*, *Boulevard* and *Street* when part of a formal street name without a number: *Pennsylvania Avenue*. Always spell out words such as *alley*, *circle*, *drive*, *road*, *terrace*, etc.

FOR BROADCAST: Use words for streets named *First* through *Eleventh*. Use numerals for streets *12th* or higher. Spell out all terms for streets—such as *avenue*, *boulevard*, *circle*, *road*, *street*, *terrace*—in all contexts.

SECTION 3: CAPITALIZATION

In general, avoid unnecessary capitals. Use a capital letter only if it is required by one of the principles listed here.

3.1 **ACADEMIC DEPARTMENTS.** Use lowercase when mentioning an academic department, except for words that are proper nouns or adjectives: *the department of sociology, the sociology department, the department of English, the English department.*

3.2 **AWARDS/EVENTS/HOLIDAYS/WARS.** Capitalize awards (*Medal of Honor, Pulitzer Prize*), historic events (*Treaty of Versailles*), periods (*the Great Depression, Prohibition*), holidays (*Christmas Eve, Mother's Day*) and wars (*the Civil War, World War II*).

3.3 **BIBLE/GOD.** Capitalize *Bible* (no quotation marks) to refer to the Old and New Testaments. Capitalize related terms, such as *the Gospels, the Scriptures*. Capitalize *God* to refer to any monotheistic deity. Lowercase pronouns referring to the deity (such as *he, his, thee*). The preferred spelling for the Muslim holy book is *Quran*.

3.4 **BRAND NAMES.** Capitalize brand names: *Coca-Cola, Cadillac, Samsung, Nike*. Lowercase generic terms: *soda; a car, athletic shoes*. Use brand names only if they are essential to a story. Do not use brand names when a generic name should be used: Use *photocopy* and not *Xerox* when referring to copying documents.

3.5 **BUILDINGS/ROOMS.** Capitalize the proper names of buildings, including the word *building* if it is an integral part of the proper name: *the Chrysler Building*. Do not abbreviate *building*. Capitalize the names of specially designated rooms: *Blue Room, Oval Office*. Use figures (for room numbers) and capitalize *room* when used with a figure: *Room 2, Room 211*.

FOR BROADCAST: Capitalize *room* and spell out numbers below 12. Capitalize numbers that are spelled out: *Room Eight, Room 213*.

3.6 **CAPITOL.** Capitalize *U.S. Capitol* and *the Capitol* when referring to the building in Washington, D.C., or to the capitol of a specific state.

3.7 **CONGRESS.** Capitalize *U.S. Congress* and *Congress* when referring to the U.S. Senate and House of Representatives. Lowercase when used as a synonym for *convention*. Lowercase *congressional* unless it is part of a proper name: *congressional salaries, the Congressional Research Service*.

3.8 **CONSTITUTION.** References to the *U.S. Constitution* should be capitalized with or without the *U.S.* as a modifier. Lowercase *constitutional* in all uses. Also capitalize *Bill of Rights, First Amendment* (and all other amendments to the Constitution). Use numerals for amendments after the Ninth: *The 13th Amendment abolished slavery.* When referring to the constitutions of states or other countries, capitalize only when used with the name of the state or country: *French Constitution, Montana Constitution.*

FOR BROADCAST: *U-S Constitution.*

3.9 **DIRECTIONS/REGIONS.** When indicating a compass direction, lowercase *north, south, northeast,* etc.; capitalize when used as nouns or adjectives to designate geographical regions, including widely known sections of states or cities: *the South, the Northwest, the Atlantic Coast states, Sun Belt, Midwest. She moved west,* but *She moved to the West Coast. The thunderstorm is heading southeast. The North was victorious. She has a Southern accent. He grew up on the East Side of New York City. The earthquake shook Southern California.*

3.10 **DO NOT CAPITALIZE.** The following generally are not capitalized, unless part of a formal name: *administration, first lady, first family, government, presidential, presidency, priest,* seasons of the year (*summer, fall, winter, spring*), and years in school (*freshman, sophomore, junior, senior*). Lowercase the common-noun elements of all names in plural uses: the *Democratic and Republican parties, King and Queen streets, lakes Michigan and Superior.*

3.11 **EARTH.** Generally lowercase *earth;* capitalize when used as the proper name of the planet: *The satellite fell to Earth. She has an earthy quality about her.*

3.12 **GOVERNMENT.** The full names of government agencies should be capitalized: *U.S. Department of Defense, Defense Department, Texas Department of Public Safety, Public Safety Department.* Capitalize *city, county, state* and *federal* when part of a formal name: *Cook County, Federal Housing Administration.* Also capitalize *city council, county commission, city hall, police department, legislature, assembly* and all other names for governmental agencies when part of a proper name: *Chicago City Council, New York Police Department.* Retain capitalization if the reference is to a specific city council, legislature, police department, etc., but the context does not require the specific name: *The City Council met last night.* Generally, lowercase elsewhere: The *council approved the ordinance.* Do not capitalize *state, city, county, town, village* or similar words when they are used as adjectives to identify a jurisdiction: *the state Department of Roads, the county Sheriff's Department, the city of Chicago.*

FOR BROADCAST: Always refer to governmental bodies by the name that is most familiar to the audience. Capitalize full proper names, and hyphenate *U-S* when that's part of the name. *U-S Defense Department.*

3.13 **HIGHWAYS.** Use numerals even for highways numbered 1 through 9. Capitalize *highway* or *route* for highways identified by number. Use *U.S., interstate, state* or a state name to differentiate highways: *U.S. Highway 6, U.S. Route 30, U.S. 36, Pennsylvania 533, Pennsylvania Route 533, state Route 533, Route 533, Interstate Highway 81, Interstate 81.* On second reference only for Interstate: *I-81.* When a letter is appended to a number, capitalize it but do not use a hyphen: *Route 1A.*

FOR BROADCAST: Spell out highway numbers *one* through *eleven*; use numerals for larger numbers: *U-S Highway One, state Route 34.* Hyphenate appended letters to show they are read separately: *Route One-A.*

3.14 **MILITARY.** Capitalize names of the U.S. armed forces: *the U.S. Army, the Navy, Marine regulations.* Use lowercase for the forces of other nations: *the French army.*

FOR BROADCAST: *U-S Navy.*

3.15 **NATIONALITIES/RACE.** The proper names of nationalities, races, tribes, etc., should be capitalized: *Arab, Caucasian, Sioux.* However, lowercase *black, white, mulatto.* Do not use the word *colored.* In the United States, the word is considered derogatory. A person's race should be identified only when it is pertinent to the story, usually when the story involves some historic event (*Sonia Sotomayor is the first Hispanic to sit on the U.S. Supreme Court*), describes a missing person or a suspect in a crime, or reports on a demonstration or disturbance involving race or civil rights.

3.16 **PLURALS.** To form the plural of a number, add *s* (no apostrophe): *1920s.* To form the plural of a single letter, add *'s.* To form the plural of multiple letters, add only *s: Mind your p's and q's. He learned his ABCs.*

3.17 **POLITICAL PARTIES.** Both the name of a political party and the word *party* should be capitalized: *the Republican Party.* Also capitalize *Communist, Conservative, Democratic, Socialist,* etc., when they refer to a specific party or to individuals who are members of it. Lowercase when they refer to a political philosophy. Do not capitalize *tea party* unless it is part of an organizational name: *The candidate said she generally supported the tea party movement. The candidate welcomed the support of the Tea Party Express.* After an officeholder's name, use this short form, set off by commas, to identify the person's home state and party: *D-Minn., R-Ore., Sen. Marco Rubio, R-Fla., said. . . .* Note that no period is used after the letter identifying the official's political party.

FOR BROADCAST: Use party affiliation only when it is relevant to the story. Do not abbreviate the name of the party or state: *Kentucky Republican Senator Mitch McConnell; Governor Andrew Cuomo, a New York Democrat, said . . . .*

3.18 **PROPER NOUNS.** Proper nouns that constitute the unique identification of a specific person, place or thing should be capitalized: *Michelle, Philadelphia, the Mississippi River.* Lowercase common nouns when they stand alone in subsequent references: *the party, the river, the city.*

3.19 SATAN. Capitalize *Satan* but lowercase *devil* and *satanic.*

3.20 TITLES. Capitalize formal titles when used immediately before a name: *Mayor, Chairman, former President George W. Bush.* Lowercase formal titles used after a name, alone or in constructions that set them off from a name by commas. Use lowercase at all times for terms that are job descriptions rather than formal titles: *movie star George Clooney; peanut farmer Jimmy Carter; Darrell E. Issa, a representative from California,* . . . Do not capitalize or abbreviate *professor* when used before a name.

SECTION 4: NUMERALS

4.1 GENERAL RULE: Whole numbers below 10 are spelled out, but use figures for 10 and above. Exceptions: Figures are used for all ages, betting odds, dates, dimensions, percentages, speeds, times and weights. Spell out a number at the beginning of a sentence, except for a calendar year: *Twenty-five students joined the club. 2008 saw the economy collapse.* Avoid beginning a sentence with a large number or a calendar year: WRONG: *Three thousand thirty-three people attended the conference.* BETTER: *More than 3,000 people attended the conference. The economy collapsed in 2008.* For ordinal numbers, spell out *first* through *ninth,* and use figures and *-st, -nd, -rd* or *-th* for larger numbers: *31st, 75th.*

FOR BROADCAST: Spell out *one* through *eleven.* Use numerals for 12 through 999. For numbers above 999, use words or combinations of numerals and words, such as *thousands, millions, billions, trillions,* but use commas to separate hundreds from thousands, thousands from millions, etc. Use hyphens to combine numerals and the words *hundred* or *thousand: Nearly two-thousand students attended the lecture. Authorities estimated 12-thousand homes were damaged by the storm. More than 85-thousand, 500 people attended the game.*

Hyphens are not needed with the words *million, billion* or *trillion: The satellite will travel eight (m) million miles. The state has a 300 (b) billion dollar budget.*

Use the same rules for ordinals. Spell out *first* through *eleventh.* Use numerals and *-st, -nd, -rd* or *-th* for larger numbers: *12th; 21st; 32nd; 43rd; 77th.*

4.2 AGES. Use figures for all ages. Hyphenate ages expressed as adjectives before a noun or as substitutes for a noun: *a 7-year-old girl, the 7-year-old,* but *the girl is 7 years old. The boy, 5, has a sister, 10. The man is in his 50s* (no apostrophe).

FOR BROADCAST: Follow the general rule of spelling out numbers less than 12: *the five-year-old girl, The suspect is 36 years old.* Do not follow a person's name with the age set off with commas. WRONG: *Smith, 26, has two children.* BETTER: *Smith is 26. He has two children.*

4.3 CENTS. Use numerals for amounts less than a dollar and spell out the word *cents* and lowercase: *2 cents, 12 cents.* Use the $ sign and decimal system for larger amounts: *$2.01.*

FOR BROADCAST: Always spell out *cents.* Spell out amounts less than 12: *five cents*; *25 cents.*

4.4 DECADES/CENTURY. Use Arabic figures to indicate decades of history. Use an apostrophe to indicate numbers that are left out; show the plural by adding the letter *s*: *the 1920s, the '20s, the Roaring '20s, the mid-1920s.* Lowercase *century* and spell out numbers less than 10: *the first century, the 21st century.*

FOR BROADCAST: Spell out centuries under 12th and lowercase *century*: *eleventh century, 19th century.* Use figures to indicate decades. Place an apostrophe after the figures but before the *s.* For the late 20th and early 21st centuries, use only the decade: *the 60's.* For earlier centuries, use the century as well as the decade number: *the 1890's*; *the 1770's.*

4.5 DOLLARS. Lowercase *dollars.* Use figures and the $ sign in all except casual references or amounts without a figure: *The dinner cost $9.75. Dollars are flowing overseas.* For amounts of more than $1 million, use the $ sign and numerals up to two decimal places: *He is worth $5.85 million. He proposed a $500 billion budget. The national debt exceeds $20 trillion.* For foreign currencies, use lowercase and spell out the name of the currency after the amount: *5 euros*; *24 pounds.*

FOR BROADCAST: Always spell out *dollars,* and never use the $ sign. Use words for amounts less than 12: *five dollars*; *500-thousand dollars.* Use commas to separate units: *five dollars, ten cents*; *135-thousand, 312 dollars.* For large amounts, round and use a *more than* or *almost* construction: *more than five (m) million dollars.* Avoid decimal constructions for amounts in the millions or billions: *three (b) billion, 200 (m) million dollars*; NOT *three-point-two (b) billion dollars.* Make references to monetary amounts as informal as possible: *two and a-half dollars.* Explain large amounts in terms people can understand, such as ratios or per-capita amounts.

4.6 ELECTION RETURNS/VOTE TABULATIONS. Separate vote totals with the word *to* (not a hyphen) for reporting results with 1,000 or more votes: *Hillary Clinton won the popular vote from Donald Trump 65,853,516 to 62,984,825.* For results that involve fewer than 1,000 votes on each side, use a hyphen: *Trump defeated Clinton in the electoral vote 304-227; The Senate voted 61-39 to pass the bill.* Spell out numbers below 10 in other phrases related to voting: *the five-vote majority.*

FOR BROADCAST: Use numbers sparingly, and use percentages rather than raw totals: *Clinton received 48 percent of the popular vote to 46 percent for Trump.* Always try to simplify.

4.7   FRACTIONS. Amounts less than one should be spelled out, using hyphens between the words: *one-third, three-fifths, nine-sixteenths.* For precise amounts larger than one, convert to decimals whenever practical: *4.25, 6.5.*

FOR BROADCAST: Spell out, using hyphens between units: *four and a-half; two-thirds.* Simplify fractions where possible: *quarter of a dollar.* Spell out decimal amounts and the word *point.* Use *oh* in place of *zero: four-point-two; point-oh-eight.* Use decimal values only when directly relevant to the story. Convert to fractions when possible.

4.8   MEASUREMENTS/DIMENSIONS. Use figures and spell out *inches, feet, yards,* etc. Hyphenate adjectival forms before nouns: *the 5-foot-6-inch man, the 9-by-12-foot rug.* Do not hyphenate in other constructions: *He is 5 feet 6 inches tall; The rug is 9 feet by 12 feet.*

FOR BROADCAST: Spell out numbers less than 12. Use commas to separate units of measure. Hyphenate adjectival forms: *He is five feet, six inches tall; The five-foot-six man. . . .*

4.9   MILLION/BILLION/TRILLION. Use numerals followed by *million, billion* or *trillion: The deficit dropped to $500 billion last year.* Do not go beyond two decimals: *8.62 million people, $3.75 billion.* Decimals are preferred where practical: *1.5 million,* not *1 1/2 million.* Do not drop the word *million* or *billion* in the first figure of a range: *She is worth from $6 million to $8 million,* not *$6 to $8 million,* unless you really mean $6.

FOR BROADCAST: For *million, billion* and *trillion* put the first letter in parentheses before the word. This helps avoid typographical errors: *15 (b) billion dollars, five (m) million miles.*

4.10   NUMBER. Use *No.* as the abbreviation for *number* in conjunction with a figure to indicate position or rank: *No. 1 team, No. 3 choice.*

FOR BROADCAST: Do not abbreviate *number: the Number 1 draft choice.*

4.11   ODDS. Betting odds should be expressed in figures and hyphenated: *The odds were 2-1. He won despite 3-2 odds against him.*

FOR BROADCAST: Use figures, hyphens and the word *to: 3-to-2 odds; the odds were 3-to-2.* Spell out the numbers when a sentence starts with odds: *Three-to-two were the odds on success.*

4.12   PERCENTAGES. Use figures: *3 percent, 4.75 percent.* For amounts less than 1 percent, put a zero before the decimal point: *The state raised gas taxes 0.8 percent.* The word *percent* should be spelled out; never use the *%* symbol.

FOR BROADCAST: Spell out *percent* and numbers less than 12: *eleven percent; seven and a-half percent.* Repeat percent with each figure unless the sentence is too cumbersome.

4.13   POLITICAL DISTRICTS: Use numerals: *1st Ward, Precinct 34, 10th Congressional District.*

FOR BROADCAST: Spell out numerals below 12: *First Ward, Tenth Congressional District.*

4.14   **PROPORTIONS:** Use figures for all proportions: *6 parts per million.*

FOR BROADCAST: Spell out numerals below 12: *six parts per million.*

4.15   **RATIOS.** Ratios should use numerals and hyphens: *The 2-1 ratio.* If the numbers follow the word *ratio*, use *to* and hyphens: *The ratio was 2-to-1, a ratio of 2-to-1.*

FOR BROADCAST: Spell out numerals below 12 and separate them with hyphens and the word *to. It was a 50-to-one ratio.* Use *ratio* or *margin* where there might be confusion between a ratio and an actual figure.

4.16   **SCORES.** Use figures for all scores. Put a hyphen between the winning and losing team totals: *The Phillies defeated the Cardinals 6-4. The Patriots scored a 21-7 victory over the Broncos. The golfer had a 5 on the last hole but finished with a 2-under-par score.*

FOR BROADCAST: Use figures only (an exception to the general rule on numerals), and use the word *to* with hyphens: *The Giants beat the Dodgers 2-to-1,* or *The final score was San Francisco 2, Los Angeles 1.* When reporting only one team's score, however, spell out amounts less than 12: *The Orioles scored seven runs in the eighth inning to beat the Twins.*

4.17   **TEMPERATURES.** Use figures for all temperatures except *zero* and spell out *degrees: The high Monday was 10 degrees.* Use a word, not a minus sign, to indicate temperatures below zero: *minus 10 degrees.*

FOR BROADCAST: Spell out numbers less than 12. *The overnight low was minus five degrees.*

4.18   **WEIGHTS.** Use figures for all weights. *The baby weighs 9 pounds, 13 ounces.*

FOR BROADCAST: Spell out numbers below 12: *The baby weighs nine pounds, 13 ounces.*

SECTION 5: PUNCTUATION

5.1   **COMMA**

5.1.1   **AGE.** Use commas before and after a person's age when it follows the name: *Barack Obama, 47, was sworn in as president of the United States.*

FOR BROADCAST: Put ages and hometowns in separate sentences rather than setting them off with commas. *The university has named Regina McCarthy dean of the College of Fine Arts. She is 52 years old and comes from Madison, Wisconsin.*

5.1.2   **CITY-STATE.** Use commas before and after the name of or abbreviation for a state when it follows the name of a city or county, unless the state name or abbreviation ends the sentence: *Thompson lived in Little Rock, Arkansas, for 20 years before he moved to Loraine, Ohio.* Use parentheses if the state name is inserted in a proper name: *the Charlotte (North Carolina) Observer.*

5.1.3 CONJUNCTIONS. When clauses that could stand as independent sentences are joined by a conjunction (*and, or, for, nor, but, so, yet*), place a comma before the conjunction: *Congress must approve the emergency funding, or the federal government will have to shut down. Childhood obesity is becoming more common, and doctors are seeing more patients with diabetes.*

5.1.4 HOMETOWN. Put commas before and after a person's hometown when it follows the name: *Sgt. Roger Walker, Houston, and Pvt. Wanda Lu, San Francisco, were the two soldiers killed in the attack.* The better practice, however, is to use an "of" construction, which eliminates the need for commas: *Sgt. Roger Walker of Houston and Pvt. Wanda Lu of San Francisco were the two soldiers killed in the attack.*

5.1.5 QUOTATION. When the attribution precedes a single sentence of direct quotation, put a comma after the attribution: *Gingrich said, "I am tired of the elite media's protecting Barack Obama by attacking Republicans."* Never put a comma at the beginning of a partial direct quotation or an indirect quotation: *Gingrich said he was tired of "the elite media's protecting Barack Obama." Gingrich said the elite media were protecting Barack Obama.* If the attribution concludes a sentence of direct quotation, change the period at the end of the quotation to a comma and put the period after the attribution. *"I am tired of the elite media's protecting Barack Obama by attacking Republicans," Gingrich said.* Remember that periods and commas always go inside closing quotation marks. *"Because of the budget crisis," the governor said, "the state will have to cut spending on the university."*

FOR BROADCAST: Use paraphrases or tape in broadcast stories rather than direct quotations. If a direction quotation is necessary for a story, punctuate it as it would be for print, but introduce it with a phrase that makes clear to listeners that the words are those of the source, not the reporter. *In the words of football coach Paul Brown, "A winner never whines."*

5.1.6 SERIES. Separate elements in a series with commas. Do not, however, put a comma before a conjunction: *His favorite teams are the Red Sox, the Braves and the Cardinals. She said she would vote for Richards, Noto or Ashton.*

5.2 COLON

5.2.1 LISTS. Colons frequently are used to introduce lists, tabulations or texts that follow a full sentence: *The candidate named three national leaders he hoped to emulate: Thomas Jefferson, Abraham Lincoln and Franklin D. Roosevelt.*

5.2.2 QUOTATIONS. Place a colon at the end of attribution that precedes a direct quotation of two or more sentences. *Obama said: "Change will not come if we wait for some other person or some other time. We are the ones we've been waiting for. We are the change that we seek."* Colons should also be used at the end of paragraphs that introduce a paragraph of direct quotation.

5.3   **DASH.** Use dashes before and after material inserted in a sentence that abruptly changes the thought: *The mayor agreed to the tax hike—one of the largest in the city's history—as necessary to balance the budget.* Dashes are also used to set off a series in the middle of a sentence: *The most valuable players on the team—Gordon, Hosmer and Perez—stayed healthy all season.*

5.4   **ELLIPSIS.** Use an ellipsis (. . .) to indicate an omission of one or more words from a direct quotation or text: *"Their pitcher . . . just dominated our batters," Wilson said.* Do not use an ellipsis at the beginning or end of a direct quotation.

5.5   **EXCLAMATION POINT.** The exclamation point (!) ends a sentence that expresses a high degree of emotion, surprise or incredulity. *"What a horrible fate!" she exclaimed.* Note that the exclamation point replaces the comma when attribution follows the quotation. Do not use exclamation points for sentences that express mild emotion.

5.6   **HYPHEN.** The hyphen (-) joins words that form compound modifiers before a noun: *man-eating shark, full-time employee.* Do not hyphenate when the modifiers follow the noun: *The employee works full time.* If a phrase that would be hyphenated before a noun follows some form of the verb *to be*, hyphenate it: *The employee is full-time.* Hyphens are also used with some prefixes and suffixes.

5.7   **PERIOD.** Use periods at the end of declarative sentences, mild imperatives, indirect questions and rhetorical questions that are more suggestions than questions: *The council voted to raise police salaries. Kline asked why Main Street had not been repaved. Why don't we take a vote.*

5.8   **POSSESSIVES.** See Appendix C for the rules for forming possessives.

5.9   **QUESTION MARK.** Place question marks (?) at the end of sentences that ask direct questions. *Who scored the winning touchdown? "What time is the meeting?" he asked.* Note that the question mark replaces the comma when attribution follows the question.

5.10   **QUOTATION MARKS.** See Chapter 10 for guidelines on the use and placement of quotation marks.

5.11   **SEMICOLON.**

5.11.1 SERIES. Semicolons separate elements in a series when at least one of the elements contains internal punctuation: *Stewart sent the plans to Allied Industries in Overland Park, Kansas; Panhandle Technologies in Pensacola, Florida; and*

Western Electronics in Bakersfield, California. In such sentences, the semicolon is used before the *and* that introduces the final element in the series.

5.11.2   INDEPENDENT CLAUSES. Use semicolons to join closely related independent clauses with or without a conjunctive adverb (*however, therefore, moreover, nevertheless*) between them: *The House passed the bill; however, the president said he would veto it. The truck swerved sharply; it hit the bridge railing.*

5.12   IN GENERAL FOR BROADCAST COPY. The rules for punctuating broadcast copy are generally the same as those for punctuating print copy. But the broadcast writer should keep in mind that the purpose of punctuation is to make it easier for another person to read the story.

SECTION 6: PREFERRED SPELLINGS

aboveboard (one word)

adviser

advisory

afterward (not afterwards)

all right (never alright)

amok

ashtray

ax (not axe)

baby-sit, baby-sitting, baby sitter

backward (not backwards)

bellwether

bloodbath

brand-new (adjective)

cellphone

changeable

check-in (as a noun or adjective); check in (as a verb)

checkout (as a noun or adjective); check out (as a verb)

crawfish

damage (for destruction); damages (for a court award)

database, data center

daylong, dayslong

daytime

dissociate (not "disassociate")

doughnut

e-book

email

e-reader

farmworker

flood plain

floodwaters

forward (not forwards)

freelancer (noun); freelance (verb and adjective)

glamour (noun); glamorous (adjective)

goodbye

goodwill

gray (not grey)

home page

judgment

kidnap, kidnapped, kidnapping, kidnapper

know-how

lawsuit

life-size

life span

lifestyle

lifetime

likable (not likeable)

livable

login (noun), log in (verb) also logon and logoff

memorandum, memorandums

menswear (not *men's wear*)

nationwide (also "citywide," "statewide" and "worldwide")

nighttime

offline, online

overall

percent (one word, spelled out)

pipeline

policymaker

politicking

pothole

primetime (noun), prime-time (adjective)

protester

questionnaire

Quran (not "Koran")

recur, recurred, recurring (not *reoccur*)
referable
sacrilegious
salable
semitrailer or semitractor-trailer
  (not *semi-tractor trailer*)
sizable
sport utility vehicle
straitjacket
successor
supersede
teen, teenager (noun), teenage (adjective) (Do not use
  "teen-aged.")
theater (except when "theatre" is part
  of a proper name)
throwaway (noun and adjective)
timeout (one word)

total, totaled, totaling
travel, traveled, traveling, traveler
T-shirt (always capitalize the first "t")
underway (always one word)
upward (not *upwards*)
U-turn
vacuum
vice president (no hyphen)
web/World Wide Web
webpage, website
web address, web browser
whiskey
whistleblower
whitewash (noun, verb and adjective)
**Preferred spellings for
broadcast copy:**
Babysitter (one word)
Teen, teen-ager, teen-age

SECTION 7: TIME

7.1 **HOURS AND MINUTES.** Use numerals and *a.m.* or *p.m.* for all clock times, except *noon* and *midnight*. Separate hours and minutes with a colon: *1:27 p.m., 8:30 a.m.* If the time is on the hour, do not use a colon and zeros: *2 p.m., 7 a.m.* The following expressions are redundant and should not be used: *12 midnight, 9 a.m. this morning, 8:30 p.m. tomorrow night.* When using both time and day, put the hour before the day: *2 p.m. Wednesday.* Use lowercase letters and periods for *a.m.* and *p.m.*

Use clock time whenever it helps the reader better understand the event or sequence described in the story. Sometimes words or phrases such as *dawn* or *late afternoon* are more effective.

FOR BROADCAST: Use numerals for clock times, except for *noon* and *midnight.* As in print style, separate hours and minutes with a colon, but use a hyphen, rather than periods with *a-m* and *p-m*: *8:30 p-m, 10:17 a-m.* An exact time of day rarely is necessary for a broadcast story. Use it only if is important to the story. Otherwise, use phrases like *shortly before dawn, early evening, midafternoon.* For some stories it is necessary to specify a time zone, such as when a story occurs in one time zone but may interest or affect people in other time zones. Capitalize the full names of time zones and the short forms as well: *Eastern Standard Time, Mountain Daylight Time, Central time, Pacific time.* Use capitals and hyphens for abbreviations of time zones: *E-S-T; M-D-T.*

7.2 **DAYS.** For an event that occurred or will occur within seven days of the day of publication, use the day of the week: *The City Council will decide on the budget at Tuesday's meeting.* Do not use *today, yesterday, tomorrow, tonight* or similar words except in direct quotations or in phrases that do not refer to a specific date: *Economic challenges today are greater than those of the 1970s.* Phrases like *last Thursday* or *next Monday* are redundant. Just use the day of the week and omit words like *last* or *next.*

FOR BROADCAST: The words *today, this morning, tonight, yesterday* and *tomorrow* may be used in broadcast copy. When referring to days within seven days of the broadcast, use the day of the week. Do not use redundant constructions like *next Wednesday* or *last Saturday*; the tense of the verb conveys that information. *The mayor spoke Tuesday. The mayor will speak Tuesday.*

7.3   **DATES.** If the story refers to something that happened or will happen more than seven days before or after the day of publication, use the month and day: *Voters will not go to the polls until Nov. 3.* Never add *-st, -nd, -rd* or *-th* to a date in Arabic numerals in print copy. Use month, date and year for dates outside the current calendar year. *The Allied invasion of France in World War II was on June 6, 1944.*

FOR BROADCAST: The dates first through eleventh should be spelled out and capitalized: *The deadline for filing for the City Council race is March First.* For dates above eleventh, use numerals with *-st, -nd, -rd* or *-th: Income tax returns must be postmarked no later than April 15th.*

7.4   **MONTHS.** The names of months are always capitalized. Never abbreviate the name of a month when it stands alone or with just a year: *The Iraq War began in March 2003 and ended in December 2011.* If a specific date is used with the name of a month, use the following abbreviations: *Jan., Feb., Aug., Sept., Oct., Nov.* and *Dec. Valentine's Day is Feb. 14.* Do not abbreviate *March, April, May, June* or *July*, even when used with a specific date. *The company's fiscal year ends June 30.*

When using only month and year, no comma is necessary. *September 2001 was filled with sadness.* When a specific date is used with the month and year, use commas before and after the year: *Sept. 11, 2001, was the date of the terrorist attacks.*

FOR BROADCAST: Never abbreviate the names of months.

SECTION 8: TITLES

8.1   **GENERAL RULE.** Only formal titles that immediately precede a name should be capitalized. The title should be abbreviated if it is one of those listed in rule 1.8: *Gov. John Kasich.* Abbreviate only those titles that have accepted abbreviations. Spell out and lowercase titles when used as appositives or when the name is an appositive for the title: *John Kasich, the governor, will sign the bill. The governor, John Kasich, will sign the bill.* Titles that follow a name or that are used alone should be lowercase and spelled out. *John Kasich, governor of Ohio, delivered the keynote address. The proposal won the support of the senator from New Mexico.* Do not use a person's title on second reference: *Sen. Shelby Watson denied the allegation. Watson insisted he had been unaware of his aide's activities.* Titles that are abbreviated when used before a name should be abbreviated when used before a name in direct quotations: *"Gov. Thatcher's tax-cut plan will deprive schools of the money they need," the superintendent said.*

FOR BROADCAST: Formal titles should be capitalized when used immediately before a name, but long titles should be avoided or condensed where possible: *Defense Secretary Leon Panetta,* instead of *Secretary of Defense Leon Panetta.* If a title cannot be easily shortened, place it in a separate sentence: *Wanda Cummings said the university's plan would help students graduate on time. Cummings is the associate vice chancellor for academic affairs.*

8.2   **BOY/GIRL.** These terms are acceptable for people younger than 18. For people 18 or older, use *man, woman, young man* or *young woman.*

8.3   **COMPOSITIONS.** Capitalize the main words of titles, including any initial articles and any prepositions or conjunctions of four or more letters. Put the title in quotation marks. These rules apply to titles of books, operas, computer games, plays, albums, songs, movies, radio and television programs, lectures, speeches and works of art: *He enjoyed "The Raiders of the Lost Ark" and all its sequels. Barack Obama wrote "Dreams From My Father." The exhibition will include Vincent Van Gogh's "Starry Night."* Never underline or italicize composition titles.

8.4   **COURTESY TITLES.** Do not use the courtesy titles *Miss, Mr., Mrs.* or *Ms.* on any reference. On first reference, identify people by first name, middle initial and last name. On subsequent references, use the last name only. A person's marital status should not be mentioned unless it is clearly pertinent to the story. Use courtesy titles only if they are part of a direct quotation or after first reference for a woman who specifically asks to be identified as *Mrs. Johnson* or *Ms. Johnson.*

The first reference to a couple should use both first names: *Barack and Michelle Obama.* Use first names and last names on subsequent references if it is necessary to distinguish two people with the same last name, such as wife and husband or brothers and sisters.

FOR BROADCAST: Generally, do not use courtesy titles. Use first and last name on first reference and last name alone on subsequent references. Do not use courtesy titles on subsequent references unless they are necessary to distinguish two or more people with the same last name. Readability should be the guide.

8.5   **INITIALS.** Middle initials help identify individuals and distinguish people with similar names: *George H.W. Bush, George W. Bush.* In general, use middle initials to help identify specific individuals. Middle initials are most important in stories reporting when people are accused of crime or casualty lists from accidents or disasters. Initials should not be used with the names of people who are widely known by first and last name only: *LeBron James, Jennifer Lawrence.*

For a person who uses only initials instead of a first name, use periods and no space between the initials: *R.W. Mahoney.* Unless it is the individual's preference or the first name cannot be determined, do not use a single initial alone: *R. Mahoney.*

FOR BROADCAST: Use middle initials only when it is essential to distinguishing a person (as in a casualty list or a report of a crime) or is the way the person is usually identified. In all other circumstances, omit initials. If a person is known by his or her initials, use both first and middle, not just the first: *A.Q. Khan*, not *A. Khan*.

8.6   **LEGISLATIVE TITLES.** The preferred form for members of the U.S. House of Representatives is *Rep.* or *Reps.* when the title immediately precedes the name: *Rep. Jeb Hensarling, R-Texas, said he would confer with his caucus.* The words *congressman* and *congresswoman* may be used in subsequent references in place of the person's name. *The congresswoman emphasized her opposition to the proposal.* For members of the U.S. Senate, use *Sen.* or *Sens.* immediately before the name on first reference. On subsequent reference, *senator* may be used in place of the name. Use *U.S.* or *state* before *Rep.* or *Sen.* as necessary to avoid confusion. Spell out *senator* or *representative* in all other uses. Other legislative titles, such as *assemblyman, assemblywoman, delegate, city councilor, commissioner,* etc., should never be abbreviated but should be capitalized when immediately before a name. Organizational titles, such as *speaker, majority leader, minority leader, chairman, chairwoman,* etc., should be capitalized before a name, but they should never be abbreviated. Legislative titles should not be used before a name on second reference, unless it is in a direct quotation.

FOR BROADCAST: Always spell out legislative titles, including organizational titles. Capitalize the title if it immediately precedes a name. Members of the U.S. House of Representatives may be referred to as *congressman, congresswoman* or *representative.* On second reference, do not use the title. Do not use party affiliation unless it is relevant to the story, and in such cases spell out the name of the party and the legislator's home state: *Senator Joni Ernst; Congressman Adam Schiff; Republican Senator John Cornyn of Texas.*

8.7   **MAGAZINES.** Titles should be capitalized but should not be in quotation marks. Capitalize the word magazine only if it is part of the title: *Rolling Stone magazine; HomeCare Magazine.*

8.8   **NEWSPAPERS.** Capitalize the names of newspapers. Do not place the names in quotation marks or underline them. If the publication includes *the* as part of the newspaper's name, it should be capitalized: *The New York Times; the Los Angeles Times.* If the name of the state is necessary to identify where the newspaper is published but is not included in the formal name, insert it in parentheses after the name of the city: *The Kansas City (Missouri) Star.*

FOR BROADCAST: If the location where a newspaper is published is not clear from its title, insert the name in the copy: *The Oregonian published the results of its investigation Sunday. The Portland newspaper said the accident could have been avoided.*

8.9 **REFERENCE WORKS.** The titles of reference works such as dictionaries, almanacs, encyclopedias, gazetteers, handbooks, school yearbooks, etc., should be capitalized. Do not use quotation marks, italics or underlining: *Black's Law Dictionary, the Encyclopedia Britannica, the Hammond World Atlas, the World Almanac.* The same rule applies to the Bible.

8.10 **RELIGIOUS TITLES.** Capitalize religious titles used before a name on first reference: *Bishop, Archbishop, Cardinal, Pope, Sister.* When coming before a name, *Reverend* should be abbreviated and should always follow the word *the*: *the Rev. Joseph Grey, the Most Rev. Joseph Grey, the Very Rev. Joseph Grey.* On subsequent references, omit all titles.

FOR BROADCAST: Never abbreviate *Reverend*: *the Reverend Joseph Grey.*

RULES FOR FORMING POSSESSIVES

1. For common or proper nouns, whether singular or plural, that do not already end in the letter *s*, add an apostrophe and *s* to form the possessive. For example:

SINGULAR	man	child	Johnson	Microsoft
SINGULAR POSSESSIVE	man's	child's	Johnson's	Microsoft's
PLURAL	men	children	alumni	
PLURAL POSSESSIVE	men's	children's	alumni's	

2. If the word is a singular common noun that already ends in the letter *s*, add an apostrophe and *s* to form the possessive, unless the next word also begins with an *s*.

   the hostess's request   the hostess' seat
   the witness's answer   the witness' story

3. If the word is a singular common or proper noun that ends in a letter other than *s* but has an *s* sound (such as *ce*, *z* and *x*), add an apostrophe and an *s*.

   the fox's den
   Butz's policies
   Marx's theories
   the prince's life

4. Singular proper nouns that end in *s* add only an apostrophe:

   Descartes' philosophy
   Hercules' labors
   Socrates' execution
   Tennessee Williams' plays

5. Plural common and proper nouns ending in *s* add only an apostrophe:

> the churches' association
> the girls' toys
> the horses' food
> the Smiths' car
> the Williamses' children
> the Carolinas' coastline

6. If a term is hyphenated, make only the last word possessive:

SINGULAR	mother-in-law	She is my mother-in-law.
SINGULAR POSSESSIVE	mother-in-law's	It is my mother-in-law's car.
PLURAL	mothers-in-law	The program featured mothers-in-law.
PLURAL POSSESSIVE	mothers-in-law's	The mothers-in-law's cars were damaged by vandals.

7. If an object is jointly possessed by two or more people or entities, make only the last noun possessive:

> Mary and Fred's entry won a prize.
> Acme Co. and Smith Corp.'s joint business is profitable.
> My mother and father's home was destroyed by fire.

8. If the objects are not jointly owned—if they are separate objects owned or possessed by different people—make both nouns possessive:

> Mary's and Fred's entries won prizes.
> The Smiths' and the Browns' luggage was lost.

9. Some special expressions that do not end in *s* but have an *s* sound use only an apostrophe: *for appearance' sake*; *for conscience' sake*. In other expressions, use *'s*: *the appearance's cost*.

10. Indefinite pronouns such as *everyone* follow the same rules. However, personal pronouns have special forms that never use an apostrophe. Personal pronouns include such words as: *his, mine, ours, theirs, whose* and *yours*.

11. Do not add an apostrophe to descriptive phrases ending in *s*: *citizens band radio*; *teachers college*. The phrase is descriptive rather than possessive if *for* or *by* rather than *of* would be appropriate in a longer form of the phrase: *a radio band for citizens*; *a college for teachers*. An *'s* is required, however, when the term in the descriptive phrase is a plural that does not end in an *s*: *women's clinic*; *people's government*.

12. Generally, avoid making inanimate objects possessives. Instead, try to rewrite the passage, either dropping the possessive or converting the passage to an *of* phrase:

> AWKWARD: the table's leg
> BETTER: the table leg OR the leg of the table
> AWKWARD: the book's chapter
> BETTER: the book chapter OR the chapter of the book

13. When mentioning the name of an organization, group or geographical location, always use the common or preferred and official spelling. Some names use the possessive case, such as *Actors' Equity Association*, but others, such as *Pikes Peak*, do not.

14. The word *it's*, spelled with an apostrophe, is a contraction of *it is*. The possessive form, *its*, does not contain an apostrophe:

> WRONG: Its higher than I thought.
> RIGHT: It's higher than I thought OR It is higher than I thought.
> WRONG: It's height scares me.
> RIGHT: Its height scares me.

CREDITS

INDEX